AMERICANA

AMERICANA

A 400-Year History of American Capitalism

BHU SRINIVASAN

PENGUIN PRESS

New York

2017

PENGUIN PRESS
An imprint of Penguin Random House LLC
375 Hudson Street
New York, New York 10014
penguin.com

Illustration credits
Part II: Library of Congress
Part IV: Andy Freeberg / Premium Archive / Getty Images

ISBN 9780399563799 (hardcover)
ISBN 9780399563805 (ebook)

Printed in the United States of America
1   3   5   7   9   10   8   6   4   2

Book designed by Amanda Dewey

For Dina

CONTENTS

PART TWO

PART THREE

PART FOUR

Introduction

When the free toy packs were being given out to children on our Air India flight that day, I was preoccupied by the sight of the deformed feet of the woman two rows in front of us. I paced the aisle back and forth to glimpse and understand how such a thing was possible. Most startlingly, her feet were an entirely different skin color than her face. Only years later would I realize that this was the visual effect of translucent women's stockings and not a mysterious Western malady that caused toes to be webbed together. But while I was fully entertained by the curiosities of my first plane trip—a one-way journey to America—my mother was anxious, quietly reciting the verses of a Hindu mantra to calm her nerves. Thirty-four years old at the time, with a doctorate in physics, she was by training and temperament a believer in rationality. But she was about to enter America with two children who didn't have proper papers, a prospect that led even her to prayer. Such was the power of the Immigration and Naturalization Services of the United States of America. At the time, some latitude existed, which allowed women traveling on work visas to bring young children without their own passports, provided that additional visas were stamped on the mother's passport. But my brother and I didn't have visas. My mother hoped to get us by on a technicality: Her visa had said "persons" rather than person, and she planned to plead and argue that the errant "s" meant all three of us. So for the entirety of our nearly twenty-four-hour journey, the uncertainty of our fate consumed her. If we were not allowed in, it likely would have ended the years of preparation, sacrifice, and savings that had gone into our American dream.

That we were dreaming of America in the first place was the result of a national tragedy. India, a poor country with hundreds of millions of people one or two steps removed from starvation, had gone to great expense to educate doctors, engineers, and scientists. Yet somehow this investment had turned the country into a third-world finishing school to provide the first world with talent. The educated began leaving India. They weren't searching for freedom or fleeing persecution—India was, and is, the largest democracy in the world. No, for decades, Indians, like millions of others, had been drawn to the dividends of American capitalism, not the liberties of its constitution. We were economic refugees.

In India, despite two college-educated parents, the sorts of goods that even poor Americans of the early '80s took for granted—the telephone, television, even refrigeration—had eluded us. An automobile, nearly as common to American adults as social security numbers, was unthinkable for us. In 1982, when we had finally saved enough for a refrigerator, it was delivered by oxcart—an indignity that I felt even as a child, especially because I had waited and hoped for some time to see a delivery truck. But we didn't need to endure this imbalance for long, this lack of purchasing power stemming from being on the wrong side of the wealth of nations. With the proper application of ambition, my mother could convert her education into a global currency, regardless of how illiquid it was in India. Ambition in this case meant the willingness to leave behind one's homeland, culture, family, and large parts of self-identity. This has always been the immigrant's price of admission.

After years of applying, my mother was offered a post-doctorate position at Roswell Park Memorial Institute in Buffalo, New York. We learned she would be entitled to $14,000 per year. According to my calculations, we were rich. But to unlock and access such largesse, we needed to borrow the money for exactly one one-way ticket to America for my mother. With generosity (and a modest amount of interest), my father's oldest brother was able to give us the loan. It was then arranged that my father's mother would look after my younger brother and me. After an overnight train from Madurai, deep in South India, we made our way to coastal Madras to send my mother off on her first plane trip. We didn't quite know how long she would be gone, but we soon began to receive her letters. Within months, one of them had the magic words. We, too, the children, would be going to America. She would be coming to get us. But my visaless father would have to stay behind. No technicalities would get him through immigration.

When we landed after our multileg flight at Kennedy Airport, it seemed that my mother's in-flight prayers had worked. We were allowed in. But one more adjustment was required of me. While my mother and four-year-old brother raced to another terminal to catch a flight to Buffalo, I was greeted by my aunt, whom I was to live with in Virginia. I had met her only once when she had made a trip to India. Visiting relatives from America were generally received as dignitaries, so my memory of her was seeded more by her reputation than familiarity. Having been settled here for years, with children my age, she provided a far better introduction to America than my mother would have been able to.

This was evident just days later on Halloween, when I was asked to put on face paint and a wig and knock on neighbors' doors, carrying a bag. Had I lived in India, that October day in 1984 would have been one of significant tumult as Indira Gandhi, the prime minister, had just been assassinated by her own bodyguards. Instead I was getting the types of chocolates—for free!—that I had tasted perhaps three or four times in my entire life. What else had I been unaware of? Not too many days later, the American election took place—my cousin was quite perturbed by a rumor that Walter Mondale was going to eliminate summer vacations. This immediately made me a single-issue Reagan supporter. I was also unaware in all of my endless daydreams and imaginations of America that anyone other than whites, and a few well-liked Indians of both varieties, lived here. For the first few days, I wondered what all these African immigrants, who seemed to know quite a lot about America, were doing around me.

Months later, during the school year, I was reunited with my mother in Buffalo. Shaped by my parents' hopes and their need to prepare me for the necessary sacrifices ahead, I was made a believer in America years before I set foot on its soil. And every step, I now believed, was a step toward betterment, each alteration of my accent a commitment to assimilation. To make things easier, I had even Americanized my name from the lengthy Bhuvanesh to the present Bhu. By 1987, my mother's work took us to San Diego; we moved again a year later when my mother joined a biotech company in Seattle. Attending nine schools over five years as I did, with the changes in the surrounding geography and demographics, it gave me an opportunity to see several Americas.

The disruptions caused by switching schools until high school made me an avid, near-religious student of the daily newspaper, the only consistent narrative I could hold on to no matter where I was. In several places, the last delivery on my paper route was my own. After the sports page, I was mostly mesmerized by the stock tables and tales from Wall Street. After high school and a short detour to New York City, I wandered back to Seattle. At the University of Washington I was fortunate to take a class taught by acclaimed American historian Richard White: a survey of U.S. history up to 1979. Our final assignment was to write an essay that weaved the implications of American history into our own family stories. Given that I had lived in America for only a decade, I was unsure of how to approach the task, whether I had any material at all.

After some direction from Professor White, I began to look at my family's decade. One theme became obvious. Our American history was economic in nature. We had spent our early years in the American Rust Belt. The roads, the disrepair, the dilapidated conditions that resulted from the fallout of American industry, especially the closure of a major steel plant, were a fundamental part of the American story. Our journey west, induced by a biotech start-up, was a familiar destiny equated in the American imagination with fortune seeking. Without the history class I would have had little sense of how to place the disparate strands of my origins into a coherent American narrative. I wanted to pursue this study much further. But as fascinating as American history was, I could not resist the temptation to participate in the greatest gold rush since the Gold Rush. The rise of the Internet—what people started calling the Next Big

Thing—was happening all around us. With the prospect of fortune, history had to wait.

While working on my own start-up, my efforts led to a role at a pre-IPO company, which then became one of the hotter stocks of the era. I raised venture capital for my own start-up in news aggregation, which eventually imploded. All this played out by the time I was twenty-four. Yet, the energy of the era, the wildness of the boom, the ease with which an idea, a blank canvas, could turn into something confirmed a central belief I had about opportunity in America. At the same time, I began to have serious doubts about the rationality of markets—in the lead-up to 2000, there were plenty of stocks that had doubled every few weeks for a year and then dropped 99 percent the next year.

Years later, settled with a family of my own, my freshman essay somehow seemed unfinished. Many thoughts had drawn me back to it, but one particular equation had intrigued me. It first came to my attention via a headline I saw while flipping through an old book showing momentous front pages of the *New York Times*. The story from January 6, 1914, had it that Henry Ford was increasing his wage levels to a minimum of $5 per day. At the time, the Model T, Ford's only car, cost $440. This meant that the wages of eighty-eight days of labor of a Lithuanian immigrant or former sharecropper equaled a brand-new car. Yet even one hundred years later, a Chinese worker earning $200 per month can barely afford an iPhone, much less a car, with three months of her labor. For many on the outside looking in, the favorable American math, this enduring contrast of first-world purchasing power, holds more allure than any civil right. Indeed, millions of undocumented immigrants affirm this, having left the democratic rights of citizenship in Mexico, to live as stateless noncitizens among the American underclass.

How, then, was I to understand and reconcile our personal history, an economic one, into the sweeping arc of America when the dominant histories are political in nature? How is it that American democracy is held as sacred, when most immigrants come here first to participate in its capitalism? Would America, and for that matter democracy, be considered great if America was not rich? Is freedom as important as prosperity? When and how did the forces of capitalism and democracy begin their myriad interactions? I did have one device with which to explore the vastness of these questions. I had witnessed firsthand the creative and destructive forces of markets—how the American spirit embraced and adapted to new ways of doing things, how its culture and geography evolved as this energy shifted from one thing to the next. And I looked to see if a series of breakthroughs, innovations, and ideas—history's Next Big Things—could help me understand the American story as it unfolded.

I began to think how the essay would have read had I started with the *Mayflower* rather than with my story at Kennedy Airport in 1984.

PART ONE

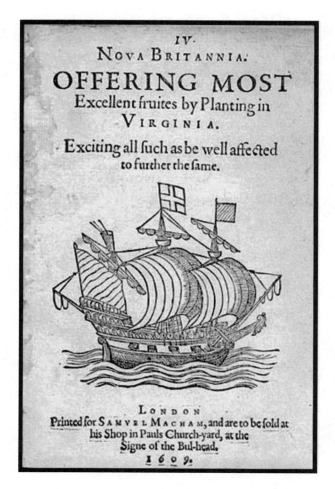

A promotion for the Virginia Company, 1609.

One

VENTURE

Lost in the American mythology of the *Mayflower* is a central
question: How did a group of disenfranchised religious separatists finance a large ship, pay an experienced crew, and provision
for a year's worth of supplies on the way to the New World? Even for
sovereign authorities of the early seventeenth century, outfitting a transatlantic voyage was no small financial undertaking. Certainly, impoverished political refugees of today, when crossing oceans, do not do so in
chartered transportation or arrive with any capacity for financial sustenance. The financial story behind this journey points to a parallel narrative, one in which the exalted sentiments of religious liberty found
themselves subordinated to economic considerations and motivations.

In 1616 the group that history would later call the Pilgrims was an
exiled community of religious separatists living in Holland. The original
members of this community had fled England in 1608, first settling in
Amsterdam for a few years before making their way inland to the city of
Leyden. In William Bradford's firsthand account of their time in Leyden, while considering it a "fair and beautiful city," the separatists were
largely limited to employment that required "hard and continual labor,"
many in the cloth-making trades.

While the full and open practice of its brand of Christianity was prohibited in England, the congregation was relatively free of persecution in
Holland. Indeed, one account held that local Dutch merchants viewed

their piety as a mark of creditworthiness, despite their relatively low economic standing. After twelve years of living in Holland, while some observed potential risks to religious freedom, the congregation began searching for alternatives primarily to improve their economic condition.

For the congregation, the initial impetus for leaving England for Holland had been to settle well and attract additional members of the church to join them. But the hard toil and "great labour" of the pioneers in Leyden proved a sufficient deterrent to these potential émigrés. To Bradford it was clear that "some preferred and chose the prisons in England rather than this liberty in Holland with these afflictions." In addition, the older members were beginning to die, with this fate often coming earlier due to the grueling work. At the same time, the congregants' children, "to bear part of their parents' burden," were forced to work in conditions similar to their elders. If all this weren't bad enough, the "manifold temptations" of Holland had drawn the older children as they entered adulthood into "extravagant" courses, away from the church, with the degenerating behavior risking "dishonor to God." It became clear to the community elders that without growth of the congregation, the experiment would likely dissipate within a generation into secular Dutch society and end quietly. In all, it seemed that challenging economic circumstances more than persecution presented the greatest danger to their religious fundamentalism.

Again the solution seemed to be relocation. Early thoughts veered to the "vast and unpeopled countries of America." The idea sparked considerable internal debate, primarily focused on the speculative dangers of climate, savages, disease, famine, and "nakedness" of the natives. After these, another risk needed mitigation: The prospect of living in any proximity to Spanish holdings in the Americas was eliminated with the view that the Catholic "Spaniards might prove as cruel as the savages in America." As most of the rest of America had been declared largely by England and to a far lesser extent by Holland, this left two choices. Either possibility required negotiations and permission.

The English possibility, of course, had a special irony: The group that had once fled England was now contemplating overtures to the same sovereignty that had once persecuted them. But this path was a circuitous one.

Dating back to 1606, England had granted a charter to a private venture known as the Virginia Company of London. While the internal operations of the New World venture were left in the commercial hands of the company, there remained an element of oversight and governance in the King's hands, exercised through his Council for Virginia. Like most new ventures, overseas or otherwise, the Virginia Company had a less than auspicious start. In its first decade, it had lost all of its money several times and needed to be refinanced each time. Worse, the vast majority of the settlers sent overseas had met miserable deaths.

A decade in, the Virginia Company was in a beleaguered state of affairs. When the Leyden congregation dispatched two men to London to explore the possibility of settling within its holdings, the company greeted them with the enthusiasm of a lonely merchant meeting the day's only customers. The profitability of Virginia as a commercial enterprise depended on viable settlements—settlements needed people willing to risk life and limb. The desperation of the men from Holland coincided with that of the company. There remained an obstacle, however. The congregation wanted explicit permission to practice their religion. The commercially motivated men of the Virginia Company, optimistic in the face of opportunity, assured them in turn that the King's blessing for this minor provision would be perfunctory. It wasn't. The process dragged on. The council's position held that an official endorsement of the congregation's practices overseas would undermine His Majesty's ability to prohibit aspects of their practice in England. With the company serving as a conduit, a compromise was reached: The King's Council for Virginia would neither endorse nor prohibit their practices overseas, provided that the Leyden congregants acknowledged obedience to the King.

With this intentional bit of ambiguity settled as a middle ground between the proxies of government and church, the Virginia Company granted a "patent" to the church in Leyden to settle in the New World. Indeed, far from needing escape from the King's persecution, as the traditional story holds, the Pilgrims voluntarily entered the business of carrying His Majesty's sovereignty overseas.

With permission in hand, church leaders in Holland now shifted to the equally complicated matters of money. While the Virginia Company had the capacity to grant permission, it no longer had any capacity to finance an overseas voyage. The congregants needed to raise capital. For prudent and conservative men of wealth, the considerable expenses of a ship, crew, and supplies were far too risky to merit investment, especially as overseas ventures proved especially prone to complete loss. The solution, then, seemed to be to find men of means given to speculation—men driven by appetites for glorious gains, who were willing to overlook the possibility of loss on a venture or two.

Just then, a rival Dutch offer seemed to emerge. Hearing of the negotiations with the Virginia Company, the Dutch group made efforts to get the Leyden congregation to venture to their own settlements in North America. But with the Virginia Company patent in hand, the role would rest with English financiers. Namely, one particular promoter named Thomas Weston, a representative of the Merchant Adventurers of London, had made his way to Leyden to ingratiate himself with the church pastor, John Robinson. With the pastor convinced that Weston was the man to "induce his friends to venture," formal terms were drawn up. In contemporary terms, this was the equivalent of a letter of intent or term sheet, an outline upon which the financing would take place subject to final negotiations. As any modern entrepreneur can readily attest, the time between the stated intentions and closing is one fraught with increasing levels of anxiety and tests of will, often heightening all the way to the final moments. The 1620 financing of the *Mayflower*'s voyage was not immune to these trials of temperament.

ADVENTURE CAPITAL WAS a phenomenon that had taken hold long before the 1600s. One group, the Fellowship of the Merchants Adventurers of England, had been formally recognized as far back as 1505. Rather than act as a formal pool of money or resources, the adventurers had always been a loosely affiliated guild in which individual members participated in the ventures of their choosing. As the century progressed, the capital requirements of overseas ventures had coincided with and propelled development of the joint-stock company—"joint-stock" implying shareholders with transferable interests as opposed to the more intimate, closed nature of partnerships.

In addition to transferability of shares, this ongoing legal evolution allowed for limiting the personal liability of any adventurer—the investor couldn't lose any more than his initial investment. The idea of limited liability, a legal invention that does not exist automatically or organically in free markets, allowed investors to have unlimited upside potential while limiting the downside, thereby making speculation in exploratory voyages more attractive. Not all concerned settlements. Sovereignties often granted exclusive fishing rights, exploration rights, and trade routes to be exploited by private entities. Governments, by granting the charters, hoped to create internal economic benefits by encouraging private capital to be deployed in risky ventures overseas.

For all of these purposes, limited liability was vital to encourage investment. By the nature of the business, investors in England were often absent from exercising any voice in the affairs of remote ships and trading missions months or years away. This strengthened the need for the corporate form in that passive investors could be assured of not being liable for unknown debts. At the same time, their distance and duration meant that such enterprises required ample levels of capital, far beyond the risk appetite of any one investor, no matter how wealthy. The joint-stock company allowed multiple investors to buy in to a venture and hold the interest. The final push to the English joint-stock company occurred in 1553 with the Russia Company, in which adventurers committed £6,000 at £25 per share, marking the first use of the corporate form for overseas ventures.

Starting then, even English privateers, state-sanctioned pirate ships looking to confiscate cargo, began using the joint-stock form to raise capital from adventurers. Privateers had another reason to spread the risk. For individual operators, the risk of being charged criminally if the political winds turned, even when sanctioned, was diffused when sufficient numbers of prominent investors were also involved. These English privateering syndicates were anything but swashbuckling men with parrots and eye patches; the accounting statements of individual ventures made careful note of ship tonnage, capital invested, men involved, and number of ships in each operation—from which Sir Francis Drake's twenty-one ships and 1,932 men stood out with invested capital of £57,000. In his thorough examination of the era's joint-stock companies, W. R. Scott suggested that the flexibility of the corporate structure lent itself to the virtues of diversification and spreading risk, particularly in matters of piracy. From privateering's tolerance for large losses emerged the basic principle of modern venture capital.

> Suppose, for instance, a capitalist was prepared to adventure 2000 Pounds in privateering, he could only fit out one ship of about 200 tons or two smaller ones. His expedition might be too weak to make any captures of importance. If on the other hand, he joined in several larger expeditions, even if one of these was a total failure, he had every prospect of obtaining handsome profits from his shares in the others.

HANDSOME, INDEED: Drake's operation provided a return of 4,700 percent—forty-seven times the capital invested. Such anomalous returns were the glimmer in the eye of every adventurer in evaluating opportunity. Staid London bankers they weren't.

At the turn of the century, after a particularly painful era of war had concluded and economic depression had taken its toll in England, opportunities for fortune seemed better everywhere but home. The East India Company was formed in 1600, the Virginia Company of London a few years later. Soon after, pamphlets were printed to entice prospective adventurers to invest. Virginia's literature managed to refrain from calling attention to any distressing factors. On the dangers of Indians: "They are generally very loving and gentle, and do entertain and relieve our people with great kindness." It detailed the varieties of trees available as lumber for bringing back to England, hills and mountains full of treasure "never yet searched," and soil that seemed immense in "lusty" potential. This was followed by a general call to one's English patriotism, proclaiming the need for "Navigation into all parts and corners of the world, to furnish our own wants, and to supply from one kingdom to another." It then pointed to the misery of the unemployed at home, the "swarms of idle persons" that such a venture could send abroad.

The pamphlet then got down to the business at hand: A single share in the Virginia Company was available for an investment of twelve pounds ten shillings to adventurers who wished to remain in England. Each planter, the men actually willing to go to Virginia, received one share at no cost, provided they work for the company for seven years in building the settlement. In addition, the company was tasked with providing the money for food, materials, and maintenance of the settlement. The company would own everything and have a monopoly on all economic activity in Virginia. At the end of the seventh year, the assets of the company, including the settled land, were to be distributed among the shareholders. For many impoverished, struggling young men, the prospect of owning land in the New World in exchange for merely providing one's labor proved enticing, especially as they saw well-heeled investors pay over twelve pounds for the same share.

Any dreams of ease were quickly dashed. The Virginia Company turned out to be a disaster. The first waves of men were struck by disease, famine, freezing cold, or Indians. Subsequent waves of supply ships, with new groups of planters, were then horrified by the appearance of the famished countrymen who had preceded them. One early group simply fled to live with the Indians. After successive iterations of failure, the company sought new investors when the old ones refused to throw good money after bad, restructuring itself multiple times in the process. As the financial circumstances became acutely desperate for private interests by 1614, and with the settlement in shambles, sentiment grew to revoke the company's patent and turn it over to the Crown. Fighting this, the Virginia Company's lawyer, Richard Martin, was left pleading with the House of Commons for financial relief, a bailout, from His Majesty's Treasury.

So when the group from Holland inquired about settling in the New World, the Virginia Company was open to any and all willing to risk death and endure misery.

· · ·

ALMOST TWO AND half years after receiving permission from Virginia and the Crown, the Leyden congregation made final preparations for the voyage. Representing the church, William Brewster and John Carver went to London to agree to the final terms.

The shares were priced at ten pounds. The structure was similar to Virginia's. A planter willing to go to the New World received one share; an adventurer willing to pay ten pounds received the same. The venture would hold all assets and economic rights in the settlement. At the end of seven years, the assets were to be distributed to the shareholders in proportion to their ownership.

But the devil was in the details. And the Merchant Adventurers changed the terms of the deal mere weeks from the proposed departure date. In the original terms, the Pilgrims were to have contributed four days per week of labor to the venture, with two days for their "private employment" and one day for the Sabbath. The investors now insisted all six days be committed to the venture's interest. Adding insult to injury, the houses that the settlers were to build for their families were now to be added to the venture's assets rather than owned by the individuals.

The church's spiritual leader, John Robinson, was indignant. He wrote to his representative, John Carver, complaining about the failure to charter a ship by this late date. Robinson found the demand to divide up the houses at the end of seven years to be particularly petty given that the profits were meant to come from "fishing, trading, etc." He then asked Carver, as he was meant to lead the voyage, to consider how it would feel to serve seven years without "a day's freedom from task." But it was too late: The agents had agreed to the terms on behalf of the congregation.

After raising £1,200, the parties quickly moved to salting beef and procuring beer, water, and other provisions for the voyage. In Holland, with some of the shares sold within the community itself, the congregation bought a small ship called the *Speedwell* with a capacity of 60 tons, which was to be kept in the New World for coastal trading and fishing. In England a ship of 180 tons, the *Mayflower*, was being chartered.

On a July day in the Dutch port city of Delftshaven (present-day

Rotterdam), the *Speedwell* stood ready to take the select congregants to meet the *Mayflower*, docked in England. One of the passengers, the future Pilgrim leader William Bradford, recounted the great sadness of the day as "mixed with an abundance of tears," with friends coming from nearby Amsterdam to bid good-bye. With their "reverend pastor falling down on his knees with watery cheeks," wishing his pioneering members a lifetime's farewell, the *Speedwell* slowly pulled away from the dock. With this, "they left that goodly and pleasant city which had been their resting place near twelve years; but they knew they were pilgrims."

Within a couple days, aided by a "prosperous wind," the Pilgrims arrived in Southampton, England. After the initial excitement of seeing the *Mayflower* for the first time, the mood quickly darkened in the face of the business at hand. The arrivals from Holland immediately took to disputing the conditions agreed to by the agents, especially the requirements of six days of labor versus four and the contribution of individual houses to the common property. Weston, the representative of the Merchant Adventurers, had come down from London "to have the conditions confirmed." The Pilgrims refused to regard the new conditions as binding even though their agents had agreed. The impasse continued for days. A final funding amount of £100 was due from Weston's group to clear the ship from port and commence the voyage. Weston refused to pay. The Pilgrims were left to sell three thousand pounds of butter, along with other sacrifices, to raise £60 quickly.

Here too the piety of the Pilgrims caused them to collectively express the reasons for their intransigence to the other shareholders, including many still in Leyden who had ventured money along with the Merchant Adventurers. They pled that the possibility of owning their homes in the New World was "one special motive," and instead assured their investors "that if large profits should not arise within seven years, that we will continue together longer with you." However conciliatory the tone, the Pilgrims would not budge on home ownership. And neither did Weston.

With the money raised by selling supplies, the *Mayflower* and the *Speedwell* cleared port and left for the New World on August 5, 1620. Due to the delays in raising the financing and chartering the ship, this was a later-than-anticipated departure. With this timeline, arrival in the

New World would occur in the early fall, leaving barely enough time for winter preparations. But the timing would get worse. The *Speedwell* failed to live up to its name—the leaking ship caused the voyage to turn to the nearest port. After an attempt to repair the leak, followed by another failed departure, the *Speedwell* was abandoned. Several of the initial passengers decided to give up on the ill-fated journey, with the remaining passengers joining those on board the *Mayflower.*

On September 5, with 102 passengers on board, the *Mayflower* started its journey to the New World. As much as the Pilgrims are recorded as religiously motivated, it should be noted that fully half of the *Mayflower's* passengers were not members of the church in Leyden but rather settlers added to the journey by the investors.

Living in Holland with relative freedom, then sailing to the New World under an English flag, with English financing, on a chartered English vessel with an English crew—all this seems an especially unlikely way to flee English persecution. Political refugees generally do not spend the final days before departure negotiating financial considerations and distribution of assets seven years into the future. But the Pilgrims were never refugees to begin with; they were critical instruments in a speculative venture, one that equally served to expand the Crown's sovereignty to the New World. Religious liberty was but one component of the overall enterprise.

But this venture, like Virginia, got off to a rough start. The *Mayflower* arrived off the coast of America in late November. Compounding this late-season arrival, the ship had missed its destination. The original charter granted by the Virginia Company called for landing near the mouth of the Hudson River. Instead, the *Mayflower* anchored within a peninsula 220 miles to the north. After sending an expedition to explore the coastline and find a place to build the settlement, the majority of the Pilgrims remained on the *Mayflower* awaiting the men's return. Simultaneously, while the *Mayflower* was en route, officials in England separated the northern parcel of the Virginia Company and placed it under the Council for New England. Without knowing it, the Pilgrims were preparing for the first winter in the history of New England.

William Bradford labeled this section in his history *Of Plymouth*

Plantation "The Starving Time." While the voyage itself saw the death of one member of the ship's crew, and no passenger deaths until the ocean was crossed, death made it onto the ship as the Pilgrims waited for the return of the expedition. Bradford returned to the ship to find that his wife had died. It was a prelude to the harsh winter that awaited them. By the end of February, the new colony had seen deaths reach "two or three a day" for a stretch of time. At the depth of their misery, Bradford noted that "there was but six or seven persons" able bodied enough to care for the rest. By March, almost half of the *Mayflower*'s passengers had died. The delays caused by the negotiations in England, combined with the failure of the *Speedwell*, had cost a full month of landfall in the New World, time that could have been well spent preparing for the cold months ahead.

After staying in Cape Cod for the winter, the chartered *Mayflower* began its voyage back to England in April. The economically motivated adventurers had expected the return voyage to bring wood, furs, or other commodities from the New World. But given the calamity of the first winter, the *Mayflower* returned home largely empty.

Mortality rates were no excuse. The investors were displeased, Thomas Weston most of all. Weston sarcastically and bitterly wrote to John Carver, who had been voted into leadership as governor by the Pilgrims: "That you sent no lading in the ship is wonderful, and worthily distasted. I know your weakness the cause of it, and I believe more weakness of judgment than weakness of hands." Weston's letter to Carver was sent on a new ship, *Fortune*, headed for Plymouth. In the event Carver missed the message, Weston added his exhortations that this ship be returned full of goods this time, threatening to cut off further financing if Carver failed. But in the time between the return of the *Mayflower* to England and the arrival of Weston's letter via the *Fortune*, Carver died.

Arriving to great relief after the winter's misery, the *Fortune* brought a replenishment of supplies along with an additional thirty-five settlers. It was left to Plymouth's new governor, William Bradford, to open Weston's scathing letter. But by that time, circumstances were slowly changing for the better. Starting with the first warmth of the spring, the colonists had spent several months building their community. More important, the settlement made direct contact with its first Native American, a man introducing himself as Samoset. Remarkably, having had some familiarity with English-speaking fishermen who operated seasonally off Cape Cod, Samoset spoke some broken English and had even offered an assuring "Welcome, Englishmen" as he strode to first greet them.

A few days following this approach, the Pilgrims were visited by Massasoit, the leader of the local tribe. This meeting marked the start of a personal relationship that would continue for another two decades, with the local Indian tribes being crucial to Plymouth's financial salvation. Namely, the Indians had access to a valuable interior commodity that commanded high prices in Europe: beaver skins. Universally desired by the wealthy in their target markets, beaver skins quickly became the commercial link between New England and the Old World. At the same time, the transatlantic trade created symbiotic economic bonds between the Native Americans and the early colonists. Rather than becoming alarmed at sharing territory, as the colonists seemed ill equipped to venture inland, the Indians looked at the English settlements as trading posts. Adept at hunting beaver over the ages as part of their own winter clothing, the Native Americans had a competitive advantage in procuring a valuable commodity that the colonists were willing to trade for. Tracking the remote beaver in distant ponds and rivers was a labor-intensive task that the colonists left to experts.

The Native Americans brought another aspect of value to the supply chain: Beaver skins needed considerable amounts of preparation. The job of dismantling and skinning the beaver fell to native women. After the meat and fat were separated, followed the even more arduous task of softening the pelts and removing the coarse bristles to leave the smooth, soft skin fit for the European upper class. At times this even entailed wearing the pelts for a year, perspiration serving as a softening agent.

This dynamic led to an early trading opportunity for the Plymouth colonists. Even before the arrival of the *Fortune*, the colonists had managed to exchange simple goods—likely items such as blankets, glass beads, knives, and utensils—for fur. The Indians, without the technical ability to forge shining knives or intricate metallic objects, were able in turn to procure such luxuries in exchange for what was to them the simple act of hunting and preparing beaver. This intersection of competencies, the comparative advantages of nations, remains the fundamental basis for all global trade.

Overlooking the indignities of Weston's letter, the colonists loaded the *Fortune* with wood in the form of clapboard and, far more important, "two hogsheads of beaver and otter skins" for a cargo worth "near £500." It was a remarkable arbitrage: These goods ready for export were procured from the Indians for a "few trifling commodities," as the Pilgrim leader noted. Given the voyage's initial investment, estimated at between £1,200 and £1,600, the value of the fur and wood would have provided a first-year dividend of over 30 percent—a solid return for financing what was at heart a group of religious fundamentalists. But providence was not in favor of the *Fortune*. As the ship crossed the seas, the vessel was intercepted by a French privateer and the cargo seized. The *Fortune*, like the *Mayflower*, sailed back to the Merchant Adventurers empty.

This disaster at once coincided with and precipitated several problems with the adventurers. If the goods had arrived safely, the sale proceeds would have been reinvested in another year of supplies for the colony. Instead, now the cost of outfitting and sending a supply ship required further investment of money for a venture that had yielded little. At the same time, Weston and one of his fellow adventurers had a falling out. Accusations flew and lawsuits were filed. The dispute constrained Weston's credibility with the adventurers, especially as an additional round of financing was needed. Before long, Weston settled matters by ceding his financial interest to the remaining adventurers.

Mirroring the disarray of their overseas financiers, the colonists found themselves with other perplexing problems. As per the initial terms, all efforts to grow food belonged collectively to the community and company. With the supply ships slow to arrive and sparsely provisioned, often bringing even more mouths to feed than food, farming took on existential importance. However, the shortages caused by the all-for-one, one-for-all ethos of collective farming proved inadequate. After much debate, it was decreed that all families would be allotted a portion of land to grow their own crops, with the product of their efforts their own to keep. "This had very good success," wrote the colony's governor, "for it made all hands very industrious. The women now went willingly into the field, and took their little ones with them to set corn, which before would allege weakness and inability." The experimental form of communism, when it came to growing food at least, ended for the Pilgrims.

At the same time, the financiers overseas came to the conclusion that there was now only a small likelihood of substantial profits at the end of the term. Compounding matters, deteriorating economic and political conditions in England had left many of the adventurers pressed for capital. Within three years of the *Mayflower* setting sail, the financial structure was unraveling. One sympathetic investor, James Sherley, wrote ruefully to Bradford: "Whereas you and we were formerly sharers and partners in all voyages and dealings, this way is now no more." Still, his concern was to ensure "our moneys be not lost." Sherley estimated that the adventurers had first claims on the assets (known as a liquidation preference in modern venture capital terms) of "not less than £1,400." A period of renegotiation ensued.

While the investors in England were engaged in acrimonious negotiations among themselves and the Pilgrims, the colony still needed outside financing to survive. To bridge this gap, the Pilgrims resorted to borrowing from trading partners and factors at interest rates exceeding 50 percent.

After nearly two years of deliberations among all of the splintered factions, a resolution started taking form. The colonists in Plymouth were loath to divide up their family homes and lands as required by the terms. Similarly, London-based adventurers had little interest in direct real estate holdings of a small, beleaguered village thousands of miles away. In a sophisticated exchange, a deal was worked out in which the Plymouth Colony assumed a debt of £1,800 to buy out all of the shares of the venture—with this, the adventurers no longer owned equity as investors. This freed the colonists to divide up the land and houses among themselves. At the same time, a group of Pilgrims, led by William Bradford, agreed to personally assume the full responsibility for the community's debt, with the £1,800 due in nine annual installments of £200 starting in 1628. For relieving the citizens of Plymouth of this debt, Bradford and his group received the exclusive fur-trading rights of the colony.

Indeed, the rights would have been immensely valuable, but for one thing: competition. By 1628 New England had received shiploads of settlers. Some, such as the Puritans, had religious inclinations. Others were itinerant traders making landfall. The Dutch, with their own settlement on the Hudson River, were building trading posts as far north as the Connecticut River. The French too made incursions. For all, fur was vital. Native Americans, continuing their role as hunters and preparers, were a key part of this transatlantic trade. None of this was good news for the local beaver. With low reproductive rates and limited migratory distance, the competition for furs rapidly killed off the beaver population in New England. With the beaver disappearing, the local Indians seemed far less useful, dangerous even.

The pressures from this market development set off additional renegotiations for Bradford and his group, deepening them into the fur trade to earn their way out. All matters were finally settled with the few adventurers who still held on in 1645. The financing of the *Mayflower*, a cross-ocean journey of weeks, had turned into a twenty-five-year venture, the contractual terms outlasting the vast majority of the Pilgrims who actually made the voyage.

Two

TOBACCO

Just as the Pilgrims were finding their initial footing in New England, the venture in Virginia was in its final days of collapse. The Virginia Company had endured repeated failures and humiliations as a commercial entity, but the 1622 Indian massacre of the English settlement in Jamestown, which killed over three hundred settlers, sealed its fate. After an investment of £200,000 over the preceding seventeen years from English adventurers, sending over one hundred shiploads of supplies and seven thousand men and women, death had left the population of Virginia numbering a little more than one thousand. In 1624, horrified by the mortality rate and the lack of prospects to grow to anything resembling viability, King James revoked the company's charter. From that point, Virginia ceased to be a company and would be governed as a colony. By not being able to keep the King's subjects safe, the company had missed a chance to control the monopoly on what turned out to be America's most valuable commodity of the seventeenth and eighteenth centuries.

Tobacco was late to arrive in England. Observed by European explorers starting in the fifteenth century, Native Americans throughout the Americas had been known to smoke tobacco through a variety of inventive methods for social, ceremonial, and medicinal purposes. By the early sixteenth century, ships and sailors returning to Spain brought with them the tobacco that they had once seen with curiosity and now used with enthusiasm. It soon became a cure-all, a remedy with doubtless therapeutic powers, on the Iberian Peninsula.

While overseas ventures had brought tobacco to England on a sporadic basis, it was with the arrival of one of Sir Francis Drake's ships with ample supplies of both leaf and seed that tobacco made its way to domestic planting. As late as 1588, an account to the Queen still had to define and describe what was to be done with this tobacco. But by 1600 the smoking pipe had become a staple of upper-class salons in London society. This led to perhaps the world's first antitobacco advocate. Assuming the throne upon the death of the childless Queen Elizabeth I, King James took aim at his subjects' seemingly insatiable indulgence.

Publishing a tract titled *A Counter-Blaste to Tobacco* in 1604—anonymously at first—His Majesty opened by questioning why honorable men would "imitate the barbarous and beastly manners of the wilde, godless, and slavish Indians, especially in so vile and stinking a custome?" Much of the rest of the admonition, however, seems to have been four centuries before its time. Countering a view that tobacco was a cure for everything, it asked, "what greater absurdity can there be than to say that one cure shall serve for diverse and contrarious sorts of diseases." It then pointed to the poisoning of the lungs and disruption in the function of the organs. Finally, it equated tobacco use with "a branche of the sinne of drunkennesse, which is the roote of all sinnes."

The King's rebuke would prove ironic. A few years later, a young man named John Rolfe would arrive in Virginia after an especially arduous journey. In 1609 a convoy of nine ships headed to Virginia. Rolfe and his wife, on board the appropriately named *Sea Adventure*, made it to within a few hundred miles of Virginia before being violently swept off course. After the ship crashed into rocks off an island near Bermuda, its passengers were stranded for nine months. Using local woods and salvaging the rest from their ship, they built two smaller boats to sail up to Virginia. After his wife's untimely death, Rolfe settled in Virginia. Seeing the tobacco of the local Indians to be "poor and weak," Rolfe planted seeds of a Spanish variety from the West Indies. "Never was a marriage of soil and seed more fruitful," wrote Joseph Robert in his history of tobacco. The Virginia soil along the river and town named for the antitobacco king proved to be the colony's salvation.

But even success brought misfortune. Seeing the miraculous growth of tobacco, the settlers, with their mercenary instincts, immediately applied the majority of their efforts to this trade. For a community that had been on the brink of starvation more often than not, this diversion of focus presented the very real risk of food shortages. For the men of Virginia, Rolfe noted, "who generally are bent to covet after gain," it would have been virtually impossible to pay attention to the "tillage of corn" with the allure of such easy profits. Remarkably, the solution seemed to be market regulation. With supply ships unpredictable and often sparsely provisioned, a collective food shortage would have been existential. Understanding this dynamic, the serving governor ruled that every man must plant two acres of corn to ensure his own food supply before planting any tobacco. The penalty was forfeiture of the tobacco.

In 1616, the first year for which meaningful agricultural data is available, a little over one ton of tobacco was shipped to England. Within four years, this grew to over sixty tons. The death and destruction in their midst cut this production in half soon after. Rolfe's discovery, however, had set the economic template, with all of its attendant consequences, for the entire southern half of English America.

IN THE YEAR before the landing of the *Mayflower*, another group made a consequential, if less than voluntary, landing on Virginia's shores. In August 1619 Rolfe recorded that a "Dutch man of war . . . sold us twenty negars." The first slaves had landed in what would become the American colonies.

But for another few decades, there was a far more cost-effective source of labor. The eventual rise of the British Empire tends to create the impression of an all-powerful England dating back to an even earlier era. But in 1620, the year of the *Mayflower*'s departure, significant elements of English society suffered from abject economic misery. One particularly chilling letter from the Virginia Company to the Lord Mayor of the City of London sheds some light on these circumstances. In it, His Lordship was graciously thanked for sending over one hundred homeless children the previous year. The company then asked the mayor to "furnish us again with one hundred more for the next spring." As before, the company offered £3 for each child's transportation and 40 shillings for apparel. Predictably, some of the "ill-disposed" children were unwilling to go, but with the city "specially desirous to be disburdened" of these would-be vagabonds, permission from the King's "higher authority" was sought to "transport these children against their will" to Virginia.

For adults, inducements to go to the New World often came in the form of indentured servitude. In exchange for agreeing to be an indentured servant for a few years, usually seven, the servant would receive land of his own at the end of the period—each adult being a microventure of sorts. With land plentiful in Virginia, the opportunity to own land presented an element of potential freedom that made the risks and indignities of servitude worthwhile. There was another benefit: The expenses of the servant's transportation to and maintenance in the New World were underwritten by his or her master. In the first year after the collapse of the company, the 1625 population of Virginia stood at 1,227, of which 487 whites were recorded as servants. Additionally, many of the free whites would likely have been former servants freed from their indentures. At the same time, the Negro population had grown by natural birth to 23 from the day of the Dutch ship's arrival.

Yet conditions in Virginia initially favored indentured servitude for its growing tobacco trade. Part of the reason was the "appalling epidemiological environment" of the Chesapeake Bay: Its swampy tidewater was a hotbed of disease that killed both natives and whites with unpredictable ferocity. These conditions made slave ownership prohibitively expensive. To purchase a slave would have required an up-front allocation of capital, and as slaves were assets entitling their owner to a lifetime of labor, Dutch and Spanish traders priced them accordingly. But with the mortality rate high, the death of a slave was far costlier than the death of an indentured servant. If an indentured servant died, it was almost costless—indeed, if the servant had served out a few years of his term at the point of death, the early demise might even be highly profitable—the master had received years of labor without giving up any land, as he would have had to if the servant survived to the end of the term. Anchored by this morbid calculus, the demand side of the labor equation favored servitude.

Conversely, the supply side of the equation had two sets of geopolitical variables, also favoring servitude over slavery. The first was that with King James's death in 1625 and the transfer of power to his son Charles I, the political conditions in England entered a new period of volatility. Within twenty years, the English Civil Wars would end the monarchy, resulting in Charles's execution by beheading. As the political tensions escalated, there was no shortage of people willing to leave for America as indentured servants.

The other factor involved England's continental rivals. For the Dutch and Spanish slave traders who controlled the transatlantic trade at the time, there were far superior markets for the sale of slaves than the backwaters of Virginia. For one, the sugar plantations in both Spanish America and Portuguese Brazil required hundreds of thousands of slaves. Given the insatiable European demand for sugar, it made little sense for slave traders to undertake the additional time required to travel up the American coast to service a small, speculative market. A slave ship could make a round-trip between West Africa and Brazil in the same time it would take just to reach Virginia one way. Compounding this cost, the death rates on slave ships being what they were, such a lengthened journey would have imposed additional attrition on the human cargo before delivery. So unless England's America was prepared to spend considerably more per slave—which it didn't need to, given the availability of white servants—the slave market's perimeter rationally ended in the sugar islands of the Caribbean.

Indeed, one man so clearly understood the allure that servitude had for England's poor that he decided to build an entire colony on the premise. This ambition benefited from England's rising religious tensions. Contrary to the generally accepted version of events, weighted by the incomplete narrative of the Pilgrims' search for religious liberty, the monarchy often sought to appease sectional interests. Equally, it was the fundamentalist Puritans and other conservative Protestants who took increasing offense at the young King Charles's conciliatory ways. For one, Charles, the nominal head of the Church of England, had married a French Catholic, Henrietta Maria of France, in the first year of his reign. A few years later, he granted the Catholic Cecilius Calvert, the second Lord Baltimore, twelve million acres touching the northern waters of the Chesapeake. Conceiving his colony to be populated by Catholics coming as indentured servants, Lord Baltimore named his vision Maryland, in honor of his benefactor's queen.

Soon Maryland and Virginia, blessed by the combination of Chesapeake soil and cost-effective labor, made dramatic gains in tobacco production. The 272,000 pounds of tobacco grown in 1631, the year before the founding of Maryland, became 15 million pounds by 1669.

But the economics of servitude shifted in favor of slavery. Of the tens of thousands of white settlers who arrived in the Chesapeake in the early seventeenth century, 75 percent came as servants. And as per the terms of their indentures, if they survived disease and overwork, they became landowners after a few years. In addition to the land granted by their masters, Maryland and Virginia for a time provided for an additional fifty acres to freedmen to encourage the overall growth of their colonies. The men went from destitution in the streets of London, through the interim step of serving their masters, to owning property in the New World. But there was only so much land. As the best land became more valuable, the generous terms of the earlier indentures made less sense. At the same time, the monarchy had been restored in England, with Charles II, the former king's son, assuming power. As political stability returned to England, the allure of overseas servitude diminished. In addition, as the tobacco country had spread farther up the Chesapeake and into the interior, mortality rates had noticeably decreased with improved immunity.

There was one additional, critical catalyst. By the late 1660s, a venture looking to establish England in the slave trade, had stalled. In 1672, seeing the trade in slaves as a vital English interest, King Charles II reorganized the venture as the Royal African Company of England and granted it a monopoly on the West African slave trade to the English colonies. In 1674 more slaves were imported into Virginia in one year than in the previous twenty-five years combined.

In the fifty years from the time when African slaves first landed in Virginia, the annual increase in their numbers had been minimal and sporadic. The year 1628 saw one hundred slaves arrive, but most years averaged around twenty or so. Along with natural increases through childbirth, the slave population numbered about two thousand in Virginia in 1670. By 1700 it would grow to sixteen thousand, composing one fourth of Virginia's population, soon to climb to far greater magnitude and proportion.

At the turn of the century, the composition and social structure of the southern colonies—factors that would divide the trajectory of slavery by geography—were becoming clearer.

THE EARLY OPPORTUNITIES in the New World that had once appealed to poor Englishmen, despite all risks, had limited attraction for the Dutch. Henry Hudson, an Englishman, was financed by the Dutch to explore America. In 1609, starting upstream from the island known to the Indians as Manna Hatta, he then claimed the areas and valleys on both sides of the river that he had sailed up for Holland. The wilds of this New Netherlands, however, failed to attract Dutch settlers in any numbers—the conditions in Holland were the most prosperous in the world. With the exception of the Pilgrims, few others wanted to leave. Conditions had turned so euphoric in the 1620s and '30s that, among other excesses, the Dutch took to speculation in tulips, where the most prized individual flower bulbs sold for the equivalent of an Amsterdam town house.

Therefore, by 1650 almost half of the settlers in the New Netherlands were not Dutch. As the Dutch were increasingly pressured by the growth of English settlements in their vicinity, the territory's governor desperately called for "homeless Polish, Lithuanian, Prussian, Jutlandish, or Flemish farmers" to help populate the Dutch possession—he knew better than to try to entice his own countrymen. It was too late. Without firing a shot, a small English fleet of just three ships caused the surrender of the New Netherlands. In 1667, after a formal transfer, the New Netherlands took the name of King Charles's brother, the Duke of York. New York, having barely grown in population over a twenty-year period under the previous management, grew fourfold by 1700. Lack of prosperity at home, ironically, helped strengthen and populate the English colonies in America.

To accelerate the English hold in the Americas, King Charles II granted the area south of the Hudson River to two aristocrats, which through subsequent transactions transformed into New Jersey and Delaware. To William Penn, a wealthy member of the English gentry, who had converted to the Quaker faith, the King awarded 45,000 square miles of land to the west of the Delaware River. An area south of Virginia extending to the northern borders of the Spanish holding of Florida was granted to eight aristocrats in England, known as the Lords Proprietors. Carolina, anchored by its first settlement in Charles Town, rounded out the English portfolio in what would become America.

As New Jersey, Pennsylvania, and Carolina looked to attract settlers, their proprietors focused on two sets of incentives: religious indifference and generous land grants. The land granted had a quasi tax placed on it, known as a quitrent. For the proprietors of vast lands, receiving the income of the quitrents, along with making the remaining land more valuable as it became populated, was the basic business model. As it turned out, the least religiously tolerant and theologically most uniform place in English America was New England; rules of Sabbath and observation were codified in most local laws. Everyone else was primarily interested in the pursuit of money, and if that meant tolerance, so be it.

The Lords Proprietors of Carolina offered an especially unique incentive. For every family member brought over, the family was granted 150 acres. But the definition of family was a generous and loose one. Looking to populate Carolina from the English holdings in the Caribbean, the Lords Proprietors counted all Africans as members of their owner's family, entitling the owner to an additional 150 acres for each slave. By 1720 this catalyzing structure led to people of African descent becoming the majority of the colony—a condition that would hold for generations.

In the North, the offer of up to hundreds of acres of land attracted full families to the new colonies, a shift that was tied to the North developing the economic characteristics of self-sustaining farms and egalitarian villages. This had to do with geography and economics, not culture or morality. Unlike Virginia's tobacco, Carolina's rice, and the Caribbean's sugar, the lack of a single, scalable cash crop in the North didn't allow slavery to flourish when more profitable uses for slaves, a capital asset, were found in the South. However, the diversity had benefits. Along the rivers leading to the ocean, small economic hubs such as Boston, Philadelphia, and New York developed populations numbering into the several thousands, enabling urban occupations such as printing, trading, and banking.

The South was entirely different. Virginia and Maryland, powered by the international demand for tobacco, rapidly grew to levels of wealth far beyond that needed for sustenance. With success, the South's defining social and economic structure became not the village nor the small town but the plantation.

IT IS HARD to overstate tobacco's role in eighteenth-century America. In 1700 the total value of the American colonial exports to ports in England was £395,000; tobacco from Maryland and Virginia accounted for nearly 80 percent of this total. Fur, the next-largest export item, accounted for around 5 percent.

By this point, earlier generations of Virginians had amassed the largest parcels of farmable land for their families and, more important, waterfront access to rivers or Chesapeake Bay, which meant the ability to load tobacco directly onto trading vessels. The most prominent among such planters, Robert Carter, had accumulated 300,000 acres of tobacco lands along with hundreds of slaves. Other men, while not as successful, had scaled to collectively dominate tobacco production. Not only did the largest tobacco farmers achieve lower costs of production than the average small farmer, but their profits were often used to add more slaves. And unlike smaller operations with two or three slaves, which inhibited family formation, the largest operations enabled entire slave communities to develop and reproduce, with each new slave birth being a human dividend of sorts.

Predictably, with such concentration of wealth, the men who grew tobacco controlled Virginia politics. In 1705 the majority of men who owned over two thousand acres were justices or burgesses, the equivalent of legislators, land and power going hand in hand. As these men died, their property and slaves were left to their heirs. One generation into the eighteenth century, Virginia's most esteemed citizens composed a landed aristocracy. These men of vast inherited wealth rarely worked: The formula of hired overseers getting the most out of slaves and land was largely set. The men and women who did the most work inherited a less fortunate condition by birth. And this too presented a developing advantage. Unlike the African-born slave, the native-born slave had never known freedom or any identity that conflicted with his owner's economic purpose, with each subsequent generation further removed from all ancestral knowledge. And the slave too now had generations of his extended family living in bondage within close proximity, making any run to freedom an impossibly large sacrifice for most, familial bonds serving the role of invisible shackles.

For the southern gentleman, inversely, ease of living by birthright became his hallmark. "In their hospitality, drinking, gaming, horse racing, and dancing," wrote Joseph Robert in *The Story of Tobacco in America*, was a "hedonism" intrinsic to the nature of growing a vice such as tobacco. Unlike a prudish New England town or a Quaker community egalitarian in spirit, the South was a place where the distinction between those at the very top and those at the very bottom was easy to see. The exalted had family crests imprinted on their china, the dark and lowly had no legal right to a family, and poor whites without slaves were masters of little but themselves. From this hierarchical society came many of the architects of American liberty.

But all this decadence had disadvantages. Much like the modern oil state that fails to develop any other economic capacity, single-commodity Virginia was highly susceptible to the overseas price of tobacco. As the revenue from tobacco sustained the high forms of living, one way to smooth out temporary price drops was to borrow against future crops. To Robert, "the tobacco planter had in him enough of the frontiersman to be incurably optimistic, and enough of the English landed gentry to desire a high standard of living. The combination meant piling on debt." The Virginia gentleman without significant debts was a rarity.

The enabler was often a London-based factor. The factor was a combination of a trader and an agent. The wealthy tobacco planter sent his tobacco to his factor in England; the factor sold the tobacco and then usually arranged to pay for the English luxury goods that were needed for good living: wine, books, tailored clothing, linens, furnishings, and china. When the tobacco crop or prices in the market were insufficient, the factor advanced money against future crop harvests at an appropriate rate of interest. To the factor, the system had the advantage of keeping the gentleman planter, no matter how wealthy or powerful, captive to both the relationship and the prices of his next year's crop. Even the two most famous Virginians in history, George Washington and Thomas Jefferson, would not escape the clutches of their factors.

This dependency on overseas factors seems to have had its roots in the geographic features of Virginia. As Chesapeake Bay offered hundreds of inlets, large plantations with water access directly loaded tobacco onto ships headed for distant ports. As a result, Virginia never developed the central port of call or commodity market that it would have had if this trade had been centralized in a single place; such a port would have easily emerged as the largest financial center in eighteenth-century America based on the trading volume. In the 1760s Virginia's largest port, in Hampton, handled a minor fraction of the tobacco exports flowing out of Virginia and Maryland, even though the port was close to the mouth of Chesapeake Bay. Despite controlling access to the Atlantic Ocean for both Maryland and itself, Virginia failed to build any lasting economic competency or significant urban center on the Chesapeake.

Thus Virginia ceded the vital functions of shipping and trade finance to cities in the North. Functions for trading hubs required the type of work known today as white collar: coordinating logistics, arranging for insurance, negotiating trade terms, extending trade capital, maintaining wholesale facilities, and others. Trading spawned other activity. Trading ports were the prime conduits of information, the aggregate of which Adam Smith would call the "invisible hand" of the market: information used by entrepreneurs and businessmen to adjust their activity to maximize profit. The more dynamic the information flow, the more fluid the opportunities were to profit from the shifting tides of the market. The more fluid the opportunities, the easier it was for new entrants and upstarts to make a name. Eventually this would lead to a far wider and greater set of urban opportunities in the North than in the single-crop colonies of the South.

In the present, however, the South dominated economically. In 1765, Virginia and Maryland's tobacco, along with Carolina's rice, combined to represent 80 percent of American exports. Leading up to the American Revolution, South Carolina by itself exported more in terms of pounds sterling than all the northern colonies combined. The South Carolina of 1770, it must be noted, while having far fewer than Virginia's 187,000 slaves, was a majority slave colony: 75,000 of its total population of 125,000 had masters. And Virginia had more blacks than the state of New York had whites. As such, the numbers were startling and undeniable: On the eve of liberty, the majority of American exports, decades before cotton entered the equation, were produced by slave labor.

Yet it was Virginia's soil that proved to be fertile ground for new ideas on freedom and governance, supplying many of the intellectual foundations, as well as the great contradictions, of the American experiment.

Three

TAXES

In 1754 the May 9 issue of the *Pennsylvania Gazette* carried a cartoon of a snake cut into eight pieces. The head of the snake was labeled "N.E." for New England, while the other seven pieces represented the various British colonies in America, with the tail South Carolina. Below the drawing was a caption in large letters: JOIN, OR DIE.

Accompanying what was perhaps America's first political cartoon was an editorial by the newspaper's publisher, Benjamin Franklin, calling for unification against a common enemy: the French. Years earlier, Franklin had elaborated on this need for a united colonial defense in private, but the events of the previous year had caused him to be far more outspoken in his drive for union.

Over the past winter, ongoing territorial disputes between the British and the French around the Ohio River had suddenly escalated beyond posturing. In addition to geopolitical prestige, at stake was control of the Indian fur trade in the American interior. The Ohio River, which flowed into the Mississippi River and could take cargo all the way down to French-controlled New Orleans, was seen as vital and strategic to French interests in North America. Located in close proximity to existing British colonies, the vast, sparsely peopled lands of the Ohio Country—sparsely populated by white settlers, that is—were equally the target of the British. Using a familiar template, the King had authorized a group of Virginians to form the Ohio Company, granting it the right to settle half a million acres and sell this land to other private investors. Given that the primary economic activity of the French in the region was trading with the Indians, they had established trading posts where Indians could bring their furs. To protect this valuable trade, they started building forts to support a military presence. In response, with commercial interests and colonial interests often one and the same, the Virginians built their own presence to rival that of the French.

In an ongoing effort to pressure the French positions, Virginia's lieutenant governor and Ohio Company speculator Robert Dinwiddie entrusted a young soldier with leading missions into the contested areas. Starting that winter in 1754, twenty-two-year-old George Washington, in carrying out his objectives, encountered both French and Indian factions in the wilderness, with each side maintaining a tenuous peace while making military moves. In the spring, much of the activity concerned a fort that the French had built on the banks of the Ohio River. On the morning of May 28, mistakenly assuming that nearby French soldiers had intentions to fight, the group led by Washington fired on the French. The incident marked the official start of a prolonged war—known in America as the French and Indian War, to include French-aligned tribal combatants—between France and Britain in North America.

Franklin's JOIN, OR DIE cartoon and editorial from weeks earlier now seemed prescient heading into the summer, as French forces took the upper hand. Blaming the military confidence of the French on "the disunited states of the British Colonies," and considering himself fully a British subject, Franklin went on to suggest that the "enemies have the very great advantage of being under one direction, with one council, and under one purse." As a remedy, a conference in Albany was planned for July to discuss a unified defense among several of the colonies. Franklin's notes from this time outline ideas on a common colonial system of taxation to fund the common interest, manage all relations with Indians, and defend the coastline—all to be approved by the British Parliament. But the conference, attended by seven of the colonies, ended without any resolution or alliance.

Namely, there already existed a unifying element—all of the colonies were a part of Great Britain, however distant, with the empire responsible for the collective security of its disparate parts. Therefore, the colonies did not need direct association with one another to bind them. Rather than a coordinated response undertaken by the colonies, each colony separately was expected to supply soldiers and tax revenues to the collective aims of the British military in North America.

In Franklin's Pennsylvania, this wartime taxation caused problems. In the American colonies, local legislative assemblies had long played an important role in governance. With governors appointed by the King, this duality of the executive and legislative functions had balanced local interests with sovereign ones. Pennsylvania, however, had a less representative governing structure than colonies like Massachusetts and Virginia, a fact that stemmed from its founding. Back in 1680, to cancel a debt of £16,000 owed by the King to the Penn family, 45,000 square miles west of the Delaware River had been granted to William Penn—this became Pennsylvania. Upon his death, the proprietorship of the colony went to Penn's sons. Though Penn had ceded some authority to a colonial assembly, all unsettled lands in Pennsylvania remained in the ownership of the Penn family. Once the French and Indian War started, Pennsylvania's assembly had passed legislation to tax its citizens to finance participation in the war, and the language included taxing the property interests of the Penns. The Penns balked. Far from unifying the colonies, Franklin found himself in a crisis, opposing the most powerful interest in his own state.

To subvert the power of the Penn family, Franklin headed to England for a period in the late 1750s to represent the Pennsylvania assembly. Ironically, in his attempt to turn Pennsylvania into a colony like Massachusetts and Virginia, Franklin looked to enlarge the power of the King and Parliament's authority in order to sever the provincial authority of the Penns as the proprietors of Pennsylvania.

By this time the French and Indian War had grown into a larger war of empires in Europe. Spain, England, and France, along with other European states in various phases of ascent and decline, entered the conflict. The Seven Years' War spread to nearly every theater that had the presence of the competing colonial empires. In 1763, when the war concluded, Great Britain emerged as a substantial victor and the world's leading power. In America it had managed to push its border substantially westward. But victory had a price: The British Treasury, despite the tax revenues collected during the war, had accumulated additional debts of over £60 million over the seven-year period.

Understandably, the British Empire now sought to pay down the sizable cost of its past war through every means available to it, including imposing a part of the financial burden on its colonial holdings. At the same time, it now needed to maintain a standing army of ten thousand troops in America to protect its hard-won gains from the war. In 1765, to finance debt repayment and the army, the British Parliament passed the Stamp Act applicable to the American colonies. Up to this point, while duties on exports and imports had been a primary tax mechanism, the colonies had faced relatively little interference in the governance of their internal affairs. The Stamp Act, however, looked to substantially alter this condition. With hundreds of individual provisions, the act called for a stamp duty—for the act of stamping an official seal on a piece of paper, not to be confused with postal stamps—to be paid when any educational degree or certificate was issued, when wine was sold, when attorneys or other professionals were licensed to practice, when land was surveyed, when documents were filed at court, when ships were commissioned, when leases were signed, when bills of sale were issued, when advertisements were placed in newspapers, and so on. Virtually any activity that required any type of contract, document, publication, or government filing had a stamp duty attached to it. The act was sweeping in its reach. In the American view it was invasive, and resistance would begin to foment.

To Daniel Dulany, the son of a wealthy Maryland politician, educated in England, the constitutional issue seemed clear. To him, the English constitution—which itself was a framework interpreted through various documents, acts of Parliament, judicial precedents, and historical understandings rather than a single document—was based on balancing three forces: "Monarchy, Aristocracy, and Democracy." Over the centuries, English law had evolved to the point where the clear role of "laying taxes" belonged to the House of Commons, "the representative of the people"; to Englishmen this vital role was a function of democracy. In one way or another, various local districts and constituencies had members in Parliament. For any bill related to taxes to become effective, the House of Commons had to approve it by a majority before presenting it to the King for approval and execution. Writing less than five months after the passage of the Stamp Act, Dulany raised a series of questions in an influential pamphlet he had printed. Calling it "an essential principle of the English constitution, that the subject shall not be taxed without his consent," which was gained through direct representation in Parliament, Dulany asked: Who represents the colonies?

Throughout 1765 and into 1766, instigated by theorists like Dulany, the objections to "taxation without representation" had hardened, especially as the American colonists saw themselves as Englishmen. In Virginia's House of Burgesses, its legislative assembly, a young Patrick Henry made his first notable agitations against the Crown, urging passage of a resolution holding that representation was the only "security against a Burthensome Taxation," that it was the "distinguishing characteristic of British freedom." Newspapers throughout America published the text of the resolution after it passed in the House of Burgesses.

Massachusetts took things a step further. Its legislature called on the other American colonies for collective action—strength in numbers—proposing a congress in New York to discuss the response. With attendance by nine of the thirteen colonies, the congress prepared a set of "Declarations of our humble opinions" as to the "Essential Rights and Liberties of the Colonists." While professing that all subjects "owe the same allegiance to the Crown," it then with greater specificity detailed its economic grievances. What the incursive threats of the Indians and French could not do a decade earlier—unify colonial interests with a single voice—intrusions into the pocketbook would. Some of the tensions spilled into the streets, with riots against royal authorities.

While the actions of this congress and legislative bodies such as Virginia's had no binding effect, the collective reaction in America led the British Parliament to actively reconsider the Stamp Act less than one year after its passage. As part of the deliberations in understanding the near revolt in America, Parliament summoned its most famous citizen, then in London, to explain the state of affairs in the colonies.

In lengthy testimony that must have lasted hours, Benjamin Franklin answered dozens of questions in the House of Commons. He took great pains to distinguish the general compliance of the colonists with external taxes, such the duties on goods and commodities, from the tension caused by internal taxes.

Q. You say the colonists have always submitted to external taxes, but object to the right of Parliament only in laying internal taxes. Now can you show that there is any kind of difference between the two taxes?

Franklin: I think the difference is very great. An external tax is a duty laid on the commodities imported, that duty is added to the cost, and when it is offered for sale, makes a part of the price. If the people do not like it at that price, they refuse it. But an internal tax is forced from the people without their consent, if not laid by their own representatives. The Stamp Act says we shall have no commerce, make no exchange of property with each other, nor recover debts; we shall neither marry nor make our wills, unless we pay such and such sums, and thus it is intended to extort our money from us, or ruin us by the consequences of refusing to pay it.

FRANKLIN THEN WENT on to subtly threaten a boycott of English manufactured goods, suggesting that America would accelerate its pace toward self-sufficiency in this regard as well. Tellingly, by the latter half of the testimony, the inquisitors asked Franklin to distinguish between American and British interests, especially in matters of security and warfare. One asked if America would submit to a tax in the event of another European war. Franklin offered a qualified "as far as their circumstances would permit" rather than a patriotic "yes."

Hearing this, prescient voices surmised that if the protests in America were able to subvert authority this time, it was foreseeable that the colonists would one day repudiate all British authority. To capitulate now in the face of "insurrections of a most dangerous nature in open defiance of His Majesty's government" would have grave consequences. Arguments against the repeal held that the entire Stamp Act amounted to less than one percent of annual wages for the colonists. Adding to the indignity was that much of this revenue was to maintain the defenses in North America, to defend the colonies. Opponents of the repeal called for the Crown to hold steadfast in the face of protests by the colonists.

But the Americans had their supporters: British merchants, traders, and manufacturers feared any boycott of their goods in America, especially as the population in the colonies continued to grow as a market at a rapid rate. In a commercial nation trafficking the trade of its empire across seas and continents, this source of British wealth had its voices in Parliament and managed to win. The Stamp Act was repealed less than ten months after it was passed in 1766. But far from defusing tensions, this marked the beginning of the end, the Americans having tasted the power of collective action.

ON A COLD NOVEMBER DAY IN 1773, the shipping vessel *Dartmouth* sailed into Boston Harbor. On board were several tons of tea from the British East India Company. Over the next twenty days, the ship's cargo would become the subject of a tense standoff.

During the seven years between the repeal of the Stamp Act and the arrival of the *Dartmouth*, issues of taxation and regulation had continued to sour the relationship between the colonies and the British. Once Parliament accepted the American aversion to internal taxes, it then attempted various methods of extracting tax revenues, as it had for decades, through traded goods upon entry into colonial ports. Seeing the extent to which Franklin had acceded to the British right to tax trade as external, the incoming chancellor of the exchequer, Charles Townshend, looked to implement a more sweeping set of duties. In 1767, the year after the repeal of the Stamp Act, the Townshend Act went into effect.

By this point, American merchants had seen the effects of the Sugar

Act, which, despite its highly specific name, had imposed a wide set of restrictions on both the export and import of goods including lumber, iron, coffee, molasses, and even textiles. By applying duties on various commodities going in and out of America, the act made clear that in addition to raising revenues, the British government would be able to regulate trade by increasing or decreasing prices. In effect, a high duty placed on incoming goods could make certain imports cost prohibitive. Conversely, a high export duty could make American exports uncompetitive in foreign markets. In either case, by controlling access in and out of America, it became clear that Parliament could adjust the duties to favor British merchants and producers to the detriment of both the colonists and foreign traders.

Within months of the passage of the Townshend Act, boycott movements against British goods gained momentum throughout the colonies. From Philadelphia to Boston, local agitators and organizers started pressuring merchants and wholesalers who sold British goods to cease the trade. In addition, towns and villages began movements to ensure citizens didn't consume British-made goods. The idea was to have British firms face substantial falls in revenue, at which point British business interests would lobby Parliament for relief. At the same time, for certain commodities such as tea, a habit that large segments of American colonists had grown accustomed to, there was the option of buying the commodity from smugglers, bypassing all duties. For Dutch traders, supplying their tea from China, America became a growth market.

By 1770 the boycotts seemed to have made an impact. The British government was barely able to collect enough revenues to pay for its civil administration in the colonies, much less its standing army. But it was an economic disaster for both sides, and while contested principles remained, the situation started easing due to financial pressures.

The coalitions of port cities such as Philadelphia, New York, and Boston, along with their respective merchant groups, had faced the growing pressure of complying with the ongoing boycott. But as the nonimportation agreement between several of the port cities was expiring, most refused to renew their obligations. Compounding the weakness of the coalition was that British manufacturers and exporters, suffering as well by having their products boycotted, were able to lobby Parliament into removing most of the Townshend duties. But not wanting to appear weak by completely reversing course, Parliament left the Townshend duties on tea untouched.

For the next couple of years, with the duties on British tea continuing, the smuggled tea from Dutch sources remained cheaper and plentiful throughout most of the American colonies.

Exacerbated by the low volumes of British tea imported into America, the mighty British East India Company's preexisting financial problems became worse. Just as the Virginia Company had once been entrusted as a commercial proxy of the King, the British East India Company had been given vast monopoly rights over all British trade to the east of the Cape of Good Hope, a point near the southernmost tip of Africa—a vast area that included China and India. One of the company's trading roles was to procure tea across ports in China and sell it to wholesalers in London. Upon the tea's entry into England, it was taxed. The wholesalers then either sold the tea internally or packaged it for export to other countries. When it was exported, it was taxed once again. With the addition of the duties upon entering and leaving Britain, British tea was already uncompetitive before it left the port in London. Paradoxically, this had a beneficial effect in America. With the addition of the Townshend duty, the price of British tea was high enough that it didn't sell as much as it otherwise could have, which then caused the Treasury to not collect much tax by way of the Townshend duty on tea.

The British East India Company, seeking relief from the British government, made a host of financial concessions in exchange for a large loan of £1.4 million. But in addition to the loan, it received one significant benefit: The British East India Company would be allowed to sell Chinese tea directly to the American market, bypassing the entry and export duties in the ports of England. The only tax the tea would face would be the Townshend duty upon entry in America. This would make British tea much cheaper and more competitive in the American market, meaning that the British government was going to collect significant sums of taxes through the Townshend duty. The first shipment under this new structure was found in the cargo holds of the *Dartmouth*, now sitting in Boston Harbor.

The issue was simple. Allowing the tea to clear customs in Boston meant acceptance of the tax. It meant acceptance of the British East India Company's role in the tea trade. Increased revenues to the royal administration in the colonies meant an enlarged presence of officials and soldiers. The cheap tea was an expensive proposition. And once it entered Boston, it would enter everywhere else. So a group of men in Boston decided to hold the ship at bay.

The ship owner's representative, on the other hand, wanted to get the goods off the *Dartmouth* to load a new shipment back to London. Each day lost was revenue forgone. But a growing dockside protest, along with prominent citizens such as Samuel Adams, John Adams, and John Hancock, wanted to force the ship to return to England with all of the tea on board. Under English law, this would have caused the tea to be surrendered—a loss for the ship owner, as he was responsible for the goods on board up to the point of delivery. To counter the seeming impasse, the customs officials and royal governor simply elected to wait the crowds out to trigger a default. Upon the ship's twentieth day in port, the customs authorities would have the right to seize the cargo for failure to pay the duties—after which the intended recipients could simply pay the past-due duties and receive the shipment of tea.

Knowing this, as the twentieth day approached, a crowd of more than five thousand had gathered. With each passing hour, the possibility of consenting to the establishment of the British East India Company's role in the American market was coming closer. By this time, two other ships, the *Eleanor* and the *Beaver*, had also made it into harbor holding as much tea as the *Dartmouth*. In the evening, groups of men with painted faces climbed aboard all three vessels. With crowds of spectators on the wharves, the men systematically took hatchets to the crates of tea. Over the next few hours, with the authorities standing down, they dumped forty-five tons of tea overboard. In the shallow areas of the harbor, mountains of tea piled up and then receded into the freezing December waters of the bay.

As the tea washed away, for many so did all hope of any reconciliation with the mother country. Within a few months, the British retaliated. Many in England, including the King, traced the boldness of the Bostonians to the repeal of the Stamp Act, a move that they now viewed as a fundamental error in the management of their colonies. This time the British closed the port of Boston, effectively putting the Massachusetts economy under siege starting in the spring of 1774. A few miles from its harbor, the first shots of the Revolutionary War would be fired within a year.

It DIDN'T TAKE long for the political ramifications of the events in Boston to be felt in Virginia. Its most privileged sons began debating, studying, and analyzing this potential call of history. While only fifteen years earlier the only common bond between Massachusetts and Virginia had been the thread that connected all parts of the British Empire, the colonies were discovering a unified identity apart from being English. The realization that unfolded through the 1760s and early 1770s was that they needed one another.

In the interior of Virginia, over one hundred miles from the colony's capital in Williamsburg, was one of the many rolling hills of Albemarle County. On one especially scenic peak stood the home of Thomas Jefferson, one of Virginia's most fortunate sons. His standing came from his inherited wealth, but his fulfillment came from the rigors of an intellectual life that few other men of gentlemanly leisure found as satisfying. From childhood Jefferson had been educated in philosophy, languages, and literature. His home, Monticello, was filled with books. He planned additions and renovations based on the most beautiful structures of Europe on a near-constant basis. His meals and domestic needs were attended to by uniformed household slaves. His wine cellar had bottles that rivaled the best collections of the finest French homes. In his younger days he too had indulged in the more routine Virginian pastimes of foxhunting, horse racing, and card playing. In short, men like Jefferson were raised to be aristocrats, the American landed gentry.

While George Washington's eight-thousand-acre estate at Mount

Vernon was a working farm that at its peak produced thousands of pounds of tobacco annually, its main residence, with its back to the soothing flow of the Potomac River, was the point of pride. Sitting amid brilliant gardens and fruit orchards, teeming with slaves trained as craftsmen and artisans, this grand home was the center of Washington's life and pleasure in 1774.

Given such material surroundings, how and why did such men become sudden revolutionaries? What was to be gained?

In the answers, ironies abound. Virginia, much like Massachusetts, had been largely self-governing for decades. Virginia's legislative body, the House of Burgesses, along with its governor, had operated the colony with limited interference from the King. At the same time, England itself was far from being an absolute monarchy. From the time of King Charles I's execution in the 1640s, the monarchy had slowly ceded most of the legislative functions to Parliament, a representative body of the people. Indeed, the poignancy of "no taxation without representation" was that Englishmen living in the motherland had some democratic ability to give or withhold consent to the taxes that they were subject to; the colonists wanted the same capacity. To continental Europeans, the unruly Englishman was far too irreverent and free to be considered the proper subject of any monarch.

Thus, the early seeds of democracy in America were not a repudiation of absolutism as much as a clamoring for the same equality enjoyed by free Englishmen across the Atlantic. But the British reaction in shutting down the port of Boston signaled a guaranteed regression of rights in the colonies. If Massachusetts capitulated in the face of British force, the Townshend taxes on tea would be fully in effect throughout the American colonies and become an opening for every other form of economic regulation. The taxes would then finance a much larger English bureaucracy, along with royal governors with far greater power and authority than ever before. In the colonists' eyes, there was no turning back to the semiautonomous days of colonial self-governance if the British subdued Boston. The British were going to dramatically increase their power in the colonies, rationally so given the political volatility, unless they were stopped.

Yet Virginia had an additional set of factors that subtly led to its involvement. Unlike Massachusetts or the northern colonies, Virginia was a net exporter: It sold more to England than it bought. Its thousands of small tobacco farmers sold their crops to be bundled with those of the largest planters. The largest planters then maintained direct relationships with agents and factors in England. Over the course of decades, however, the relationship had turned into one of dependence. The wealthiest planters had become nearly captive to their overseas factors, especially when tobacco prices were weak, but the relationship had often been smoothed out by the laxity of English credit granted to the planters. The planters, in turn, used this credit to procure the English luxuries that had become the standard mode of Virginia living at the top. By the 1770s, individual Virginians were deeply indebted to British creditors. Nearly half of the £4 million owed by the colonies to British lenders was owed by the tobacco planters of Tidewater Virginia.

Washington, in letter after letter to his British factor, Robert Cary, complained about both the low prices offered for his tobacco and the high prices of luxuries charged to his account—the combination resulting in such debts as to be "an irksome thing to a free mind." This state of affairs put the "high-tempered" tobacco planter in the "comfortable circumstance of squaring his political convictions with his economic interests," meaning liberty from England also implied freedom from its creditors.

With the port of Boston under siege by British forces as a result of the Boston Tea Party, the colonies called for a Continental Congress to assemble in Philadelphia in September 1774 to discuss a collective response. To prepare for the event, as a representative in the Virginia House of Burgesses, thirty-one-year-old Jefferson began work on a document titled *A Summary View of the Rights of British America*. In contrast to the Mayflower Compact signed by the Pilgrims, which called for absolute obedience to both God and King, Jefferson's piece called His Majesty merely "the chief officer of the people, appointed by the laws, and circumscribed with definite powers, to assist in working the great machine of government." Jefferson went on to recount that the initial American settlements had been financed entirely through private funds of "individual adventurers," with the risks borne by private interests and the lives of men. Yet as the colonies had made themselves into territories of some commercial importance, the power of the King in the colonies had grown. And at this hour, a century and a half later, this growth was culminating in the perverse fate that the men in the colonies an ocean away had more limited rights than the free men in England. The document made its way to the Virginia House of Burgesses, to interested readers like John Adams in Massachusetts, and then to the First Continental Congress, which dissolved soon after.

From here sentiment hardened into momentum, but shots were yet to be fired. Many intended to prevent this civil war, while others saw bloodshed as inevitable, most resoundingly in Patrick Henry's stark terms, "give me liberty or give me death." In the meantime, a Second Continental Congress of the colonies was called to meet later in the spring of 1775. But on Wednesday, April 19, in the Massachusetts towns of Lexington and Concord, after months of tension, British troops and the colonists fired on each other. Despite what would later be considered the opening act of the Revolutionary War, political forces in the colonies were more than a year away from fully coalescing and declaring independence.

Perhaps more than the shots fired in Massachusetts, events hundreds of miles to the south in Virginia seemed to cross the point of no return, beginning with an act by the colony's royal governor, Lord Dunmore, that threatened the most valuable property of the Virginians.

One day after the battles of Lexington and Concord, but without any possible way of knowing about the conflict, Dunmore ordered a large cache of gunpowder removed from the control of the Virginians and onto a Royal Navy vessel. At the time, the Virginians had been far more concerned about a slave insurrection than about any impending British hostilities. With slaves composing two fifths of Virginia's population, this was no idle fear. And a few recent actions by militant slaves had caused the Virginians to be on alert. When Dunmore removed the gunpowder, the Virginians took it as a blatant effort to diminish their capacity to put down a potential revolt. A group of Virginians then marched to the home of Governor Dunmore to protest. Dunmore, angered at the prospect of having his authority questioned, threatened to liberate Virginia's slaves, the labor force of southern fortune.

The liberation of slaves by the British had been a festering concern of the Virginians since 1772. In *Somerset v. Stuart*, a case before Britain's highest court, the ruling dramatically limited the rights of British slaveholders in England. The decision was regarded by slaveholders in America with considerable alarm. To many of the slaves themselves, hearing gossip of the more progressive view of the British court, the British seemed the liberators and the Americans the oppressors.

Within weeks of Dunmore's seizure of the gunpowder, the men of Virginia had managed to intimidate Dunmore to the point of fleeing his home to the safety of a navy ship. When the Second Continental Congress prepared to convene in Philadelphia in May 1775, significant hostilities, independent of each other, had taken place in both Virginia and Massachusetts, the two most populous colonies in America. Attended by Washington, Adams, Franklin, Jefferson, Henry, and the other leading men of the Revolution, the conference this time saw the rhetoric escalate and coalesce into plans for a collective colonial defense. Washington, with his military résumé, in a hall of men primarily skilled in the letters, was selected to assume supreme command of the unified Continental Army.

The Declaration of Independence, authored by Jefferson, was more than a year away. But the war had started. Dunmore, reacting to the developments, issued a proclamation declaring all slaves taking up arms against the colonial agitators to be free. As the war raged on for the next few years, a number of Jefferson's slaves at Monticello and Washington's at Mount Vernon would seek their liberty by fleeing to British ships and encampments. Even at the late hour of 1781, months before the British surrender at Yorktown, when the British naval ship *Savage* docked at Mount Vernon, seventeen of Washington's slaves fled to freedom. After the Treaty of Paris in 1783 gave official British recognition of the independent American colonies, Washington was tasked with asking the British to return all of the slaves who had escaped. Despite British reluctance to the further surrender of their honor, eight of Washington's escaped slaves were returned to him.

The sanctity of this property translated directly into political power for the Virginians. The next phase of negotiations among the colonies, to form a more perfect union through the American Constitution, allowed each slave to count as three fifths of a person for purposes of allocating representatives to each state. Propelled by the electoral math of free men and slave property, given that Virginia was nearly as black as it was white, Virginia went on to control thirty-two of the first thirty-six years of the American presidency. Washington's eight years were followed by four years of John Adams from Massachusetts. Then three more Virginians—Jefferson, his protégé James Madison, and his neighbor James Monroe—would each serve for eight years, extending into 1825. Thirty-six years later, Virginia would again declare its independence, this time from America itself, choosing to preserve its economic interests over the Union.

Four

COTTON

A t the time of the American Revolution, there was another
revolution taking place across the ocean, the implications of
which were far more global. With the dawn of the Industrial
Revolution in Britain, the loss of the American colonies, economically
speaking, turned out to be a minor hiccup, a blow more to Britain's vanity
than to its pocketbook. And while the political severance was made
permanent by one revolution, the economic link between Britain and
America only deepened with the other.

At the heart of the Industrial Revolution was power, not the political
variety but rather the type of energy that made physical things move. For
centuries man had devised increasingly clever ways to harness the wind
and water. Windmills in the countryside were often the settings of small
industry. As the wind turned the giant wheel, gears and machines
worked to crush stones, grind grain, or saw wood. The same logic applied to water power. Set next to a rushing river, a wheel placed in the
water supplied the motion required to turn the machines inside the
facility. A simple sawmill could endlessly turn the blades on a saw as
men fed in lumber to be sliced into uniform sizes. With the components
built by blacksmiths, iron makers, or carpenters, these methods of using
nature's power to save labor were well known.

But nature imposed limitations. A windless day or a dry season had
dramatic effects on productivity. Such mills and factories could be placed

only in favorable locales. And the facilities could be only so large; one windmill or watermill could power only so much activity. The steam engine, however, eliminated these limitations and allowed power to be generated at a previously unimaginable scale.

The principle was simple. Steam was created by heating water in a sealed enclosure. Once the steam pressure built, it could be released in such a way as to move a machine. Conceptions of the steam engine had been a long experimental process. But the techniques for scaling the theory into increasingly large units and dimensions led to an evolving series of breakthroughs and insights in the middle of the eighteenth century. The critical break came from James Watt, a Scotsman employed as an instrument maker at the University of Glasgow. Watt was obsessed with finding a solution to the loss of energy from traditional approaches to manipulating heat and steam. His idea to create a separate chamber for the steam, where the contact with a functioning piston would occur, magnified the power of the steam pressure. Watt's steam engine, which created power on demand, became a central driver of the Industrial Revolution.

The first great application of steam power was in the production of cloth. Clothing had several virtues that lent it to this revolution. One, everyone needed it. Two, the process of creating it had multiple simple but labor-intensive steps that made it perfect for mechanization. At the heart of the transformation were the miraculous natural properties of the fluffy white cotton boll, valued for millennia in the hot climates where it was grown, including the areas of present-day Africa, India, and Mexico. Despite the distances between these places, the methods of turning cotton into cloth were both familiar and similar. Once the cotton was removed from its plant, the seeds were pulled from it. Then the cotton was beaten down and smoothed out. The fibers of the cotton then were combed through and painstakingly spun into thread. Finally, the thread was woven into cloth. As each step required arduous effort, the cost of cotton cloth was a simple reflection of all this human input, making it expensive and unattainable to most.

In England, on a limited scale, many of these functions had first become mechanized through the power of water mills that turned the machines: One individual sitting at a machine could turn raw cotton into thread at rates that would have seemed magical to the generation before his. With the power of the steam engine, the scale and scope of factories became much larger. As the functions became widely mechanized, increases in this labor productivity reduced the price of finished cloth, making it far more affordable and accessible. Lower prices meant much greater demand for cloth, which in turn grew the demand for labor needed in the textile factories. Counterintuitively, great labor savings through mechanization created the need for more labor overall. This became humanity's first dividend from the Industrial Revolution.

Remarkably, a friend of James Watt at the University of Glasgow best understood how this phenomenon of labor savings would unfold. Making a wide set of observations and predictions about specialized industrial processes—in which each laborer focused on a particular task rather than creating the whole as craftsmen and artisans did—Adam Smith advanced the idea of "division of labor" as a central concept in his 1776 *Wealth of Nations*, the treatise that defined the contours of market capitalism. As people specialized and the work needed for a given task decreased, the overall need for human labor would not fall as was feared. Instead, standards of living would increase as more people could afford more, widening the market for all sorts of new goods, which would create new forms of work. To Smith, this endless discovery of efficiency gains was the catalyst for all economic growth. The ability for humanity to collectively rise above a day's work for a day's sustenance, by definition, required the economy to get more out of mankind's collective labor. At the same time, Smith argued that these newly discovered efficiencies that caused men to lose their livelihoods would seem cruel, but were inevitable as new ways replaced old. The interdependencies caused by industrialization, where one man's effort was tied to that of another and then another, were an abstraction. As people left the self-sufficient village farm, where shelter, food, and clothing were simple domestic responsibilities, the idea of losing one's place in the specialized economy was a danger that few had been exposed to.

To MAXIMIZE EFFICIENCY, just as people specialized in narrowly defined tasks in the English factories, nations fell into specific functions. America's place in this global supply chain came about by accident on a

1792 boat ride. On it was the widow of Nathanael Greene, a notable general from the Revolutionary War. A woman of society, Catharine Greene was making her return home to South Carolina from her annual summer in Newport, Rhode Island. On the leg of the voyage from New York City to the port of Savannah, traveling with her family, Mrs. Greene became acquainted with twenty-seven-year-old Eli Whitney, a recent graduate of Yale. Postgraduation, Whitney had arranged to serve as a tutor for a wealthy family in the South while preparing to study the law in his spare time.

Upon arriving in Savannah, Whitney traveled with the Greene family to their South Carolina plantation, Mulberry Grove, a short distance away. His original plan, as he recounted in a lengthy letter of explanation to his father, was to spend a few days at the Greenes' and then be on his way to his scheduled occupation. One account has it that the position had been filled, and in the time that it took for messages to travel in those days, Whitney couldn't be notified. Whitney's letter, however, pointed to a distraction presented by a "very respectable gentleman" who had pulled his attention away from pursuing both a paying occupation and his study of the law.

In the aftermath of the Revolution, with significant disruptions in trade between the revolting colonies and England, southern planters had looked to diversify away from rice and indigo. In the coastal areas around Georgia and South Carolina, a variety of fine cotton known as Sea Island seemed to grow especially well, but it required the soil variety found close to shore. Another variety, upland cotton, seemed to grow virtually anywhere in the Carolinas and Georgia, even in soil types unsuitable for much else, but the "extreme difficulty" of separating the seeds from the cotton made it close to useless, much to the respectable gentleman's lament. Therefore, America had never been much of a cotton producer. Making idle conversation, gentleman neighbors of the plantation had expressed longing for the invention of a machine created for the task.

Hearing this, Whitney, possessing considerable mechanical aptitude that he had exhibited even as a child, now set his imagination to the task of separating cotton from its seeds. After coming up with a few designs, Whitney brought his ideas to Phineas Miller, the manager of the Greene

Plantation and future husband of Mrs. Greene. Miller offered to finance Whitney's experiments and share the profits if anything came of the efforts. Within ten days, Whitney came up with a model; after a few more attempts, he had a fully functioning prototype for his cotton engine, shortened to "gin." It wasn't much of an actual engine—the cotton gin was a simple hand-cranked device that pressed the raw cotton against comblike metallic "teeth," with the seeds staying on one side of the teeth and the cotton fiber separated to the other.

As this prospect presented a "great thing for both the country and the inventor," Whitney let his father know that he was abandoning his career plans and "had concluded to relinquish my school to perfecting the machine." To assure his "Dear Parent" that such a decision was neither hasty nor foolhardy, he explained how the machine worked in detail, concluding: "How advantageous this business will eventually prove to me, I cannot say. It is generally said by those who know anything about it, that I shall make a fortune by it. . . . I am now so sure of success that ten thousand dollars, if I saw the money counted out to me, would not tempt me to give up my right and relinquish the object." His father, it could be surmised, was likely less than thrilled.

As time went on, the path to Eli's fortune turned out to be less than straightforward. However, his invention's impact on the lives of people, nations, and war and peace was staggering. At the core of its value was the gin's efficiency. In Whitney's estimation, with his machine one man could now do the work of fifty men. He exulted that not only did it make "labor fifty times less," but since almost no one was currently employed in America separating upland cotton, it would do so "without throwing any class out of business." This turned out to be the understatement of the century. Rather, the breakthrough of the cotton gin put the entire American South, powered by millions of black hands, in the business of growing cotton.

TWO YEARS BEFORE Whitney made his journey south, the Carolinas and Georgia had produced 3,000 bales of cotton, much of it the satinlike Sea Island variety. Ten years after he invented the cotton gin, annual production stood at 136,000 bales of cotton—equal to 68 million pounds in weight—almost all of the upland variety. This number too would be dwarfed in the coming years.

While the results of the efficiency gains were immediately clear, Whitney ran into issues in attempting to profit from his creation. Within months of building the prototype, he had applied for a U.S. patent. The framers of the American Constitution had understood intellectual property protections as fundamental to the "progress of sciences and useful arts." Before addressing the freedom of speech or religion through amendments, the American Constitution relegated to the federal government functions such as minting money, maintaining a postal service, and declaring and financing war, and the granting of copyrights and patents to protect "writings and discoveries." When granted, this formal recognition of the government in effect created property rights out of thin air, based on ideas and abstractions.

In 1793, when Whitney petitioned for protection, the task of evaluating patents fell to the Department of State. Remarkably, with the nation's population numbering less than four million, Secretary of State Thomas Jefferson himself took up the review of Whitney's patent. Replying to Whitney's application, Jefferson requested a working model be sent to him. But the correspondence turned more personal after the opening paragraph—Jefferson offered that as a Virginian, he considered the arduous separation of cotton from seed "one of our great embarrassments." He then asked Whitney a series of questions: Has the machine has been "thoroughly tried"? "What quantity of cotton has it cleaned?" "By how many hands?" "What will be the cost of one of them?" and then offered that "favorable answers to these questions" would induce him to buy one.

Whitney, like any entrepeneur, would have found this interaction highly encouraging, as the secretary of state had more or less asked to be an early customer. Whitney, along with Phineas Miller, his partner from the Greene plantation, now searched for the business model to turn the idea into the coveted fortune. One idea was to build the machines and operate cotton gins themselves, where the Miller & Whitney operation would separate the cotton from the seed, keeping one third of the cotton as their profit and giving the remainder of the cotton back to the grower or forwarding for further sale. This was an unfortunate scheme for several reasons, a victim of its own success. Whitney did not have the capacity to build enough machines to keep up with the pace of demand, which created incentive for even "honorable planters" to use the technique by creating their own devices—it was a lot to ask of a planter to restrain himself from separating cotton by a simple mechanical method that by now everyone knew and understood. Once a man had grasped Whitney's method, it was simply inconceivable to do it by hand. Yet Whitney didn't license the patent freely as a part of his business model, wishing to remain in control, an approach that seemed to guarantee widespread patent infringement.

Whitney's strategy faced another problem: To build and operate machines in the proprietary manner Whitney proposed was highly capital intensive. One option was to borrow money at high rates of interest. When searching for funds through a friend in Boston, he received a reply relaying the onerous terms of "one of those vultures called brokers, who are preying on the purse strings of the industrious." As Whitney had retreated to New Haven, Connecticut, to build a facility to manufacture gins, his partner in South Carolina sent panicked letters asking for "fifty to one hundred gins" before the next harvest of 1795. But the gin, being so simple to replicate by anyone with tools, allowed modest improvements in technique to bypass the patent with competing models. At the same time, the manufacturing concern of Miller & Whitney faced a more immediate catastrophe. Whitney's New Haven facility burned to the ground through an accidental fire—he was in debt to the tune of $4,000 without an operation. Miller consoled Whitney:

> It will be very extraordinary, if two young men, in the prime of their life, with some share of ingenuity, with a little knowledge of the world, a great deal of industry . . . should not be able to sustain such a stroke of misfortune such as this, heavy as it is.

Miller asked Whitney to rush to rebuild the facility and to borrow more money as rapidly as he could. In a last bit of counsel, he suggested to Whitney the importance of maintaining confidence in negotiations, of not seeming desperate, as the line between "the prospect of large gains and the approaches to bankruptcy" were rather thin. If it seemed things couldn't get any worse, they did. London traders complained about the impurities contained in the cotton ginned by Miller & Whitney. With a Georgia operation consisting of real estate and thirty operating gins in 1796, Miller & Whitney had picked a business model that left them unable to take full advantage of their intellectual property rights. They were left to borrow a final $1,000 at 30 percent—even this only due to a family connection through marriage. Even after a tour in England mollifying London traders and ongoing corrections to the device to increase the purity of the cotton, the infringing units in wide circulation in the South meant their operation had no real competitive advantage.

Facing such financial obstacles, Whitney then decided on a final business model: the threat of litigation. After winning one lawsuit in Georgia, Miller & Whitney began to focus instead on collecting licensing fees from any use of the Whitney techniques found in the South, essentially abandoning the idea of building gins or processing cotton on their own. This was met with resistance from southerners. By 1800 the technique of separating cotton with a simple machine bordered on common knowledge in Georgia and South Carolina—it seemed preposterous to pay fees, in essence an idea tax—for simply using one's own tools, property, and slaves to get cotton ready for market. Indeed, the entire nature of intellectual property rights such as patents, copyrights, and trademarks was in essence a restriction on someone else's physical right to copy something "protected." But even though protection of intellectual property was codified in the American Constitution, southerners demonstrated some early trouble respecting federal law.

In light of the apparent impossibility of collecting royalties from individual cotton planters in South Carolina, Miller & Whitney came up with another plan. They asked the legislature of the state of South

Carolina to license the patent rights to Whitney's invention for the whole state. "We will not go into any detailed calculations of this invention, but only to observe that the citizens of South Carolina have gained, and will gain, many millions of dollars by the use of this machine, which they never could have acquired without it." Miller & Whitney asked for $100,000. In 1801 South Carolina passed an act granting $50,000 to Miller & Whitney—$20,000 up front and three payments of $10,000 to be paid on a deferred basis. Now anyone in South Carolina had the right to gin cotton. The entirety of the sum would have barely enabled Whitney to pay the debts he had accumulated.

North Carolina, a state with a climate not as amenable to cotton production, was more progressive. It levied a small tax on every farmer ginning cotton by weight, with the proceeds going to Whitney after the expenses of tax collections. Tennessee levied an annual tax of 37 cents on every gin in operation in the state for four years as part of licensing the patent for the entire state.

But within two years, seeing an opening with a conflicting patent, South Carolina refused to make the three installment payments and sued for recovery of the initial $20,000; it eventually backtracked and rescinded the suit, but not before Whitney was made to feel like a "felon, a swindler, and a villain." While this was going on, Miller died, never getting the full satisfaction of the final settlements. The state of Georgia went even further. It accused Whitney's patent rights of being the device of Yankee "extortion." Whitney's interests would be litigated in Georgia courts for the better part of a decade.

By now, however, Whitney was on to a more lucrative venture altogether. Starting in 1798, having come to terms with the fact that little money would come to him from the cotton gin, he had turned his attention to weapons. With his skill in manufacturing and fame as inventor of the cotton gin, he received an initial order for ten thousand muskets for $134,000 from the U.S. government. His long-awaited fortune eventually came from guns. In doing so, Whitney set the stage for the Connecticut River Valley to become a leader in arms manufacturing, a competitive advantage for the North that poetically would be felt by South Carolina and Georgia decades later.

. . .

SEVEN YEARS AFTER he had received Whitney's application with enthusiasm, Thomas Jefferson became the third president of the United States. One federal purchase by Jefferson would dramatically enhance America's role in the global production of cotton. Within weeks of assuming the presidency, Jefferson heard rumors that Spain had recently transferred, via a secret treaty, a large portion of its North American territory to France. This territory, beginning in New Orleans, traced its footprint deep into the American interior in a large tract defined by the river system of the Mississippi. With the secretive Spanish transfer, Napoleon's France now owned a territory of 530 million acres, larger than what the United States itself constituted with all of its states and territories combined.

By the following year, the rumor had been confirmed. Jefferson then spent much of 1802 contemplating the implications of neighboring a large French holding. His immediate concern was access to New Orleans, where the Mississippi River emptied into the Gulf of Mexico—small streams and rivers as far north as Pennsylvania and New York merged and flowed into the vital Mississippi. Jefferson decided to dispatch James Monroe as a special envoy to negotiate with France. Once in Paris, Monroe was to join the American minister to France, Robert R. Livingston, to negotiate the purchase of New Orleans and territories near it. Jefferson authorized up to $10 million. Monroe and Livingston, however, were shocked at the French willingness to cede the entirety of the French holding in North America. As transoceanic communication was only as fast as that of a sailing vessel, and relaying the message back to Washington raised the risk of Napoleon changing his mind, the American negotiators went beyond their mandate and agreed in principle to pay $15 million for the territory ranging from New Orleans up to Canada, with a natural western border ending at the foothills of the Rocky Mountains. The news of the agreement took well over a month to reach the president. With the details finalized through the remainder of 1803, the United States more than doubled in size.

As America's rise in cotton production was just starting, it is doubtful

that Jefferson or anyone else could have foreseen the impact of the Louisiana Purchase, but it was immense beyond all estimation. The story
unfolded in geographic stages. It became clear soon enough that cotton
would not be spreading to Virginia and North Carolina in any meaningful
way—production was headed farther south. Climate was one limitation.
But after nearly a century and a half of tobacco farming, the Virginia soil
was substantially depleted.

In terms of labor supply, however, Virginia remained the leader, with
a surplus of idle hands due to the Revolutionary War's initial disruption
and subsequent decline in tobacco production. In addition, in a bid to
maintain the value of their slave property, slaveholders had acceded to
restrictions on the importation of new African captives, competing supplies of labor in an already saturated market. As a result, within twenty
years of adopting the Constitution, the United States prohibited the entry
of new slaves from Africa. As the last of the African slave ships unloaded
their advertised cargoes of "choice Gold Coast negroes" or "prime Man-
dingo Africans" in 1808, a vibrant internal slave market—the sale of slaves
from the old tobacco upper South to the new cotton lower South—was
born. If there had ever been an era of gentility or concepts of patriarchy or
Christian civility that men used to soften slavery's image to themselves,
the cold economics of cotton ended all such delusions.

With Whitney's gin invented there, meaningful cotton production
had first started in South Carolina and Georgia. By the 1820s, production had expanded to Alabama and Tennessee. By the 1830s, fast-rising
producers were added along the Mississippi Delta—Louisiana and
Mississippi—as South Carolina and Georgia faded in importance.
Virtually all of it was headed to mills in England. Cotton constituted
well over half of all American exports by midcentury—it grew into by far
the biggest sector of the economy—and the American South was soon
supplying over 70 percent of the world's raw cotton, producing well over
one billion pounds annually.

Mirroring this geographic shift, Maryland, Virginia, and the Carolinas became the leaders in slave exportation, selling hundreds of thousands of slaves to cotton plantations in Louisiana, Alabama, and
Mississippi. Soon the New York and London prices of cotton developed a

noticeable relationship to the price of slaves in the American Deep South. But during heated auctions for the best slaves, the relationship sometimes broke down; one trader noted on his era's frothy market conditions: "The old rule of pricing a negro by the price of cotton—that is to say, if cotton is worth twelve cents, a negro man is worth $1,200—if at fifteen cents, then $1,500—does not seem to be regarded."

One price was more predictable: As British industry became increasingly efficient at spinning cotton into yarn and weaving yarn into cloth, the price of cloth dropped dramatically decade after decade. The luxury of an occasional change of clothing became an affordable necessity for millions across the globe—industrial efficiency had turned desires into fundamental needs.

Five

STEAM

In the 1780s, as if propelled by magic, John Fitch's experimental boats went up and down the Delaware River to the dropped jaws of sailors and rowers as he passed them by. Fitch was an obsessive inventor. His first models did not scale or travel far, but his years of tireless advocacy for the steamboat had drawn him into the acquaintance of notable men including George Washington and Benjamin Franklin. Over time, Fitch's models improved. Investors supplied the capital that allowed him to build increasingly large models able to ferry handfuls of passengers across and up rivers for short distances. The steam engine, applied to a boat, allowed for on-demand propulsion for the first time in human history.

To that point in history, travel had been limited to organic modes: water current, the wind, animals, or one's own feet. Traveling upstream was an especially arduous and slow process. To go against a strong downstream current, boats often required poles pushing off riverbeds or ropes pulled along the sides of riverbanks. As a result, the great American rivers on the eastern seaboard such as the Hudson, Delaware, and Connecticut remained underutilized.

As word spread, Fitch's early accomplishments were credible enough for state governments to pay close attention. To encourage Fitch to attempt his operations in New York, the state legislature granted Fitch a fourteen-year monopoly on the exclusive use of the steamboat in New

York if he created a commercially viable model that could run for long distances. Just as King James's patent grants to the Virginia Company induced private investment in the New World, grants of monopoly rights drew private capital to risky ventures.

But Fitch faced two related problems: power and weight. He had to figure out how to generate enough steam power while carrying the large amount of energy needed for longer journeys. The weight of the energy source, dried pinewood at the time, was enough of a drag on speed to make most journeys unviable for the transportation of commercial goods. And stagecoaches, even on the crude roads of the time, could transport passengers alongside the rivers at lower rates. The steamboat's lack of immediate commercial viability meant little money for the ongoing research and development of improved models. Adding insult to injury, Fitch lost his shares in the venture as more money had to be raised.

Penniless, Fitch was unable to improve his steamboat to take advantage of his monopoly. New York then revoked the monopoly on the grounds that Fitch had not "made any attempt in the space of more than ten years for executing the plan for which he obtained an exclusive privilege." Unlike with Eli Whitney, there was no recovery for Fitch, no saving grace for the inventor of the steamboat. With the disappointment of his setbacks playing a role, Fitch killed himself in 1798.

The state of New York, however, remained undeterred. Starting on the west side of Manhattan the Hudson River was the primary artery into the vastness upstate with its endless acres of farmland. Pioneers, along with Old Dutch and German families, continued to settle the frontiers, but a trip from New York to Albany, an upriver stretch of 150 miles, could take as many as seven days via sailboat. Such a trip, with its costs in money and time, was often a one-way journey to settle the river valley. It was this constriction on commerce and communication that had led the New York legislature to encourage the development of steam power for river travel.

The state then turned to Robert R. Livingston. A member of a prominent and wealthy New York family, Livingston had played a role at the Continental Congress during the drafting of the Declaration of Independence, while another member of his family had signed it. The exclusive terms granted to him were contingent on performance: If within one year Livingston developed a steamboat with twenty tons of capacity and capable of upstream speeds of four miles per hour, the state would grant Livingston's venture a monopoly on New York waters for a period of twenty years. To maintain the twenty-year term, Livingston needed to operate a commercial service between New York and Albany.

Livingston, sufficiently induced by the prospect of a monopoly, proceeded to invest in the research and development to build a viable steamboat. It would be a sizable gamble. Steam travel had barely achieved a four-mile-per-hour speed at any weight, and never at a weighted capacity as high as twenty tons, as required by the terms of the state legislature. From the state's perspective, a grant of monopoly cost nothing from its treasury, but were it successful, the state's citizens and landowners would benefit economically, even if the operator extracted monopoly rates for a period of time.

But Livingston failed to meet the one-year deadline. For this favored son of New York, the legislature then extended it. This pattern of failure and extension would be repeated several times, especially as Livingston had taken on additional responsibilities: He became the American minister to France, a role of such strategic importance that it had been filled by both Thomas Jefferson and Benjamin Franklin in the country's short history. In 1803, as Livingston was negotiating the Louisiana Purchase to significantly expand America and add the Mississippi River in the process, the New York legislature extended his time to meet the conditions for another two years.

Livingston found his solution in France.

A PORTRAIT ARTIST turned self-styled engineer, Robert Fulton had thought up several concepts for a steamboat that would have fit Livingston's New York mandate. But as with many things Fulton touched at the time, "concept" remained the operative word. The thirty-six-year-old Fulton had spent the second half of his life splitting time between Paris and London, having left America in 1786. His London sponsor at one time was notable artist Benjamin West, who had encouraged Fulton as a painter and sculptor. But Fulton's imagination wandered after not achieving any substantial success in the arts. A true polymath, Fulton turned to the sciences. He became increasingly obsessed with mechanical engineering, specifically anything having to do with water. And unable to suppress his myriad enthusiasms and theories, he maintained an energetic stream of correspondence with politicians back in America filled with ideas.

After a few years, Fulton left London for Paris. Once there, he painted. He designed. He philosophized. And he lobbied. Among his preoccupations, Fulton was busy tinkering with designs for all types of water-based inventions, including torpedoes and submarines based on the use of compressed air.

His maritime experiments brought him the favorable attention, temporarily, of both the French and British navies. His experiments eventually failed but had gained enough traction that they attracted the interest of another notable innovator in Napoleon. The Emperor's interest didn't lead anywhere either. Besides, Fulton had a different motivation than his would-be customers. Fulton's primary mission was to invent weaponry so powerful that it would render naval warfare futile. He envisioned submarine-fired torpedoes creating a mutually assured destruction scenario among the parties that would "put a stop to maritime wars" and free the seas for peaceful, "humane" pursuits.

He continued to spend many years peppering people like Thomas Jefferson with letters and drawings. He pressed the secretary of the navy. For a man committed to ending naval warfare, Fulton seems to have spent enormous energy trying to sell weapons. In the end, all of his marketing efforts with both domestic and foreign navies failed. But another member of Jefferson's government offered Fulton his best prospects.

Livingston, while in Paris on diplomatic duties, had heard of this expatriate American experimenting with maritime designs. In 1803, with Fulton maintaining his substantial gap between genius and achievement, Livingston's overtures arrived just in time.

With the statesman as a benefactor, Fulton turned his attention to steamboats. Fulton, being Fulton, had some familiarity with most of the earlier methods of harnessing steam power for propulsion. Through this point, much of the effort had involved a screw propeller, the fanlike device at the back of a boat—the steam pressure captured by the engine turned the propeller to make the boat move. When engineers considered other techniques, their efforts tended to veer toward moderate increases in the size of the vessels.

To Fulton, moderation seemed the wrong approach. Reflecting on his observations of other efforts in Paris, Fulton came to the realization that a giant paddle wheel attached to the side of the vessel, rather than a screw propeller at the back, might be the answer. The variables of power, distance, speed, and capacity all had to be made to work in order to take advantage of Livingston's monopoly grant—by now Livingston had added Fulton's name to it. Larger size meant the need for a larger engine; the larger engine required more coal to operate; more coal added to the weight. By the time Fulton came to his conclusions, his design called for a steam vessel considerably larger than anything built before. On using the previously overlooked paddle wheel, Fulton offered modestly "that the fault has not been in the wheel, but in the ignorance of proportion, velocities, powers, and possibly mechanical combinations."

Livingston asked for a model of small scale to be built in Paris. Fulton complied. It showed enough promise for Fulton, with Livingston's backing, to order a large engine from James Watt's company in England to be delivered to America. After twenty years away from America, Fulton came home to see his vision built. In America, Fulton began construction of a vessel 133 feet long with a tonnage of 160—eight times that required by New York. The engine itself was twenty feet long, seven feet high, and eight feet wide. It dwarfed all previous efforts. And it was a massive financial bet.

On a Monday in August 1807, Fulton's boat, the *North River Steamboat*, was ready for its trial run to Albany. It was docked in lower Manhattan, where crowds had formed to see the boat slowly move from the wharf. Fulton heard the snickers and "sarcastic remarks" of "ignorant men." He estimated that "there were not thirty persons in the city who believed that the boat would ever move one mile an hour, or be of the least utility." With smoke plumes tracing its course, the *North River* slipped past view after a few minutes, headed north on the Hudson. It was a triumph. In thirty-two hours the boat had reached Albany, averaging close to five miles per hour upstream. It then turned around and came back down in thirty hours.

Vindicated, Fulton wrote a letter to a friend that made no mention of commercial success. In his moment, he thought in terms of national glory:

> Having employed much time, money and zeal in accomplishing this work, it gives me great pleasure to see it answer my expectations. It will give a cheap and quick conveyance to the merchandise on the Mississippi, Missouri, and other great rivers, which are now laying open their treasures to the enterprise of our countrymen; and, although the prospect of personal emolument has been some inducement to me, yet I feel infinitely more pleasure reflecting on the immense advantage my country will derive from the invention.

Fulton was right. The Mississippi, the Ohio, and every major river would soon have steamboats churning up and down their waters, moving goods and people. And just as remarkably, Livingston, the same man who played a critical role in negotiating the purchase of Louisiana, had now played a central role in making the territory accessible.

With the success of their steamboat, Livingston and Fulton triggered their monopoly rights in New York, now set to expire in 1827. By the fall of the first year, the *North River Steamboat* had an established pricing schedule with an overnight passenger fare of $7 from New York to Albany. Within a few years, the venture added ferry service between Manhattan and other points and built and operated a fleet of vessels, some almost twice the tonnage of the original. With his fame, Fulton even finally managed to sell something to the U.S. Navy during the War of 1812; a steamboat built at a cost of $320,000, it was named *Fulton the First*.

SUCCESS FOR BOTH MEN was short-lived. Livingston, after a long and storied career in politics, succumbed to old age and died in 1813. Fulton, considerably younger, died at forty-nine two years later. His death was front-page news, with obituaries celebrating his genius. He had fallen sick after spending a day in New Jersey engaged in a legal matter that went on to have significant constitutional implications. The question at hand: Since the North River Steamboat Company owned the monopoly rights on New York waters, was a New Jersey operator then prohibited from operating a service between New Jersey and Manhattan, since such a service would enter New York waters?

When Livingston passed away in 1813, his heirs inherited the monopoly rights for steamboats on New York waterways. Rather than litigate, almost all independent operators of steamboats conducted business under license from Livingston's family. With New Jersey sharing waterways with New York, new operators that wished to run steamboats to New York required consent from the Livingston monopoly.

But a man named Thomas Gibbons refused to cooperate.

Sharp, combative, and physically imposing, Gibbons was a wealthy former plantation owner from Savannah who had recently moved to New Jersey. He had leased a steamboat pier on a property he owned to his neighbor, Aaron Ogden, who had received a license from the Livingstons after suing them. A dispute between the neighbors, however, came to a boiling point, and Gibbons decided to enter the steamboat business. Gibbons, sixty years old in 1817, first preferred the simpler methods of a duel to settle the dispute, challenging Ogden at his home, but times had changed in New Jersey from when an incumbent vice president had killed the nation's first treasury secretary. Neighbor Ogden, a former New Jersey senator and governor, refused to duel and had Gibbons arrested instead.

Gibbons resorted to plan B. He purchased a small, secondhand steamboat called the *Stoudinger* and started to ferry passengers between Elizabethtown, New Jersey, and lower Manhattan. As Gibbons had the benefit of owning his own dock, which he had rented out to licensed operators like Ogden, he had a unique option. But Gibbons did not ask for or seek any license from the Livingston monopoly. He simply began operating his service.

But he soon had a labor problem that needed solving. When the captain of the *Stoudinger* quit suddenly, Gibbons found himself on the wharves of New York, where he learned of the reliability and courage of a twenty-three-year-old ferry operator. Young Cornelius Vanderbilt would become a key participant in the battle to end the monopoly on the Hudson. One day the proudly uneducated Vanderbilt would become the richest man in America. For now, he was looking to make a switch from sail to steam.

Born to a working-class family with Dutch roots dating back to 1650, Vanderbilt ran small sailboats between Staten Island and Manhattan. His work was of a brutal, physical nature, pitting him and his boats against the wind and frigid waters. As a young man, he was a sailor through and through in temperament, physique, and profession. While Vanderbilt was making a good living and saving up his profits as an operator of his own boats, his income was still largely tied to his individual physical effort. Seeing the gleaming new steamboats, largely immune to weather conditions, he could sense that wind would soon entirely give way to steam. But he couldn't enter the capital-intensive steamboat business on his own.

Hearing Gibbons's overture, Vanderbilt took command of the *Stoudinger* for what he expected would be a temporary position. But Gibbons thoroughly impressed the usually unimpressible Vanderbilt, who in late-life reflections assessed his employer as "the strongest I ever knew," a high honor of commercial tough-mindedness. For the next season Gibbons planned to launch another vessel, the *Bellona*. To keep Vanderbilt enticed, Gibbons agreed to pay his young captain $60 per month and half of the profits from the operation of the bar on board. As a side benefit, Vanderbilt watched a master of litigation and confrontation openly defy New York law; this tutorial, of course, would come in handy.

Beyond any ambitions for steamboat dominance—he was sixty and already rich—Gibbons seemed to thrive on the visceral thrill of satisfaction, of avenging his honor. Had his rival Ogden acceded to a trial with pistols, the battles of the courtroom and marketplace could have been avoided. On his route Gibbons could and did charge considerably less than Ogden and other licensed rivals; he didn't have to account for the cost of a license from the monopoly. Predictably, Gibbons was served for violating the monopoly—a New York court promptly issued an injunction against further operation of the *Bellona*. Gibbons, a trained lawyer himself, had known this would happen. With sage advice from Aaron Burr, the former vice president, Gibbons planned his appeal. At the center of the strategy was to have all state monopoly grants on waterways ruled unconstitutional. To do so, he sought and received permission to navigate all waters under a federal act. With this in hand, Gibbons looked to invalidate the Livingston monopoly, pitting federal authority against the power of the individual states.

Gibbons then sued Ogden in federal court with the help of another lawyer of considerable oratorical skill experienced in such matters: Daniel Webster. Webster's argument was that the steamboat monopolies granted by the individual states violated the commerce clause of the Constitution. In 1824 *Gibbons v. Ogden* was decided by the Supreme Court in the aging Gibbons's favor. *Gibbons v. Ogden* went on to become the landmark case affirming that only the federal government had the right to regulate interstate commerce. Waterways and roads connecting states all fell within the framework, as ruled by the court: The era of monopoly grants was over. Indeed, it fell upon the native southerner Gibbons, a plantation owner from Savannah, to affirm the superiority of federal rights over the states' rights in matters of interstate commerce.

BUT THE ULTIMATE beneficiary of the court's decision was Gibbons's irascible captain. John Fitch's frustrations, which led to his swallowing a bottle of opium pills; Fulton and Livingston's short-lived period of glory before their deaths; Gibbons's genius in opening up the waters on constitutional grounds; and countless investors and theorists dating back to the 1780s all contributed to the making of one of America's greatest capitalists. He was no scientist or engineer. Legal scholarship and affairs of state were not his bailiwick. Vanderbilt's contribution was his commercial orientation. "Truly a creature of the market," noted his biographer T. J. Stiles, "law, rank, the traditional social bonds—these things meant nothing to him. Only power earned his respect, and he felt his own strength gathering with every modest investment, every scrap of legal knowledge, every business lesson."

To start, Vanderbilt had all the habits of thrift and parsimony that Benjamin Franklin preached in his *Ways to Wealth*, although it was most unlikely that he would have read a word of it. Vanderbilt saved his money. Even with a strong wage and ample profits from the bar on the boats, the accommodations he provided for his family left much to be desired. Soon the family moved to a residence that served as an inn for passengers coming off the steamboat *Bellona*, Bellona Hall. Vanderbilt's wife, Sophia, managed the inn while raising her growing family—she eventually gave birth to fourteen children. One account held that Vanderbilt virtually lived on Gibbons's boats, tirelessly working, and the income from Bellona Hall provided for the household expenses.

The family's parsimony, even as Vanderbilt's share of Gibbons's profits grew, created the basis for his ascendance. When Gibbons died in 1826, his son inherited the fleet of boats. Rather than have Vanderbilt on salary, William Gibbons leased the *Bellona* to him for a flat fee. Gibbons then gave Vanderbilt one of his routes. With all of the money he had accumulated, thirty-three-year-old Vanderbilt commissioned the construction of a steamboat of his own, the *Citizen*. With the now-ubiquitous side paddle wheel, the *Citizen* was smaller than Fulton's original, but it was Vanderbilt's own a full eleven years after meeting Thomas Gibbons for the first time. Back then, he had willingly given up his entrepreneurial independence to enter a field he could not otherwise afford to. Now he was his own man—he had side businesses, to be sure, but they were ancillary to his daily commercial activities. A year later the younger Gibbons sold his assets to someone else. With this, Vanderbilt shed all past ties.

Over the next decade, the steamboat business grew in the number of routes and volume of passengers. Vanderbilt, his thrift enabling him to be the perpetual low-cost operator, practiced a simple strategy. When he decided to compete for a route, he offered fares 50 percent or even 75 percent below the incumbent. He sold his first boat, the *Citizen*, for $30,000 after three years of use to a competitor who simply wanted to avoid price wars. For a venture, called the Dispatch Line, that he formed with stage-coach operators between Philadelphia and a harbor across Manhattan, he bought the old *Bellona* back into his fold for $15,000. This process repeated itself a few times: enter a market, undercut prices to the point of causing pain, and get bought out. Other times, when Vanderbilt operated a route as an incumbent, competitors avoided entering the market.

In all this Vanderbilt cast himself as the antimonopolist—a man who looked down on established men unable to compete, to the same degree they looked down on his predatory behavior as unseemly. At one point he even wore the mantle of social justice, advertising one operation as "People's Line—FOR NEW YORK—No Monopoly" with a cut-rate fare of $3 from Albany to New York. Within a few months, the company he accused of being monopolistic paid him $100,000 and guaranteed him $5,000 annually to remove his People's Line from service.

Indeed, in a time before bridges, the island of Manhattan, a city growing rapidly in importance, could be accessed from the mainland only by crossing water. In the waters around this island, Vanderbilt built the first wave of his fortune and prepared to meet new threats on the horizon.

Six

CANALS

While steam travel had conquered American rivers, another geographic feature continued to present a substantial obstacle to commerce. The mountain range known as the Appalachians cut through most of the early colonies, including New York, Pennsylvania, Maryland, Virginia, North Carolina, South Carolina, and Georgia, creating an eastern seaboard confined by mountains on one side and the Atlantic Ocean on the other. Areas west of the mountains were largely inaccessible, sparsely populated frontier lands.

With the rapid adoption of the steamboat, the costs of water-based transportation had contracted to a fraction of those of land-based transportation. Via land, the considerable exertion of horses, oxen, and people, along with rough roads, made for a time-consuming, exhausting, and expensive proposition. Even in flatlands, the capacity to carry goods by carriage, if pulled by a team of horses, was limited to a few tons per effort. Through the mountains it was virtually impossible. As a result, land-based commerce between the eastern and western parts of states like New York and Pennsylvania was nonexistent. When it was possible, with the products of the interior lands primarily grains or perishable crops, the transportation costs due to weight or spoilage caused by time eliminated coastal markets. On water, much more was possible.

Waterways made accessible by steam power now meant that areas along the Mississippi River were in position to develop quickly. But it also presented a significant dilemma to eastern states. It was cheaper to transport goods from Pittsburgh to New Orleans than across the state to Philadelphia. As the Allegheny River proceeded south from its origins in western New York, grain could theoretically travel downstream to Pittsburgh, where the river merged with the Monongahela River to form the Ohio River; the Ohio then flowed into the Mississippi all the way to the Gulf of Mexico. This meant that areas in the vicinity of the Great Lakes were commercially more connected to the American South than to their neighbors on the Atlantic shore. The eastern seaboard, however, had millions of people. An easier route to the eastern ports from western territories would mean new opportunities. For the large land speculators holding inaccessible land in the West, access would mean skyrocketing values on millions of acres. But the stakes were not solely commercial. Inaccessibility meant disconnectedness. For a young nation, especially a republic of near-sovereign states, such physical separation meant risking a rupture of fragile political bonds.

A bold plan that had seemed to be the key to unlocking the American interior, despite repeated failures in the past, kept resurfacing. The idea's potential had even once managed to captivate and then stymie the greatest of American heroes, George Washington. In the immediate period after the Treaty of Paris, which resulted in British recognition of American independence, General Washington expected to retire to life as a private citizen. His needs at once became ordinary: He needed to earn money to make up for the years he had given up to command the Continental Army. One venture soon consumed him. Well before the war, Washington had accumulated tens of thousands of acres for speculation in the Ohio Country, the areas of present-day West Virginia through which the Ohio River briefly runs before veering farther west. Washington's plan in 1785 was to build a canal that would connect the Potomac River to the waters of the Ohio River.

At its core, a canal is a narrow man-made ditch that, once filled with water, connects two other natural bodies of water through an artificial river of sorts, making it possible to transport people and goods from one body of water to the other. The purpose of Washington's canal was to create water navigation from the western territories to the Atlantic with the Potomac, passing by Washington's backyard at Mount Vernon, as the final conduit. It would have made his beloved Virginia the primary American gateway to its vast interior.

To make this happen, the Virginia and Maryland legislatures, with Washington as an advocate and supporter, jointly formed the Potomac Company. General Washington was appointed head of the company. As gratitude and to serve as "durable monuments of his glory," as the forming documents stated, the Virginia state legislature granted Washington fifty of the five hundred shares to be sold to private investors in the company. Once the canal was built, the toll revenues from canal boats would go to the private benefit of the company and its investors. For the states of Virginia and Maryland, the public benefit would be derived through the commercial opportunities presented by goods flowing through the states—at the same time, leaving the task entirely to a private entity meant none of the public's money would be used for construction.

Washington would undoubtedly have benefited from the surge in land values of his Ohio Country acreage. However, given his public standing, he was reluctant to have his motivations be seen as financial: When the state of Virginia enacted legislation granting Washington his fifty shares, Washington postured hesitantly. He requested that he be able to bequeath his shares in the future to a cause of a public nature if he chose to, a middle ground that allowed him to own the shares but maintain the dignity of being above material interests. Given that the fifty shares were of the same class of shares that others were subscribing to at $444 per share, Washington's ownership stake was nominally valued at $22,000.

If the Potomac Company was successful in building a canal connecting the Ohio and Potomac rivers, it would have been the largest private project yet completed up to that point in American history. All of the stars seemed aligned. James Madison and Thomas Jefferson were both in favor of the Potomac Company and its future impact on the fortunes of their Virginia. Wealthy planters on both sides of the Chesapeake in Maryland and Virginia looked forward to this transformative feat to restore their lost tobacco fortunes. The Potomac Company's leader was the greatest American hero and an international celebrity. Labor was cheap—thousands of slaves from tobacco plantations were idle. If private financing for a large-scale infrastructure project could ever be willed at the time, the Potomac Company's circumstances were as right as they could be.

Of course, it didn't happen. The Potomac Company stalled out of the gate. The plan had been that the venture would need to raise ongoing capital in addition to the initial investment to complete construction. A common practice at the time was to structure ventures as subscriptions, so when investors committed to buying shares, they paid a part of it upfront with an obligation to pay the remainder as the company called for it. But the initial subscribers seemed to have second thoughts. Both the Virginia and Maryland legislatures had to repeatedly enact legislation imposing penalties on investors for failing to come up with the money that their subscriptions required. By 1789 General Washington's personal window for a major commercial success had passed: He became the president of the United States. The Potomac Company, ultimately, would fail to accomplish its mission.

WHILE WASHINGTON WAS PRESIDENT, he heard from the young Robert Fulton, as did seemingly everyone who had access to a national or military budget. Before Fulton found acclaim with commercial steamboats, he had once been obsessed with canals. In 1796, while in London, he published his dense 100-plus-page manifesto titled *Treatise on the Improvement of Canal Navigation*. Fulton, awarding himself the title of civil engineer, went on to detail the geography of multiple nations, centuries' worth of history on the canals of Europe and China, and the economic advantages of free-flowing commerce, along with technical detail after technical detail about a locking system that would enable large-scale canals. Fulton had tables detailing the unit economics of road-based transportation versus the projected costs via canals.

His final chapters, however, offered some specific ideas for his native country. Addressing the governor of Pennsylvania, Thomas Mifflin, Fulton argued for a canal of massive scale in America. Years before his concept for the steamboat, he called for a wide canal favoring large boats of capacity exceeding twenty tons. His argument was that it would cost as much to traffic a small boat as a large one. If the canal favored large boats, though the initial capital requirement for construction would be much larger, the long-term costs to transport each ton of goods would be far lower. The *Treatise* would have left few readers doubting Fulton's immense intellect and range, while raising plenty of new questions regarding his sense of practicality or proportion.

President Washington, having received a copy, wrote a letter to Fulton acknowledging the logic of it. In response, Fulton, in a letter addressed to "His Excellency George Washington" in the waning months of his presidency, guaranteed that if his ideas were pursued in earnest by each of the states, it would "in less than a century bring water carriage" accessible to "every acre of the American States."

For starters, Fulton called for the longest canal in the history of the world: a 360-mile canal connecting Philadelphia to Pittsburgh, right through the heart of Pennsylvania. At the time, the idea must have seemed preposterous to almost everyone except a few people like Washington, who had spent years in a similar attempt.

One of the major challenges of long canals was the height of the mountains. Unless a canal wanted to zigzag inefficiently for miles, it had to scale mountains. It is simple in principle to connect two bodies of water at the same elevation—just dig a ditch. It is quite another to impose a canal through mountains connecting bodies of water with an elevation difference measured in the hundreds of feet. In addition, the water source at the higher elevation must be especially strong, so as to maintain adequate flow of water through the canal.

In America small-scale canals bridging a few hundred feet to a mile or two existed, but these were largely to make an existing waterway more efficient or to go around a waterfall or other obstruction. These efforts were not the fulfillment of Washington's or Fulton's vision of opening up the western territories to the Atlantic. But by 1805, during Jefferson's presidency, the case for federal financing of large-scale projects was being strongly considered. Jefferson, not one to assert federal supremacy in most matters, saw firsthand that private financing was not wholly reliable for large-scale infrastructure—public improvements, as they were known—even in the most favorable of circumstances. There was another reason that Jefferson was open. The federal government was running large budget surpluses. This was due to revenue from federal land sales to private citizens and companies. To Jefferson, it made sense to allocate this surplus to public improvements benefiting the Union.

He authorized his treasury secretary, Albert Gallatin, to come up with a plan. Gallatin, in his report, made an argument that continues to serve as the rationale for infrastructure spending in the United States. There were infrastructure projects whose revenues might not be sufficient to cover the direct costs, yet such projects carried significant benefits to consumers, farmers, manufacturers, exporters, cities, and the country as a whole. Additionally, he argued that each state and community executing projects exclusive of the other deprived the economy as a whole of the benefits of cohesion. This cohesion could come only through federal planning.

Using this rationale, Gallatin called for large-scale building of canals and roads. He proposed and budgeted for numerous canals of approximately twenty miles, each with a digging cost of $20,000 per mile. To be fair to all states, the public works were carefully apportioned to be largely equal. But Gallatin found the notion of a large-scale canal hundreds of miles long, connecting western rivers with the Atlantic, to be impractical. Even if it were practical, through which state would this massive canal be constructed? In early America, federal financing of just one state's large canal to the exclusion of other states would have been a political nonstarter, contrary to the idea of a republic of equal states. So the idea of a large canal stalled.

ON A SUMMER DAY IN 1807, close to the day when Livingston and Fulton's *North River* stunned critics and the age of the steamboat dawned, Jesse Hawley was entering debtors' prison in a small town in western New York hundreds of miles away. Hawley, a small grain trader, had run into financial difficulties due to a partner, and had run off rather than face his debts. He was eventually found and, being indebted beyond his capacity to pay, was sentenced to debtors' prison. This was in the days before entrepreneurs could freely, without any special permission, set up corporations that limited their liability. With a lot of time on his hands,

Hawley decided to have a few of his essays published in a local news-paper, the *Genesee Messenger*. Understanding his lack of credibility as a prisoner, Hawley decided to write under the pen name "Hercules." For six months starting in the fall of 1807, Hercules published a series of essays detailing his ideas for a canal going through New York.

Using maps from the Holland Land Company and his imagination, Hawley detailed how a canal starting at Lake Erie and finishing across the state at Albany would be viable, carefully noting the distance between various points and elevations along the way. In his first essay, he recognized that the "magnitude of this improvement is beyond the reach of individual capital in America." He then suggested that the federal government be called upon to finance it: "The common purpose of government is protection. But can it not be made to do more?" He projected that an immense amount of goods would flow through such waters, new fertile lands would be opened, and animal and manual labor used for local land-based transportation would be freed up for cultivation.

Rivaling the past visions of Washington and Fulton, the canal proposed by this Hercules would open up the entire Great Lakes to New York City and the Atlantic Ocean. His tone in each subsequent essay became more strident and detailed. Remarkably, the ideas in his pseud-onymous essays resonated enough to influence power brokers throughout the state. Men including the mayor of New York and the future governor recalled years later hearing of the concept for the first time through Hawley's columns in the *Messenger*.

Two forces gave the idea its initial momentum: The success of the steamboat that summer opened up a new, exuberant sense of possibility in New York, and state politicians at the time maintained hopes of federal financing. But one prominent Virginian objected. Jefferson called "making a canal of 350 miles" through the wilderness "little short of madness." Besides, Jefferson pointed out, even General Washington had been unable to raise a mere $200,000 from the various investors involved—private-market rejection seeming to invalidate the idea overall—while this Hercules's unschooled estimate, which became a nominal benchmark, stood at a preposterous $6 million.

Undeterred, the state of New York was determined to build the canal, but it would take years. It had a political champion in DeWitt Clinton. Clinton was the mayor of New York, a former U.S. senator, and a member of a prominent family. Understanding the impact of a canal on the finances of his city, which would serve as the primary access point to the entire Northwest, Clinton pressed the New York legislature. Predictably, he met resistance from political opponents.

But the momentum was building. Anticipating surging land prices, major landowners in western New York, including the Holland Land Company and the Western Inland Company, predictably expressed a strong interest in having such a canal built. Before their deaths, Livingston and Fulton, enjoying their fame and fortunes from their steamboat monopolies, were in full support, understanding the value of increased steamboat traffic from Albany, where the proposed canal was to end at the Hudson River, to Manhattan. Farmers saw the potential of having new markets within easy access of the water.

Clinton would fail at various legislative points repeatedly. Newspapers scoffed at the plan's expense and impracticality. Various provincial interests throughout New York needed to be mollified, lobbied, and coalesced. The basic issue was how to pay for the canal, which, it turned out, was going to cost very close to what Hawley (Hercules) had projected from prison. To put in perspective the more than $6 million that Clinton proposed New York take on, it is worth noting that the entire federal budget for 1811 was $8 million. But Clinton's stature had grown; he was elected governor of New York in 1816. He immediately made the Erie Canal his primary objective.

Unlike the efforts of Maryland and Virginia, however, Clinton's New York was going to take on the project as a public initiative. Private ownership of the canal was ruled out, however, private financing was not. To raise the capital, the state of New York created the Canal Fund, which would borrow money by selling public bonds to private investors. The bondholder would be entitled to interest payments from the Canal Fund; the fund would pay this interest from toll revenues collected from boats that passed through the canal. In Clinton's first year in office, the bill passed.

On July 4, 1817, construction began on a 363-mile canal.

.   .   .

THE PLAN WAS to dig all the way from Lake Erie to Albany. The construction relied on a series of locks, gated sections underneath that locked out and released water, which would gradually allow vessels to descend into the Hudson River at the other end of the state. Thousands of men would be put to work. While the plan for Washington's ill-fated canal to the Ohio River would have had slaves digging, New York used a cost-saving innovation: explosives. Mountains would be blasted with the powder from a Delaware outfit named E. I. du Pont de Nemours; this powder was DuPont's only product for the first sixty years of its existence.

The efforts needed another tool. In addition to buying tens of thousands of acres of land from companies including the Holland Land Company, the state authorized the Canal Commission responsible for construction to exercise the right known as eminent domain, which allowed the state to compel a private property holder to sell land that the government needed for a public purpose. Indeed, if the canal were a private effort, private holders would have been forced to sell their land to a private company, perhaps a less politically palatable exchange than a transfer to a public entity. Once completed, the plan projected 500,000 tons of annual traffic moving through the proposed canal. At a toll rate of $2.50 per ton, the planners calculated revenue of $1.25 million per year.

In financing the canal, New York brokerage houses sold Erie Canal bonds to wealthy individuals, overseas investors, and savings banks, making it one of the first public projects to raise money for a specific purpose tied to a revenue stream—"revenue bonds" in contemporary municipal finance terms. After eight years of construction, the total debt stood at $7.8 million.

But the Erie Canal opened in sections as it was being built. Every section became instant proof of the canal's value as a propeller of commerce. Traffic grew immediately every time a section opened. When the full canal opened in 1825, its revenues from tolls vastly exceeded all expectations. The initial projection of 500,000 annual tons of goods within twenty years was exceeded within ten. Within twenty years of its opening, over a million tons per year were being transported on the Erie Canal.

Overnight, the commercial implications were clear. Goods from Cleveland could end up in New York within days. Chicago was completely accessible by water from New York through the Great Lakes. With the Mississippi River already the conduit to New Orleans, a very large part of the United States could now be accessed by waterways. The Erie Canal's financial success set off canal mania in other states, which saw that it had cost the state of New York nothing financially—the tolls were more than sufficient to pay off the bonds—while transforming the state economy and driving down the price of grain. It was the model of successful public infrastructure.

To emulate New York's success, canals became the rage for states and private operators. Maryland sponsored a canal between the Chesapeake and the Delaware River. Starting construction in 1826, Pennsylvania looked to one-up New York with a canal to Pittsburgh; it would be a hybrid called the Main Line that included turnpike roads, tunnels through mountains, and other conveyances. Outside of New York, the impact of canal mania was greatest along the Ohio River, which formed the southern border of three states: Ohio, Indiana, and Illinois. To the north, these three states had access to either Lake Michigan or Lake Erie. In Ohio, with Lake Erie to the north and the Ohio River to the south, numerous canals formed interior arteries that opened up the entire state. A canal named the Ohio and Erie Canal went from Cleveland to the Ohio River 350 miles to the south. Another, the Miami and Erie, went from Toledo to Cincinnati. With these two long north–south canals connecting Lake Erie to the Ohio River, the Ohio Country that George Washington and his peers had invested in more than eighty years earlier rapidly gained in value. Indiana, with access to Lake Michigan, resembled Ohio by 1840. Water transport was within a dozen miles of millions of previously inaccessible acres.

In an agrarian society, as America was at the time, the intrinsic value of land was based on crop yield. How much could be grown and how much could be sold? For a long time the answer to the latter question was limited, as little could be transported. Land had always been abundant, but its utility less so. Now people moved in. The prospect of farming much larger parcels of land meant a significant increase in economic opportunity. For young men and their families, fertile land was still cheap, provided that they were willing to move. As many were new immigrants with no roots in America to begin with, they were. With steamboats operating along natural waterways, the population of the Northwest had grown from 292,000 in 1810 to 859,000 by 1820. By 1830 the population of the Northwest doubled to 1.6 million and doubled again ten years later to 3.3 million. The canals had opened up the West.

For New York City, with the Erie's bond issue as a success story, bond sales for other canals, infrastructure projects, state governments, and the federal government started flowing through its growing banking houses, a start that would eventually cement the city as the nation's leading capital market. As a shipping port, and with people and goods moving between the American interior and the city, New York's economic trajectory would lead it to dwarf the competing centers of Philadelphia and Boston. By 1850 the two major ports of the United States were New York, with all its diversity of goods and occupations, and New Orleans, situated at the mouth of the Mississippi, with its endless supply of cotton. But unlike the organic cotton economy, the modern economy taking shape in New York City was the beneficiary of years of government intervention, from the steamboat to the canal.

Seven

RAILROADS

As expensive as they were, canals turned out to be both a critically important and a wholly temporary commercial conduit: Their dominance lasted less than one generation. Fulton's vision of "water carriage" throughout America came true, but it failed to foresee the Industrial Revolution's propensity to destroy past innovations with new ones—even his steamboat would find itself ceding its role to this next big thing. The century appeared to be turning into capitalism's equivalent of the Renaissance—a tightly compressed period of expanding knowledge, only with its applications grittier, dirtier, and more practical. The purpose of this revolution, as Adam Smith put it in 1776, was the "great multiplication of productions" that would eventually turn into a "universal opulence" touching even the "lowest ranks of the people."

This "great multiplication" started with steam power. And generating steam power often started with coal. With England's industrialization a couple of decades ahead of America's, demand for cheap coal drove innovation across the Atlantic in the late eighteenth century. English coal mines were being worked at full capacity, but transportation costs posed an impediment. For the most part, coal transportation from the mines involved horse-drawn carts across often wet, muddy roads. A new idea came to the forefront: tracks. Rather than risk unpredictable road conditions, teamsters could rely on wood tracks upon which a cart could be pulled easily, allowing for the efficient movement of coal. The tracks improved. Then it became common practice to apply a layer of iron on the wood tracks to make the rails smoother and faster. To keep the tracks stable and in place, wood logs were placed below the tracks, perpendicular to the rails, and staked into the ground. Before long, horse-drawn trains seemed to be the most efficient way of transporting coal from mines to the nearest waterway or factory.

This led to a search for an even better solution. Coal was powering the steam engines of modern industry, yet the transportation of the coal itself on railroads relied on farm animals. The owners of coal mines turned to the possibility of using steam engines to pull the trains. As with steamboats, the main issue to overcome was power to weight. While the weight of the steam engine on waterborne vessels no longer prevented self-propulsion, even the most powerful engine of the day could not overcome inertia to propel itself on land. Engineers tried hybrid approaches, such as a combination of horses and steam power. Each approach led to subsequent permutations and improvements, ultimately yielding a steam-powered engine able to propel itself on iron-laced tracks. A short period of years after the initial breakthrough, the "iron horse" was moving at speeds approaching thirty miles an hour in the English countryside. Humanity's fastest speeds on land, up to this point, had been limited to the galloping stretches of a good racehorse.

In England the railroad was developed to serve industry, mainly to bring coal, the Industrial Revolution's fuel source, to textile mills. In preindustrial America, an agrarian nation with vast farmland that had just been unlocked by the system of canals, the railroad's effect was far more pronounced. Here the railroad was the catalyst for industrial capitalism, where the system of transportation itself became the nation's first great industry. And in a circular turn, railroads would soon become the biggest users of coal.

The railroad arrived in America via a series of experiments. One began on the Fourth of July, 1828, in Baltimore, where local businessmen first broke ground to lay tracks to keep up with neighboring efforts in canals. The planned railroad, the Baltimore and Ohio, was to extend all the way from the port of Baltimore to a town on the Ohio River. The B&O Railroad Company started as a public/private partnership—a for-profit company serving a public purpose—with the state of Maryland especially interested, as rival Pennsylvania was constructing a large canal system. To start, the company issued shares to raise $1.5 million, with the state of Maryland and city of Baltimore each purchasing $500,000 and private investors subscribing to the rest. But the B&O Railroad Company, while committed to laying hundreds of miles of iron tracks, planned on horses providing the actual horsepower.

At the time that the B&O started laying track, no locomotive had ever made a successful run on American soil. This, incongruously enough, would happen the following year for an experiment by the Delaware and Hudson Canal Company. Seeing how a short rail line might be used to bypass a stretch of its canal, the company ordered a locomotive from England. Once delivered, the *Stourbridge Lion*, operated by engineer Horatio Allen, seemed to be proceeding well on its maiden run until the wooden tracks on a bridge seemed to crack and wobble under the seven-ton locomotive. While the train made it back, this turned out to be its first and only run.

Horatio Allen then made his way south to South Carolina. In a bid to stimulate cotton traffic from deep within both Georgia and its own state to the ports of Charleston, South Carolina had chartered a railroad known as the Charleston and Hamburg. In 1830 the Charleston and Hamburg commissioned the West Point Foundry in New York to build the first American-made locomotive. Called the *Best Friend*, it made its inaugural run pulling two hundred shareholders and politicians on board, achieving speeds of thirty-five miles per hour, with the dignitaries feeling the exhilarating future for the first time. This southern railroad officially became the first locomotive-drawn line in America. The Charleston and Hamburg continued to add track, culminating in a 136-mile route that made it, for a short period, the longest line in the world. But the South, with its most fertile cotton-growing areas now in the Mississippi Delta, didn't have an immediate need for a vast railroad network when its most dominant cash crop could be floated down the great river to New Orleans, with ships taking the cotton across the ocean. Despite its pioneering railroad effort in Charleston, the favorable geography of cotton made the railroad a less than critical part of the southern economy.

. . .

DESPITE THE OBVIOUS benefits of locomotives, speed being the first, the development of the American railroad industry took some time. The effort stalled in the North for a different reason: Canal mania continued to consume much of the speculative bond capital available in the financial markets for infrastructure or internal improvement, as it was known then. The states themselves had guaranteed millions of dollars' worth of bonds for canals in trying to emulate New York's success with the Erie. Additionally, American locomotive manufacturing was considerably behind that of the British—it had just started in 1830 with the launch of *Best Friend*. Lastly, American iron making was significantly underdeveloped in the 1830s compared with that of the British. But with Britain in the midst of a railroad boom, British imports were for a time cost prohibitive. The combination of all of these factors kept the lid on railroads for most of the 1830s. By 1837 the total mileage of railroad track had grown to less than fifteen hundred miles; at $20,000 per mile, the construction of tracks alone had cost $30 million—seemingly significant, but a fraction of the investment in canals.

While the future may have seemed clear in the early 1830s to a few—seeing their iron horse reach speeds of thirty, forty, even sixty miles per hour on land—the canal construction projects started in the late twenties could not be stopped once under way. And since states had guaranteed the repayment of bonds financing the canal projects, sponsoring competing railroad projects would essentially serve to diminish future toll revenues for the canals under construction. While some canals, such as the Erie and many in Ohio, were of vital importance, many of the projects that followed were driven by a provincial need to compete. The last of the canals were being opened at precisely the point of their obsolescence.

But there were important developments for railroads outside of actual construction. The rise of railroads in the 1830s spawned the first widespread use of the corporation. To form a corporation in the early nineteenth century meant obtaining a charter with a specific purpose from the state. Generally states granted charters only for infrastructure, banking, and insurance. Just as it once had for New World ventures, the corporation shielded passive investors from the potential liabilities of the enterprise. This feature of the corporation in turn served to encourage wide and transferable shareholdings. A share was much harder to sell if it also conferred unlimited liability for past debts or actions. Thus, for large-scale private projects that required raising large amounts of capital, states saw the need to limit the liability of shareholders. Stock markets, requiring frictionless and anonymous share transferability to function, benefited from the wider use of the corporate form. As one consequence of this development, railroads would eventually be financed through sales of stock, unlike canals, which were financed through sales of bonds.

"Eventually" was the operative word. Dozens of railroad companies were chartered throughout the 1830s, but most remained empty shells for years while the promoters looked to put the pieces together. The first was getting permission to build a railroad on a general route. In exchange for the exclusive rights, the state required some controls over fares and route specifics. This was a minor concession for most railroads, given that they could barely finance a mile of track privately. Perhaps even more important than providing the corporate charters, states provided these private companies with a right that would seem anathema to the property rights of private citizens.

The experience of the Erie Railroad was typical. Chartered in 1832 as the New York and Erie Railroad, the company was granted the right to build a railroad from Albany to Lake Erie by the state of New York. In addition to the charter, this private railroad was granted the right of eminent domain, making its track construction rights superior to those of the private landowner in its proposed way. Under the rationale of eminent domain, once a plan was agreed upon and chartered by the state, the private company had the right to force any private property owners to sell the railroad their land. In the Erie Charter, if a dispute over the fair value occurred, the appeal went to the vice-chancellor of the circuit to determine the valuation. Just as with the government-owned Erie Canal, the state once again saw a greater public purpose in having infrastructure built over the conflicting rights of property holders.

The central logic was that eminent domain made railroad development more efficient. To build hundreds of miles of track cost effectively, a straight line made the most sense. But what if a landowner or series of landowners obstinately held out against selling their land right in the middle of a route?

This would allow a major infrastructure project, private or not, to be extorted or inefficiently detoured, ultimately imposing a cost on the commercial and consumer interests of the state. And there was another related factor: Once it was announced that a railroad was planned through a certain town or locale, the price of the land would go up speculatively based on the information. Essentially, a railroad's announcement of construction plans would be its own detriment, as this would increase its land-acquisition cost. Eminent domain preempted what might have been an endless series of negotiations and gamesmanship among private property owners, speculators, and the private builders of infrastructure, all to the detriment of the public purpose, which was low-cost infrastructure.

Despite the state incentives, including in many cases large amounts of direct financing, railroad construction grew slowly in the 1830s. By 1837 there were only 1,497 miles of track, barely ten times the length of South Carolina's Charles and Hamburg, throughout the entire country. But track construction accelerated right after the Panic of 1837, the deep recession of the era, while other sectors felt lingering effects for far longer. The scarcity of capital in the markets caused the final death of canal financing, diverting it to its more efficient replacement, with the slowdown serving as the metaphorical step backward making two steps of progress possible. As track construction sped up, so did production of rails at new ironworks, manufacturing of locomotives and railcars, construction of train stations, growth of small towns along routes, and formation of hubs for gathering produce and grains.

Railroads became the arteries of American capitalism, the circulation system of its commerce, even information—a letter or message or rumor could travel only as fast as its messenger, which now invariably was a train. Yet the railroad's development makes clear that even early American capitalism was never the same as laissez-faire capitalism: Various forms and forces of government were instrumental to its development, its trajectory, and its eventual implications. And what was the notion of corporate limited liability but a legal abstraction created and recognized by the state? As important, the early development of financial markets was propelled by bond guarantees of the various states, enticing private capital to underwrite American infrastructure.

In all, the next big things of the early nineteenth century—enabling man to travel through and over nature in new ways, with steamboats, canals, and railroads—began as intricate public/private partnerships. The government activities of setting in place the infrastructure, reconciling federal and state laws, permitting limited liability, and defining and balancing the conflicts of property rights, evolved into the operating system of its economy, upon which was placed the dynamic layer of free-market creativity and the vibrant applications of entrepreneurial activity.

AND ONCE MODERN American capitalism started its momentum, men who knew how to impose their will conquered markets. To Adam Smith, these emerging industrial artists were "philosophers," enterprising men whose role in society was "to observe everything" and by so doing become "capable of combining together the powers of the most distant and dissimilar objects."

It is unlikely that anyone who knew him would have called Cornelius Vanderbilt a philosopher. By 1840 the unschooled Vanderbilt had bought and sold steamships and routes enough times to amass a fortune, estimated at half a million dollars by some. His waters now extended well beyond the Hudson River and around Manhattan. His new battleground was the waters between Long Island and Connecticut, known as the Long Island Sound. Cutting through the Sound, Vanderbilt had his fastest boats taking passengers from New York to Providence, Rhode Island, and Boston Harbor. As New York City didn't yet have bridges connecting it to the American mainland, any act of coming or leaving the island of Manhattan involved water transportation.

In the 1830s he took notice of one class of potential usurpers of his trade. For decades, ferryboat operators had partnered with stagecoach operators on land, timing their arrivals and departures in a coordinated fashion to benefit passengers with seamless transfers. Now, starting at a Connecticut town, a railroad, known as the Stonington, had formed to take passengers up to Providence and Boston. Taking a steamboat from New York to the Connecticut seashore, combined with a fast train ride to Boston, was much faster overall than even the fastest steamboat curling around Cape Cod. "The first time I ever traveled over the Stonington, I made up my mind" to enter the railroad business, Vanderbilt said, understanding the immediate threat.

And Vanderbilt had a stroke of luck. The financial Panic of 1837 was especially severe; the outgoing Jackson administration had earlier shut down the equivalent of the central bank. Credit had seized in the economy and prudent men now demanded hard currency, silver or gold. As Vanderbilt's business collected an endless stream of silver coins from passengers, he seemed resistant to the afflictions caused by this economic retrenchment. Aided by the particularly effective combination of being debtless and ruthless, the Panic gave Vanderbilt an opening.

The Stonington, on the other hand, had come into rough times. The railroad had partnered with a steamboat rival of Vanderbilt's to transport passengers from Stonington, Connecticut, to New York City. Unable to match the combined speed of the railroad and his steamboat rival, Vanderbilt went to his tried-and-true playbook. As a perpetual low-cost operator due to his thrift, Vanderbilt used his solvency to charge such low fares as to cause large losses to his rivals, already under deep financial pressure. Faced with the prospect of large ongoing losses from Vanderbilt's pressure, the steamboat partner of the Stonington chose to pay Vanderbilt to not compete with it further. After receiving the payment, Vanderbilt moved on, but his eyes were still set on targeting the railroad itself.

He then partnered with the emerging Long Island Rail Road, which ran trains from Brooklyn to near the end of Long Island. The Long Island Rail Road had trouble finding suitable steamboat partners to provide a connection from the end of Long Island up to Boston through the Atlantic Ocean. In his first entry into the railroad business, Vanderbilt sold three of his steamboats for a large portion of Long Island Rail Road stock and bonds. This railroad, with its new steamboats, now competed with the Stonington. With the competition, the troubled Stonington's share price continued to fall.

At the same time, Vanderbilt ran boats to connect with another railroad, the Hartford and New Haven. Before long, he sold another three steamboats in exchange for a major stake in this railroad. With his stake, the stock market received the message that rates would likely come down on the New York-to-Boston route, dropping the Stonington to battered levels. With this, Vanderbilt finally accumulated enough shares in the open market to assume control of the Stonington.

Starting with his one steamboat, the *Citizen*, Vanderbilt had grown his operation into a fleet. A dozen years later, without founding a railroad or taking on the trouble of laying a single mile of track, Vanderbilt had maneuvered his way into the railroad business, exhibiting the adaptive skills and precision of a man who saw the world in terms of dollars and cents. The commercial frustrations that plagued the mechanical genius of Whitney with his cotton gin, or thwarted the ambitions of polymath Fulton before his steamboat, were foreign to Vanderbilt's innate sense of the transactional world. Conversely, the patrician sponsors of American democracy, including Jefferson, Washington, and Livingston, who were equally transfixed at times with commercial ambitions, needed to maintain noble appearances—detours of pretension that Vanderbilt had little need for.

At the same time, it is unlikely that Vanderbilt would have been in his element dealing tactfully and patiently with state legislatures and government officials in organizing the construction of tracks, or diligently maneuvering toward the economic incentives as the early men in steam and railroads had. Yet here was Vanderbilt, a pure and primal inhabitant of the marketplace, where the only rules were supply and demand, using his operating expertise in one endeavor to leverage himself into the other. For him, the market was a more egalitarian master in many ways, simpler for the man without aristocratic bearing or intellectual polish to access and understand.

Mastery, however, required new forms of sophistication. The tactics open to the free-market entrepreneur of the age included every type of transaction and agreement possible: collusion, price-fixing, rebates, cross-ownership, and stock market manipulation. Here too, nothing in natural law suggests any of this was immoral—in these evolving, unregulated free markets, people were free. For a man who came from nothing and was largely uneducated—called "illiterate and boorish" in one credit report—to be able to weave through all of the abstractions of this new paper jungle was in many ways an affirmation of the nation's republican values.

FOR MILLIONS OF MEN OVERSEAS, sharp-elbowed conquest was not the objective. Fleeing famine was. The rise of the American railroad coincided with a flood of immigrants such as the United States had never seen before. The first year in American history when more than 100,000 immigrants arrived in a single year was 1842. Five years later, the number from Ireland alone exceeded this. Over the course of the next eight years, almost 1.2 million Irishmen came to America, leaving the scarring horrors of the potato famine behind. In percentage terms, the numbers are even more startling: In the two decades of the 1840s and '50s, 20 percent of the entire population of Ireland crossed the Atlantic. These immigrants left in far humbler and more desperate circumstances than the Pilgrims had: The *Mayflower* had been a proactive, planned financial venture supplied with rations, while the Irish faced the existential choice of either leaving in rags or risking starving to death. And they were Catholics leaving for a decidedly Protestant nation.

During this same span, another wave of people from the European mainland were fleeing revolution and counterrevolution. A spirit of revolt had captured Germany along with other European nations—"we are sleeping on a volcano," warned Alexis de Tocqueville—and this same 1848 spirit led two exiled German thinkers, Karl Marx and Friedrich Engels, to pen their *Communist Manifesto* in London. But the radicalism of the revolutions, which had overthrown governments from sovereign France to the princely states of Italy, was overturned in time. Upon the defeat of revolutionary elements in Germany, half a million Germans left for America in the three-year period from 1852 to 1854 alone.

While the doctrine of Marx and Engels failed to gain political ground at the time, the egalitarian engine of American capitalism absorbed both the Irish and the Germans. How did a sudden surge of two million immigrants make it in America? Some evidence is found in the physical placement of iron rails. In 1846, the year before the impending boom of new people, railroad mileage in America stood at less than 5,000 miles. Eleven years later it had grown to nearly 25,000. At a rough estimate of $20,000 per mile of track, this represented a collective capital investment of close to $400 million in rails alone. Quite simply, upon arrival, the Irish and Germans found ready work building railroads, and the influx of all this raw labor made this rapid expansion possible. As famine gripped Ireland and revolution gripped Europe, these foreign transplants began the work of transforming their new nation.

And nowhere in America was this transformation more evident, more spectacular, than in the newer states of Illinois, Indiana, and Michigan. While the country had an incoming wave, it also had been in the throes of a decades-long internal migration, with families leaving the East to move to the cheap, fertile lands known at the time as the American Northwest. As Ohio had risen to vital importance with its river and canals, railroads would make Illinois a rising power.

In 1851, with a land grant from the federal government, Illinois chartered a railroad known as the Illinois Central. Raising over $5 million in bonds, the railroad set to work on building a 705-mile network in the state. Almost immediately, with the entire nation under construction, it found itself with labor shortages. It employed labor agents in New York City who advertised for the newest immigrants. Paper circulars screamed WANTED! 3,000 LABORERS, guaranteeing $1.25 per day in wages. It promised good meals and board for $2 per week. And then, understanding the need to transport the workers from the wharves of New York to the prairie, the Illinois Central offered to subsidize the fare of $4.75, a simple three days' wages: "This is a rare chance for persons to go west, being sure of permanent employment in a healthy climate, where land can be bought cheap." Even in its solicitation of unskilled labor, the railroad understood the promise of America—a chance to improve and build upon the first opportunity offered.

The Irish and Germans soon revealed different characteristics and preferences. The Germans, to the lament of the Illinois Central, barely stayed until they saved up enough to buy land. The Irish, with the freshness of the trauma caused by being dependent on the land, preferred the constancy of industrial labor. Remarkably, the Illinois Central needed to continually increase wages even as it finalized construction, despite the American population growing at a rate of well over one thousand new immigrants per day. Within five years, the Illinois Central assumed its place as the longest railroad in America. From this point, Chicago started rising as the railroad and agricultural hub of America, where railroads bringing grain, meat, and live animals from the plains were unloaded, processed, and reloaded for their destinations.

By the end of the decade, the Northwest had grown by nearly four million people, nearly equaling the size of the South and the Northeast; many of its nearly nine million people, pioneers and immigrants, would play a decisive political role in the future of the country, becoming the strongest base of support for a local country lawyer, Abraham Lincoln, who often did work for the Illinois Central.

Eight

TELEGRAPH

Before political systems, economic theories, businessmen, capital, and labor enter the picture to magnify the effects of some next big thing, science is generally crucial to the moment of inception, with subsequent breakthroughs and feats of engineering becoming the building blocks of material progress. Some inventor, somewhere, has often paid the price of seemingly endless frustration, dispiriting self-doubt, and years of thankless toil. And this frustration is usually layered upon a foundation of centuries of other men's fruitless trials and errors. Such men usually die before their work crystallizes into any practical application. But when such a miracle actually comes together as some dreamer designed it, the attainment of such elusive glory for one keeps another generation of tinkerers and thinkers hopeful and hopeless at the same time. Such is the nature of research and development. American capitalism's redeeming quality was, and is, that when those rare epiphanies prove to work, the system deploys to bring them to the people faster than any other.

But sometimes the system misfires. With the development of American railroads, the ability to reach New York from Washington DC within a day or two was a significant alteration of time and space. Once upon a time it had taken nearly a week for New Yorkers to learn of George Washington's passing. Communications had been able to travel only as fast as men could, in that if a man could travel from the capital to

New York in hours via train, of course, so then could a letter. But in the 1830s, less than a decade after ground had been broken in Baltimore for horse-drawn trains, an artist came up with a system that would enable information to travel at nearly the speed of light.

This development had been almost a century in the making, the critical breakthrough occurring in 1749. In the same Dutch town of Leyden where the exiled Pilgrims had once planned their voyage, two scientists had discovered a way to store electricity. At that point in history, common observations of electricity were not a complete mystery, as even simple friction between the body and wool clothing often caused static and sparks. In the century preceding the Leyden discovery, inventors used a variety of methods in an attempt to not only create electricity but, more important, store it. The Leyden duo used a simple jar, filled with water and insulated inside with foil, and found that it held a charge, becoming a simple battery. The Leyden Jar started a new wave of experimentation with electricity.

Before long, the idea of sending an electric current to a recipient to signal messages emerged as a prospective theoretical use. In the simplest form, a sentry on guard duty could be made to hold a copper wire, through which he could then be alerted to danger by a shock of electricity—binary, but effective. At this point the idea of communicating with visual signals was already known as telegraphy. Militaries had often used fire signals, airborne fires, and other cues to send signals quickly. With the emergence of the telescope, the visual signals could be seen from much greater distances—for example, where a series of strategically placed posts could relay information in a time of war. By the late 1700s, in many parts of Europe, advanced techniques of communication were in place using nonelectric methods. The problem, of course, was that inclement weather such as fog or rain prevented any signals from being passed.

By the early 1800s, hundreds of simultaneous experiments had emerged, each taking an incremental step forward from previous ones. Many patents were issued, and storage techniques advanced considerably; so did knowledge of wires and conductivity. While the pieces were there, however, no system or technique designed to this point had brought them all together to transmit messages in a repeatable, scalable way. It fell to an American artist of some notable achievement, Samuel Morse, to do what decades of scientists and engineers didn't or couldn't. Morse proved that good product design could make technology practical.

This is not to say that Morse had no scientific background. As a fifteen-year-old, he had enrolled at Yale University. In letters to his father, he often recounted the experiments and classes of a favorite professor of chemistry. In later years, during patent disputes, this professor would testify to Morse's exposure to theories of electricity. His talent and disposition, however, led him to fine arts. During his time at Yale, he often painted portraits of his wealthier peers to help defray his expenses. After graduating, he made his way to Europe, where his talent drew him into a community of American artists abroad. Noticed by Benjamin West, the same artist who had mentored Robert Fulton decades earlier, Morse was encouraged to pursue his art. Eventually, one of his works was displayed at an exhibition of the Royal Academy in England, a prestigious honor for any artist. He had found recognition, but not a secure living.

In the 1820s Morse returned home and married. In New England he found work as a portrait artist painting individuals and families, including notable men like his fellow Yale alumnus Eli Whitney. His work even led to a sought-after opportunity to paint the sitting president, James Monroe. A few years later, while engaged in one of his most significant works in Washington, he learned that his wife had died. Compounding his sadness, Morse received word that he had not been selected as a part of the commission of paintings for the Capitol and again left for Europe. On his return voyage, Morse found himself gripped by an idea that sprang to his mind during a conversation on board regarding the use of electricity to communicate messages. Morse, in his diary, devoted all of his energies on his transatlantic voyage to designs of possible methods.

In Morse's view, the recipient's ability to see the electricity was the missing piece. Eventually he sketched out a device that would, in essence, mechanically tap paper to confirm the electricity being passed. After making his way to New York, starting in a teaching position at New York University in fine arts, he committed to improving the concept. His mind wandered to create a system of sequential taps to represent numbers and letters. Soon this system gave way to one of lines and dots. A quick tap of current would be a dot. A longer tap of current would be a line. The dots and lines, representing currents of electricity, would constitute an entire electronic alphabet. The combination of rolling paper to record the taps of current, the abstraction of an entire alphabet based on taps, and the mechanical drawings themselves were Morse's proprietary combination. It was simple, brilliant, and revolutionary.

But after his breakthrough in 1832, he spent five years designing and making models in his apartment while continuing to teach, with his remaining attention turned to completing his immense painting, in terms of size, the *Gallery of the Louvre*, for which he expected commercial success. It should have been the immediate beginning of the modern age of telecommunications. Instead the idea languished in the hands of an artist with resoundingly poor commercial instincts. Vanderbilt he wasn't.

FIVE YEARS LATER, to Morse's dismay, two Frenchmen announced a reliable method of communication across vast distances faster than man could travel. The men claimed that messages could be sent from New York to New Orleans in less than half an hour. While the press seemed enthralled, Morse was incredulous. Acclaim was being given to a technique of using telescopes to see and relay distant visual signals, not electricity. His attention refocused, Morse quickly turned to filing a patent.

Adding to Morse's sense of urgency were accounts from Europe, where competing inventors claimed methods of using electricity to transmit information—to this Morse suggested that his competitors demonstrate actual messages being sent through prototypes, not unverified boasts. To prove his own claim, Morse arranged for wires stretching one third of a mile, 1,700 feet, back and forth across a lecture hall at New York University. From one end of the hall, Morse relayed the message to the receiving end. At this public demonstration, the results astounded those who saw it. It led him south to demonstrate the telegraph in early 1838 to the Franklin Institute in Philadelphia. Here Morse upped the scale to a ten-mile circuit. The institute immediately passed along a glowing report to Washington. By February 15 Morse was presenting his device to

President Martin Van Buren and his secretaries of the navy, war, and state. Other demonstrations were conducted for roomfuls of senators and congressmen, who in their awe deemed it "impossible and visionary." It was nothing short of the erasure of time as a fundamental aspect of communication, vast distances compressed to mere seconds.

The possibilities of this technology as a national strategic asset were too significant to let the moment pass. A congressional committee was formed. It recommended appropriating $30,000 immediately to allow Morse to build a fifty-mile test in an actual ground environment, against the elements. It must be noted that $30,000, even then, was not an astounding sum of money, as laying just two miles of railroad track cost more than this. Considering the matter settled in his favor, given the scope of his achievement, Morse headed to England to ensure his patent rights there. To finance his travel and interim expenses, he sold off a meaningful share of his interests for an exceedingly small amount.

Both efforts failed. The appropriation in Congress failed to pass, and the patent filing in England was rejected. A British journal had published details of Morse's invention based on his U.S. patent earlier in the year. Consistent with modern patent law, once the methods of an invention were publicly known, the right to file a future patent claim was nullified. While in Europe, through acquaintances, Morse had even managed to have the czar of Russia consider placing the telegraph on an experimental route. This deal too fell apart over a matter of weeks. Other nations similarly passed.

When Morse returned to the United States, he found his professorship reduced to a nominal role. He was broke and broken. His notes indicate that at times he missed meals. He was despondent, recounting how even with his very basic standard of living, he was unable to afford food. At the same time, he was sourcing basic materials for his telegraph: wire here, iron there. He did much of the mechanical work himself. Over a dinner paid for by one of his students, he provided his young host the following advice, laced in self-pity:

> This is my first meal in twenty-four hours. Strother, don't be an artist. It means beggary. A house dog lives better. The very sensitiveness that stimulates an artist to work, keeps him alive to suffering.

. . .

MUCH ABOUT MORSE'S behavior is baffling. After failed overtures to governments, why didn't he make any attempt at raising private capital in New York City? Wall Street, with its issuance of railroad and canal securities, was mere blocks from him. He surely had some access. By this point in his life, Morse had met with multiple American presidents face-to-face. He was a prominent artist in touch with wealthy, cultured patrons, including New York politicians like DeWitt Clinton. At the same time, given the merits of the telegraph, in the midst of the tens of millions of dollars that made their way into canals and railroads from lower Manhattan, how was it that a few thousand dollars weren't offered to Morse by some opportunistic Yankee? In many ways, the fact that Morse wasn't exploited in his desperate circumstances constitutes a form of market failure, a missed opportunity in recognizing a revolutionary invention in plain sight. Next, it points to the bias of commercial participants against investing at speculative stages of science and technology and toward investing at the stage when implementation and scale are clearer.

Gathering his energy, scrimping for travel money, Morse decided to lobby once again in Washington. Six years after he had first dazzled the nation's most important politicians, in 1843 the House of Representatives passed a measure to grant Morse $30,000 to build a line of significant distance to test his telegraph. The measure then passed the Senate. Out of the $30,000, Morse was allowed an annual salary of $2,000. His long, dark winter was over.

AT FIFTY-TWO YEARS of age, Morse set to work on building an outdoor line: a proposed route from Baltimore to Washington. Morse's plan called for digging a trench and submerging the wire. To execute the subterranean approach, a contractor whom Morse had hired subcontracted the digging to a young man named Ezra Cornell. Cornell had recently failed at selling plows to farmers but was industrious enough to have invented a specific tool for digging a deep incision, simultaneously layering in the wire, and filling the dirt back in. But the underground

wiring resulted in failure—it didn't conduct electricity reliably. For someone who had struggled for years to make the idea a reality, the anxiety of
going back to the drawing board must have been daunting. Cornell
stayed on. They tried again.

The next iteration called for installing poles in the ground and running
the wires above ground. As each interval was confirmed to work, the miles
between Baltimore and Washington were prepared for a testing event. By
May 1, one device had been installed in Washington and the other near
the 1844 Presidential Convention of the Whigs in Baltimore. As men in
Washington waited for the results to be brought by train, a Morse associate
telegraphed the message that the Whigs had selected Henry Clay to be
their candidate. Crowds of people swarmed into the makeshift messaging
room to hear the details from the convention floor coming in. Immediately
the clamor and disbelief caused by both the medium and the message set
off requests for more information, causing a delighted and vindicated
Morse to tap and receive messages at his machine with the "rapidity almost
of common conversation." When the official announcement arrived via
train an hour later, confirming what had first been sent via this mysterious
machine, the commercial era of the telegraph began.

The reaction was one of wonder. It must be remembered that electricity, up to this point, had no commercial application; the only form of
electricity that touched people's lives was lightning followed by thunder.
The average person did not have any frame of reference that would lead
him to believe that such a thing was possible. One Morse biographer
noted that an early impression equated telegraphy with teleportation,
where people imagined the physical movement of words through time
and space. And in many ways there was nothing incremental about the
buildup. It was a startling, overnight revelation. One day it was taken for
granted that words, in the form of physical letters, moved as parcels did.
The day after, it was learned that messages could move through wires
instantly.

The marketplace made up for lost time. Newspapers understood the
value of getting news stories wired in from the capital. Stock market
operators, seeing the same securities trade in both the Philadelphia and

New York markets, could find arbitrage opportunities by buying cheaply in one market and selling higher in the other. Railroads could track hourly and daily progress as lines were being constructed and, on existing lines, learn of exact places on routes where tracks had to be repaired.

Morse, benefiting from a great self-awareness about his commercial limitations, took the opposite strategy of cotton gin inventor Eli Whitney. While Whitney attempted to manufacture the devices and process the cotton in his own facilities, Morse decided to license his patent liberally. He had no lack of suitors. But old habits were hard to break—Morse's initial instinct was to sell the entirety of what he owned to the federal government. But he changed course and decided to have Amos Kendall, a former postmaster general, act as his agent. Kendall then licensed the patent rights to a variety of regional ventures with exclusive territorial rights. Each license created a revenue stream for Morse.

So began a rapid transformation of the American landscape. By the late 1840s, the telegraph and railroad were developing in lockstep. Many times telegraph wire was connected at faster rates between key locales than the track was being laid. There was a key difference between a mile of railroad track and mile of telegraph wire. Railroads were extremely capital intensive: Public financing, bond guarantees, and land grants were required to build the actual tracks. For the telegraph the pattern was the opposite. The initial grant to develop a commercial version came from the government, but the rest came from private capital with little government support, local, state, or federal. The reason was simple: The copper wire and wooden poles needed to build a mile of telegraph cost less than $200 in many cases, one hundredth of the cost of a mile of track. A line from Philadelphia to New York could be built for less than $20,000. Private investors could easily afford to speculate at these levels. Additionally, unlike a single mile of track, two hundred miles of telegraph could be operational quickly and start producing immediate revenue, charged by the letter or word.

The relatively low capital costs of the world's first telecommunications infrastructure compared with transportation infrastructure created a set of unique conditions. Often competitors rapidly built lines next to each other. In the frenzy, entrepreneurs of all types quickly chartered, organized, and financed telegraph lines throughout the states, between any two points that could plausibly require them.

Within seven years, with the overinvestment in telegraph operations, a wave of consolidation would create another beneficiary. While Morse had been content to collect checks, his young ditch digger, Ezra Cornell, had managed to negotiate from Morse a substantial patent license that he then leveraged into royalties from multiple telegraphic ventures from Buffalo to the growing Northwest. Partnering with people like Henry Wells, who would go on to found both American Express and Wells Fargo, Cornell retained shares in many of these telegraph companies, forgoing cash payments. One of his largest stakes was in what ultimately turned into the Western Union Telegraph Company. By the end of the century, Western Union would have more than one million miles of wires under operation, transmitting more than 200,000 messages per day. Cornell was its largest individual shareholder for a brief time, but by the time he turned forty-nine, he had decided to retire from the business. Denied much of a formal education growing up, he provided $500,000 to found a college in Ithaca, New York, bearing his name.

BY THE 1850s a considerable synergy seemed to exist between railroads and the telegraph. Though the telegraph industry developed independently and privately with ample capital for the laying of wires, ongoing maintenance costs turned out to be significant in proportion to the initial capital outlay. At the same time, the biggest industrial users of the telegraph were the railroads themselves. Before the telegraph, a stationmaster would not have any idea about the status of a train due to arrive. As a result, a train waiting to depart on the same line in the opposite direction could be delayed for hours as a precaution to avoid a head-on collision. The possibility of instantaneous information altered the entire logistics of the railroad industry. In many cases the larger railroads directly licensed Morse's patent and established a line alongside their railroad.

For the telegraph operators, the benefits were obvious. The telegraph company would hoist its poles along the tracks. The railroad would then provide ongoing maintenance of the telegraph wire. Since railroads monitored their own tracks and were highly dependent on the telegraph to coordinate movements, this was a straightforward proposition. In turn, the telegraph company granted priority usage for the railroad at no cost.

The growth in wires led to hundreds of local telegraph offices throughout the country. Most times the offices were located at or adjacent to a railroad station. These were staffed with intelligent telegraph operators who needed to record messages coming in via Morse code accurately and quickly. Messenger boys would then deliver the messages by hand to the local recipients. Interestingly, deciphering telegraph messages opened up opportunities in the office setting for women, who proved to be as "neat, accurate and hard-working" as men, but with the added benefit that their wages were "considerably lower than men's."

Similarly, for a few men from the lowest social strata, the telegraph office provided an opening to a white-collar world, a window of opportunity that hinted at possibilities of class mobility, of rising beyond one's assigned station. One notable young immigrant, engaged in blue-collar child labor from the time he set foot in America, made the most of such a chance. Starting as a messenger at the telegraph office at the age of fifteen, he reflected later in life upon what this entry into office life meant to him:

> From the dark cellar running a steam-engine at two dollars a week,
> begrimed with coal dirt, without a trace of the elevating influences
> of life, I was lifted into paradise, yes, heaven, as it seemed to me,
> with newspapers, pens, pencils, and sunshine about me. There was
> scarcely a minute in which I could not learn something. I felt that
> my foot was upon a ladder and that I was bound to climb.

The boy's family had migrated from Scotland. His father was one of the last of generations of weavers in the town of Dunfermline. With the advance of industrialization in England, their piecemeal livelihood, based on the loom in their living room, had faded to the point of no return.

Displaced by the Industrial Revolution, the family made its way to America, ending up in Pittsburgh, where the boy and his father went to work in the hard conditions of industrial life. Life in this promised land ended the formal schooling the twelve-year-old had known in his homeland.

From the engine room, a fortuitous opening led the son to his position in a Pittsburgh telegraph office. Here he was exposed to the commercial activity of the city. After dropping off messages to notable businessmen throughout Pittsburgh, he came to learn telegraphy in bits and pieces at the office; eventually he became skilled at the rare technique of making out messages by the sound of the clicks alone. While employed at the office, he came to the attention of the Pennsylvania Railroad, as the railroad needed an operator to assist its superintendent in the logistics of its own telegraph office. For a teenager only a few years removed from Dickensian conditions, this stroke of fortune elicited emotions from his normally taciturn father. It seemed an assurance that his son might never need to return to hard labor, an early indication that the promise of upward mobility in America might in fact be real:

> My father was usually shy, reserved, and keenly sensitive, very saving of praise lest his sons might be too greatly uplifted. He upon this occasion, grasped my hand. . . . He murmured slowly "Andra, I am proud of you." The tear had to be wiped from his eye, I fondly noticed, as he bade me good-night and told me to run back to the office.

THE FATHER, WILL CARNEGIE, died soon after. He wouldn't live long enough to see his son go beyond the telegraph office. But young Andrew Carnegie was in full possession of the entrepreneurial genius that had eluded Samuel Morse—he was exactly the type of "philosopher" vital to the wealth of nations of whom his fellow Scotsman, Adam Smith, had once written.

Nine

GOLD

Their indictment was clear. "The bourgeoisie, during its rule of scarce one hundred years, has created more massive and more colossal productive forces than have all preceding generations together," wrote Marx and Engels in 1848. "Subjection of Nature's forces to man, machinery, application of chemistry to industry and agriculture, steam-navigation, railways, electric telegraphs, clearing of whole continents for cultivation, canalization of rivers," in their telling, had ripped apart the old social order in Europe, leaving "no other nexus between man and man than naked self-interest." The evolution of modern industry, the marketplace, had allowed an upper middle class and capitalist class to usurp much of the political power of monarchs and nobility, of feudal societies, while assuming none of the traditional social obligations that had bound "natural superiors" to their fellow man. The parallel development of political freedoms, alongside industrialization, was mere subterfuge to gain consent for a system that put the workingman at a natural negotiating disadvantage; he was only free to compete against his fellow man in the sale of their labor, with the man who was willing to work longer and harder for the lower wage proclaimed the winner.

As methods of production improved at what seemed to be breakneck speed, they introduced "everlasting uncertainty" into the workingman's place in the economic order, replacing "the little workshop of the patriarchal master" with the "great factory of the industrial capitalist." Owing

to the "extensive use of machinery and to division of labor," all charm for
the workingman was lost, turning him into "an appendage of the machine" of whom only the most simple, most monotonous task was required. Most appalling, in this free-market system, were the "epidemics
of over-production," the force that mysteriously and suddenly appeared,
causing the economy to contract; the sudden loss of jobs and subsistence
caused painful, lasting crises among industrial laborers. This too was a
new development. In the agrarian age, there was rarely such a thing as
overproduction of food. In short, political systems did not keep up with
the unpredictability of the rising industrial age; the governments of Europe failed to provide the social shock absorbers for this new, volatile age
of surplus and calamity. Just as 1776 had introduced the seminal works of
capitalism and democracy—Smith's *Wealth of Nations* and the American
Declaration of Independence—1848 was marked by the February publication of *The Communist Manifesto,* which coincided with the spirit of
revolution that in the following month convulsed France and the small,
princely states of Europe, including zones that eventually united as Italy
and Germany. But while the events of 1848 were widespread, the revolutions were ultimately unsuccessful. However, when royal authorities
across Europe soon gained back their power, the dramatic unrest had
instilled enough fear that governments accelerated efforts to regulate the
direction of capitalism in Europe.

But 1848 in America was a time of unabashed exultation. The nation
was celebrating the achievement of its great destiny, a final territorial
conquest on its continent. Four years earlier, when Samuel Morse
received the famous telegraph message that announced Henry Clay as
the Whig nominee for the election of 1844, it sparked a national debate.
The central issue of the presidential campaign that year was the fate of
the independent Republic of Texas. Democratic candidate James Polk
favored annexing the state to make it a part of America. Clay took the
opposite position, seeing the annexation of Texas as doubly troublesome,
in terms of provoking Mexico into war and bringing the complications of
adding another slave state to the Union.

The geopolitics of the 1840s could equally be traced back to the
Louisiana Purchase. A couple of years before Napoleon's sale of the Lou-

isiana Territories to the United States in 1803, Spain had transferred the territory back to France—a consequence of its alliance during the Seven Years' War of the earlier century. But Spain, in control of Mexico and territories to the west of the Rocky Mountains to the Pacific Ocean, had stipulated that France not transfer any of the land to any other party without its consent. With the prospect of receiving $15 million for his military, Napoleon had overlooked this limitation.

Spain therefore refused to recognize the Louisiana Purchase as legitimate until 1819, when the Monroe administration acquired Florida from Spain and in turn recognized the Spanish holdings in California, adjoined to Mexico, as legitimate. With Spain agreeing to a northern border of California at the 42nd parallel, the United States then negotiated with Great Britain for dual possession of the Oregon Country, today's Pacific Northwest.

But the Mexicans seemed to have a mind of their own. In 1821, less than two years after the agreement between the United States and Spain, Mexico claimed and won independence, taking California with it; Spain's presence on the North American mainland was suddenly over. The Republic of Mexico then made a strategic mistake: In an effort to populate its territory of Texas, it encouraged white settlers to effectively emigrate from America. Before too long, the sparsely settled Texas had a white population that exceeded its Hispanic population. As the Texans were ostensibly American citizens living in a foreign land, simmering conflicts between these opportunistic expatriates and Mexico called upon the pride of American nationalism.

With numbers on their side, the Texans declared themselves an independent republic, seeking freedom from Mexico, which in turn responded with force. Seeing ongoing war with the Mexicans as futile, the Texans pleaded to join their territory with America. Once James Polk won the election of 1844, the issue was decided: The United States annexed the Republic of Texas as the twenty-eighth state days before he took office the following year. The question then became, Where exactly did Texas end? When it was a part of Mexican territory, there hadn't been a pressing need to so closely define a border within that republic, given that Texas was largely uninhabited. Once Texas became a part of the United States, however, this boundary needed to be defined with the utmost precision. President Polk dispatched General Zachary Taylor to establish one. The efforts started the Mexican-American War.

Nationalism, predictably, lent itself to wartime sloganeering—Americans were presented with the idea of westward expansion, starting with Texas, as "the fulfillment of our manifest destiny to overspread the continent allotted by Providence," as New York's *Democratic Review* put it in 1845. The American desire expanded in scope to contest Mexico's California. All of this played out via new telegraph dispatches from the South—it had been less than two years since Morse's trial. Daily transmission of news from the battlefield to readers in Boston and New York, who followed the action in print, allowed heroes to emerge. Before the war was over, it became clear to newspapers that rather than each paying for reporters on the battlefield and taking on the costs of telegraphic dispatches, it made sense to pool their efforts—these pioneers, in the process of making war entertainment, formed the Associated Press. And getting information at such speeds served only to reinforce the sense of modernity, and therefore moral superiority, of the Republic itself. America spreading was the spread of progress, the force of civilization.

By late 1847, it was clear that Mexico had lost the war. With the signing of the Treaty of Guadalupe Hidalgo in February 1848, everything to the west, including all of California, became a part of the United States. The terms of surrender called for an American payment of $15 million for the territory, the same price tag applied to the Louisiana Purchase forty-five years prior. With it, the project for the continental United States had been completed. Destiny had unfolded in Polk's first term, just as the campaign rhetoric of 1844 had prophesied.

The proponents of Manifest Destiny had always attempted to invoke a certain providential quality: The nation's unstoppable westward momentum was an ongoing affirmation from the heavens. That the defeated Mexicans were Catholic, of course, didn't disturb this nativist narrative. But Providence had been even kinder than anyone could have possibly prayed for. At almost the exact time of the Mexican surrender, gold was discovered in a remote riverbed in northern California. And when the news of this discovery in California came to the eastern seaboard of America by the end of 1848, to the most fervent believer in God's will in matters of war and conquest, this immense treasure must have seemed ordained proof that, yes indeed, God did love America more than any other nation in the history of humanity.

CALIFORNIA, despite its natural beauty and temperate climate, had remained largely uncontested by European powers, primarily due to its inaccessibility. The Spanish, starting in the eighteenth century, had built a series of missions close to the coast to administer the region, but the effort had stimulated no great influx of people. Despite the advances in steamships and railroads in the East, the territory west of the Mississippi remained the frontier. By land it was months away from the East Coast. To reach southern California meant crossing a desert; to reach northern California meant crossing mountains, both the Rockies and the Sierra Nevada. On sea the nautical distance from Charleston, South Carolina, to Santa Barbara, passing below the southern tip of South America, was greater than the distance between Monterrey, Mexico, and Shanghai.

In short, anyone headed to California had to be either highly motivated or highly desperate. Some were both. John Sutter had made it to California from Switzerland in 1839. Fleeing creditors and leaving his wife behind, Sutter had managed to curry favor with the Mexican authorities and started life anew with some land in northern California. From his base on the Rios de los Americanos—American River even before it became one—Sutter had looked to erect a sawmill. A few miles north of the base, Sutter's hired overseer, James Marshall, had spotted an area that appeared to be the most suitable place.

During a routine check of the construction, Marshall saw sparkles in the ground below the trickling water. His camp was notably startled but dismissed the small find of yellow, metallic flakes. After a few days, Marshall took his discovery downriver to his boss. After some investigation using scales and nitric acid, Sutter was convinced: It was gold.

The riverbeds around both the American River and the Sacramento River contained one of the largest gold deposits discovered in human history. That this accident happened within days of the Mexican surrender only added to the improbability of it all. Predictably, the news spread quickly despite Marshall and Sutter's wish to keep it quiet. Men from around California made their way to the rivers to dig and pan for gold. The young men on the few ships that docked periodically in San Francisco— whaling ships and merchant ships on overseas voyages—abandoned their current occupations and rushed to the chance at fortune, leaving empty ships in the bay. By the spring of 1848, the riverbeds of California were full of men.

Reports of "Gold! Gold! Gold!" soon reached the U.S. Army officers who had remained in California after the war. It fell to William Tecumseh Sherman to report back to Washington that upwards of $50,000 per day in gold was being dug out of the riverbeds. Some accounts had the average man earning $20 per day working shovel and pan, nearly fifteen to twenty times a laborer's daily wage in the East. To corroborate his report, Sherman purchased two hundred ounces of local gold to send along to his superiors back east. "I have no hesitation in saying that there is more gold in the country drained by the Sacramento and San Joaquin river," wrote Sherman, to offset the cost of "war with Mexico a hundred times over." If this wasn't advertisement enough, he continued, "no capital is required to obtain this gold. . . . Many frequently pick out gold out of crevices of rock with their butcher knives in pieces from one to six ounces." The Californians were picking up gold pieces weighing over a third of a pound.

Upon hearing the report from Sherman's messenger, the outgoing president decided to alert his countrymen. In the annual presidential message to Congress, which took place in December in that era, Polk wove in Sherman's findings as a part of an overall report on the Mexican-American War. Polk confirmed that the "abundance of gold" in California was of "such an extraordinary character" that "ships arriving on the coast are abandoned by their crews" and that "labor commands a most exorbitant price," as the "whole of the male population . . . have gone to the gold districts." Newspapers across America published Polk's address the next day, many in full.

Just like that, after centuries of colonial empires scorching the earth in search of gold, America stumbled into the greatest discovery of gold up to that point while building a sawmill. As the final days of 1848 passed into the New Year, thousands of hopeful Americans—the forty-niners—started heading west.

THE GOLD RUSH attracted all types of fortune seekers. Some left their families, jobs, futures, and farms. Others had little to leave. While the steady movement from the East to the American Midwest promised stable and secure futures with ample land, the far West promised instant riches, attracting a different type of settler more mercenary in his desires.

Over a dozen whaling ships left from Nantucket with the intention of docking in San Francisco Bay, taking the circuitous route around South America to then head back north thousands of miles. For the more affluent, the faster route was to take a steamer to Panama on the Atlantic side and have local Indian guides point the way through malarial swamps and jungles to the other side facing the Pacific, and then take a ship up north. From places inland, like Missouri and Texas, the overland journey was inexpensive but arduous. Failing to make it over a mountain pass before the winter had fatal consequences.

Once in the California hills, the incoming men drove the prospecting to levels of extreme competition. The ones who arrived early enough to claim good land had significant advantages. Sherman, witnessing the conditions with the victorious soldiers from the recent war under his command, couldn't help but envy the easy fortunes all around them: "Many men have already become rich, and others are growing so fast. All have pockets full of gold, and everybody gets more than ten dollars daily for his personal labor, save those in the employ of the government— we are the sufferers." Newcomers often went to work for those lucky, early few as wages continued to climb. The wages, which were paid in gold, were often enough to lure men away from their independent efforts. The prices of anything a forty-niner could buy with the gold that he mined or received as wages were equally inflated. The months required to transport even the most basic goods, along with the high labor costs, led to high prices. And for young men with gold in their hearts and in their pockets, the high cost of essentials came with similarly high-cost amusements: gambling and women.

It soon became apparent to some that to endure the hardships of digging for gold, only to face exorbitant costs for basic essentials once successful, was a losing proposition. Many simply stayed in San Francisco, choosing to sell supplies to incoming prospectors arriving via ship rather than digging for gold themselves. As President Polk had noted, the ships themselves were often abandoned—the bay was filled with hundreds of anchored ships without sailors. In this frenetic atmosphere, "little stores were being opened at every point, where flour, bacon, etc. were sold; everything being a dollar a pound, and a meal usually costing three dollars." Sherman reported, "I have seen blankets worth one or two dollars in New York sell for $50. Shoes of the coarsest quality sell for ten dollars a pair, and the best of it is, all consumers are able to pay down in gold for these articles." The opportunity to sell shovels to gold miners became its own draw soon enough.

Within the first couple of years of the Gold Rush, the scale of mining operations had entirely changed. All of the easy gold had been picked off all the riverbeds and hill surfaces. The days of pans and shovels gave way to blasting the earth with gunpowder. Other operations used hydraulic pressure to strip away the faces of hills where gold was reputed to be in abundance. Thus the men who came in the aftermath of the immediate wave, deterred by the capital costs of the new mining operations, simply came to set up a supporting trade—these men never had any intention of digging for gold. Once they arrived in San Francisco, they found a fast-growing town with every trade thriving. These arrivals added to the thousands of Chinese immigrants who had made San Francisco home. The Bavarian immigrant Levi Strauss, a general goods merchant, arrived to set up his store in this climate, eventually creating the blue jeans that went on to become an enduring symbol of Americana.

Yet other men came with the idea of setting up links between the East and the West. In 1850 Henry Wells and his partner, William Fargo, were operating American Express, an express company in the burgeoning city of Buffalo. An express company's business was to ship things quickly but expensively. Messages, banknotes, and valuables were the primary goods transported by express companies. To hedge against the risks to his express company from the instant telegraph, Wells had invested in local telegraph companies, including Ezra Cornell's. Sensing the opportunity in the West, especially as laying telegraph lines across a desolate country was a practical impossibility, Wells and Fargo proposed expanding their company, American Express, to the West. Their investors balked. So starting in 1852, Wells and Fargo set up a new company to provide express services to California. In addition to simple messages, Wells, Fargo & Co. ventured into the business of bringing gold back east. And since an express company was already entrusted with valuables, it soon made sense for Wells, Fargo & Co. to also offer banking services locally.

Others missed success altogether, only to rise again. At thirty years old, George Hearst had inherited a Missouri farm from his father. Upon hearing the stories coming from California, George left his mother and sister to pursue gold but largely struck out well into his middle age. After years of making a living on the periphery, Hearst learned of a silver strike over the border in Nevada about one hundred miles away. Upon hearing the initial results of soil tests in 1859, Hearst felt that the owner of the property, Henry Comstock, along with early claim holders, was unaware of the true value of the property. Raising money quickly to buy claims from other holders, George Hearst soon held a substantial claim on the Comstock Lode. He would become one of the wealthiest men in California, seeding the fortune that served as the base for his only son, William Randolph, to venture into newspapers.

Some men never made it to the West Coast but simply profited from men going west and gold coming east. Given the steady flow of steamships to Central America from New York City and from Nicaragua and Panama up to San Francisco, Cornelius Vanderbilt entered the trade. With the growing competition among enterprises to control the flow of passengers to California and the safe carriage of gold and mail back to the East, capital allocated to launching new, fast ships led to dramatic improvements in the use of steam for oceanic voyages—within years, transoceanic voyages by sail would be obsolete. The business had been so strong that private operators, including Vanderbilt, had considered raising private capital to build a Nicaraguan canal to speed up the connection between the West and East Coasts of the United States. To the lasting regret of the Nicaraguans, the proposed construction of a canal through Central America would not come to pass, for now, though this too became an idea cemented by the Gold Rush. But the allure of gold was only the beginning. For the next century and a half and counting, American movement westward would become a metaphor for progress, symbolizing both ambitious restlessness and internal mobility—a dynamic search for greener pastures.

THERE WAS A CERTAIN PARADOX in this sudden release and movement of human energy—from continents away, no less—all to dig in the dirt for a shiny metal that, once dug out successfully, was melted into neat rectangular bars and made its way back into darkness, in bank vaults, never again to see the light of day.

Yet this arbitrary construct underpinned the entire monetary system of the United States and the world. The same primal attraction that had once led pirates, conquistadores, and medieval sovereigns to search for gold was now being mirrored in an age when wires transmitted words at near the speed of light. The value of gold then, as now, was largely based on a seemingly universal agreement, an article of faith: that gold is valuable because others see it as valuable. Why should the discovery or non-discovery of a yellow metal in the dirt in California have any impact on the utilization of industrial capacity, growth of crops, transportation of goods via rail, improvement of the telegraph infrastructure, or any other economic activity? But its religious effect, regardless of its logic, was undeniable. The flood of gold helped unleash significant economic activity throughout the world.

Banks, large and small, that issued paper money did so on the basis that the bank, at any time, would be willing to exchange the paper for physical gold. But carrying around physical gold was cumbersome. In coin form, it was bulky. And when used endlessly in transactions, gold being especially soft and malleable, parts of it slowly eroded away. And if simply buried in one's backyard, the gold did not collect interest. To hold large amounts of physical gold required security, which in essence caused gold to be a negative-interest-bearing asset—it cost money to protect and did not grow into more by itself, unlike the compounding interest on paper money. Hence, gold-based paper money and banking. But despite misconceptions, paper money backed by gold—the gold standard—never meant that there was literally a quantity of gold for every bit of paper. It still required faith. Banks assumed that not everyone with a paper bank-note would to want to withdraw the physical gold all at once, and as long as people were confident holding paper, only a fraction of physical gold actually had to be held in proportion to the outstanding printed currency or banknotes. With the large amounts of gold coming in from California, confidence in paper money boomed—few needed to worry if their banks held adequate gold. With this confidence came the surge of economic activity. The close to $300 million in railroad tracks laid down throughout America in the immediate aftermath is one bit of evidence. At the same time, the return to normalcy in Europe in the aftermath of 1848 was much the result of optimism and economic growth fueled by increases in the world's gold supply.

Without the Gold Rush, industrial economies would have been forced to turn to more sophisticated forms of central banking to keep up with advances in technology, production, and science, just as legal frameworks governing eminent domain, patents, copyrights, bond indentures, and the limited liability of corporations had propelled economic progress. Instead, due to this accidental discovery, banking for the industrial age would continue to be based on metals found in the ground until the next century.

But the political consequences of the Gold Rush dwarfed the monetary ones. President Polk's confirmation of the existence of gold set off a political crisis. Interestingly, the events of 1848 had far graver consequences in America—great fortune being a prelude to bloodshed—than the revolutions of the same year in Europe. The question, an unforeseen detonation, became that of California's statehood. Before the proverbial ink had dried on the Mexican surrender, the new citizens of California wanted to rush to become a U.S. state. They organized themselves quickly, with unelected but prominent delegates from various areas of California, and prepared a state constitution. In late 1849 these Californians presented themselves for statehood in the Union.

To make California a state would require an act of Congress. And Congress was divided. Ever since the Missouri Compromise, the proportion of slave states to free states had been carefully calibrated. The count now stood exactly at fifteen free states to fifteen slave states. For the South, this balance was vital. The populations of the Northeast and the South were more or less equivalent in 1800—but in the five subsequent decades, the burgeoning Northwest and the Northeast had combined to nearly double the population of the South. What this meant in practical political terms was that the majority of the U.S. House of Representatives came from states without slavery. Presidential elections, with the Electoral College system based on state populations, would also decisively favor Northern candidates soon enough. Control of the presidency, in turn, would ultimately mean Supreme Court appointees with a northward bias.

The only remaining political safety valve for the South was the equality in the Senate, with two senators per state; the North and the South had an equal number of senators at thirty each. In the House, the overwhelming population advantage of the North could, theoretically, tilt every issue against the South's interests, with immigration waves from Europe only hastening this condition further. The math was simple: Famine in Ireland and political turmoil in Europe meant more people. More people simply meant more power. And the cotton economy being entirely dependent on slave labor, the South was not as inviting to new immigrants as the economically diverse North.

Since 1820 the Missouri Compromise had set the terms of slavery in the territories that composed the Louisiana Purchase. But as the United States had expanded farther west, each new state had set off a battle of political will. Texas entered as a slave state in 1845. Iowa and Wisconsin were added as free states in 1846 and 1848. And here was California, with a state constitution presented to Congress, asking for admission as a free state. The issue might have been stalled for years but for one factor: California seemed to possess unimaginable riches.

Great debates ensued among the old lions in the Senate: Henry Clay,

Daniel Webster, and John Calhoun. And the existential fissure of the Union was plain to see during the debates on California statehood. The language was ominous, the pleas desperate. Predictably, the entire South opposed California's entry. And geography was adding insult to injury. California was large, and southern California was of the same latitude as Louisiana, Alabama, and Georgia. To some it seemed logical and fair to split California into two—one slave, one free. But California had already decided on its identity as a free state. A different compromise was required, an olive branch to southern slaveholders, assuring them that California's addition as the thirty-first state would not weaken slavery in the Union. The price was the elaborate Compromise of 1850 and, within it, the Fugitive Slave Act. California would not have become a state without it. And the Union would divide further because of it, the victory lap of Manifest Destiny, of gaining California and all its gold, serving as a very clear beginning of the end.

Ten

SLAVERY

Not too far from the South Carolina plantation where Eli Whitney first conceived of his cotton gin back in 1793 stood Butler Island, another plantation on the Georgia side of the border. Almost seventy years later, in 1859, the lasting consequences of his invention would be felt through three generations born and bred on this island. Once owned by Major Pierce Butler, a signer of the American Constitution, the plantation had one particularly distinguishing characteristic: The slaves there had rarely, if ever, been sold. Over time, slaves there had come to number in the hundreds, now resembling a village of grandparents, aunts and uncles, mothers and fathers, and children.

Through inheritance the plantation had been passed down to Butler's two grandsons. But one of the grandsons, also named Pierce Butler, had reportedly lost a fortune via speculation in the recent Panic of 1857: He now owed large debts and needed a way to appease his creditors. And so the 436 slaves of Butler Island packed their meager belongings of a lifetime, tearfully departed the only home and community most of them had ever known, and were loaded onto freight cars. While this community on the move was filled with anxiety about what future awaited them, another community of men was filled with eager anticipation, excitement even, at the prospect of one of the largest slave auctions in American history.

In preparation, the unlucky inhabitants of Butler Island were led to temporary housing next to the racecourse in Savannah, where the auction was set to take place in the early days of March. For now, in the holding pens that usually housed prized racehorses, they awaited their fates. In their despair, they couldn't have known that all this was happening as the nation's fate itself hung in the balance. Indeed, Butler Island's long-dead namesake had much to do with the current condition of four million slaves in America. As one of the nation's Founding Fathers, Butler's grandfather had been one of the leading men who had negotiated the language governing slavery at the time of the Constitution's drafting.

Indeed, the Compromise of 1850, including the Fugitive Slave Act, only added a dramatic layer of clarity to the words in the American Constitution. As part of the debates and politics of the Constitutional Convention of the 1780s, the nature of slaveholding had been especially important to southern states, where the majority of slaves existed. To unite these thirteen colonies and become one country required some safeguards for the wealthy southern delegates. As slavery either was abolished or its future tenuous in several of the northern colonies at the time, the question centered on the nature of property rights. If slaves were property, to what extent could that property be recovered? As property, a runaway slave had essentially stolen himself away from his rightful owner. What, then, happened when this runaway property, a fugitive slave, fled into a state where slavery was prohibited? Escaped horses or cattle would need to be rightfully returned to their owner; it only made sense to remove any ambiguity and apply this principle across all property.

So Article IV, Section 2 of the final draft of the Constitution made it clear: Slaves escaping into another state needed to be returned "upon claim" back to their owners. In the event that there was any future debate about the founders' intent, the tireless young James Madison's handwritten notes highlighted the sentiments of one southern delegate, Major Pierce Butler, as to what he expected: "Fugitive slaves and servants to be delivered up like criminals." And understandably so. Butler was one of the largest slaveholders in the South, representing South Carolina, a state that had more blacks than whites. To Butler and other

South Carolinians, it would have made little sense to join a union if the bulk of one's property could run away to another part of it and gain freedom as persons.

Here too the southerners managed to be shrewd negotiators. As the Constitution awarded congressional power and Electoral College votes based on population, the southern states wanted all slaves to be counted as "persons," even if they had no rights; the delegates finally settled on a slave counting for three fifths of a person when it came to allocating political power. When it came to economics, slaves would be counted as property. It was considered the best of both worlds.

But despite the sanctity of the Constitution and its nuances, several northern states had refused to catch runaway slaves. By 1850 their repudiation of their constitutional obligations had become especially offensive to southerners. Of thousands of runaways, the six New England states had managed a grand total of two captures over the preceding twenty-five years. Worse, runaways like Frederick Douglass in Massachusetts were made into celebrated figures among abolitionists. Given this, the price of allowing California in as a free state was that the North needed to accept the enforcement provisions of this new Fugitive Slave Act, giving real teeth to the clause in the Constitution. The sorts of sentiments that Douglass said he felt when he first reached a free state—"a moment of the highest excitement I ever experienced"—could not be allowed to endure. This new federal law extended the recognition of slaveholders' rights everywhere. But the compromise was the political equivalent of gasoline on inflamed tensions.

THE LARGE PATCHES of ice on the Ohio River were the steps to freedom in *Uncle Tom's Cabin*. From her home in Cincinnati, Harriet Beecher Stowe had heard a number of accounts through the years of escaped slaves from neighboring Kentucky crossing the river to emancipation in Ohio. Until the Fugitive Slave Act, the pursuing slave catcher could not readily count on the support of Ohio law enforcement to secure his target.

Starting in 1850, he could: The state of Ohio was now compelled by federal law to hunt escaped slaves, with local courts and magistrates having the power to conduct hearings and compel local marshals to assist slave catchers throughout the United States. The act even created a financial incentive for magistrates ruling on whether a slave could be transported away or not—$10 for expenses when the court ruled that the accused was an escaped slave, $5 when the accused slave was set free. And "good citizens" were asked for "faithful observance of the clause of the constitution," but in the event their patriotic conscience failed them, federal law now made it clear that helping escaped slaves was a criminal offense subject to indictment. Lastly, if it needed to be stated at all, the voice of the accused fugitive slave had no bearing: "In no trial or hearing under this act shall the testimony of such alleged fugitive be admitted in evidence."

Alarmed by this expansion of slaveholders' rights, Stowe began writing *Uncle Tom's Cabin.* Just as the lives of slaves on the Butler plantation were tied to their owner's debts, the fictional Tom's fate was tied to the credit woes of his owner, Mr. Shelby. To raise cash, Mr. Shelby reluctantly agreed to sell Tom to a slave trader, but the trader insisted on additional value, asking for a four-year-old boy to be added to the bargain. Upon hearing this, the boy's mother runs away with the child. The novel tells the parallel stories of Tom, as he is sold south, and the boy with his mother, as they escape north before the slave catcher can get them. The story sold hundreds of thousands of copies through the 1850s, including 300,000 in its first year. Even Queen Victoria was sufficiently moved to write Stowe a note of appreciation. Of course, British industry was highly dependent on southern cotton, highlighting the conflict between morality and money.

While Stowe and other northern abolitionists argued against slavery on a variety of moral grounds, the demographics of the North were strengthening the average American's economic interests against slavery too. Namely, the flood of immigrants in the early 1850s from Europe had added to working-class concerns about future wage pressures. At the same time, the white easterner with hopes of settling in the new territories in the West did not find the prospect of competing with slave owners to be a fair one. In any place where slavery was legal, the white farmer not wealthy enough to own slaves, forced to use his own hands for labor, was a second-class citizen. Alexis de Tocqueville, in his travels in the 1830s, had observed that in Kentucky, "work is connected with the idea of slavery," making it a "source of humiliation" for poor whites who, despite tending their own soil, "dread to look like slaves." As families with nothing more than their own labor had largely settled the entire Midwest, the idea of slavery in economic terms was an affront to the spirit of egalitarianism, of the vitality of self-sufficiency.

At the same time, the liquidity in the economy propelled by the Gold Rush had enabled a steady expansion of thousands of miles of railroad construction, rapidly adding new bands of iron tracks throughout the Northeast and Midwest. With each mile of track, each new immigrant—2.9 million people from overseas in just the preceding nine years to 1854—and each new settler from the East to the Midwest, the identity of the majority of Americans was separating from that of whites in the South, but it had yet to fully crystallize. From the perspective of the mid-1850s, the commercial telegraph was only ten years old—notions of modernity and an industrialized North were still unsettled concepts.

Politically, things in the North were unsettled as well. Rather than ease tensions, the Compromise of 1850 had pushed southern members of the Whigs into the hands of Democrats, who dominated the South, leaving the party in shambles it would not recover from and forcing former northern Whigs to forge new coalitions. For a moment some aligned with the new American Party. With the members professing to not know of the party's existence as an element of surprise saved for the polling booth, the "Know Nothings" attempted to rise as a native-born workingman's party. It was anti-immigrant, to ease pressure on the American workingman. It naturally was anti-Catholic as a part of being anti-Irish, given that the influx of cheap labor came from Ireland. And a few even looked to add an anti-alcohol component to the platform, casting the Germans and Irish immigrants as drunkards. And lastly it was antislavery, as owned labor was antithetical to the idea of the free workingman.

But the political unraveling led to political crises. In debates about how new states should be allowed into the Union as the vast American territory out west continued to be settled—how the balance between slave states and free states could be maintained—an idea known as popular sovereignty gained currency: Prospective new states would decide through popular referendum—elections within their territories—whether to enter as slave states or free. The Kansas Territory tried it out with the Kansas-Nebraska Act, but the attempt ended in disaster: Settlers on each side of the slave debate rushed in to settle the territories ahead of the election and routinely clashed in the bloody battles of a minor civil war to become known as Bleeding Kansas.

Violence even made it to the Senate floor. During an incendiary floor speech casting slaveholders as rapists of the American soil, Massachusetts senator Charles Sumner insulted an aging senator from South Carolina. Offended, the southern senator's cousin, Congressman Preston Brooks, saw Sumner sitting at his desk on the Senate floor some time later and nearly beat him to death with his cane. While Sumner spent the next three years recovering, his Senate seat was left empty as "mute testimony to the wages of violence," writes historian David Goldfield. Men across the South sent Brooks new canes to replace the one that he had damaged in beating Sumner.

From this climate emerged a new party, the Republicans. Eliminating much of the exclusionary politics of the Know Nothings while seeking common ground among the interests of free workingmen, immigrants, abolitionists, and prospective western settlers, the party's founding platform coalesced neatly into an antislavery position. Its first presidential candidate in 1856 was California's John Frémont, running with the slogan "Free soil and Fremont." He lost.

The antislavery interests would lose again the next year. Days before president-elect James Buchanan took office in March 1857, the chief justice of the Supreme Court, Roger B. Taney, personally notified him of a momentous decision. The case involved a slave named Dred Scott. Scott's owner had brought him to Illinois and the Wisconsin Territory, where Scott would live for some time. When his owner died, Scott sued for his freedom. Scott's essential claim was that as his owner had no right to maintain a slave in a free state in the North, he had relinquished his rights of ownership. The Taney court didn't directly rule on the issue of Dred Scott's freedom as much as it did on the nature of his humanity, his citizenship. In his majority opinion, Taney asked: "Can a negro whose ancestors were imported into this country and sold as slaves become a member of the political community formed and brought into existence by the Constitution of the United States, and as such become entitled to all the rights, and privileges, and immunities, guaranteed by that instrument to the citizen?" Taney argued that the founders did not intend this, and declared that even free blacks—in the North or South—could not ever be considered citizens of the United States, therefore denying Dred Scott the standing to pursue legal recourse in federal court. In addition, the decision enabled a new interpretation that a slave could be moved to any state in the Union, kept permanently there by his owner, and recognized forever as property. In a further blow, the decision held the Missouri Compromise, with its federal limits on the expansion of slavery, to be unconstitutional. At this late hour, from the abolitionists' perspective, the rights of slave owners were expanding.

In Illinois the entire 1858 Senate race between former congressman Abraham Lincoln and Senator Stephen Douglas centered on slavery. The Lincoln-Douglas debates hardened Lincoln's logic, his "belief that this government cannot endure, permanently half-slave and half-free." Lincoln lost the election, but the language that he used in the campaign would resurface. He would return to practice as a lawyer for another year or so before emerging on the national stage.

Despite the North's unease, the 1850s featured a series of political victories for slaveholders. There was only one national party of importance, the Democrats. The Supreme Court was sympathetic and sweeping in prohibiting federal limitations on slavery. And through equality in the Senate, southerners maintained legislative blocking power. All of this was very good for slave prices going into 1859.

AS THE BUTLER SLAVES waited for the hour of the auctioneer's gavel near the stables, all of the politics of slavery were far removed from the world that they knew. Their immediate concerns were focused on who their next master would be—Would he be humane? Would any of their extended family members be joining them? Would grandmothers see their grandsons ever again? Would sons see their mothers or aunts? How should the last days and hours be spent with people whom they would likely never see again?

For Joseph Bryan, on the other hand, the occasion was a highlight of his professional career. Bryan had risen to the status of a preeminent slave trader over a short period of five years, after retiring from eighteen years in the U.S. Navy. Known primarily through newspaper advertisements for slave sales, Bryan was a familiar name to those who followed the market in Georgia and Florida. While the vast majority of his offerings, presented in classified ads offering up to a dozen slaves, could be sold in the local market, receiving the large Butler consignment required far wider efforts. Starting in early February 1859, Joseph Bryan advertised his upcoming auction to prospective buyers as far away as New Orleans, Richmond, and points in between. The rarity of such a large lot of hundreds of slaves offered at a single time turned the auction into a notable southern event, a place to meet other large traders and speculators and glean the conditions of the market firsthand.

The news of this great sale had made it all the way up to New York, reaching Horace Greeley, the publisher of the *Tribune*, the city's largest newspaper. Greeley's abolitionist views were well known—editorials in his paper had seethed with anger as slaveholders won major political battles through the fifties. The publisher sent a correspondent, Mortimer Thomson, to report extensively on the details of the sale. As southerners were especially sensitive to prying northern eyes, Thompson took the guise of a slave speculator in an effort to gain complete access.

As the days of the auction approached, Savannah hotels were filled with men who had arrived for the event. "Nothing was heard for days in the bar-rooms and public rooms but talk of the great sale and speculations as to the probable prices," Thomson wrote. During the days, many, including Thomson, ventured to the outskirts to visit the holding pens before the auction. He saw the desperate pleas of the enslaved to prospective buyers—most wanted their extended family members to be purchased with them. In a bit of humanity, Butler had insisted that married couples and their children be sold together, but this left out many others—aunts and uncles, grandparents, generations of extended relatives—and courtships that had not been consummated in slave marriage.

For the buyers, more technical issues prevailed during their visits to the stables. The sixteen-page catalog produced by the auctioneer could tell a seasoned trader only so much. Proper due diligence required an examination of the teeth, musculature, and limbs of the human assets for signs of deformity, disease, and overall health. Thomson noted that there was great showmanship among the speculators during this routine, with several showing off with hostile interrogations of the incarcerated, peppering the slaves with scores of questions and indignities intended to show other traders that they "knew all about niggers."

In quieter moments, Thomson observed the slaves in their silence:

> On the faces of all was an expression of heavy grief; some appeared to be resigned to the hard stroke of Fortune that had torn them from their homes, and were sadly trying to make the best of it; some sat brooking moodily over their sorrows, their chins resting on their hands, their eyes staring vacantly, and their bodies rocking to and fro, with a restless motion that was never stilled; few wept, the place was too public, though some occasionally turned aside to give way to a few quiet tears.

Then the final hours came. After several days of inspections, posturing, and revelry among the buyers, the sale began on the morning of March 2, 1859. The proprietor of the trading house turned matters over to his auctioneer, T. J. Walsh, a man experienced in the art of creating energy among buyers to elicit top dollar.

The first family presented, lot number 1, was a family of four:

1. George	age 27	Prime Cotton Planter.
2. Sue	26	Prime Rice Planter.
3. George	6	Boy Child.
4. Harry	2	Boy Child.

The final bid was $2,480: the man for $1,200, his wife $900, and the young children for less than $200 each, according to the reporter's notes.

Each sale, along with its descriptions, provided deep insight into the value of slaves.

Jeffrey, lot number 318, age twenty-three, prime cotton hand, sold for $1,310.

The term "prime" meant the highest grade of field hand, the slave benchmark. It meant there were no visible physical deformities, impairments, or history of running away. The term was an enforceable seller representation—if a trader or buyer found otherwise, he could sue the seller for damages. The sale continued.

Guy, lot number 419, age twenty, prime, sold for $1,280.

Fielding and Abel, lot numbers 354 and 355, aged twenty-one and nineteen, both prime, sold for $1,295 each.

Wooster and Mary, lot numbers 103 and 104, sold for $300 each. Age was the discounting factor. Wooster was forty-five; Mary was forty.

Dembo, lot number 322, age twenty, had recently married Frances, lot number 404. The young couple sold for $1,320 each. Though women as field hands were generally worth less, a factor in the valuation was the expectation of children. Another factor, which enhanced the value of married prime hands, was that marriage reduced the risk that a slave would run away.

On and on the auction went. As could be expected, the most valuable slaves were young men in their late teens and early twenties, when a lifetime of productivity was ahead of them. For children, the maintenance cost of the first several years of ownership generally outpaced the yield. For older hands, the risk of a long, unproductive life on the plantation took their value back down to that of infant children, with older women often put in charge of young children while the mothers went to the fields. Very old slaves had negative value. Two dozen had stayed behind at the plantation for this reason.

When the final gavel landed, the auction had turned out to be a resounding success. The 436 slaves from the Butler plantation were sold for a total of $303,850, or an average price of close to $700. The composition of the Butler auction, since it was an entire community for sale, was an accurate approximation of the general slave population of children, the elderly, and working adults. At an average price of $700, the nearly four million slaves in the American South in 1859 can be estimated to be worth $2.8 billion collectively.

To put this in perspective, the longest railroad in America, the 705-mile Illinois Central, had recently been completed at a total cost of $25 million, with an average cost per mile of $35,000, which included all land acquisition, labor, and iron. Using this per-mile cost, which was on the high end, the thirty thousand miles of American railroad track, the most valuable industrial asset in America, were worth $1 billion. And it should be remembered that one third of the track mileage was in the South.

Similarly, slaves were worth several times more than all the gold found in California over the prior decade. All this suggests the impossibility of the lingering narrative that the federal government could have avoided bloodshed by compensating all slaveholders. The federal government's total expenditure for 1859 was $69 million—at this scale, even forty years of the entire annual federal budget would not have covered the market value of the slaves. Despite the rising tide of industry in the North, the numbers are beyond dispute: Slaves were the single most valuable asset class in America. Preservation of principal, not principle, formed the basis of every argument ever made in defense of slavery.

And the next year, 1860, slave prices went up even further—newspapers dubbed the speculative climate "Negro Fever"—making the institution worth defending at all costs all the more.

It might seem incongruous that slaves in the South represented the most valuable form of American property in the industrial age, but its link to industry overseas needs to be seen fully. This black labor was essential to growing the white gold that was cotton. And raw cotton was still the industrial lifeblood of England. Even in states where cotton wasn't grown, the slave's value was pegged to what he would be worth on a plantation that specialized in growing this most global of commodities. Given that the labor force involved in the production of cotton could be owned, it was valued accordingly. With the United States producing the vast majority of the world's cotton, cotton was its most valuable export, with no close second. In 1859 cotton production made up well over half of total U.S. exports. This too had significant implications for the American trade balance.

The northern states, contrary to their historical reputation for having an advanced economy in comparison with the South, imported far more manufactured and industrial goods from England than they exported. Throughout the 1850s, British iron rails, for instance, had come into the North in increasing quantities as America added thousands of miles of track. The northern trade deficit caused by such importation was offset by cotton exports from the South, keeping the American balance of payments whole. This delicate calibration of cotton exports and industrial imports was done through British creditors and New York investment houses, making New York City a vital nexus of the cotton trade. Ships that brought goods from England to the American North, rather than return home empty, took cotton back to England. Since New York investment houses were coordinating British capital investments in America, they were well positioned to convert the trade surplus created by cotton exports from the South into investment capital for the North. In short, the North was industrializing but had not industrialized—it too was largely an agrarian society, just far less so than the South. Unmistakably, the majority of what America actually sold to the world was grown in the South.

In this context, for slavery to unwind itself on the basis of morality or righteousness was a tall order. To the contrary, there is ample evidence to suggest that slavery had morphed from simply being a pool of owned labor to becoming, in effect, the monetary base of the South. In most farming societies, the most valuable asset was the land. The yield—what was and could be grown—was the basis of income. The South was different. Not only could the land be owned, but the lifetime value of labor inputs, human beings, could also be owned with clear and transferable legal title. Most important, just like land, slaveholders could pledge their slaves as loan collateral. Indeed, slaves made for a much better form of collateral than land. Land prices had far greater variability based on size of parcel, location, microclimate, crops grown, soil depletion, water access. And unlike a slave, land could not be moved. For the borrower, it was easier to sell one or two slaves than to break off a portion of their land. For a distant creditor, it was easier to lend against a group of twentysomething slaves than against unknown land—upon a default, a pledged slave could be taken quickly, moved, and sold in the market that fetched the best prices. The Tennessee land of a defaulting borrower could not be easily assessed and sold by a New Orleans lender, but his slaves could.

That slaves were easy to borrow against, conversely, made it easier to buy a slave. Just as at the Butler auction, few buyers needed to pay cash up front. Most borrowed. When a slave was borrowed against, the slave became a security, a note that could be traded among financial interests even without the slave changing hands. This degree of liquidity allowed a slave owner to borrow against his slaves on an ongoing basis. And as slave prices went up throughout the 1850s, there was a noticeable and growing confidence among southerners, one journal holding that "this alliance between negroes and cotton, we will venture to say, is the strongest power in the world."

On many plantations, slave-backed loans were used for working capital, the purchase of materials for the planting season, and capital improvements. At the center of this need was the dramatic growth in the production and demand for cotton. In 1840 the South produced 674 million pounds of raw cotton. By 1859 this had tripled to over 2 billion pounds in a single year; cotton was now a crop valued at well over $250 million annually, four times the federal budget of the United States. This growth needed infusions of capital to support the clearing of new lands to be converted to cotton production. Just as with tobacco in the eighteenth century, the capital made its way to cotton planters through layers of intermediaries starting with the men known as factors.

The factor was essentially a middleman who arranged for financing secured against future delivery of the upcoming season's crop. Upon advancing money to numerous planters, the factor aggregated the contracts on expected crops and bundled them for sale to a shipping merchant or agent in New Orleans. The money advanced to the planter, like all cash advances, carried with it some level of interest. When the cotton was harvested, the factor would settle the remainder with the planter. Even though he was technically an agent for the planter's cotton crop, the factor's primary profits came from brokering financing from the wholesalers, banks, and the world market at large to the planter—an agrarian investment banking activity of sorts.

Over time, the role of factors and agents grew into broader financial intermediaries. The factors, since they were already in the business of advancing funds, evolved into guarantors, cosigners, on larger loans made to planters. The factor would agree to endorse a note for a planter. Often, the planter would pledge a group of slaves as collateral. With the guarantee of the factor, a bank or merchant would then loan money to the planter. The factor earned his fee by brokering the loan without providing any actual capital but guaranteed that his client planter would pay the loan. By 1860 endorsed notes collateralized by slaves had a wide secondary market. Merchants who loaned money to a planter could sell the note to other parties; such a note often served as a currency in itself. Far more than land, the most widely accepted collateral at the base of this monetary system was either future cotton deliveries or mortgages on slaves.

Predictably, when a plantation owner died, the executor of the estate often liquidated the slaves to pay the creditors. Some banks even had slaveholding pens for situations when they had to repossess collateral on nonperforming loans. This legacy of slave collateralization is not completely removed from the American corporate lineage: Though it existed neither as a brand nor as a business at the time of slavery, Chase bank discovered in its history of acquisitions two banks, Citizens Bank of Louisiana and the New Orleans Canal Bank, that had together collateralized over thirteen thousand slaves before the Civil War.

Culturally, owning a slave became a financial rite of passage, an indication of having made it. Just as owning land conferred social standing and respect, owning slaves, even one, marked an elevating factor from being a slaveless poor white. Land could be depleted. Cotton prices could change. But owning a few slaves, even a family, capable of having slave offspring signaled a renewable source of wealth. For a young man of ambition, given that cotton was the center of most large fortunes, the highest station in life, which conferred ease of living, social status, and financial stability, was that of the large plantation owner. With a mansion and surrounded by one's "people"—the gentleman's euphemism for slaves—the southerner who made it rose to the level of landed aristocracy, which had no equivalent in the North. In emulation of the financial acumen of these achievers, slaves were "considered the best investment for persons of small means and for trust funds for widows and orphans."

But what appeared to be stability was distorted by leverage. Just as a person with a credit card may feel their purchasing power to be greater than it is, looseness of credit fueled the final act of American slavery. Despite the rising tensions in the North, slave prices continued to climb into the presidential election year of 1860. Months away from the breaking up of the Union, the collective wisdom of the market seemed to see little threat to the institution of slavery. The evidence could be seen at another auction. A little more than a year after the Butler auction came an even bigger sale.

Joseph Bond, a wealthy southerner, was killed while confronting a former overseer over a personal affront. A few months after his death, his estate was compelled to sell the entirety of his lands and slaves: over nineteen thousand acres and over 500 slaves. By January 1860, conditions in the slave market had become so euphoric that the prices seen at the Bond auction were even higher than those at the Butler auction—566 slaves of all ages sold for a total of $580,150. Top field hands fetched over $2,000. The average price had exceeded $1,000, a level that implied that the four million slaves in America were now collectively worth $4 billion. Remarkably, even young children and young mothers commanded good prices. On the eve of America's great cataclysm, the prices of the young suggested that buyers and financiers felt confident in the long-term future of slavery—long enough for the children to grow into productivity. Or buyers, fueled by ample credit, simply viewed slaves as continually appreciating assets, assets that could be sold to the next buyer at even higher prices. Credit was always the final enabler of speculative frenzies.

But credit also corrupted morality, complicating slavery with layers of paper. Was a widow left with five hundred acres, six slaves, and $10,000 in debt in any position to free her slaves? Her creditors would have objected. Was a man who in his youth had been bent on financial accumulation and had borrowed heavily to build his estate, but was now having a change of heart about the source of his wealth, in any position to embrace enlightenment? Widespread borrowing, the credit structure of the entire South, was based on its most valuable asset. Credit was intertwined within and interlaced through every aspect of slave society. Southerners could no sooner free their slaves voluntarily than contemporary Americans could donate their mortgaged homes to charity. Debt limited action. It took a person without debts, without heirs, and with high principles to voluntarily give up a valuable personal asset. And even here, principles could be subverted by political considerations. Roger B. Taney, the Supreme Court chief justice who ruled that Dred Scott and all African descendants could never be considered American citizens, had freed his own slaves as a young man decades earlier.

In the final months of the first iteration of the United States, the political issue that the American Constitution could not solve came down to money. The trigger was the bubble in slave prices. And as slave prices kept going up in the speculative mania of Negro Fever from the late 1850s into 1860, there was more to protect and more to lose. The market made the South perceive that slavery was worth far more than it actually was, decoupled from the cotton prices with which it had once been strictly correlated. And rationally and ironically, southerners did not want to let go of an institution that the market irrationally valued at well over $3 billion and growing. Unfolding political events seemed to point to only one rational option. The illusion of rising fortunes caused by the deep, abiding faith in market valuations, with all its accompanying bravado, sealed the American fate.

PART TWO

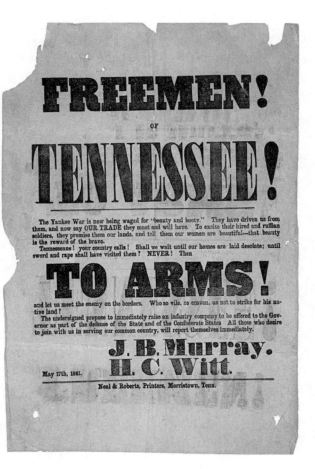

*A Confederate recruitment
poster, 1861.*

Eleven

WAR

In the dark evening hours of a Sunday in October 1859, Bill Smith and his adult sons made the move for which they had been preparing patiently. For months, in the small Virginia town of Harpers Ferry, the Smiths had been seen diligently running errands through town. Having rented a farm across the river in Maryland, the men had seemingly been developing a small mining venture. But Smith's preparations had nothing to do with any commercial activity. In an age before the wide availability of photographs, it was easy for a figure of some notoriety to pose as a generic Bill Smith. Had the Virginians known that this Bill Smith was actually John Brown, their manners would have been far less welcoming.

Brown's reputation stemmed from the aftermath of the Kansas-Nebraska Act, when he had made his way west to Kansas to fight against the proslavery settlers there. He and his sons had reputedly hacked several such men to death in front of their families. Having fallen significantly short of his ultimate goal, Brown made his way to Virginia to lay the groundwork for his latest plan to free slaves. In Harpers Ferry stood a federal armory. Brown, along with a few men he had enlisted to the cause, planned to seal off the town, seize the armory, and lead a slave insurrection with the armory's weapons and bullets. Over the course of the first evening and early morning, he managed to take over the armory, along with several hostages, explaining to one of his prisoners, "We are abolitionists from the North, we come to take and release your slaves." The effort failed when federal troops, led by Robert E. Lee, responded within hours, forcing surrender after a standoff.

In the North many now considered Brown a hero, expressing "astonishment at the insane undertakings of the insurgents." In the South he was considered a terrorist; Brown's actions and the sympathy he garnered were an indictment of the entire North, its subversion of the law, and its refusal to respect either the Constitution or the terms of the Union. Over the next few weeks, telegraphed daily accounts gripped Americans everywhere. The trial of John Brown, along with the voices of northern supporters and the seething anger in the South, all blended together to occupy newspaper front pages for weeks. Convicted by a court in Virginia within days, Brown was sentenced to death, leading to widespread paranoia among Virginians that northern vigilantes or an abolitionist army would liberate him. The governor of Virginia considered invoking martial law in the days leading up to the execution, and over three thousand federal troops were ordered to guard Charlestown, where Brown was being held. "Panic pervades all classes," the *New York Times* reported, "every eye is anxious, and even the presence of a large body of troops does not allay the apprehension of an invasion."

In death, John Brown became a symbol. Henry Ward Beecher, Harriet Beecher Stowe's brother and the pastor at the Plymouth Church in Brooklyn, suggested that a power far greater than the Constitution redeemed Brown: "A man who will not suffer for his country does not love his country. . . . It was the martyrs who walked into the fires—who thrust their hands boldly into the flames—who died singing as they expired. . . . Hence the progress of all causes that could find martyrs." Two months after Brown's hanging, in the early months of 1860, Beecher invited an improbable presidential candidate to speak at his church.

When Abraham Lincoln received Beecher's invitation, he had been out of political office for nearly ten years. Even that early accomplishment was underwhelming—he had served as a congressman for a total of two years. Mostly he had made a living as a lawyer in Illinois. He did, however, have a national reputation stemming from published transcripts of his debates with Stephen Douglas. Though he had lost that Senate race, the text of Lincoln's speeches had resonated enough that he viewed the nomination of the nascent Republican Party as a possibility. Other candidates for the nomination included William H. Seward and Salmon P. Chase—both men, who were far more esteemed and established than Lincoln, had been equally strident in their opposition to slavery. But Lincoln had one advantage: He was a vastly superior speaker by all accounts.

By the time Lincoln made it to New York, the venue for the speech had been changed from Beecher's church to the cavernous hall at the Cooper Union. There Lincoln dissected the slavery question constitutionally, politically, and historically, but in closing he boiled it down to the one question that made it unsolvable:

> If slavery is right, all words, acts, laws, and constitutions against it, are themselves wrong, and should be silenced and swept away. . . . If it is wrong, they cannot justly insist upon its extension. All they ask we could readily grant if we thought slavery right. All we ask they could readily grant if they thought it was wrong. Their thinking it right, and our thinking it wrong is the precise fact upon which depends the controversy. Thinking it right, as they do, they are not to blame for desiring its full recognition . . . but thinking it wrong as we do, can we yield to them?

Decades of compromises, contrivances, and stopgap measures could no longer give this stark issue politically negotiated cover.

Lincoln, of course, went on to win both the nomination and the general election in the fall of 1860. Unsurprisingly, he did it without winning a single southern state. The fact that Lincoln could put the issue of slavery in such stark terms and still win the election meant, in Southern eyes, that the final hour of the Republic had arrived. A little more than a month after Lincoln's election, South Carolina seceded. The American Constitution, a political document as venerated as the founders, was invalidated and held to be a bad bargain, its binding effects abrogated. In its official declaration of the causes of secession, the South Carolinians' equivalent of the Declaration of Independence, the state pointed explicitly to the "election of a man . . . whose opinions and purposes are hostile to slavery."

Then in January, before Lincoln took office, Mississippi seceded, followed quickly by Florida, Alabama, Georgia, and Louisiana before the end of the month. Among this group, Mississippi and Georgia detailed the causes of their secession. In Mississippi's declaration, after a long list of grievances related to the attacks on slavery, it listed the real reason in closing: "We must either submit to degradation, and to the loss of property worth four billions of money, or we must secede from the union framed by our fathers. . . . For far less cause than this, our fathers separated from the Crown of England." Indeed. But the Georgians were more modest. In their valuation of the four million Southern slaves, they claimed their seceding principle to be the Southern defense of only "$3,000,000,000 of our property." Regardless of a billion here or there, all of this was fundamentally true. Slaves were worth billions of dollars. It merits mention that despite later invocations of individual states' rights as the superseding principle, when it came to calculating monetary damages, Georgia and Mississippi counted all slaves across the South as one collective institution. And if they were freed somehow, all this property would be worth nothing.

By the time Lincoln took the oath of office, six states in the Deep South, along with Texas, no longer considered themselves a part of the United States. While the rebel spirit of 1776 was once again alive, with states declaring independence, the constitutional experiment of forging a more perfect Union had failed.

At the same time, a dominant strain of Southern thinking suggested that secession by itself did not necessarily mean war. Could the new, untested, and inexperienced president even mobilize forces? During the Mexican-American War more than a decade earlier, tens of thousands of men had volunteered for the national cause with great enthusiasm, but manifesting the destiny of the Republic westward was a call for national glory. There was no prospect for glory in a civil war—just a return to the former status of the Union. Would the North send its sons to keep the South? Would men be willing to die to hold onto the idea of a unified nation, a political abstraction, when Southern citizens of that very Union dissented by the millions? The only guarantee was that both victory and defeat would leave the same bloody, bitter aftertaste. Why spill blood to cement the states when the ink on the Constitution couldn't? Where was the northern incentive to fight, given these factors?

But the South miscalculated. Between Lincoln's election in November and the official start of his term in March, rebel forces in South Carolina surrounded Charleston's Fort Sumter, a federal military outpost, one of the last that had not come under Southern control. Responding to the developments through his inaugural address, Lincoln asserted that the federal government had a right to all of its property, whether in seceded states or not. He concluded by saying, "In your hands, my dissatisfied fellow-countrymen, and not in mine, is the momentous issue of civil war. The government will not assail you. You can have no conflict without being yourselves the aggressors." Thinking it unnecessarily provocative, Lincoln had even deleted the final few words from an earlier draft, where he would have asked simply, "Shall it be peace, or a sword?" Nevertheless, he received the answer to this unasked question a few weeks later.

The army major holed up inside Fort Sumter had passed along a message to the White House. He would run out of food in six weeks, at which point he would have to surrender unless resupplied. After notifying the governor of South Carolina of its intentions, despite the state's secession, a U.S. naval vessel was dispatched to resupply the fort. Sometime after the ship's arrival, to prevent replenishment of the fort, Confederate forces fired on Fort Sumter. After a barrage starting overnight and lasting over a day, on April 12, Major Robert Anderson surrendered his forces and was allowed to walk off with his men to the nearby naval ship. No one died. But the end of the standoff, caused by the act of firing on a federal fort, had just started the civil war.

WARFARE IN THE INDUSTRIAL AGE, it would become clear, was not going to be waged by brave soldiers and stoic generals alone. Rebel spirits and patriotism could only instigate—matériel and money would become as vital as, perhaps much more so than, blood and men.

Within days of the attack on Fort Sumter, the North mobilized its response. Immediately it became clear that American business would play a central role in the effort. One of the first orders was to get a telegraph and railroad system operational for war. Having been in office for mere days, Secretary of War Simon Cameron called on the Pennsylvania Railroad to dispatch an executive to Washington at once. The executive, Tom Scott, was then made the assistant secretary of war in charge of all railroads and telegraph operations. Scott, in turn, delegated many of his responsibilities at the War Department to the young boy he had once recruited from a local telegraph office. Just twenty-five, Andrew Carnegie was tasked with initial preparation of the telegraphic and railroad infrastructure for the Union Army. A week after Fort Sumter, Carnegie found himself traveling from Pennsylvania to Washington, supervising a contingent of Pennsylvania Railroad employees tasked with bridge building, track maintenance, and railroad operations in advance of the troops that the president had called to Washington.

As the train pressed through Maryland, a slave state in the Union, Carnegie needed to fix a sabotaged stretch of track and get it ready for trainloads of incoming troops from the North. After this was completed, he noticed that a portion of the telegraph wire had been cut by rebel sympathizers. Carnegie, in his attempt to fix the damage, suffered a laceration when a released wire struck him in the face. His deputies in his telegraph department would later joke, with some truth, that Carnegie's injury and bloodied face had made him one of the first casualties of the Civil War.

Upon reaching Washington, Carnegie was given the immediate job of overseeing the extension of the Baltimore and Ohio Railroad from its depot in Washington into neighboring Alexandria, Virginia. Over the course of a tireless seven days, Carnegie and his men extended rails across Long Bridge over the Potomac River. Soldiers from various state militias arrived at the capital through a transportation network that hadn't existed twenty years earlier. But the private interests of railroads had left a patchwork of uncoordinated railroad lines, where tracks from one system didn't connect with those of another, an incompatibility that had often required passengers and freight to switch trains to different operators when venturing to out-of-state destinations. Over the next three years, the federal government would mandate significant efficiencies:

Fast mobilizations of the Union Army and its supplies required complete standardization of many aspects of the nation's railroad system, the most basic being track gauge, a measure of the width between railroad tracks.

While the Long Bridge was being readied, Carnegie called for four telegraph operators from the Pennsylvania Railroad to set up a makeshift telegraph office in Washington. Before long, this group would expand to become the U.S. Military Telegraph Corps. For the first few months, Carnegie helped establish the office, set protocols, and open facilities next to areas where advancing troops set up camp. Before long, an executive from the largest telegraph company, Western Union, took over as the military's head of telegraph operations. Staffed by dozens of operators, the office would receive continual dispatches related to enemy movements, coordination of logistics, and news from the battlefields. For the first time in history, a war was conducted with near-real-time information "employed to direct widely separated armies in unison." Lincoln himself, to get news and reports from the battlefield, spent a part of nearly every day in his telegraph office.

The South had its own railroads and telegraphs as well. In fact, one subsequent analysis conducted by the U.S. Army Combat Studies Institute reasoned that both armies' movements, so heavily dependent on the logistics of railroads, led to prolonged warfare, as the use of railroads tended "to diminish the significance of victory or defeat" of any single battle. "When defeated, an army supplied by rail often could be reinforced before the victor, traveling on muscle power, could exploit his success. Thus tactical victories rarely led to strategic gains." At the same time, a stalemate was the same thing as a Southern victory, achieved simply by holding on to the South's new independence and resisting any invasion. A Union victory, however, required invasion into Southern territory—where Northern railroads and telegraphs would be of no advantage—and needed to compel complete capitulation. In defending Southern territory, large Confederate troop movements in the first half of the war relied heavily on the railroad, moving up to thirty thousand troops in shifts to the battlefield. Given the South's defensive advantage, "had the war ended in 1863, historians might well list the Confederate railroads as a decisive element contributing to Confederate victory," writes army historian Christopher Gabel.

But maintenance of railroad tracks, which deteriorate within months in times of heavy use, required ongoing inputs of iron. And the South ran out. Gabel estimates that the South needed nearly 50,000 tons of iron rails per year to replace worn-out tracks on its nine thousand miles of railroad. By midwar the North had produced over 200,000 tons of iron rails, while the South had produced about one eighth of this amount. By 1863 "rail was wearing out all over the South, and stockpiles of new rail were gone." The South then began cannibalizing iron tracks from other lines to support the most essential military supply lines. This disrupted flows of food from low-traffic routes as railroad tracks began contracting in agricultural areas. This modern warfare was a battle of two economies.

Indeed, many histories of the Civil War touch on the superiority of Northern industry as a causal factor that led to eventual Union victory. But this line of reasoning presents an incomplete picture and misses a central data point. The North, in the decade before the war, was not wholly self-sufficient when it came to iron either. Throughout the 1850s, America was by far the biggest market for British iron makers, including over 138,000 tons in 1860 alone.

Lost is the perspective that flows from the South having controlled nearly 60 percent of America's prewar exports. If the South continued selling cotton to British textile mills, couldn't it in exchange get whatever industrial or military goods it needed? Britain, compared with the American North in the mid-nineteenth century, was the far superior industrial power. And since Britain needed raw cotton to keep its own mills running at capacity, a large part of its economy was entirely dependent on the American South, the world's dominant cotton producer. The South, then, didn't need to have its own industrial capacity when it could so readily use cotton as currency for British iron or manufactured goods. Iron for cotton would have been a natural trade, a simple war-financing mechanism as endless as the cotton fields in the Mississippi Delta.

This, of course, did not happen. Seven days after the Confederate attack on Fort Sumter, around the same time Carnegie and his boss, Tom Scott, began their early preparations for the army, Lincoln ordered his navy to blockade the Southern ports. Indeed, there is a case to be made that the Civil War was not won on land at all.

. . .

THE NORTH'S BLOCKADE almost risked starting another war. In the first few months, as it became clear that the Union Navy had effectively cut off the South from trade, British newspapers grew increasingly vitriolic. British cotton mills and ironworks both suffered substantially. Understanding the strategic importance of Britain and looking to exploit the sentiment to its advantage, the Confederacy appointed two ministers, James Mason and John Slidell, with the mission of establishing direct diplomatic ties with Great Britain. Even before the war, one confident Southern posture held that the economic bonds of King Cotton could be converted to diplomatic and political bonds with Britain, and soon extended into full sovereign recognition of the Confederacy.

The two ministers, escaping the blockade, made their way to Cuba, where they boarded the British steamship *Trent* to present their case to officials in London. Enforcing the blockade, but inadvertently breaking protocol, the USS *Jacinto* stopped the ship in international waters. The ship's commander, after searching the ship, captured the two men and sent them as prisoners to Fort Warren in Massachusetts. The British protested the search of their flagged vessel as a breach of international law—an affront to their sovereignty—and demanded the release of the Confederate diplomats along with an apology. The Lincoln administration refused on all fronts—a bit of nationalism that played well with Northern newspapers, especially as initial battles, starting with the First Battle of Bull Run, had gone the South's way.

The British, however, had a significant point of leverage. Since the 1600s, India had been the world's leading producer of saltpeter, or potassium nitrate, the key ingredient in gunpowder. Like the Chinese tea of the British East India Company, the saltpeter then made its way to Britain for export to the rest of the world. In the fall of 1861, while the Trent Affair was playing out, the Union's primary supplier of gunpowder, E. I. du Pont de Nemours and Company, had been instructed to buy massive quantities of saltpeter. The company's head, Henry du Pont, then dispatched his nephew Lammot du Pont to England to coordinate the purchases. But Lammot's purchases were of alarming scale, comprising nearly all of the saltpeter on hand in England at the time. The company, without directly stating that it was buying for the U.S. government, then purchased the entirety of a future shipload due to arrive from India. Collectively the nearly three thousand tons on order and its hastily arranged departure caught the attention of the British foreign secretary, who wrote a note warning, "The very rapid way it is being shipped off within three days [is] altogether unusual." While Lammot was having one of four large ships loaded with his order, given that the Confederate diplomats were still being held, the British government ordered the ships to remain in port.

As Lincoln's first Christmas in the White House approached, tensions had reached a fever pitch. Several London newspapers called for war with America. British troops were mobilized to Canada. A high-ranking British diplomat then presented an ultimatum to his American counterpart to release Mason and Slidell, or the British Embassy in Washington would be closed and diplomatic relations severed, such breaks often a prelude to more serious hostilities. Highlighting the centrality of American companies in the conduct of the war, DuPont company officials conferred with Secretary of State Seward as to the logistical consequences. Meeting with his cabinet on Christmas Day, and then the next day, Lincoln agreed to both the release and apology. Soon after, the gunpowder was released to DuPont. Pleased, a Union general noted that the ninety thousand barrels would last three years based on the scale of the war at the time, but the scale would escalate beyond imagination.

For the South, the release of Slidell and Mason turned out to be a moral victory only; the blockade continued for the remainder of the war. The presence of U.S. naval vessels in the waters outside major ports such as Charleston, New Orleans, and Savannah shut off the South's ability to finance its war. Far more than any other military strategy, this opening gambit may have been most fundamental to the Union's victory. The effect was immediate and severe. In 1861 the Southern cotton crop was even higher than the previous year at 4.4 million bales, each bale weighing about five hundred pounds. But the cotton could not leave Southern ports. With millions of bales of unsold cotton sitting on Southern docks, cotton production the following year declined by nearly 70 percent. By

1864, cotton production in the South had fallen by over 93 percent from its prewar level. Without the ability to sell cotton overseas, the South had no way to pay for or import its wartime needs.

Despite the administration's capitulation, Britain did its part to avoid offending the administration overtly. Earlier in the year, Seward had warned that any British support for the Confederacy would make America, "as we have twice before been forced to be, enemies of Great Britain." But bluster alone was not the deterrent. British industry suffered, as did European nations to varying degrees, quite dramatically due to the American Civil War. Not only did many cotton mills come to a near standstill, but iron exports to America fell nearly 80 percent in the first two years of the war, causing substantial slowdowns in the foundries as well. Through 1862 the Confederacy had tried to use this economic wedge to garner support in global capitals. But British colonialism ruined the South's remaining leverage. Cotton production dramatically increased in British India and Egypt, growing from less than 450 million pounds of raw cotton in 1860 to nearly one billion pounds by 1866. Seward understood how this dynamic would play out, calling the Confederacy "blind to their own welfare if they do not see how their prosperity and all their hopes are passing away, when they find Egypt, Asia Minor, and India supplying the world with cotton, and California furnishing the gold for its purchase." The shift was so significant, writes Sven Beckert, that "historians of Egypt rank the American Civil War among the most crucial events in that country's nineteenth-century history."

BUT SOUTHERN RUIN was a far cry from conditions in the North. There the war was more profitable than anyone could have imagined. While the profiteer of the South was perhaps best exemplified by future fictional characters such as *Gone with the Wind*'s Rhett Butler, a blockade runner who evades the Union naval patrols with his contraband—a sole wealthy miscreant in a sea of desperation—in the North the businessmen molded by the war would be of a less fictional nature.

In contrast to the Confederacy, which shrank its own railroad infrastructure due to iron shortages, the North was in the midst of a booming commercial renaissance, a complete transformation. The Civil War introduced a vast variety of modern elements to American statecraft and governance. Indeed, in light of the secession, the United States no longer needed to maintain any placating pretenses that the nation was made up of strong individual states. In its emergency, it needed the full weight of federal power and coordination to conduct the war. The Civil War could even be considered the final act in the Darwinian competition between the competing visions of government: The Jeffersonian precepts of limited government finally gave way to the Hamiltonian vision. Modernity required a government that could operate at scale, one that could bypass provincial interests quickly and forcefully. But even this realization came slowly.

For much of 1861, the North was shell-shocked. Rebel forces seemed to have the upper hand. And the incoming Lincoln administration was anything but sure-footed. The federal government's expenditures in this first year had barely changed from peacetime—$66 million compared with the previous year's $68 million. Companies, including Western Union, simply provided services with the expectation of payment in the future. By early 1862, it had become clear to Secretary of the Treasury Salmon P. Chase that the federal government's ability to borrow was significantly curtailed by the uncertainties of war. It had experimented with a paper currency, popularly called the greenback, the previous summer, but the initiative had been widely scorned. The idea of paper that was not convertible to gold was a foreign concept. But the government tried again. In February, Congress passed the Legal Tender Act, authorizing the issue of $150 million of currency that was not backed by gold to pay for wartime expenses. To ensure that the currency would achieve wide circulation, the Legal Tender Act mandated that all parties in the United States, public and private, accept the paper to satisfy all debts. All taxes, except for import duties, could be paid using the greenback. To increase its acceptance among people fearful of paper, recipients of this paper could convert the money into five- to twenty-year bonds, with 6 percent interest paid in gold. With this currency, 1862 expenditures went up to $474 million—a 620 percent increase in federal spending.

The federal government, whose largest peacetime activity had been to operate the postal service, was now unshackled financially to prosecute the war in full. By the middle of 1862, as the Union was ramping up its efforts to bring hundreds of thousands of soldiers into its forces, it needed to borrow hundreds of millions of dollars. It enlisted a friend of the treasury secretary, Jay Cooke, to act as an agent to sell bonds to the public. Cooke, employing hundreds of traveling bond salesmen over the years, marketed these bonds to local savers throughout the North by going town to town. Federal debt would ultimately grow to nearly $3 billion by the end of the war. But there was nothing illusory about all this paper—it stimulated a significant amount of economic activity. Indeed, some of the activity had little to do with the war but reinforced big-picture ideas of the modern Republic, continental ambitions that predated the conflict.

From the time of the Gold Rush, the idea of connecting the Pacific Coast to the East via a large railroad had been a dream of both capitalists and politicians. But there had been a problem: Southerners wanted the route to run through the South. With larger political issues looming, the transcontinental railroad had not been approved during the 1850s. But in the summer of 1862, the emboldened federal government, in the absence of Southern elements in the House and the Senate, approved the Pacific Railway Act. While the South was rationing its iron, here was the North embarking on a railroad experiment to connect the continent. The Pacific Railway Act, with a combination of land grants and bond guarantees, allowed for private interests to begin the construction of a railroad. Starting from the West, the rights to build fell to a group of Sacramento merchants, led by Collis Huntington and Leland Stanford, men who had arrived and prospered with the Gold Rush. By the end of the decade, the transcontinental railroad would allow a passenger embarking in New York to arrive in San Francisco in less than a dozen days. But the lingering effects of the Gold Rush benefited the North in another way. With paper currency used internally, the federal Treasury and eastern banks had ample physical gold holdings that had made their way to the East Coast during the gold rush. This was then used to pay for overseas purchases; over $100 million worth of physical gold left the Union in 1864. In the same year, imports of British iron went back up to over 100,000 tons.

But the idea of laying down track in barren areas was hardly a match for the prospect for profits geographically closer to the war. John D. Rockefeller, a young Cleveland produce wholesaler barely in his twenties, had achieved a small fortune brokering shipments of food throughout the war. Andrew Carnegie, from his vantage point as a young railroad executive, found himself pursuing investments and side ventures, including a bridge-building company, a telegraph line, and other start-up efforts. Noticing that iron was fetching as much as $130 per ton, Carnegie then organized a rail-making concern, his first foray into iron. For 1863, the same year that Lincoln's Emancipation Proclamation asserted the liberty of slaves, the twenty-eight-year-old Carnegie reported a personal wartime income of $42,260.67; this dwarfed by many multiples the amount he still earned as an official employee of the railroad.

Of course, there was a fundamental mechanism that allowed such pursuit of personal gain during inestimable bloodshed. The Union Army allowed wealthier men who were drafted to pay $300 for a substitute to fight in their place. This had even boiled over into a dramatic bit of class warfare with the Draft Riots in New York City, where "$300 man" was the invective used by the have-nots in occasionally accosting the haves. One $300 man, J. P. Morgan, the son of America's top banker in London, noted in his account book that he had spent about the same amount on cigars in 1863.

Still, even the prospect of fighting in an American war was a unique economic opportunity for many overseas. At the tail end of the war, the Union continued to look for soldiers, with agents recruiting across the ocean. The proposition was alluring: free passage to America, payment for service in the Union Army, American citizenship, a signing bonus, and money to start one's life in America. For men like Joseph Pulitzer, fighting seemed more attractive than his prospects in Europe. Altogether unfit for service and speaking few words of English, he made his way to a Union regiment. But the war would be over before he saw battle.

It was all a prelude to the next American age—an era from which the names history would remember most would stand in stark contrast to the signatories of the country's founding documents. These men would be conquerors of industry, builders of brands, inventors and makers, and masters of economic organization who together marked the rise of America.

Twelve

OIL

In America's whaling capital, the seaside Massachusetts village of New Bedford, thousands of spectators assembled for a large send-off in the opening year of the Civil War. In the harbor stood nearly two dozen whaling ships, all outfitted for what would surely be their final voyage at sea. But there would be no search for whales this time. The ships' owners had sold them to the U.S. Navy. The vessels, sold for scrap at $10 per ton, were procured as a part of the Union's effort to blockade the South. The ships had been painted to look like warships and loaded with stones—granite, cobblestones, and old rock walls—in preparation to sail to Savannah, Georgia. Once there, the ships were to be sunk in the shallow harbor, effectively closing off one vital Southern port. Under the headline THE GREAT STONE FLEET, the *New York Times* gleefully held that this armada of a once-vital industry was now on the mission of delivering "terror and dismay" to the rebellion.

Unfolding as it did during the Civil War, the fate of the whale ships seemed an especially apt signal of the end of early America and the rise of industrial America. Whaling's final decline had started with an 1859 discovery in Pennsylvania, which precipitated another rush similar to the one for gold—only in this case men were soon covered head to toe in a slick, black substance as evidence of their daily fortune seeking. Oil quickly brought an end to the era when ships full of hardy men had battled giant creatures of the ocean for their economic value, primarily as a clean-burning source of evening light. Now the ships were almost worthless. It was fitting that this industry, which had been captured in countless fictional forms—most notably Herman Melville's *Moby-Dick*—would maintain its romance with a bit of theater even in its hour of sunset.

Unlike the Gold Rush, which had started from a single momentous discovery, the oil rush was the product of dozens of experiments. The final series of trials centered in one region of western Pennsylvania, where oil was so rich that it practically seeped out of the ground or from streambeds. Where it was present, it was largely viewed as an unavoidable, foul-smelling nuisance. Notably, it had obstructed one entrepreneur, Samuel Kier, who had started a venture to drill for salt water to make salt, only to have his efforts yield more of this useless oil. But knowing a bit about local Indian tribes' veneration of its therapeutic uses, Kier began selling the oil for 50 cents per small bottle, cleverly marketing it as "Kier's Petroleum or Rock Oil, Celebrated for its Wonderful Curative Powers." Others, such as George Bissell, a thirtysomething Dartmouth graduate, came to see potential in the flammable properties of this surface oil and organized a venture called the Pennsylvania Rock Oil Company to capture it in larger quantities.

At the same time, another venture called the Kerosene Oil Company had invested heavily in a process to extract a flammable liquid out of coal. As coal was required for steam engines of all types, it was mined in abundance—speculating on this alternative use, numerous ventures had committed to the idea of extracting this "coal oil." Coal oil, soon synonymous with its trade name, kerosene, made its way into American homes, with over two million coal-oil lamps sold in America by 1859. But the Kerosene Oil Company had realized independently that compared with extracting fluid from coal, oil from the ground yielded kerosene far more easily.

But despite Kier's accidental success, drilling this oil out of the soil was not at all a reliable process. Even with wholesale prices for crude oil hovering around 50 cents per gallon, ventures such as Kier's barely yielded two to ten barrels per day—enough to market as expensive bottled potions, but not plentiful or cheap enough to light homes across America. But Bissell's Pennsylvania Rock Oil Company kept at it and, after a bit of difficulty, reorganized as the Seneca Oil Company. It then hired the man universally credited with the starting the oil rush. The company dispatched Edwin Drake to the small Pennsylvania town of Titusville, nearly forty miles from the nearest tracks of the Erie Railroad. After months spent organizing and procuring equipment, including a small steam engine, Drake started drilling into the ground in May 1859, laying iron pipe as the drill made progress. Churning slowly every day for weeks, with locals amused for much of this time, Drake had his drill lowered to over 60 feet. Then one Saturday afternoon in August, with his drill touching 69½ feet, he hit a pocket of oil—the pressure in the earth pushed it through the pipe into a fountain ten feet aboveground. With this discovery of a viable drilling technique, oil would make basic, cheap lighting possible for millions of Americans.

At the princely sum of 50 cents a gallon, a forty-two-gallon barrel of oil sold for over $20—similar to the price of an ounce of gold then, but far easier to extract in volume. As the nation was going through the tense election of 1860, the first of the men looking to strike it rich in oil spared little time for politics and started setting up oil derricks throughout Titusville, the epicenter of the area that prospectors knew as the Oil Regions. Farmers made fortunes, too, simply by selling rights to drill for oil on their properties, whether it was there or not. The men with the rights needed other men to drill for oil, capture it, and barrel it up. The rush was on.

And for well over another century, it would cement America as the leading oil producer on earth, a data point often overlooked in narratives looking to attribute the country's economic success solely to the ideology of free markets, freedom and democracy, or the ingenuity of its entrepreneurs. Starting with oil, the nation's rise was propelled, in no small way, by its immense natural-resource wealth. Still, American culture must be credited for encouraging the exact form of behavior that maximized this national advantage.

"On every rocky farm, in every poor settlement of the region, was some man whose ear was attuned to fortune's call, and who had the daring and the energy to risk everything he possessed on an oil lease," wrote Ida Tarbell. With this influx of men, along with Drake's technique, "oil poured forth in floods." Tarbell's father was such a man. He was a schoolteacher in

Iowa visiting the roots of his childhood in Erie County. One visit to the oil region pointed to a new career. But her father did not look to speculate on an oil lease. To Franklin Tarbell, getting oil out of the ground seemed to be the easy part. Getting it out of the isolated, hilly region of western Pennsylvania was much harder. With the army competing for resources, "there were not enough barrels to be bought in America," wrote his daughter a generation later. The oilmen had used "every sort of barrel" meant for turpentine, molasses, and whiskey but still lacked adequate storage. Without storage, men who had risked everything were forced to dump the oil back into the ground. Sensing opportunity, Franklin Tarbell proposed building large tanks for interim storage. Within months, with some investment money from large local producers, "the school teacher was buying thousands of feet of lumber, employing scores of men, and working them and himself—day and night," recounted Ida with no small hint of pride in her father's timely opportunism.

Others sought minor fortunes transporting the oil: The local farm boys with their horses and wagons made for ready teamsters. Teamsters, so called for their handling of teams of horses, took to transporting the oil via makeshift, muddy roads to railroads tens of miles away. Others operated vessels on a stream leading to the Allegheny to transport the oil downriver to Pittsburgh. But the stream was shallow and seasonal, and even in the best of circumstances, only the smallest vessels could navigate it effectively. Visitors to the fields would see oil caravans of a hundred wagons or more leaving the Oil Regions, carrying wooden barrels filled with oil. A good rainfall would leave the narrow main road impassable, with a stuck horse cart loaded with several tons of oil. The long line of stopped carts behind, however, would not stop for long. Neighboring farms would be overrun with teamsters improvising a road where there wasn't one. Tarbell noted with some admiration that "not even a shotgun could keep the driver from going where the passage was least difficult."

Remarkably, this boom was happening as the North was mobilizing its war efforts. During the first year of the war, improved drilling techniques had resulted in some individual wells sprouting 2,500 barrels of oil per day. But nothing else in the industry had kept up. The nearby creek bottoms were flooded with oil. It was so expensive to transport from the point of production, and the product so abundant, that the previous year's $20-per-barrel price had fallen to a laughable 10 cents at the source of the wells—all one had to do was move it dozens of miles, each barrel of this black gold weighing several hundred pounds. Then, of course, the price climbed again. The spike in price invited a flood of new prospectors. This then led to an immediate oversupply. In addition, prices were subject to whim, rumor, fundamentals, weather conditions, teamster temperaments, and manipulation. In a temporary period of high prices, an enterprising prospector might pay a neighboring farmer a small fortune for an oil lease, only to find the farm dry, bankrupting the prospector. Or the price would have fallen to such a degree that the barrel rental and transportation costs ate up all the profits. The ability to thrive in such a climate, to be repeated in plenty of other oil regions over the decades, gave the successful American oilman that rough-hewn, swaggering reputation: "They loved the game, and every man of them would take his last dollar on the chance at striking oil," concluded Ida Tarbell. To her there was something heroic in the character of such men, both winners and losers, and their willful and enthusiastic participation in this rugged, wild form of individualistic capitalism. But Tarbell was also one of the great critics of industrial capitalism, and her preamble of the early days of oil was a setup to contrast earnest men like her father with the prime object of her criticism.

So her pen turned to a man whose character was the opposite of the inveterate oilman—a model of sobriety who abhorred the region's social life of gambling, women of easy virtue, and strong drink, a culture that seemed to follow the energies of speculative prosperity and mercenary men. But this man's rise was another signal of America's upcoming industrial age, an era in which organizational skills in harnessing entrepreneurial activity into giant enterprises were rewarded above all. The ability to think through layers of abstractions and capital and ownership structures, maximize pricing power, and scale down costs, all to insulate the enterprise from the vagaries of the market, defined America's most incongruous oilman.

. . .

IN 1859, when Edwin Drake struck oil with his drill, the Cleveland firm of Clark & Rockefeller had just been formed. The younger partner, John D. Rockefeller, was barely twenty years old. Seeking independence, he had just left his position at Hewitt & Tuttle, a small firm that sold wholesale produce on behalf of farmers. Rockefeller had started there as an apprentice bookkeeper four years earlier.

Beginning with $4,000 in capital—Rockefeller's $2,000 coming half from his savings and half from a loan from his father—the firm took produce on consignment from farmers and sold it to wholesalers and other large buyers. Cleveland, being strategically positioned on Lake Erie, was an efficient point from which to get produce to New York City via Buffalo and the Erie Canal. The market for food and provisions was influenced by one especially large and consistent customer: the Union Army. The timing was good. Clark & Rockefeller thrived during the war. By the end of its second year in business, the firm's profits for the year were $17,000. As a part of their business, the men found themselves occasionally consigning barrels of oil from the men of western Pennsylvania.

By 1862 Clark & Rockefeller, with a steady stream of profits rolling in during wartime, decided to participate more directly in the oil trade. The firm, along with two of Maurice Clark's brothers, backed a young Englishman named Samuel Andrews in setting up a small oil refinery in Cleveland, the Excelsior Oil Works, to take the thick crude oil and refine it into kerosene. Many enterprising men in Cleveland and Pittsburgh, looking to get in on the oil boom, thought refining oil to be more consistently profitable than actually drilling for oil. Predictably, in the early days, refining operations were often as crude as the oil. With "a cast-iron still, usually surrounded by brick work, a copper hose, and two zinc-lined tanks," Rockefeller wrote, anybody who had the inclination and modest start-up capital could set up a refinery, with the early profits in refining large compared to the cost of entry. A forty-two-gallon barrel of crude oil priced at 35 cents, depending on market conditions, once refined, could fetch 35 cents for each gallon. Profitability was determined by the efficiency of the refining process—how much refined kerosene could be yielded from every barrel of crude oil. But with the early profit margins, even the most wasteful and least efficient refiner made money.

By 1864 the operation Clark & Rockefeller had set up as a sideline venture was turning into Cleveland's largest refinery. Andrews, their technical expert in refining, had managed to experiment his way into high yields of kerosene from every barrel of crude. At the same time, the young Rockefeller began demonstrating his innate knowledge of economies of scale. In the judgment of rivals and contemporaries, Rockefeller was often derided as a bookkeeper, a mere technocrat who watched every penny. He did profess to "have great respect for figures and facts, no matter how small they were," but to Rockefeller, the road to operating savings came through large capital expenditures. Only bigness saved money: The larger and more modern the refinery, the cheaper it would be to refine each subsequent barrel of oil.

And he wanted to borrow endlessly, forgo current profits, and expand the facilities to do it. His partners, Clark and his two brothers, did not. The final falling-out occurred when Rockefeller presented yet another set of loan documents for Clark to sign, and Clark refused. At the same time, to restrain Rockefeller's ambitions, Clark suggested caustically that perhaps they should dissolve the firm. Calling his bluff, Rockefeller called a partners' meeting of the three Clark brothers, Andrews, and himself. At the meeting the men formally expressed their desire to dissolve the refinery operation. As per the partnership agreement, either Clark or Rockefeller could buy the other's interest at auction.

Conducted by Clark's lawyer, the bidding started at $500. Rockefeller recalled: "I bid a thousand; they bid two thousand; and so on, little by little, the price went up. Neither side was willing to stop bidding, and the amount gradually rose until it reached $50,000, much more so than we supposed the concern to be worth." Yet Rockefeller did not want to start from scratch in the oil business, which he saw as the future, and he was willing to overpay for strategic position. "Finally, it advanced to $60,000, and by slow stages to $70,000, and I almost feared for my ability to buy the business and have the money to pay for it. At last the other side bid $72,000. Without hesitation, I said $72,500." His partner relented: "I'll go no higher, John; the business is yours." That Rockefeller would have access to this amount of capital in 1865 was evidence of both the Union's expenditures reverberating through the broader economy and the introduction of the greenback, the paper money unlinked from gold.

Such rising fortunes during wartime would have been unthinkable in the South, yet the North seemed to be able to launch an entirely new industry even as it fought. Five years removed from borrowing seed capital from his father to go into business for himself, and now twenty-five years old at the war's closing shots, Rockefeller was in control of Cleveland's largest oil refinery, a term that was a bit grand for an operation that could only refine five hundred barrels of oil per day. But it would grow rapidly into an organization that rivaled the size of government's. And with federal power receding to a peacetime posture, over the next thirty-five years to the close of the century Americans would become increasingly anxious about the rise of industrial power, of which Rockefeller was seen as an ominous proxy, a silent force every time a rural living room struck a match to start its evening light.

WHILE COTTON was a global commodity and the initial growth of American railroads had relied on British iron, oil became the first industrial supply chain to grow to a full scale entirely within America itself. Layered upon the infrastructure of the railroad—the earlier next big thing of railroads enabling the new next big thing of oil—came the intricacies and intrigues of the nineteenth-century oil business.

The intermediary layer in the basic supply chain between the producers, who drilled for oil, and the refiners, who turned crude oil into kerosene, was transportation. The question that remained was how best to get the oil extracted in western Pennsylvania to the refiners in Pittsburgh, Baltimore, New York, and Cleveland. For the first few years, the most expensive cog in the machinery was often the first few miles of transportation, provided by the teamsters from the oil wells to the river or rail hub. While the railroads could efficiently transport any quantity to the major refining cities in a day, the teamsters and their horse carts could barely keep up with the gushing wells of the early era. And the railroads, despite the building of tracks to get closer and closer to the oil regions, could not quite make it to the exact point of a gushing well.

Within a couple of years of the oil boom, producers had the idea to send the oil via pipes to large tanks nearby, rather than having to barrel the oil up on location. The original pipes relied on gravity along with a pump at the source, but the pipes kept bursting or leaking or having other equipment failures. Then in 1864, a well-to-do entrepreneur named Samuel Van Syckel came to the Oil Regions hoping to strike it richer. While brokering and overseeing shipments of oil from the wells to the railroads, Van Syckel saw his profits eaten up time and again by the teamsters. His simple solution was to build a two-inch pipe all the way to the railroad terminals. To make it work, he added relay pumps along the way, which helped the oil flow with adequate pressure. To the producers, a single pipeline was one of the "most wonderful of the many wonders" in that it replaced three hundred teams working ten hours a day.

The teamsters resisted. As with any technological innovation that quickly displaces a class of worker in the name of efficiency, their livelihoods were immediately threatened. Their protest involved routinely digging up and destroying the pipeline. Other times teamsters targeted the oil wells that used the pipeline, or they threatened the wildcatter. In response, the pipeline operators soon stationed guards along the line. At one point, when this proved to be inadequate, the governor of Pennsylvania was finally called upon to intervene. The use of the state's forces too would set the upcoming era's template for governments intervening on behalf of property owners, a reminder that free markets needed not just written laws on paper but the enforcement authority of the state to function.

Within a few years, two major pipeline operators emerged and dominated the flow from the wells to the railroads. The Empire Transportation Company and the Pennsylvania Transportation Company, both started in 1865, took the oil from their pipelines into large tanks for holding oil and then transferred them to railcars. By the late 1860s, railroads preferred the efficiency of large, standardized railroad cars in the now-common long, cylindrical form, which replaced the lengthy process of loading barrel after barrel into freight cars. This more or less eliminated the option for small producers to fill up and sell barrels independently to distant refiners as railroads wanted to fill tank cars.

With the end of the war, the railroads were desperate to replace their primary source of predictable and consistent revenue: the U.S. government. And as railroads were the main securities of the American stock market, Wall Street was attuned to every dollar of revenue gained or lost, as reported to shareholders, with shifts in perception playing into the hands of one set of stock operators or the other. The transportation of oil, an industry growing at a rapid pace, was seen as critical to railroad profitability.

To any railroad, each additional dollar of incremental revenue had very high margins. To run a train, an engine had to be operated, conductors paid, tracks maintained, and stations kept open. Whether the engine pulled twenty railcars behind it or thirty, the operating cost of that train was more or less the same. Therefore, if a route was at break-even, the revenue from each additional car went directly to the bottom line as pure profit. As railroad profitability was under substantial postwar pressure, the fight for this additional revenue made the railroads a central actor in the oil business. A great refiner of oil not only paid for rail transportation in bringing crude oil from the fields, but also, once the refining process was completed, contracted to send railcars of refined oil back to the market.

John D. Rockefeller understood this dynamic, this interdependency, better than even the railroads did. Within a couple of years of buying the controlling interest from the Clark brothers, he had taken on additional partners in his refinery. He then invested in a second refinery with his brother, William. In June 1870 he combined his interests into an entity called the Standard Oil Company. At the time, the entire oil industry was refining a little more than 45,000 barrels of oil per day. Standard Oil was responsible for about 1,500 barrels of this capacity—just over 3 percent market share of refined oil. But it was a competitive business, and declining prices for refined oil dramatically pressured the profits of Standard Oil's business. Given that oil was a commodity that every refiner paid more or less the same for, Rockefeller understood that the one area of competitive advantage was to reduce the transportation costs. And the only way to gain any negotiating leverage with the railroads was through size—to refine efficiently and transport more oil than anyone else.

But the era's business tactics were never quite that simple or transparent. In 1872, when the industry was not even one tenth of 1 percent of its eventual size, a group of the largest oil refineries, including Rockefeller's, met with a group of railroad executives to collectively negotiate rates. The refiners agreed to have their interests represented collectively as the South Improvement Company. Structured as a de facto refining cartel, the South Improvement Company guaranteed a percentage of the oil traffic of the major refiners to three railroads: 27.5 percent to Jay Gould's Erie, 27.5 percent to Vanderbilt's New York Central, and 45 percent to Tom Scott's Pennsylvania. But there was a complicated catch. On the surface, the member refiners would agree to pay listed rates to the railroads, as would smaller refiners who were nonmembers. But in exchange for guaranteeing the large volume of business, the members in the South Improvement Company would secretly receive back from the railroads a portion of all the shipping fees paid by the nonmembers. This would guarantee that all refiners outside of the cartel would have higher shipping rates than the members, an insurmountable competitive advantage.

As the plans were being formalized, Standard Oil started to talk to other, smaller Cleveland refiners. By cryptically presenting the impending power of the South Improvement Company, Standard Oil implied to other Cleveland refiners, about twenty-six in total, that refiners outside the system would not be able to compete. With the refining business intermittently profitable due to too much supply, and facing the sudden threat of increased pricing pressure in shipping rates, the refiners sold out to Standard Oil. Over forty-five days, twenty-two of the twenty-six Cleveland refiners agreed to be acquired by Rockefeller. This acquisition spree would one day become the source of much dispute as to what pressure the sellers felt and whether fair prices were paid, but the indisputable fact is that the vast majority of Cleveland refineries sold out to Standard Oil within an alarmingly short time frame. To Ida Tarbell this was Standard Oil's original sin that tainted all future achievements. Rockefeller often defended the transactions by saying that he offered stock in Standard Oil to anyone who preferred equity, which many did; those who chose to take stock instead of cash became overwhelmingly wealthy. Regardless of the perspective, Standard Oil, within a few short weeks, took its daily refining capacity from less than two thousand barrels to over ten thousand barrels, approximately 20 percent of the industry's capacity.

Soon after, word leaked of the South Improvement Company's plans, leading to widespread anger in the oil fields. Even in the Darwinian jungle of the era's capitalism, the plan seemed audacious. Its participants quickly backtracked, tried to deny involvement, and attempted to soften its purpose. And the South Improvement Company unraveled.

Standard Oil didn't—it emerged as a beneficiary. The ominous impending reality of the South Improvement Company, before the plan was scrapped, led to Rockefeller's control of almost all of Cleveland's refining capacity. Standard Oil, by itself now, had enough capacity to guarantee regular, large shipments through certain railroads. Predictably, in exchange for the guarantee, it negotiated for its own secret rebates when others shipped oil on the same routes. But the logic and leverage of a company asking for a discount when it guaranteed shipments of sixty railroad cars of oil per day, thereby subsidizing multiple railroad routes and creating efficiencies, were sound and obvious. Standard Oil owned its own railcars and loading facilities, making it even easier and cheaper for the railroads to transport Standard's freight.

Standard Oil soon applied its scale to a consumer marketing and distribution arm. It had thousands of towns receiving shipments of Standard Oil. Customers knew to buy kerosene in the recognizable, ubiquitous Standard Oil cans to light homes and to use as fuel for cooking. The price of crude oil, and with it the price of kerosene, kept dropping throughout the 1870s. New oil fields became active. Along the way Standard Oil kept consolidating the industry—its eventual breakup yielding the modern brands Exxon (derived from Esso), Mobil, Chevron, Amoco, and others. Rockefeller, beginning his ascent without drilling for any oil, came to completely dominate the industry by assembling the layers of a supply chain.

But all this began to hint at the apparent paradox of American capitalism. Rather than being a marketplace of countless independent entrepreneurs drilling, refining, and distributing oil, competing ruthlessly, evidence seemed to point to the efficiencies of consolidation, where the small operator in a large, growing sector was soon at a distinct disadvantage. Modern capitalism seemed to favor giant entities, which could coordinate activities through standardized policies and central planning, achieve economies of scale, borrow more cheaply and access the large capital markets, and insulate themselves from the volatility of the business cycle. In spirit, free enterprise was akin to other democratic freedoms, but in practice over time, the function of the individual practitioner was often superseded and replaced by the large institution. At the same time, industrialization, through its corporate proxies, rapidly and undeniably increased the standard of living in American households. Low prices delivered by large enterprises, fearful in concept, made basic things far more affordable. Unlike the spermaceti candles of decades prior, sometimes wrapped in tissue paper fit for jewelry, cheap tin cans filled with kerosene now allowed the common man to light his home.

Thirteen

STEEL

In 1873, several years before introducing the world to Tom Sawyer and Huckleberry Finn, Mark Twain gave the era its enduring label with the title of his novel *The Gilded Age*.

The novel begins with the story of Si Hawkins and his family. Si, an otherwise dutiful husband and doting father, is stricken with the seemingly incurable impulse to speculate on what he feels is his American destiny. Perpetually enraptured by thoughts of vast riches from one venture or another, Si manages to risk and squander his family's livelihood repeatedly. At the center of the Hawkins family misfortune is family friend and promoter extraordinaire Colonel Beriah Sellers. Before the war, Sellers had brought Si into a foolproof venture to corner the slave market, only to be foiled by a failure to change a few laws. Sellers then lured Si on a venture to create a perpetual-motion machine, but it failed with just one small part of the equation remaining to be solved. Finally, Si dies leaving vast, worthless acreage that soon carries the hopes of his descendants, with Sellers lending a helpful hand.

Through the appropriately named Sellers, Twain offered a caricature of the euphoric American promoter and striver. To this man, expectations were indeed gilded. All opportunities held promise. Failure was only a temporary setback. The nation was on the move. The young man who once ran to the gold fields upon the slightest evidence or went to sea for a chance at a successful whaling voyage's purse, now had a wide range of opportunities close to home. With the Union off the gold standard, the monetary base of the United States was far larger than it had been before the war. Credit was plentiful. And in the North, most sensed the inevitability of the nation industrializing, of railroads bridging the entire country ocean to ocean with an iron web, of final frontiers being discovered and settled. The early days of this Gilded Age, before the term came to its fuller historical meaning, were ones of palpable excitement and speculation as to what tomorrow would bring America.

Nowhere was this spirit of modernity expressed in finer form than on Wall Street. With ownership stakes of real companies traded back and forth on paper, the stock market operator became a recognized archetype. It was here in this paper temple that the best operators of the era, such as Jay Gould, could—without leaving the island of Manhattan— end up controlling far-flung enterprises that had taken the toil of thousands to build. Through dealings in the stock market, Gould engaged in corporate gamesmanship of the highest order and ended up in control of major railroads and telegraph operations. Gould's boardroom battles and intrigues—which included the Erie Railroad, Western Union, and one half of the first transcontinental railroad, the Union Pacific—often played out in the newspapers, highlighting the power of the knowing men on Wall Street to determine the fate of so many through the control of financial instruments. At the same time, even the young prospector who might have ventured to the oil fields in search of easy money could participate by taking sides, by buying his own few shares of stock.

The idea of Wall Street could even be found in uplifting literature meant for young boys and adolescents. Starting in 1866, Horatio Alger Jr., a Harvard-trained divinity scholar turned writer, found a theme that gained footing in the marketplace. Over the decades, various Horatio Alger novels and series, such as *Ragged Dick*, *Luck and Pluck*, *Brave and Bold*, and *Tattered Tom*, served as a call for young men to rise above their station in life, to strive. In one of the earliest Horatio Alger stories, *Ragged Dick*, the unkempt fourteen-year-old Dick is a shoeshine boy charging 10 cents a shine. He has a few bad habits: He smokes, gambles, goes to the theater, spends every cent he earns, and loves playing practical jokes on ignorant country folk coming into the city. But Dick has financial aspirations beyond shining shoes; he wants to own shares of the Erie Railroad. It was a sign of the times that Alger could casually reference the stock market in novels intended for school-age boys across America. When Dick manages to come into $5 of his very own, Alger writes of his young protagonist's feeling of arrival as "for the first time, he felt himself a capitalist."

The characters in the Horatio Alger stories—nearly all of them boys in challenging financial circumstances, including homelessness in some cases—rose to respectability in *Strive and Succeed*, *Bound to Rise*, *Slow and Sure*, and *Strong and Steady*. In adapting his roots in religious studies to the times, Alger pointed out to his young readers that the path to morality and grace was through the honest dollar. The stories played to the optimism that anything was possible in America, even for an immigrant boy who shined shoes on the street. But there was an element of Gilded Age truth, of legitimate possibilities, that sustained the narratives. And truth sometimes surpassed the boundaries of fiction. Compared with the path of Alger's typical character in *The Telegraph Boy*, the tale of one real-life telegraph boy, Andrew Carnegie, was far beyond what even Alger or his readers would have considered realistic.

LIKE ROCKEFELLER AND GOULD, Carnegie came of age in the 1860s. At the start of the Civil War, he was an assistant superintendent at the Pennsylvania Railroad—which already represented a startlingly fast rise for an unschooled, immigrant child laborer who had ended up in a local telegraph office—but during the war, his myriad side investments had prospered into an independent fortune. Days before the South's surrender, Carnegie, at thirty, bade his railroad colleagues and his days as an employee farewell.

But the farewell, in many ways, was a technicality. During much of the war, Carnegie's start-up investments had included stakes in a maker of railroad cars, a bridge-building company whose bridges were capable of supporting the weight of railroad traffic, a telegraph company, and an ironworks. Many of these ventures were directly related to some aspect of the Pennsylvania Railroad's business. Often acting with the complicity of his superiors, Tom Scott and Edgar Thomson, Carnegie became a conduit for arranging deals where the railroad executives would invest in new companies, and the new ventures in turn sold services to the Pennsylvania. Upon his official retirement from the railroad, Carnegie continued to leverage his connections with the Pennsylvania Railroad, but without being encumbered by any obligation as an employee.

His first venture, the month after he resigned, was to reorganize the Keystone Bridge Company. The company, with the Pennsylvania Railroad as its major customer, took on the role of converting old wooden bridges into far sturdier iron. The railroad's president and vice president were both silent investors in Carnegie's bridge company and thus had a vested interest in pushing the Pennsylvania's bridge-building needs his way, no small thing, as most railroad track systems of any importance had dozens of bridges. The bridge company, of course, needed iron. This was conveniently purchased from Carnegie's iron-making venture. One investment in a start-up sleeping-car company was eventually parlayed into an interest in the dominant Pullman Palace Car Company—acquiring Carnegie's venture was the only sure way to sell sleeping cars to the Pennsylvania Railroad. Tellingly, the only field he dropped was one where he enjoyed little advantage. After making an early killing in an oil venture during the war, far more than Rockefeller had made at the time from oil, he found the business too volatile for his interest.

Yet Carnegie was an entirely different breed from his diligent, singular contemporaries like Gould and Rockefeller, or railroad executives, or the myriad entrepreneurs who worked tirelessly to make their way in this postwar industrial order. Not long after signing his first postwar venture's formation documents, Carnegie embarked on a nine-month grand tour of Europe, leaving the management of his enterprises to his brother. He visited the great capitals and opera houses, keeping thorough and detailed notes of his observations. Presciently, even in late 1865, he expected the world to see a unified Germany eventually "taking the lead in Continental affairs."

In his international travels, Carnegie discovered another avenue of service to both the Pennsylvania Railroad and his own companies: selling bonds. By the late 1860s, the appetite of British and European investors for American investments had fully returned, attracted by the growth rates and higher rates of interest in the unified Republic. Having maintained the highest of confidences with his former employer, Carnegie was enlisted by the Pennsylvania Railroad to sell its bonds in London. In addition, he sold bonds for the bridges he was building, including the St. Louis Bridge. Carnegie benefited in multiple ways: He received commissions on the bond sales themselves, and his company then received the construction contract to build the bridge. The bridge-building company then paid Carnegie's other company for iron. Carnegie, with his bond issues of the Pennsylvania and well-known projects, became a favorite of Junius Morgan, the eminent American banker based in London. Other times he would be relegated to dealings with Junius's son, J. P. Morgan. The latter relationship, though often frosty, would last decades.

Yet Carnegie, for all his financial success, questioned his own commitment to commercial matters. Just three years into his independence, he had an income of $50,000 and had amassed assets of $400,000. In the waning days of 1868, he wrote himself a letter, setting a limit of two more years to secure his fortune:

> Beyond this never earn—make no effort to increase fortune, but
> spend the surplus each year for benevolent purposes. Cast aside
> business forever . . . settle in Oxford and get a thorough education
> making the acquaintance of literary men. . . . The amassing of
> wealth is one of the worst species of idolatry. . . . To continue much
> longer overwhelmed by business cares and with most of my
> thoughts wholly upon the way to make more money in the shortest
> time, must degrade me beyond hope of permanent recovery. I will
> resign business at thirty-five.

This conflict between the ease with which he made money and what he saw as his elevated purpose would arise time and again. But the letter, in tone and content, was more pessimistic and stark than the refined, exuberant Carnegie philosophy that would ultimately emerge. He would eventually appoint himself the unofficial industrial spokesman of the American Republic. For the secular Carnegie, the fact that an immigrant, starting as a child laborer with no connections, no capital, and no formal education, could end up on this trajectory was the essence of the American gospel. There was nothing debased about such liberating possibilities.

There would be no retirement at thirty-five.

CARNEGIE'S CHANGE OF HEART had much to do with a newfound focus. In his earliest travels, Carnegie had witnessed a process that could manufacture steel at a fraction of the former cost, and he had acquired the American rights to it. While iron making had existed for centuries in crude form, steelmaking was newer and more specialized. Steel was far superior to iron in terms of malleability, tensile strength, and durability, but the science and technique to scale production remained elusive. As a result, until the mid-nineteenth century, steel took on the qualities of an almost semiprecious metal, used for knives, precision tools, and instruments. Just as iron making had once been increased to industrial scale, a race was on now to do the same for steel.

Similar to how iron was first coated onto wood tracks until all-iron tracks became the norm, the initial concept was to apply a steel coating to iron rails to allow the iron rails to last longer. As rail shipments became heavier with the growth of industrial traffic, iron tracks proved too brittle, especially in extreme weather conditions, a problem that was more common in America than in England. Around areas where the tracks curved, they sometimes wore out within months. However, the process Carnegie had acquired was inadequate despite its early promise, and he went deeper into iron ventures.

But across the Atlantic, steel continued to make progress, and Carnegie saw that, far from securing his fortune as he had told himself to do, his largest and most valuable investment, the Union Iron Mills, faced risks. Track mileage during the decade had increased by over 70 percent from the 1860 level. Each mile of track meant repeat business for the hundreds of American iron mills, as the rails wore down. But steel, the next big thing, was replacing iron in England.

Iron making, at its most basic, depended on removing impurities from iron ore, a basic mineral found readily in rock formations in much of the world. The search for steel started with iron. The substantial breakthrough in achieving industrial quantities ultimately came from Henry Bessemer. Bessemer had invented a converter that allowed air to quickly rush through the molten iron, which caused combustion that allowed the iron to remain in a prolonged liquid state, which then allowed it to be manipulated into steel.

But there was an obstacle to bringing the Bessemer process to America. The initial Bessemer process required a high-quality iron ore that was relatively phosphorus free. By the late 1860s, even England was left importing high-quality ores from Europe to feed its steel mills. With no proven source in America, it was far cheaper to import finished steel from England as opposed to bulky iron ore—rocks—from across the ocean. This lack of a basic input not only cast doubt on the prospects of steelmaking in America but also caused anxiety among iron makers.

But again the natural-resource wealth of the vast American continent fulfilled the needs of industrial capitalism. In 1845 a young Michigan prospector named Philo Everett was leading a scouting mission in the Upper Peninsula of his state. His Indian guides soon pointed him toward a mountain—a 150-feet-high formation extending into miles of pure iron ore. Everett named it Iron Mountain. The remoteness of Iron Mountain limited its use due to transportation costs until an 1868 test showed it to be home to some of the most phosphorus-free ore in the world. As a catalyst for American steel manufacturing, this turned out to be the industrial equalizer. With domestic supplies of ore secure, several iron makers around the country started licensing the Bessemer patents and building the expensive steel plants, which were far more capital intensive than ironworks.

The final prompt for Carnegie to enter the steel trade came through his St. Louis Bridge Company. The bridge's designer and engineer in chief, Captain James Eads, insisted on using steel for major components of the bridge, whereas Carnegie looked to sell the bridge iron from his mills. Eads refused to compromise and continued to escalate his demands, causing Carnegie to complain that the engineer had "the pride of a mother for her first-born," who looked to "bedeck the darling without much regard to his own or other's cost." While he derided Eads's requests, Carnegie started seeing the writing on the wall. The age of steel had arrived.

Once committed, Carnegie began organizing a venture to build one of the world's largest steel plants from scratch. It would manufacture one product: steel rails. To design the plant, Carnegie hired the best-known Bessemer steel mill designer of the time, Alexander Holley. He then looked to find a location to build his plant. For steelmaking, access to transportation was critical: Heavy components such as iron ore, limestone, and coal needed to be freighted in, and finished steel needed to be freighted back out. Despite years of dependence on the closeness of his relationship with the Pennsylvania Railroad, Carnegie hedged his risk. He decided to buy a site that provided access to the Monongahela River, the B&O Railroad, and the Pennsylvania—each serving as a defensive measure against any one entity exerting power over his works. Lest this move be seen for the cold economic decision that it was, Carnegie ingratiatingly asked for permission to name the plant in honor of Edgar Thomson, head of the Pennsylvania Railroad. With a total of $700,000 in capital, of which $250,000 was Carnegie's personally—a very large portion of the fortune accumulated from his dozen years of enthusiastic enterprising—the Edgar Thomson Steel Works broke ground in early 1873, with plans to open in two years.

The timing could not have been worse.

"ALL WAS GOING WELL for us," wrote Carnegie, "when one morning in our summer cottage, a telegram came announcing the failure of Jay Cooke & Co." For Northerners, Jay Cooke was the patriotic pitchman behind the Union's war bonds, responsible for helping the government borrow over $2 billion during the war. Eight years later, Jay Cooke & Co. was regarded as one of the strongest financial houses in America, but it had overreached with investments in the transcontinental railroad. Its failure set off a panic. As was often the case, what happened next was a self-fulfilling prophecy. When depositors panicked, they tended to withdraw deposits, which increased the insolvency of the institutions. Seeing the run on banks, other creditors called in loans to ensure that they had capital on hand. Without a central bank or source of emergency liquidity, rumor fueled the panic. "Almost every hour brought news of some fresh disaster. . . . Every failure depleted the resources of some other concern. Loss after loss ensued, until a total paralysis of business set in." The growth of the American economy came to a complete, sudden halt. Carnegie's own shrinking liquid resources caused him to enter crisis mode—the collective liquidity of his ventures down to two weeks' worth of the capital needed for payroll and expenses as he negotiated with banks, sold stock in unrelated ventures, and bought time.

Years of wartime spending, then expansion, easy credit, and speculation—all had led to more than a decade of robust economic activity. And like any period of prosperity, the years had masked the residues of corruption, waste, inefficiency, and leverage that accompanied good times. For many years, railroads laid track in an effort to show growth in some form. Capital markets encouraged fast growth, as new miles of track meant the expectation of future revenues. But the fundamentals didn't keep up; people often didn't move to where the tracks were. For a while, this reality could be ignored. In the era's heady climate, shareholders got rich when railroad stocks went up, not when people actually used the railroad. When Jay Cooke failed, the moment of clarity set in. Men rushed to liquidate holdings of value to get their hands on cash, financing for speculative and incomplete projects was frozen, and banks called in loans or refused to extend terms. Carnegie too was forced to liquidate. He would sell shareholdings wherever he could to maintain liquidity for his steelworks. Even then, construction had to be suspended for a brief period. He was able to stay solvent. Barely, as one history has it—his personal cash balance falling to under $5,000.

The Gilded Age, published mere months before the collapse, looked in retrospect like a prescient warning, comeuppance wrapped in satire. The United States entered what was known then as the Great Depression. It would last six years, but its effects, especially on wages, would linger far into the future. For Carnegie this would be a period of personal reinvention. While the postwar years had drawn him into the varied ventures of his economic environment, now approaching forty, he pulled his sails in. In later years Carnegie would note for posterity that when it came to wealth accumulation, "the proper policy was to put all eggs in one basket and then watch that basket."

Perhaps. But equally likely, the period after 1873 simply didn't lend itself to the schizophrenic wildness of the postwar boom. The bubble had burst. Capital was scarce. Prompted by necessity, Carnegie would focus on steel for the remainder of his career.

Carnegie adapted well. He could not have known it, but he was building a steel plant to open at the start of a twenty-year period of deflation—the prices of labor and commodities were headed down, which had implications for how Carnegie managed his operations. When the Edgar Thomson opened in 1875, it was the biggest steel mill in America. While demand in other areas of the economy was tepid, steel had one thing going for it: It was dramatically more cost-effective for railroads to use steel rails than iron. It was stronger, it lasted longer, and as it held its shape better, it cost less to maintain prior to replacement. And depression or not, railroads needed to replace tracks often. As iron tracks wore out, the country's entire network of railroad track was being redone in steel. As the economy slowly recovered to normalcy, excess gave way to efficiency: Companies became ruthlessly cost conscious.

For Carnegie's new plant, the first order for two thousand tons of steel rails came in almost immediately—an order of well over $100,000. By October 1875, the cost structure for a ton of steel at Carnegie's plant looked like this:

OCTOBER COSTS—COST PER TON OF RAILS

Labor	$8.26
Metal	$40.86
Lime, fuel, etc.	$6.31
Bessember & Siemens Royalties	$1.17
Total	$56.64*

In an accompanying note, his manager reported that the rails were "sold at an average of $66.32 per ton, so our profit of $9.86 per ton is

* The numbers, with their minor discrepancies, are directly reproduced from Carnegie's memoir.

pretty good for second month." It would get better. Carnegie would seek efficiencies in terms of cost at every turn. Where at an earlier time he could head off to London and use his charisma to sell something, this era called for watching every penny. And steel rail was in such demand that it sold itself, provided that it was cheap enough.

For Carnegie the deflationary climate proved to be equally suitable to his temperament. His new mantra—applicable to all commodity businesses then and now—became "Watch the costs, and the profits take care of themselves." But as much as steelmakers could watch their costs, supply was only one side of the equation. On the demand side, where customers drove hard bargains, free-market competition sometimes compressed margins to unprofitable levels, especially for the inefficient operators. In a business in which most steelmakers had made large capital investments prior to the crash, the competitive strategy of the steelmakers of 1875 was simple: Collude and fix prices.

Within a year of the opening of the Edgar Thomson plant, Carnegie was invited to join the newly formed Bessemer Steel Association. The association was a cartel, and in the days before antitrust laws, completely legal. Rather than compete tooth and nail for every bit of railroad business, it made far more sense for the steelmakers to establish quotas to limit the total supply in the market. By agreement, each firm was to produce its quota and sell into the market at agreed-upon prices. Carnegie insisted on a higher quota, citing far greater efficiency at his plants. After a bit of chafing at the upstart's bravado, the men of the more established steelworks reluctantly gave in.

The postulates of classical free-market economics notwithstanding, the most efficient operator with the lowest costs did not always look to eliminate competition. Such a strategy would take too long, would require forgoing larger profits in the interim, and might not even work out in the end, as customers would be used to low, unprofitable prices. The more immediate opportunity was to lobby for a larger share of a cartel's quota. But as with most informal, contractually unenforceable pooling operations such as cartels, suppliers often agreed to limit production, only to then cheat on the quota and sell as much as they could. Carnegie often violated his quota, preferring to partner with another large steel operation, Cambria, to bid jointly on large contracts. But Carnegie had the final advantage. As the low-cost producer was profitable at any price level at which his competitors could only break even, cooperation and competition suited him equally.

One area where all American steelmakers could maintain absolute, almost religious agreement was on the topic of British steel. British steelmakers were more efficient, and as a result, their rails were cheaper even than Carnegie's. As with the iron industry before, the Americans' collective strategy was equally simple: tariffs. Congress complied. The tariff on a ton of imported British steel started at $28 per ton. Given that Carnegie's first-ever order was fulfilled at $68 per ton, the British would have had to sell steel at $40 per ton, with overseas shipping included, to pay the tariff and match the price in the market. In an era without a personal income tax or corporate income taxes, the federal government relied on duties and tariffs for a significant portion of its revenues—many years the tariff generated more than 50 percent of the total revenues. Given the federal government's dependence, the tariff schedule played an essential role for domestic producers, especially when foreigners were more competitive.

Even Carnegie, with all his competitive, Darwinian pride, granted that tariff protection "has played a great part in the development of manufacturing in the United States." But he also spun this indirect subsidy as not a helping hand but a tool that enabled him to engage in a "patriotic duty to develop vital resources." And in fairness, there was policy rationale in encouraging capital investment in the American steel industry, with the hope that the nation would develop the competency. Such policies were successful in diversifying and growing the industrial base: America did emerge as the largest steel producer in the world by the end of the century. From here the growth of the American steel industry paved the way for a variety of ancillary and dependent industries over the next few decades. Even military might in the next century would be firmly rooted in steelmaking capacity. But laissez-faire capitalism it was not. The invisible hand of Adam Smith's free market was accompanied by the guiding hand of government policy.

Fourteen

MACHINES

The Gilded Age had a philosopher who seemed perfect for the times. Herbert Spencer built upon his fellow countryman Charles Darwin's observations on natural selection and developed a social treatise that flowed from this evolutionary spirit. Spencer even claimed credit for coming up with the phrase "survival of the fittest," which then made its way into subsequent editions of Darwin's *Origin of Species*. While Darwin concerned himself with how organisms adapted to their environment, Spencer applied theories of natural selection to the man-made, industrial world of individuals, societies, and organizations. Long before Max Weber linked Protestantism with the spirit of capitalism, Spencer was arguing the opposite: that in this industrial age, when science was unraveling the mysteries of the past, the "irrational doctrines" of religion and "the carpenter-theory of creation" had little place.

To Spencer, channeling Darwin, nature ran continuous experiments. The superior methods of doing things—of organizing, of living—eventually won out over the inferior in nature's marketplace of ideas. Based on observation, mankind's trajectory was a move from the simple to the complex. It applied to governance: Whereas the "barbarous race" needed "despotism capable of the necessary rigour," or absolute "celestial rule" through the word of God, the most advanced societies moved to the "substitution of free institutions" that were more complex in their administration. It applied to languages: From a time when ideas were "conveyed through a single sound" to the present, when "civilized races express minute modifications of meaning" through verbs, adjectives, pronouns, and prepositions, expression itself was evolution in action. Here, citing its depth and endless variations, Spencer, naturally, declared English to be superior to all other languages. And linguistically, as America was now home to the largest number of English-speaking people on earth, surpassing that of English-speaking subjects across all of Britain's colonies, Spencer may have found this reason enough to declare America the fittest.

But Spencer's line of reasoning resonated most strongly when it came to the spread of capitalism. In this, Spencer drew upon Adam Smith's observations regarding the division of labor: that as economies advanced, the number of professions and occupations varied and multiplied. In contrast to the nomadic tribes in which "every man [was] warrior, hunter, toolmaker, builder," a factory setting improved productivity through high degrees of specialization, where multiple hands each worked on an aspect of the larger task. Natural selection, survival of the fittest, and division of labor: It all meant that the superior culture was going to spread and the inferior culture was going to submit—this was nature's way. If people and governments wanted to accelerate such destinies, they were only hastening the inevitable. Modern civilization was a complex machine driven by an evolutionary algorithm.

The Plains Indians missed this memo. Ever since the white man had arrived, the Native American lived in ways that defied every principle of capitalism. Property rights were a fluid concept at best—how could man own nature? Just as the evolutionary theorists could argue that religion provided no answer to who or what came before God, the natives could equally ask who held the first legal title to the mountain range that was a hundred million years old or the great prairie that seemed to come before all human life. Did the first property rights simply transfer from nature to man, or was man a subset of nature, just as the animals and birds were? And in this civilized world of rights and organizations, of elaborate checks and balances, of declarations and constitutions, why was there so much bloodshed involved? No Indian war had ever killed as many as the Civil War, coordinated by steam engines, railroads, and telegraph, and fueled by abstractions of paper money and bonds and fought over the fate of four million souls of human property. And yet at the end of it, free blacks were back to picking cotton as sharecroppers, with cotton production even higher a decade after the war than before it. No, these Indians would not submit to a force they neither controlled nor understood. The machine would have to kill them.

At the heart of the last Indian wars was the forward face of capitalism: the transcontinental railroad. The effort that began during the Civil War was finally completed in 1869, when the final stakes were driven into the ground in Utah, a celebrated event connecting the tracks of the Central Pacific from the west and the Union Pacific from the east. But the final years of the Union Pacific's construction had included intermittent Indian attacks on advancing railroad men. The Sioux, Cheyenne, and Arapaho had roamed the plains of the Dakotas and Nebraska for unnumbered generations—along with tens of millions of buffalo and ample wildlife. For the hunting tribes, the richness of the ecosystem provided for a vigorous life. At the same time, it had cemented their ways away from farming and made them especially resistant to any stationary mode of living. Being far removed from eastern civilization, these Plains Indians had been left alone for decades while tribes on the coasts had been subjugated to the reservation. But each new foot of railroad track was the iron staple that confirmed that this land too belonged to this new industrial America.

Of course, white progress into Indian land led to brutal agitations on both sides. U.S. Army forces at times fired upon women and children. In addition to raiding white settlements with ferocity, Indians routinely tortured and mutilated the bodies of soldiers after successful battles. To William Tecumseh Sherman, the Union general who had led the Civil War's final and decisive march through the South, keeping the Indians "far away from the Continental roads" was now the top priority of the American military. Writing to his brother John, a U.S. senator, Sherman concluded, "I suppose they must be exterminated, for they cannot and will not settle down, and our people will force us to it." By "settling down" Sherman meant on the reservations that the federal government offered the Indian tribes—millions of acres in total—but accepting that fate meant surrendering their way of life.

Once the celebrations of the transcontinental railroad had concluded at Promontory Summit in Utah, the iron horse crossed the Great Plains with its thundering roar all the way to the Pacific Ocean and back. For thousands in the East, this became their first chance to see the West. For years the railroad workers had relied on buffalo meat, as the Indians did, as a primary source of food. The Union Pacific had even once hired a hunter named William Frederick Cody, "Buffalo Bill," for the purpose of supplying meat to the labor force. In his year of service, he reputedly killed 4,280 buffalo. Soon delighted tourists riding on the train began shooting buffalo for sport while in motion, leaving the carcasses to rot on the plains. With the plains now accessible, others soon came for the delicacy of buffalo tongue, to be smoked or salted for shipment back east, or for buffalo skins at a couple of dollars wholesale. With buffalo herds at times appearing to be dozens of miles long, the trade seemed unlimited. Nearly four million buffalo were killed between 1872 and 1874 alone. The U.S. Army understood the impact of hunters destroying the Indians' food supply. Exterminating the buffalo meant exterminating the Plains Indian, the infliction of a final catastrophe upon their ecosystem. By 1889 the buffalo was nearly extinct, down to a few hundred in total from tens of millions just a quarter century earlier, a final surrender to progress.

NOT ALL CULTURES were broken by the wheels of industry. Some thrived. During the twenty-five-year period between 1850 and 1875, close to 2.5 million Germans arrived on American shores, over ten times the Indian population living in America. Tens of thousands made their way inland to the American frontier, to cities such as Chicago and Milwaukee, along with great numbers down the Mississippi to St. Louis. Unlike the Irish who had fled famine, the Germans escaping their political crisis were often middle class, leaving trades and land back home, equipped to take advantage of a full range of economic opportunities in America.

The Germans were the first large group of non–English speakers to immigrate to America voluntarily. Rather than an impediment, this turned into a compounding advantage. When a set of middle-class Germans made their way into a city, they moved close to communities of other Germans, and they naturally entered a trade or business along the lines of what they had known back home, resuming life as mechanics, craftsmen, and smiths. Germans, at the least, could serve other Germans, with the prospering tradesman hiring his countrymen, most often the younger newcomers. And language, in turn, kept the German community unified. With adequate capital in their community, Germans had a relatively soft landing as far as immigrant experiences went. Indeed, rather than assimilate, the Germans managed to impose their culture on America.

Wherever Germans settled, breweries and beer halls followed. In 1840 the American taste for beer was not nearly as prevalent as that for distilled spirits. Americans were known to prefer strong drink, its consumption common enough that it caused no less an observer than Alexis de Tocqueville to conclude that in America, "drunkards are in the majority." Alcohol consumption was equated with inebriation. For many evangelical Christians, drunkenness was the most significant social ill. With some legitimacy, it was equated with domestic violence, poverty, financial recklessness, family breakups, and general social disorder. But the strength of the German communities in maintaining families and achieving commercial prosperity was one counter to the absolutism of the temperance position. Indeed, one New York court found that the lager Germans preferred was not a "spirituous liquor capable of producing intoxication," protecting it from a local liquor law.

The Union Army had bought this logic as well. While liquor of all forms was banned in the camps, lager was both permitted and encouraged by the U.S. military—after noticing German regiments consuming liberal amounts of beer, the army came to view it as an aid to keep soldiers in proper digestive order. Other than amiable soldiers, there were several significant beneficiaries of this growing element of German culture.

Adolphus Busch, the son of an affluent family in Germany, arrived in St. Louis in 1857 as a teenager. Within a couple of years, Busch had set up a company to supply the numerous breweries around St. Louis. And as one of the earliest Union mandates had been to secure a hold on the city, with its large federal armory, and maintain control of miles along the Mississippi River, the presence of soldiers was undoubtedly to Busch's benefit. One of the breweries that Busch supplied belonged to Eberhard Anheuser, a soap factory owner who had taken the brewery as payment for a debt. After marrying Anheuser's daughter, Busch ended up operating his father-in-law's brewery. But brewing was not an especially difficult or capital-intensive business to get into. By definition, every brewery was micro.

But several factors allowed German culture to scale beyond local confines. With Louis Pasteur's discovery, pasteurization allowed for a longer shelf life, making wider distribution possible. Next, following the initial use of large blocks of winter ice, new innovations allowed for more refined techniques of refrigeration in railcars. Using both, Busch was one of the early pioneers in taking his beer farther west and south, all to avoid the large Milwaukee brewers fighting over Chicago and other midwestern markets. But the innovation that contributed most to his initial wave of success was bottling. Glass bottles allowed his product to appear directly in the customer's hand with the implicit guarantee of quality, since only the more expensive brews were worth bottling.

And then there was the matter of taste. Carl Conrad, a local St. Louis beer and wine distributor looking to expand his market, contracted with Busch to brew a proprietary product for him. Under the terms of the deal, Conrad would underwrite the costs of development and own the rights to the beer—Anheuser would do the brewing on contract. The goal had been to come up with an alternate recipe to the darker lagers that German immigrants preferred. Conrad wanted a lighter beer to expand American tastes. Early sentiment showed that American drinkers liked the beers based on the brewing tradition of Bohemia, a region now in the Czech Republic. Several pilsners, based on brewing methods from the town of Pilsen, made it to market. For Conrad, Anheuser Brewing came up with a recipe from the lesser-known town of Budweis. The new beer would be bottled as Conrad Budweiser.

Almost immediately, the American beer market saw the introduction of numerous lagers that were light golden in color, rather than brown like the Bavarian varieties. Larger brewers, such as Pabst in Milwaukee, seeing customer demand shift, started introducing lighter beers. Less-established brewers did so as well, but many simply called their versions Budweiser too. The basic belief was that as "Budweis" was the name of the place where the beer's tradition was rooted, no one could own the name "Budweiser." Conrad's argument was that he had incurred a sizable initial investment in developing the formula and in marketing the Budweiser name; if it hadn't been for Conrad's efforts in the marketplace, there would have been nothing inherently profitable in the Budweiser name worth copying. For years Conrad's agents would report of competitors selling their own Budweiser. He won in court, but due to unrelated losses elsewhere, Conrad needed money. To raise cash, he allowed the newly named Anheuser-Busch to maintain and operate the Budweiser brand. He would never find the means or methods to get it back. With Conrad's misfortune, the Budweiser name would become the flagship brand of Anheuser-Busch.

Before long, it would become clear that the brand was worth more than all of the brewing facilities, refrigerated cars, bottling machines, and warehouses combined. This idea of the trademark was less important when businesses were largely named after their local proprietors serving local markets, but this era of national markets would see the widespread use of invented names for products, often pulling clever derivatives and amalgamations from the English language. And just as patents and copyrights protected ideas and thoughts, trademark rights meant that even words and illustrated symbols used in commerce could be owned—an intangible property right that the Sioux would have found as bizarre as owning a folktale told by the fire. But this heightened abstraction of brand, built upon the industrial infrastructure of science and mechanization, saw a whole new way of conceptualizing and valuing companies take hold.

THE BEST-KNOWN BRANDS of the early Gilded Age were machine makers themselves. And for companies and their machines, adaptability seemed to be as vital to survival as it was for natural beings. For one company in the midst of an especially large revenue drop-off, salvation was found in a machine designed for the English language.

In the years after the Civil War, even as the economy boomed,

E. Remington & Sons saw its fortunes decline. The company made guns. Soldiers needed them and then, at war's end, they didn't. Based in the small town of Ilion, New York, Remington was one of many well-known gunmakers in the North. Following in the footsteps of Eli Whitney— who after his endless frustration in monetizing his cotton gin turned his mechanical genius to gun making—manufacturers in New England, including Samuel Colt, Smith & Wesson, and Remington gave the Union Army a decided advantage in arms. To meet the demands of war, the gunmakers became especially skilled machinists, using the latest in tooling techniques to make precision weapons. Seeing some synergy, an inventor approached E. Remington & Sons with a functional prototype of a new kind of machine for the written word.

Rather than propelling bullets through the air, the typewriter fired letters at paper. Developing the machine had been a long process. As with many inventions, a fortunate series of events needed to converge to create momentum for the final breakthrough. In this case, three men became inspired by an article about a theoretical writing machine in 1867. After repeated trial and error, they found an investor by demonstrating a functional prototype. After some frustration, two of the initial founders left, leaving the third, C. Latham Sholes, to develop the successful permutation: Each key, when pressed, caused a corresponding inked hammer to imprint the character on a piece of paper.

Up to that point, unlike printed works like newspapers, for which a typesetter set the individual letters by hand for the printing press, business correspondence had remained handwritten, prone to error, misinterpretation, and inefficiency. Seeing an opportunity to completely alter business communication, Remington took the prototype and, with its machinists and toolmakers, perfected the typewriter for market. Introduced in 1875, followed by a much bigger launch at the Centennial Celebrations in 1876, the Remington typewriter soon set the standard in offices across America, and Remington became a brand rather than a family manufacturer's name.

It was to "the pen what the sewing machine is to the needle," held a contemporary magazine. In the mid-1870s American sewing machine manufacturers, led by the Singer Manufacturing Company, were selling over 500,000 machines per year—a remarkable number considering that the overwhelming majority were for commercial use. While the sewing machine's ease of use and contributions to efficiency were immediately obvious, the typewriter presented an obstacle: Few knew how to use it— making it inefficient compared with the pen due to its learning curve— and it wasn't clear if typing was a skill that just anyone could develop.

By 1880 specialized typing schools had begun to offer training. Remarkably, even though the typewriter was destined for the office environment, a place where very few women had roles, the position of typist was open to both men and women from the very beginning. The profession drew in hundreds of women in major cities. With good typists in New York City making as much as $15 to $20 per week—nearly $1,000 per year—the pay was higher than that of many blue-collar men and that of women schoolteachers with years of education. "The excellent feature of this new profession for women," read an account in a literary journal in the 1880s, was that "any bright girl in from three to six months may obtain sufficient facility with the typewriter to make herself valuable in an office." As the telegraph office once had done in more limited form, the Remington became the machine that brought thousands of women into the modern office setting.

WHILE WOMEN'S ENTRY into the office coincided with, and was perhaps stimulated by, the era's push for universal suffrage, the neighborhood saloon also became an unlikely, and indirect, catalyst for women's right to vote. The saloon became the target of temperance forces—prohibitionists who detested the presence of hundreds of thousands of saloons, local bars, across America where all manner of vice originated and thrived. For decades, advocates of local temperance laws had enlisted the voice of women. While they lacked voting rights, this was one political issue where the woman's perspective had credibility in the public arena. As alcoholism was associated with violence, misspending on liquor, hungry children, and other household consequences—all detracting from the woman's ability to maintain Christian values in her home—expression of domestic concerns led to a political voice for women.

Before the Civil War, there was some effort by the most strident evangelical reformers to combine the issue of temperance with what they felt were three other American ailments, no matter how tenuously linked: slavery, immigrants, and Catholicism. The newly formed Republican Party, however, focused on slavery. The overwhelming majority of American voters—men, that is—liked to drink, and alienation was no way to build a party. After the war, temperance forces found a new, potent voice in the Woman's Christian Temperance Union. Founded in 1874, the WCTU soon boasted hundreds of thousands of members, some undoubtedly riveted by the prospect of political participation. Soon its leader, Frances Willard, was openly declaring that alcohol prohibition, critical for the betterment of society, was not possible without the votes of women. Just like that, temperance forces and the women's suffrage movement converged.

The WCTU's members may have been legion, but the major American brewers had hundreds of thousands of saloons, found in every nook and cranny of the Republic's geography. The German brewers had changed the economics of the saloon. It was no longer a mere neighborhood business started and owned by a proprietor. The beer makers, in addition to their vast industrial scale, co-opted the saloons as the final outpost in the machinery of distribution. By pledging affiliation with brewers such as Anheuser-Busch, Pabst, or Schlitz, local saloonkeepers could finance fixtures, get supplies of free goods like beer mugs, and borrow start-up costs. In places like New York City, the tightness of space in living quarters made the saloon an extension of the workingman's living room. While this social element would remain a fundamental appeal, the saloons of the nineteenth century also provided practical services, such as cashing paychecks and serving as a mailing address for new arrivals. Employers and politicians soon took notice of the saloonkeeper as a central organizing figure in working-class culture, a broker of jobs and votes.

As important, a saloon next to a factory served as the midday cafeteria as well. Most saloons offered a spread of meat, bread, and soup—the free lunch provided to workingmen along with purchases of beer. Propelled by the saloon, the two million barrels of beer produced in the second year of the Civil War grew to over 24 million barrels twenty-five years later—beer became the new "national beverage."

But there was an element of political power for beer makers that went far beyond voters. With each passing year, beer increasingly became one of the most important pillars of revenue for the federal government. Without a personal or corporate income tax at the federal level, the tax on beer sales, as well as tobacco and distilled spirits, had grown to nearly one half of the federal government's tax revenues, rivaling the revenue from duties and the tariff on imported goods. And with every dollar of growth for Anheuser-Busch, Pabst, or Schlitz, the industry's lobbying group, the United States Brewers' Association, grew in political power.

Yet for jaded observers of American democracy, who tend to equate political power with money, the fate of alcohol would eventually present an effective counterexample. Just as the economic importance of slavery and the cotton trade did not save either from disruption, the millions of beer-chugging male voters, along with a vast distribution network of local entrepreneurs, coordinated machine politics, and a dependent federal government, would eventually run into the temperance forces. Following the Woman's Christian Temperance Union, the Anti-Saloon League would look to fight one of America's most powerful industries with an army that couldn't vote. It wouldn't be a fair fight. Decades later, two constitutional amendments, one prohibiting the sale of alcohol and the other giving women the right to vote, would pass within months of each other.

For men of industry, the concept of survival of the fittest once had a certain congratulatory ring to it—any survivor in the market, by defini-tion, was fit—giving philosophical and scientific purpose to those who otherwise were content with making money. Yet survival increasingly required business to adapt to changing political conditions—to abide by the sentiments of society in addition to responding to the simple signals of the marketplace. Much like the complexities of temperance politics, the unfettered growth of industrial power in the late nineteenth century would spark countermovements in labor, consumer safety, banking, and social relations. At stake was nothing less than the answer to a beguiling question: How would American capitalism absorb the myriad competing interests and still reap the dividends of its economic engine?

Fifteen

LIGHT

Scientific American, already one of the nation's oldest continuously published magazines at the time, dedicated its April 2 issue in 1881 to the enchantment of the electric light. On its cover was a sketch of the recently placed lights on the sidewalks of New York City's Broadway. Even in the more than three decades since Samuel Morse's invention, telegraphy remained electricity's only large commercial application. Other uses were either experimental or for entertainment, such as amusements at traveling carnivals, of the touch-this-and-see-your-hair-stand-up variety. So the prospect of seeing the cityscape glow, with faces and objects as fully visible at night as during daylight, suggested immense promise to the magazine's editors.

Broadway owed its lights to the breakthroughs of a young Cleveland-based inventor named Charles Brush. Brush represented a new generation of Americans—one that had entered adulthood after the Civil War, that had been born into a modern world with railroads and telegraphy. By the time he graduated from Cleveland High School in 1867, he had already spent years studying natural phenomena as a pastime, often experimenting with magnets and batteries. At the University of Michigan, he intermittently indulged his curiosity while studying engineering. After graduation and a brief detour into a business venture, Brush went back to the laboratory. His attention turned to a series of conceptual advances in light generated by electricity.

. . .

THE TELEGRAPH, as ubiquitous as it was, used a minimal amount of electricity. Therefore, the improvements in telegraphy did not equate to deep advances in the understanding of electricity. And there did not seem to be great need to explore this energy source. Coal provided the significant energy needed to move machines. And burning coal in industrial settings offered a derivative benefit: The gas emitted in the process could be captured as coal gas, able to be piped out for another use. In the burgeoning industrial economy of postwar America, the abundance of gas offered a cheap way to light gas lamps on street corners and urban homes. While the economic rationale for light by electricity was not clear, it did not stop experimentation by inventors.

In 1877, layering his insights upon the era's latest achievements, Brush came up with a significant advance in electrical design. Up to this point, mechanisms used to generate electricity could power one single lamp. The lamp itself relied on a principle known as arc lighting: Two carbon rods with a gap between them would be electrified, and the transfer of electricity between the rods through space produced a very bright light. Brush devised a system through which multiple lamps, connected by wires, could be lit up at the same time through a single power source. Almost immediately, seeing the implications, the Telegraph Supply Company of Cleveland agreed to license the American rights to Brush's patent, guaranteeing Brush a royalty.

Years before Edison's incandescent bulbs, the Brush system would dominate this new field of light by way of electricity. This innovation led to the start of companies looking for similar breakthroughs or applications. Predictably, investors who wanted to bet on lighting's future found eager promoters willing to organize lighting companies. The press was similarly delighted by the prospect of bright, endless illumination for the night sky. Industrialists marveled at the prospect of running all manner of factory operations twenty-four hours a day. Urban planners looked forward to a time of safe, lighted streets and bridges that would reduce crime and accidents. Wealthy households envisioned a future without malodorous gas lamps in their gilded living rooms and dining rooms—not to mention the dark stains left on walls after just a few months of using gas lamps. To Americans familiar with the developments, the future suddenly looked bright, clean, and modern.

For a brief period, Brush's system dominated the field. With 98 percent market share, the Telegraph Supply Company of Cleveland, reflecting its new success, changed its name to Brush Electric Company and formed a subsidiary operation to expand the business to the East. Headquartered with a large electric generator at 133 West Twenty-fifth Street, the New York operation attended to its first order of business: to light Broadway from Fourteenth Street to Thirty-fourth Street with twenty-one arc lights. With this permanent demonstration right in the heart of the city, the company advertised the capability of running wires from its generating station "to any point within a two-mile radius, putting up the light in any desired place." Seeing the night sky now immune to darkness, New Yorkers marveled. For most, this marked their first exposure to artificial light.

But New York was actually late to electric light—over six thousand individual lights had already been installed in other places. Several small towns across America had purchased the Brush system, being in closer proximity to the Brush Company's Cleveland factory. In Wabash, Indiana, town leaders installed a total of four lights on top of the courthouse, enough to provide illumination for the streets of the entire town. Enterprising factories, mines, city streets, docks, stores, hotels, churches, and theaters had also become early adopters.

All this success led *Scientific American* to issue an enthusiastic early verdict that the Brush Company, despite the efforts of competitors, had effectively "monopolized the field" of electric light for the foreseeable future. But, of course, the assertion was premature. Charles Brush's system would not have the final word. Indeed, the man to whom much credit would ultimately be given was not significant enough to warrant a mention in an entire magazine issue devoted to artificial light. But it was Brush who would be forgotten.

RECORDED HISTORY WOULD be kinder, perhaps too kind, to an equally youthful inventor thirty or so miles removed from the bustling thoroughfares of New York City. In the New Jersey township of Raritan, Thomas Alva Edison had set up a laboratory in the Menlo Park section of town. At the peak of Brush's acclaim, Edison was working on experiments in incandescent lighting, the lightbulb. An arc lighting system, while extremely bright, required daily maintenance and replacement of the carbon rods—it was also unstable at times, throwing off sparks from its high-voltage wires. Its brightness and related costs relegated its use to the outdoors and cavernous indoor spaces visited by large numbers of people. Edison's experiments were structured to discover a bulb that would be far cheaper to maintain, longer lasting, and appropriate for indoor use.

Edison himself was a bit of a late bloomer relative to Charles Brush. While Brush had been obsessed with chemistry and electricity since his adolescence, Edison was a less-than-stellar student. Born in 1847, Edison had been kicked out of the first school he attended by the age of seven. His mother, after a period of homeschooling, enrolled him in another school. But young Alva didn't fare well there either. The chronically daydreaming boy found the rigid structure of grammar school too constricting for his energies. Edison's relief from the drudgery of school came through a job hawking newspapers on a train that connected Port Huron to Detroit. With this change, Thomas Edison's formal education was over.

While spending a few teenage years working on the railroad, Edison engaged in a variety of misadventures made possible by his independent financial means, a creative imagination, and the freedom of roaming through destination towns. Generally, the adventures involved either store-bought chemicals for conducting crude experiments or schemes for making money to supplement his newspaper-sales income. After a few years, his family steered Alva to proper trade work in a telegraph office. Unlike the teenage Carnegie, Edison was only marginally competent at telegraphy, but not inept enough to be fired and lose his monthly $75 paycheck—the war economy of 1863 required all the telegraphy help that it could get. But for an unschooled boy the telegraph office was a ticket to the broader world. Carnegie's talents led him to valuable interactions with the recipients of the messages. Edison's time at the telegraph office introduced him to the mechanics and operations of the telegraph machines themselves, exposing him to electricity, chemicals, mechanical tickers, and wires.

From here his imagination wandered, but never too far into the realm of the theoretical. Edison, with the newspaper hustler still in him, was always on the lookout for opportunities to make money, keeping his creativity in sync with the strictures of commercial application. At the same time, he made for as poor an employee as he had been a student. Told not to touch the equipment and to focus on sending messages, Edison went into the equipment room anyway, with his unauthorized antics leading to a large quantity of battery acid spilled on the floor. He was fired.

At a subsequent posting, Edison came upon a solution to a vexing problem in telegraphy. A given telegraph message, after being transmitted two hundred or so miles, had to be received by an operator and retransmitted. This was due to the electricity becoming weaker after traveling such a distance, to the point of risking the message being lost. Edison developed a breakthrough known as a "repeater": Through perforated paper recording the message, the device relayed the message without having to be reentered. Edison patented it—one of the first patents among the more than one thousand he would file in his life. With this bit of success, entrepreneurs and promoters increasingly came into Edison's acquaintance, allowing him independence from all further employment. For his next act, he invented a system whereby two messages could be transmitted along a wire at the same time, rather than sequentially, thereby doubling the capacity of a telegraph wire. Edison's reputation grew rapidly. Not only was he a great talent, but he was immensely practical—he was inventing techniques that had potential for immediate economic impact, real cost savings, at an industrial scale. Along the way, Edison licensed his patents and sold partial interests to various partners. Each time, cash would come Edison's way to fund further innovation in his laboratory. With the fees coming in, Edison, in a sense, became a fully independent research-and-development outfit.

Again, as was the case with Eli Whitney and Samuel Morse, the U.S. Patent Office was the great equalizing force of the thinker and tinkerer. Edison's patents protected his intellectual property, giving him a monopoly over the use of his inventions. The development of American capitalism relied to a large degree on government recognition of a unique form of property; the patent transformed the product of an inventor's imagination into a set of legal rights, creating new property out of nothing. With this property right in hand, such upstarts were able to attract capital to commercialize their inventions. But unlike physical property like land or buildings, where title can be clear and ownership permanent, grants of patents had a large degree of subjectivity. What exactly merited giving the inventor exclusive commercial rights over a line of thinking or concept? Indeed, even the duration of a patent grant was limited to an arbitrary seventeen years—why not four or fifty? On one hand, with scientific experimentation being usually fruitless and expensive, a grant of exclusivity over viable breakthroughs made sense to encourage the risky expenditure of capital, time, and effort toward the unknown and unproven. On the other hand, the period needed to limit exclusive ownership of knowledge and new techniques for only so long, ideally enough to allow the inventor time to profit from his risk and breakthrough.

With his telegraph patents in hand, Edison thought himself every bit the equal of his newest negotiating counterpart, the president of Western Union. In a recent period, the telegraph giant had laid down sixty thousand miles of additional wire at an investment of over $5 million, mostly along existing routes to accommodate for increased messaging traffic. It was one of the fastest-growing companies in America. Sensing a large opportunity, America's richest man, Cornelius Vanderbilt, along with his son William Henry, had taken control of the company as large shareholders. As the postwar American economy went into overdrive, commercial communication and coordination required increasing use of the telegraph. Commodity and stock markets transmitted pricing information almost constantly. The use of the wires by newspapers and newspaper wire services grew exponentially. To accommodate the use, Western Union needed massive ongoing capital expenditures to add new wires across America to support the messaging volume, many times doubling and quadrupling wires across existing routes. For Western Union,

Edison offered a significant breakthrough that he had yet to commercially license: the Quadruplex. This innovation allowed two messages to be sent on a telegraph wire at the same time while also enabling it to receive two incoming messages simultaneously, doubling his previous groundbreaking effort. If such a technology could be implemented going forward, and if it worked, Western Union could support four times the volume on its new wires. With such immediate potential savings in capital expenditures, Western Union was receptive.

Historians and biographers have often discounted Edison's business acumen, but he was no fool. Even in his early years, he was shrewd in extracting value for his inventions from the biggest of the big—he was savvy enough to get to the negotiating table in the first place. But he was simply more interested in inventing than in managing any enterprise. His near-term fortunes allowed him to indulge in finding the next new thing rather than maximizing value from his previous new thing. Now, just ten years removed from hawking papers on a train, having started with no education and no connections, he was demanding close to $500,000 from Western Union for something he had developed independently in a lab.

But Western Union, assuming endless leverage due to its stature, dragged the process out. Edison, hard up for money with his lab expenses mounting, asked for an advance while the parties negotiated. Western Union's president demurred and left for Chicago under the impression Edison had nowhere to turn. It was a mistake. Edison's genius was by now well recognized in the close-knit telegraph industry. It fell upon an old Vanderbilt rival, Jay Gould, to step in on behalf of his own telegraph operation, the Atlantic & Pacific. The opportunity was alluring enough that Gould left his confines in the city to venture to Edison's laboratory in New Jersey. Edison demonstrated the Quadruplex. After a very short visit, Gould left impressed. Days later, Gould offered a cash and stock deal, which Edison accepted.

Western Union, missing the opportunity, would find itself in conflict with Gould's smaller operation, which now controlled a vital technology. The scope and limitations of Edison's patents would become the source of much dispute between the rivals. Edison himself, however, with his check and shares in hand, moved on unscathed. His decade in telegraphy had brought him in touch with the principles of electricity, power generation, wiring, and instrumentation. In Samuel Morse's personal estimation, Edison's contributions to telegraphy were second only to his own in inventing it.

MOVING ON, Edison set his ambitions on the next realm of electricity. challenged by the sight of Brush's and other arc lights, he looked to create a lightbulb that would be long lasting, odorless, and intimate enough for an indoor environment. But unlike inventors who struggled through years of desperation in finding capital, his talent was now held in high esteem by many of the richest men in America. Normally the leading capitalists, such as William H. Vanderbilt, the recent inheritor of 95 percent of his father's fortune, stayed away from investing in new technology unless it had a role to play in an existing industrial enterprise of theirs. But with Edison the Vanderbilts made exceptions. Within a year, even the austere and somber J. P. Morgan took a special interest in underwriting Edison's efforts to produce not only a lightbulb, but also a power generation and distribution system that Edison envisioned to go along with it. And with access to capital, Edison scaled his imagination accordingly. The venture would be incorporated in New Jersey as the Edison Electric Illuminating Company.

Still, it was no sure thing. *Scientific American*'s article on Brush offered a resoundingly negative assessment of incandescent lighting. It was the reason that Edison's name wasn't mentioned despite his acclaim in telegraphy. This omission would prove to be an anomaly. Matching his genius as an inventor, Edison had strong instincts for giving reporters a good story, usually with him at the center. And with the lightbulb, Edison's turn would come, and make him one of the most famous men in America in the 1880s.

But Edison's most optimistic projections didn't come to fruition. It took him a couple of years to develop a lightbulb that could last more than a few days. The entire system he had conceptualized was far more complicated than the Brush lighting system, which used a simple power generator with miles of wire connected to lamps. In addition, unlike the arc light system, where every light on a wire needed to be powered on at the same time, Edison's system planned for switches, which would allow an individual lightbulb to be turned on or off, on demand. Edison imagined a power grid with centralized power generation and metered use. To top it off, Edison went with the costly option of underground wires.

By the end of 1881, the Edison lighting system existed in prototype form at Menlo Park as his company was hard at work digging underground around the nexus of American finance: Wall Street. Edison then purchased a building on Pearl Street to serve as the site for a central power station for the grid. Dismayed residents soon complained about the endless drilling, especially for such a speculative purpose. And newspapers turned skeptical with the ongoing delays—the criticism might have been even more pronounced, but President Garfield's assassination had occupied American attention through most of the summer. It seemed to validate *Scientific American*'s failure to even mention Edison by name in that 1881 issue. The streets of Broadway were already lit up with Brush's system, while Edison's grid had yet to illuminate a single bulb in New York City.

While the fourteen miles of planned digging around the streets of lower Manhattan continued, a couple of investors indulged in a unique privilege before the central grid was operational. William H. Vanderbilt asked Edison to arrange for electric light at the new Vanderbilt mansion under construction. Considering that it was miles from where the subterranean efforts were taking place, Edison installed a generator—a loud power-generation system to power a total of one home—and the mansion was wired for light. But the men overlooked a key factor in all their enthusiasm: Mrs. Vanderbilt. She refused to move in upon hearing the sound of power generated from her basement. It probably didn't help that a small fire caused by the wiring had threatened to burn down the house during construction. In the end, it was financier J. P. Morgan, with his far more acoustically tolerant wife, who would own the first residence in New York City wired for electric light. This development also was not without its trials. His rich neighbors, relying on quiet gas lamps themselves, complained repeatedly about the noise. Then his library caught on fire.

In the meantime, the digging in lower Manhattan had finally come to a halt. And genius, it seemed, came at a price. Edison had managed to exceed his original cost estimate of $160,000 by an additional $320,000. With an entire electric grid placed in the ground, several office buildings, including those of Drexel, Morgan & Co. and the *New York Times*, were wired for light, with a total of eight hundred lamps. On September 4, 1882, Edison turned the power on at his Pearl Street station. The remarkable event was not indoor light—factories, cavernous spaces, and the Morgan residence already had it—but an entire system of electricity that flowed into offices, revealed by the flick of a switch powering a small bulb.

A DILIGENT READER of the *New York Times* in 1883 would have noticed an almost daily dose of articles related to some minor development in light, electricity, or the telephone. The articles by now demonstrated a more matter-of-fact tone than the reverential one of less than five years earlier: BASE-BALL BY ELECTRIC LIGHT gave an account of the first night game from Fort Wayne, Indiana. The *Times* headline from June 23 noted that GOULD BOAT GETS ELECTRICITY, in reference to Jay Gould's grand yacht *Atalanta*. Churches, starting with one in Elizabeth, New Jersey, started introducing lighting. There was even a curious mention of a horseless streetcar powered by electricity.

Light was installed on the new steel bridge connecting Manhattan and Brooklyn, which, having been under construction for years, had opened in May. A few months before the opening of the Brooklyn Bridge, the contract for lighting was opened for bids, but Edison lost out to the United States Illuminating Company when the builder felt that arc lights were more suitable. Edison's proposal of incandescent bulbs also came in several thousand dollars above the winning bid of $18,000. When it opened, the bridge became the tallest point in New York City, an observation deck appropriate for a Sunday stroll. For New Yorkers of the 1880s taking in this scenery, progress seemed to be all around this steel bridge, and at tantalizing new heights, as the daylight stretched into the evening.

But progress was not always progress. Horse manure from the busy, unceasing traffic piled up in the city streets. The city's population had far outpaced its ability to build. And it became worse each year. Tens of thousands of immigrants ventured no farther than a few miles from where they first arrived. Sidewalks meant crowds. And a slight upward look from the streets revealed a mishmash of wires running here, there, everywhere—endless, intricate spiderwebs in the sky. Any business that wanted to have a telegraph, electric wire, or arc lights simply had the installer add to this unregulated web.

Prior to the 1880s, the vast majority of electric wires covering the streets were for the telegraph, alarm companies, and other applications that used minimal electricity. If they fell, the passerby might get a good shock but avoided fatal harm. Headlines and editorials suggested nuisance and aesthetics as the primary reasons for complaint. With time, this view changed. With the higher voltage of the arc lighting systems increasingly occupying the sky, the danger was more substantial. The city's dozens of newspapers, in a bare-knuckles competition for readership, added the electrical mayhem to the potpourri of murder, robbery, and salacious stories on their pages. The headlines in 1883 alone included TOO MUCH ELECTRICITY FOR COMFORT, THE HORSE INJURED BY ELECTRICITY, NUISANCE OF POLES AND WIRES, and ALMOST A PANIC AT RIDLEY'S, the last of which described an incident at the recently lit Ridley's department store, where a large section of the lights in front of the store dropped to the ground. Women panicked and rushed to the door. A hasty bystander yelled "Fire!" assuming all electrical failures caused fires—not an unsafe assumption. Local fire officials restored calm. There was enough tension and anxiety over electricity that even this event warranted coverage.

Edison Electric's underground wires proved prescient in terms of public safety. But the biggest challenge to rapid electrification was posed by gas. Gas companies, using the by-product of industrial coal or natural gas piped in over hundreds of miles, had full-scale infrastructure in most major cities to provide metered gas to American urban homes. The light wasn't clean, it smelled, and it darkened the furniture and walls with use, but it was plentiful and cheap. Not to mention that in New York, as in other places, there were constant rate wars among competing gas companies. In rural America, the ubiquitous Standard Oil gas can provided the kerosene needed for illumination and cooking. While household adoption was limited, electricity did spread quickly to office buildings and commercial establishments. With this growth, Edison established central power stations in multiple cities, with investors providing the capital. Each new dollar of investment further diluted Edison's ownership of the various entities using his name.

By 1887 another form of competition had arrived by way of George Westinghouse. The men would begin the first great commercial battle over an industrial standard. In an ecosystem such as electric power, where hundreds of companies and vendors were expected to participate in building an electrified world, there was efficiency for all if everyone agreed on a common standard. Eventually Westinghouse's alternating current, which enabled more cost-effective power transmission over longer distances, would become the standard over the direct-current system that Edison had pressed for. And while much is made of the history between Edison and Westinghouse, as with his previous ventures in telegraphy, Edison didn't last long in the electric transmission business either.

Around the time of Westinghouse's entry into the business, Edison had authorized the consolidation of all his patents and his electric company interests throughout the nation into a company known as Edison General Electric. New Jersey had just passed a law, the first of its kind, allowing a corporation formed in the state to hold shares in out-of-state companies. The new company then looked to further consolidate Edison's market share, proposing a merger with another electric company known as Thompson-Houston. Initially reluctant, Edison's primary financier, J. P. Morgan, eventually saw the benefits of organizing the consolidation. Through his firm Drexel, Morgan & Co., he raised a few million dollars to capitalize the combined interests of Thompson-Houston and Edison General Electric. Along with J. P. Morgan, Edison received a seat on the board of directors of the new company. But the merger contained a final blow to the fame-loving Edison's vanity: Going forward, the new company would be known simply as General Electric.

Still, for all of its promise, electricity made its way to fewer than 650,000 total customers, household and commercial, by 1900. Department stores, office buildings, electric streetcars, and commercial spaces were the places where Americans enjoyed the benefits of electricity. But less than 5 percent of American households had electricity at the turn of the century. The inferior alternatives in the market, gas and kerosene, still enjoyed substantial pricing advantages. From the lighting of Broadway, it took five decades for the majority of American households to be electrified.

In time, Edison's glory would grow into that of a full-blown American hero—his fingerprints would be found on improvements to Alexander Graham Bell's telephone, the lightbulb, telegraphy, the phonograph, and even motion pictures. Financial glory, however, belonged to others. The consolidation of various firms into General Electric would be the opening act to a financial era headed by J. P. Morgan.

Sixteen

RETAIL

Nearly twenty years after writing *Uncle Tom's Cabin*, Harriet Beecher Stowe joined her older sister's effort in an altogether different genre. Catharine Beecher, also a writer, had focused for decades on the education of women, becoming a notable author on the topic of domesticity. Though unmarried and childless, she was not without some experience. While Harriet was writing *Uncle Tom's Cabin*, much of the household management and care of the Stowe children had fallen to Catharine. After the war, she published an essay in *Harper's* titled *How to Redeem Woman's Profession from Dishonor*. In it she argued that the woman's role as a homemaker had significant economic value on par with that of men's work and that its execution was "a science and art as much as law, medicine or divinity."

The Beecher sisters themselves were as empowered as women could be. Both earned substantial incomes as published authors. Harriet was arguably a historical figure—her novel had played a role in the building of antislavery sentiments in the North. With the passage of the Fifteenth Amendment giving African American men the right to vote, it seemed that the next battle would be to extend voting rights to women. Here the Beecher sisters departed somewhat from the suffragist viewpoint, not seeing the right to vote as absolutely central to the woman's role in society. The Beecher view was that the moral sphere of the home and the political sphere of statecraft were distinct but equally important. Indeed, running a household was more than equal to merely making a living. The woman's task went further: She was to instill moral values in her household, starting with her children, to infuse society with the qualities necessary for harmony. In the Beecher understanding, the functions of cooking, cleaning, and homemaking were not trivial matters—they were the building blocks of clean, healthy Christian living.

Predictably, when the Beecher sisters brought forth ideas on domestic economy and household governance, they packaged the full force of their piety and rigor in a pragmatic manifesto. Published first in 1869, *The American Woman's Home* was authoritative, not sunny. It included sections on cooking meat properly, the role of fresh air and ventilation in health, the deodorization of commodes, equipping a kitchen, and selecting home furnishings. The manual went further in exhorting women to have calm and commanding dispositions in managing their homes. It warned against stimulants such as coffee and tea for both adults and children. There was a chapter devoted to gardening and growing crops. Each chapter offered clear, concise reasoning behind the Beecher formula.

The book also hinted at a widening gulf between the upper middle class and the working class. In a nod to the prevalence of immigrant women employed by affluent households, *The American Woman's Home* devoted considerable space to the training and management of servants. Given that many of these women were poor Irish Catholics—"with all the unreasoning heats and prejudices of the Celtic Blood"—the need to acclimate the help to decent Christian practices was of no small concern. In addition, its pages casually referenced a wide variety of household products and furnishings that were deemed necessities. A generation earlier, such a book on domesticity would have guided a woman toward self-sufficiency with advice on sewing, home therapies, and churning butter. This new America pointed to specialization and consumption— simply buying what one needed.

This prescription coincided with the emerging wage structure of the industrial economy. Unlike those of farmers, the earnings of wageworkers and salaried men of growing middle-class professions meant predictable monthly household incomes. At the same time, this new type of household, unlike a farm, was no longer an income-producing unit—it sold nothing to the market. The middle-class home of the salaried man was a consumptive unit; it purchased almost everything that it needed. Given this interdependency, household expenses took on a new dimension as a larger part of the domestic economy. And household purchasing decisions, in the course of managing the home and raising children, fell to women. While American democracy took its time in recognizing the full citizenship of women, the marketplace of American capitalism was decades quicker in recognizing the power of the purse, the source of domestic spending.

ON APRIL 11, 1876, nearly the entire front page of the *New York Times* was devoted to the death of one of the city's richest men:

> At 1:50 o'clock yesterday afternoon, Alexander Turney Stewart died at his residence on Thirty-Fourth Street and Fifth Avenue. The flags upon many private and public buildings, including City Hall, were at half-mast. There was a general feeling that these marks of respect were not paid to the man of enormous wealth, to the successful merchant, to the man of vast designs and achievements, but to one who had by his career illustrated, perhaps more than anyone else, the capabilities and opportunities of American citizenship.

IT WAS AN APT, wholly American obituary, perfectly suited for the Gilded Age. This wealthy man was celebrated not for his wealth but for the affirmation that anyone could achieve anything in this undivided America, an idea so central to the nation's self-identity.

A. T. Stewart left Ireland as a teenager and arrived in America around 1820. Having graduated from Dublin's Trinity College, Stewart started his career in New York as a teacher. Soon after, he lent money to a friend to start a small dry goods store. The friend, unable to pay back the loan, offered ownership of the struggling store instead. With no experience in retail, or any business for that matter, Stewart found himself a merchant by default. After a trip back home to Ireland, he steered the store toward specializing in Irish linens. From here, Stewart kept expanding his presence in the city until he became a well-established merchant by the 1840s.

At the time, American retail, as practiced nearly everywhere, was a pragmatic, transactional affair. Goods were stocked at general stores behind the counter. Clerks, usually male, brought out merchandise for the customer to review, and negotiation ensued. Prices were based on the customer's savvy. Larger cities like New York had smaller specialty retailers for every type of good: toys, fabric, china, furnishings, and so forth. There, as at the general stores, customers did not roam the floors in a leisurely manner. Nothing about the retail experience could be deemed experiential or entertaining in itself. Stewart changed this.

On the corner of Tenth Street and Broadway, he decided to begin construction on a vast new structure for his thriving operation. Built over a five-year period, Stewart's Cast Iron Palace had reportedly cost almost $2.5 million by the time it opened in 1862. It was America's first department store, both opulent and cavernous—at least five floors set over a city block. Counter stools were upholstered in luxurious fabrics. The staff was trained to be deferential to one and all. Departments for each class of goods, from clothing, kitchen utensils, and bedding to home furnishings, were neatly organized, each intended to demonstrate the material life open to the American household. Even during wartime, well-heeled Northern consumers, such as Mary Lincoln, made the store an instant success. Indeed, the First Lady may have found A. T. Stewart's too enticing; she had spent so much at Stewart's, among other places, to redecorate the White House that a chagrined President Lincoln had to ask for a special congressional appropriation to cover the overage. But the department store was open to everyone. As time went on, the environment of the department store became an accessible opulence, a taste of the Gilded Age for the residents of major American cities.

In a reverential tone, the *Times* obituary outlined Stewart's contributions to retailing and consumer culture. Starting in his little store, he had created "absolute honesty between the buyer and the seller" by not allowing salesmen to exaggerate the quality of the merchandise. His next innovation was "selling *at one price*" to everyone, removing haggling from the shopping experience. Lastly, "any one could wander for hours if he liked through the labyrinth of goods without once being asked to buy or even accosted by a clerk," the welcoming atmosphere offering an egalitarian dignity to even those who could not afford to buy anything.

While estimating Stewart's fortune at between $40 million and $50 million, the obituary took care to note that though Stewart was not especially known for his philanthropy or generosity, his contributions were significant. The *Times'* treatment highlighted the distinction between the American public's sympathies for men of industrial fortunes, who sold goods to other businesses, and the men who amassed fortunes from products and services that touched the consumer directly. The mechanics of Stewart's fortune were clear and plain for the public to understand—he made money when people bought things from him. It had none of the mysteries of backroom dealings, science, politics, tariffs, or finance. Stewart orchestrated his form of capitalism to provide the consumer with value. Hard-won concessions from suppliers and employees all served to lower prices. With the consumer now the beneficiary of the policies and practices pioneered by the retailer, the fortune was venerated as honestly earned and deserved, a formula whose yield it was un-American to begrudge.

But the value went beyond good-quality merchandise at good prices. Stewart's Cast Iron Palace trained the urban middle-class consumer to conceive of shopping as leisurely entertainment without specific intent— a destination in and of itself.

For a few of the older retailers, Stewart's success meant adapting to changing consumer appetites or suffering a slow decline. Aside from creating a more indulgent experience for the customer, the small general store or specialty retailer had little purchasing power due to its lack of scale. As in other industries, economies of scale—the principle of lowering operating costs through large volumes—were being applied to retail. A large store or multiple stores gave the retailer negotiating power with his suppliers. The more sophisticated aspects of retail, such as international sourcing, were beyond the scope of small operations to engage in at all. Transatlantic steamers could cross the Atlantic within a week or two to let a buyer look at merchandise directly from European manufacturers. Retailers could communicate with European suppliers of fine goods through telegraphic messages over the transatlantic cable. But these travel and communication costs could be borne only by retailers selling in larger quantities.

Stewart inspired enough entrants with their own cast-iron buildings—named for the type of iron that initially made such cavernous spaces possible—that the commercial area around Broadway, where Charles Brush's arc lights first lit the night sky, was christened Ladies' Mile. Retailers such as Macy's, Lord & Taylor, Gimbels, and others opened their storefronts. The inducements for shoppers to enter, including novelties such as Lord & Taylor's steam-powered elevator, one of New York's first, multiplied with the competition.

Other cities produced even grander efforts. After Stewart's success, the center of nearly every major American city would soon feature at least one anchoring department store. In Philadelphia, a successful merchant named John Wanamaker gambled his entire reputation and credit on a new location, sensing that the proportions of the business were changing. Wanamaker had visited with Stewart at his Cast Iron Palace to take notes on the pioneer's methods. Stewart had graciously walked the younger merchant through his store, where Wanamaker witnessed the older man's attention to detail department by department. Inspired by seeing this concept in action, Wanamaker purchased the site of the Pennsylvania Railroad's freight depot on the edge of Philadelphia to attempt his own version. When it opened in 1876, within months of Stewart's death, the ornate Grand Depot debuted to the foot traffic of seventy thousand Philadelphians. Its acres of indoor retail space made it the largest store in the world.

Wanamaker's contribution to retailing, beyond the predictable one-upping in scale and grandeur, was in advertising. Wanamaker believed in the primacy of newspaper advertising above all. He wrote his own copy, promoting shopping events and sales through newspapers. In the early days, Wanamaker took a significant portion of each day's sales receipts to allocate his next day's advertising budget—yesterday's sales driving growth the morning after. For the next century, department store advertising would remain one of the largest sources of revenue for city newspapers throughout America. His effort proved successful enough that twenty years after the Grand Depot opened, Wanamaker expanded to New York with the purchase of Stewart's old Cast Iron Palace.

BUT IT WAS WANAMAKER'S ROLE as a public servant that would lead to the expansion of the retail experience to all Americans. Given his visibility as a businessman, during Benjamin Harrison's one-term presidency starting in 1889, Wanamaker was appointed the postmaster general of the United States. The role was not without significance. Until the Civil War, one of the only major functions of the federal government had been the delivery of mail. And it had a Philadelphian provenance. Benjamin Franklin himself had served as the nation's first postmaster. Wanamaker's tenure was marked by his tireless advocacy of an experimental service eventually known as Rural Free Delivery, beginning a fundamental change in how mail was delivered to rural Americans. His successor at the Postal Service, with the help of Congress, would implement Wanamaker's plans.

Until Rural Free Delivery became codified, farmers would have to go into distant towns to collect their mail. Similarly, to send a letter might mean a half-day trip to a country store. Given that millions of American farmers lived miles from any small town or village, the lack of home delivery isolated these households further from the modern energies of their country. Rural Free Delivery brought the mail to rural households at mailboxes along country roads. Rather than dozens of farmers coming into town, each spending time away from the farm, one mail carrier delivered the mail to dozens of farms. It took years to fully implement this system across America, but it soon added one more element of participation in the American consumer economy. The U.S. Postal Service opened up the market for consumer goods to the 70 percent of Americans who lived hours from a big-city department store.

Other than rural Americans themselves, the two biggest beneficiaries of such advances in the mail system were based in Chicago. As far back as the 1860s, working for a variety of wholesale merchants as a sales agent, Aaron Montgomery Ward was aware of the deep frustration of farmers at being able to buy only the simplest of goods. In most instances the farmer was essentially captive to the one or two country stores within an accessible distance. Given the lack of customers, the stores had limited quantities, high prices, and generally poor-quality merchandise. In addition, the stores served as quasi banks, extending goods on credit. This made the store susceptible to credit risks and nonpaying customers in the community, which the store made up for by passing on even higher prices to local customers. Compounding this, country stores were themselves captive customers of wholesale merchants that charged prices commensurate with the stores' remoteness. All in all, the consumer dividend stemming from the output gains of industrial capitalism bypassed rural America.

The farmers had made attempts to pool their purchasing power to some modest effect, forming local cooperatives in which the larger orders of the group helped bring down prices. Ward's retail innovation would tap into this form of collective action perfectly. Losing his first name, he printed a one-page "catalog" with 163 items under the name Montgomery, Ward & Co.—the insertion of the comma likely to cause the inference that more than one person was involved. Initially he targeted local farmer groups that belonged to a national order commonly known as the Grange. He subsequently moved up to a thirty-two-page pocket catalog. In the pages of the catalog, used as his primary marketing tool, Ward transparently outlined his logic: Eliminate the middleman, buy directly from manufacturers, and sell for cash, not credit. Farmers, being businessmen themselves, particularly understood the savings to be gained from not having capital tied up in extending credit, along with having no retail location. The savings from the business model were likely better appreciated by farmers' wives, who as managers of their household budgets were subject to the whims of the commodities markets in a way that the wives of wage laborers and salaried men, with more predictable household incomes, weren't. And as important, they had ready access to a wide variety of goods for the first time in their lives. Everything else they needed to know about any business model was found in the prices of the goods listed in the Montgomery Ward catalog. The prices were so low that they elicited cries of fraud—"Don't Patronize Montgomery, Ward, & Co., They are Dead-Beats"—from local country merchants.

Indeed, mail fraud and hucksterism grew alongside the legitimate practitioners of the catalog trade. Victims often were told to send money in for this product or that cure and, when they received nothing or something worth nothing, were left without recourse. Distance from their customers, the anonymity of a post office box, and the small amounts involved in each transaction allowed this breed of schemer to operate. Yet even with the healthy doses of skepticism, Montgomery Ward continued to grow. To counter the customer's perception of risk, Ward offered a full money-back guarantee on virtually everything that he sold. This most consumer-friendly practice of liberal refunds—a true American original, both in department stores and in catalog retail—hastened the pace of mass consumerism in America. It also served to strain the relationship between local merchants and their local clientele. The small store could rarely match the prices, selection, or refund policies offered by those with scale.

By 1895 Ward's catalog business had grown by leaps and bounds, operating out of large warehouses in Chicago. The catalog, which cost 15 cents, exceeded six hundred pages, detailing thousands of products accompanied by sketch drawings. Within the catalog was the evidence of the consumer revolution. The catalog opened with thirty pages of fabrics of every type and design starting at 4 cents per yard for cotton to 50 cents or more per yard for Chinese and Japanese silks. This was followed by dozens of pages of books for sale: the decades-old *Uncle Tom's Cabin* was 18 cents plus 7 cents for postage, a series of six Horatio Alger stories for boys could be had for $3.50 or 88 cents for a single story, and the memoirs of President Grant, which he finished at a feverish pace before his death in order to leave money for his wife, sold for $3.25. For 85 cents the toy section included "The Yale-Harvard Game: A high-class game for thoughtful players," featuring a football field as a checkered board and helpfully noting for those unfamiliar with the sport, "the idea of each side being to carry the ball into the opposite goal." The hand camera at $3.50 brought "the possibilities of picture making within the reach of all."

Other practical offerings included farm implements, pianos, furniture, silverware, clothes, and guns. The latest Winchester repeating rifle, among dozens listed, sold for $10.96, while a Smith & Wesson .38-caliber nickel-plated five-shot pistol set one back $12. Even the wonder of electricity had made the cut, with two pages of rudimentary products—all battery powered, as electricity via wires had not made it into even most urban homes. The Magnetic Telephone Company had a unit listed for $18 or two for $35 with a connection between the units. The majority of the electric products, however, were designed to shock—"when doctors fail to effect a cure with drugs and medicines, electricity often cures." This sizzling marvel of modern medicine offered cures "in even the worst cases of paralysis and in fact, all nervous diseases." The miracles started at $5. Perhaps less miraculous was the last item listed in Electrical Goods: a vibrating undergarment available in an assortment of colors, which, according to the copy, "never fails to fit and give satisfaction"—$2.25 for the silk version.

SEEING WARD'S SUCCESS, other established retailers such as Bloomingdale's entered the catalog business with varying degrees of success. But its greatest practitioner emerged not from the sophisticated retailing of the city, but from a small midwestern railroad station.

Richard Sears was a freight agent for a railroad in Minnesota. Among other things, a freight agent's role was to get goods at the station forwarded to the local recipient in the community, usually a merchant or businessman, and collect the money due to the sender. In a common practice at the time, manufacturers and wholesalers would send merchandise without notice to a local retailer, hoping to make a sale. At one point Sears was tasked with forwarding five hundred gold watches to a jeweler; the jeweler turned them down and refused to pay. Sears relayed the message. The sender then offered the watches to Sears at a further discount. Sears, already in possession of the watches, succeeded in selling them for a quick profit. Enlisting other station agents, Sears ordered more watches and sold more while still employed at the railroad station. He earned

enough to pursue the business on a full-time basis. To sell watches directly
to customers, he started running newspaper ads, which proved effective
in luring increasing numbers of customers to his low-priced watches.

In 1886 Sears decided it would be cheaper to buy the watch components
and assemble the watches in house as R.W. Sears Watch Company. To
start, he placed an ad for a watchmaker, which led him to hire Alvin
Roebuck. Within eight years, in 1894, Sears, Roebuck & Co. was producing a catalog about half the size of Montgomery Ward's. Sears, however,
had twice the exuberance in terms of colorful language, especially in its
watch section. "Hampden Watches Slaughtered" read one page. "We say
slaughtered because we are offering Hampden for less money than any
other wholesale house in America." Another description, channeling the
economic populism in the air at the time, screamed: "Down with Monopoly! Down with Watch Trusts! Down with Prices!"

Like Ward, Sears often went to some lengths to describe his business
to his customers, layering the language of radical transparency within
the hyperbole. About an improbably cheap watch: "We do not guarantee
or recommend this case as it is impossible to say how long it will wear."
In a catalog filled with similar items at multiple price points, Sears clearly
conveyed that the lowest-priced items were priced that way for a reason.
Other times the copy dived into the reasoning behind the price. Marketing an entry-level bicycle at $11.90: "We made a contract with a large
manufacturer for their entire product, and by so doing we have got the
prices so far below all others that there is no room for comparison." In
this most commercial of nations, the customer of the 1890s was expected
to understand wholesale purchasing power.

At one point Sears discontinued the practice of collecting cash on
delivery, finding too much of his working capital tied up in the process.
To protect against any backlash and to diminish the customer's perceived
risk in paying cash up front, Sears added the policy of free shipping on
all returned goods—no questions asked.

But some things were far beyond the customer's ability to evaluate
properly, free returns notwithstanding. Sears, Roebuck's, drug section in
its 1902 catalog, for one, highlighted the shortcomings of an unregulated
market. Within a few years, the federal government would step in with

the Pure Food and Drug Act, the precursor to the Food and Drug Administration. Until then, trusting consumers used to seeing scientific and technical progress in all walks of life, could not be faulted for assuming such progress was being made in areas of health as well. The Cure for the Opium and Morphine Habit was guaranteed to be "perfectly harmless." The Sure Cure for Drunkenness and the Sure Cure for the Tobacco Habit, in addition to curing vice, promised to "make weak men strong again and impotent men gain weight and vigor." For women in search of improved complexion, there was Dr. Rose's Arsenic Complexion Wafers, which, "taken in the manner directed is absolutely innocuous." Not only that, but they "guaranteed a sure cure for freckles, pimples, vulgar redness," and a host of other facial maladies.

The eighty-gauge Heidelberg Electric Belt, worn around the waist for brief periods, assured men that the "invigorating current of galvanic electricity" was a "wonderful cure for seminal or vital weakness." "Have you perhaps written to some quack, so called institute, or self-styled men's physician without getting any help?" For men who had endured such fruitless efforts to cure their impotence, use of the "magical" eighty-gauge guaranteed "health, strength, superb manliness, youthful vigor" by carrying "life giving electric fluid straight to the affected parts."

American medicine, while making legitimate advances, straddled the line between boastful witchcraft and sound practice. Still, there were moments of surprising enlightenment. Catalog text related to alcoholism stated boldly that "drunkenness is a disease and must be fought and counteracted by proper medical methods the same as any other disease." If the Sears catalog was any guide, the moral judgment was reserved for sellers of alcohol rather than habitual drinkers. Even Sears had limits. In a policy portentous of events yet to unfold, while the company sold everything else, it refused to sell perfectly legal spirits on moral grounds.

This collision of morality and markets, even as expressed by businesses, as in Sears's case with alcohol, reflected the era's growing apprehension about the direction of capitalism, about where the market's border ended. Its most successful agitators would find a collective label as Progressives, co-opting the term "progress," which Herbert Spencer had equated with evolution. In the consumer realm, the argument was simple.

Yes, industrial capitalism produced a consumer dividend that was plain for many to see in terms of choice, price, and quality. But the complexities of new products and new materials left the consumer, among others, increasingly vulnerable without some basic protections. Functioning free markets required informed buyers and sellers. While the consumer's power to evaluate a plow or baseball glove was perhaps sufficient, other products, such as drugs, were difficult to evaluate, especially given that the seller could say anything to make a sale. And many times the consequences of faulty or inaccurate representations materialized only years in the future.

It became clear that the unscrupulous operator who spent the least on safety considerations was the biggest beneficiary of the unregulated landscape—he could price his products even lower and claim equal measures of safety in marketing. Correcting for all this required a force outside the market. The calls for consumer protection laws would grow stronger as the era progressed. Yes, regulation increased costs—it most certainly added to the producer's burden—but any lasting, systemic mistrust between consumers and producers would have a halting effect on commerce, while increased trust in the marketplace would accelerate economic growth. As these realizations emerged, American capitalism would increasingly create a role for the government as a referee.

Seventeen

UNIONS

On a spring night in 1886, off the corner of Chicago's Desplaines and Randolph streets, a bomb was thrown into an assembled troop of policemen, killing several, injuring dozens. Immediate suspicion turned to a movement that called themselves Anarchists, a breakaway order of Marxists. For years the American establishment of businessmen, newspapers, and politicians had been concerned by their talk of dynamite and revolution, of inciting workers to bring down the institutions of capitalism.

To the burgeoning American middle class of farmers, merchants, professionals, and teachers, with a stable foothold on the economic ladder, the message of the Anarchists did not resonate. Despite a couple of years of economic slowdown, these American households had little interest in wholesale disruption of an economic system that was transforming their country into an industrial giant. Remarkably, this rise had come so quickly, merely one generation removed from one of the bloodiest conflicts of the nineteenth century. The material abundance could be seen both within American homes and on the streets in arc lights and steel bridges. This Gilded Age had seeded a consumer revolution, aligning the interests of the consumer class—the middle class and above—with those of the capitalists. Low labor costs were reflected in the prices of goods at stores and in catalogs. For millions of Americans, the excesses of capitalism seemed forgivable by-products of its very success.

Indeed, how bad, really, were the working conditions in industrial settings?

They did not seem to dissuade the hundreds of thousands of immigrants who washed up each year on these shores, who expected to head directly to the factories. If so many wanted to come here, was it not proof that the system worked, that the system was fair? And one could move up in America. The titans of the Gilded Age had not gotten there by birthright. Andrew Carnegie had been a child laborer and now owned his own industrial empire. Rockefeller's father, Big Bill, had been known to tour through villages under a second identity selling patent medicines and cure-alls. When he was alive, old Vanderbilt could not be mistaken for anything but the unread and uncouth sailor he had once been. Edison, Wanamaker, Westinghouse, and Singer with his sewing machines, all had earned their place at the top. Harvard and Yale had not produced these conquerors. And wealth being the ultimate mark of survival in the economic jungle, to begrudge the dominance of the fittest was to argue against nature. If anything, Founding Fathers such as Jefferson, Washington, and Madison had been far more pedigreed—an aristocratic landed gentry—than these gritty, hustling Gilded Age capitalists. Those celebrated presidents owned and traded slaves; these modern men paid wages for an honest day's work. Judging by how far these men of humble origins had climbed, this capitalism was more meritocratic than the founders' democracy.

To Richard Theodore Ely, one of the first to document the rise of the American labor movement, such a defense of the American way—that the idea that anyone could rise to the top justified all ruthlessness and cost management in labor relations—entirely missed the point. The vast majority of laboring men were always going to be laboring men. Indeed, the suggestion that the only way to improve one's condition was to move beyond that of a lowly worker diminished the very dignity of the workingman, as if there were no intrinsic self-worth in performing the needed basic work of industry. And mathematically, as there would be far more at the bottom of the pyramid than the top, the question now facing society was how to improve the conditions of employment, not how to inspire laborers to escape them through ambition. Writing his book as the developments of 1885 and early 1886 were happening, Ely explained to his readers that this rapid rise of unions and labor organizations was meant to "remove disadvantages under which the great mass of workingmen suffer" by collectively bargaining for shorter hours and better working conditions.

The need for such an approach somewhat conflicted with the market principles outlined by Adam Smith. In his *Wealth of Nations* he had argued that freedom of contract, two parties in a negotiation, was enough to obtain a fair outcome between any buyer and seller. But the negotiating leverage of the vast modern industrial enterprises controlled by millionaires—the buyers of labor—was far greater than that of any individual, uneducated worker—the seller. The only leverage came through strength in numbers.

Simple enough, but another writer's words, which inspired the most spirited defenders of unions, presented some deep cause for concern. The final line of the then-decades-old *Communist Manifesto*, "Working men of all countries, unite," meant that communism was the equivalent of one large union of the world's working class, calling for "the overthrow of bourgeois supremacy" and "to do away with private property." Along with the rise of industry, themes from the *Manifesto* were increasingly embraced by radicals in America, with the most strident being the Anarchists, in an effort to differentiate themselves from the more muted aims of rival socialist groups. Thus anarchy, in the way these Anarchists meant it, was entirely different from the conception of statelessness that the term may now evoke.

The central conceit of the Anarchists was that no true change could come through the American electoral process, as the system had been built entirely by the hands of wealthy and powerful men. Given that man is generally incapable of acting beyond his economic self-interest, the political system that surrounded this industrial empire would serve only to protect its benefactors—private property was an instrument of the state, not distinct from it. Change could not come from within. Just as slaveholders did not willingly give up slaves, nor the South the institution of slavery, neither would industry cede its hold over the wage laborer. In struggle, power respected only power.

For years the Anarchists seemed to be more bark than bite. But the risk assessment changed on May 4, 1886, when the bomb exploded.

.   .   .

THE FINAL CHAIN of events had started at Chicago's McCormick
Reaper Works earlier in the year. McCormick's mechanical reaper had
once transformed harvesting practices on American farms, lowering the
cost of grain for consumers nationwide. By the 1880s the company, now
led by Cyrus McCormick Jr., was a large American exporter of farm
equipment. A labor union began enlisting segments of McCormick's
employees who were pushing for an eight-hour workday. McCormick,
feeling he had conceded too much in an earlier negotiation on wages,
was resolute, annoyed at the intrusion of this external organizing force.
Digging in, he fired a group of workers to demonstrate his resolve. Looking to the throngs of new immigrant men coming into the city each day,
he quickly replaced them.

But the move backfired. Rather than halting the spread of his men's
efforts to unionize, it spurred two unions, the United Metal Workers
and the Knights of Labor, to enlist nearly all of his workers. Unable to
come to terms with the unions, McCormick moved to temporarily shut
down the entire factory, locking out his workers. Immediately McCormick set about looking for new men with whom to reopen the factory.
With his strikebreakers, he reopened the factory with locked-out workers protesting outside. This maneuver, however, required escalated
protection in the form of hundreds of Chicago policemen. Seeing the
government firmly on the side of factory owners and property holders,
the union men were vulnerable to the entreaties of the Anarchists and
socialists who railed against the state.

For radical political elements, the large pool of laborers served as a
necessary proxy for their nascent political movements. While the message resonated in parts of Europe, the world's largest functioning democracy was more resistant to the voices and appeals to overthrow the
government: The people here had a voice at the polling booth, and as a
matter of identity, Americans believed themselves to be the most free
people in the world. In addition, the big-city newspapers almost universally sided with law and order and not with recent immigrants who
barely spoke English. In addition to the revenues from middle-class

readers buying their papers, the other revenue source of nearly all news-papers, advertising from businesses, meant favoring the commercial establishment to a large degree. Not to mention, strikes disrupted lives, inhibited commerce, canceled trains, and so on.

The year 1885, however, seemed to be a tipping point. America's largest union, the Knights of Labor, had 52,000 members in 1883. Since then, the growth had been so sudden and dramatic that rumors suggested that several hundred thousand members, perhaps more, now belonged to the Knights of Labor. Other smaller unions specializing in specific trades and sectors, such as typesetters, ironworkers, or railroad workers, were growing as well. Each work stoppage in the country seemed to be marketing for joining or forming a union. Throughout April, English-speaking middle-class-and-above newspaper readers saw daily headlines related to strikes by railroad workers, carriage makers, messenger boys, ironworkers, and more.

Workingmen's lack of a voice in mainstream politics and media played into the hands of socialists and anarchists. In Chicago, the epicenter of the agitation, the German Anarchist newspaper *Arbeiter-Zeitung* and the English-language *Alarm* strove to become the unofficial, collective organ of striking workers. While the unions were focused on practical considerations such as working hours, safety conditions, and wages, the intellectual framework of ideological movements proved to be an organizing factor. In Chicago, vows of solidarity with the locked-out McCormick workers started spreading.

Each day, hundreds of workers in unrelated businesses demonstrated their support by walking out of work collectively after eight hours—short of their mandated workday. Sensing the opportunity to build the disparate strikes into even greater collective action, the editors of *Arbeiter-Zeitung* called for a general strike on May 1, 1886, asking workers everywhere to stop work on that day. The sentiment for the general strike spread to other cities such as Cincinnati and Milwaukee. At the same time, the Knights of Labor, which had been entangled with Jay Gould's Texas & Pacific, had increased calls for strikes across a much larger system in the South. Unlike the smaller unions that represented specialized crafts, the Knights had the ability to incite far wider collective action to express worker solidarity. When Gould employees, deputized by a local sheriff, shot and killed seven unarmed strikers in April, it added to fuel to the fire.

Predictably, violence elsewhere increased the tensions at McCormick's. As May 1 approached, workers sensed that a large-scale collective action in Chicago could permanently alter the workday to eight hours. Enrollment in the Knights of Labor dramatically escalated. And lurking beneath this momentum was the threat of even greater violence, of terror. Anarchists had often spoken of dynamite as an equalizer against the police power of the state. In Chicago, which in 1871 had suffered a scarring fire that had virtually destroyed the city, the notion of Anarchists using dynamite in the context of striking workers added to the sense of danger.

When May 1 arrived, a working Saturday, Chicago came to a standstill. Tens of thousands of workers either took the Saturday off or cut their hours. Freight handlers disabled the railroad traffic, shutting down the Chicago economy and thus ensuring that nothing could come in or leave from the nation's commodity hub for grain and meat. With these laborers being the intermediate layer between the market and the source, even days of stoppage would have quickly impacted both middle-class consumers and farmers as suppliers of grain and meat. The plan was to continue the action into Monday and beyond, forcing a full recognition of the eight-hour day throughout the nation.

On Monday, May 3, the editor of *Arbeiter-Zeitung*, August Spies, spoke at a rally of Chicago's lumbermen. His speech took place within a few hundred yards of the McCormick factory, which continued to operate with strikebreakers. A couple of hundred locked-out McCormick workers joined the crowd to hear Spies. As he spoke, the bells at the McCormick factory rang, signaling the end of the shift. The locked-out workers, frustrated after months of being out of work, took it as their moment for escalation. They rushed to confront the nonunion workers leaving work after their shift. The police guarding the facility opened fire.

Six men were killed by the gunfire. Spies was enraged. Retreating to his newspaper's office, he quickly went to press with a one-page message calling for a mass meeting at the area known as Haymarket Square. The next day his issue of the *Arbeiter-Zeitung* suggested that if the

McCormick men had carried weapons, the police would have been reluctant to fire upon them. Then, fatefully, he suggested that a "dynamite bomb" would have been even more effective. On May 4 a flyer circulated calling for an outdoor meeting that evening to protest the police violence. With the city on edge, the police stood at a distance to monitor the developments. Spies once again spoke. As the night progressed, other speakers took the podium. Shortly after 10:00 p.m., the police moved in to disperse the crowd of a few hundred. A smoldering shell was thrown into the oncoming police contingent.

With the blast, any trace of sympathy for labor among the middle-class, mainstream newspapers, law enforcement, and government was effectively dead. CRUSHING ANARCHY, read the next day's headline in the *New York Times*. In the nation's leading papers, the Anarchists—and, through guilt by association, organized labor—were deemed terrorists. In the following day's *Chicago Tribune*, the big paper closest to the source and therefore a template for others to follow, headlines included HOW WILL IT END, RIOTOUS SCENES, and MOB RULE IN MILWAUKEE.

The assailant who had thrown the bomb would never be identified. The police rounded up a group of eight Anarchist leaders involved in the past weeks' organizing efforts. While no link to the actual bomber could be asserted, the state alleged a conspiracy led by Spies. Two of his acquaintances in the movement were bomb makers discovered to have been assembling bombs for weeks, including on the day of the explosion. With the trial sensationally covered in newspapers across America, the verdict was a foregone conclusion. Seven of the eight defendants, within months, were sentenced to death. Spies was defiant to the end. The *New York Times* exulted, VIOLATED LAW VINDICATED, but it warned in another article on the front page "that the murderous spirit of the Anarchists has not been subdued by the hanging of four of their brethren." Equally, it was a severe blow to the labor movement; the Knights of Labor receded as quickly as they had risen.

The events of the Haymarket would reverberate for some time. The Anarchists went underground. For one teenage girl, Emma Goldman, the sacrifice of the "martyrs" would be a further call to arms. For others, such as Samuel Gompers, the new head of the nascent American

Federation of Labor, it highlighted the political realities and limitations of the labor movement. Any formal links to anarchists or socialists were detrimental to the practical aims of labor unions. Labor's gains in the era of industrial capitalism would have to come from negotiation and regulation, not ideology or revolution. Political power for labor would eventually come through becoming a voting bloc. But the politics would only get more complicated. And violence would not disappear.

FOR NOW, capital had won. By the late 1880s, Carnegie's place as one of the wealthiest men in the United States was cemented, so much so that Carnegie did not bother spending much time in Pittsburgh, where his company was based, with its smokestacks and perpetually darkened skies. He left his executives to concern themselves with daily commercial matters, preferring world travel and the salons of New York. With the free time afforded him as the controlling shareholder, Carnegie put forth theories on capitalism, the human condition, and the American Republic. In 1889 Carnegie wrote an article simply titled "Wealth"—it would soon become known as "Gospel of Wealth"—that was published in the *North American Review*. In it he offered an unapologetic defense of the system that enabled great wealth such as his. He started with a comparison of his era to the past: "Today the world obtains commodities of excellent quality at prices which even the preceding generation would have deemed incredible. The poor enjoy what the rich could not before afford. The laborer has now more comforts than the farmer had a few generations ago. The farmer has more luxuries than the landlord had. The landlord has books and pictures rarer and appointments more artistic than the king could then obtain." The price for this material progress—"cheap comforts and luxuries"—was great wealth inequality.

The man with the ability to operate at the largest scale would invariably outcompete all others, Carnegie continued. "The Socialist or Anarchist who seeks to overturn present conditions is to be regarded as attacking the foundation upon which civilization itself rests, for civilization took its start from the day when the capable, industrious workman said to his incompetent, lazy fellow, 'if thou dost not sow, thou shall not reap.'" Any thinking person, Carnegie surmised, would conclude "that upon the sacredness of property civilization itself depends—the right of the laborer to his hundred dollars in the savings bank, and equally the legal right of the millionaire to his millions." But his defense of capitalism was a setup for a most startling conclusion.

In the article Carnegie argued that the greatest of men, capitalists, should be unencumbered to accumulate wealth. But once great wealth was achieved, these men should, during their lifetimes, give it away. As the possession of wealth was proof to society of great achievement, aptitude, industriousness, and ability, it made little sense that it should be bequeathed to descendants. Inherited wealth would undermine the argument that those with wealth earned it, deserved it. Next, he held that if men waited until death to give the money away, less competent men unused to large sums would squander it thoughtlessly, however well intentioned. While Carnegie viewed wealth as a symbol of intellectual mastery, the actual possession of it should be considered only a trust fund, with "the man of great wealth becoming mere trustee for his poorer brethren, bringing to their service his superior wisdom, experience, and ability to administer, doing for them better than they would or could for themselves." The unreligious, atheistic Carnegie closed with a most biblical decree: "The man who dies thus rich, dies disgraced." Carnegie was hailed by newspapers, socialists, workingmen, and, more discreetly, even his fellow capitalists, namely John D. Rockefeller, for such enlightened views.

But Carnegie was not necessarily unique in his aspirations to philanthropy. Just weeks before Carnegie's "Gospel of Wealth" was published, John D. Rockefeller himself had funded the University of Chicago with $600,000 of seed money. He didn't do it for public acclaim—he refused to have any building or the university itself named after him. It was typical of Rockefeller, who had given away money secretly and silently even as he was climbing. A few years earlier, in 1883, he had funded Atlanta's Spelman Seminary, named for his abolitionist in-laws, to provide education for black women. Johns Hopkins did something similar with his railroad fortune from the B&O Railroad. Leland Stanford did the same in California. Stanford's wife had to liquidate assets to meet her other commitments, as her husband had died, having bequeathed vast sums to the university during his lifetime. A generation earlier, Ezra Cornell and even Vanderbilt had financed universities bearing their names; Vanderbilt had given more to the university than to most of his children. Later, tobacco baron James Duke and dozens of others would follow suit.

Carnegie's giving was more egalitarian. In a nod to the free library that he had frequented on Sundays as a youth, he funded libraries throughout the country. Small libraries as far away as San Anselmo, California, bear his name on plaques to this day.

Just as the simple ideology of free markets offered an incomplete understanding of an increasingly complex system, men who seemed driven by the values of capitalism were far from one-dimensional, with motivations beyond easy caricature. Still, libraries and universities were abstractions to the miners and factory workers putting in twelve hours a day, six days a week. Wages, hours, and working conditions remained pressing concerns. These workers wondered why such vast surplus wealth, accumulated profits, could not be distributed in the form of higher daily wages among the men who performed the physical work as the great fortune was being created. If it was all going to be given away anyway, why not now?

HENRY CLAY FRICK did not have time for theoretical questions. He was the founder of the H. C. Frick Coke Company. Coke, short for "coal cake," was processed coal that was a critical ingredient in modern steel manufacturing. He was a detailed taskmaster in the way that Carnegie was not. Over time, Frick slowly sold his holdings to Carnegie, making Carnegie the majority owner of the Frick Coke Company. Frick would stay on as a smaller shareholder of a much larger enterprise. Carnegie, recognizing his talent, made him the head of all of the Carnegie interests.

At Carnegie's newest and most modern plant, Homestead, which had unionized, the contract with the Amalgamated Steelworkers was due to expire on July 1, 1892. From Homestead's very modernity stemmed some of the paradoxes of labor negotiations. As a result of ongoing capital investments and new technologies, the production capacity at Homestead increased, needing fewer skilled men per ton of steel produced. In addition, the union contract contained a scale through which wages were a function of the productivity of the plant and the price of steel in the market. But the market price of steel had dropped dramatically. And while productivity per worker was better than ever, Frick and Carnegie, with some sound logic, attributed this to the new technological processes in use at the plant. There was no way to avoid the zero-sum equation: The large investments in the latest equipment were meant to reduce labor costs. For labor, this would be the toughest pill to swallow in modern capitalism: Increased productivity often resulted in either lower wages or fewer jobs.

At Homestead the math would get messy. Frick, in the words of Carnegie biographer Joseph Frazier Wall, had a "simple, uncomplicated attitude toward labor, to regard men as a commodity like anything else used in manufacturing—something to be bartered for as cheaply as possible, to be used to its utmost capacity, and to be replaced by as inexpensive a substitute as was available." Carnegie was far more conflicted. He had the difficult task of reconciling his socially progressive views with his highly competitive nature. And while he personally wanted to be respected and admired as a thinker, a man of the people, he was still the reigning king of steel.

Frick's modus operandi would prevail—perhaps by design, as Carnegie retreated to his estate in Scotland and his annual summer travels despite the trouble brewing. After a couple of preliminary overtures were met with resistance, Frick started fortifying the facilities in preparation for either a lockout or a strike "behind 11-foot-high fences, with portholes just large enough for guns to stick through," along with "giant searchlights of 2,000-candlepower." As the expiration date loomed, Frick's strategy appeared to be to secure his plant, lock out the workers, and bring strikebreaking workers into Homestead. But Homestead was more than just a factory—it was a town of twelve thousand people. Families lived there. Understanding that this reality heightened the sensitivity of his workers, Frick contracted for a small private army. When the local police were not up to the task or were unavailable, industrialists often called upon Robert Pinkerton to send his "Pinkertons." For Frick,

Pinkerton dispatched three hundred of his men. In the days leading to the arrival of the Pinkerton men, the factory went silent. Parts of the plant were locked out and, in retaliation, workers in other areas walked out. The Pinkertons were set to arrive by barge up the Monongahela River at a landing that led to the factory. Their task was to secure the property.

There was a dichotomy to these industrial mercenaries, who for a wage that was less than that of the factory workers, but wearing crisp blue uniforms with regal brass buttons, worked to put down working-class agitation. For the people of Homestead, with the temporary loss of livelihood, the arrival of this private army was akin to an invasion. And the arrival was met with violence. The workers fired on the Pinkertons. The Pinkertons fired back from the safety of their barge. The battle continued for hours. Several steelworkers were killed, along with two Pinkertons. Overpowered and unable to disembark, the Pinkertons surrendered.

The workers, with their large numbers, had effectively cordoned off the property. The state of Pennsylvania immediately intervened. What three hundred Pinkertons could not do would now have to be done by eight thousand troops from the state militia dispatched by the governor. Management took back the factory and began a strategy of waiting out the increasingly desperate strikers. New workers, strikebreakers, soon started working at the factory.

The actions of the Pennsylvania government, aiding property owners with the full force of the state without imposing any obligation on the company to negotiate, did not sit well with observers sympathetic to the workers. For a young couple, Alexander Berkman and Emma Goldman, it seemed time to foment a revolution. Ever since the events of the Haymarket bombing in Chicago, Goldman had found her life's passion in the Anarchist cause. She would go on to achieve notoriety as a speaker and agitator for the movement. Berkman, inspired and in love, plotted to go to Pittsburgh. On July 23, posing as an employment agent to supply Frick his needed nonunion workers, Berkman was able to enter Carnegie Steel's Pittsburgh headquarters. He then barged into Frick's office and fired two bullets—both hitting their target, with one scraping Frick in the neck, before being wrestled to the ground by another executive in the office. Frick survived. After receiving medical attention, as a show of determination and resolve, he finished his workday at the office.

After months, on November 18, Frick cabled a one-word message to Carnegie, "Victory!" The strike was over. Capital had won. Carnegie's reputation, however, would be tainted both at home and abroad. The establishment in England particularly reveled in the state of labor in its old colony. In industrial England, whose monarchy and liberties Carnegie had repeatedly disparaged as inferior to America's, violence didn't seem to accompany labor strife as it did in the boastful young Republic that professed freedom at every turn.

Frick's victory, of course, was not the final chapter in American labor relations. The pace of young men leaving farms for industrial towns, of old cobblers giving way to shoe factories, would only accelerate. Far more Americans were going to become a part of the industrial workforce. And given the intermittent violence, and the free-market capitalists who didn't repudiate protectionist tariffs or the use of police, state militias, and even federal troops to protect private property against their workers—"the people," in the language of revolutionaries—the ironies and contradictions could not last. For capitalists it was possible to win every battle and yet, if some revolution resulted, lose the war. Indeed, Haymarket in Chicago or Homestead in Pennsylvania or any number of others could have been a mark in history like the Boston Tea Party or Fort Sumter, had the central grievances of labor been allowed to fester.

But American capitalism was not ideologically rigid. It was never the laissez-faire laboratory of purist, principled imaginations. The strength of the system came through its pragmatism and flexibility, juggling competing and contradictory ideas, just as Carnegie did personally, and eventually finding political solutions to seemingly intractable issues, especially after the scars of the Civil War. Just as successful species adapted to changes in their environment, democracy would shape capitalism to adapt to social conditions, with compromise emerging as the best form of insurance against any risk of revolution. This middle ground, forged by the clashing interactions of capitalism and democracy, a free people acting to check free markets, would give rise to the regulatory framework that would govern its economic system.

Eighteen

PAPERS

While the violent events at Carnegie's steelworks played out, Grover Cleveland had been readying himself for the election of 1892. Four years earlier, he had lost his presidency to his Republican opponent, Benjamin Harrison. He would have better luck this time, becoming the first and only former president in American history to gain back the White House after losing it.

The Democrats' victory, however, had been no easy task. Many Americans remained wary—they were the party of the Confederacy and the South—and the evidence would be seen in election results. For fifty-two years, from 1860 until 1912, New York's Grover Cleveland would be the only Democrat to win the presidency. As the Republicans had nearly constant control of the presidency during the rise of industrialization in America, Gilded Age business interests naturally gravitated to the party in power. This was especially logical given that the Union's Army had served as a financial catalyst for the North, business having been a vital part of the war effort. The Republican Party began life as the antislavery party before the war and became probusiness during it. Though Democrats had a lock on southern voters, as they would for a century, the party needed new constituencies to be competitive—a survival mechanism—voters being the political equivalent of customers.

As a result, the platform would evolve to become a check on business and capital. As capitalists wanted endless cheap labor in the form of new immigrants, which suppressed wages for workers already in America, the Democrats during their convention in 1892 asserted their commitment to stop this "foreign pauper" immigration in an effort to gain the labor vote. Labor factions, seeing their economic aims in practical terms, were in the process of severing themselves from the ideological clutches of socialists and anarchists into the mainstream arms of Democrats. But the evolutionary process of American politics would be messy.

In the four years that Cleveland was out of office there was the contentious issue of taxation. Since the end of the war the federal government had funded itself through a combination of taxes on alcohol, tobacco, and the tariff, the last of which represented the majority of the federal government's revenues. At the same time, as the tariff was a tax on imported goods, it was a major benefit to American manufacturers, who saw it as a protective subsidy. This led to the main question. Was the tariff's role simply to generate revenues for the government or to protect American business? Cleveland, in his first presidency, had wanted to cut the tariff, having seen large budget surpluses for nearly twenty years. In his 1887 address to Congress, which was almost entirely dedicated to the issue, he argued that the tariff was a substantial and indirect tax on the consumer passed on through higher prices, which had resulted in revenues that the federal government didn't need and wasn't spending. To reduce the tariff, cutting taxes, was an antibusiness position, as it made foreign imports more competitive. Helpfully, Cleveland lost his reelection bid in 1888.

With his loss, the ongoing suppression of foreign competition allowed domestic producers to charge more for goods than they otherwise would have been able to. The net effect was that consumers not only indirectly paid the tariff when they bought foreign goods, but also subsidized the profit margins of domestic producers. The tariff was not a simple tax rate. It was a list of thousands of specific items known as a tariff schedule. Each industry had specific desires and requirements to impose on its foreign competition. The rate on a ton of foreign steel, on linen towels, on a box of cigars, on prunes, on leather goods, and so on were set by a bill spearheaded in 1890 by Republican congressman William McKinley of Ohio. Even Carnegie, usually absent from day-to-day business affairs, made sure to keep diligent tabs on happenings in Washington as the 1890 tariff schedule was negotiated, as did representatives of the nation's business interests. It would be known as the McKinley Tariff, cementing him as a great friend of American business.

But the tariff had a great enemy: farmers. American farmers, who still considerably outnumbered industrial workers, were exporters of grains and foodstuffs to foreign markets. In addition to facing a higher cost of living and of agricultural inputs, they stood to suffer the retaliatory measures of other countries in closing off their markets or applying their own tariffs. At the time, exports of American food and grain were more than double those of manufactured-good sales to overseas markets. Despite allegiance to the Republican Party dating back to the war, farmers increasingly saw themselves paying the price for the protection of American manufacturers.

With Cleveland back in the White House, farmers expected relief, as the Democrats had for years committed themselves to treating the "tariff for revenue only," meaning that the tariff's sole purpose was to collect revenues for the Treasury, and not to protect business interests from foreign competition. But Cleveland was unlucky. Only months into office, the Panic of 1893 struck and with the slowdown sharply reducing tax revenues, his agenda was derailed.

CHINAMEN CUT BY A JAP read the headline in the left-most column on the front page of Joseph Pulitzer's *New York World* on the eve of election day back in 1888. Though it was a simple tale of an angered Japanese man who had stabbed two Chinese men on New York's Mott Street, Pulitzer's writer managed to tenuously link the event to the candidates, pointing out that the assailant supported Harrison, while the victims had been in favor of Cleveland. Column one, as the *World*'s readers had come to know, was generally reserved for murder or mayhem. That one of America's most politically astute and interested observers would waste space on such salaciousness on the eve of a major election was no accident. In the five years that he had owned the *World* up to that point, Pulitzer had gone from running a money-losing paper with a circulation of 15,000 to declaring that 260,030 copies had been sold the previous Sunday. By the 1890s, circulation would climb further still. To have power, Pulitzer understood as well anyone, meant that one must have constituents, and to dive into the minutiae of tariffs and regulation was no way to win them. And the marketplace of newspaper buyers provided him with a daily poll of exactly how much influence he had, to be used as and when he needed.

Pulitzer had come a long way from his days as a Hungarian recruit for the U.S. Army during the Civil War, enticed to service by the free passage to America. Speaking minimal English, he started his rise in St. Louis, finding work as an entry-level reporter for the German-language *Westliche Post*. Tirelessly covering St. Louis politics, Pulitzer became the editor soon after. In 1872, with borrowed money, he bought a stake in the paper, only to sell it for a profit within a year. After another opportunistic acquisition and sale of another German-language paper, Pulitzer looked for an opportunity in English-language papers. As newspapers were the only media of their day, there were countless single-sheet newspapers in every town. With some capital and a reputation in the St. Louis publishing community, Pulitzer won an auction for the money-losing *Dispatch*. The paper was one of several newspapers attempting to seize the new opportunity of evening readers, a market that the widening use of gas lamps and evening light in the home made possible. Combining his *Dispatch* with another challenged newspaper, Pulitzer created the *St. Louis Post-Dispatch*, promising his readers a minimum of four pages per day of content.

Pulitzer had ambitions for political office but would soon realize that he could achieve far greater power and influence through his paper. Far more than having commercial objectives, Pulitzer was a political creature. To satiate his need for the broadest reach, he looked east to New York City. In 1883 Pulitzer made his way to the city and met with the type of man whom his newspaper would generally demonize. Pulitzer and Jay Gould sat down at Gould's offices at Western Union, which he had taken control of, to discuss the *New York World*. Gould had owned it for four years. Not only did its editorial posture not suit him politically, but unforgivably worse to Gould, the middling paper lost him money every month. He offered the paper to Pulitzer for $346,000 with 10 percent down and Gould carrying the remaining 90 percent as debt. Pulitzer, even with his success in St. Louis, now carried a large debt load that only rapid success in New York could hope to pay back.

In New York City, rapid success would mean reaching a market that the large newspapers of the city ignored. The average newspaper of 1883 was a dense, dreary affair loaded with small text, contained within rows of undistinguished columns, often with deep detail into the mechanics of legislation or political speeches published in full. Almost instantly, as one competitor wrote years later, "Mr. Pulitzer quickly succeeded in demonstrating that the newspapermen of New York had been writing over the heads of a very large portion of the public, and in getting down to this level of the public, he had his reward."

Pulitzer went for the working class and immigrants, often one and the same. As he had once been an immigrant speaking little English, Pulitzer had a deep sense of this learning curve. His writers wrote in simple English. His headlines were of varying font sizes and used white space to stand out. And the stories themselves attempted to add a bit of theater to any household, a welcome respite from a long day of work. The formula was simple. Rather than focusing on endless politics, mechanics of the legislative process, and even more politics when there was little else to report, as the majority of other papers tended to do, Pulitzer's front page generally offered a large cartoon to grab the reader; a good account of a murder, court case, fire, or salacious crime; weather reports that took into account how the city's heat or cold affected the lives of the working class, such as BROILING HUMAN BEINGS—NO RELIEF TO BE EXPECTED; and results of horse races and probable winnings. In this mix Pulitzer introduced populist elements. To reach the widest base of readers, he soon reduced the price to a penny, causing other New York papers to drop their prices. The *Times* held its price at 3 cents to signal a higher status than Pulitzer's.

While Pulitzer's *World* delivered a far greater visceral sense of the streets of New York, with all of their crime, thrills, chaos, corruption, gossip, and thriving energy, it wove in a core sense of empathy for the workingman and his family—it was a mirror of their world, publishing articles such as one that called for public streetcars to be subsidized for poor schoolchildren, so they could go to schools outside their crowded districts. Equally, it understood the material dreams of its readers and the escapism of fantasy. One column solicited reader responses to the question "If you were a millionaire? What would you do with the money and yourself?" publishing dozens of answers ranging from the charitable to the grandiose. Populism made for good business, gave its publisher power against far wealthier business magnates, and started the media's rise to become a check on the power of both government and business, a power unto itself rather than mere agitator.

But Pulitzer, powerful and wealthy during Cleveland's second presidency—often cocooned on his yacht or in Europe suffering from a variety of physical maladies including the onset of conditions that would lead to his blindness—finally misread the mood of his readers, his status blunting his instincts.

THE ECONOMIC EXPANSION that had started in the late 1870s, after the fallout from the crisis of 1873, and gained momentum in the eighties had been a long one, despite its hiccups. The American household had been transformed. For most, standards of living had markedly increased. But all this material prosperity produced speculation and overbuilding based on endless confidence about the future. As the Gilded Age economy was highly interconnected, a pause in any major sector was enough to reverberate into a broad economic slowdown, a recession. Railroads that overbuilt track mileage paused on steel purchases, which in turn affected coal shipments, as coal was an input in steel production, and so on. At some point in this silent chain of events, when a critical mass of businessmen came to the conclusion that the economy was contracting, it created a "panic," the apt nineteenth-century term for what was often the opening act of recessions and depressions. Panic meant businessmen and capitalists running to the financial exits at the same time to seek safety, sell assets, call in debts, pull money out of banks, or raise cash to meet their obligations.

With money essentially backed by gold, this retreat generally led to great demand for the gold in the vaults of banks. Depositors brought in their paper notes to banks to exchange them for actual physical gold, rather than trust the bank's paper. Banks and institutional depositors, in turn, looked to turn in dollars and retrieve gold from the U.S. Treasury. As a result, the government's gold reserves were often depleted to alarming levels.

While gold kept the value of money sound and stable, it also heightened money's scarcity and made it increasingly valuable during market panics. At the time, both the Republican and Democratic establishments took the view that the government's primary responsibility at such a time was to maintain sound money. The policy response of strengthening the gold reserves in the U.S. Treasury, in effect becoming a competitor to private interests by trying to hold on to gold, reduced the supply of money in the economy even further just as private banks and businessmen were also scrambling for gold. This constriction of money supply was the monetary equivalent of bleeding the patient to cure him of disease. And as the supply of money dropped precipitously, the prices of assets, goods in stores, and crops all fell. Deflation set in.

For a time, until 1873, both silver and gold could be minted into legal tender. Large holders of either metal could bring it to the mint and have it converted into silver or gold dollars to take back to bank vaults. Back then, the ratio of silver to gold was set at sixteen to one, meaning an ounce of gold was sixteen times as valuable as an ounce of silver. But large discoveries of silver in the western states drastically increased the supply. Holders of silver could technically have it minted into silver dollars and then take the silver dollars and exchange them for one sixteenth their weight in gold. Shrewd speculators realized that with the discoveries, silver was far less valuable relative to gold than what the previous ratio of sixteen to one implied. If the Treasury continued to treat silver and gold at the same historical ratio, it would be only a matter of time until the Treasury found its vaults full of the newly minted silver and emptied of its gold. This reality caused the United States to suspend the coining of silver into dollars. Starting then, apart from periodic efforts to mollify silver interests and the silver-producing states, the gold standard became de facto American policy. But ever since, there had been a "Free Silver" movement to restore silver to its rightful place alongside gold.

The Panic of 1893 hit American farmers especially hard. Farmers often had large mortgages on their farms. To pay the mortgage and support their livelihood, they relied on the sale of annual crops. But the scarcity of money caused deflation, the opposite of inflation. This meant receiving lower prices for their crops in the market, while the monthly mortgage payments and principal balance stayed the same, making the debt servicing more burdensome in proportion to the income—each dollar became more valuable and harder to earn. But President Cleveland, despite his party's platform to restore silver as a currency medium, which would have dramatically loosened the dollar, instead affirmed the government's commitment to gold due to the economic crisis. Being from New York, Cleveland was seen as yielding to eastern banking interests, which did not want the gold-backed dollars that the banking system lent out paid back with silver-backed ones.

Cleveland then alienated another voting bloc: labor interests. The Pullman Palace Car Company, maker of railroad cars, suffered a strike when Pullman tried to cut wages dramatically. In the starkly deflationary climate of 1894, it was hard to get a man to understand that a wage cut could still be a raise, as the prices of food and goods had dropped even more. Deflation in many ways was incompatible with human psychology. Seeing a chance to make a stand, railroad unions across America, led by the American Railway Union, joined the Pullman workers by refusing to unload or service trains that carried any Pullman-manufactured cars, which was essentially every passenger railroad in America. The collective union action effectively halted railroad traffic. In response, Cleveland secured a federal injunction on the basis of guaranteeing delivery of the mail, a constitutional function of the U.S. government. The unions ignored the injunction. Cleveland then ordered federal troops to put down the strike. Of course, this lost him the support of labor.

Cleveland then lost another political battle that he had seemingly won in Congress. As Congress was amending the tariff schedule, the budget surpluses of the 1870s and 1880s were now a distant memory. With the economy having slowed down, the tariff had failed to produce enough revenue, yielding deficits. To get a new source of revenue—one that the Democrats felt would ultimately end the government's reliance on the tariff and open up free trade, a benefit to farmers—Congress approved the first nonwartime personal income tax in history: 2 percent on incomes over $4,000. The following year, however, the Supreme Court ruled the personal income tax to be unconstitutional, holding that the direct tax on citizens caused high-income states, such as New York, to bear a disproportionate per capita share of the federal burden.* The new tariff schedule, however, remained intact.

To his detractors, the only Democratic president since the Civil War now looked as probusiness as any Republican of his day. Even Carnegie started inquiring about President Cleveland's health. The support for gold, use of force against labor, and protecting industry with the tariff increase—all to the benefit of the eastern establishment—set off a revolt within the Democratic Party. And it opened the door for two great forces in the history of American politics.

WILLIAM RANDOLPH HEARST was a Harvard dropout from San Francisco. At Harvard his suite included room for his butler and a maid, and by all accounts he lived like the son of a potentate. The roots of the Hearst fortune came from the silver mines of Nevada. His father, George Hearst, who had made it to California to look for gold, ended up in Nevada, striking silver instead. The Hearst fortune was soon diversified across vast mining interests. George developed few affectations, keeping his chewing tobacco habit, along with the ritual spitting it entailed, throughout the workday. His wife, Phoebe Hearst, was more refined. George's fortune supported Phoebe in her world of the arts, literature, and travels, giving young Will exposure to a world beyond mining. She was as literary and cultured as her husband was coarse. George, however, did manage to move up socially in his own way later in his life: After years of giving to Democratic politicians, he eventually managed to get the California state legislature to appoint him as one of its two U.S. Senators.†

On the day George Hearst became a senator, the *San Francisco Examiner*, a minor newspaper holding of his, changed its masthead to show the name of the twenty-four-year-old William Randolph Hearst as the

* The Constitution would be amended in the next century.
† At this point in American history, U.S. senators were appointed by state legislators—not directly elected by the people.

new publisher. His exasperated mother and father hoped Will would take the paper more seriously than he had his studies. Throughout college, Hearst had peppered his father with ideas and plans for the *Examiner*. His trips to New York had given him ideas to follow and copy.

Dissecting every aspect of Pulitzer's paper, Hearst dived in to emulate as much of the New York formula as possible in his market. This included illustrations, murder and mayhem, political exposés, and stinging and withering criticisms of establishment forces. Hearst added fiction, sports, and news for businessmen. In short, everything and anything to achieve the widest possible circulation. But just as Pulitzer had found St. Louis too provincial, Hearst had his eyes set on New York.

With his father's passing, Hearst made his move and started scouting for opportunities to buy a newspaper in New York. George, prudently mistrustful of his son, however, had left the entirety of his wealth to his wife. With his mother's consent, Hearst found a willing seller in the owner of the *New York Morning Journal*, a paper that Pulitzer's younger brother had founded. The younger Pulitzer had just sold the paper to Cincinnati publisher John McLean when the gravity of the Panic of 1893 forced McLean to sell the *Journal* to Hearst. Purchasing the *Morning Journal* for $150,000 in the fall of 1895, Hearst now had a foothold in New York.

Given that Pulitzer's paper had cornered the market on the sensational, along with advocacy for working-class interests, there seemed to be little opening at the lower end of the market—plenty had tried to match Pulitzer. Hearst, however, announced his arrival boldly, calling the revamped *Morning Journal* REVOLUTION IN JOURNALISM, in a full left-column advertisement that ran on the front page of the *New York Times*, which at this point desperately needed the revenue. He guaranteed a "beautiful art supplement" with pictures every day and eighteen pages of coverage. Then, just months into his ownership, Hearst had an incredible stroke of luck and the aptitude to understand exactly how to play his hand.

THIS GOOD FORTUNE came in the form of the meteoric ascendance of William Jennings Bryan. Just two years earlier, in 1894, Bryan was a

fiery thirty-four-year-old congressman in the final year of his first and
only term representing Nebraska. His populist platform caused repeated
embarrassments and consternation for the Democratic establishment,
including President Cleveland. But by the middle of 1895, a movement
was afoot.

The tariff revisions of the previous year had been passed in conjunction with passage of the federal personal income tax. But in April, when
the Supreme Court ruled the personal income tax unconstitutional, it
was clear that the legislative agenda of big business had won. To Bryan,
not only did banking interests keep their gold standard and industry its
tariff protection, but also the courts had done away with even the modest
equalizer of the income tax.

Bryan now took multiple strands of economic frustration and wove
them all into a simple message of Free Silver, the elixir of inflation. This
was antithetical to creditors and the nation's financial interests, who
wanted strong dollars lent out in the past to be paid back with equally
strong dollars in the future. And the agreed-upon way to maintain the
strong gold-backed dollar was for the government to show its commitment and retain ample levels of gold in its Treasury. With government
purchases of gold in the Panic's aftermath making the metal even scarcer
in the private economy—gold and paper money being proxies for each
other under the gold standard—debtors continued to see their economic
noose tighten.

After he left Congress, Bryan's star rose with each denunciation of the
gold standard. The obscure topic of the return of monetary silver and
bimetallism, understood by few, found a messianic orator who made it
into an existential issue. For farmers, the loose money of the silver standard would not only make it easier to pay back debt but would also increase crop prices with inflation. Laborers felt deflation when their
nominal wages declined, reductions that felt incompatible with the
American promise of economic advancement. Most others understood it
metaphorically: The Free Silver movement was a repudiation of the power
of manufacturers, railroads, and bankers. It was a referendum on monopoly,
the political establishments of both parties, Wall Street, city elites, and the

largeness of an economic system that seemed to favor one class of people over another.

By early 1896, with economic recovery tepid at best, President Cleveland was fully sidelined. At the Democratic Convention that summer, the now thirty-six-year-old Bryan, barely meeting the constitutional age requirement for the American presidency, was the standard-bearer of a white-hot political movement. Whatever hope the party establishment had of neutralizing Bryan was extinguished with one of the most famous speeches in American history. He opened with a preamble that described how the Free Silver movement had grown so quickly, noting that "old leaders have been cast aside when they refused to give expression to the sentiments of those whom they would lead, and new leaders have sprung up to give direction to this cause of freedom." This rebellion, led by Bryan, cast the gold standard as the enemy of liberty itself.

When rival Democrats at the nominating convention declared that the gold standard was instrumental to the industrial interests of the nation, Bryan took issue:

When you come before us and tell us that we shall disturb your business interests . . . we say to you that you have made too limited in its application the definition of a businessman. The man who is employed for wages is as much a businessman as his employer. The attorney in a country town is as much a businessman as the corporation counsel in a great metropolis. The merchant at the crossroads store is as much a businessman as the merchant of New York. The farmer who goes forth in the morning and toils all day, begins in the spring and toils all summer, and by the application of brain and muscle to the natural resources of this country creates wealth, is as much a businessman as the man who goes upon the Board of Trade and bets upon the price of grain. The miners who go 1,000 feet into the earth or climb 2,000 feet upon the cliffs and bring forth from their hiding places the precious metals to be poured in the channels of trade are as much businessmen as the few financial magnates who in a backroom corner the money of the world.

We come to speak for this broader class of businessmen . . . those hardy pioneers who braved all the dangers of the wilderness, who have made the desert to blossom as the rose—those pioneers away out there . . . are as deserving of the consideration of this party as any people in this country.

HIS SOARING RHETORIC made him an instant star, a man who appeared capable of toppling the institutional forces assembled against him. To his enraptured audience, he made his closing argument with one theme that would become the fundamental issue of nearly every peacetime election well into the twenty-first century.

There are two ideas of government. There are those who believe that if you just legislate to make the well-to-do prosperous, that their prosperity will leak through on those below. The Democratic idea has been that if you legislate to make the masses prosperous their prosperity will find its way up and through every class that rests upon it.

He then thundered biblically:

You come to us and tell us that the great cities are in favor of the gold standard. I tell you that the great cities rest upon these broad and fertile prairies. Burn down your cities and leave our farms, and your cities will spring up again as if by magic. But destroy our farms and the grass will grow in the streets of every city in the country.

. . . If they dare to come out in the open field and defend the gold standard as a good thing, we shall fight them to the uttermost, having behind us the producing masses of the nation and the world. . . . We shall answer their demands for a gold standard by saying to them, you shall not press down upon the brow of labor this crown of thorns. You shall not crucify mankind upon a cross of gold.

It was a defining speech in American political history. From then on, the labor vote belonged to Democrats and Republicans solidified their role as the party of business. Bryan won the Democratic nomination, an outcome that would have seemed impossible at the start of 1896. But the speech and the nomination left the Democratic establishment reeling: Papers such as Pulitzer's, which had risen as a friend of the common man, refused to support the insurgent Bryan, seeing him as an aberration, a revolutionary when one wasn't needed.

But Bryan did have one ally in New York. Less than a year into his paper's ownership, Hearst bet everything on Bryan for a simple reason: Bryan sold papers.

JUST AS WITH HEARST, Bryan's timing and messaging created the perfect opportunity for another publishing insurgent to make his way into New York City, a man who would outlast both Hearst and Pulitzer in the city's newspaper wars. Originally from Kentucky, Adolph Ochs was the thirty-eight-year-old publisher of the *Chattanooga Times*. While Pulitzer and Hearst both had started their newspaper careers in relatively large cities, Ochs began his in Chattanooga, a small city in a small state. Its population was a little over thirty thousand. Ochs had come a long way. Leaving school and formal education at the age of fourteen, Ochs was apprenticed as a printer for the *Knoxville Courier*. From there he moved into other roles in the actual production of the paper. By the time he turned nineteen, he had partnered with two others to found a small paper called the *Chattanooga Daily Dispatch*. The paper failed within months. Ochs diligently used the presses for odd printing jobs to pay back creditors. This bit of rectitude brought him an opportunity to buy a half interest in a struggling newspaper with a circulation of 250. Borrowing $250 as a down payment on the required $1,500, Ochs became the publisher of the *Chattanooga Daily Times*.

As Chattanooga grew, as cities generally did in the Gilded Age, so did the fortunes of Adolph Ochs. Within a decade, he had bought the other half of the paper for $5,500 using the profits and was the prosperous publisher of the city's main newspaper, propelling his *Times* with ample revenues from real estate advertisements along with growing circulation revenues. By 1892 Ochs had built a six-story building that signified his and his paper's status in Chattanooga. But it was built with borrowed money. When the Panic of 1893 struck, Ochs's finances became strained to the point of desperation. To secure loans and restructure his finances, he headed to New York to pitch banks and investors in order to remain solvent. Instead, he found an even bigger target.

Just as the *Chattanooga Times* was suffering from the conditions in the broader economy, so was the *New York Times*. In a city with multiple newspapers with circulations of over 100,000, led by Pulitzer's *World*, the *New York Times* had an aging formula that exacerbated its financial woes. After the death of its last founder, it was now on the block and on the brink of going into receivership in early 1896. Ironically, its shareholders were some of the most powerful financiers in America, including J. P. Morgan and men from the banking and insurance communities. The *New York Times*, even then, was a vehicle of prestige and stature, the newspaper of record.

This gravitas, in 1896, seemed to be needed to counter the cyclone of the Free Silver heresy that threatened the New York banking establishment. Ochs, in a great act of salesmanship, persuaded shareholder after shareholder to entrust him with the operation of the *New York Times*. The old shareholders would get shares in the new company. Ochs would serve as publisher, and if he managed to operate the paper profitably for three years, he would receive control of the majority of the shares of the *New York Times*. Less straightforward was that the Equitable Life Assurance Company would secretly retain a call on the majority of the shares for a couple of decades, meaning that the insurance company could buy Ochs out at any time, a condition Ochs was desperate to keep secret. Accepting this condition from Equitable, and with the consent of numerous financiers on Wall Street, Ochs came into nominal control of the *New York Times* without investing a penny of his own. Less than three months before the election of 1896, on August 17, he appeared on the masthead for the first time as the publisher of the *New York Times*, which has remained in his family's control to this day. There is little question that if Ochs had been a Bryan supporter, or in any way editorially ambiguous about the sanctity of the gold standard, none of this would have been possible. When it came to acquiring the *New York Times* in the summer of 1896, the political leaning of any potential buyer on this single issue was more important than his personal balance sheet.

Hearst, on the other hand, who never had to worry about his or anyone else's balance sheet, had little to worry about in supporting Bryan—so much so that the *Journal*'s offices were virtually the New York campaign headquarters for the Bryan campaign. Bryan had nowhere else to turn in New York. His earlier attacks on President Cleveland, a favorite of New York's Democratic Party, had made Bryan a pariah in New York. Hearst, when faced with advertisers pulling out due to his support of Bryan, responded that it was for the best, as he needed more space in the paper to support him further. But Hearst's defiance was strategic. With Pulitzer tied to establishment Democrats, Hearst owned the market that saw Bryan as a savior.

While history tends to acknowledge the newspaper wars between Hearst and Pulitzer, it has virtually overlooked the similarities between Hearst and Ochs. Both men acquired their New York City papers within months of each other as upstarts; each was in his thirties, entering a market with heavyweights, while Pulitzer was months away from turning fifty and already owned the most profitable paper in America. And with Bryan's candidacy, the younger men had their first chance to cement their approach to journalism, business, and politics. Ochs, despite having personal capital that was a fraction of Hearst's, resisted all temptations to chase the stylistic and colorful flourishes of either the *World* or the *Journal*, choosing to keep his paper nearly as gray as ever and enjoying history's verdict.

While the *Times* would eventually become an institutional power with a footprint far beyond its income statement, weeks into his initially tenuous ownership, Ochs operated the seventh-ranked paper in New York City heading into the election of 1896. With Ohio Congressman William McKinley, the proud advocate of the tariffs of 1890, as the Republican candidate, the stage was set for the most consequential election since 1860.

Nineteen

TRUSTS

O n Election Day, Hearst went for a particularly innovative bit of spectacle. While the *Times* remained its usual calm ocean of small text, *Journal* readers were instructed to look up to the night sky for instant election updates. Hearst announced that he planned to launch a giant hot air balloon over Manhattan at sundown and invited his readers to see this "inflated monster rise heavenward from the roof of the Grand Central Palace." The balloon featured two sets of colored electric lights placed on the outside, large enough and bright enough for hundreds of thousands of people in Manhattan, Brooklyn, Queens, and New Jersey to see. As Election Night proceeded, telegraphed results from the various states would come to Hearst headquarters. From the ground, updates would be sent up by a wire that ran along the rope that tethered the balloon to the ground, where blinking red lights for William Jennings Bryan or blinking green lights for William McKinley would indicate which candidate was leading as the election results came in. If either color light went steady, it meant that the election was over.

Despite Hearst's best efforts for Bryan, before the night was over, the light went to a steady green. McKinley won the election by taking the entire eastern seaboard north of Virginia. He even won in states like Illinois, where labor had most visibly collided with business, winning a silent majority that remained alarmed by the recent agitations and the Bryan insurgency. Hearst won too: He sold 1.5 million papers among his morning, evening, and German editions. To Pulitzer's shock and dismay, Bryan's defeat didn't discredit Hearst. If anything, it enhanced Hearst's reputation as the bold upstart willing to stake new ground. Within a few years, aided by the paper's coverage of the Spanish-American War, he would take the circulation lead in a costly battle with Pulitzer's *World*.

In addition to McKinley and Hearst, the election produced another winner. Operating at the nexus of American finance and industry, J. P. Morgan would reach enormous peaks. Elections had consequences. With the probusiness McKinley in the White House, a four-year window of opportunity coincided with a broader trend in the American economy toward consolidation. The deflationary economy of 1893 and onward saw major industries buckle under the tremendous pressure of their debts. A large percentage of the railroad mileage in the United States found itself in receivership. Operators in commodity businesses dealt with one another with endless price competition—a cutthroat race to the bottom. Gentlemen's agreements, otherwise known as price fixing, did not hold up under the pressures and risks of insolvency. In addition, the Sherman Antitrust Act prohibited competitors from most types of cooperative behavior that would have maintained pricing power.

The act was passed weeks before the McKinley tariff bill in 1890. It was an effort to soften the Republican's probusiness appearance and mollify opposition to the tariff. John Sherman, an Ohioan like McKinley, had drafted the legislation, which was intended to curtail abusive practices like collusion and price-fixing. But this had a dramatic, unintended consequence.

With cooperation between two or more companies to coordinate prices now illegal, the simple solution seemed to be for the largest companies within a given industry to merge into one entity, which could then do as it pleased legally. The orchestration of these mergers often fell to the preeminent financier of the era.

J. P. Morgan was a banker. He was not a speculator, industrialist, or trader. His objective wasn't even solely to accumulate personal wealth—he had been wealthy since birth—it was to impose financial order, to remove the volatility caused by endless industrial competition in the free market. He was not an upstart like Gould, Vanderbilt, Carnegie, or

Rockefeller. His father, Junius Morgan, had been a London-based banker who sold bonds and other securities to British and European investors. His father had even bought railroad bonds from the young Carnegie before his entry into the steel business. Unlike mere financial salesmen, however, the Morgans were trusted as prudent guardians, men who remained obligated after the sale—a valuable and necessary characteristic, as they were often selling securities of companies to clients an ocean away. When a security or company was in trouble, the Morgans intervened to secure their client's interests. Starting from here, the younger Morgan, based in America, had built a long career operating on Wall Street. Morgan had a patrician's view of the marketplace: Free-market competition often resulted in irrational price wars that led to volatility, insolvency, and default. As it affected the entire market, such behavior was the opposite of the stability that large investors needed and that Morgan, as a guardian of the capital markets, was especially keen on having. Over time, Morgan assumed the role of an unofficial intermediary between the financial interests on one side and the industrial interests on the other. And he had his fair share of dealings at even higher levels of power—even governments and sovereigns needed to borrow money in the capital markets.

The outgoing Cleveland administration had relied heavily on Morgan to support the gold standard during the aftermath of the Panic of 1893. When the U.S. Treasury started running dangerously low on gold, it was Morgan whom the Treasury Department called on to raise money for an emergency bond issue, proceeds from which the government used to buy gold. When McKinley assumed office in early 1897, the economy was slowly recovering; despite the emphatic defeat of Bryan and the Free Silver movement, the entrenched dogma of the gold standard had done little to ease credit conditions.

But the American economy got lucky. The needed monetary jolt came from Alaska. When the United States paid Russia $7.2 million for all of Alaska in 1867, it was considered folly, the territory considered a valueless frozen tundra. But just months into McKinley's term in 1897 came this fortuitous and succinct headline: GOLD! GOLD! GOLD! GOLD! This bit of excitement from the *Seattle Post-Intelligencer* on July 17 had to do with the arrival into Seattle of a steamship from the Klondike region of Alaska. Additional subheadlines provided the color: STACKS OF YELLOW METAL!; THE STEAMER CARRIES $700,000; SIXTY-EIGHT RICH MEN ON THE STEAMER PORTLAND. The next day the *New York Times*, in a characteristically subdued tone, detailed the riches of the passengers:

> William Stanley . . . He went to the Klondike last year and is now returning with nearly $90,000 in gold.
>
> William Sloan, formerly in the dry goods business, sold his claim for $52,000 and with the gold he took from the mine has come back to civilization.
>
> Richard B. Lake of Dungeness has been successful, and is coming back to the place where he was born with a big sack full of nuggets.

Even the *Times* could not resist placing an uncharacteristic eye-catching headline halfway down the column: MORE THAN A TON OF GOLD.

Eight months after an election campaign decrying the scarcity of gold, gold was suddenly not so scarce. Ongoing discoveries in Western Australia added to the world supply, loosening money everywhere. In America the amount of gold coins sitting in local bank vaults, which had fallen to $454 million in 1896 as people withdrew them to hoard, suddenly grew to $657 million by 1898. Credit conditions in America changed almost overnight.

When the large amounts of gold were discovered and the rumors confirmed, the expectation among holders of gold immediately shifted. Since the new supply was expected to find its way to banks, the appeal of keeping physical gold diminished. As the gold supply eased, prices of goods relative to gold started increasing. At the same time, holding physical gold had its limitation: Gold paid no interest. In bad times, physical gold was a safe haven. In good times, however, because it didn't earn anything, holding onto gold was not as attractive compared with other opportunities. Depositing gold in a bank, converting it into a paper note, and leaving the note at the bank earned interest. By way of Alaska, the economy had its lubricant and sudden stimulus.

Industrial production surged. Production of pig iron, a step needed to produce steel, grew to 29,000 tons in October 1897, almost double the previous October's 16,000 tons on the eve of the election. Railroads, the largest buyers of steel in the economy, again began to add new mileage and replace old tracks.

Economic growth returned. American industry once again went to the capital markets to finance large factories and expansion. The scars of what were known then as the depression years of 1893–1896, however, had a lingering and undoubtedly instructional effect. A prudent invest-ment in a factory, for instance, required the assurance that the products of that factory could be sold profitably. In a variety of commodity businesses, there was a large risk of making capital investments only to see all profits eroded by relentless price competition in the market—it would be far safer if one company owned all the competition in a sector. Given that capital was rushing to find opportunities, the logic of maintaining pricing power through consolidation made sense. Starting in McKinley's first year in office, industry after industry began to get folded into enterprises, some at previously unimaginable scale. With each consolidation, the public would increasingly become wary of these entities, known as trusts.

THE TERM "TRUST" was a throwback to an earlier era. Until 1888, when New Jersey adopted a new incorporation law, it was not possible for a corporation in one state to own shares in a corporation formed in another state. Before the law went into effect, when multiple firms based across state lines wished to consolidate into one, the workable method was for the shareholders of each company to contribute the entirety of their shares to a trust. The trust then owned the shares of multiple companies, with the beneficiaries being the former shareholders. The trustees could then direct the activities of the multiple firms in terms of pricing and cooperation. With the New Jersey law in place, the trust mechanism became obsolete: Entities such as General Electric and Stan-dard Oil of New Jersey incorporated to hold subsidiary companies across multiple states.

Still, in the public imagination and colloquial usage, the term "trusts," now technically imprecise, evolved to mean large, monopolistic corporations. Starting in late 1897, the trust movement gained momentum. Some companies consolidated large industries; others focused on niche sectors. But almost always, the industry was a commodity or generic good where one supplier was as good as another. For instance, with a total value of $16 million, American Thread Company was known as the "Thread Trust," a small consolidation of thirteen small thread makers in New England, formed to control 50 percent of the U.S. cotton and wool thread market. American Sewer Pipe Company, the "Sewer Pipe Trust," combined thirty-three firms with a collective market share of 40 percent—the company was capitalized at $9.5 million. American Ice was formed, combining 80 percent of the U.S. ice market. American Caramel controlled 90 percent of its market. National Biscuit Company was known as the "Cracker Trust." The prevailing convention of naming these new companies became to use the generic American, United, National, General, International, or Standard to signal each entity's desired dominance in a commodity category.

Many of these consolidations, however, were quite insignificant, including categories such as school furniture, grass twine, and writing paper. If anything, just as companies a century later would add "dot com" to their names to receive market favor, these efforts were likely attempts to benefit from the favorable investor sentiment that came with an implied monopoly position. It was easier to attract investors in the capital market when one posed as a dominant "trust" in a given category. The formula was simple. A promoter, usually a banker or entrepreneur, would reach out to a number of firms in a category, usually family-owned firms. The promoter incorporated a company in New Jersey or another state where the holding-company structure was permitted. With the incorporation in hand, all of the companies that wished to be a part of the company would settle on a price at which they would agree to sell to the trust. With commitments from ten, twenty, or even thirty firms in hand, the promoter would then finance the transaction on Wall Street with the aid of one of the top merchant banks. At the close of the transaction, the purchase price to each seller would be paid in a combination of cash, common stock, preferred stock, or bonds of the new company. And the goal of a monopoly was not winked at or whispered in hushed tones—it was the primary selling point to public investors. In 1898 investors clamored for the chance to own shares of these companies that purported to have monopoly positions in their markets. In addition, with the vast majority of the market value of the American stock market being railroads, investors welcomed the opportunity to diversify and bet on other sectors.

The era marked a significant transition point in American capitalism. It represented the first time many founding families and builders of industrial firms gained liquidity. The thirtysomething upstart during the Civil War was now in his sixties close to the end of the century. In addition, the emergence of modern accounting methods, a growing public securities market, and professional management meant that single-factory firms were increasingly at a distinct disadvantage in terms of scale. For men and families who had achieved some success after a generation or two of hard work, these new organizations offered an exit strategy for the sale of their business.

If the nature of the movement had been limited to smaller family-owned firms methodically consolidating into medium-sized public corporations, the reaction might have been muted. But the speed of hundreds of consolidations across sectors in a few short years, along with the dramatic size of a few large corporations, heightened the public anxiety.

But McKinley had a booming economy and another object of public fascination that overshadowed the initial concerns. His quick victory in the Spanish-American War, which brought the Philippines, Guam, and Puerto Rico into the American fold, had Americans feeling confident. Whatever Americans thought of the mechanisms of their progress, their country was now the largest economy in the world.

With the election of 1900 looming, McKinley's old foe once again looked to secure the Democratic nomination. William Jennings Bryan stubbornly held to the same domestic platform as he had in 1896. Hearst implored Bryan to put the Free Silver issue on the back burner—the new supplies of gold had eased monetary conditions almost entirely—asking him to emphasize his anti-imperialism or take on the trusts as his main campaign issue instead. It likely would not have mattered. The incumbent president, backed by prosperity at home and military victory abroad, was going to be difficult to beat. To ensure victory, McKinley added forty-one-year-old Theodore Roosevelt, a war hero who was less than two years into his stint as governor of New York, to his ticket as vice president. Adding to the sting of a second defeat, Bryan this time failed to win even his home state of Nebraska.

Wall Street took the election results as a green light to go even further in terms of scale. In 1898 a number of players in the steel and iron trades had taken advantage of the opportunities to merge their interests. In the steel industry, even smaller consolidations resulted in substantial firms. Capitalized at $40 million, American Steel & Wire folded in firms in the wire business. Federal Steel, even larger at $100 million, brought in over 150,000 acres of iron ore fields, the Illinois Steel Co., and a variety of feeder railroads needed to make its steel operations work efficiently. The American Tin Plate Company consolidated over one hundred mills, resulting in 95 percent control of the country's tin box manufacturing. The next year saw the formation of the National Tube Company, which consolidated 90 percent control of steel tube manufacturing. Rounding out the frenetic activity was National Steel and American Bridge Co. The largest firm, Federal Steel, had the backing of a syndicate formed by Morgan.

One man was conspicuous in his absence from the rounds of deal making. Andrew Carnegie, unperturbed by Federal Steel, remarked that his new rival's specialty was "manufacturing stock certificates" rather than expertise in the actual production of steel. By 1901 J. P. Morgan had come to his own conclusion. Unlike Morgan or anyone else, Carnegie knew the economics of steel intimately, even if he was physically absent. He had the full force of conviction that in any pricing race to the bottom, Carnegie Steel would be victorious. With over $100 million structured by Morgan for the Federal Steel consolidation, the risk of having Carnegie operating independently was significant. It would be impossible to control pricing or production with the largest producer out of the fold.

To compound matters, Carnegie was an enigmatic financial force with few boundaries. When the McKinley administration, as a part of the terms of Spain's surrender, agreed to pay $20 million for the transfer of the Philippines to America, the antiwar Carnegie offered to reimburse the American government the same $20 million to give the Filipinos their independence, rather than having the nation become an American protectorate. And Carnegie Steel was private, with the majority of the shares safely in one man's hands. Carnegie answered to no one. Still, approaching sixty-five, Carnegie faced a pressing matter: In the time left in his life, he wanted to give away the bulk of his fortune.

This was Morgan's opening. In January 1901, Morgan met secretly with the president of Carnegie Steel, thirty-eight-year-old Charles Schwab. Having worked his way up from the factory floor as a teen, Schwab was a professional manager who understood cost containment in steel production and distribution. After sharing his idea of forming a giant steel company, Morgan asked Schwab to see if Carnegie would be interested in selling and, if so, at what price. Schwab dutifully made the trek to see Carnegie to disclose Morgan's interest. After a winter round of golf in Westchester, outside Manhattan, Carnegie asked Schwab to come see him the next day. Carnegie wrote out his terms in pencil with all the formality of a golf scorecard. The final number: $480 million.

Schwab immediately took the terms to Morgan's offices at 23 Wall Street. Morgan, after a quick glance, accepted the price. This seemingly casual bit of deliberation, it should be noted, was the beginning of Morgan's efforts—it wasn't his money going to Carnegie. Carnegie agreed in his penciled terms to accept the bulk of the proceeds in the form of $160 million in bonds and $240 million in stock of the new entity, and $80 million in other consideration. And indeed, there was no new entity as of yet. Morgan would have to create a new corporation now that Carnegie had agreed to merge his interests with all of the steel interests previously mentioned. For the time being, a handshake sufficed, with Morgan spending a total of fifteen minutes at Carnegie's home on West Fifty-first Street. Even if they weren't particularly close, the men had done business together for more than thirty-five years. At the visit's conclusion, indulging in a final bit of salesmanship for the pending transaction, Morgan congratulated Carnegie on "being the richest man in the world."

A few weeks later, the United States Steel Corporation was formed. It was a testament to the power of Morgan, and the entirely unregulated securities market, that he could go from a handshake to a public company in less than eight weeks. As the syndicate manager, Morgan's firm deposited $25 million to execute the mechanics of the transaction. Morgan's role was to organize the consolidation, sell shares to the public, and serve on its board of directors. Morgan himself was not a major shareholder of any of the consolidations he sponsored or underwrote. His compensation generally came in the form of fees for arranging these massive transactions. U.S. Steel combined every major steel consolidation of the previous three years, along with Carnegie Steel, into a super-consolidation. On March 29, when the shares were brought to market, U.S. Steel became the first company to be valued at over $1 billion.

Almost immediately Carnegie made good on his "Gospel of Wealth" thesis. Grants from Carnegie started flowing to libraries, universities, and institutions. His first gift, made within days, was $4 million for a fund for his workers, as an "acknowledgment of the deep debt which I owe to the workmen who have contributed so greatly to my success." He then gave another million to maintain the workers' libraries and halls that he had built during his ownership. Over $5 million followed for sixty-eight branch libraries in New York City. Another $10 million went to found the Carnegie Institution; $15 million went to pensions for university professors; $5 million went to pensions for families of heroes who had sacrificed their lives trying to save others; $600,000 went to the Hampton and Tuskegee Institute to "promote the elevation of the colored race we formerly kept in slavery." And on and on it went.

If American capitalism ever found itself on trial, Carnegie's career would have been defense exhibit number one. Here he was, living testimony to the egalitarian spirit of this economic system—a man who had risen from economic deprivation as a child laborer, a working-class immigrant who fed his intellectual soul at free libraries, to a place at the very top, only to give it all away. Was this not proof enough that class in America, far from being a defining castelike characteristic, was a temporary and fluid economic station? What about the half million poor and unwashed immigrants who landed on these shores every year? Were they not more proof that this economic engine offered great allure and promise that the Old World could not match? Who would want to disrupt such an order?

. . .

IN THE SUMMER OF 1901, an old ghost from Carnegie Steel's past would return. While Alexander Berkman, the man who shot Carnegie's junior partner, Henry Clay Frick, was serving out his jail term, his partner and lover, Emma Goldman, continued her activism. She became an underground organizer and a sought-after speaker in anarchist circles. Hearing a speech earlier in May in which Goldman railed against capitalism and its excesses against labor, a young man named Leon Czolgosz became inspired to action. In September he headed to Buffalo, New York, for the Pan-American Exposition with a mission. After a couple of days of tracking his target, Czolgosz made his way to a receiving line to shake hands with the honored guest. When Czolgosz reached the front of the line, rather than shake the outstretched hand offered by the president, he pulled out his pistol and shot him. After a few days when he seemed to be on the verge of recovering, McKinley died on September 14.

Less than six months into his vice presidency, Teddy Roosevelt was sworn in as the youngest president in American history. As the industrial interests that had favored McKinley over the years would soon learn, the Roosevelt presidency was to be a complete departure from business as usual.

This outcome was wholly unexpected given Roosevelt's upbringing. Roosevelt had grown up in New York City as a member of a wealthy household. His doting father had taken his family on safaris in Africa. The young Roosevelt had visited the capitals of Europe. He went to Harvard. In addition to his classwork, he took it upon himself to write a definitive history of American naval warfare during the War of 1812. It took him a couple of years after graduation to finish the volume. Soon afterward, he decided to run for local office to represent a district in the state assembly in New York. He was appointed police commissioner of New York City. A couple of years later, he was a colonel in the U.S. Army, leading forces known as the Rough Riders to victory in Cuba. Returning a hero, he easily won the governorship of New York in 1898. He was still in his thirties.

When McKinley selected him as his running mate, Roosevelt's

worldview was entirely consistent with his president's. America had become a great world power just a generation after its existential conflict. And the base of this power was economic. The country had no great naval fleets or standing army. America made things. It invented new methods. One look at the White House stables, with their new horseless carriages, made this clear. America's people were strivers, tinkerers, and builders. And this outlook was not reserved to elites: The American people had explicitly affirmed it with McKinley's reelection in the face of a distinct alternative. But Roosevelt's view transformed with startling immediacy as events unfolded. And as it did, it became the final, emphatic end of the Gilded Age.

On November 14, a few weeks after McKinley's death, the headline in the *New York Times* screamed: PEACE FOLLOWS WAR IN NORTHERN PACIFIC. In the event readers were confused about the happenings of some unknown military conflict, the subheadline cleared it up: $400,000,000 SECURITY-HOLDING COMPANY FORMED BY FACTIONS. The chief combatants had been the railroad interests represented by Morgan and those of another capitalist, E. H. Harriman. Rather than engage in ongoing rate wars, the Northern Pacific, Great Northern, Union Pacific, and parts of the Burlington were to be rolled into a company incorporated as Northern Securities Company. Combined to control over twenty thousand miles of track, the company was positioned to become the second-largest company in the country after U.S. Steel, which itself was barely eight months old. The orchestrator, again, was J. P. Morgan.

As big as U.S. Steel was, the combined value of American railroads exceeded $10 billion. While no single company was as large as the new steel giant, there were six large groups that controlled over 80 percent of the railroad mileage in the United States. The systems consisted of hundreds of smaller railroads held through one of these affiliated groups. Many of the groups themselves had over $1 billion worth of "independently run" railroads, along with tens of thousands of miles of track, under their control. Until Northern Securities, none had tried to merge large groups under one corporation. If Northern Securities was successfully brought to market, it was virtually guaranteed that additional railroads would consolidate.

However, the young new president's leanings indicated to the seasoned observer that things might not be smooth sailing. On December 3 Roosevelt delivered the era's equivalent of a State of the Union address, the Annual Message, to Congress—following the protocol of that time, it was read out loud by a clerk rather than the president himself. In near-perfect proportionality, half was dedicated to economic affairs and half to foreign policy. After a short excoriation of McKinley's assassin and the anarchist movement in general, Roosevelt held that "the nation is to be congratulated because of its present abounding prosperity." He brooked little doubt that the welfare of the nation rested on "individual thrift, and energy, resolution, and intelligence." He defended the competitive principle that resulted in wealth inequality and large individual fortunes:

> It is not true that as the rich have grown richer the poor have grown poorer. Successful enterprise, of the type which benefits all mankind, can only exist if the conditions are such as to offer great prizes as the rewards of success.
>
> The captains of industry who have driven the railway systems across this continent, who have built up our commerce, who have developed our manufactures, have on the whole done great good to our people. Without them the material development of which we are so justly proud could never have taken place.

But Roosevelt's preamble was leading to a conclusion, in many ways *the* conclusion, about the role of government in the new century:

> The tremendous and highly complex industrial development which went on with ever accelerated rapidity during the latter half of the nineteenth century brings us face to face, at the beginning of the twentieth, with very serious social problems. The old laws, and the old customs which had almost the binding force of law, were once quite sufficient to regulate the accumulation and distribution of wealth. Since the industrial changes, which have so enormously

increased the productive power of mankind, they are no longer sufficient.

And then he addressed the basis for both his and the public's anxieties:

There is a widespread conviction in the minds of the American people that the great corporations known as trusts are in certain of their features and tendencies hurtful to the general welfare. This springs from no spirit of envy or uncharitableness, nor lack of pride in the great industrial achievements that have placed this country at the head of the nations struggling for commercial supremacy. It is based upon sincere conviction that combination and concentration should be, not prohibited, but supervised and within reasonable limits controlled; and in my judgment this conviction is right.

AMERICAN BUSINESS HAD a countervailing power. He justified this role with a simple bit of irrefutable logic: The corporate form that limited the personal financial liability of its owners and managers was itself a government-sanctioned, statutory creation—how would it make sense that the government should not then have the power to regulate corporations? Corporations, just like patents, copyrights, or trademark rights, did not exist in nature.

In this Republican, startlingly, Progressive voices now had an ear in the White House.

After the two polarizing elections between McKinley and Bryan, it seemed as though fate—an anarchist's bullet—had brought American capitalism to a happy compromise in Teddy Roosevelt. While financiers and industrialists had accepted that certain activities are best engaged in at large scale, this new president had come to the same conclusion regarding the scope of governmental activities.

Perhaps there was some predictability in this outcome. The Spanish-American War and the speed with which the nation had acquired overseas territory had created the conditions for a strident nationalism. All Americans, in both the North and the South, rooted for the same flag. But nationalism also meant rooting for the government in prosecuting a war. The notion of an overseas, imperialistic adventure was incompatible with the notion of a limited federal government back at home. Just as the Northern economy thrived during the Civil War, military affairs were not disconnected from economic ones.

Roosevelt's affinity for the military was on full display in his first message. He called for massive expansion of the American navy. He dived into the proposed American role in building and securing the Isthmian Canal, known later as the Panama Canal. Within four years, during peacetime, the Navy Department's budget would escalate to over $117 million—more than 20 percent of total federal expenditures. In 1896, when McKinley first took office, the navy required $27 million.

The growth of the military, by definition, meant the growth of the national government and its budget. Once the government became a consumer of industrial output—ships required steel, for instance—policy regarding labor laws could be dictated through federal contracts. As it happened, federal contractors were soon prohibited from night work for women and child laborers. Other than mere legislation and enforcement, larger government expenditures gave policy makers the lever of the purse to influence industrial behavior. Thanks to the navy, the government became one large, demanding customer. But Roosevelt preferred even more direct maneuvers for federal authority.

In February Roosevelt and his attorney general, Philander Knox, had announced that they viewed the consolidation of three major railroads into Northern Securities to be a violation of the Sherman Antitrust Act of 1890. J. P. Morgan was shocked and assumed it was a misunderstanding that could be smoothed over at the White House. Once face-to-face with the president, Morgan approached the meeting as a business negotiation over a technical issue, telling Roosevelt, "If we have done anything wrong, send your man to my man and they can fix it up." When the attorney general interjected, "We don't want to fix it up, we want to stop it," Morgan understood the gravity of the administration's position. He then asked if his other consolidations, such as U.S. Steel, were at risk.

The answer was the equivalent of a stunning "not yet." After the financier's chastened departure, Roosevelt remarked with amusement that Morgan seemed to view the American president as simply a "big rival operator." Morgan would proceed with the merger anyway. The case would go to the U.S. Supreme Court. In a 5–4 vote, the court sided with Roosevelt, affirming that the combination of firms into Northern Securities restrained trade and the company would have to be dissolved.

But Morgan's view of the president as an equal might have been reasonable given the circumstances: U.S. Steel's revenues that year were $560 million; the federal government's total revenues through all its taxation powers amounted to $562 million. And Morgan had interests in multiple companies, while poor Roosevelt was a proxy for but one government.

But Roosevelt, as Morgan now understood, was just getting started on balancing the equation.

ALMOST IMMEDIATELY ROOSEVELT'S ideas on federal power would be tested. As corporations and Wall Street increasingly consolidated industries and sectors, so did labor unions. The same advantages of economies of scale and professionalized management that corporations argued were the benefits of specialized bigness were used by labor unions to pool the strength of workers in similar fields. A few weeks after Morgan's fateful meeting, a large union engaged in conflict against one of the largest industries in the country: 147,000 workers from the coal mines went on strike.

The men were members of the United Mine Workers. Their work was vitally important to modern life: Millions of American homes in the Northeast relied on anthracite coal for heating. Anthracite coal, a variety consisting of high-carbon quantity, was largely mined in a 496-square-mile region of Pennsylvania. By 1901 anthracite coal production amounted to sixty million tons annually—more than a ton per every living adult in the United States. Since coal was largely used for winter heating, the strike had a benign quality given that it started in May. Unlike previous large strikes, in which local unions stopped work in sympathy, the UMW was one large, fully coordinated union. Its demands were simple: more money, an eight-hour workday, and better working conditions.

This last demand was especially important. Mining was dangerous. Death had multiple calling cards down in the shafts. Suffocation, collapse, blowouts, and explosions were the most common, not to mention the general atrophy of the lungs from breathing in coal dust during the majority of one's waking hours. And there was evidence that American working conditions were generally more dangerous than those in British or German mines. Of the 147,000 workers in the anthracite mines, 513 died at work in 1901. More than 3 out of every 1,000 miners died each year. To bring the math home, a worker had approximately a one-in-thirty chance of dying over a ten-year period. A family with a father and three sons down below tempted fate.

The mine owners refused to negotiate. A couple of the larger operators had voiced their concerns to United Mine Workers president John Mitchell, stating that increased wages would mean increased prices to consumers. In their opinion, the market would not support it. Mitchell, with the leverage of being able to shut down the entire industry, pressed the issue. Before striking, however, Mitchell offered to abide by the results of binding arbitration. Given the prevailing sentiment against trusts, it was perhaps sensible of the mine operators to refuse this overture.

By the time Roosevelt was marking his first full year in office, the American public had become a bit more nervous, a feeling undoubtedly hastened by the arrival of the first crisp chills of autumn. The strike placed front and center a central question that faced the nation for the century ahead: What was the government's role in a private battle between a union and an industry, especially in one that was almost as vital as food? In earlier times, neither the industry nor the union would have had enough coordinated power to bring total production to a standstill. As Roosevelt knew, and as his countrymen could feel in cold homes, times had changed.

Still, federal intervention in commercial negotiations between two private parties had little precedent. The mine operators simply believed that the striking workers would eventually fold when their living conditions were dire enough. Unfortunately, the living conditions of nonstriking Americans seemed to be in similar peril. Roosevelt called a meeting of the heads of the largest mining operations, along with Mitchell. One Roosevelt biographer, Edmund Morris, has noted sardonically that the meeting's balance of seven businessmen to one all-powerful union head suggested to conservatives "Mitchell's monopolistic power," referring to his control of the entire labor supply of anthracite mines.

But in person this labor monopolist appeared far more conciliatory in the president's eyes. In contrast, the mine operators seemed to be incensed at the prospect of having the president neutralize their negotiating position by calling the meeting in the first place. The operators stated that twenty thousand nonunion workers stood ready to go into the mines, but to guard against violence by the striking workers, the labor replacement would require federal troops to act in the protection of property. Conversely, the union's leverage stemmed from its physical ability to prevent, through the threat of violence, entry by strikebreakers to work on private property. But Roosevelt wasn't comfortable with the use of federal force against labor. Anyway, it would not exactly be the free market at work, as the mine owners implied, if federal troops were needed. The trust movement had galvanized public anxiety against the power of capital—to augment this further with federal troops would indicate a tin ear in the White House. Such an action seemed especially preposterous given that Mitchell offered to agree to any finding by a neutral panel appointed by the president.

But the temperature in the East kept dropping as the days became shorter. The president, frustrated, had his secretary of war, Elihu Root, put a force of ten thousand army regulars on alert, in case no resolution came to fruition and the mines had to be opened as a matter of national emergency. Root, however, had the idea to call upon the one power that could force reconciliation where the president could not. All coal mines were dependent on railroads. They also depended on access to capital markets. So Root went to see J. P. Morgan on his yacht, the *Corsair*. Using *Corsair* stationery, Root and Morgan sketched out a set of terms that would allow the operators to save face and accept federal intervention.

Within days, Roosevelt appointed a presidential commission, a panel of five members. Both the operators and the mineworkers' union agreed to abide by the eventual findings. While the commission investigated their working conditions, the workers returned immediately to work. By November the coal mines were once again in full operation. When the commission came back with its report and judgment, the workers received a wage increase of 10 percent and a workday of nine hours. However, the report also debunked the cries of great deprivation among the miners—the commission's investigation found conditions in the mining areas to be good, the public schools in the mining towns of decent quality, and homeownership rates among the miners on par with the rest of American society. But the implications went well beyond a simple labor dispute. The president's intervention was the harbinger for twentieth-century regulation of American capitalism.

Starting in his second year on the job, Roosevelt would continue to shape the role of government as the regulating force balancing the interests of labor, capital, the public, journalists, and his own party's establishment. If his party had known who he was, he never would have been nominated.

Twenty

FOOD

F or much of his life, good health and prosperity had eluded Charles William Post. But in 1891 the strain of a failing business venture had compounded his health problems. For most of his life, Post had been afflicted with stomach ailments. At one point, failing health had caused him to leave a good trade selling farm implements in the Midwest. With a recommendation that a warmer climate might do him some good, he headed to Texas. There he dabbled in real estate and looked to sell plots to prospective homeowners, which yielded him only financial distress coupled with physical exhaustion. Hoping to find a reprieve from both, Post, with his wife, Ella, and daughter, Marjorie, arrived at Michigan's Battle Creek Sanitarium seeking wellness.

By 1891 the Battle Creek Sanitarium was a wellness spa with some of the functions of a hospital. An imposing building set amid bucolic grounds, the place was the brainchild and mission of Dr. John Harvey Kellogg. Even Kellogg's spelling of "sanitarium," a derivative of the existing word "sanatorium," was new. Unlike many of the medicine men of the era, Kellogg was a legitimate doctor, and what's more, he was a thinker and a writer. Beyond his medical training, he was influenced by the other major Battle Creek institution that had preceded his own: the Seventh-day Adventists. His parents had been some of the earliest adherents to the church as it was being formally established. Kellogg's medical education itself was paid for by a $1,000 loan from the White family, widely influential in the founding of Adventism. One of the unique aspects of this denomination, in addition to the absence of eternal suffering, was the emphasis on maintaining a clean diet and the avoidance of pork, shellfish, and other "unclean" meats. Many adherents went further and embraced vegetarianism.

To this body of dietary thought Kellogg added his own—one that vilified most forms of human sexuality. Barely twenty-seven years old and a few months removed from his medical studies, he made his views clear in an 1879 treatise titled *Plain Facts for Old and Young*. He covered topics such as "Infanticide and Abortion," pointing to the scourge of patent medicines intended to induce miscarriages. He attributed promiscuousness to a genetic quality. "Indulgence during pregnancy" was one of the worst forms of marital excess and drained the resources from the fetus—it even abnormally enhanced the sexual instinct of the unborn child. Even in otherwise conservative men and chaste women liberated by marriage, he found that, shockingly, "intercourse is engaged in night after night, neither party having any idea that these repeated sexual acts are excesses which the system of neither can bear." Some ignorant couples even believed that "indulgence may increase powers, just as gymnastic exercises augment the force of muscles." It all stemmed from Kellogg's main view that the sexual function was solely "for the purpose of producing new individuals to take the place of those who die." Unnecessary sexual acts led to monstrosities like abortion. Much of this pleasure seeking he attributed to meat eating. Nothing stimulated animal impulses like eating animals.

To prevent unnecessary sexual acts in adulthood, Kellogg surmised it was best to start early by preventing masturbation. Having "no parallel except in sodomy," it was "the most dangerous of all sexual abuses because the most extensively practiced." To Kellogg, even "lying upon the back or the abdomen frequently leads to self-abuse by provoking sexual excitement." Aside from a whole host of evil influences from schools to servants, a risk factor in even the most virtuous home came from the pantry. "Candies, spices, cinnamon, cloves, peppermint, and all strong essences, powerfully excite the genital organs, and lead to the same result." By watching out for a list of thirty-nine behaviors and attributes that included rounded shoulders, acne, clay eating, confusion of ideas, mock piety, or unnatural boldness, parents would be able to diagnose the prevalence of "solitary vice" in their children. The fate of the Republic depended upon curtailing this menace. Look at Rome.

Despite his sexual prudishness, Kellogg's actual practices at the sanitarium were minimally invasive and impressively modern. Quackery it wasn't, at least not entirely. The Battle Creek philosophy was to create a pleasant environment where the body would heal largely by itself. Kellogg focused on making sure that the sanitarium served vegetarian foods, with a focus on whole grains along with fresh vegetables and fruits. He was not a nativist—he acknowledged the benefits of Japanese seaweed and Mediterranean yogurt for the digestive system. He believed that drugs should be used minimally, if at all. His recommendations to patients almost always included fresh air, exercise, and water therapy, such as swimming. He offered a variety of massage therapies to comfort his patients. In developing a fully cooked, easily digestible form of grain for his patients, Kellogg created a form of granola and then a "toasted flaked cereal, in which each grain was spread into a thin film and toasted slightly brown." Kellogg's cereals were meant for the patients of the Battle Creek Sanitarium.

C. W. Post was impressed. Before long, he caught an entrepreneurial second wind while recuperating at Kellogg's facility and scrambled together funds for a tract of land in Battle Creek. He then started his own, much smaller wellness center. For his patients Post developed a liquid-based breakfast concoction known as Postum. A year or two later, he developed a granular cereal based on techniques he had seen at the sanitarium and named it Grape-Nuts, based on its resemblance to grape seeds. Of course, it was made from neither grapes nor nuts.

UNLIKE JOHN HARVEY KELLOGG, though, Post had few reservations about marketing widely beyond his wellness center. He was a businessman, not a doctor. To promote Grape-Nuts, Post gravitated to the burgeoning art of newspaper advertising. As an incentive for local grocers to stock his merchandise, Post offered to generate in-store demand for retailers through advertising, a novel tactic. Post's company was offering to

spend money to advertise a product that it did not directly sell to consumers. The first beneficiary of the consumer's demand would be the
grocer; Post's benefit would follow from the wholesale demand stimulated
through this concept of promotional branding. And without any medical
degree holding him back, Post was able to make bold claims about the
potent and wholly unverifiable effects of Grape-Nuts. According to the
copy, Grape-Nuts was the best brain food on the market. Eating it cured
appendicitis and even improved blood quality. With the strength of
newspaper advertising, Post, within a decade of being Kellogg's patient,
had built the first dominant cereal franchise in the Grape-Nuts brand.

Kellogg, seeing Post's and other imitators' successes, started marketing
the sanitarium's cereals under the brand name "Sanitas" to limited effect.
After a few years, he allowed his younger brother William Keith to establish a cereal brand under the Kellogg name. The separation of interests was
to some degree prompted by William Keith's insistence that he be able to
add sugar to the cereals to appeal to a wider market. John Harvey, being
solely interested in wellness, disagreed. To segregate their approaches, the
signature of W. K. Kellogg accompanied advertisements for his company's
Corn Flakes. But John Harvey soon had second thoughts about the use of
the Kellogg name for his flaking cereal. Litigation over the dual use of the
Kellogg brand name ensued, with W. K. Kellogg's interests ultimately prevailing. Just a few years into the new century, this small Michigan town
had given rise to two great cereal makers, Kellogg's and Post, inspired in
part by a nascent religious order headquartered in the same town.

To his older brother's alarm, W. K. Kellogg's advertising soon shed
the restraint that could be expected from a practicing Seventh-day Ad-
ventist. John Harvey couldn't let Post slide either, noting with some
bitter pride that "the numerous imitations and piracies" of his wholesome
health food now bore the corrupt messaging of marketing.

Post's product may have drawn its inspiration from Kellogg's
sanitarium, but his marketing ideas came from the playbook of patent
medicine sellers, the most prolific newspaper advertisers of the era. If
one took them at their word, the patent medicine industry collectively
had cured every disease and malady known to man, and these cures
could be had by anyone for the mere price of a few bottles. Newspaper

advertisements ran ads along the lines of CANCER CURED, RHEUMATISM CURED, and THE GREATEST DISCOVERY OF THE 19TH CENTURY as a "sure cure" for tuberculosis. By 1905 a significant portion of the newspaper revenues of the country came from advertisements for patent medicines. Even the term "patent medicine" was a misrepresentation. There was almost never any patent. To receive a patent, a medicine man would have to disclose his ingredients and the methodology of manufacture to the patent office, and perhaps even prove the efficacy of his claims. This was a lot of unnecessary trouble. It was far easier to get a trademark such as "Dr. Haines' Golden Treatment" to treat drunkenness, "Nicotol" to cure smoking, or "Actina" to cure deafness. Not only could a proprietor build a brand, but he could imply that there was a secret formula behind it, adding a mystique that mere transparency most certainly would not.

Even the most famous trademark in American history, perhaps the entire world, started with firm roots in the patent medicine industry. The thinking behind the brand started with John Pemberton, a former doctor in his midfifties who had converted to the more lucrative field of pharmacy. The 1880s for the Atlanta-based pharmacist had been challenging. But despite bankruptcy, fires, and failures, he had had just enough past financial success to merit ongoing speculation in his laboratory. The aim for Pemberton, as it was for many, was to develop a formula or drug plausible enough to be marketed—as he had once done with Dr. Sanford's Great Invigorator, Eureka Oil, Triplex Liver Pills, and Lemon and Orange Elixir before sales faded. With the barrier to entry low and the cost of the chemicals and ingredients a fraction of the selling price, breaking into the consumer's imagination as a medicinal panacea was no simple task—it was intensely competitive.

With his age advancing, Pemberton decided to focus his attention on a new plant-based ingredient that seemed to have rather miraculous properties. The plant's attributes were a Western rediscovery of sorts by German scientist Albert Niemann. Natives in the Andes of South America, including the Inca, had chewed the plant's leaves for millennia, finding them beneficial for digestion, energy, and mental alertness, and as an aphrodisiac. Now scientists had come to learn about the magic of the coca leaf. Sigmund Freud raved poetically about it in his 1884 text *Über Coca*.

Freud primarily referred to cocaine, the leaf's naturally occurring chemical compound that gave it its fame. Pemberton first saw coca in product form when it was added to wine and marketed as Vin Mariani. Seeing a good idea, Pemberton came up with his own derivative wine-and-coca concoction. His formula doubled down with the fruit of another exotic plant, the African kola nut, which gave Pemberton's product the added benefits of caffeine.

But he ran into the age-old buzz kill of entrepreneurs everywhere: regulation. Just as Pemberton was getting going, Atlanta passed a prohibition law. Pemberton complied and stripped out the alcohol content but was now left to do with only cocaine and kola. The wine content and flavor had disappeared. After experimenting with sweeteners and other ingredients, Pemberton came up with a sugared syrup that blended the kola and coca. He then looked to distribute the syrup through a southern institution: the soda fountain. Offering carbonated water with myriad flavors of fruit, drugstores pioneered an ample seasonal business for cold beverages in the hotter months. Pemberton's syrup found its way into the soda fountains in the summer of 1886. Soon Pemberton's "temperance drink"—powered by the cocaine of coca and the caffeine of kola—was named descriptively "Coca-Cola."

Pemberton, staying true to his roots, marketed Coca-Cola for its medicinal properties more than he touted it as refreshment. After some initial success, however, the aging Pemberton needed both cash and a succession plan. The Coca-Cola trademark and formula, through a labyrinth of transactions originating from the Pemberton Chemical Company and the Pemberton Medicine Company, ended up in the hands of another patent medicine man named Asa Candler. But Candler saw that Coca-Cola's appeal went beyond the market for therapies and curatives. In some ways, the choice was made for Coca-Cola. When the federal government instituted a tax on drugs to help pay for the Spanish-American War, eager revenue agents deemed Coca-Cola a drug rather than a beverage. Years of messaging such as "ideal brain tonic," "sovereign remedy for headache and nervousness," and "It makes the sad glad and the weak strong" brought Candler to a crossroads. By 1900 Coca-Cola had deemphasized its medicinal properties altogether, at once

avoiding the tax on drugs and eyeing a bigger market. It gave up on cocaine, increasingly seen as less than benign, soon afterward. It then moved
beyond the drugstore soda fountain, granting independent operators the
right to bottle Coca-Cola throughout the country.

But Coca-Cola was the exception. Most other patent medicines had
no such transition points. And the princes of the industry understood the
legislative risks to their golden geese. Not only were most drugs grandiose
in their claims, but many contained ample undisclosed doses of alcohol,
opiates, morphine, and cocaine. Some cures marketed to treat alcoholism,
for instance, contained strong inebriating doses of alcohol. The risks of
use or misuse went beyond the consumer being separated from his or her
money for an ineffective drug. Fatality, serious impairment, and addic-
tion were often the results of a patient's desperate search for cures.
Following Teddy Roosevelt's 1904 election victory, aided by his reputation as a trust buster, provocateurs in the media became emboldened to
take on other powerful interests, with magazines such as *Harper's*, *Collier's*, and *McClure's* leading the charge against big business. The previous
year, Ida Tarbell had eviscerated John D. Rockefeller and Standard Oil
in a series of articles in *McClure's*. As if on cue, *Collier's* found a target in
the patent medicine industry with a startling series titled "The Great
American Fraud."

The author Samuel Hopkins Adams looked to expose a secret co-
conspirator to the patent medicine industry: American newspapers. Adams pointed out that $40 million of the industry's revenue was spent on
newspaper advertising, by far the single biggest expenditure. Indirectly
getting a lion's share of patent medicine revenues, the newspapers netted
more money from selling advertising to these firms than did the patent
medicine firms from selling their potions after expenses. "Should the
newspapers, magazines, and medical journals refuse their pages to this
class of advertisements, the patent medicine business in five years would
be as scandalously historic" as past financial follies and frauds. He
pointed out that Hearst alone generated over half a million dollars from
patent medicine advertising. But as Adams knew well, the economics of
publishing was such that once the printing cost of an edition was met,
each incremental advertising dollar generated was nearly all margin and

dropped right to the bottom line—neither Hearst nor anyone else was likely to turn away from the industry's largesse.

But the allegations, and Adams's documentary evidence, went much further. As the series continued into 1906, it shed light on a simple, genius scheme orchestrated by the head of the Proprietary Association of America, the patent medicine industry's trade association. The leader, F. J. Cheney, was the president of the Cheney Medicine Company, which advertised in over fifteen thousand newspapers across America, many with circulation in the hundreds. As a large advertiser, Cheney found a simple technique that applied some leverage to the editorial policies of the newspapers. In all of his advertising contracts, he applied a simple one-sentence addendum that read as follows: "It is mutually agreed that this Contract is void, if any law is enacted by your state restricting or prohibiting the manufacture or sale of any proprietary medicine."

From his position of influence, he then recommended that every major patent medicine vendor add the same sentence to his or her advertising contracts. To his peers he outlined his simple logic that "when you touch a man's pocket, you touch him where he lives. That principle is true of the newspaper editor." This new clause had its intended effect. Newspaper editors and publishers, understanding that a large portion of their contracted revenues could be canceled at a moment's notice, made sure to apply the lightest touch with all editorial and legislative matters concerning patent medicines. The concerted action of major advertisers, exercised through one simple clause, compromised much of the newspaper industry's editorial integrity. As evidence, Adams pointed to legislative sessions on patent medicine regulations in numerous states, known as "pure food laws," which failed to merit even a footnote in most local newspapers.

While the *Collier's* series was well received, just months later it was overshadowed by another author's words, which jolted the American psyche, and stomach, much more forcefully.

JUST AS *UNCLE TOM'S CABIN* had once described life among the most subjugated class of American society, a novel titled *The Jungle* found its protagonists among the recent, desperate arrivals on American shores.

The year 1905 marked the first time that more than one million immigrants arrived in America in a single year—even for a nation of immigrants, this growth was sudden and immense. In 1900 the number had been less than 450,000. The composition of the immigrant pool had also changed dramatically. Germans and Irishmen now made up less than 10 percent of arriving immigrants. The turn of the century saw an unrelenting wave from Italy; Eastern Europe, including Poland, Czechoslovakia, and Hungary; and Russia and its bordering countries, such as Lithuania, Latvia, and Ukraine. Unlike the Irish, this wave didn't speak English. Unlike the Germans, they had little education and money to start life with. American society faced the immediate challenge of absorbing this endless influx. Never had so many different languages been sizably introduced into the country at the same time.

Upton Sinclair's novel told the story of a broad-shouldered, bull-like Lithuanian immigrant named Jurgis Rudkus. Fueled by optimism and lured by tales of endless wealth, Jurgis and members of his family land in New York and make their way to Chicago. The family begins life in America in a tenement community called Packingtown. Beyond rows and rows of shacks and boardinghouses, set amid open sewers and fetid ditches with odors "of all the dead things of the universe," stood the smokestacks, stockyards, and rail tracks belonging to the meatpacking industry.

It is easy to imagine that the worst of America's living conditions would naturally fall to its most recent arrivals, longing for an economic foothold. For Sinclair, *The Jungle*'s twenty-eight-year-old author, the stark environment in which these families found themselves resembled a desperate third-world country, an urban dystopia, set within an industrial powerhouse. To Sinclair, Packingtown was not a temporary stepping-stone on the way to the American dream—it was the place where industrial captives lived out their lives. The fictional Jurgis, though, was delighted to find work almost immediately upon arrival at one of the dominant meatpackers.

There was enough truth in Sinclair's novel to keep it credible. The meatpacking industry did have two large packers in Chicago: Armour and Swift, which he fictionalized as Durham and Brown. Meatpacking did transform meat into an industrial product. And in this there was a redeeming quality. Up to then, at no point or place in human history had meat been so available to so many as it was in America. The prevalence of meat at multiple weekly meals was an unthinkable luxury throughout much of the world, whereas in America a meat-based diet was commonplace. By no means was this a small thing: A lack of food had once led to 20 percent of the entire population of Ireland emptying into America over an eight-year span. The industrialization of agriculture and meat production had guaranteed food security and produced ample surpluses. By the time Sinclair's novel was released, the meatpacking industry made up almost 20 percent of all U.S. exports. Unless a person was morally opposed to killing animals for food, the industry served an essential purpose.

Meatpacking itself had emerged from a confluence of factors. In the decade preceding the Civil War, meat was largely a local product. Cattle or hogs were grown on local farms, and the farm family slaughtered one or two of its animals in the winter, kept some meat for itself, and sold the rest to a local grocer or butcher. As the American population increasingly crowded into cities, growing and slaughtering enough meat locally, especially on the eastern seaboard, became challenging. Cattle ranching and raising hogs evolved into more specialized affairs falling to entire states and regions in the Midwest and western United States. For a time, railroads would then transport live cattle or hogs to local slaughterhouses close to the consumer. With the advent of refrigeration, it became possible to slaughter animals centrally in industrialized settings. Once the animal was killed, the meat could be sent to markets everywhere without spoiling.

Within a decade or two, Chicago became the national center of meatpacking. It was the largest railroad hub in the country, and as such, it was the central hub for grain distribution. The nation's commodity markets, where futures prices on crops were shouted and fought over with elaborate hand signals, were located in the city. By the turn of the century, millions of hogs and cattle made their way into the Chicago stockyards. The meatpackers were the buyers, and farmers and ranchers were the sellers. The live animal was the raw, wholesale industrial input; each day, tens of thousands of pigs and cows stood in the stockyards around Chicago waiting their final hours. In 1905 over 54 million hogs and 13 million cattle—one large animal for every adult American—were slaughtered in the United States, many of them in Chicago.

The industry's margins were tight. After being shipped in and paid for, the bulk of the industry's working capital was tied up in live animals. The way to maximize yield in a highly competitive business was to take every part of every animal and convert it into something useful. And if an animal had to be killed, it was somewhat commendable to not be wasteful. The era's most prominent packer, Philip Armour, marveled at his industry's advances:

> So recently as twenty-five years ago, the blood was allowed to run into the river, and men were paid five dollars a load to cart the heads, feet, and other wasted material upon the prairie and there bury it in pits and trenches. Today, a large packing plant depends largely for its profit on the intelligent utilization of those so-called waste materials. The large packing establishments of today manipulate their own horns, hoofs, bones, sinews, hide-trimmings, etc.

THIS MINIMIZE-ALL-COSTS, maximize-all-yield approach did serve to reduce the market price of beef and pork, the primary beneficiaries being the working family that spent a relatively large portion of its income on food. As always, a little savings went a long way in a household that had little. Ironically, this compelling need to utilize every part of the animal served as the basis of the indictment in Sinclair's novel. Meatpackers did not just cut costs; they cut corners. Sinclair's account might have been readily dismissed as the ramblings of a socialist—which he very much was—but for one factor: Sinclair actually worked at Swift & Company's facility to research his book. He painted a chilling picture of the modern slaughterhouse:

> Here was the chute, with its river of hogs, all patiently toiling upward . . . and then through another passageway they went into a

room from which there is no returning for hogs. At the head there was a great iron wheel, about twenty feet in circumference, with rings here and there along its edge. Upon both sides of this wheel there was a narrow space, into which came the hogs at the end of their journey. They had chains, which they fastened upon the leg of the nearest hog, and the other end of the rings upon the wheel. So, as the wheel turned, a hog was suddenly jerked off his feet and borne aloft. At the same time, the ear was assailed by a most terrifying shriek. . . . The shriek was followed by another. And meantime another was sprung up, and then another, and another, and then there was a double line of them, each dangling by a foot and kicking in frenzy—and squealing. It was all so very businesslike that one watched it fascinated. It was pork making by machinery, pork making by applied mathematics.

SINCLAIR DESCRIBED a disassembly line of sorts, where a living, breathing, functioning animal was converted into a series of parts, the sum of the components being worth more than the whole. Hundreds of men worked in highly specific functions, each operating in some way on the hog as it came his way, from the initial wheel to the boiling water where the hair bristles were taken off. At the end of this process, in which not the "tiniest particle of organic matter was wasted," the various parts made their way onto the railcars to the marketplace. Sinclair's protagonist, Jurgis, marvels at this splendor of specialization, this division of labor to extract all value, and takes pride in his place within this economic machine.

In the bitter cold of Chicago winters, Jurgis works in an unheated facility filled with freezing, misty blood. At mealtimes "Jurgis had either to eat his dinner amid the stench," or he could find his way to Ashland Avenue or Forty-seventh Street adjacent to the factory, where he could choose from over a hundred saloons at Whiskey Row and Whiskey Point. The American saloon's special feature: As long as a man bought a drink or two, he could enjoy a free lunch. Nourished and inebriated, "as he went back he did not shiver so. . . . The deadly brutalizing monotony of it did not afflict him so,—he had ideas while he worked, and took a more cheerful view of his circumstances." And on payday, "where in Packing-town could a man go to have his check cashed but to a saloon, where he could pay for the favor by spending a part of his money?" But Jurgis soon loses his place in the machine by getting injured. After a series of events, he is exploited, corrupted, forced into criminality, and de-stroyed spiritually—Sinclair's rapturous metaphor for the price of in-dustrial capitalism.

But it was Sinclair's accounts of the meat quality that touched the far deeper nerve. "Scraps of meat and odds and ends of refuse" were scraped out and added to the meat for market. Steers with tuberculosis and hogs that had died of cholera were loaded up to Indiana, "where they made a fancy grade of lard." A fancy brand of potted chicken was made up of "fat of pork, beef suet, and the waste ends of veal." "All of this inge-nious mixture was ground up and flavored with spices to taste like some-thing." With its imagery of filthy floors, dead rats, acid, and chemicals to take away the stench and color of rotten meat, *The Jungle* detailed the price the American consumer paid for being so trusting of the modern market.

But Sinclair's story missed its intended target. Dedicating *The Jungle* "to workingmen of America," he had hoped to shed light on the working conditions in American factories. The novel's prescription and conclu-sion was for men to find strength in unions, and then socialism. To Sinclair's dismay, sympathies gravitated to concern for the American stomach rather than any concern for the plight of immigrant workers.

This lack of empathy was understandable for many reasons. Labor unions themselves, which had grown by 400 percent in the past decade, were wary of foreign workers; the endless supply of cheap labor willing to work for low wages under the worst working conditions did not help the negotiating power of native-born workers. Others were suspicious of political agitation—an anarchist had shot the president just five years ago, after all. For Americans in their forties and fifties, born just before or during the Civil War, the greatness of their nation's achievement in becoming a transcendent economic power was a matter of no small pride. Shortcomings came with the territory. At the same time, urban residents understood the impossibility of housing hundreds of thousands of new arrivals on an annual basis. What else was possible but overcrowded, ramshackle tenements? Lastly, the most strident nativist might have posed a question to Sinclair: How many of the newly arrived, upon seeing their initial conditions, would have accepted a free one-way ticket back to where they came from? Yes, the face of capitalism had blemishes, but few Americans saw the sense in cutting off free enterprise's nose with socialism to spite it.

But the issue of food quality was something else. To again balance the public's interests against the excesses of capital, a skilled political surgeon was required.

WHEN *THE JUNGLE* was published, much of the story had already been serialized, published in installment form in a socialist journal. The socialists having considered Sinclair a genius, it fell to mainstream book reviewers to corroborate the judgment. When the *New York Times* reviewed Sinclair's work on March 3, 1906, it not only dismissed the work as merely clever but also missed any hint of its almost immediate future impact. The review focused entirely on Sinclair's socialism and the industrial conditions: The lengthy critique did not mention pork, meat, or cattle, or touch on a single food-related issue, thinking them, with good reason, literary devices of a larger point. The *Times* stuck to examining Sinclair's work on its political and literary merits. In its sobriety, it missed the story.

The Roosevelt administration found *The Jungle* to be a bit more credible. Roosevelt himself viewed much of the strident and holier-than-thou investigative journalism that accompanied his administration's term as poisonous to civil discourse. To an audience in March, he even resorted to a reference from *The Pilgrim's Progress* to label this sort of journalist "the man with the muckrake, the man who could look no way but downward with muckrake in his hand." With one speech, Roosevelt made the term "muckraker" a professional specialty. It was fitting that Roosevelt would use an obscure passage from a seventeenth-century novel to describe modern journalism pejoratively. Yet it was even more fitting that he could look past his own prejudices and remarks to see the value of *The Jungle*'s exposé. To many, this only cemented Roosevelt as a seeker of truth no matter his opinion of the source.

The timing helped. *The Jungle*'s release happened to coincide with a policy objective Roosevelt had outlined in the previous December's address to Congress. In addition to calling for regulation of railroad rates and justifying his administration's intervention in commercial affairs, he had called for strong regulation of food, asking for legislation related to "misbranded and adulterated foods, drinks, and drugs." Reasonably enough, he wanted to outlaw "debased" food that had the power "to injure the health or to deceive purchasers." Even for Roosevelt this was a tall order. The newspapers with their reliance on patent medicine revenues, the meatpackers along with the agricultural states that supplied hogs and cattle, and the nation's commercial interests in general did not want to see an ongoing, active expansion of federal authority. Socialist messenger or not, in *The Jungle* Roosevelt found the form of propaganda he needed. If the *New York Times* reviewer failed to be revolted by the unsanitary conditions of meatpacking, the president made sure no one else did.

Sinclair, decades later, would lament that his book ultimately did little to evoke sympathy for workers. Ironically, Sinclair's own immediate activism after the book was published played some part in that outcome. Seeing a political opening for change, as it synchronized with the policy aims of the administration, Sinclair focused on publicizing the health hazards of meatpacking rather than pressing wider issues of working conditions. In a series of remarkable letters between the author and the president, Roosevelt asked, "Is there anything further, say in the Department of Agriculture which you would suggest my doing?" In response, Sinclair laid out how the president should proceed: a secret undercover investigation.

I would suggest the following: Find a man . . . whose intelligence and integrity you are absolutely sure [of]. Then let him go to Packingtown as I did, as a workingman; live with the men, get a job in the yards, and use his eyes and ears; and see if he does not come out at the end of a few weeks feeling . . . that the conditions in the packing-houses constitute a "menace to the health of the civilized world."

INCREDIBLY, THE PRESIDENT did exactly as Sinclair suggested, soon appointing two men to carry out the undercover investigation. Within months Roosevelt had the report of his investigators' findings at the meatpackers. But the president didn't immediately release the report. In the U.S. Senate, Senator Albert Beveridge of Indiana had introduced a bill calling for meat inspections and sanitary standards for meatpacking facilities, a dramatic step in the escalation of federal power. The president wanted to give the senator time to operate politically and move the bill along.

Sinclair, however, was unhappy that the report was being kept secret, arguing in a major May 28 *New York Times* story that the people "must be put in possession of the facts contained in the report of the President's special commission." In addition, he was concerned about the meatpackers' views of the proposed federal intervention's constitutionality: "Will they allow it to go unchallenged after Mr. Roosevelt is succeeded by another President?" Sinclair deftly applied public pressure to force the release.

Sinclair undoubtedly also wanted his allegations to be corroborated with a presidential seal. Within a week, they were. The report was far worse than anything contained in *The Jungle*. Small newspapers as far away as Eugene's *Register-Guard* in Oregon led with headlines such as HORRIFYING CONDITIONS IN PACKING HOUSES: "The packers have generally displayed a disregard, not only of the common rules of sanitation, but even of decency." For the vast majority of the American public that hadn't read *The Jungle*, it was all but impossible to miss the excerpts of the commission's report splashed on covers across the country. It gave the president all the momentum that he needed. Within weeks, Congress passed the Federal Meat Inspection Act. It was perhaps the first time the interests of consumer protection coalesced in a uniform way against the financial interests of an industry. The federal government, at the packer's expense, would soon have inspectors at every major meatpacking facility in America. This development was far different from rules regarding commercial practices. The federal government was now actively in the quality-assurance business of a private product for private consumption.

After passage of the Federal Meat Inspection Act, the Pure Food and Drug Act quickly followed. This legislation, having been on the back burner for almost a decade, flew into law with the public calling for whole-sale federal regulation of what they put into their bodies. It would eventually lead to the establishment of the Food and Drug Administration. In the space of six months, two of America's most powerful industries ran into the coinciding agendas of a socialist author and a Republican president, resulting in sweeping legislation.

Roosevelt's transformative presidency did much to defuse the antag-onisms among capital, labor, and consumers that had festered and grown over the previous decades. American capitalism, if there had been any doubt, by now had fully diverged from the laissez-faire doctrine. To Americans, market forces alone had not been enough to guarantee clean meat or safe drugs. Capitalism's future was contingent upon the democratic ability to correct for excesses, with regulatory oversight being the price of consent of the governed. And as this balance became refined in the un-folding century, the American's stake in capitalism as a consumer would grow to become as important as his citizenship in its democracy.

PART THREE

An early Ford Model T advertisement, 1908.

Twenty-one

AUTOMOBILES

While the Progressive era introduced government intervention across a wide range of commercial activity and in regulating market behavior, including activism in areas like conservation and land management, the free market emphasized that it was private hands that made the useful and transformative things, the ingredients of modern society and ease of living. When the *Horseless Age*, a trade publication for the nascent automotive industry founded in 1895, published its first edition of 1900, it proclaimed that "revolutionary inventions" were no longer needed to "make the motor vehicle a success." The *Horseless Age*'s readers were mechanics, inventors, and engineers and its advertisers were carriage makers, bicycle parts manufacturers, and engine builders. The publication focused on covering the ecosystem of parts suppliers feeding the countless workshops that built crude but functional motor vehicles, of which about four thousand were sold that year throughout the United States.

That an entire publication could be focused only on automobiles indicated a rapid pace of development. Just eight years earlier, in 1892, one of the industry's pioneers, Ransom Eli Olds, had appeared in a small article in *Scientific American* in which his steam carriage was noted as being able to travel up to forty miles, achieving speeds of fifteen miles per hour. Interestingly, Olds had used gasoline to heat the water necessary to create the pressure for his steam engine, despite having deep familiarity with internal combustion as a builder of gasoline engines for boats on Lake Michigan. The steam-powered automobile, the article pointed out, had the virtue of silence, not scaring horses upon passing. Olds subsequently sold a model to the Francis Times Company in India, America's first export of an automobile. After several more years of tinkering, backed by investors in Michigan, he formed the Olds Motor Vehicle Company.

Much like Olds's efforts, attempts at building automobiles were often a combination of putting together available parts and engineering new parts, rather than scientific breakthrough. Functionality was measured in terms of how far and how fast given combinations could go. As electric trolleys and streetcars were in use in major cities, electric cars were also seen as a viable option in the early days, but lack of battery storage needed for long distances made the automobile a contest between internal combustion and steam power. In a large advertising supplement in 1900, the Mobile Company of America announced that it was building, somewhat speculatively, the largest automobile factory in the world—capable of turning out twenty carriages a day, each priced at $650, powered by odorless and noiseless steam engines. But gasoline-powered engines had the advantage of producing more power at lighter weight, despite the noise and odor. In gasoline-powered vehicles, the venture formed by Ransom Olds soon took the lead. In 1902 one third of the nine thousand cars sold in America were Oldsmobiles.

But Olds, after having raised over $200,000 in capital, owned very little of the company, and he soon left the company. This pattern repeated itself at other automotive ventures, where capitalists with large sums at risk pushed out less-than-compliant inventors and tinkerers, implicitly holding the view that the principles of business were universal, better known to men of capital than to myopic engineers. Seeing the local success of Oldsmobile, a Detroit plumbing supply entrepreneur named David Buick started the Buick Manufacturing Company. After selling just sixteen cars in 1903, Buick's finances were stretched, and two brothers from the sheet metal business, who had provided the metal to Buick on credit, assumed majority control of Buick. The business then switched hands to James Whiting of the Flint Wagon Works, a traditional carriage maker, who saw that the horse would give way to the automobile. Whiting then partnered with a man who had significant prior success in carriage works and had now turned his sights to organizing an automobile venture, eventually for Wall Street as much as for the public. Billy Durant, inspired by the great consolidations of the trust movement, came into control of Buick as his first building block in 1904 for what would eventually become General Motors.

Just as Ransom Olds and David Buick were sidelined as investors gained control, the chief engineer and founder of the Detroit Automobile Company, Henry Ford, met a similar fate. Having left a secure job at the Edison Illuminating Company in 1899 to focus on his sideline passion, automobiles, Ford had managed to find investors to fund his vision. But the path to a viable product had been a tricky one. After selling only a handful of cars, the company was reorganized in 1901 as the Henry Ford Company, but with Ford granted only a sliver of ownership and control. But the name change didn't prevent Ford from parting ways from his own company the following year after disputes with his controlling shareholders. Writing years later of this departure, he dismissed the former venture in terms that he considered most pejorative, calling it "merely a money-making concern," a capitalistic purpose entirely distinct from building cars.

After being pushed out, however, Ford didn't immediately move on to the practical matter of building a car for the people. In the fall of 1902, he was preoccupied by the spectacle that had gripped much of the sporting public: auto racing. In the early days, every race seemed to offer a chance to see some speed or distance record broken. It was loud, noisy, and exciting. And unlike in horse racing, there was the very real prospect of serious injury or death, which only made the whole thing all the more thrilling; the courses were often set over a distance of miles, allowing spectators to watch in close proximity as the cars sped by. Before any awareness of consumer utility set in, automobile racing made newspaper headlines both in America and in Europe.

Armed with a keen sense of public perception, Ford decided that it made sense to build his reputation by building a race car to set speed records first. In his memoir, he reflected that the public at the time believed that "a first-class car ought to be a racer," and given that the average consumer was not going to be buying either a racer or a first-class car, nuanced attributes such as luxury or dependability were not as easy to showcase as pure speed, which suggested quantifiable technical prowess on the part of the builder. This precedent carries forth to this day as large automakers invest in racing programs to demonstrate speed as a central aspect of engineering superiority. That Ford did this before incorporating his next company suggests his long-term view that the broad public would eventually be buying cars, and that to cement a reputation in racing was, in effect, an investment in marketing.

Ford, in a short-lived partnership with professional cyclist Tom Cooper, built two cars, the "Arrow" and the "999." The single-seat 999—"one life to a car was enough," quipped Ford—produced over eighty horsepower from four cylinders, along with enough noise to "kill a man." But neither Ford nor Cooper wanted to run the car as fast as it could go, especially around corners. To find a suitable driver to demonstrate their car, the men reached out to a stuntman and cyclist, Barney Oldfield, who had never driven a car before but compensated by being fearless at the prospect of fatal danger. After giving Oldfield just a week of training, Ford entered Oldfield and the 999 in a five-mile event against three other racers. Oldfield beat the field and lapped one of the other drivers, finishing the five miles in five minutes, twenty-eight seconds. Rushing fans, in their elation, carried him out on their shoulders to the judges' stand. In December Oldfield would set a record time on the same track.

The races launched two great careers. Oldfield would become one of the two most famous race car drivers in the world, along with the Swiss-born Frenchman Louis Chevrolet, who would lend his name to an American car brand. The other was Henry Ford, who, with the visibility of the demonstration, was able to raise capital immediately from a coal magnate named Alexander Malcomson. Ford then contracted with the Dodge brothers, John and Horace, to supply engines in exchange for equity in the venture. All of the relationships were further formalized in 1903 when the Ford Motor Company was incorporated with a total paid-in capital of $28,000, with Ford and Malcomson receiving 25.5 percent ownership each and the Dodge brothers 10 percent, along with smaller interests to other shareholders. Even in 1903 this was modest to the point of undercapitalization. Olds had been funded with several times this amount years before. Even Ford's earlier ventures had been better capitalized. But the Ford Motor Company would never raise capital again in Ford's lifetime.

That Ford, having gone through two automotive failures and on the verge of turning forty, looking to compete with dozens of new entries in the automotive field each year, could still raise any capital at all was an affirmation of the principles laid out by Adam Smith, and every classical economist since: That despite the risk of total loss, money finds its way to opportunity when the potential rewards are high enough. In this, the birth of the automobile was the pure free market at work. Unlike the steamboat, which developed out of a monopoly grant; or the railroad, which needed the state's power of eminent domain to provision the land needed for tracks; or the telegraph, which received $30,000 from the federal government to prove its viability; or cotton, which grew into America's top pre–Civil War export with state-sanctioned slavery; or steel, which needed tariff protection for decades to compete with British imports, the automobile was the product of the tinkerer and inventor, the iteration of thousands of mechanical minds like Ford's.

Yet paradoxes were unavoidable as capitalism advanced. In contrast to government regulation of producers to protect consumers such as in the meatpacking industry, as the automobile made its way onto roads, the government would find a more immediate need to regulate the consumers of automobiles rather than the manufacturers. Drivers on American roads, with their automobiles, were increasingly able to cause death and dismemberment to pedestrians, horse-and-carriage passengers, and one another. While the development of the automobile industry was capitalism at work, the consumer had to be regulated for the industry to thrive.

Regulation of the roads was an apt metaphor for the regulation of markets—it was possible that, left to their own devices, motorists, pedestrians, street trolleys, and horses and buggies would have come to a complex set of social understandings that morphed into traffic rules, enabling traffic to flow smoothly without the heavy hand of any new laws. Or the automobile could have added total chaos to road conditions, stifling the industry's growth and stalling its eventual immense contribution to the American economy. Rather than take a chance that this new traffic would regulate itself, it seemed far more sensible and expedient for the local authorities to put new traffic rules in place to keep up with the times—to limit the excessive speeds on roads that the new cars were capable of, for instance—much like the always-evolving set of laws that adapted to the increasingly complex commercial interests of the nation. States moved to require that automobile owners register their vehicles, that chauffeurs submit to eye exams, and that drivers get official permission in the form of driver's licenses to operate their free-market purchases. Ironically, as the cars became cheaper to own through market forces, it made the need to regulate drivers all the more urgent, to protect the public from the "class of persons who buy the cheap scrap-heap machines" as opposed to wealthier owners with their trained chauffeurs. To make matters worse for ideological free-market purists, the century's first great act of consumer capitalism, perhaps its greatest, seemed to call for the central planning of bureaucrats at various levels for the needed roadways and stoplights to make it all work, to fuse society and markets.

"He was contemptuous of money-making, of money-makers and profit seekers, yet he made more money and greater profits than those he despised. He defied accepted economic principles, yet he is the foremost exemplar of American free enterprise. He demanded efficient production, yet made place in his plant for the physically handicapped, reformed criminals, and human misfits in the American industrial system," wrote Charles Sorensen, one of Henry Ford's long-serving lieutenants. As Carnegie and Rockefeller entered their sunset years, Ford would soon become the iconoclastic titan of the first quarter of the century.

Starting with his modest amount of capital, Ford began his work on the Ford Motor Company's first car, the Model A, starting in 1903. And from the start, contradictions abounded. Ford didn't believe that the customer was always right. Indeed, he attributed the difficulties of his early competitors to their slavish need to listen to customers. To Ford this was a trap. The customers willing to pay the absolute most for a car were ones who wanted customization. But an automaker willing to customize, to cater to individual requests, lost the opportunity to scale his operation, which rested on repeating the same thing over and over again. To reduce the cost of production, a manufacturer needed to standardize components and processes. Customization, in Ford's words, led to "the habit of grabbing at the nearest dollar as though it were the only dollar in the world." Customers needed to be led, not followed.

Yet Ford invited constant feedback starting with the Model A, with the improvements affecting every car that he made in the future. The Model A was a fast success. Within the company's first nine months, the company sold 658 units, generating $354,190. From this Ford netted a profit of $98,851. For the next model year, the company introduced new models, the luxurious and large twenty-horsepower Model B, priced at $2,000, the utilitarian eight-horsepower Model C at $950, and the sportier Model F at $1,000. Sales for the fiscal year 1905 approached almost $2 million on over 1,700 cars. Ford's net income was $289,000—ten times the amount of cash invested in the company in 1903. But the strategy to move to higher price points troubled Ford, who felt that the largest part of the market existed at lower levels.

After another year of similar revenues, Ford decided to focus entirely on lower-priced models. Using a more advanced four-cylinder engine than what was in the $2,000 Model B, the Ford Motor Company promised a new model priced at close to $500. Predicting large unit volume, Ford retooled his work in anticipation. The Model N was to weigh 1,050 pounds and travel as fast as forty-five miles per hour. At the same time, Ford's relationship with his other large shareholder had become strained. After posturing on both sides, Ford, using his share of the dividends and by personally borrowing additional funds, bought out Malcomson's 255 shares for $175,000. On the brink of the Model N's launch, Ford owned 51 percent of his company.

Powered by the Model N, priced at $600, 1907 sales grew to over eight thousand cars. Ford had 20 percent of the American car market for the year. Less than five years after founding it, Henry Ford controlled a company with revenues of almost $5 million and profits exceeding $1 million. Unlike other carmakers, the immediate profitability of Ford kept its capital structure and ownership immune to outside forces. And Ford, unique in the history of American titans, kept *growing* his ownership stake as his company became larger, cementing his control to that of absolute status over time. His majority control allowed him the freedom, despite the commercial success of the Model N, to scrap everything for a new model, the Model T, for 1908.

For the first five years of the Ford Motor Company, the company introduced eight different lettered models at various price points. For the next nineteen years, the Model T would be its only product, a feat of focus that would have been impossible to pull off had there been shareholders to please. In many ways, Ford's company was the anticorporation. Whereas the corporate structure was meant to allow more investors to come in as a company grew, Ford saw this as a dilution of his vision, impairing his ability to execute. At a trial in future years battling the Dodge Brothers in a shareholder suit, one that prompted him to buy everyone out, he even disputed the notion that a company was primarily in business to make money. He expressed the inverse: Profits were the fuel of the industrial artist to make the products that he chose to; money was an ingredient, not the purpose. This rise of the Ford Motor Company, powered by the Model T's profits, into a de facto sole proprietorship, stood in stark contrast to another automotive entity that embodied exactly what it meant to be a corporation.

In the same year of the Model T's launch, Billy Durant of Buick mapped out his vision of an automotive corporation. After Durant became involved with Buick, it grew from producing a few dozen cars in 1904 to over eight thousand per year by 1908. Operating out of the largest automotive plant at the time, Buick's production exceeded Ford's. Given that Buick's cars were priced higher than Ford's, his revenues exceeded Ford's as well. But Durant never had full control of Buick and, in order to grow, had brought in ongoing infusions of capital from shareholders. And temperamentally, Durant wanted to build a large enterprise for economic gain, a more traditional purpose. He envisioned a structure similar to what he had seen the trust movement produce. After reaching out to Olds Motor Works, which had seen better days for its once-market-leading Oldsmobile, Durant proposed merging Buick with Oldsmobile. To facilitate his vision, Durant had a law firm in New Jersey incorporate General Motors, a generic name for a company that looked to consolidate car brands.

As late as 1909, a year that saw automobile sales grow from a little over 60,000 the previous year to over 120,000, the stock market had yet to see a prominent automaker list its securities. The vast majority of manufacturers were too small to merit much consideration by themselves. Durant used this market need for a car company to invest in to roll up over a dozen firms in a single year. It included parts makers such as the Champion Ignition Company, Dow Rim Company, Michigan Motor Casting, and Michigan Auto Parts; automakers included Weston-Mott, Welch Motor Car, Cartercar, Rapid Motor Vehicle, Rainier Motor Company, and Ewing Automobile Company. Most deals were in the tens or low hundreds of thousands of dollars in stock. And most were duds. The selling shareholders were enthusiastically relieved of the burden of unprofitable companies. One of the better transactions was Cadillac, which had a car priced at $1,400 that sold more than seven thousand units in 1908. Its owner, the Leland family, wanted $4.5 million in cash, which Durant couldn't pay. Ultimately the parties agreed to a little over $5 million in preferred stock and $500,000 in cash. With the strength of Buick and Cadillac, General Motors had a stellar first year ending in October 1909: gross sales of $29 million with profits of over $9 million.

General Motors and Ford would eventually become one of the great corporate rivalries, but there was no enduring icon behind the faceless General Motors, or even a great financial beneficiary. Durant, diluted down to a small ownership stake in GM when his acquisition spree was completed, found himself at the mercy of Wall Street. When GM's 1910 results had a reversal of fortune, Durant was pushed out. Resourceful and opportunistic, he would return to the fold after taking over Louis Chevrolet's nascent firm, which looked to compete with the Model T, selling the company to General Motors. Eventually General Motors would surpass Ford Motor Company in sales, but it was Ford who became the billionaire, the torchbearer of the great American fortunes, who, rather than managing an enterprise of countless brands, plants, and models, focused on building one car, available only in black.

. . .

THE MODEL T was a technological marvel. It had four cylinders producing twenty horsepower. It was light and strong: The Model T pioneered the use of vanadium steel, which had several times the tensile strength and greater flexibility than the traditional steel used in automobile bodies. Ford introduced a new gearing system for his transmission. According to the account of Ford's most trusted engineer, Charles Sorensen, the Model T had been a four-year, secretive project in development from the company's founding, an unprecedented level of research and development spent on a car that was designed to retail for less than $1,000.

But the Model T, upon its launch, was not particularly cheap. Ford's vision had not been to build an inexpensive car but to build an advanced, reliable, easy-to-use car and then lower its price. There were plenty of alternatives in the 1908 car market that were cheaper than the Model T, which was priced at $850 upon its launch. Ford's own Model N sold well through 1908. And in the magazines of the time, such as *Popular Mechanics* and *Motor Age*, in addition to thousands of newspapers, plenty of advertisements ran for crude automobiles priced below $500. The Sears catalog had one for $495. However, the technological difference between cars using the technology of 1900 and that of 1908 was significant, as it is with modern electronics and computing products.

But the Model T was far more than a product. It became the foundation of a system that, with the car's success, extended into the founder's vision of industrial and social order. In 1911 the automobile was on the verge of becoming a mainstream product with almost 200,000 vehicles purchased in 1911. As others introduced new products, Ford focused on incremental improvements and, by not changing his car dramatically, made it a car familiar to service-station mechanics nationwide, which was no small matter in the total cost of ownership. Beyond this, Ford looked to continually reduce the price of his car, surmising that as Americans shifted from the horse to the automobile, as millions did in the 1910s—over ten million cars were sold in total during the decade—basic utility and reliability, at a good price, would be the paramount considerations for most buyers, just as much as they once had been when buying a family horse. The more familiar the Model T was on American roads, the more assured a first-time buyer felt in buying it, a compounding advantage.

As his prices dropped, Ford would sell 168,000 cars for the 1912–13 model year—almost a 40 percent share of the entire American car market. But the demand strained his production methods. The scale of production meant that parts piled up at one end of the factory. Finished components in one area, such as a radiator or engine, had to be taken down to the point of final assembly. A radically different approach was needed to keep up with demand and keep costs down. Rather than assemble the large components in one location, one idea was to move the major components through the factory as they were being worked on. In Ford's recollection, he experimented with his first assembly line in April 1913. The trial involved radiators that dangled overhead and moved along the factory floor as workers welded, bolted, and hammered them along to a finished assembly. As to his source of inspiration, Ford credited as the unlikely pioneer of the moving assembly line "the overhead trolley that the Chicago packers use in dressing beef," the efficient dissection of dangling cows now inverted to making cars.

The results from the assembly of just one component, the flywheel, astonished Ford:

> With one workman doing a complete job, he could turn out thirty-five to forty pieces in a nine-hour day, or twenty minutes to an assembly. What he did alone was then spread into twenty-nine operations; that cut down the assembly time to thirteen minutes, ten seconds. Then we raised the height of the line eight inches—this was in 1914—and cut the time to seven minutes. In short, the result is this: by the aid of scientific study one man is able to do what four did only a comparatively few years ago.

This method soon found its way into every process at his factory. The final chassis assembly went from twelve hours, twenty-eight minutes down to one hour, thirty-three minutes.

In the chassis assembling, there are forty-five separate stations. The
first men fasten four mud-guard brackets to the chassis frame. The
motor arrives on the tenth operation . . . the man who places a part on
does not fasten it. The man who puts in a bolt does not put on the nut;
the man who puts on a nut does not tighten it. On operation thirty-
four, the budding motor gets its gasoline. On operation forty-four, the
radiator is filled with water, and on operation forty-five the car drives
out onto John R. Street.

It was marvelously efficient, yes, this division of labor, but it was also
mind-numbingly monotonous. The satisfaction that a man got from fully
assembling an engine over the course of a day was replaced by a single
repetitive function—it was more efficient for man to become a machine
than to act as a craftsman. But men responded in ways machines did not:
They quit often. Looking to limit turnover and keep his men attentive
on the job, Ford considered a range of compensation options. His operation had about fourteen thousand employees with a minimum wage of
26 cents per hour, or a little over $2 per day. His profits for 1913 had
been staggering: $27 million resulting from revenues of approximately
$90 million. Ford already had in place a generous eighteen-day vacation
policy from which sick days, tardiness penalties, and workplace errors
were deducted. But on a January day in 1914, Ford announced that he
was doubling the minimum wage of his employees—blacks included, but
women excluded—to $5 per day as part of a profit-sharing program. He
also reduced the workday to eight hours and instituted three shifts at
his factory. Ford's move captured front-page headlines throughout the
country, thrilling workers and alarming industrialists, who in turn had
to increase wage levels in Detroit and elsewhere.

In doing so, he gained significant leverage with his workmen to extend
both his nativism and his paternalism. He mandated English-language
lessons for his workers, many of them recent immigrants. He created a
sociological department staffed with company personnel who visited men's
homes to inspect living conditions and ask about savings rates and drinking and gambling habits, with admonitions and probationary periods given
for noncompliance. Unlike his counterparts facing unionized factories,

which prevented management from changing work rules without consent, Ford paid so well he could enter his workers' homes.

The surge of automobile production also had geographical consequences. Historians have generally regarded the 1910s as the starting point of the Great Migration, the decades-long move of African Americans from rural areas in the South to urban centers in the North. Ford's policy of applying the $5 day equally to African American men was significant— American manufacturing promised the first meaningful hope for African Americans to escape the subsistence of sharecropping in the South.

As the price of the Model T Touring model dropped to $360 by 1916, the American equation for prosperity came into focus: A mere seventy-two days of labor, less than three months, at the $5 wage per day equaled the purchase of a brand-new car. The formula made Henry Ford a national hero and an international celebrity, a man who directly touched the people through the sturdiness of every chassis assembly and door hinge, who made owning an automobile a fundamental mark of citizenship, an essential characteristic of what it meant to be an American. That an economic system would be able to provide automobiles to virtually an entire nation in the opening decades of the twentieth century was a staggering achievement, access to the open road symbolizing another form of freedom.

The widespread adoption of the automobile was industrialization's valedictory moment, a triumphant equalizer that converged the workingman and the consumer, making them one and the same, and turning him into a full participant in the dividend of American capitalism. He was only an industrial input, a wage laborer, a cog in the machine—more so than ever, perhaps—but equally, he was a beneficiary of the system's efficiency in that his purchasing power, unmatched anywhere else in the world, allowed him ownership of a car, the product of his own output in the Marxian sense. This egalitarianism, a counterargument to the Upton Sinclairs of the world, cemented capitalism as the American way, its defenders to be found across economic strata.

Twenty-two

RADIO

By 1912 Philadelphia's Wanamaker's department store was well settled with its New York outpost after taking over the operations of A. T. Stewart, the pioneer of the American department store. Looking to gain every promotional advantage in the highly competitive New York market, Wanamaker added a floor exhibit that aroused the curiosity of shoppers and satisfied the practical needs of the store's operations at the same time. It was usually manned by David Sarnoff, a twentysomething employee of Guglielmo Marconi, the inventor of wireless telegraphy. Focused intensely on the device in front of him, with a pair of headphones over his ears, Sarnoff was tasked with communicating wireless messages in Morse code to the Philadelphia store. Through the air, the messages transmitted everything from daily sales receipts to orders for resupplying items of merchandise; in addition, it handled occasional wireless transmissions from third parties.

The idea of wireless messages was not new. Newspapers throughout America, including the *New York Times*, ran stories labeled as wireless dispatches from across the Atlantic. But the technology on display at the store was still mostly novelty; the practical, wider advantages of wireless telegraphy weren't all that clear.

To begin with, the transatlantic cable laid under the ocean had been operational for decades. Its use had standardized messaging across the ocean. Wireless telegraphy, while significant in terms of technical and scientific achievement, had a limited set of uses for which the ubiquitous fixed-wire telegraphy was not a substitute. In addition, wireless messages could be picked up and deciphered by anyone with a receiver. For most communications that required any degree of confidentiality, wireless telegraphy was not an option. The one area where wireless telegraphy had immediate implications, where no fixed-wire substitute was available, was for ships out at sea.

Benefiting from a budget that had expanded significantly under Roosevelt, the U.S. Navy had outfitted a number of its vessels with wireless transmitters. A few other merchant ships and passenger steamers did the same. But the technology was by no means rapidly adopted. The equipment was expensive and required a trained radio operator to be on board. Both the American and British governments had looked to pass legislation requiring ships, at least ones carrying passengers, to have wireless equipment, but the passenger lines resisted the imposition of additional costs on their operations. But starting on a mid-April evening in 1912, sentiment changed overnight.

On April 10 the White Star Line's newest steamship, *Titanic*, the largest ship in the world, set out on its maiden voyage. Days later, it ran into an iceberg. Built at a cost of $7.5 million, it was equipped with the latest in wireless technology. Using it, the *Titanic*'s crew sent out a distress signal at 10:25 p.m.; a Marconi Wireless station in Newfoundland, Canada, received the message, along with others. It then transmitted the signal to other ships in the area. The *Virginian* was 170 miles away and was expected to reach the *Titanic* by the morning steaming at full speed. *Titanic*'s sister ship, the *Olympic*, also immediately headed to the scene, as did the *Carpathia*. By the time the *New York Times* went to press in the very early morning, the subheadlines reported the *Titanic* as SINKING BY THE BOW AT MIDNIGHT; LAST WIRELESS AT 12:27AM BLURRED. Morning readers could only guess at the likelihood of the rescue missions' success and the passengers' fates.

David Sarnoff had assumed his position at the Wanamaker's receiving station sometime during or shortly after the initial distress messages from the *Titanic*. By 2:27 a.m., Sarnoff, along with a few other operators awake at the time, had received the message that the ship had sunk.

Starting in the early hours of the next morning, the names of rescued passengers trickled into Sarnoff's post, as did the names of passengers who were confirmed deceased. The newspapers had circulated the start of the story in print, but the fact that the operator at Wanamaker's was receiving real-time updates from the middle of the ocean was news in and of itself. Crowds, not wishing to wait for printed editions carrying old news, rushed to the department store. Others made their way to Times Square, where a lighted bulletin board displayed news in real time. In the enclosed booth at Wanamaker's, the sons of two prominent men on board the ship, Isidor Straus and John Jacob Astor IV, watched over Sarnoff's shoulder. Straus was the head of the rival Macy's department stores, and Astor was the reigning patriarch of one of America's most storied fortunes. For three days the names came in. The *Carpathia*, after rescuing many of the freezing passengers, began heading to New York. Before long, it was clear that the death toll was going to far exceed the number of survivors. Straus and Astor, choosing to not take up precious lifeboat seats, had perished along with more than 1,500 others. About 700 survived.

Before the final fate of the *Titanic* was clear, its collision had set off an isolated financial panic. The insurance syndicate Lloyd's of London had underwritten risk for centuries through a loose affiliation of wealthy men, simply known as "names." Names collected insurance premiums in exchange for agreeing to pay up if an insured risk manifested in losses. Many names had come together to underwrite the *Titanic*'s policy. But given that the great ship had been built with watertight compartments, the risk of loss had been deemed minimal when the ship was insured. Once wireless communication with the ship was lost, underwriters scrambled to sell off portions of their exposure to others. Each passing hour that it took for rescue ships to reach the scene increased the tension and speculation.

But all was not loss. In addition to insurance companies, the press and the public both came to immediately understand the lifesaving implications of wireless technology. So did speculators and stock promoters. By Friday of the tragic week, Marconi Wireless Telegraph Company shares had jumped from $170 to $245. Not wishing to squander the opportunity made possible by tragedy, the company announced that it was increasing its capital base to $10 million—as the current holders of shares would have the first rights to purchase the new shares, this had made the existing shares even more attractive, propelling their rise. Another catalyst for the rise of Marconi's fortunes came from the developments in Washington. Within forty-eight hours of the initial news, President William Howard Taft had been alarmed at the extent of interference with important news by amateur wireless operators; he issued an emergency directive ordering all operators to stop transmitting. In the completely unregulated environment, when two or more operators attempted to communicate at the same time, the frequencies would get jammed, making coherent communication impossible. The fact that wireless was still limited to telegraphy, where the long and short sounds of Morse code were the entirety of the protocol, compounded the problem. Within days, the administration called for the nation's airwaves to be placed under federal control. The specter of drastic regulation in the wireless business, ironically, added to the dramatic rise in Marconi's shares. Chaos in the air was not good for business.

In a situation perhaps unprecedented in the annals of American capitalism to that time, it seemed clear to the patent holders, investors, and governments that the early development of the industry called for a form of absolute authority. If anyone with equipment was allowed to transmit anything at any time, there would be no way for viable commercial practices to develop. If the nation's airwaves were clogged by transmissions, it would limit the opportunities of the medium. Its growth exposed the private market's conundrum with regard to radio frequencies: They were an exploitable, invisible medium that no one owned or had exclusive right to—who owned the air?—but that suddenly had immense practical value. Yet if everyone exploited the right simultaneously, the right would continue to have no value, as no one could effectively use it. For frequencies to become an actual property right, the laws of the applicable government had to recognize them as a form of property, not just a scientific phenomenon. To maximize the utility of the wireless spectrum, the simple solution was for the government to assert complete ownership of the nascent airwaves, after which it would ration and allocate transmission authority to private parties. Officials from the Marconi Wireless Telegraph Company, the exclusive holders of the most important wireless patents, helped shape this authority. Marconi wanted to sell equipment and license stations—the less haphazard its development, the more profitable the industry was likely to be. The stock market agreed.

Within a week of the sinking of the *Titanic*, the entire U.S. regulatory approach to wireless telegraphy, which would carry into broadcast media and frequencies of all types, came into focus. It made invisible airwaves a form of property to be owned, leased, licensed, or sold.

THE SINKING of the *Titanic* was the biggest news event of Taft's last year as president. Undercut by his predecessor, Teddy Roosevelt, who ran as a third-party candidate of the Bull Moose Party, taking away valuable votes, Taft lost the 1912 election to Woodrow Wilson. Wilson became just the second Democratic president, after Grover Cleveland, elected since the Civil War. Remarkably, the sinking of another ship would define Wilson's first term.

America by now had achieved its standing as the undisputed economic power among nations. It led the world in the production of food, steel, oil, and automobiles. It had the most miles of railroad track. Of the large nations, it boasted the highest wages. It maintained this position despite absorbing up to one million new immigrants per year. But it was relatively isolated. Across the oceans, other nations too had grown in strength relative to their Old World neighbors. Germany, once a loose federation, had coalesced into the leading industrial power in Europe. Japan had made such remarkable strides that the world had been shocked at its victory in its war with Russia in 1906. Territorially, colonial powers such as Great Britain and France maintained influence across the world, but other old empires, such as the Ottoman, had been waning for decades. The centuries-old Habsburg Empire, as Austria-Hungary, had receded to being a secondary power in central Europe. China, after centuries of dynastic rule, had dethroned its last emperor. These powers, along with their challengers, didn't have oceans as barriers, as America did.

Instead they had alliances. When Austria-Hungary's Archduke Ferdinand and his wife were assassinated in Sarajevo in June 1914, it set off a sudden, cataclysmic series of events. Given that the assassin was a Serbian nationalist, Austria-Hungary threatened Serbia, which had allegiances with Russia, which incited Austria's ally Germany. On Wednesday, August 3, the *New York Times'* multi-line headline described the culmination:

RUSSIA INVADES GERMANY; GERMANY INVADES FRANCE,
BUT DOES NOT DECLARE WAR; ENGLAND'S DECISION TODAY;
BELGIUM MENACED, LUXEMBOURG AND SWITZERLAND INVADED;
GERMAN MARKSMEN SHOOT DOWN A FRENCH AEROPLANE

The world's great powers were at war, with the United States as the neutral exception. America had paid its own internal price a half century earlier, when it had shed its blood to keep its vast territory together through warfare. American grandfathers and former soldiers, now in their seventies, remembered the Civil War, as did Carnegie and Rockefeller, who were still alive. Since those dark days, these men had seen their country's exhilarating, unceasing growth. What's more, America's natural ally in the conflict overseas was not all that clear. Much of industrial America had been built by millions of Germans and their descendants. Millions of Americans had Irish blood and no great love for Great Britain. In the new century, millions upon millions of immigrants had come here from Russia, Eastern Europe, Italy, and the Slavic countries. The melting pot seemed to have a created an ethnic hedge against participation in foreign wars.

But the hedge wore down over time. In the waters off Britain and northern Europe, the British navy was policing an embargo to shut off the seas to German trade, which the Germans countered with submarines. As a neutral party, American-flagged vessels were permitted to sail unobstructed even in contested waters. But according to the German allegations, the British passenger vessel *Lusitania* had deceptively and repeatedly sailed under the American flag. Understanding the dangers of inciting an American response accidentally, the Germans had even taken out advertisements in American newspapers, below the travel timetables of ocean liners, warning Americans against traveling in contested waters. In May 1915, with the Great War less than ten months old, torpedoes fired by a German submarine destroyed the *Lusitania*. Along with almost a thousand others on board, dozens of Americans died. The Germans, with some evidence, claimed that the *Lusitania* had carried munitions on board, including explosives, a practice that eliminated its immunity as a passenger ship.

With memories of the *Titanic* still fresh, intentionally sinking a passenger steamer was regarded as a shocking and unforgivable act. Still, President Wilson, a scholar and historian, resisted the calls to action. From the sidelines, Teddy Roosevelt seethed at what he considered a weak and tepid response. Yet others felt that American passengers, in a sense, had been used as shields by the British to transport weapons and materiel. William Jennings Bryan, the three-time Democratic nominee and Progressive icon, was one of these men. Appointed by Wilson as secretary of state, Bryan resigned his post to protest Wilson's partiality to the British posture. Still, for now, the official position of the United States remained one of neutrality.

But an unofficial position started developing commercially. With British industry unable to keep up with wartime demands, Britain and her allies turned to America. In 1916 American exports doubled to $5.4 billion from the previous year's $2.7 billion. American factories became the engine for Europe's war. America's trade surplus grew to over $1 billion. It received a net transfer of over $500 million in physical gold, mostly from British vaults. Soon Britain and France were borrowing significant sums of money from American financiers to finance purchases of American goods. Exports of finished manufactures of all kinds tripled to $2.6 billion from 1915's $800 million. While businessmen and companies found a most willing set of customers overseas, Wilson's reelection campaign featured the slogan "He Kept Us Out of War."

But the slogan couldn't hold. A few days before the start of Wilson's second term, under pressure to win the war, the Germans announced an escalation of submarine warfare, declaring all areas accessible to England and France via water subject to submarine attacks. But a German declaration of open warfare in international waters, including upon American ships, not only was an affront to American sovereignty but also was going to cut off American commercial ties to Britain and Europe, now worth billions of dollars. Then another shoe dropped. In the midst of their own prosecution of the war, the Russians had an internal revolution. The czar abdicated his throne. The largest nation in the war, by population, effectively ended its participation. Two weeks later, understanding the dramatic disruption in the balance of forces, Wilson called for a declaration of war. Over the course of 1917, America began its role in European affairs and the communists filled the power vacuum in Russia.

Overnight, America began to add a military dimension to its economic identity. It had virtually no standing army. It had few bases. It needed to raise billions of dollars almost immediately. The Progressive Era had led the federal government to become a counterforce to the rising power of corporations. Now the federal government was tasked with harnessing the industrial capacity of corporations to intervene in the conflict among the world's great powers. But something would be permanently lost. Every idea of limited government was, in the context of militarization, drained of its power. Patriotism paved the way for an all-powerful government, and much of the productive engine of American capitalism became an instrument of the state.

Most corporations put up little resistance. War paid well. In 1918 war spending would push total federal expenditures to $12.7 billion. In 1916 the government's budget was $734 million. Even once peace was declared, however, annual spending would never again fall below $3 billion. War had enlarged the state permanently. To finance this massive escalation, the government had two mechanisms: first, the issuance of bonds, aptly named Liberty Bonds, advertised to savers through magazines and newspapers; second, the authority granted by the first constitutional amendment in over fifty years. The Sixteenth Amendment, passed by Congress in 1909 and ratified by the states in 1913, authorized the income tax. When the income tax was first challenged in 1895, the Supreme Court's majority opinion held that with direct federal taxation of income, states with a concentration of wealthy individuals and corporations bore a disproportionate share of the federal burden. This made it unconstitutional until Progressive elements, during a Republican presidency, finally succeeded in amending the constitution. When America mobilized for war, revenue from the income tax quickly exceeded all other previous sources of tax revenue—namely the tariff on imports and taxes on liquor, beer, and tobacco.

With this money, the government became the largest customer of many of the largest industries. Steel was diverted to shipbuilders, gunmakers, and armorers. Railroads were in effect nationalized on a temporary basis as a part of wartime logistics. Food production went into overdrive to feed the American and foreign armies. Americans were encouraged to have a day a week without meat, another without sweets, and another without heat. A draft was instituted—ten million men received a number for a lottery to determine who went—demonstrating that in times of national need, the state even owned the individual. And unlike in the Civil War, a man couldn't pay for an alternate to take his place.

Some of the money was spent on scaling new technologies. The military asked the automobile industry for aircraft engines. Since the Wright Brothers' flight in 1903, total production of aircraft in the country had barely exceeded 100 in many years. It reached 416 in 1916. In 1918 over 14,000 aircraft were produced in the United States, 13,991 for the U.S. military alone. Much of this effort started with a contract for the Liberty motor, an aircraft engine. Packard, Cadillac, and Ford received orders in the thousands, in addition to their other wartime contracts. The new Lincoln Motor Car Company, founded by Henry Leland in 1917 after he had left Cadillac, produced the Liberty motor before it ever produced an actual car. In addition to aircraft, the government took over the airwaves. The navy ordered all radio patents and technologies to be put into its service for the duration of the war.

By November 1918, the war was over. The worldwide death toll was in the millions. American participation had lasted less than eighteen months and resulted in over 100,000 deaths. France, Russia, Germany, and Austria lost over a million men each. The late entry of fresh American troops and unlimited American resources, when all other economies had been stretched and exhausted, proved to be the decisive factor.

WAR ALSO PROVED to be a laboratory, an urgent stage upon which technology advanced in remarkably compressed time frames. Wireless telegraphy, going by "radio" during warfare, made considerable strides during the war years as a vital mechanism for coordinating troop movements and naval deployments. Developments on the seas were transmitted back to Washington in real time. With the help of the private sector, General Electric in particular, the navy financed the development of the world's most powerful transmitters. Since the Marconi patents were not exclusive or proprietary to the United States, the transmission technology owned by GE was an American edge. Other American companies, such as GE's rival, Westinghouse, and American Telephone and Telegraph, seeing opportunities in wireless, developed their own radio patents during the war years.

Most incongruously, so did the United Fruit Company, which primarily grew bananas. Before the war, the company was perhaps the largest industrial user of wireless telegraphy. Across countries in Central America and islands in the Caribbean, the company owned millions of acres on which it grew fruit. Employing large native populations in these "banana republics," the company matched its landholdings with the equivalent of a private navy. Unlike other industrial goods, fruit was perishable. Once an area was picked of its fruit, say, bananas in a remote part of Jamaica, the fruit needed to be placed on board a steamer with refrigeration. The ability to communicate with ships at sea and route them to the right location eliminated costly spoilage and allowed fruit picking to be optimized. In a real sense, radio communications lowered the cost of bananas for consumers in New York. As every degree of efficiency impacted the bottom line, the company had developed its own proprietary methodologies.

But the secretary of the navy, Josephus Daniels, felt security considerations were more important than the cost of bananas and other private interests. He resisted the idea of the radio patents and technologies going back to private hands, a stance that set the trajectory of the radio industry. Immediately after the war, Guglielmo Marconi himself had met with Owen D. Young, then a senior executive at GE. Negotiating for Marconi's American and British operations, Marconi wanted to license GE's transmission patents and buy the most powerful transmitters in the world. After agreeing in principle to the terms, Young notified the navy as a courtesy. But the undersecretary of the navy, Franklin Delano Roosevelt, immediately ordered the negotiations stopped. The navy offered an alternative. It had purchased a vast assortment of patents in the buildup to war. It suggested to GE that a new company be formed, to which the government's radio interests would be contributed. This way, leadership in the field of radio would not fall into foreign hands.

With the navy's message clear that GE was not to act as a seller, Young reversed the transaction with Marconi, proposing to buy his operations in America instead. Marconi shareholders, understanding the risks of confronting an operator with a large portfolio of patents and the American government on its side, agreed to sell. With this deal in hand, GE then sponsored a new company called the Radio Corporation of America that combined GE's patents and the navy's, along with the receiving stations of Marconi Wireless. The new corporation, RCA, consisted of many of the old Marconi employees, including David Sarnoff, the young operator at Wanamaker's department store during the fateful night of the *Titanic* disaster.

Sarnoff, with his star quickly rising at RCA, saw radio's potential beyond its use as a wireless telegraph. Enough technology existed at the time to enable audio to be emitted through the air with increasing clarity. It was less clear what business model would merit investment in this line of expansion. Sarnoff was aware that experimental transmitting stations had occasionally played music, which amateur operators heard through headphones. Sarnoff wrote out a plan for his boss that suggested RCA sell music boxes capable of receiving radio signals. If the existing RCA stations, outfitted for telegraphic transmission, could transmit music, news, or other forms of entertainment on a consistent basis, the American household would eventually buy a box that was capable of receiving the broadcast. At $75, Sarnoff projected RCA could sell 100,000 boxes in the first year; by the third year, Sarnoff projected that the sale of 600,000 music boxes would generate $45 million in revenues.

With GE's endorsement, Sarnoff took the concept of the music box to Dr. Alfred Goldsmith, an inventor known to the former Marconi executives. To Sarnoff's delight, Goldsmith had a particularly suitable device in an advanced experimental form. Built out of wood, with a speaker encased inside, Goldsmith's "radiola" had a dial each for volume and frequency tuning, along with a place for batteries.

But there was a problem: The ability of wireless equipment to play audio was covered by patents owned by AT&T. With over ten million household and business customers and hundreds of millions of dollars in revenues from its telephone business, AT&T was actively looking to bring wired music into homes through telephone wires. With GE's transmission technology looking more viable, it decided to cede the opportunity to RCA. In exchange for about 10 percent ownership of RCA, AT&T agreed to cross-license the patents.

Next Sarnoff ran into another giant's ambitions. An inventor named Edwin Howard Armstrong had come up with a tuner that heightened the sensitivity of the wireless signal, resulting in far clearer sound. Armstrong, however, had sold his patents to Westinghouse Electric for $355,000. Westinghouse had even operated a couple of stations in Pittsburgh and was looking to enter the radio device market—it had started broadcasting to create demand for a potential market. But Westinghouse needed the patents that AT&T and GE owned to complete its portfolio. RCA made a deal. In exchange for giving Westinghouse a 20 percent ownership stake in RCA, RCA received the Westinghouse patents. In addition, Westinghouse received the right to manufacture 40 percent of all of the radio sets to be sold under the RCA brand, with GE manufacturing the other 60 percent. Lastly, United Fruit Company bought a 4 percent ownership interest in RCA for $1 million in cash and the contribution of its powerful looping antenna technology.

The era of broadcast communications was launched by these rounds of deal making, and RCA became the exact opposite of the archetypal American start-up. Its founders were giant corporations GE, AT&T, and

Westinghouse under the direction of the U.S. Navy. These three corporations, founded to magnify the respective visions of Thomas Edison, Alexander Graham Bell, and George Westinghouse respectively, had now become institutional powers, durable enough to move beyond iconic innovators and financiers such as Morgan, who had put GE together. In the birth of the radio, the modern corporation—which had been birthed by New Jersey law just one generation earlier—highlighted that it could both be an instrument of the state and grow vastly beyond the power of any one individual.

To PROVE the allure of radio, Sarnoff needed a spectacle. Baseball was the American pastime, but no sport could match the thrill of the heavyweight championship bout, fought in grueling three-minute rounds. Boxing's heavyweight champion, by default, was the most famous athlete in the world—Babe Ruth and baseball meant nothing across the ocean. In 1921 the heavyweight champion, Jack Dempsey, was set to face French challenger Georges Carpentier in a highly anticipated match. The bout, to take place at a facility known as Boyle's Thirty Acres in Jersey City, was expected to shatter all known attendance records. Understanding the significance of the event, Sarnoff asked his bosses for permission to broadcast the event. After making a deal with the fight promoters, Sarnoff borrowed transmission equipment from the navy and GE and strung up a makeshift broadcast operation. He then arranged to equip a few local facilities and theaters with speakers for fans to listen to the fight.

In front of this record crowd of ninety thousand, Dempsey would knock out Carpentier in the fourth round. Moments after the knockout, the broadcast transmitter melted, but it had worked for the fifteen important minutes that it needed to. Thousands of people in the specially outfitted locations, including one in Times Square, heard a live audio account of the fight in amazement.

Within a year, the radio industry was booming. It even had its own trade magazines full of advertisements for tools, components, batteries, and advice for radio merchants starting in the industry. The premiere issue of *Radio Dealer* noted that over 25,000 amateur broadcasters had set up transmitting stations on allowed frequencies. Dozens of radio manufacturers raced to install radios in homes. At the same time, the *Radio Dealer* warned its commercial readers of an emerging scourge: "Any attempts to put over 'advertising stunts' should be nipped in the bud." The industry's assumption was that the future of the business was in the sale of transmission equipment and home radios, antennae, and installation services. The fear was that attempts to commercialize the actual content away from amateurs would destroy the airwaves and thereby the radio equipment business.

Others saw things differently. David Sarnoff, now RCA's general manager, described content programming as a job for "specialists" with "expert knowledge of the public's taste." In his view, with the audience for broadcast potentially larger than for any other medium, the business of broadcasting needed to be separated from the business of manufacturing radio equipment. Still, Sarnoff didn't see far enough. He expected radio makers to directly fund the operations of professional broadcasters as a public service. Sarnoff had the content model right but the business model wrong.

A few stations, starting with one owned by AT&T, started broadcasting messages for advertisers. Within a couple of years, AT&T's broadcast activities had become far more professional. Baseball games and highlights, news reports, music, and other forms of entertainment soon made their way onto the air. AT&T, as the nation's telephone company, owned an advanced wiring system that enabled small and distant radio broadcasters nationwide to pick up programming from hundreds of miles away—with this, a small station in Maine could pick up a signal from Washington DC via a wire and broadcast the signal to a local audience. Rather than have countless stations develop their own expensive programming, AT&T's primary station, WEAF, allowed other local stations to broadcast a programming block. With its national infrastructure and early entry into broadcast advertising, AT&T's national broadcast operation was profitable. For RCA, GE, and Westinghouse to compete with AT&T in national radio, they ironically needed actual physical wires connecting distant stations.

In the midst of ongoing patent disputes with AT&T, Sarnoff now looked to merge the experimental broadcast interests of RCA, Westinghouse, and GE into a new broadcast company. After protracted negotiations and subtle maneuvering detailed in countless letters, RCA persuaded AT&T to sell its broadcast operations in exchange for other concessions. With AT&T's assets, in 1926, GE, Westinghouse, and RCA together formed the National Broadcasting Company, a national network that produced programming for pickup by local affiliates throughout America. Within a few years, William Paley, an entrepreneur with no technical roots in radio, would cobble together his own network of local stations, calling it the Columbia Broadcasting System, CBS, to compete with NBC.

Throughout the twenties, Americans bought millions of radio units, with thousands of radio stations broadcasting all manner of programming. For millions of rural Americans, the battery-powered radio was often the first electric device in the household. Even at the end of the war in 1918, strikingly, only half of American homes had been wired for electricity, with rural households largely left out. Before the pleasures of Edison's lightbulb and the alternating-current standard propagated by Westinghouse became ubiquitous, the next generation of their respective corporations brought pop culture to the nation's living rooms, where Americans in the city and out in the country huddled to spend their evenings—often in a collective trance, listening to the same thing at the same time for the first time in history.

Twenty-three

BOOTLEGGING

Just as government influence set the trajectory for the development of the radio, federal action set into motion another defining element of 1920s America: Prohibition. It was one of the most improbable political achievements in history. A democratic nation with millions of drinkers who could vote, 300,000 locally operated saloons serving as the hub for workingmen, and the nation's fifth-largest industry were all powerless to stop a perfect storm of political forces.

The storm had been building from multiple directions for decades. Women found the temperance movement to be a fertile outlet for their rising political voice. Moral crusaders argued that the use of alcohol was destructive to the social fabric and to American productivity. Other factions associated saloons and alcohol consumption with the lowly immigrants who formed the urban base of America. Progressive icons, including William Jennings Bryan, had been vociferous about the need for betterment of society through the absence of alcohol. Business leaders like Henry Ford discouraged its use by their employees. Even the navy had been ordered alcohol free on ships and bases early in Wilson's administration. The problem, as framed by Prohibition's advocates, was that America had become a nation of drunkards. The only people in favor of alcohol seemed to be people who liked to drink and the business-men who had made fortunes serving them.

But since the 1860s, there had been one other constituent that was very interested in the ongoing flow of liquor and beer: the U.S. Treasury. Before the First World War, a full one third of the entire budget of the federal government was financed by taxing beer and spirits. In effect, America had a regressive tax system. Workingmen with a taste for drink spent a greater portion of their incomes on alcohol than did the wealthiest men. And with the government dependent on this base of revenue, the brewers and distillers held the most effective weapon against the risk of federal legislation.

But with the American entry into the war, the weapon lost its potency. The new income tax that was used to finance the war immediately dwarfed the importance of all other sources. Suddenly the couple of hundred million dollars from liquor and beer taxation didn't seem as significant—the new income tax was delivering revenues in the billions. The ethnicity of the brewers didn't help either, given that America was now at war with Germany. The most powerful lobbying group in the industry, the United States Brewers' Association, was so true to its roots that it still conducted much of its internal business in spoken and written German. The Busch family, in control of Budweiser, up to the war held a large annual celebration for the Kaiser's birthday every year. In addition, the Brewers' Association was aggressive politically. They financed newspapers and their share of politicians. But the brewers overplayed their hand given the changed circumstances.

In the initial months of the war, a petition representing nearly six million women was presented to the president calling for a temporary ban on beer, suggesting that the grain used for beer could be diverted to making millions of loaves of bread daily for the Allied war effort. This argument was not without precedent: Britain, vitally dependent by then on American grain production, had placed limited restrictions on beer when it first became engaged in the war and, mirroring the efforts in America, saw renewed attacks on beer in Parliament calling for a full ban. Soon afterward, a funding bill made its way through Congress, detailing a wartime prohibition until the cessation of hostilities. Predictably, the Brewers' Association attacked it with their full force, causing congressmen to capitulate in the face of the powerful lobby and attempt to water down the legislation. This backfired on the brewers. Supporters of the original bill were outraged enough at its stripping down that Congress passed a more stringent bill, which called for total prohibition via a constitutional amendment. Given the patriotic backdrop and anti-German sentiment that came with American engagement in the war, many representatives and senators felt compelled to go along with the amendment, taking comfort in the belief that the next step was all but impossible: three fourths of the individual states would have to approve the measure to actually change the Constitution.

The first states to ratify this dramatic expansion of federal power were in the South, the same ones that generally claimed the supremacy of states' rights when it came to matters of race. South Carolina, just as it had done during the income tax amendment, this time along with Mississippi and Virginia, was among the first five states to approve federal authority over an entire industry. The South as a whole, as the nation's strongest Democratic constituency, enthusiastically appreciated the merits of federal authority when it came to matters of taxation and Prohibition—every member of the former Confederacy ratified both constitutional amendments.

Shockingly, by January 1919, three fourths of states had approved the Eighteenth Amendment. It was flawed from the start. It didn't prohibit Americans from consuming beverages—it was a supply-side modification, banning only the "manufacture, sale, or transportation" of alcohol. The amendment then left the legislative details to Congress. The National Prohibition Act, commonly known as the Volstead Act for its author, Andrew Volstead, specified restrictions on beverages containing more than one half of 1 percent alcohol. Enforcement and investigative authority would fall to the commissioner of internal revenue.

Less shockingly, the political bargaining process led to some exemptions. When the act went into effect in 1920, it allowed homemade "fruit juices" and cider for consumption exclusively in the home. It also carved out an exemption for syrups and extracts that contained alcohol but were not beverages at the time when they were sold. Sacramental wine, lobbied for by rabbis and Catholics, was allowed on religious grounds with virtually no restrictions. Given the need for alcohol in certain medicines, physicians were permitted to issue prescriptions for remedies that happened to contain intoxicating substances. Ever adaptive, Americans would learn to drink to God and health.

GOD'S WORK STARTED in earnest in the fertile fields of northern California. Anticipating enforcement of Prohibition, an enterprising editor named H. F. Stoll had decided to start publishing a trade magazine called the *California Grape Grower* to keep farmers updated. Within a year, the grape business was booming. The Italian-American Bank, to be known later as Bank of America, advertised its services with the headline HOW TO FINANCE DISTANT SHIPMENTS OF GRAPE PRODUCTS. It offered to help growers, getting newly acclimated to the wider market, collect proceeds from "far-away" sales. A trading firm in Pittsburgh, Leo G. Altmayer, marketed itself to the Californians as a broker in fresh and dried grapes with the ability to reach sixty million people in the East within twelve hours from its warehouses. Equipment makers advertised distillers, extractors, and high-vacuum evaporators to convert the grape into a concentrated form.

Stoll, judging by the tone of his editorial on his publication's one-year anniversary, was exultant. When the act's fruit juice exemption was finalized, "as if by magic, California became the Mecca for grape speculators." Growers and speculators in the grape districts had already sensed the enthusiasm over the summer of 1920 when prices were a healthy $50 per ton. But by the end of the growing season, trading had produced "unheard of prices," jumping to "$75, $100, $125, and $150 a ton for ordinary wine grapes." The "700 wineries of California have been supplanted by millions of home manufacturers of wine," who needed grapes and grape concentrate.

His editorial turned more philosophical: "Men who are otherwise law-abiding citizens have no respect for this particular law." And in his telling, the federal government was not going to spend the appropriate resources on enforcement. Weakening Prohibition further, the states refused to help enforce the federal law that they had ratified into a constitutional amendment. The politics had inverted. Drinkers, disorganized and outmaneuvered, had been blindsided—there was no prodrinking political movement. With federal law now firmly on the side of temperance forces, drinking Americans on the opposite side made sure to exert themselves at the state level, pressing local and state officials to render Prohibition toothless.

The growers had become emboldened to the point where Stoll ran columns on branding syrups with "winning trade names." He suggested that growers look to the soft-drink industry to come up with names, as the grape brands Zesto, BoneDry, and Whistle had just done. One grower decided to take a more biblically taunting approach with "Forbidden Fruit." Other growers were more concerned that "consumers remained woefully ignorant" of grape varieties such as the petite sirah, vastly preferring zinfandels. Still, California sold 250,000 tons of grapes in 1921. Bad law had made for such good business, the *Grape Grower* couldn't help but publish some euphoric poetry:

> The season opened with a whiz;
> From every angle looked like biz.
> The yield was fair, quality grand;
> Prices established, bids on hand.
> O happy day, happy day
> When booze was banned and grape held sway.

Prohibition provided less cause for celebration elsewhere. The urban saloon, which had served as the afternoon cafeteria with its free lunch and the evening living room, was gone. Large companies such as Anheuser-Busch, Pabst, Schlitz, and others that had financed and supplied the saloons were shells of their former selves. Some attempted to market nonalcoholic beers or carbonated beverages. And homemade wine, by itself, did not satiate the market previously supplied by the legitimate liquor and beer industries. In 1921, the first full year of Prohibition, in one analysis, alcohol consumption dropped to 30 percent of the pre-Prohibition level.

Many wealthy men and institutions, however, had legally stocked up on alcohol before the law went into effect. Since the act did not prohibit consumption, basements in many of America's elite neighborhoods had personal caches comparable to modest liquor stores. The Yale Club in New York had procured a supply that would last fourteen years. For the less affluent, physicians with their prescription pads were more than accessible. In a concession to rural states at the time of the Volstead Act's passing, farmers had been given an exemption for hard cider for home use. The urban working class, living paycheck to paycheck, was shut out from the neighborhood saloon, which provided a social reprieve from the tight quarters of urban housing, but kept the private members-only clubs in continued good spirits. To the moralists in the temperance movement, removing the scourge of alcohol from the American underclass had been one of the main objectives. In that regard, Prohibition appeared to be working.

But the pendulum had swung too far the other way. The progressive crusade to limit what people put in their bodies had led to food and drug laws. Curtailments of corporate power had balanced interests with equitable labor laws. To many, it was now clear that any power or political movement, no matter how well intentioned or righteous its origins, would grow until its momentum was stopped.

If the Progressive era had marked a growing appreciation and respect for the power of the government as a check on free markets, Prohibition marked a time when Americans rejected government with every sip of strong drink. Millions came to appreciate that the market, conversely, could act as democratic check on legislative overreach. Restrictions merely added a price premium to account for the risks of the seller and inconvenience of the buyer, but then again, booze was now tax free. Outlaw heroes mocked the Constitution instead of earnestly adhering to it. To the workingman, politics looked privileged and unrepresentative. The president could serve scotch in the White House, but a free man couldn't have a beer? Even the communists in Russia had rolled back the czar's restrictions on vodka. Moral living was perhaps desirable, but the liberty to be immoral seemed vital. Prohibition added a defiant edge to American culture. The Republic reasserted itself. And if one law could be openly and widely broken, why not a host of social conventions along with it?

. . .

ONE OF AMERICA'S most famous men faced a conundrum regarding the fate of his second career. In his first career, Jack Johnson had stood distinct as the least popular heavyweight champion in American history. His sins were numerous. He was black. He was articulate. He was prideful. Troublingly, Johnson dated white women, which had made him the target of law enforcement. Adding to the litany of affronts, he looked rich with his tailored suits and sports cars. In attempts to unseat this most detestable champion, the sport had proffered up Jim Jeffries as the "Great White Hope" to take the title back to the right race. But Johnson shattered this hope in fourteen rounds. Eventually, with age, Johnson lost the title. Like countless other African Americans, Johnson made his new home in Harlem, opening a nightclub there in 1920.

By then, Harlem had become the center of an African American renaissance, a point of cultural arrival. In a triumphantly worded essay in 1925, the executive secretary of the NAACP wrote that Harlem had become "the greatest Negro city in the world." The author, James Weldon Johnson, recounted with no small measure of pride that 175,000 African Americans now occupied "twenty-five solid blocks" of New York City. This takeover had unfolded with astonishing speed. The vast majority of Harlem's population had been born in the South and taken up residence in New York over the past decade, at the start of African Americans' Great Migration north. And Harlem's location as a "city within a city" in America's cultural capital attracted "the enterprising, the ambitious, and the talented of the whole Negro world," wrote Johnson. Notably, Harlem attracted artists and musicians, which, as Prohibition took hold, were the ingredients for thrilling, illicit nightlife that soon attracted whites.

One of its biggest and most notable nightclubs started as a transformation of Johnson's dining club, which Johnson sold to a gangster named Owney Madden, who then changed its name to the "Cotton Club." Presumably, the last thing the former champion needed was to be the proprietor of a club as criminal elements entered the business. Under Madden's ownership, the now-exclusive Cotton Club didn't allow blacks to mingle with whites. But its stage did. With this door opened, black musicians stood in command with an energetic, free-flowing genre called jazz. Modern jazz, as enjoyed at the Cotton Club, was a dazzling combination of playing, singing, and dancing with the full sounds of clarinets, trumpets, and trap drums. Jazz came to define the age, an emerging art linked to Prohibition. Unlike in the minstrel acts and subordinated roles blacks often took on in front of whites, jazz had black artists pushing a vibrant art form to the forefront of culture. Considering that every establishment serving alcohol was already breaking the law, the venues lent themselves to experimentation of all sorts, including the mingling of races in many clubs.

Nightlife and the "speakeasy" became synonymous—to get into one of the countless speakeasies that popped up during Prohibition, one was expected to "speak easy" and discreetly. And speakeasies brought in the growing presence of women as a central part of nightlife. To traditional America, still living on farms, the idea of a liberated urban woman, as portrayed in silent films, radio programs, and magazine articles—single and able to work, drive, drink, and listen to jazz—signaled a new modern age. Set against this cultural vitality, the temperance movement seemed to be moving toward comical levels of stridency. With alcohol beaten back, the Woman's Christian Temperance Union had set its sights on Coca-Cola. Asa Candler, Coke's great organizer, had once been a temperance advocate. Whether this view was commercially motivated is not known, but the commercial results were less ambiguous. Coca-Cola sales started skyrocketing immediately after Prohibition. The thousands of miles of new roads in the twenties brought Americans into frequent contact with service stations. Along with gasoline, many served ice-cold, refreshing Coca-Cola. Coca-Cola signs, adorned with pretty young faces, were ubiquitous. But Coca-Cola contained caffeine. It had once been targeted for its cocaine content, but now the "dope"—as some anachronistic southerners still called Coca-Cola—was being assailed for its addictive properties. This charge went nowhere. If anything, it exposed the addictive nature of having a political voice, where one victory was a stimulant to seek another.

Others understood the times much better—indeed, they defined them. Already a celebrated author, F. Scott Fitzgerald touched on the moral ambiguities of the law and the marketplace in his 1925 novel *The Great Gatsby*. His protagonist, Jay Gatsby, is the mysterious and ostentatiously wealthy neighbor of the story's narrator. As the story moves through its characters' inherited wealth and casual immorality, the source of Gatsby's fortune comes under some scrutiny by the story's antagonist, Tom Buchanan, who insinuates that the too-polished Gatsby was in the drugstore business in Chicago. Without the need for further elaboration, readers of the era understood well that drugstores, fueled by prescriptions for alcohol and sometimes fronts for bootleggers, were booming during Prohibition. The drugstore chain Walgreens, with twenty-two stores at the beginning of Prohibition, had more than five hundred stores by its end. But Tom's attempts to discredit Gatsby ring hollow. In Fitzgerald's prose, the high society of drinkers and revelers were given no greater moral standing than the sellers of their pleasure, gangsters included.

To many it seemed obvious that the crusaders behind Prohibition had created a new class of commercial aspirants beyond drugstore operators and grape growers. The legitimate industry that had thrown off billions of dollars in profits over the years might have been sidelined, but the consumer demand seemed as strong as ever. To supply the thousands of speakeasies an alternative supply chain emerged, making a mockery of the Eighteenth Amendment. This one relied on paying off judges, police, and politicians in place of liquor taxes and licenses. In this new, unregulated market, its most notable practitioners often resorted to less orthodox weapons to win market share and settle business disputes.

For men of a certain disposition, Prohibition was a combination of the Gilded Age and the Gold Rush. Compared with prostitution, gambling, or extortion, the business of alcohol was bigger by orders of magnitude. The day before Prohibition went into effect, it had been the legitimate source of wealth for some of America's richest men. Now they were out of business. Cities like New York were overflowing with young first-generation immigrants from Italy, Eastern Europe, and Ireland who, with little standing to lose, gravitated to fulfill market demand.

Leaders in ethnic communities, many in the gray area of the law to begin with, had been instrumental in delivering up the votes of their precincts to local politicians, part and parcel of the Democratic Party's machine politics in big cities. When Prohibition came around, this system allowed many to seamlessly leverage the local political infrastructure to efficiently counter federal authorities by putting local authorities on the payroll.

The activity wasn't limited to the bustling cities. Even small towns played a role. In one small suburb in the Midwest, local politics and crime simply merged into one. The *Chicago Tribune* in 1924 marveled at how the neighboring small town of Cicero, with a population of 55,000, could simply "withdraw from the general operation of law and become an independent principality." The state authorities, and Cook County's, seemingly had no power to regulate the happenings in this small bedroom community. Cicero's saloons, brothels, and gambling joints operated openly in what the article headlined as THE FREE KINGDOM OF TORRIO. John Torrio, a gangster transplanted from New York more than a decade earlier, had effectively taken over the town. Rather than cementing any negative impressions of Torrio, however, to many readers of the *Tribune*, the editorial likely served as an enticing advertisement for Chicagoans wishing to experience Cicero for themselves. And Cicero's most prominent citizen had been actively making efforts to expand his reach into Chicago. To do so, Torrio would increasingly rely on his young associate Alphonse Capone.

Just a few years earlier, Torrio had brought Capone to Chicago, aware of him as a tough twenty-year-old from his old neighborhood in Brooklyn. Within months, Capone had a business card that referenced his trade as a secondhand furniture dealer with a storefront located at 2220 South Wabash Avenue. It is safe to assume that not much furniture was sold. Next door at 2222, a building known as the Four Deuces, was the actual location of Capone's apprenticeship.

From this vantage point, Al Capone saw his mentor expand his operation. From the beginning of Prohibition, Chicago was on the verge of violence. Dion O'Banion and his large Irish clan, with some Jews mixed in, controlled much of the bootlegging in the northern parts of the city. The Sicilian Genna brothers, six of them, were pioneers in using the residents of Chicago's Little Italy to craft a near-toxic brand of whiskey. Poor Sicilian families, who were paid $15 a day to oversee a still within their home, found the nearly effortless work to be a blessing. In addition, the Gennas ran an industrial alcohol factory with a government permit. The product of this operation was then converted to bootleg whiskey.

Torrio's distribution operation initially focused on product from a brewery that he had purchased from a legitimate brewing family. After some time, he brought in O'Banion as an equal partner to maintain distribution peace. Soon O'Banion looked to sever the brewery relationship and offered to sell his share back; Torrio assented and paid O'Banion the asking price of $500,000. Within days of the transfer, the brewery was raided with Torrio on-site. Torrio, facing indictment, suspected that he had been betrayed and defrauded. With the consent of the Genna brothers, he plotted to have O'Banion killed, risking a large-scale war. On a late-fall day in 1924, O'Banion was killed in a flower shop he owned. Torrio, understanding the likely retribution, tried to keep a low profile, but O'Banion's successors were able to fire at him a few months later. He survived with minor bullet wounds.

The likelihood of future attempts on his life, along with his pending trial, led Torrio to an intelligent decision: Retire immediately, serve time in prison on the brewery charges, and then leave town. While still in the hospital recovering from the injury, he summoned Capone. In the presence of Torrio's lawyers, the two huddled for several hours, and Torrio transferred the entirety of his Chicago operation to twenty-five-year-old Capone. Starting in May, three of the six Genna brothers were killed within weeks of one another—the other three went into hiding. By the end of 1925, Al Capone emerged as the bootlegging power in Chicago.

The public was both riveted and revolted at the same time. Thousands of mourners attended Angelo Genna's funeral. A silver casket, flowers costing tens of thousands of dollars, and a lengthy funeral procession led the *Tribune* to conclude that for Italians "a bandit leader is the prince of heroes," highlighting the community's sympathy as a moral gulf between Americans of northern European stock and the new olive-skinned invaders.

But the appeal of gangsters would grow beyond that of provincial, nativist heroes into full-blown celebrity. And Capone eagerly embraced this role. He was known to refer to himself by his alias, Al Brown. The knife scars on his face from a bar brawl as a youth added "Scarface" to his titles. With Capone, American pop culture had a new archetype for celebrating criminality. Unlike bank robbers or daring criminals, Capone was a capitalist and an organization man. He had management responsibilities and negotiations to attend to. Many of his calculations were no different from those of the head of any business marketing a product that people wanted. But unlike that of most businessmen, the bootlegger's daily life did not seem boring—it lent itself to endless public fascination.

And Capone himself was refreshing: He openly admitted that he was a bootlegger. In December 1927, as the cold winter was setting in, Capone threatened the people of Chicago with retirement in a front page *Tribune* story. "Let the worthy citizens of Chicago get their liquor the best they can. I'm sick of the job—it's a thankless one and full of grief." He seemed exasperated that law enforcement and elements of the public appeared to take the gangster's sacrifices for granted. His feelings were hurt. "Public service is my motto. Ninety-nine percent of the people in Chicago drink and gamble. I've tried to serve them decent liquor and square games. But I'm not appreciated." After a couple of weeks in the Florida sun, however, Capone returned to Chicago full of Christmas cheer. The boss, it seemed, had just needed a vacation.

None of this sat well with two diametrically opposed factions. The U.S. Treasury, with uncooperative local law enforcement elements, was unable to link Capone with any of his self-professed activities. Capone owned nothing. He didn't have a bank account, a house in his own name, or virtually any other asset. In Chicago, he was never indicted for any violence committed directly by him or on his orders. But the Treasury Department, through a Capone bookkeeper, was able to link him to a total of $1 million of income over a seven-year period. His reign would end at age thirty-one with an indictment for income tax evasion. It seemed fitting that the income tax mechanism, which had made Prohibition financially possible in the first place by reducing the government's reliance on alcohol taxes, was now used to cement Prohibition's most public victory.

For the criminal elements in New York that had tasted fortune during

Prohibition, Capone was a cautionary tale on how not to operate a criminal enterprise. Capone's national stature—he had made it to the cover of *Time*—had far exceeded his actual power. He barely controlled all of Chicago. And worse, he brought unnecessary attention to himself by courting fame. The mission of the New Yorkers was to build a national organization, aspiring to institutional permanence, based on Sicilian traditions. To suit the geography of the United States, it was decided that rather than have one national head like in Sicily, a boss of bosses, this syndicate should have a ruling family in each major American city with the exception of New York, which would have five families. All in all, it was a democratic approach to American criminality. To coordinate and settle interfamily disputes, there would be a commission of nine members. Behavior would be highly codified, with entry limited to members whose parents were both of Italian origin. The killing of any member needed to be sanctioned by the head of the family. The killing of any family head needed to be sanctioned by the other family heads, the commission. With this plan, Charles "Lucky" Luciano established the blueprint for the American mafia, La Cosa Nostra. It seemed that even in the criminal markets, rational actors tended to collude, form cartels, and create local monopolies, rather than ruthlessly compete for every last dollar to everyone's detriment.

Law enforcement would not learn of the extent of La Cosa Nostra's intricate existence for decades. As silent as Capone was loud, the institution was Prohibition's lasting contribution.

Twenty-four

BANKING

T he country is in the midst of an era of prosperity more extensive and of peace more permanent than it has ever before experienced," concluded outgoing president Calvin Coolidge in December 1928, in his final address to Congress. The 1920s had blessed Americans with "tranquility and contentment," courtesy of the "great wealth created by our enterprise and industry." In material terms, it was indisputable that American capitalism had delivered a standard of living unsurpassed in the history of the world. The industrial infrastructure put in place in the late nineteenth century with steel, oil, and railroads had led the way to a consumer age. Entering 1929, there were nearly 26 million registered vehicles on the road, nearly one for every five Americans, with millions of small trucks supplementing railroad commerce. The twenty million electrified American homes had new appliances such as washing machines and vacuum cleaners. The war efforts had made way for the rise of commercial aviation, with thousands of small aircraft operating scheduled service. And Americans continued to push the boundaries of their own breakthroughs: Charles Lindbergh crossed the Atlantic and became an international hero. American ingenuity was even putting radio into cars.

Despite the loss of alcohol taxes due to Prohibition, the income tax had led to years of postwar budget surpluses. During the eight years of Republican presidencies under Warren Harding and Coolidge, the country had paid down vast amounts of debt incurred during the war. It exported far more than it imported, resulting in substantial trade surpluses. American vaults could not help accumulating large reserves of gold and foreign currencies. A decade after rising to its role as the pivotal factor in the Great War, the United States stood as the world's great creditor. Germany owed reparations to France and Great Britain, who in turn were deeply indebted to the United States.

Given the economic success, Coolidge's commerce secretary, Herbert Hoover, won the election of 1928 promising continued prosperity. Implicit in the election of Hoover was the electorate's affirmation of its deep faith in markets, in allowing commercial interests to operate with minimal interference. Indeed, Coolidge, earlier in his presidency, had once called taxes a "species of legalized larceny" and pointed out that industrial production had boomed every time taxes were cut. While neither Coolidge nor Hoover—being of the law-and-order variety of Republicans—looked favorably on ongoing widespread lawbreaking due to Prohibition, Americans, on the other hand, saw that even the criminal free markets served people efficiently, as judged by social hour. Hoover's tenure, however, would not be as charmed as Coolidge's.

The year 1929 started well enough—it even looked as if prosperity were accelerating. Automobile production was at record levels, as was steel production, which was used across industrial settings and served as a useful gauge. Reflecting the optimism of the era, the stock market was especially buoyant, continuing its climb. Redolent of the euphoria of 1872, when Twain and Warner were finishing *The Gilded Age*, this era saw the stock market operator as a clairvoyant, a species so deft at moneymaking that both awe and emulation were warranted. The allure of stock market fortunes was the same as ever: Unlike building a factory or starting a business, stock speculation seemed so tantalizingly simple, an enticement that rising prices only compounded.

Articles such as the one headlined, "RADIO" HAS MADE A NEW MILLIONAIRE added to the allure. "Radio," as everyone knew, meant RCA, one of the highest-flying stocks of the twenties. And few readers of the era's financial pages would have been foolish enough to assume that this new millionaire actually built radios. The story described how thirty-seven-year-old Michael Meehan, who had been a streetside ticket seller for Broadway shows, was now "master of the market" in RCA shares. In these days of unregulated markets, the tool of the operator such as Meehan was to coordinate with other investors to buy a given stock simultaneously, creating the illusion of a price rise for other reasons, which enticed other investors, then sell as the unwary investors bought in. Some renowned pool operators, such as GM founder Billy Durant, found the market to be an easier source of fortune than building companies such as Chevrolet. Women's magazines contained tales of homemakers compulsively watching stock tickers at New York City brokerage offices. At the same time, Wall Street investment banks had sponsored new vehicles—the predecessors to today's mutual funds—that were expressly created to buy stocks, generating another buyer in an already frothy market. By September 3, 1929, the Dow Jones Industrial Average, an index of the nation's industrial companies, including U.S. Steel, Standard Oil, General Electric, Sears Roebuck, RCA, and Westinghouse, had climbed to a record level of 381.17.

It should be noted that much of the frenzy was experienced vicariously: There were only 1.3 million brokerage accounts in the United States, with 600,000 of those margin accounts, cleared to borrow against the value of their shares. To the millions following the headlines, an appreciating stock market was an ongoing affirmation of economic greatness, of the rational market forces of national destiny expressed daily in the Dow Jones average, with all of the scientific and mathematical precision of two decimal points. Through this real-time gauge of economic health, the public was psychologically vested in the financial exposure of a few hundred thousand investors. At the same time, their fellow countrymen speculating in the market had managed to borrow $8.5 billion in hard dollars, a significant percentage of the nation's banking assets, pledged against their stock holdings.

On September 18, AT&T climbed to over $307, a level implying that the company was worth $4 billion. But as in any market rise, the momentum runs out when the last of the buyers stops paying even higher prices or enough existing shareholders look to take out profits by selling; the greater this imbalance, the more precipitous the fall in price, which then causes even more shareholders to rush to sell. Starting on Monday, October 21, the stock market began to show the first tremors of what would be a rapid descent, a shift in sentiment ending the "long dance of advancing and inflated prices." Companies with the loftiest rise were its most notable victims: RCA, which had been at 114 earlier in the year, dropped 11 points to 68, then the next day to 58, then a few days later to 40. The prices of the nation's largest companies were not immune either, despite the best efforts of Wall Street banks to inject optimism into the market, the cheery language masking desperation. The market no longer seemed under the control of the men who professed a near-religious faith in market verdicts. Instead, the market collapsed. Over six days, culminating on October 29, 1929, the Dow Jones Industrial Average shed one third of its value, closing at 230—it had been at 380 in September. But these drops, however dramatic, were just the beginning of a painful new American story. Within three years, the Dow would be a fraction of even this.

GIVEN THAT THE 1929 stock market crash occurred within just over six months of Hoover assuming office, his administration's response was blamed for the course of events. But history had few lessons to draw upon. Economic progress had been such that history was not repeating itself; the modern industrial state was far removed from the policy choices of prior eras, just as much as modern warfare could not be wholly patterned on that of the past. Compounding this, the Hoover administration's simple orthodoxy—that markets were self-correcting, that excesses in supply and overbuilding would sort themselves out, and financial failures were moral lessons for irrational market actors—suggested that the best course of action for the government was to let events play out.

But nothing about the American economy was simple. It was a vast, complex, specialized, interconnected, and interdependent system. Just as the man on the assembly line putting in the bolt needed the next man to put on the washer and tighten the nut, every function affected the chain of subsequent actions. One drunken worker—an irrational labor input to the technocrat—could slow down an entire factory of the most conscientious workers. The worker's wife didn't churn butter or sew her own clothes, either. She bought things. Every man's wage was continually circulated through the economy. The concept of economic independence, of freedom even, was purely philosophical. The American's high standard of living relied on the simultaneous execution of millions of jobs—that most of this happened without any planning or direction, the continuous intersection of supply and demand curves, seemed remarkably natural. But the phenomenon had a shortcoming: Money retreating suddenly and rapidly due to speculative failure caused collateral damage, where activities throughout the economy were impacted, not just the reckless ones. The comeuppance was collective.

Throughout the twenties, even to Coolidge and Hoover, some need for a regulatory system had been more than clear. Everything from air routes to radio frequencies to driver's licenses were allocated or rationed by government; laws governing labor, corporations, food safety, drugs, and utilities were regarded as legitimate by men of most political stripes. Yet to simply intervene when the markets were oversupplied with goods and demand dried up was not seen as the legitimate role of government. To perform triage and resurrect markets, how should that work? One man's influence carried disproportionate weight on this issue. Treasury secretary Andrew Mellon, under Hoover, was then serving his third straight Republican president, having been in the same role in both the Harding and Coolidge administrations. Given his continuity in the role, the prosperity of the 1920s had propelled him to receive favorable comparisons to Alexander Hamilton, the nation's first treasury secretary. To Mellon, an austere banker in his seventies, backed by a banking fortune made in industrial Pittsburgh, recessions and panics were nature's way of washing out speculative excesses, of economic misjudgments meeting their verdict. To not allow pain to take hold would blunt the implicit lessons of the market. As demand and asset prices fell, shrewd investors would pick up the pieces, or so went his thinking.

But the economy was not recovering by the middle of 1930. Instead, the sudden hiccup from the previous year's stock market crash had started a slow-building avalanche, reverberating in unpredictable ways. The amount lent out against stocks at the market peak was nearly one third as

large as the total savings deposits of $28 billion in American banks. Bor-
rowers with losses in the market, who were generally more affluent than
the average American, had to sell other assets such as real estate in addition to withdrawing their savings deposits to cover losses. Banks had less
to loan out; as real estate prices dropped, the collateral on loans was no
longer as strong; and given that deposits were not guaranteed by the
government or any authority, prudent depositors often wanted to withdraw funds, weakening the banks further.

While the difference between being insolvent and being illiquid is a
vast one, to anxious depositors this distinction was irrelevant anytime they
couldn't get their money out instantly. Most banks had loans outstanding
that substantially exceeded what they owed depositors—meaning people
owed the bank more than what the bank owed depositors—however, if an
unexpected stream of withdrawals was triggered by emotion or rumor, few
banks could demand that borrowers pay back their loans immediately so
that the banks could then pay their depositors. While most of the larger
banks were a part of the Federal Reserve system, in which member banks
could quickly lend one another excess reserves—excess cash that a bank
had, beyond what was needed for expected withdrawals—thousands of
smaller banks were in effect isolated. In November 1930 alone, 256 small
banks with an aggregate deposit base of $180 million, less than $1 million each, failed.

But the next month, a far more psychologically scarring event occurred in New York City. There had been rumors among depositors
about the strength of the Bank of United States, which, despite its
official-sounding name, was an entirely private affair. It had no more
affiliation with any form of the U.S. government than did A. P. Gianni-
ni's Bank of America. With 400,000 depositors, the bank had a deposit
base of nearly $200 million even after a rush of earlier withdrawals, which,
as the *New York Times* reported, was "small savings of comparatively poor
people." With fears stemming from the hundreds of small bank failures
that had occurred earlier that year, and aware that the Bank of United
States was less liquid after the initial wave of withdrawals, depositors
began to withdraw money before others got the same idea, with rumors
making it everyone's idea at the same time. The bank's assets were largely

in the form of mortgage loans collateralized by New York buildings and land; the loan book was performing, meaning borrowers were paying on time. But the bank could not borrow from other banks readily given that its collateral was in mortgages. Despite desperate efforts by the state of New York's superintendent of banking, Joseph Broderick, to get private banks to provide emergency funds against collateral, he was unable to coordinate a response, a failure he regarded as "the most colossal mistake in the banking history of New York."

At 9:00 a.m. on December 11, 1930, Broderick announced that the operations of Bank of United States were suspended until its assets could be liquidated. Around the bank's fifty-nine branches throughout Manhattan, the Bronx, and Brooklyn, "large crowds of bewildered depositors, many of whom did not understand English, stood determinedly in the rain, hoping that something would turn up to get their money." No one turned up except the police to disperse the crowd, who were effectively the opposite of bank robbers—these were people who couldn't get their own money out of the bank. Not only was the Bank of United States a member of the Federal Reserve with substantial assets dwarfing all of the bank failures in November combined, but it produced a contagion effect due to the official impression of its name, which the economist Milton Friedman later noted substantially exacerbated the impact of the closure. More than a year after the 1929 stock market crash, readers in America and around the world read ominous headlines to close 1930: The Bank of United States had failed.

The American role on the world stage at that critical time was especially significant. While America had transitioned out of the war quickly, Europe in the 1920s had not fully recovered. Britain attempted to restore itself to its prewar financial standing but suffered stagnation instead. Wild inflation took hold for a brief period in Germany, after which the German economy remained burdened by the weight of reparations to Britain and France imposed by the Treaty of Versailles. In turn, Britain and France owed billions of dollars to the Americans from wartime borrowing. But the Germans defaulted, which caused Britain and France to voice concerns about the money they themselves owed America.

Finally, an American delegation met with German, British, and French counterparts at the conclusion of which, in 1929, the Germans agreed to pay $492 million per year for thirty-six years and another $375 million for twenty-two years to cover British and French debts to the United States. The perception created by the strength of the twenties was that America was an untroubled economic oasis.

In addition to the Treaty of Versailles, the postwar framework had led the major powers back to the gold standard, which all of the countries had suspended during the war. Since each nation's currency was fixed in value to a corresponding amount of gold, the exchange rates between the gold-backed currencies were also fixed. For instance, if four British pounds and twenty U.S. dollars both were pegged to equal an ounce of gold, the exchange rate between pounds and dollars was set as well. Interestingly, the most market-oriented economies of the day did not allow their currencies to trade freely in the global market. To maintain a currency on the gold standard, a nation's central bank had to possess large reserves of physical gold to create confidence in major holders of its currency, such as foreign central banks and major institutions, that the paper could be redeemed at any time. This ended up causing substantial problems.

After the failure of the Bank of United States in late 1930, bank failures in the United States accelerated dramatically the next year. As American banks failed, the American government faced a stark choice. Modern policy options to help stimulate the economy include reducing taxes, which may create temporary budget shortfalls but leaves money in the private economy; having the Federal Reserve buy bonds to infuse cash into the economy and increase the supply of money; engaging directly in public works programs, effectively acting as a buyer of the nation's goods and services; and/or lowering interest rates by allowing member banks to borrow cheaply. At the time, however, if the government did any of this, the looseness of such a policy would likely have caused overseas governments to withdraw their dollar deposits in the form of physical gold. The alternative choice was to defend the gold standard at all costs—to project financial strength and stability by adhering to a balanced budget and maintain the dollar's value in gold. This required increasing interest rates in the face of a recession to make dollar deposits attractive enough to retain international deposits. America chose gold.

Religiously adhering to the gold standard tightened the money supply and significantly limited the Hoover administration's policy options. For a few months, it worked. Overseas investors and banks, seeing the American commitment to gold, brought over bullion from countries perceived to be faltering. In England this led to dramatic withdrawals of gold to the point where the Bank of England was on the verge of exhausting its supply. In September 1931 England left the gold standard, as did numerous smaller countries in the fall of 1931. No longer was the British pound convertible to gold as a matter of government policy. With its currency weakened, loosening money, the British economy started its recovery.

There was no recovery in America. By the end of 1931, 2,294 small banks had failed, spreading anxiety in pockets throughout America. The Hoover administration could not provide relief to the banks and maintain the gold standard—the move would have been seen as weakening the currency. With the strong dollar and weak economic demand, deflation set in. Unlike inflation, under which a weaker currency pinches people through higher prices, the negative effects of deflation are difficult to see and manifest themselves in opaque, systemic ways. Prices are lower, but dollars are harder to come by. For debtors, the effects are the worst. An amount of debt, such as a home or farm mortgage, is fixed at the time that it is borrowed. However, if a person's wages or the price of crops fall with deflation, the debt becomes relatively greater in proportion to the falling income. At some point, the falling incomes of the debtors can no longer service the debts, wreaking havoc on banks and their depositors.

At the start of 1932, unemployment climbed to over 15 percent, with seven million primary breadwinners out of work. Total income in the country fell dramatically. The year would get significantly worse. New residential construction plummeted to a value of $462 million from over $1.2 billion the previous year, meaning the nation's construction workers and contractors were out of work. At its high point a few years prior, the industry had generated over \$4.5 billion in annual revenue. Automobile production was similarly devastated. From almost 2 million cars built in 1931, production nearly halved to a little over 1.1 million. Automobile production had been four times higher in 1929. Revenues on American farms dropped by 33 percent from 1931. Millions of idle hands were added to the already alarming unemployment rolls.

Despite the substantial decline in farm revenues, the number of declared farms actually grew slightly. The farm—the ability to grow one's own food—seemed a safe place in the midst of the economic unraveling of modern industrial society and wage labor. Food production in 1932 stayed remarkably steady: Butter, milk, slaughtered cattle, hogs, chickens, and eggs were similar to 1929 levels, but prices were half of what they had been. The harvested acreage and bushel quantity of oats, barley, corn, and wheat stayed flat, as did the yield of pears, grapes, and oranges. This flew in the face of economic logic with its fancy supply and demand curves: Dramatic drops in prices should have altered production. But they didn't. Country logic seemed a better fit. What else was a farmer going to do but farm?

Likely the \$9 billion of farm mortgage debt owed collectively by American farmers left them with little choice—it had barely dropped from the 1929 level of \$9.7 billion. Though 1932 farm revenues had been cut in half from 1929, farmers carried virtually the same level of debt as before. Just as this had once served as the basis of William Jennings Bryan's candidacy in 1896, the American farmer once again stared at the consequences of deflation and the gold standard.

Even Al Capone, the night before his sentencing, was perplexed over the intricacies of public policy. "I'm not complaining, but why don't they go after all these bankers who took the savings of thousands of poor and lost them in bank failures? How about that? Isn't it a lot worse to take the last few dollars some small family has saved—perhaps to live on while the head of the family is out of a job—than to sell a little beer?" It was too late to counter views such as Capone's with the intricate points of preserving the gold standard or the nuances of the balance of payments—the verdict was on display at the soup kitchens for all to see. The men of the shantytowns named "Hoovervilles," full of makeshift homes that assaulted the dignity of the once-proud workingman, father, and husband, understood this economy as well as any economist.

It was clear that America's most famous gangster had a better read on public sentiment than America's most famous banker, Andrew Mellon. Hoover sensed disaster. With an election looming and unemployment headed to 20 percent and higher, Hoover transitioned his treasury secretary out of the job into an ambassadorship to England. It was too late. The Hoover administration's policies had failed miserably by any objective measure. The administration's failure was due to a lack of action fueled by an unwavering faith in the free market to restore itself. Contributing equally was the dogma and inflexibility of the gold standard: The need to project strength led to policy weakness.

As conditions grew worse in 1932, the decision to stick with gold backfired further. Initially, foreigners felt safe keeping gold in American vaults due to the administration's commitment. But in 1932 the American Treasury was no longer seen as a safe haven for gold—a shrinking economy with high unemployment and dislocation was a recipe for social unrest, or worse. Just as depositors looked to withdraw printed currency during local bank runs, central banks and large investors started a run on American gold. Now Hoover was stuck with the worst of both worlds: Escalating withdrawals of gold required even more monetary tightening, paying higher interest rates, to entice international depositors to not withdraw gold. And in an effort to signal greater fiscal responsibility, he raised income taxes in the summer of 1932. All of these actions took capital out of the private economy, worsening conditions.

By the eve of the 1932 presidential election, though Hoover's record seemed indefensible, he presented the choice in sweeping terms: "The fundamental issue in this campaign, the decision that will fix the national direction for 100 years to come, is whether we shall go on in fidelity to the American traditions or whether we shall turn to innovations, the spirit of which is disclosed to us by many sinister revelations and veiled promises." His Democratic opponent was Franklin Delano Roosevelt, the governor of New York. The "innovations" Hoover railed against included paper money and Roosevelt's allusions to a "new deal." The details really didn't matter. By now, Americans would have taken any deal from anyone not named Hoover. Other than a smattering of smaller states in the Northeast, Roosevelt won the rest of the country as one large, unbroken bloc.

Hoover was right. The decision did permanently alter the national direction.

DURING THE TRANSITION period between Hoover's defeat in November and Roosevelt's inauguration in March 1933, the nation's banking system, and therefore its economy, was nearing calamity. Central banks and foreign holders assumed that Roosevelt was not committed to the gold standard and began withdrawing gold ahead of the president-elect's assuming office. Small depositors rushed to withdraw money from banks. Banks in the countryside found themselves in an increasingly untenable position: Foreclose on the homes and farms of defaulting borrowers to raise proceeds to pay depositors, or refuse to pay the depositors wishing to withdraw their money.

Foreclosing on a farm was no simple task. Farmers often banded together to physically prevent farms from being sold at auction. Potential bidders too faced hostility, and given that a successful bidder could not physically move a farm, the community's threat was a sufficient deterrent. Sometimes the violence was real. Sixty-seven-year-old Luther Marr, who was found on the side of the road in a car full of bullet holes, had been returning home after successfully buying a foreclosed farm at auction. The head of the Farm Bureau Federation warned a Senate committee of a "revolution in the countryside." Around the time of Marr's death, sensing unrest, Prudential Insurance, the largest holder of farm mortgages in the country, declared a moratorium on foreclosures. Small banks too could not foreclose farms to raise cash, but nevertheless, depositors lined up to drain what was left.

With one week left to go before Roosevelt's inauguration, a full-scale contagion had taken hold. States began declaring bank holidays, ordering banks to collectively suspend customer withdrawals; Michigan, California,

Ohio, and most of the South suspended all bank operations by March 1. A handful of other states severely curtailed operations, such as limiting withdrawals to small amounts. With days left in power, the Hoover administration was in a full panic and made repeated overtures to the president-elect for joint action, but Roosevelt refused any responsibility for anything until he assumed the office. With less than forty-eight hours to go, the situation worsened. Gold withdrawals by foreign holders, governments, and central banks accelerated to such alarming levels that Hoover called the president-in-waiting at eleven thirty at night and again at 1:00 a.m., asking Roosevelt for consent to suspend the gold withdrawals. By the time Roosevelt awoke on March 4, a few hours from becoming president, New York had declared a banking holiday.

Hours later, his opening remarks, given the climate, cautioned Americans that the "only thing we have to fear is fear itself—nameless, unreasoning, unjustified terror," which had unrelentingly, over the past weeks, caused the nation's already-depressed economy to go into cardiac arrest. The fear Roosevelt pointed out illustrated a central paradox in free-market societies: In economically uncertain times, it was rational for an individual to act cautiously, cutting spending and withholding currency from the economy, but collectively, prudence caused even greater economic slowdown and job losses and risked lasting damage—a hundred million rational actions becoming irrational in the aggregate, a destructive antisynergy that "fear itself" propelled.

But Roosevelt also understood his countrymen's mood and refrained from painting a rosy picture:

> We face our common difficulties. They concern, thank God, only material things. Values have shrunken to fantastic levels; taxes have risen; our ability to pay has fallen; government of all kinds is faced by serious curtailment of income; the means of exchange are frozen in the currents of trade; the withered leaves of industrial enterprise lie on every side; farmers find no markets for their produce; the savings of families are gone.
>
> More important, a host of unemployed citizens face the grim problem of existence, and an equally great number toil with little

return. Only a foolish optimist can deny the dark realities of the moment.

To resuscitate the economy, "to meet the unprecedented task before us," Roosevelt told his inaugural audience, he planned to ask Congress for near-dictatorial authority, equal to the greatest of wartime powers—"broad executive power to wage a war against the emergency, as great as the power that would be given to me if we were in fact invaded by a foreign foe."

After three years of economic failure following nine years of growth, that the principles of limited government should now include active management of a market-based economy—something that America's founders, Adam Smith, and Karl Marx all would have considered an ideological departure from capitalism—seemed to Roosevelt a practical application of power, of government evolving to meet the complexities of the age.

The day after his speech, Roosevelt issued a presidential proclamation ordering all banks throughout the nation to be closed for four days and then obtained further authority from Congress to open them at his discretion. He froze all gold withdrawals and shipments, invoking powers under the Trading with the Enemy Act. Given that the banks were closed, the New York Stock Exchange stopped trading. Using new powers granted to him by Congress in his first week, he authorized his Treasury Department to compel "hoarders" to turn in gold and gold certificates in exchange for Federal Reserve notes, which could not be converted back to gold. America was off the gold standard.

After one week on the job, with all banks in America still closed, the president decided to take his case directly to the living rooms of the anxious American people. CBS Radio's Washington station introduced Roosevelt's address as akin to a "fireside chat." It turned radio into a modern form of participatory democracy as people listened to their president outline his thinking during crisis, especially on the mysterious subject of banking.

"First of all let me state the simple fact that when you deposit money in a bank the bank does not put the money in a safe deposit vault," began

Roosevelt. The bank loaned money to others "to keep the wheels of industry and agriculture turning." As Americans panicked and raced to withdraw their money, even the soundest banks couldn't liquidate assets fast enough to satisfy the withdrawal needs of depositors. The banks kept only a small amount of people's deposits on hand and loaned the vast majority of it out. Over the course of the Fireside Chat, Roosevelt patiently walked his countrymen through the basics of banking, explaining why he had ordered all banks closed.

To the relief of millions of Americans, he announced that the first waves of banks would open the next morning, with additional openings each successive day.

With the first banks opened on Monday, the afternoon brought another request from Roosevelt. Stating that he needed the tax revenue, he asked Congress that beer with alcohol content of up to 3.2 percent be made legal; the Eighteenth Amendment did not specify the percentage that constituted an intoxicating beverage. Congress complied. The House passed the bill the very next day with a vote count of 316–97, pushing it to the Senate. Wednesday brought good cheer: The stock market opened for the first time in Roosevelt's presidency. In a single-day record, the Dow Jones Industrial Average gained over 15 percent—a gain in total market value of $3 billion. By Thursday, for increased fiscal prudence, the Senate had added an exemption for wine to go with beer, but negotiated the alcohol content down to 3.05 percent. Throughout the week, banks were receiving net deposits rather than facing panicked withdrawals.

Over the following weeks, the administration developed a sweeping farm package designed to "increase purchasing power of our farmers" and "relieve the pressure of farm mortgages." To guarantee the safety of bank deposits, the Federal Deposit Insurance Corporation was created. To regulate the entire American stock and bond markets, the Exchange Act of 1933 required companies to report their financial condition accurately to the buying public, establishing the Securities and Exchange Commission. Safety nets such as Social Security for retirement and home loan guarantees for individuals would be added to the government's portfolio of responsibilities within a couple of years. It was the largest peacetime escalation of government in American history.

The worst of the Depression was over and economic output started growing again. The stock market, as reflected by the Dow, rose 66 percent in 1933—its best year on record. It went up another 40 percent in 1935. Automobile production doubled to over 3 million cars by 1935 from fewer than 1.5 million in Roosevelt's first year. The prices of eggs, meat, and grain went up, benefiting farmers. Gross national product, the sum of economic activity in the United States, jumped 53 percent from the 1933 level of $55.8 billion to $90.2 billion in 1937. The general historical impression of the thirties is that the Depression lasted throughout the decade. To some degree, the fact that the economy fell back into a recession in 1937–1938 gives credence to this view. However, the economy's output of $84.7 billion even in the lull of 1938 was a significant improvement from 1933. Without the disastrous period between 1929 and 1933, the appendage of "Great" preceding "Depression" would be an exaggeration. And the election of 1936 reflected the American public's verdict on Roosevelt's economic management and his performance in turning around the economy. He won forty-six out of forty-eight states against Republican Alf Landon, an unlikely margin of victory had the outlook not been substantially better than when he first took office.

The election made it clear that the American understanding of government had completely transformed. Intervention in times of recession from here on would be expected. In the American electorate's eyes, given the trauma of the early thirties, the legitimate role of the federal government was now as the economic actor of last resort. Prolonged economic disruptions in the future would be seen as the policy failure of the government, not the failure of markets, with economic growth rates and levels of employment serving as report cards for future presidents.

Twenty-five

FILM

As the nation was in the midst of recovery, one industry rebounded better than the rest. Even in silent form, film had been a growing industry for two decades. Actors had emerged as full-blown stars. But the technical breakthrough of being able to couple full vocal dialogue with music and sound effects brought the film industry to new heights. Residents of remote country towns, far away from the vaudeville acts of bigger cities, had access to the same moving imagery as their urban countrymen. Unlike the theater or even sports that had provincial followings, the movies had a national scale. Even the greatest Broadway show could take place at only one time for a few hundred people—a widely distributed movie could reach fifty million people. And actors on Broadway needed to be paid for the next day's act. The economics of the movies were different: The majority of a film's expenses were incurred up front, so the revenues that followed had high margins without ongoing costs. A hit made a fortune.

But the economics of other industries predictably relied on natural resources, scientific methods, production processes, or distribution logistics—rationality and utility determined profitability. Hollywood was more idiosyncratic. The film industry's core ingredient was the enigmatic written word. The ability of millions of moviegoers to be entranced, to have their emotions and imaginations gripped for two hours, almost always started with the words of a lonely writer somewhere. For the film industry's greatest financial success, somewhere happened to be Atlanta, Georgia.

FAR AWAY FROM the studio stages and cameras of Hollywood, starting in the midtwenties, Margaret Mitchell had spent seven years writing her novel, set during the Civil War. Even with the bulk of the writing completed by 1929, Mitchell had not been confident enough to submit it to publishers, preferring to improve her work sporadically. In the spring of 1935, an editor at the New York publishing house Macmillan, while on a scouting trip through the South, was introduced to Mitchell and signed her to a deal for her untitled book. Upon its release in the summer of 1936, the *New York Times Book Review* declared it "one of the most remarkable first novels produced by an American writer." Priced at $3, *Gone with the Wind* was a blockbuster. By the end of the summer, Macmillan had sold over 500,000 copies.

A few days prior to the gushing review in the *Times*, an almost desperate telegram originated from New York reading, "I beg, urge, coax, and plead with you to read this at once. I know that after you read the book you will drop everything and buy it." The sender, Kay Brown, in this missive to her boss, the movie producer David Selznick, asked to purchase the book's movie rights before its release. But Selznick waited. On July 15, seeing its reception, Selznick bought the film rights to *Gone with the Wind* for $50,000. Within a year, sales of the book had exceeded one million copies.

Almost immediately Selznick looked to assemble the pieces needed to turn the book into a movie. At the time, he was one of a handful of major independent producers (including Frank Capra, Alfred Hitchcock, and Walt Disney) who had access to the resources to make films. Few others could break into a system controlled by the major studios. After producing films as an employee of major studios, including Paramount and MGM, the thirty-seven-year-old Selznick had branched out to helm his own productions. He had been a highly paid salaried employee throughout the thirties. His career included producer credits on dozens of films, but nothing as big as what he had now taken on.

As the producer, Selznick needed to figure out how to take a lengthy book and translate it onto the screen. To do this, Selznick International Pictures needed to hire writers and a director, cast the characters, get the sets and the costumes designed, set a budget, put together the financing by giving investors profit-participation interests, arrange the distribution plan for theaters, and oversee the marketing to bring audiences to see the film.

Selznick's bigger problem was the projected cost. His independent outfit had limited capital. To faithfully execute his vision for the book, he needed a budget that was likely going to exceed $2 million, or even $3 million. Up to that point, the most expensive film ever made had been *Ben-Hur*, eventually costing over $4 million to make. It had been so expensive to complete that it was one of the prime factors in the sale of Goldwyn Pictures to the theater chain Loew's, which would eventually finance the film's completion. Selznick was aware of the damage an inordinately costly production could do to his finances, regardless of how well a film turned out.

But *Gone with the Wind* was different. Macmillan had to keep re-printing the book to stock bookstore shelves with enough copies. The movie had built-in marketing before the cameras shot a single scene. The major studios, sensing a sure thing with the film adaptation, now looked to partner with Selznick. Selznick, looking for financing and distribution, could not escape the grip of the cartel known as the studio system.

THE SYSTEM in many ways was a necessary one. Each film was entirely different, but all were expensive. Unlike a factory, a lavish movie set might be used just once, especially if the scene called for a fire or explosion. The key employees, writers, actors, and directors were known to be volatile. Even an expensively produced film that got everything right, however, could not guarantee that audiences would actually pay to watch it. And if a movie was well received by audiences, very little of this knowledge could be directly applied to another film. It was art posing as business. The rise of major studios resulted from an ongoing search for an economic formula that could make the movies work as an industry.

MGM, Selznick's eventual studio partner for *Gone with the Wind*, was one of the five major studios in the midthirties. Its roots went back a full generation. Starting in the early 1900s, a theater owner named Marcus Loew had looked to expand beyond live plays and musical acts. Primarily he operated a few vaudeville houses, where a number of variety acts ranging from comedians to short dramas took place within one evening's billing. The first motion pictures were shown as short additions as part of the variety of vaudeville shows. Few expected motion pictures to eventually eclipse their host. As filmmakers in the silent era expanded their output, along with the films' length and sophistication, several pioneers repurposed or built new theaters specially outfitted for motion pictures. By the twenties, Loew's theaters had grown into a large chain in New York; his cavernous main theater on Forty-fifth and Broadway alone had seating for 3,200 guests, a mini stadium. The major capital investment was in the theaters—the exhibition end of the business—not in the films themselves.

With the expensive real estate committed to films, Loew needed consistent product. In addition, the mentality of the old-line theater and vaudeville bosses, as they shifted to film, was to compete with other theaters by offering an exclusive product that no else could show, just as a play was. For Loew, the best way to guarantee the quantity of the exclusive films he needed was to buy a studio. In Metro Pictures he found a small studio with a strong distribution operation. Distribution was the part of the film business that took a finished film from a studio or producer and made sure it was shown in theaters across the country. It would have made little sense for a filmmaker or producer making one, two, or five films per year to maintain the field staff needed to sell and service theaters—this function fell to distributors. But Metro was a weak studio in terms of actual filmmaking. A year after buying Metro, Loew was offered Goldwyn Pictures. Goldwyn owned a large 4,500-seat theater in New York, but it had a large studio in Los Angeles where it brought some efficiency to film production. To operate the combined

Metro-Goldwyn studios, a Loew's executive became acquainted with Louis B. Mayer, a Jewish immigrant from Russia, who had made his mark operating small theaters in New England. Mayer, thirty-eight, had moved up to filmmaking with his own Louis B. Mayer Productions. For $75,000 Loew's, Inc., acquired Mayer's company and had him manage the Los Angeles operations of Metro-Goldwyn. In the midtwenties, Metro-Goldwyn added "Mayer" to its name and became MGM. Mayer had a large degree of autonomy as a studio boss, but the ownership remained firmly in New York.

As theaters were the first point of revenue collection for the entire industry, this side of the business often had insights on how to keep the halls full every weekend and therefore needed some control of the product, the films themselves. Unlike a producer, who usually hired people one movie at a time and could scale down expenditures, a theater owner had substantial leases or mortgage payments on his real estate and faced ongoing pressure. Further, theater owners suddenly had to spend large amounts of capital to upgrade their facilities for a new technology.

In 1927 Warner Brothers, a second-tier operation, took a major risk and produced *The Jazz Singer* at a cost of $500,000. It was the first feature film with spoken dialogue. The four immigrant brothers, Harry, Albert, Sam, and Jack, had been modestly successful in the film business for years. But their fortunes had soured. Needing a differentiated offering for their theaters, Warner Brothers invested in a sound technology that enabled the film reel to contain an embedded soundtrack. At the same time, for an audience to be able to hear the audio, theaters had to be outfitted with speakers and the equipment to play sound. With makeshift arrangements in theaters, the film grossed $3 million. Sensing the demand for sound, Warner Brothers pushed ahead with sound studios for filmmaking and installation of sound speakers in all of its theaters.

The rest of the industry followed. The novelty of sound initially made box-office receipts immune to the economic slowdown, but by 1931 revenues declined. Theater owners, with leveraged capital structures, had trouble making the debt payments with the lower revenues. Several of the major operations or their theater subsidiaries went into receivership, with the banks leading the restructuring. Twentieth Century Pictures was merged with William Fox's Fox Film Corporation. Bankrupt Paramount ended up in the temporary control of New York investment bank Lehman Brothers. Chase National Bank ended up with a stake in Loew's and its MGM Studios. Even RKO, a company spun off from RCA to make use of the radio company's sound technology, ended up insolvent. Rounding it out, Columbia and Universal ended up with Bank of America as a shareholder.

The only group left relatively unscathed was Warner Brothers, with the namesake family retaining ownership and control. With the initial success of *The Jazz Singer*, Warner Brothers' early bet on sound conversion for all of its theater acquisitions paid off. The initial wave of talking-picture revenues allowed Warner Brothers to emerge from the worst years of the Great Depression as a major studio. By 1935 Hollywood's studio system included five major studios that owned their own theaters—Twentieth Century–Fox, MGM (Loew's), Paramount, Warner Brothers, and RKO—and three submajor studios that didn't own their own theaters, Universal, Columbia, and United Artists.

The system looked to bring some economies of scale to a business in which every product, the film itself, was unique. Large multiacre lots allowed for virtually any setting and scene to be shot right in Los Angeles. Each studio employed cameramen, directors, writers, and sound and lighting technicians as salaried staff. Most important, each studio had a stable of stars on contract. Fox had arguably the midthirties' biggest star: Shirley Temple. MGM had Clark Gable and Norma Shearer. Errol Flynn was at Warner Brothers. The studios then fed their pictures first and exclusively to theaters they owned in competitive markets like New York, Chicago, and Boston. A caste system among theaters developed in which first-run pictures went to certain chains and second-run pictures—reruns, essentially—went to another tier of chains. In dealing with independent theater owners, distributors used the leverage of stars and major pictures to bundle their slate of minor pictures—for a theater owner to get the big blockbusters, he had to agree to show the harder-to-market films. The studio system's purpose at every step was to smooth out the economics of an unpredictable business. The outcome was a functioning cartel.

Even for the fiercely independent David O. Selznick, who had left the majors to do things his own way, the road to producing *Gone with the Wind* led back to his former employer, MGM. There were two good reasons: For one, Louis B. Mayer was his father-in-law. And two, Selznick needed the perfect star to play Rhett Butler. MGM had Clark Gable on contract. MGM agreed to allow Gable to play the male lead in exchange for the distribution rights going to its parent, Loew's. In addition, MGM invested $1.25 million in financing for 50 percent of the profits, including the 15 percent distribution fee for Loew's. With the deal in place, Selznick started filming before he even cast the film's main character, Scarlett O'Hara. The latest and most expensive cameras from Technicolor were deployed. The set included facades of Atlanta and Tara, Scarlett's plantation home. When Selznick was watching his Atlanta being set on fire, the reenactment of the Union's final blow to the South, his brother Myron Selznick introduced him to Vivien Leigh, a largely unknown British actress. Within days, she was cast as Scarlett.

Selznick went through three directors to get his film made. His first director, the acclaimed George Cukor, was quickly deemed ineffective. His next director, Victor Fleming, didn't capture the epic nature of the material in line with Selznick's vision and kept Selznick's high-paid stars idle while he filmed ancillary scenes. Selznick was particularly perturbed that the brilliant colors of the costumes in the prewar scenes didn't come through enough to contrast with the destitution of the postwar scenes. He eventually replaced Fleming with Sam Wood, who stepped in from work on MGM's *The Wizard of Oz* to complete the film. This ability to interchange directors and borrow personnel from other studios was one of the benefits of the system—the process was akin to trading sports stars among teams. In casting Olivia de Havilland to portray Melanie Hamilton as the moral counterweight to Scarlett, Selznick had to make concessions to Warner Brothers to borrow her, offering to trade Paulette Goddard.

In the midst of these anxieties, Selznick was alarmed to learn that Clark Gable refused to apply any type of accent for Rhett Butler— Selznick was left pleading with Gable for the "occasional accented word." Selznick, watching every detail, was equally appalled by the initial slovenliness of Rhett's suits and switched tailors in costuming. By the time *Gone with the Wind* was completed, its cost had exceeded $4 million. The initial cuts of the movie ran to almost four hours, a mark that MGM's chief quipped was enough for an audience to lose its patience even if the film revealed the Second Coming of Christ. Selznick confided that they needed "the largest gross any picture has had in the last ten years simply to break even."

Despite production problems, Selznick remained optimistic—most days he expected to set the needed box-office records for his film to be financially successful.

THERE WAS ONE MAN in the movie business immune to the usual pressures of dealing with actors, directors, set design, and union contractors. He created stars who never aged, never complained, never walked off the job, and never demanded salaries. By 1937 Walt Disney was already a dominant parallel force to the studio system, "the Horatio Alger hero of Cinema." He did need distribution, but his company's work had such a strong draw at the box office that the distribution arms needed Disney more than the other way around. He controlled the biggest star in the world, Mickey Mouse, who had debuted in a short seven-minute cartoon *Steamboat Willie* in 1928. Even better, Mickey was a commercial phenomenon away from the box office.

In the midst of an economic recovery, Mickey Mouse's licensed image could be found on watches, stuffed animals, food, pencils, notebooks, cups, hairbrushes, and hundreds more items. Just six years after his creation, Disney had Mickey Mouse licensed to eighty different entities in the United States, forty in England, and another eighty in Europe. Lionel, the maker of toy trains, credited the Mickey Mouse license with pulling it out of receivership. Ingersoll Waterbury, a Connecticut watchmaker, sold two million Mickey Mouse watches during a two-year period starting in 1933—the additional $5 million in retail revenues helped increase the company's employment rolls from 200 to 3,200.

Even the communists were impressed. When the head of the Soviet motion picture industry visited Hollywood over a period of six weeks in

1935, he most notably came away taken by Walt Disney's cartoons and cleared them for Soviet audiences. Thinking them satire aimed at the shortcomings of America, a Russian newspaper critic held that "Disney is really showing us the people of the capitalist world under the masks of pigs, mice, and penguins." The American reporter cabled back a different take: "Not since the days of the food shortage have the streets of Moscow witnessed such queues."

By the time he was thirty-three, Disney himself was as famous as many of the biggest movie stars. He was certainly more renowned than any studio executive or director. But Mickey, Minnie, Donald Duck, and even his recent Three Little Pigs all graced the screen for a fraction of the time of feature-length films. Generally, Disney cartoons were shown as a package of short films that ran consecutively to fill up a block of time. For some time, Disney had wanted to push the envelope of the art form to see if it could support a feature film. Starting in 1934, he publicly hinted at a possible feature involving a Grimm brothers fairy tale. Disney surmised that *Snow White* might cost as much as $250,000 to make, would take eighteen months, and could clear $1 million if it was successful.

Unlike a studio with giant sets and stages, Disney's operation resembled a scientific art school. Animators experimented with every aspect of motion and emotion. Live animals were brought in to help capture the nuances of the forest. Ink and paint ran through thousands of hues to give each of the seven dwarfs their individual identities. Writers continually tweaked the dialogue that would be cued to the animation. Color cameras had to be set and set again to pan over the drawings to give each shot the right amount of depth, light, and dramatic tension. *Snow White* was then set to an original symphony score and voice-overs. Over three hundred animators created two million celluloid sheets— hand drawn and hand painted—of which 250,000 "cels" were shot successively to create the animation of Snow White.

The original $250,000 that Disney estimated as the cost was way off the mark, and his revenues from Mickey Mouse were not enough to cover the overages. After investing much of the company's profits on the initial phase of the production, he turned to Bank of America for loans.

Mortgaging all of his company's assets, including the trademarks of Mickey and all of his other characters, Disney borrowed $630,000 in 1936 and another $650,000 less than a year later. A few months later, being equally off on the time needed for completion, he borrowed another $327,000. *Snow White* ended up costing well over $1.5 million, which meant that the film's revenues, in essence, belonged to Bank of America— unless Disney's original revenue expectations of $1 million were also wrong.

And he was. The public was eager to see what this most commercial of American artists had been up to. *Time* magazine featured Disney on its final cover of 1937 with seven small statues of his dwarfs, with the accompanying story comparing him to Rembrandt. Disney had planned to release the film nationwide for Christmas, but only the Los Angeles market got to see it. *Snow White* dazzled audiences there—Clark Gable and Carole Lombard were spotted wiping away tears when Snow White was poisoned. The ability of the film's drawn figures to elicit the full range of emotions made it a masterpiece of modernity.

In January the film premiered in New York at Radio City Music Hall. Theater management estimated the total audience at 800,000 people over its first four weeks in this single theater. *Snow White* went on to set box-office records throughout 1938. Making its gross receipts even more remarkable was the fact that children, a significant portion of the audience, were charged half the price of adult tickets or less. *Snow White*'s first-year record, however, would be broken the next year.

ONCE *GONE WITH THE WIND* was in the distribution pipeline, bringing to an end Selznick's consternation with his directors and stars, his attention shifted to the distribution and marketing of the film. MGM expected to open at the major first-run theaters, the movie palaces in major cities, and then distribute the film to regular theaters nationwide. Selznick disagreed. Unlike in film distribution today, the price of a movie ticket varied by film. As the film made its rounds, prices were reduced over time to stimulate demand among audiences that had missed the initial run. One common strategy was to stage major openings in big cities followed by a "road show" across the country over a period of years—limited engagements to maximize exclusivity and revenues. After the revenues from all of the pent-up demand were extracted, the film would then be distributed to regular theaters with wide distribution and cheaper tickets. Selznick wanted MGM to experiment, restricting the showings and setting prices high, whereas MGM wanted to distribute widely and quickly. In his arguments with MGM, he countered that a high price was a form of marketing and signaled an exceptional product. Finally, MGM agreed to set a minimum price of 75 cents for morning and matinee performances, $1.00 for evening shows with unreserved seats, and $1.50 for reserved.

But Selznick had a much bigger problem in the midst of holding his ground with MGM. Since the midtwenties, individual states had started to subject Hollywood's product to varying degrees of censorship restrictions. To defuse the provincial efforts and standardize practices, the motion picture industry adopted its own code to censor itself. The Motion Picture Producers and Distributors of America, headed by Will Hays, established a set of studio practices that prohibited overt allusions to sex, ridicule of religious beliefs or public officials, glorification of vice, and swearing. It was enforced so strictly by the MPPDA's head that it was known as the Hays Code. For Selznick the problem was swearing. The code had caused *Gone with the Wind*'s ending to be put on hold by one of Hays's lieutenants. After hearing suggestions that he change the ending to "my dear, I don't care," Selznick wrote to Hays, pleading that "the punch line of *Gone with the Wind*, the one bit of dialogue which forever establishes the future relationship between Scarlett and Rhett, is, 'Frankly, my dear, I don't give a damn.'"

Hays relented, perhaps understanding that he had little leverage in the matter. The entire South, the Democratic stronghold of the sitting president, had high expectations for *Gone with the Wind*. Selznick had been repeatedly lobbied to ensure that the film stay as true to the book as possible—insisting on changing the final line to "my dear, I don't care" would have backfired.

To debut the film, Selznick chose to arrange a gala celebration in Atlanta. Atlanta and the state of Georgia went through preparations as though it were a victory march for the Confederacy. Georgia's governor declared a statewide holiday. Atlanta's mayor called for a three-day festival. *Time* magazine suggested that "to Georgia, it was like winning the Battle of Atlanta 75 years late, with Yankee goodwill thrown in." When the film's stars arrived at the airport, they were brought into town along a seven-mile procession route lined with an estimated 300,000 people—"crowds larger than the combined armies that fought at Atlanta in July 1864 waved Confederate flags, tossed confetti till it seemed to be snowing"—many in tears as they imagined welcoming Scarlett O'Hara "back home."

As revisionism, and given the film's benign portrayal of the Confederacy, the southern reception made sense. Everywhere else, the film's story of once-carefree days, filled with plenty and then shattered by larger forces that seemed unpredictable and endless, resonated given the economic troubles of the thirties. Americans could take solace that their once divided nation had survived and built itself into a power.

Gone with the Wind was a story of economic endurance as much as it was about war. Much of the film centered on Scarlett's amoral opportunism in saving her plantation, and her transformation from a decadent young woman into a gritty survivalist was understandable to the larger American audience.

In garnering empathy for the South, the film, and the book, did manage to get away with a glaring obfuscation. All moral judgment of slavery and its aftermath was suspended. This burdensome legacy, even in the giddy atmosphere of the premiere, wasn't difficult to find. One of the film's stars, Hattie McDaniel, who played Mammy, Scarlett's caricaturized Negro caretaker, wasn't welcome at any event in Atlanta celebrating the film.

Seventy-five years after emancipation, she would win an Oscar for best supporting actress for her role, but she couldn't enter the movie theater where *Gone with the Wind* premiered. Had she tried to go to Atlanta anyway with her costars, she would haven't been able to stay in any hotel worthy of Gable or Leigh or even the lighting director. This humiliation was not all that she suffered. Her portrayal of a devoted and subservient former slave made her the target of black newspapers. In Chicago film openings of *Gone with the Wind* included protesters who derided its sympathetic treatment of slavery. Ironically, Hattie McDaniel was the most authentically southern of all of the film's stars: Gable refused to sound like a Southerner, Vivien Leigh and Leslie Howard were British, Olivia de Havilland was born in Japan and would live most of her life in Europe—but this black Oscar winner had her southern roots revealed right down to her Irish last name, McDaniel, the enduring legacy of some slave owner somewhere.

But a few protests notwithstanding, *Gone with the Wind* shattered all box-office records. Selznick International Pictures' profits were as large as those of any of the major studios in 1940 on the basis of one film alone. Adjusted for inflation, it remains one of the highest-grossing movies of all time. But the escapist pleasures of film would be sharply circumscribed. As millions of Americans flooded the theaters to catch a story set during America's greatest conflict, the opening act of the world's greatest conflict began unfolding an ocean away.

Twenty-six

FLIGHT

Around the time Roosevelt first assumed office in 1933, Adolf
Hitler was a few months into his own consolidation of absolute
power in Germany. Just as the New Deal and the rise of federal
power were the stimulant for the American economy, the authority of
Nazi Germany restored the industrial order of Europe's largest economy.

While the New Deal gave birth to social programs, minimum-wage
laws, restrictions on working hours, securities regulations, farm subsidies, and large-scale public works, German economic stimulus in the
thirties was simpler. Hitler focused on a vast expansion of his nation's
military. Politically, this approach was consistent with Hitler's priorities
of restoring German pride and repudiating the final terms of the Treaty
of Versailles. In addition to the financial reparations, the treaty explicitly
prohibited the remilitarization of Germany. But the uncertain fortunes
of the Great Powers during the thirties did not make enforcement a
priority—internal economic problems were the paramount concern. In
particular America, in many ways the epicenter of the Depression, did
not seem eager to intercede.

If anything, a sizable proportion of Americans sympathized with the
Germans and felt that their own country had been duped into intervening
in the Great War. Even if it had the political will, an impossible "if" at
that, what could America do? In 1934 defense spending as a portion of
federal expenditures dropped to its lowest level in decades. In the

budgetary balance between guns and butter, the former was considered especially wasteful in peacetime. This made perfect sense considering that America's two most formidable defensive assets didn't cost anything to maintain. As long as the Atlantic and Pacific oceans remained vast and filled with water, America was going to be tough to invade. This conception of warfare left America with old ships, old guns, old planes, and a small standing army.

In the late thirties, to one American living in England, the fate of Europe seemed sealed. Charles Lindbergh had done more than any living person to shorten the time and space separating Europe from North America. His 1927 crossing of the Atlantic Ocean had made him an American hero and international sensation, with President Coolidge dispatching a warship to retrieve both Lindbergh and his plane. But celebrity had crushed Lindbergh. In America, faced with his reluctant country-boy shyness, the press had hounded him for pictures and sound bites, something and anything for an adoring American public. Reluctance turned to reclusiveness. And this reclusiveness was touched by tragedy. Lindbergh's twenty-month-old son was kidnapped from his bedroom and killed as part of a ransom attempt. The sensationalism this brought on furthered the cruelty. Once the child's body had been discovered and then prepared for burial, news photographers managed to open the coffin to snap pictures.

Lindbergh and his wife, Anne, left America to seek refuge in Europe. Through the midthirties, the Lindberghs spent time in both France and England, living in relative peace. From his vantage point in postwar Europe, Charles's conclusion hardened to what he viewed as the inevitable rise of Germany. To the technical and practical judgment of the aviator, the Teutonic efficiency of the Germans was superior in every way to the Old World methods of his two host countries. For Lindbergh, as for many others, the rise of Germany was less a source of geopolitical anxiety than it was cause for admiration. As far as the Nazi high command was concerned, the feeling was mutual. This great young aviator, with a most German-sounding name, no less, was soon invited through Truman Smith, the American military's attaché in Germany, to be an honored guest. Cynically playing to his hosts' vanity, Smith predicted that the Germans would be eager to show off their latest advances in aviation to Lindbergh.

The Lindberghs arrived without public ceremony, per Charles's wishes. In private Lindbergh was feted and hosted by Hermann Göring, at the time the chief of the Luftwaffe, Germany's air force. Afterward the Germans gave Lindbergh tours of their factories and demonstrations of their aircraft. Sufficiently impressed by the staged orchestrations, Lindbergh sent his observations through Truman Smith back to the States, conveying a belief in German superiority in all matters of aviation. For the Germans, Lindbergh's first and subsequent visits were compounding propaganda coups. Each admiring visit by the most famous aviator in history served as a signal to all rival powers of the futility of attempting to match German technical and scientific superiority. Most critically, Lindbergh put forth his view that the few miles of the English Channel offered little buffer against German aviation, an assessment that added to German negotiating leverage in subsequent events.

By September 1938, hostility had returned to Europe. Hitler looked to claim the Sudetenland, a region of Czechoslovakia mainly populated by Germans. The ostensible reason was to allow the German-speaking populace of Sudetenland the right of self-determination. To apply sufficient leverage, Nazi Germany mobilized troops to the Czech border. Such offensive movements had multiple governments, including the French and British, preparing their citizens for potential conflict. At the same time, British prime minister Neville Chamberlain led the efforts for a negotiated solution by engaging in direct diplomacy with Hitler. Meeting him multiple times in Germany over the course of weeks, including marathon negotiating sessions, Chamberlain pressed for compromise to avert war. On the night of September 30, Britain and Germany, with the assent of Mussolini's Italy and France, made a breakthrough. Under the Munich Agreement among the four powers, German troops were allowed to enter Czechoslovakia and occupy a portion of the Sudetenland. In exchange, the Germans were to refrain from further military action.

On October 1 London and Paris rejoiced. The French premier, Édouard Daladier, returned to wild, cheering crowds on his entire route from the Le Bourget airport all the way to the Ministry of War building. Chamberlain, facing equally elated crowds in London, celebrated, saying that "for the second time in our history, a British Prime Minister has returned from Germany bringing peace with honor."

With war averted, Lindbergh was back in Germany less than three weeks after the agreement. At a formal dinner at the American Embassy, Hermann Göring presented Lindbergh with a medal, the Service Cross of the German Eagle. The pair then retreated for private discussions. After Göring pressed for details on Lindbergh's summer visit to the Soviet Union, the Nazi *Reichsmarschall* invited him to see Germany's latest aircraft, boasting that one of his planes was "far ahead of anything built." As detailed in Lindbergh's remarkable and thorough journal entries from the time, he then spent the next few days flying and testing the Luftwaffe's fighters and bombers, likely the first and only non-German ever to do so. He was impressed to the point of being smitten, going so far as to look at Berlin real estate: "I am anxious to learn more about this country. The Germans are a great people. The future of Europe depends upon the strength of this country. It cannot be kept down except by war, and another European war would be disastrous for everyone."

By March, Germany had seized all of Czechoslovakia.

With war on the horizon, Lindbergh and his family returned to the United States. Once home, he found a new cause that required his reentry into American public life: keeping America out of war.

ROOSEVELT, THE ASSISTANT secretary of the navy during World War I, knew firsthand how events had escalated then and how American intervention had been vital. But he was headed into an election year in 1940, and the politics were tricky. The Depression and the uneven economic recovery hardened American sensibilities, with public sentiment firmly opposed to any participation or alliance. Official government policy reflected this. The president, to his now-considerable regret, had tied his own hands by signing the Neutrality Act in 1935—a time when the dangers and probability of any serious conflict seemed remote.

As many Americans initially saw it, there were no natural allies that merited unconditional defense on moral terms. The Europeans had been fighting for centuries. In the late twenties, a large segment of Americans had sympathy for the Germans, feeling that the postwar conditions imposed by the French and British were unnecessarily humiliating. When the British finally came to the conclusion that collecting German reparations was a lost cause, the British simply turned around and asked for debt forgiveness on the amounts that they themselves owed America. These final wartime debts were forgiven even as the American economy was spiraling downward in 1932. And now the British and French, who couldn't police their neighbors even after one hundred thousand American soldiers had died in Europe in World War I, wanted American intervention again? No, thank you.

For technocrats like Lindbergh, the anti-interventionist perspective was forward looking. German dominance was inevitable. In their eyes, Germany was far more like America than were the colonial empires that had discovered the New World. The arguments that Britain and France were the last strands of democracy held little merit. While the sun never set on the British Empire, did everyone under this British sun vote in the elections? The hundreds of millions of Africans and Indians who were ruled by this colonial power seemed more subjects than citizens. The French too had colonies as far away as Indochina, later to be known to Americans as Vietnam, Cambodia, and Laos. In contrast, the Germans had virtually none. Did it not seem logical that modern nations should surpass old colonial empires weighed down by pride and territory? Wasn't the justification for colonialism based on the material progress and productivity of the colonialist, the idea that superior cultures should be entitled to spread their ways, making everyone better off? Was the rise of Germany not then the natural order of things?

Then one evening, a few weeks after the Munich Agreement, events

took an ominous and sudden turn for the worse. After an evening of ri-
oting and looting, the Nazis announced a "liquidation" of the Jews. But
the word had yet to take on the full weight of its history—at the time, it
denoted a full elimination of Jews from German economic life. Detailing
the damage to Jewish homes and businesses, the *New York Times* guessed
that almost half of Jewish assets in Germany had been seized, destroyed
in "this week's holocaust." Jewish business owners were forced to sell
their holdings almost immediately. The palace of the Catholic Church's
archbishop in Munich was ransacked when he spoke out in defense of
Germany's Jews. To many on the fence, the character of the German rise
now seemed less nationalistic than something altogether different. At
these early developments, former president Hoover publicly voiced his
alarm, stating presciently that "these men are building their own con-
demnation by mankind for centuries to come."

Others had a more distant, and chilling, reaction. Lindbergh found
the evening of German terror against Jews "so contrary" to the German
"sense of order and intelligence. They have undoubtedly had a difficult
Jewish problem, but why is it necessary to handle it so unreasonably? My
admiration for the Germans is constantly being dashed against some
rock such as this." But it wasn't dashed permanently.

This same reluctance to fully reject Germany applied to segments of
American industry. The growing German economy in the thirties had
been good to some of America's largest companies, especially the automakers. Ford had established its second-largest plant outside of North
America in Cologne. General Motors' wholly owned subsidiary, Opel
AG, happened to be the largest automaker in Germany. Combined, the
U.S. automakers constituted the majority of German automotive production. This was especially critical as German automakers Daimler-
Benz and Bavarian Motor Works (BMW) had shifted from passenger
car production to the service of rearming Germany. The operating subsidiaries of GM and Ford, however, could not take their profits out of
Nazi Germany. Just days before the Munich Agreement, the president of
General Motors, fifty-nine-year-old William Knudsen, arrived in Berlin
to check on the status of his operations. Upon his arrival, Reichsmarschall Göring summoned Knudsen to his country estate to discuss a

matter vital to German security. At Göring's estate, heavily fortified and guarded by storm troopers, it soon became clear to Knudsen that he had not been brought there to talk about the trucks that Opel was building for the German military. Göring had learned of a top-secret twelve-cylinder aircraft engine GM was building in America, and Germany wanted a full factory built by GM for the production of similar engines. After getting over his initial shock that Göring obtained knowledge of the secret engine, Knudsen agreed to discuss the German overture with his board.

But as 1939 progressed, it became clear that General Motors was not going to be building aircraft engines for the Nazis. The ownership of German subsidiaries dissolved to being in name only—the Germans took control of the factories and kept their American owners out of further deliberations. All this played into a stunningly prescient analysis by an author writing under the pseudonym of Max Werner. In *The Military Strength of the Powers*, published in 1939 on the eve of war, Werner held that Germany, Japan, and the Soviet Union were the three countries that had sufficiently militarized their economies in the thirties. With this advantage, "the aggressor country can begin with the mass production of the latest and best weapons of war, and it will begin hostilities not only with much more powerful armaments than its enemy, but also with a war industry fully mobilized."

Werner concluded that of all the powers, the least prepared was the United States: "The industrial potential of the U.S.A. is enormous, but her preparedness as a land power is negligible: A weak war industry . . . very little prepared for war mobilization, and very few trained reserves." Independently, Roosevelt came to the same conclusion. To the president, the American military needed to be strengthened regardless of the direction of events. Hitler's boldness in Europe was due in large part to his air force: The Luftwaffe's potential strength in opening corridors for an army on the move and debilitating the enemy's war-making capacity was an essential element of Germany's war machine. Less than a few weeks after the Munich Agreement, and more than three years before the eventual American involvement in war, Roosevelt summoned his secretary of war, secretary of the treasury, and top generals to the Oval Office to call for a dramatic escalation of military strength in peacetime. The president's plan centered on the mass production of planes.

According to the man ultimately credited with building the American Air Force, Hap Arnold, "the president came straight out for air power—now—and lots of them!" To justify such an abrupt expenditure, Roosevelt cynically raised the prospect of having to defend against an attack on the Western Hemisphere. One attendee at the meeting, Brigadier General George Marshall, objected to the seeming illogic of a plan to build planes without the supporting airfields, barracks, bases, artillery, or much else. Indeed, the War Department had just called for a carefully balanced increase in investment across the board. But Arnold was elated as Roosevelt held firm, paraphrasing the president's response as "A new barracks at an army post in Wyoming, or new machine tools at an ordnance arsenal" on American soil "would not scare Hitler one blankety-blank-blank bit!" Roosevelt wanted planes years before the eventual American entry into war. And left unstated was another element of FDR's strategy: He didn't need bases or airfields in America, because he planned to send the planes to old American allies, if they became engaged in a war with Germany.

To build them, private industry would be called into service. But as his military prepared production plans and budgets, Roosevelt had to maneuver politically. The first days of his presidency, when his authority to address the economic crisis was virtually absolute, were a distant memory. He needed two things: money to build planes and authorization to send them to Great Britain and France. Fortunately for Roosevelt, once Czechoslovakia had been taken by Hitler, who had not waited a full year to violate the Munich Agreement, public sentiment had nominally shifted to the British and French, with 66 percent approving the sale of arms in a Gallup poll.

But the fight in Congress did not fully reflect the public's support, at least in terms of selling weapons. The central question was this: If Britain and France were in a state of war with Germany, could the United States supply either country with arms? According to the Neutrality Act stifling Roosevelt, the answer was no. Thirteen senators, both Republicans and Democrats, vowed "an uncompromising fight." "Are we to replace those factories in the arming of Europe? Are we to become the arsenal of the world?" asked the incredulous Republican report. Roosevelt's efforts ended in humiliation as Congress headed for its summer recess in late August, 1939. Lacking confidence in the president's "meddling in foreign affairs," one leading Republican senator held that the "repeal of the embargo" would itself precipitate conflict in Europe.

Two days later, war came anyway. On September 1, 1939, Germany invaded Poland. In response, France and England declared war on Germany.

IF ROOSEVELT HAD expected the events in Europe to unite his nation behind him, he was mistaken. By no means did the growing anti-German sentiment mean a new softness on the part of the American people toward Jewish refugees or support for any military intervention. Instead, the onset of war sparked isolationist sentiment in Congress and in America.

But in the days immediately following Britain's entry into this new war, Roosevelt could not shake his earlier loyalties. He found himself communicating with Prime Minister Chamberlain, pledging his hopes to repeal the arms embargo. Roosevelt also opened up communication with a man who had reemerged in Chamberlain's cabinet to assume the same role he had held earlier in the First World War—Winston Churchill was once again the first lord of the admiralty, the civilian head of the British navy.

But before he could make his arguments to Congress, the president found his position attacked by a man every bit as resolute as him. Lindbergh, having returned from exile, took to the radio to argue the case against any intervention. "If England and France had offered a hand to the struggling Republic of Germany, there would be no war today." After pointing out the complicity of the two powers, he deviated to make another point: "Our bond with Europe is a bond of race and not of political ideology. If the white race is ever seriously threatened, it may then be time for us to take our part for its protection, to fight side by side with the English, French, and Germans. But not with one against the other for our mutual destruction." Considering the mainstream acceptability of such a racial argument at the time, much of Lindbergh's speech was seen as intellectually coherent and sophisticated. He found the thought of arms merchants profiting from warfare repugnant. He argued that granting credit to the belligerents would leave Americans feeling that it was "more important for that country to win than for our own to avoid the war." Still, Lindbergh conceded two points. One was the legal flexibility to sell defensive weapons to favored nations. Two, with his strong ties to the aviation industry and Army Air Corps, he tacitly approved the buildup of American defenses with the logic that "a neutrality built on pacifism alone will fail."

Unimpressed with all the nuances of the aviator's speech, Roosevelt concluded to his treasury secretary, "I am absolutely convinced Lindbergh is a Nazi."

Lindbergh's position, however, provided enough of an opening for Roosevelt to get the arms embargo lifted. There were limitations. No credit could be granted. American ships were prohibited from entering the seas of warring nations. Immediately after signing the bill, the United States was in the business of war, if not yet in the act of fighting one.

As Roosevelt had predicted, there was one product all of the belligerents wanted: planes. On the same morning that the embargo was reported as lifted, the *New York Times* reported estimated orders of 2,600 planes for 1940. Along with explosives, guns, and trucks, $2 billion in sales were expected to the approved nations, including Belgium and Holland.

Wasting little time or momentum, Roosevelt announced that he would seek $1.3 billion over the next few years to build ninety-five ships, including three aircraft carriers, fifty-two destroyers, and thirty-two submarines, along with a fleet of six thousand aircraft. He had waited for over a year from his Oval Office presentation to his secretaries and generals to press Congress for the funds. American industry was going to not only supply the war in Europe but also engage in the then-to-date largest peacetime buildup of the American arsenal, an effort surpassing Roosevelt's cousin Teddy's initiative in the first decade of the century. About nine hundred planes had been built annually for the military in the United States from 1936 to 1939. In 1940 production jumped to over six thousand. Even this would be a mere fraction of what was to come.

While American war production had started in earnest, the isolationist forces had grown stronger. Lindbergh continued for the next two years as the most active and energetic voice of this movement. Despite accusations that he was a Nazi sympathizer, he maintained his credibility in several important corners. High-ranking military officials credited Lindbergh with giving them "the most accurate picture of the Luftwaffe, its equipment, leaders, plans, training methods, and present defects." In addition, Lindbergh served as a consultant at the Ford Motor Company as the automaker bid on defense contracts.

As 1940 progressed, the German military took over Holland, Belgium, and Denmark. By early June, the German military was thirty-five miles outside Paris. Less than two weeks later, France surrendered. "The French Army, despite its 3,500,000 men, proved inadequate. French deficiency in air power, to a large extent, explained the subsequent disaster" was the analysis of the American secretary of war, Henry Stimson. With all of Continental Europe neutralized, the Germans turned their power to daily air bombings of Britain. Around the same time, Germany formed an alliance with Japan, which had transformed itself into an imperial force on the Asian mainland.

But America continued to exist in a paradoxical and perplexing vacuum. It was preparing for full-scale war even though public opinion was set against intervention. Ever resourceful, using a statute from 1916, the president reconvened the Council on National Defense to call for production of fifty thousand warplanes per year. Roosevelt then enlisted William Knudsen, the president of General Motors, to take over all matters of military production. Less than two years before this appointment, Knudsen was being entertained and coaxed for information by Hermann Göring. Now he was tasked with bringing mass production to the American military. Knudsen turned to Ford, his former employer, to coordinate production plans. Henry Ford, like Knudsen, also had dealings with the Germans. In 1938 Ford had received the Service Cross of the German Eagle, a similar honor to Lindbergh's.

A few months later, Roosevelt faced his most formidable challenger to date in the election of 1940. His opponent, forty-eight-year-old Wendell Willkie, was a former corporate executive. To him, the New Deal had destroyed the competitiveness of America, the commercial energy needed to safeguard democracy. In the final stretch of the campaign, indicating the centrality of the issue, Willkie derided the president's call for fifty thousand planes per year. "Anybody that knows anything about production will understand after years of neglect and abuse by the New Deal that goal cannot be reached short of a period of years." Roosevelt's predecessor, Hoover, declared that the unprecedented attempt for a third presidential term had an "odor of totalitarianism." Willkie closed with a final election-eve plea to women voters, pledging "not to send your husbands and sons and brothers to death on a European or Asiatic battlefield." The polls provided a referendum on the New Deal, the economy of the 1930s, and Roosevelt's handling of foreign affairs. It was Roosevelt's smallest margin of victory—after eight years in office, he won thirty-eight out of forty-eight states. The message sent by the electorate was, once again, resoundingly clear: The American people trusted this crippled man, who could not walk across the Oval Office without assistance, in all times of crisis.

ROOSEVELT'S VICTORY WAS less than pleasing to some. Henry Ford had become increasingly paranoid that the government was looking to take over his business. Even before Roosevelt won a third term, the mere mention of the president's name could send the aging Ford into a rage. Knudsen—called the "Defense Commissioner" by *Time* magazine— found this out firsthand to his great embarrassment. Knudsen's task was to bring the mass production capabilities of the Detroit automakers to the airplane. The plane makers, used to the high levels of precision required for aviation, had never had to build at the volumes that the escalating government contracts mandated. The standard manufacturing process involved parts being brought to the airplane frame. At the same time, the aircraft industry had balked at the suggestion that the automakers build planes using an assembly-line method. As a compromise, Knudsen started asking automakers to build components and parts for final assembly by the aircraft makers.

Knudsen tasked Ford with building six thousand aircraft engines designed by Rolls-Royce. Ford initially agreed, until he heard reports of a British lord discussing the order. Refusing to make anything for any foreign military, as it appeared he was doing, Ford pulled out. Knudsen implored Ford to keep his word, but he made a mistake by invoking Roosevelt's pleasure at Ford's initial consent. Knudsen left empty-handed and enraged. The New Deal had been especially tough for Ford to weather. Once hailed universally as the friend of labor with his five-dollar day, he had found himself in a losing battle with unions throughout the 1930s. He blamed Roosevelt's union policies for severing his direct connection to his labor force. Now his life's work, his plants and method of manufacture, were being summoned by the government for a cause he didn't believe in. He was, perhaps above all other men, the most important contributor to the American way of life. Yet he was being asked to tolerate a most un-American approach to protecting America.

But Ford's petulance presented his chief deputy, Charles Sorensen, with a dilemma recounted in his memoir: "On one side, a mightily determined old man racked by hallucinations; on the other hand, a Franklin Roosevelt administration able, even eager, should occasion rise to take over Ford Motor Company." In the deputy's mind, open defiance risked nationalization. So Sorensen, who had been with Ford before the very first assembly line was put together, led the company's participation in Knudsen's plans.

In early 1941 Sorensen found himself in San Diego reviewing the B-24 Liberator, a four-engine bomber manufactured by Consolidated Aircraft. The air force was displeased at the "snail's pace" of production of the Liberator. As the man from Ford saw it, "here was a custom made plane, put together as a tailor would cut and fit a suit of clothes." The parts were so sensitive that changes in the temperature required further adjustment before final assembly. Producing parts in Detroit for assembly in California made little sense. He returned to his room at the Coronado Hotel to review his company's possible contribution to the effort.

Inspired, he outlined and sketched methodologies for the remainder of the day and well into the night. Taking into account the requirements of each of the major parts, the time required for assembly, the floor space required for each operation, and the sequence of operations, Sorensen began to develop a plan to significantly increase the production of the B-24. The bomber's size, almost sixty-six feet in length with two large engines mounted on each side, presented a challenge that exceeded anything he had tackled in the automotive trade.

The next day at breakfast, he shared his plan with Henry Ford's son, Edsel. The air force's intermediary proposed that Ford build one thousand wings for Consolidated Aircraft. Sorensen countered: The air force should give the Ford Motor Company $200 million to build the largest industrial facility in the world to build complete B-24s. Based on the earlier day's sketches, Ford's production chief called for a plant "a mile long and a quarter mile wide." If the government approved this, the automaker promised one bomber per hour for eighteen hours each day. While the air force reacted enthusiastically, Sorensen had to convince his increasingly erratic boss. Perhaps sensing the futility of resisting or marveling at the challenge of an immense facility, Henry Ford gave his permission. Within a month, the government approved the plan. Less than four full months from pencil drawings, steel was being erected at the new Willow Run facility. Ford was in the airplane business.

Other automakers were similarly retooled. Knudsen's former employer, General Motors, converted three factories to make machine guns to augment Colt. Chrysler was commissioned to produce thirty-ton tanks in a new $20 million facility. American Car & Foundry and Baldwin Locomotive were in the business of building heavy tanks. A top Sears Roebuck merchandising executive was placed in charge of getting the "fairest price, fastest delivery, and best quality in everything the Army and Navy" purchased, from "safety pins to 16-inch guns." The chairman of U.S. Steel resigned from his $100,000-per-year job at the steelmaker to oversee all procurement of industrial materials, from steel to rubber to tin. By 1941 the federal government's expenditures in its War Department, mostly in rearming America, amounted to $3.9 billion. In 1939 the department had spent less than $700 million. But despite the fivefold increase, America was not yet at war.

The other hemisphere, however, was being entirely reordered. In June 1941, a year after the surrender of France, German forces invaded the Soviet Union. The communists had formed an alliance of convenience with Great Britain; the Soviets made the first request for American supplies of arms. In the Pacific theater, the Japanese government's puppet regime in Japanese-occupied China was recognized as the legitimate government by Germany, Italy, and the minor Axis powers. In response, just as with Great Britain, America planned on sending planes and pilots to unoccupied China.

The likely course of events became clear to the administration. The master politician in the White House started preparing his countrymen subtly and psychologically. He no longer answered the question of whether America could stay out of war in the soothing manner of his fall campaign. Confronted with a new poll that revealed that Americans remained overwhelmingly against war, Roosevelt dismissed it, suggesting that it was like asking people if they were against sin.

The debate raged on in the newspapers, which carried near-daily editorials and speech excerpts of antiwar forces, including Lindbergh's. As the leading figure in a movement called America First, Lindbergh sought to reassure Americans of the safety they derived from the oceans.

But the aviator had miscalculated. As Japan mobilized its forces across Asia, it found one potential threat. American bases on islands from Hawaii and Guam to the Philippines were the dots that connected the American mainland to Asia. As tensions rose in the Pacific theater—a conflict that stood secondary to the war in Europe—the war came closer. After a week of negotiations that took place in Washington, the special envoy of Emperor Hirohito was invited to meet with Roosevelt on November 27. The parties, America and Japan, remained far apart. Upon hearing of Japanese troop movements toward Burma, Roosevelt appealed directly to the Emperor. On December 7, Japan bombed the U.S. naval base at Pearl Harbor and declared war on Britain and the United States. The Senate voted unanimously to authorize war. In the House there was one dissenting vote.

"We have brought it on our own shoulders; I can see nothing to do under these circumstances except to fight," Lindbergh conceded in his journal. "If I had been in Congress, I certainly would have voted for a declaration of war." With Germany allied with Japan and the Japanese declaration of war on Britain, by the end of the week, America was at war with Germany, too.

With America called into war, capitalism effectively stopped. For the next three and half years, the government was the primary actor in the economy. It channeled the previous decades of American private efforts to the purpose of winning a two-front war. The next big things from America's past—from the exploration of oil fields to steel production, mass production of automobiles, radio applications like radar, even the film studios—would be called upon to serve the national cause. Hollywood was ordered to create morale-boosting propaganda films for a nation that needed to produce at maximum rates at home and fight abroad. A country that had produced almost 4 million passenger vehicles in 1940 produced 222,000 in 1942; this figure dropped to a grand total of 139 new cars for public consumption the next year. Within twelve months of Pearl Harbor, auto and aircraft makers collaborated to produce almost 48,000 planes—2,000 short of Roosevelt's prewar target. Production would double to almost 100,000 planes the following year—a credit to Roosevelt, who had readied his nation militarily even when it lacked the political will to fight.

And there was another element of American power—one that Hitler understood. Thanks to its geography, America had endless natural resources. It was beyond self-sufficient in energy, minerals, and food. While fuel shortages plagued the Nazis, natural gas and petroleum production in America grew throughout the war. Similarly, there were no shortages of iron ore, copper, zinc, or lead. Beef, pork, wheat, and dairy production were at all-time highs. But this geographic bounty buffered by two oceans was no accident of history. The purchase of the Louisiana Territory, displacement of the Indians, the westward movement of Manifest Destiny, winning the Mexican-American War and the California coastline with it, and the American Civil War to hold it all together—each played a role in this strategic advantage that now powered and insulated America.

Yet the tireless production of all of these armaments—Liberator bombers and Liberty ships—masked the fact that liberty all but disappeared during a state of war. Just as the cliché holds that crisis reveals character, war revealed the nature of the modern state. Any man, even in arguably the most democratic and capitalistic country on earth, could be drafted to fight and forced to serve his country, which suggested that the individual only truly owned himself in peacetime; in wartime, he belonged to the government. Equally, World War II established that the entire industrial capacity of free-market capitalism could be taken over; property rights too were not immutable. War seemed to be the great eraser of all ideological constructs.

At the same time, war had also shown that central planning could not only coordinate the resources of a large economy but also force rapid innovation. The Manhattan Project, which developed the nuclear bomb, was as innovative as anything private industry had ever produced in American history. Numerous military technologies, including advances in television, jets, and computing, rose from the research-and-development laboratory that was World War II; efforts intended to help destroy would be repurposed in the future by the private sector for more humane uses. Indeed, the expensive science that often yielded transformation would increasingly come from government-funded research, which ironically could be conducted without regard to its commercial prospects. The notion that only the profit motive could lead to invention or maximize production was contradicted by the performance of America during wartime.

But after victory, the paramount American ideology that emerged again was its steely pragmatism: one that could contract the principles of both democracy and capitalism in times of crisis but was rooted in its ability to revert to its traditional conceits when threats dissipated—a Darwinian mode of internal and external statecraft that adapted to shifting conditions.

In this era of modern weapons able to bring horror through the sky, Americans understood that there could be no retreat from global affairs. With its victories over Germany and Japan, America established permanent military bases in both countries and wrote their constitutions, imposing demilitarization and democracy. But remarkably, America embraced its vanquished adversaries with magnanimity and money:

Japan and Germany would reemerge as the second- and third-richest countries on earth in short order, with American markets open to both. Ironically, it would be America's allies, France and England, that would recede from the world stage, relinquishing their colonial empires and thereby shifting the bloody decades of European wars to conflicts within the newly independent former colonies, each now free to mix its own potion of ideology, religion, cult of personality, militarism, and economic theory. America's other wartime allies, the Soviet Union and Nationalist China, the latter falling to its internal communists shortly after the war, emerged as the vanguard of a competing ideology.

In opposing and differentiating itself from communism—in the race to export the American template to the free world and beyond—free-market capitalism would become an article of faith elevated in standing to that of democracy. Like freedom of speech and religion, free enterprise would be presented as an intrinsic aspect of human freedom and creativity, a system of economic liberty justified on philosophical grounds beyond its mere ability to deliver high standards of living.

Twenty-seven

SUBURBIA

To Bill Levitt, America had been a little too good at war production. In his time in the Pacific as a naval officer, he had seen a navy deprived of little. "My outfit had so many electric refrigerators," he recalled in a speech, "that many of them were never uncrated. We had so many tins of coffee that it was a toss-up as to what made us more nervous—Japs or caffeine. And as for cigarettes: Well, somebody in logistics must have confused cartons with packs because we had enough to make us rival the open-hearth furnaces of Pittsburgh." The implications of Levitt's colorful anecdotes were clear: Such waste was a natural outcome of central planning and government regulation, a fate that his industry audience of home builders now needed to resist. But at the time of this 1950 speech, Levitt was no disinterested observer. As a home builder himself, he was perhaps the biggest beneficiary of the return and acclimation of American soldiers to civilian life.

Over fifteen million Americans had served in the military in World War II. Starting in 1944, the first waves began their return home after their final tours of duty. Older soldiers returned to their wives and children, towns and villages, homes and farms, and resumed their adult lives. But the youngest of the men who had served had come of age entirely during wartime. The typical young soldier born in, say, 1920, had been all of nine when his country had started on its descent to its worst economic trauma. He had seen the hardships of the Great

Depression grip the only America he had known. By the time he turned eighteen, the headlines had turned to impending conflict overseas. Before being able to vote in any presidential election—the voting age was twenty-one then—this boy had been called to serve. For his older brothers and cousins born in the 1910s, the narrative might have even been starker—they had reached working age in the early 1930s.

This generation had not seen the land of plenty, the seemingly endless upward trajectory endemic to the American way of life. He didn't marvel at the automobile and radio, because they had been commonplace as far back as he could remember; these were items that Americans, even in times of deprivation, took for granted. Even in John Steinbeck's 1939 tale of poverty, the Joad family travels across America in their own car as economic refugees from Oklahoma to California, a believable story that would have been unbelievable just about anywhere else in the world—where by definition poor people didn't own cars. Nevertheless, this America of the young soldier's adulthood was one of economic dislocation at home in the thirties and death abroad in the forties. The coordinating institution at the center of American life for more than a decade—the one that had triaged the economy back to life and won two parallel wars in the Pacific and Europe—had been the federal government. But private America was returning.

During the last year of the war and his life, Roosevelt had shifted some attention to the reintegration of millions of men back into the economy. Officially titled the Servicemen's Readjustment Act when he signed it, the GI Bill covered a range of programs, including housing, education, and employment for returning soldiers. It started with fifty-two weeks of unemployment pay at $20 per week. For soldiers looking to attend college or receive training in a trade, the bill offered $500 per year for tuition and $50 per month for living expenses for four years—$75 for married soldiers. Taking full advantage of the subsidy, millions of soldiers enrolled in colleges and vocational training programs. Lastly, the government provided for loan guarantees on loans made to veterans for buying houses or starting businesses.

But despite the access to mortgage financing for returning soldiers, there were few homes to buy. Victory was coupled with "the frantic search for accommodations which do not exist," said a columnist at the *Chicago Tribune*. In bigger cities like Chicago, this was a full-blown crisis. A *New York Times* editorial urgently called for the construction of five million homes across the country. Several factors compounded the problem. Residential construction had peaked in 1925. New construction had dropped to a fraction of that level during the thirties. But just as housing was recovering, the war began and shifted men and material away from home construction. In total, a twenty-year period had passed during which the nation's housing stock had not kept up with population growth, family formation, or the decay of existing housing units. People had made do. As millions of young men and women who had postponed getting married due to war looked to start work and families, the need for housing became acute. The solution set off a complete transformation of the American landscape.

BILL LEVITT, like hundreds of other home builders throughout the country, ended up building not just homes but entire towns. At war's end, two years shy of forty, Levitt had returned from military service to the family business, Levitt & Sons, which his lawyer father, Abraham, had founded. Levitt had played only a junior role in the company's large development in 1934. Set on Long Island, Strathmore at Manhasset was a development of two hundred houses priced between $9,000 and $18,000. At these price points during the Depression, the homes were affordable only to the upper middle class.

This project had been the beneficiary of legislation passed in the first days of Roosevelt's presidency. Starting in 1933, to address the national economic emergency, Roosevelt had sought to create two federal agencies to help urban homeowners. The agencies, the Home Owners' Loan Corporation (HOLC) and the Federal Housing Administration (FHA), were intended to prevent a crisis of foreclosures and encourage home building by making new loans. Until the New Deal, the vast majority of mortgages in America were of relatively short duration, up to ten years in most cases, and many were not fully amortizing. This meant that at the end of the loan's term, the homeowner still owed money, for which he generally needed another new loan. During the Depression, with the collapse of home values, such loans were not easy to come by—banks did not want to loan money against an asset whose value was falling.

The HOLC and the FHA stepped in to provide loan guarantees on a large scale in the housing market. With the government guaranteeing repayment of the loan, the bank or savings-and-loan association could make the loan to the borrower without worrying about default. At the same time, to reduce the borrower's monthly burden and create stability, the loan terms were stretched out to up to thirty years. In addition, the FHA guarantee allowed banks to lend up to 95 percent of a home's value. By 1939 the housing market had considerably accelerated due to the loan guarantees, only to be stopped by war.

At war's end, even the down-payment requirement was waived for returning veterans. Anyone with a job could technically buy a home. The question then became one of location: Where were these millions of new homes going to be built? In a nation that had become saturated with cars by the end of the twenties, the answer was the open countryside surrounding every major city in America, such as potato fields on Long Island. In 1947 Levitt & Sons, led by Bill, gambled on 1,200 flat, less-than-verdant acres of farmland set in the center of the island. Set about thirty miles from the Empire State Building, beyond the dense boroughs of Brooklyn and Queens, stood this parcel of land, seemingly a world apart from the vibrant, dense urban street life filled with trolleys, vendors, and pedestrians. Levitt viewed this prospective transition in evangelical terms: "You marvel at the rebirth of man, man with his own piece of the good earth, his own share of light and air and sunshine." To this reborn man, Levitt planned to sell single-family, detached houses in the suburbs.

On this land Levitt would build an entire suburban town from scratch. His vision called for homes of solid quality and practical design, and at price points never before seen in new construction. Mass production of houses was not a new concept. Sears and Montgomery Ward had sold homes via catalog for decades. Each retailer, using its immense purchasing power in lumber, metal, and porcelain, was able to offer families on the frontier a full set of materials for assembly on-site; the homeowner simply needed to buy the land and hire a local crew. But anything that varied, such as design options or land type, added to costs and time. As the Ford Model-T had once shown America, to achieve good quality at the best possible price, the only formula was to build the exact same thing over and over.

Within months, Levitt's potato fields were converted into the equivalent of a large factory. Convoys of trucks stopped at identically divided plots of land, dropping off "identical piles of lumber, pipes, bricks, shingles, and copper tubing—all as neatly packaged as loaves from a bakery." Earth diggers stood nearby to dig out dirt in rectangles of twenty-five by thirty-two feet for the bases of the houses. Cement trucks immediately followed to lay the foundations. When the cement slabs dried, specialized crews of two or three men arrived, each one tasked with executing one specific function, such as laying bricks at the base, raising the frame, nailing the sideboards, putting on the roof, painting, and so on. After its particular job was complete, each crew moved to the next plot, while the crew on the adjacent plot came over to perform the next task. Unlike an automobile assembly line, where the chassis of the car moved through the factory, here the crews quickly moved through Levitt's outdoor factory assembling homes.

The more homes that were built, and the more efficient managers and crews became, the lower the cost of each home. The homes were small. Designed by Bill's brother, Alfred, they were modern renditions of the humble ranch house: a single floor with a twelve-by-sixteen-foot living room, two small bedrooms, a kitchen, and a bathroom, all placed under a sharp-angled roof. The homes were set on sixty-by-hundred-foot plots of land, with the front door set thirty feet back from the road and an additional thirty feet in the back for a yard. Within a year, Levitt had built four thousand homes, more than any other developer in America. He named the development Levittown.

He was as adept at selling houses as he was at building them. Pricing each home identically at $7,990, he included a refrigerator, bookshelves, and a washing machine. Making Levittown even more accessible, Levitt offered to rent the homes for $65 per month. When homes went up for sale, news photographers captured people camped out overnight for a chance to buy one. Since the price didn't adjust to demand, it instead created frenzy, which made for good marketing. In 1948 Levitt expected

to build another four thousand homes. In addition, he planned on adding community swimming pools and shopping centers. Given his stature,
the significance of Levitt wasn't his dominance of suburban
construction—even thousands of houses added up to less than 1 percent
national market share—but his template: producing and selling homes at
a scale that turned farmland into communities virtually overnight.

With additional advances in federal support of private housing initia-
tives, spearheaded by Republican senators like Joseph McCarthy, the
United States adopted a policy of encouraging the construction of fifteen
million new homes over the coming decade. By necessity, these homes
had to be built where land was cheap, but the compounding factor was
that to employ Levitt's mass-manufacturing techniques, a builder needed
vast, wide-open spaces. This technique didn't work in urban areas or in
high-rises—a builder would have to customize building plans for the
unique parcels available in the city. The major advantage of a suburban
development from a cash-flow perspective was that each home could be
sold as soon as it was built. With a multistory building, the builder needed
to wait until the entire building was completed before finalizing the sale
of units and allowing buyers to move in.

The effect was that an entire generation of new families was being
formed within driving distance of a city, but without being a part of one.
The suburban ethos and the impending baby boom coincided in spirit
and function. The profile of these towns took the shape of male com-
muters, housewives at home, and communities entirely centered on
raising children, family factories of a sort. The patterns of life, family,
and commuting—the bland and conforming sameness of it all—alarmed
social and cultural critics as it became apparent that the energies and
aspirations of young families, the renewable source of people, were going
to be drained from the American city.

In his seminal work on American suburbs, *Crabgrass Frontier*, Kenneth Jackson relayed the critics' view of the suburb as "offering neither
the urbanity and sophistication of the city nor the tranquility and repose
of the farm"—the suburb was a "cultural, economic, and emotional
wasteland." But this collective critique, not necessarily Jackson's own,

had the stinging tinge of elitism. To many, the countryside was not all that bucolic in the first place. Farm life was notoriously tough. Any dairy or hog farmer would dispute the idyllic vision of the country that New York writers and academics held of it. And the charms of the city? When one spent eight hours each day in a noisy factory with all of the glamour of hard, physical work, the cultural attractions of the city held little allure compared with a cold beer. A cramped apartment, with the sounds of one's own children mingling with the muffled conversations of neighbors through shared walls, didn't seem that sophisticated. And when the hot weather arrived, unlike the cultured literati, the ordinary man could not choose to leave the city to "summer" elsewhere. Having four walls of one's own, a patch of grass in the back, a grill for hot dogs, and the ability to see the sky didn't seem that bad. And what was this culture the critics were so fond of? Most Americans went to the movies, not poetry readings. Couldn't a few of these theaters be built out here too? And didn't a baseball game on the radio sound just as good anywhere?

Enticed, factory workers, truck drivers, shopkeepers, and junior professionals left their rented and often cramped urban settings and became Levitt's "proud country home-owners." For decades, sons of farmers had flocked to the cities, mingling with immigrants from all parts of the world. Now they headed back out. For the young man who had come of age on the battlefields of Normandy, with parents who had struggled during the Great Depression, it would have seemed the height of ingratitude to not think of this as the American dream.

SUBURBIA WOULD SOON become the central driver of American culture. In the period before World War I, it was not uncommon to have single years with over one million immigrants. But for more than fifteen years, from 1931 to 1945, a total of fewer than 700,000 immigrants arrived in America. The slow trickle of immigration for almost an entire generation meant that the vast majority of newly married couples in postwar America were native born. They spoke American-accented English, and the war had further solidified their Americanism in place of their ethnic parents' nativism. Increasingly, white Americans intermarried regardless of their ethnic roots. A postwar couple's offspring might be a mix of Irish, German, Scottish, and English blood without anyone taking offense. If the inner-city neighborhoods and tenements of their parents' reinforced ethnicity, suburbia was the new America that fully washed away ethnic roots. This happened so successfully that the grandchildren of most white Americans could no longer place a single, dominant ethnic hyphenation before "American." Incongruously, the uniform whiteness of suburbia was actually the melting pot at work.

In addition to blending ethnicity among whites, the lack of immigration eroded class divisions. No longer did a million hungry and desperate souls land on these shores to undercut wages for the workingman. For well-to-do households, no longer did the wives and daughters of the newly arrived provide an endless supply of cheap domestic servants such as maids, governesses, and cooks—they had aged without replacement by newcomers. The differentiating factors between an upper-middle-class home and a lower-middle-class home increasingly came down to which suburb one lived in. By 1954 the simple and wide definition of "middle class" could have been owning one's home but not being able to afford a servant.

Similarly, suburbia unified taste. In *The Organization Man*, a wide-ranging analysis of suburban household behavior, William H. Whyte pointed to "inconspicuous consumption" as a central precept of acceptable behavior in the middle-class cul-de-sac. While material comforts and luxuries were to be energetically pursued as a part of the good life, it was a part of an observed social contract to not stand out too much relative to one's neighbors. It was a delicate balancing act between showing that one had a little more taste or money versus maintaining the "strong impulse toward egalitarianism." And when a family's capacity for consumption significantly outpaced their neighbors,' they upgraded suburbs. What might have been seen as an obscene or vulgar show of upward mobility in one neighborhood might be normal in the next development over.

This mobility had broad implications. While the 1954 entry-level Levittown homes were advertised for $8,490—calling for $440 down and $65 per month—families with growing incomes could jump to the successively more affluent brackets. New developments in the New York area, with names like Gedney Meadows, Forest Acres, and Rolling Hills evoking peaceful pastures, had price points that suggested gradations of middle class. A home in Yorktown Heights started at $11,560, while a home in Forest Acres in Rye, New York, started at $30,450. Unlike the implied permanence of the family home, the new American dream required periodic and opportunistic shifting. The white-collar worker's promotions and transfers normalized this transience for everyone else. In many developments, the average homeowner owned his home for less than seven years. The ease of home purchase made it equally easy to sell to others—this suburban liquidity washed away the quaint idea of the multigenerational hometown.

All of these forces created a predictable homogeneity in attitudes. But unappreciated is the extent to which the move to suburbia put millions of Americans in touch with democracy. Unlike the big cities, with their century-old political institutions and settled constituencies, these newly built suburbs needed local governance. They did start as outdoor factories building cookie-cutter homes, but with time they coalesced into communities and towns that needed essential services. Fire and police departments needed to be chartered. Residents needed to set aside land for parks and argue about the placement of stoplights. Discussions on local zoning for shopping and commercial real estate had a tangible immediacy. And most important, at the center of all politics was the paramount issue of suburban existence everywhere: schools.

If buying cheap land, subdividing it a hundred times, hiring teams of men to quickly build homes, and selling each at a substantial profit was the essence of capitalism, the public school district that unified each of these homes was the essence of socialism, perhaps even communism— what else to call free education for all? When the new communities took over responsibility for maintenance from the developers, the future was in the collective hands of homeowners. Invariably, local communities got together, held referenda, and voted to tax themselves on their properties. The bulk of local taxation, as is still true today, was for the children. The school became the center of all community affairs. How much should we spend on classrooms? How much do we pay teachers? Do we really need that new building? Keeping up with the Joneses turned into a competition among towns to keep schools up to par. There was an economic rationale beyond pride in all the little Johnnys and Wilmas—almost all prospective suburban buyers would learn to look at schools as a primary measure of a community's quality. A degraded school district affected resale value.

Earmarking taxation primarily for schools kept these communities young—it often made little sense for retired couples to absorb the tax burden of educating neighborhood children. It also meant that even if the obligations of one's mortgage ended, the local town's annual tax bill was attached to the property—the community owned a residual, permanent interest in the home as much as the homeowner did. For an entire class of people to once again be involved in the political process, to directly vote on taxes and financing matters, was a level of participatory democracy at which Alexis de Tocqueville would have marveled: "To have a hand in the government of society, and to talk about it," wrote Tocqueville in his *Democracy in America* in 1835, "is the most important business and so to speak, the only pleasure an American knows." As the economy of the nineteenth century progressed beyond the small towns of Tocqueville's observations, Americans' ability to affect politics diminished with the move from the country to the big city, with its varied, complex interests. Yet here it was in the sterile, boring, lily-white suburbs of postwar America: the rebirth of local democracy.

BUT THIS SUBURBAN DEMOCRACY, the new American dream, was not open to all.

Before the final homes were completed in New York, Bill Levitt turned his attention to a housing development even larger than Levittown, set in the meadows of Bucks County, Pennsylvania. His plan was to again turn thousands of acres of farmland into a community of tens of thousands of people. The impetus was an announcement by U.S. Steel. Decades after it had been formed from a merger of Carnegie and other major steel interests, the company's outlook remained a bellwether of the American economy. Everything from buildings to automobiles needed steel. If U.S. Steel was optimistic, it meant conditions were good. And in the early fifties, U.S. Steel was very optimistic.

In what the *New York Times* called the "largest steel expansion project ever undertaken," the company was in the process of spending $400 million to build a large plant on the banks of the Delaware River. Seven thousand construction workers were working six-day weeks to get the plant up and running. The plant itself, partially constructed, already employed thousands and expected to employ thousands more in the blue-collar jobs that defined the heart of the middle class. The regional economy, with its supporting railroads, was projected to entice a total of $4 billion of other industrial investment. In all, it was a good place to build homes.

The first stage of the new project by Levitt & Sons, set on a two-thousand-acre plot, saw the sale of 3,500 houses before a single one was completed. Some of the sales were stimulated by Levitt's reputation alone. In a *Time* magazine cover story, Levitt had characterized his ambitions simply as "I wanted to make a lot of money." The purity of his intentions, achieved through well-priced homes in well-planned neighborhoods, was an advertisement in and of itself. A man was always telling the truth when he professed his self-interest. Equally important, home buyers relied on another assurance from Levitt: He would not sell to blacks.

He was not alone. Many home builders throughout the country, in the North as in the South, practiced a strict policy of not selling to blacks. And it made economic sense. To Levitt, a man who didn't "like to be associated with anything that doesn't make money," the market was the master. His role was to serve a demand. And the aspiring homeowners of Levitt's entry-level product did not aspire to live next to blacks. "If we sell one house to a Negro family," he suspected, "then ninety to ninety-five percent of our white customers will not buy into this community." Prices would fall to the point where it would not make sense to build anymore. His view was that home builders could either "solve a housing problem, or we can try to solve a racial problem, but we cannot combine the two." Regardless of Levitt's personal views on race, he was a rational economic actor who simply wanted to sell houses. If that meant excluding blacks, so be it.

To be sure, dirty hands also belonged to the federal government. When the FHA was first formed in the thirties and restructured the entire nature of American housing finance, the government entered the business of insuring mortgages. When a mortgage lender made a housing loan to a veteran or young couple, in a technical sense it was loaning money with the same level of safety as U.S. government bonds. If a borrower didn't pay back the mortgage, the government guaranteed the difference between the foreclosed value and the value of the loan. Given this dynamic, the government now had a vested interest in making sure the value of residential real estate did not fall. Since lenders making FHA loans might make reckless loans with the government holding the bag, the FHA put out an underwriting manual on the types of loans it would guarantee.

To make it simple, the FHA asked its underwriters to gauge the quality of residential neighborhoods before guaranteeing loans. Quality was determined by economic stability, access to utilities, level of local taxation, transportation, and adequacy of shopping and commercial centers. But the second-biggest factor, after economic stability, was "protection from adverse influences." This clause was intended to prevent underwriting in areas that had the potential for "infiltration" by "inharmonious racial groups." It recommended that neighborhoods and communities adopt covenants to prevent home sales to certain racial groups, much as zoning ordinances kept out undesirable commercial elements like factories in residential neighborhoods. Item 233 of the manual was clear as day that "a change in social or racial occupancy generally leads to instability and a reduction in values." Considering that almost all homebuyers needed a loan, it was best to prevent infiltration in the neighborhood; otherwise, prospective buyers might not be able to borrow to buy when it came time for older owners to sell. Eventually a Supreme Court ruling made the old guidelines illegal, but old habits were hard to break.

By 1957 Levitt had successfully completed his Pennsylvania development. With over sixty thousand people in the community, spread across 15,500 homes, spending their days in playgrounds and swimming pools, Levitt had once again delivered on his promise. He had even managed to name one of the elementary schools after Walt Disney, an act notable enough to prompt a visit from Walt himself to one of America's most famous suburbs—a creation of scale, if not imagination, that Disney could relate to. With this, Levitt's work was done. All the demand had been more than met and the market cooled off.

But in the spring the suburban fantasy was disrupted. Two Jewish families, like Levitt's, had taken matters into their own hands. As some of the earliest residents in Levittown, they had watched a neighboring home languish on the market, a light pink one on Deepgreen Lane similar to their own. Lew and Bea Wechsler's neighbor, Irv Mandel, was in a financial bind and desperately needed to sell the home. When Mandel approached the Wechslers, he asked reluctantly if they would mind his house being shown to a larger pool of buyers, one that included blacks, perhaps. The Wechslers, being socially conscious types, decided to help find a buyer. After a few nights of deliberation, the couple learned of a black family in a neighboring community that wanted to move into Levittown.

Within days, understanding the rarity of the opportunity, Bill and Daisy Myers had agreed to buy the home from the Mandels for $12,150, just $150 more than the price Mandel had paid four years earlier—a sign of how well the housing shortage had been satiated by developers. To prevent any pressure from other neighbors, all of the parties operated quietly and expeditiously. Thirty-four-year-old Bill Myers, a veteran, quickly qualified for a GI Bill loan with his income as a refrigeration engineer. After spending a few days preparing their new home for move-in, the neighbors assuming Bill to be a worker, the couple moved in on a hot August day. What happened next were scenes that put Levittown in the national news.

An angry mob formed outside of the Myerses' home. The couple, inside with the drapes drawn, were subjected to an evening of screams and epithets. The crowd soon grew into the hundreds. Even among the dissenters, segregation was many times an economic consideration. In a *Life* magazine pictorial covering the angry scenes, titled "Integration Troubles Beset Northern Town," one neighbor gave voice to this inescapable plight: "He's probably a nice guy, but every time I look at him I see $2,000 drop off the value of my house." Even when personal prejudice was absent, the cold economics of one man's rationality reinforced his neighbor's racism. Made up of a combination of people who disliked blacks, people who disliked depreciation, and people who disliked both, the crowd outside the Myerses' American dream turned violent. Rocks were thrown through the windows. The state police were called in. A local police sergeant was knocked unconscious by a thrown rock. But within days, order was restored. Levittown had its first black family.

But given this level of resistance in the pleasant suburbs, it seemed to many that it would take great levels of courage to break this barrier, to gain access to the American dream. And even if a pioneer wasn't met with outward violence, what about social isolation the next day and the day after that? For a people escaping the Jim Crow South, as millions were doing, the last thing many needed was a new battle in the North. Blacks would find the cities, which young whites were leaving, to be more readily accommodating. And as more blacks moved in, more whites moved out. In an era when immigration was a fraction of previous eras, America was marked by two simultaneous waves of internal migration.

The children of the immigrant tenements, the sons and daughters of the peasants and refugees from Lithuania, Italy, and Ireland, successfully moved up and out in just one or two generations. The children of share-croppers and grandchildren of slaves, after three hundred years, made it to the city blocks that had once been reserved for the newest immigrants.

Twenty-eight

TELEVISION

I ntegration might have been slow to come to the neighborhood, but inside the living room, a shift as dramatic as the move to the suburbs was taking place. Throughout the fifties, Cuban-born Desiderio Alberto Arnaz y Acha and his white American wife, Lucille Ball, managed to find a warm and enthusiastic welcome in their weekly visits to American living rooms. They entered through a new window that was altering pop culture with a rapidity never seen before in American history.

In a sense, television was an overnight success twenty years in the making. Its most optimistic proponents had anticipated that the medium would make its way into households by the mid-1930s. The radio pioneers, including RCA, spent tens of millions of dollars investing in technology in preparation to manufacture the sets needed to receive experimental broadcast signals. Just as it was on the verge of overcoming technical hurdles, the war sidetracked the effort; RCA's manufacturing capabilities were fully called into war production. During the run-up to war, television technology—with its ability to transmit pictures through radio waves—was recognized as applicable for a wide range of military uses. Experimental uses turned to attaching "eyes" to missiles and torpedoes, with television envisioned as a tool for guiding the projectiles to the point of impact.

. . .

SIMILARLY, given that it seemed television sets would not be appearing in households anytime soon, the radio broadcast networks NBC and CBS suspended their own research efforts and allocated all of their reporting and programming resources to covering the war. News of World War II was delivered via radio broadcasts, newsreels at movie theaters, and newspaper accounts. By the time the war ended, every component of television technology had progressed significantly with wartime research and development, but the industry was as nascent as it had been before the war.

Within two short years, there was little that was experimental about television or its possibilities for the civilian market. The regulatory structure, due to radio, was already in place for the nation's airwaves. The large broadcasters had a business model that worked well in radio: a national network underwriting expensive programming and local affiliates augmenting it with lower-cost, local programming. The courts had even intervened to force NBC to divest its sister network, NBC Blue, for antitrust reasons. NBC Blue was soon rechristened the American Broadcasting Company (ABC) to form a third national network. All of the messiness that typically accompanied the birth of new markets didn't apply. Starting in 1947, television entered America with the anticipation of a future that had once been put on hold.

When Bill Levitt started promoting his 1950 model home in Levittown, televisions were cheap enough that he included the latest Admiral television set in one promotion as part of a $7,995 home—the lowest-priced TV sets, mimicking the formal look of wood cabinetry, started at $149. In 1946, fewer than 10,000 television sets had been produced. By 1955, ten years from the war's end, 26 million households had televisions.

It seemed clear that television was going to encroach on radio's turf. The consumer, for the one-time cost of a television set, would soon expect free movies, baseball games, soap operas, political coverage, and news beamed into their living room. To CBS boss Bill Paley, who had come of age building his radio network to rival NBC, the simple formula to keep up was to transfer his radio stars to TV. The transition worked for America's most famous newscaster, Edward R. Murrow, who had become famous for broadcasting from London during the Battle of Britain. But two far bigger stars would emerge in a different genre. In the late forties, Lucille Ball had been a star of a CBS radio program known as *My Favorite Husband*, a situation comedy that chronicled the domestic life and squabbles of an all-American couple. When Paley proposed adapting the program for television, the radio star insisted that her real-life Cuban husband, Desi Arnaz, play the role of her television husband. To convince Paley, the couple agreed to forgo a network salary and opted to produce and own the television program through their company, Desilu Productions (short for "Desi and Lucy"); their company would sell finished episodes to CBS rather than CBS hiring them as actors.

In October 1951, *I Love Lucy* introduced to America the TV couple Ricky and Lucy Ricardo, with Arnaz playing Ricky in a hard, Spanish-accented English. And nothing else about the show was consistent with the caricaturized version of the idealized fifties family life. The Ricardos lived in a rented apartment in New York. In the first season of the show, the couple was childless. Ricky Ricardo was a bandleader in a nightclub, not the typical factory or office worker. And Lucy's primary onscreen ambition, to the endless consternation of her husband, was to become famous. Usually some minor disaster ensued, pushing Ricky beyond the limits of his English and degenerating "into a torrent of Spanish epithets." Other times, "Lucy, you goh suhm esplainin' to do" was the punch line heard by millions of viewers every Monday night at 9:00 p.m. The show became an instant hit. Halfway into the second season, the biggest television event of 1953 featured Lucy giving birth to the Ricardos' first child, little Ricky. Its audience vastly exceeded that of the following day's coverage of President Dwight D. Eisenhower's inauguration.

The audiences, for *I Love Lucy* and everything else on TV, led total television advertising revenues to surpass those of radio in less than nine years. After less than two seasons on the air, the genius of Arnaz and Ball's insistence on ownership became clear. Philip Morris, the show's original sponsor, agreed to pay $8 million to underwrite another two and a half seasons of the show. Half of the money went to Desilu to produce the show—Desi and Lucy's salaries, in addition to all production expenses, came out of the $4 million. The other half went to CBS to pay for the airtime. While CBS gained $4 million without incurring any of the expenses of production, all of the rights to reruns and second airings belonged to Desilu. Outside of the prime-time premiere of each episode, CBS or anyone else needed to pay Desi and Lucy every time any episode of *I Love Lucy* ever aired.

As the show progressed, the Ricardos gained a stronger foothold on the American dream. TV's most famous family—an interracial one—packed their bags and moved up to Connecticut.

FOR A ONETIME radio star like Lucille Ball, television was a step up. For Ronald Reagan, television was a step down. On the big screen, Reagan was a well-known actor who never quite broke into A-level stardom. By the 1950s Reagan was coming to the realization that he was fighting Father Time in his chase after coveted leading roles.

Reagan's life had up to that point been uniquely reflective of the changes, trials, and successes of the American century. He was born in 1911 in a small town in Illinois. His father, who worked in a shoe store, held out hope of one day owning his shoe shop. The Reagans, as Ronald was growing up, rented and moved often.

As a young boy, he played in the streets when the horse-drawn carriage was still a primary mode of transportation, seeing firsthand the transformative effect of the automobile. After a fairly uneventful childhood playing sports and going to school, he looked to attend college; with loans, some deferred tuition, a partial football scholarship, and summer jobs lifeguarding, Reagan made it to Eureka College, with its combined student body of 250.

His father's dream had come true with his Fashion Boot Shop, but he would soon become a victim of the Depression. When Reagan graduated in 1932, the American economy was in an unrelenting downward spiral. His father was out of work, and Reagan was desperate himself, looking at bleak career prospects to start his adult life. In the 1932 presidential election, the first he was eligible to vote in, he enthusiastically cast his ballot for FDR and then watched the government's emergency measures resuscitate the economy. His father was a prime beneficiary, becoming the local head of the Works Progress Administration, which put people to work building roads and bridges. Reagan, as he came of age, saw the depths of misery afflicting the small-town merchant and the beleaguered farmer and, at the time, approved of the government's role in easing the crisis.

Soon after graduation, Reagan applied for a job at a local Montgomery Ward to head up the sports department, but he lost the job to a fellow basketball star from his high school. Without any serious prospects, he decided to pursue a passion: He wanted to be a radio sports announcer. Radio in the thirties was one of the few bright spots in the economy as local stations were still being formed in rural areas. After a few days of driving around in the family's thirdhand Oldsmobile, stopping at radio station after radio station, a small one in Davenport, Iowa, offered Reagan $5 and bus fare to announce the Iowa-Minnesota football game. Satisfied with the effort, the station offered him $10 to call the next three games. Before long, the station called him back for a full-time role when one of its radio hosts quit.

He worked his way up, becoming an announcer for the Chicago Cubs within a few years. As a part of his role, Reagan was sent to Catalina, an island off the coast of Santa Barbara, to see the Cubs in spring training. The Wrigley family, the team's owners, had built facilities there close to their winter home. Unable to make it out of Los Angeles to the island due to inclement weather, Reagan looked up an old friend from his hometown who was trying to make her way in Hollywood. She then pointed him to her agent. After a screen test, aided by his good looks and six-foot-plus frame, Reagan was offered a contract by Warner Brothers at $200 per week. At twenty-six, Reagan had made it to Hollywood.

He didn't become the next Cary Grant or Humphrey Bogart. But he did ascend quickly in other ways. During the war, Reagan helped oversee propaganda films for the newly created U.S. Air Force. After the war, his leadership and organizational skills led him to become head of a labor union, the Screen Actors Guild, representing the interests of Hollywood actors. In this role as head of the union, he saw government antitrust actions separate ownership of studios from ownership of theaters,

effectively ending Hollywood's studio system. Yet even in this role representing the interests of actors, in which he often locked horns with
powerful studio heads, Reagan considered the government's intrusion
into the marketplace unwarranted. "You had seven companies who were
always competing with each other to turn out a better movie than the
guy down the street," he recounted in his autobiography, "and if people
didn't like a picture, they'd show it by voting with their feet."

With studios no longer able to guarantee and control theatrical
distribution, the stabilizing system of keeping stars on contract unraveled. Every actor soon became a free agent. For someone who was a self-
declared "New Dealer to the core" and a Hollywood liberal, it was the
start of a slow erosion in his faith in government. Had the government
waited just a couple of years, it would have seen the studios face the
competitive pressures of television from the three networks, where audiences could watch programs for free from their living rooms.

FEELING THE IMPACT of government action as an actor, Reagan found
his way to television. General Electric was looking for a new host for its
weekly theatrical program that it had started in 1953. Would Reagan be
interested? As he no longer had a steady studio paycheck, the opportunity
was compelling. But there was a risk. The industry's view of the small
screen was that once a known actor went to television full time, there was
no coming back in a meaningful way. But he went anyway.

The business model was simple. General Electric paid CBS for a
block of weekly airtime and then paid to produce the program. Evening
television seemed a great fit for GE's consumer business, which was
marketing the latest ovens, refrigerators, dishwashers, washing machines,
and televisions that Americans considered essential aspects of modern
living. Starting in the fall of 1954, Reagan took over the hosting duties
for the year-old *General Electric Theater*. For eight straight years on Sunday night at nine, the half-hour program followed the highly rated *The
Ed Sullivan Show*, a variety program that was a rebirth of vaudeville.
Reagan benefited from Sullivan's viewers, who stayed tuned to watch
whatever was on next.

After a pleasant introduction by Reagan, *General Electric Theater*'s content consisted of short theatrical dramas performed on minimalist stages, featuring many of the biggest stars in America making one-time appearances. James Dean starred in one where he regretfully put on false airs to impress a young woman. Sammy Davis Jr., James Stewart, Fred Astaire, and Tony Curtis were cast over the years. Other companies had similar offerings in the inaugural years of prime-time television, such as *The Colgate Comedy Hour, Goodyear Television Playhouse, Pabst Blue Ribbon Bouts, The Buick Circus Hour, Gillette Cavalcade of Sports*, and the enticing *U.S. Steel Hour*. Almost all would disappear within a decade.

During its run, *General Electric Theater* performed remarkably well, making Reagan a weekly presence for millions of Americans. For a brief period during the 1956–57 season, it was the third-ranked show on television, following only *I Love Lucy* and *The Ed Sullivan Show*.

Along with his hosting role on *General Electric Theater*, Reagan was tasked with an internal responsibility at GE of visiting plants and talking to employees. Reagan would later estimate that this contractual obligation, along with providing him with substantial financial security, brought him into contact with over 250,000 people. Each stop at a factory or power plant allowed him to hone a political message that would eventually lead to his next career after television. The very act of leaving Hollywood for television started the transformation of a self-described "liberal Democrat" and a union head, an actor once mistrustful of business, into America's most famous political proponent of free enterprise and limited government.

WHILE IT TOOK some time for Reagan to arrive on the national stage as a political figure, one ideologue found early television to be the perfect vehicle for grandstanding in front of millions to root out communists in America. Wisconsin senator Joseph McCarthy saw the postwar world as a deep, fundamental struggle between totalitarianism and democracy, which was not guaranteed to spread. Equally, McCarthy viewed it as plausible that people within free societies, even Americans, might choose communism with their political freedoms. Rather than some Red Army assembling on the border of Canada or Mexico, the ideas of communism could invade from within, which made it all the more insidious and dangerous.

It was easy to understand why Americans were fearful and susceptible to anticommunist hysteria. America had won a war against an imperial army in the East and fascists in the West. But soon after, the Nationalist government in China, an American ally, fell to Mao's communists. Compounding this, the Soviet Union had demonstrated its own nuclear bomb. Fearing the spread of communism, five years after the end of World War II, the United States was once again the prime actor on the Korean peninsula in an effort to stop an ideology on the move. This forgotten war in Korea would cost tens of thousands of American lives, just as the next war in Vietnam would. At the same time, the Depression and World War II had cemented the government as the major actor in the economy. It was not a stretch for conservative Americans to think that liberal Americans, along with labor unions, could fall under the sway of communist dogma here at home: If central planning and coordination was a good enough system of organization to recover from the Depression and win World War II, why couldn't such a system work in peacetime, all the time? And wasn't America allied with the Soviets, with Stalin presented stateside as friendly "Uncle Joe"? American propaganda itself had softened the people to the red menace.

To McCarthy, communist sympathizers needed to be uprooted from all parts of American society, and from his position as a first-term senator, he accused the State Department of harboring communists in 1950. McCarthy's initial efforts came months after the conclusion of the sensational Alger Hiss trial, in which a handsome high-level employee of the State Department had been tried and convicted of being a Soviet spy. Given that Hiss had access to the highest levels of government, the conviction by a jury stood as evidence that the Soviet Union had an active espionage program in America. Predating both the Hiss trial and McCarthy, the House Un-American Activities Committee had started its ongoing investigation of Hollywood for its association with communists, with Reagan, Ayn Rand, Louis B. Mayer, and Gary Cooper among dozens called to testify. Reagan, as the head of the Screen Actors Guild during this period, often had to vouch for individual members' disavowals of communist leanings. In a private conversation with Olivia de Havilland—*Gone with the Wind*'s Melanie Hamilton—he laughingly let her know that he had once suspected the actress of being a communist, only to have her respond seriously that she had once suspected Reagan of the same. So when McCarthy took the stage to fight communism in America, he was by no means a pioneer but a political opportunist who found a platform from which to build his profile.

By 1952 he was a national figure. As that year's presidential election propelled Eisenhower and his vice president, the staunchly anticommunist Richard Nixon, to office, McCarthy had fully emerged as a parallel power in the Senate, subordinate to no one. McCarthy had taken the stalemate of the Korean conflict, where the North was ceded to the communists, as a reason to heighten investigations into the allegiances of Americans at home. As chairman of the Permanent Subcommittee on Investigations, the senator's daytime interrogations and allegations made the nightly evening news.

In January 1954 employees at General Electric were suspended when they refused to answer questions from McCarthy's committee, professors at Harvard were forced to admit to being members of the Communist Party, and McCarthy started in on the U.S. Army, his biggest target yet. With bipartisan support, despite any misgivings, the Senate appropriated an additional $214,000 for McCarthy to continue his efforts by a vote of 85–1.

In this climate, it fell to Edward R. Murrow at CBS to challenge McCarthy. Once America's most famous radio reporter, Murrow now produced and starred in a television show called *See It Now*, a public affairs program that brought the news alive in an analytical magazine format, an early preview of the format that would emerge in later decades.

During one particularly searing episode from his half-hour prime-time slot on Tuesday nights, Murrow painstakingly assembled a case using clips of McCarthy contradicting himself. Morrow's plan to take on McCarthy had caused a considerable bit of anxiety at CBS in the days leading up to the broadcast. But Murrow was allowed to proceed. Accusing McCarthy of "operating as a one-man committee" and "terrorizing" his targets, he moved to a montage of four years of McCarthyism, concluding that the senator's stock-in-trade combined his "Congressional immunity" with "half-truths." While countless newspapers had attempted to editorialize against McCarthy and his committee, Murrow had brought to bear the irrefutable power of one's own words through the moving images of television, discrediting and unraveling McCarthy to a national audience.

By the end of the Eisenhower presidency, television had become inseparable from national politics and presidential campaigns. The average American household had owned a television set for less than ten years when, in 1960, Massachusetts senator John F. Kennedy and Vice President Nixon faced off in the first-ever televised presidential debate. While the polio-afflicted FDR could not walk and Eisenhower was a less-than-charismatic speaker in public, the new visual medium granted no allowances. Starting with the debate, presidential elections were now a form of performance art in which every grimace, eye roll, and hand gesture counted toward the outcome—democracy subject to the rolling cameras of capitalism's next big thing.

EVEN GOD AND baseball weren't completely safe from the competitive pressures of television. By the time of Kennedy's election, Sunday audiences increasingly found themselves captivated by a gladiatorial spectacle seemingly made for television.

Pro football's growth would have seemed improbable in 1950. Dating back decades, the professional version had always been a nonfactor compared with the collegiate variety. Ironically, even with college reserved for the elite, it was the college game that had a hold on pop culture. At the turn of the century, the Harvard-Yale game had been a subject of substantial intrigue and coverage—the Sears catalog of the era even carried a board game based on the rivalry. College football also made its mark in other ways: Reagan's most memorable role as an actor was his portrayal of the dying George Gipp, a player on the Notre Dame football team of the twenties. College football's appeal didn't, however, translate to the pro game. Unless subsidized by the traditions of a college or university, it was a poor business. This was partly due to the structure of the sport. The required preparation and on-field violence, with resulting injuries, limited each team's output to one game per week. With half of any team's games played on the road, this effectively meant half a dozen games where it could collect ticket revenues. In contrast, professional baseball gave each team 77 home games in the era's 154-game season. The economics of attendance alone were not enough to make pro football a profitable business. And even the rules were in flux—the forward pass was being tinkered with as late as the 1930s.

Besides, baseball was the national pastime. Boys played hooky to catch one of the dozens of day games during the typical baseball season. During the summer, a day at the ballpark was arguably the most American way of spending a few hours. But as people moved to suburbs, farther from urban baseball stadiums, and with the new choices on television, attendance fell throughout the fifties. Football, on the other hand, benefited enormously from television.

By the late fifties, the sport's professional version was soaring in popularity. It was a stark contrast to twenty years earlier, when even the best college football players passed up the chance to become professional football players. Now few, if any, would turn down the chance for gridiron glory played in front of millions. The biggest beneficiaries of this rapid turn of fortune were the owners of the twelve National Football League teams. As recently as 1950, the league's viability had been in question. That year a rival league completed its collapse and its three most successful teams were folded into the NFL. Of the three, the Cleveland Browns and San Francisco 49ers were marginally viable, but the Baltimore Colts were soon dissolved. A new NFL franchise, the Dallas Texans, failed quickly thereafter, and was converted into a team known once again as the Baltimore Colts. The team's reluctant new owner had to put up $25,000 up front—the price of three entry-level Levittown homes—with the remaining $175,000 of the purchase price deferred. It turned out to be a good investment.

Along with San Francisco, Cleveland, and Baltimore, the major markets of Washington, Chicago, Los Angeles, New York, Detroit, Pittsburgh, and Philadelphia were covered. Chicago had both the Bears and the Cardinals. And Green Bay, by far the smallest market, with its hometown fans in religious attendance, filled out the league. In 1955, to introduce its readers to the rise of the league, *Life* ran a pictorial with the title "Savagery on Sunday." The brief story had an unnamed quarterback lamenting that "the game is getting rougher every year. It's war rather than sport." But there was more to the game than simple brutality. The evolution of the pro passing game, along with player specialization, added a degree of strategic complexity to the game, with coaches resembling generals as they patrolled the sidelines. Given these factors, football made for great television, with the game often better seen at home than from within a stadium. Needless to say, Americans were sold on all counts.

Seeing football's growing appeal to audiences, it didn't take long for television executives to start paying up for local television rights. The NFL allowed each team, as an individual business, to largely negotiate its own TV and radio deals. CBS and its affiliates won most of the rights.

Within a couple of years, the team that almost couldn't be given away, the Baltimore Colts, was scheduled to play in the NFL's 1958 championship game. The game, pitting the New York Giants against Johnny Unitas's Colts, took place at Yankee Stadium in late December with sixty thousand people packing the stadium. A Colt field goal tied the game at seventeen in the closing seconds, and then they won in sudden-death overtime with Unitas leading the Colts on an eighty-yard drive capped by a one-yard touchdown run. But the victory was really the NFL's. Forty-five million people saw the game at home.

Broadcast television had the outline for what would become its most important programming franchise, one that would endure well into the next century. Football's schedule of weekly games fit the episodic cadence of the television week. Its limited number of games heightened the importance of each one; for fans, the biggest games even during the regular season took on the importance of can't-miss events. The earlier limitation of few games per football season, which had limited attendance revenues, turned out to make a perfect season-long programming package for fall television.

Sensing its growth, others wanted in. The thrill of owning a football team captured the imaginations of wealthy men across the country, such as Lamar Hunt, a twentysomething scion of one of the richest oil families in America. Seeing that Dallas, where the Hunts were based, didn't have a team, Hunt reached out to the NFL inquiring about its plans for expansion.

From his overtures, he learned of a possible opportunity to relocate the Chicago Cardinals, but the owner remained elusive and cool to Hunt. Instead, in the process of either posturing or trying to rebuff Hunt, the owner made the mistake of bragging about another interested oilman in Texas, Houston-based Bud Adams, who also wanted the Cardinals. In the end, neither man succeeded in buying the team. Then the NFL gave Hunt a definitive answer that it wished to stay at twelve teams and, seeing no other possibility of NFL team ownership, Hunt went to plan B and contacted Bud Adams.

With Adams and a group of other men, Hunt founded the American Football League. Along with Barron Hilton, the son of Hilton Hotels founder Conrad Hilton, and Ralph Wilson, an insurance executive in Detroit, the AFL quickly formed an eight-team league for 1960, composed of the Boston Patriots, Buffalo Bills, Los Angeles Chargers, Denver Broncos, New York Titans, and Oakland Raiders, along with Adams's Houston Oilers and Hunt's Dallas Texans. The NFL was incensed and shocked. To retaliate, the older league hastily announced a two-team expansion, including a team slated for Dallas to specifically punish Hunt.

Predictably, the start-up league had its share of financial woes. Hunt's Dallas team lost so much money, as did the NFL's new Dallas Cowboys, that Hunt moved the team to Kansas City, renaming it the Chiefs. But Hunt did have one financial innovation up his sleeve that perhaps saved his league. Unlike the NFL, the AFL started out by bundling its entire league as one television package. Rather than each team negotiating, the equal revenue sharing among the AFL teams helped the teams in smaller cities, and it increased each owner's vested interest in the collective enterprise. The rights for the AFL ended up on ABC—derided as the "Almost Broadcasting Company"—a network looking to compete on more equal footing with NBC and CBS. With the ABC deal guaranteeing each AFL team $170,000 per season, these new start-up teams were already earning more than some of the individually negotiated deals of the NFL teams—the storied Green Bay Packers only received $75,000 from theirs.

In early 1962, copying the AFL's template, the NFL then negotiated a leaguewide deal with CBS for $9.3 million over two years, providing each team over $300,000 annually. With the rapid audience growth, successive deals for both leagues would escalate. On the day CBS and the NFL announced their next deal in 1964, NBC offered the AFL a five-year, $36 million deal. With the revenues from this deal, AFL teams were competing for the best talent along with the NFL. The final measure of equality came the following year when Alabama star Joe Namath, regarded as the top prospect in the country, passed up the NFL to play for the AFL's newly renamed New York Jets.

Within a couple years, the upstart AFL was able to force the NFL to a merger of equals. Its championship game, which featured the winner of each league, became the Super Bowl, which then grew into a national television holiday, joining the Fourth of July, Thanksgiving, and Christmas in terms of faithful observance. It was uniquely American, with endless commercials for beer, cars, potato chips, and soft drinks becoming a much-anticipated event within the event, a metacelebration of capitalism as people embraced how businesses advertised their products to consumers. The Super Bowl also hinted at American exceptionalism: Its winners were proclaimed "world champions," even though almost no other country played the sport.

Twenty-nine

ROADS

As the summer of 1956 approached, Harland Sanders's long career seemed to be on the brink of ruin. At sixty-five, his great misfortune seemed to be one of location. His gasoline station, roadside diner, and motel were situated at a fork on Highway 25 in Corbin, Kentucky. As a part of the Depression-era works programs, the construction of US-25 had once presented a golden opportunity for Sanders. The Shell Oil Company financed him to set up a service station selling its gas. In time, using profits to acquire nearby land, Sanders added a motel to board weary travelers stopping over en route to Atlanta, Knoxville, or Asheville, North Carolina. Sanders was doing well enough with the motel until it caught on fire in 1939. While rebuilding using insurance proceeds and a bank loan, an epiphany struck: "You can sleep a man only once in twenty-four hours, but you can feed him three times." He added a restaurant. A decade and a half later, a simple announcement from Washington DC would unravel his life's work.

For months the House of Representatives and the Senate had been considering a bill that would have far-reaching consequences for the course of American enterprise. The simple free-market forces of traffic, the flow of customers to roadside services that men like Sanders built their lives around, would be utterly distorted by a new objective of the federal government. In June 1956, the final contours of a nearly $33 billion highway bill reached President Eisenhower's desk for his signature.

Even Eisenhower couldn't resist superlatives, calling the National System of Interstate and Defense Highways the "greatest public works program in the history of the world." The 41,000 miles of fast, smooth, and federally funded interstate highways were designed to connect all the major cities in America with populations of over fifty thousand.

To get the appropriation to its final staggering level, its proponents offered the cold war rationale that military equipment needed to be mobilized across the country with speed and efficiency. To pay for it all, in addition to a tax on tires and truck sales, the government added a 1-cent-per-gallon gas tax. Construction companies, home developers, mall builders, automakers, and oil companies, in addition to legislatures in nearly all states, looked at the proposed infrastructure as a tremendous boon, a platform that would stimulate new levels of commerce and growth.

But the proposed interstate highways had a distinctive feature that existing American highways and country roads largely didn't have. These new roads had on-ramps and off-ramps, runways for cars to speed up to and slow down from highway speeds, and these access points prevented existing roadside businesses from taking advantage of the traffic. The new highways had immediate and severe consequences for the economies of small towns that were built around the traffic patterns of the old highways. Corbin, Kentucky, was one of the towns Interstate 75 was going to pass by on its outskirts, away from the center of town. Sanders, who had been offered $164,000 for his business just two years earlier, was forced to sell it at auction. With the $75,000 in proceeds covering debts and taxes, the motel owner and restaurateur resigned himself to a fate of collecting Social Security checks.

But Sanders did have one bit of intellectual property, an asset that would carry him forward yet again: a fried chicken recipe that he had perfected over the years in his restaurant. Initially, fried chicken had been an ancillary item on the menu, a means of using leftover chicken. However, customers on long drives didn't want to wait the time it took to pan-fry the chicken. Another cooking method, immersing chicken through a wire basket in oil, was fast but didn't meet Sanders's exacting standards. It took an accidental experimentation with a pressure cooker to give Sanders his old restaurant's special item: Kentucky Fried Chicken.

Now without a restaurant, Sanders hit the road to try to franchise his Kentucky Fried Chicken—specifically his secret recipe of eleven herbs and spices. It wasn't a traditional franchise—Sanders expected road-side diners and varied restaurants to simply offer his Kentucky Fried Chicken as a menu item. He charged nothing up front. Sanders would supply the prepared spice concoction, along with the strictures of his technique, and receive royalties on every chicken sold—4 to 5 cents per chicken. To aid his marketing, Sanders started using the honorific title of "Colonel," which men of esteem in Kentucky often received from the state governor.

The Colonel's recipe was a hit. Within a few short years, over two hundred restaurants were offering up Kentucky Fried Chicken, earning Sanders over $100,000 in profits. But Sanders didn't own any actual lo-cations or even have a proper office. He hosted prospective franchisees at his five-bedroom home and cooked samples in his home kitchen. The restaurants, his franchisees, were often full service, with dishware and myriad menu items. According to Sanders, his daughter Margaret came up with the idea of freestanding Kentucky Fried Chicken outlets that exclusively focused on his recipe. After franchising a few locations, Colonel Sanders began building his loose confederation of fried chicken outlets. In 1964, nearing seventy-five, he decided to sell. A few franchi-sees, along with a wealthy businessman, raised the capital to buy Sanders out for $2 million, along with a lifetime employment contract and resid-uals from TV commercials that featured the Colonel.

While Sanders came into late-life success by parlaying a specific roadside recipe, it fell to another man to fully develop the system of fast food, restaurants built for cars and roads as much as people.

IT WAS ONLY fitting that entrepreneurs would bring the assembly line to food preparation. Earlier in the century, Henry Ford had credited the meatpacking industry and its disassembly of an animal into parts as an inspiration for his method of putting together a car. Now an America being built for cars, with billions of dollars committed to roads, needed the speed of the assembly line applied to roadside dining.

Like Colonel Sanders, Ray Kroc stumbled into his opportunity—one that would become arguably the most widely known symbol of postwar Americana—through the winds of economic tumult and years of hard experience. He had started in the 1920s as a traveling salesman selling housewares to housewives door to door. He graduated to selling a new innovation, the disposable paper cup, for the Lily-Tulip Cup Company. Soda fountains and ice cream parlors served milkshakes and sodas in glasses that needed to be washed after every use. This was initially a difficult sale as vendors were reluctant to pay 1.5 cents for a disposable cup. Fountain owners soon came around when they noticed the urban customer with the "to go" cup didn't need to wait in the restaurant to finish his drink and return the glass. Disposable cups led to jumps in revenue by turning over customers much faster.

Kroc's biggest customer, fast-growing Walgreens with its soda fountains, saw the potential labor savings and bought millions of the Lily-Tulip cups. During the height of the Depression, Kroc was a top salesman in a growth industry. On one of his prospecting travels through the Midwest, he ran into a dairy creamery that seemed to have a booming side business. In Battle Creek, Michigan, the proprietor had devised a way to freeze milk, sugar, cornstarch, vanilla flavoring, and a stabilizer in place of ice cream to make milkshakes. To customers it presented a smoother, colder drink. Kroc had an insider's view of the sales volumes of this trend—he could gauge growth by seeing how many cups were ordered. The one challenge, as he saw it, was to quickly mix the shake out of its frozen state and get it into a paper cup. Along with another of his restaurant customers and his paper-cup employer, Kroc formed a venture to start selling milkshake machines, known as Multimixers, that could quickly mix six milkshakes at once.

Before long, he took out a second mortgage on his house to build what he felt at the time to be his "personal monument to capitalism." But the effort led to financial stress, unraveled his marriage, and upended his relatively affluent life. He survived the war years selling milkshake powders and, left without much choice, returned to selling his Multi-mixer in the postwar years to customers such as the A&W Root Beer drive-ins, Dairy Queen, and other similar restaurants. Kroc, however, sensed an irreversible trend: Ice cream parlors and soda fountains seemed to be on the way out. Compounding the problem, once a restaurant bought a Multimixer, it often never needed another. Few restaurants needed to prepare more than six milkshakes simultaneously.

But the Chicago-based Kroc learned of a drive-in in San Bernardino, California, that used eight of his Multimixers. He wondered what kind of an operation could possibly need the capacity to make forty-eight milkshakes in rapid order. He went to find out. In 1954 two brothers, Dick and Maurice McDonald, operated a single drive-in that seemed to be the model of simplicity and efficient execution. Unlike other drive-ins of the era, McDonald's had three base items: hamburger, French fries, and drinks. It had no seating. The hamburgers were priced at 15 cents, an extra 4 cents for cheese. Fries cost 10 cents, a milkshake 20 cents.

This formula by itself was not earth shattering, but what made Kroc feel like "some latter-day Newton" was seeing the lines form around the block at lunchtime. As each order came in, it was relayed in a system that made the burger, fries, and drink converge at the cashier's stand within a minute. Kroc proposed becoming a franchising agent for the brothers. Ironically, Kroc envisioned more McDonald's locations as primarily benefiting him with more Multimixer sales. The McDonalds brothers had tried their own hand at franchising, but the haphazard effort had re-sulted in franchisees supplementing the menu with enchiladas, pizza, and so on.

With Kroc, the brothers insisted on exact replicas of their San Ber-nardino location, with any changes to be approved in writing. Kroc was authorized to charge up to 1.9 percent of sales as a fee to each franchisee, with 0.5 percent coming to the brothers as a license fee.

With the master franchising agreement in hand, Kroc returned to Chicago. To start, he first built his own McDonald's in Des Plaines, Il-linois. From here Kroc's earliest franchisees came from two pools, one significantly more promising than the other. He belonged to the Rolling Green Country Club, whose membership was made up of owners of small businesses and midlevel corporate executives. From the membership rolls of the club, the assorted owners of a cemetery, a car dealership, a heating and ventilation service, and a home builder became among the first owners of McDonald's franchises. Along with the land and building, the initial setup costs averaged around $80,000. With the bulk of the cost being real estate, most of Kroc's friends were able to borrow from local banks using the land and building as collateral. But soon Kroc found that experienced businessmen made for poor franchisees, unable to faithfully follow a system without adding their own ideas or operating techniques. And even worse, as relatively successful men, they were almost never found behind the counters.

To Kroc, the ideal franchisee was more like Betty Agate. In Kroc's first year as McDonald's franchising agent, Agate had walked into his offices trying to sell Bibles. Kroc's secretary and eventual large shareholder, June Martino, finding humor in the Jewish Agate selling Catholic Bibles, proposed she look into a McDonald's franchise. Along with her husband, a printing press operator, Betty signed up to open a McDonald's in the Chicago suburb of Waukegan. Sinking their life savings of $25,000 in the business, along with a bank loan on the real estate, the Agates opened their location in the spring of 1955. Having little choice but to work day and night, the couple braced themselves for struggle. On opening day, sales came in at $450. By the weekend, daily sales had crossed $800. By the end of the first year, the Agates' McDonald's had grossed over $250,000, netting $50,000 in profits for the couple.

Kroc now had his best sales tool for recruiting other franchisees. He also cemented his policy of zero tolerance for deviation from the McDonald's operating formula. The Agates' success proved that the best franchise operator was a person who unwaveringly executed the system. The Agates themselves attracted relatives and neighbors in Waukegan into the McDonald's system, with each taking McDonald's into the burgeoning suburbs of Illinois, Wisconsin, and Indiana. To keep his tight control, Kroc licensed franchisees in one location at a time. Unlike other franchisors, which granted large territories to wealthy businessmen, Kroc opted for discipline, with each location a test of operating faithfulness. The reward for a good franchisee was the award of another McDonald's location. The efficiency of the assembly line in constructing a burger from a meat patty, lettuce, and bun was combined with a model of replication. Franchising revealed a duality within capitalism, one where the businessman, franchise owner, and executive could be seen as temperamentally distinct from the entrepreneur, the latter of whom was most in his element experimenting with new ideas rather than in maximizing gains from proven techniques; in fast food the thousands of creative, entrepreneurial experiments by various drive-ins had yielded a handful of brands that could be scaled by business owners with unyielding rules.

By 1961 Kroc had made it. A *Time* magazine story marveled at the growth of these "294 highway stops stretching from Connecticut to California" serving a conforming, predictable burger at each stop. By then, road construction had reached such a fevered pace, each suburb was indeed an interstate highway stop.

Kroc soon rooted out another set of nonconformists, buying out the McDonald brothers and largely writing them out of the company's history, except for their name. By the end of the sixties, McDonald's had grown to over two thousand locations with annual revenues approaching $1 billion. In time American capitalism in the form of golden arches, would be received in the capitals of China, Vietnam, Russia, and Saudi Arabia with more enthusiasm than would be shown for American democracy.

IN THE SUMMER OF 1960, a green GMC pickup truck with camper attached was delivered to John Steinbeck's home in Sag Harbor, New York. Years after writing *The Grapes of Wrath*, he had countered his country's migratory pattern west by leaving California to settle in this former fishing village on Long Island. Having crossed middle age, and insulated by financial success and literary acclaim, Steinbeck had felt a need to reconnect with America. To once again see and feel his country in the flesh, rather than through news accounts and television footage, Steinbeck embarked on a road trip with his dog, Charley.

After a few days on the country roads of New England, doing his best to avoid interstate highways, Steinbeck was forced to take his green truck onto I-90, "a wide gash" through the wilderness that seemed to him the new "carrier of the nation's goods." Efficient but without distinction, the interstate led him to lament the possibility of driving from New York to California "without seeing a single thing," as the highways were completely removed from local life, a sterile arterial system made up of endlessly paved tar with new, long freight trucks speeding along. The national sameness both struck and distressed him, evoking the feeling of an America lost, of efficiency as the paramount cultural thread as infrastructure changed the landscape.

The nation's most dominant industry at the turn of the century, railroads, had finally ceded its supremacy in moving commerce. In 1945 railroads carried five times the freight of commercial trucks. In less than twenty-five years, revenues from shipping via tractor-trailers—each one the size of a single railcar—exceeded the railroad's. This made perfect sense. With each new housing development in suburbia, entire local economies needed to be built around it. Movie theaters, shopping centers, and chain grocery stores, along with local services such as doctors and dentists, started filling out the commercial ecosystem. Instead of quaint town centers with intersections and sidewalks, the new commercial center of America was typified by large parking lots. In the back, suburban stores often had loading bays that made it efficient to pull up a giant truck. Rather than unload railroad freight at a hub onto local trucks, a preloaded freight truck sent across the country point to point was far more cost-effective in many instances.

This had repercussions for old small towns, communities that already had thriving Main Streets of cobblers and toy stores, bookstores and furniture showrooms. Starting in the late fifties, retailing spawned the idea of the discounter. Just as the railroads had once enabled catalog merchants like Sears and Montgomery Ward to erase the markups on goods due to distance, the interstate highway opened up logistical possibilities to this new class of entrant.

Unlike the multistory retail palaces of the downtown department stores or the variety stores that peddled low-cost goods, the new category of discount stores sold everything from appliances to detergent to lawnmowers. The fundamental consideration of the discounters was price. The philosophy was to do away with all aspects of costly service and fixtures, sell goods as cheaply as possible, and do so in volume. In erecting their stores on the peripheries of cities, the stores reflected the economics of the merchandising strategy. Bright fluorescent lights, linoleum floors, cash registers in the front of the store, shopping carts, and limited floor personnel, all accompanied by the most important feature of all: acres of blacktop with hundreds of painted lines for the parked cars.

In the age of postwar American affluence, the retail trend that was sweeping the nation was the opposite of gilded. The department stores of the late nineteenth century had served as a glimpse of luxury for Americans of all economic strata, but the consumer of the 1960s gravitated to the illusion of thrift, of maximizing value, at a time of unprecedented middle-class prosperity. The obsequious salesman waiting on the customer was considered not a luxury but an unnecessary intrusion and overhead expense. What assured customers was the names of the brands sold in the stores—the same brands advertised on TV and in magazines. If the price was the same, what difference did the retail environment make? As a result, discount stores in the suburbs were built to the lowest cost specifications allowed by building codes.

As in many phases of American capitalism, the early winners were not the final winners. In mid-1962, the giant Woolworth's announced a new chain called Woolco. S. S. Kresge, an operator of similar variety stores, opened a new discount concept called Kmart the same year. Both were overshadowed momentarily by the discount king of the era, Eugene Ferkauf, the founder of the arbitrarily named E. J. Korvette. The company operated just seventeen stores, but its revenues had climbed to $230 million. It profits, holding with the principle of low margins, were a little over $4 million. The industry as a whole had grown to four thousand stores and several billion dollars in sales by the early sixties.

Low margins, however, were a double-edged sword. The simplicity of leasing or building a large warehouse-type space, stuffing it with goods trucked in from distributors, and selling the best-selling items at close to or below cost left little room for error. Be it a mistake in ordering, shrinkage from shoplifting or employee theft, shortages at a distributor— anything could turn a low-margin business from profitability to losses. Indeed, the industry suffered a dramatic shakeout, with weaker stores closing. But the weakness was operational: The stores rarely closed due to lack of sales, but usually from an inability to generate profits from those sales. The onetime leader E. J. Korvette sold out to a garment maker and ceded the discounting market to Kmart, which was on its way to becoming the leading retailer in the country.

But the intense competition among discounters had other casualties. Small mom-and-pop shops often had little pricing power in competing with stores that literally sold everything. Contemporary criticism often suggested that this was a distorted free market at work. In 1965's *The Great Discount Delusion*, Walter Henry Nelson pointed out the fallacies of low prices and their impact on small businesses. Often the discounter, in an advertisement, listed a price below cost on a highly popular good such as a new toy or popular brand of toothpaste. The "loss-leader" served to drive customers into the store, where the discounter then made up the difference on other goods. For a small shop focused on selling one category of product, such as toys or books, to compete with the loss-leading practices of a discounter on best sellers was particularly devastating—there was no place for this specialized retailer to make up the loss. Loss leaders also served to cement the belief among consumers that the discounters generally offered lower prices across the board. This then served to attract shoppers from long distances, drawing commerce away from the Main Streets of small-town America.

But while the discounters in the Northeast, such as Dayton-Hudson's Target and Kmart, expanded in the Midwest and Northeast suburban markets, an operator in the South understood that rural customers would drive even longer distances to get low prices. Sam Walton's Wal-Mart, based in Arkansas and starting in towns with populations as small as six thousand, grew to dominate the entire South. Walton understood the discount business to be one of information and logistics, of using the roads to maximize efficiency in attracting customers and procuring goods. With his old plane, he would scout for locations where he could see advantageous traffic patterns, positioning stores at a distance so that one didn't cannibalize another. And once this system was established, semitrucks roving the country saw little difference in stopping in rural Arkansas versus suburban St. Louis to supply their merchandise.

· · ·

FIFTY YEARS EARLIER, American economic vitality had been so strong that even an immigrant family, with a couple of years of hard work, could afford its own car. By the midsixties, postwar affluence meant that even the American teenager with a part-time job at McDonald's could entertain prospects of his own car, the driver's license becoming a rite of passage like a bar mitzvah. Children of the baby boom, largely raised in the suburbs, had turned the two-car household from a rarity to a necessity—even as late as 1950, only 4 percent of households had more than one car. But the wives needed an additional car at home while the husbands commuted to work. When the teenaged baby boomers started driving in the sixties, the growth in the number of cars on the road, incredibly, outpaced population growth. While the population from 1960 to 1970 grew from 180 million to 203 million, an addition of 23 million people, American roads added over 27 million registered passenger vehicles during the same time, with much of the growth found in high school parking lots.

Some saw this affluence as a form of hollow prosperity, a mindless and fundamental alteration of society, where people served the economic engine, moved by the momentum of commercial events, rather than the other way around. To Jane Jacobs the evidence suggested that the cultural vibrancy of the city was being lost to remote, metallic islands traveling at seventy miles per hour. At the time of her book *The Death and Life of Great American Cities*, reflecting the move to the suburbs, the urban core of nearly every American city had started declining. Cities in the East and Midwest had once been bustling centers of activity, but the idea of the city would come to be associated with decay.

To Jacobs nothing about this death of her beloved cities was "economically or socially inevitable" due to market forces. To enable the "freshminted decadence" of suburbia, she argued, "extraordinary governmental financial incentives have been required to achieve this degree of monotony, sterility, and vulgarity." Thanks to federal appropriations that ultimately used private contractors, "highwaymen with fabulous sums of money" had little incentive to make automobiles and cities compatible. In addition, she pointed to central planners who guaranteed housing loans in the suburbs but did not do the same in the city, which then resulted in greater blight due to little credit being available. Kentucky Fried Chicken and Kmart were entrepreneurial reactions layered upon federal policy, not organic outcomes of either free markets or civilization's progress, which for hundreds of years had caused people to crowd into denser living conditions. Poetically, the largest American city to feel the full scale of this trend reversal was Detroit, the epicenter of the automobile industry. The definition of the city instead now included a geographically unspecified, undefined "inner city," which meant any urban core where there was a concentrated presence of blacks who had stayed behind.

But the federal policy of highways was itself a product of one overlooked source of American success: oil. For well over a century, from the time that oil had first been successfully drilled from the Pennsylvania earth in 1859, America had been the world's largest producer of oil. By 1970 oil production in the United States had gone up to nearly ten million barrels of oil per day, not far from Saudi Arabia's present production levels. For most of American history, oil was never a foreign product and never needed to be; real-life men like John D. Rockefeller, John Paul Getty, and the founders of the American Football League, as well as fictional ones such as J. R. Ewing and James Dean's character in the movie *Giant*, had always symbolized oil as a source of great American wealth. Wide roads, suburbia, and tens of millions of large cars, many with fuel-inefficient automatic transmissions that are still uncommon in Europe, were all reflections of this seemingly limitless natural endowment. But despite America being the world's top producer through the 1960s, the unrelenting American growth into distant suburbs had consequences. The country consumed every drop of oil it produced and turned to the cheap global markets for more. Soon, when a few countries in the Middle East learned the extent of their pricing power given the American demand, an oil crisis was at hand—the postwar growth came to a screeching end. Starting in the seventies, for the first time since 1893, America started running trade deficits—importing more from the world than it sold to the world.

PART FOUR

Steve Jobs and Bill Gates, 1985.

Thirty

COMPUTING

J ust seven weeks into his job as the president of the Ford Motor Company, forty-four-year-old Robert McNamara was already contemplating his next job. In December 1960, on a cold morning in Michigan, his secretary had brought him a note saying that Robert Kennedy, the brother of the incoming president of the United States, was on the line. By the end of the day, McNamara had been offered one of two cabinet positions: heading up either the Department of the Treasury or the Department of Defense. He was then summoned to Washington to meet with John F. Kennedy the following day. After initially refusing the offer, McNamara would soon resign from his job at Ford to become the nation's secretary of defense.

Less than five weeks after the fateful phone call, millions of Americans turned on their televisions to see Eisenhower offer his departing words to his countrymen. With the halting cadence of an aging grandfather, the onetime general, who had personally accepted the official surrender of Nazi Germany, now offered a warning of a stark internal threat. If the cold war suddenly turned hot, given the nature of nuclear weapons, there would be no time to convert the nation's industrial capacity for the purposes of warfare as in times past. Yet to Eisenhower, remaining in a permanent state of preparedness itself posed a danger to democracy:

Until the latest of our world conflicts, the United States had no armaments industry. American makers of plowshares could, with time and as required, make swords as well. But now we can no longer risk emergency improvisation of national defense; we have been compelled to create a permanent armaments industry of vast proportions.

. . . This conjunction of an immense military establishment and a large arms industry is new in the American experience. . . . We recognize the imperative need for this development. Yet we must not fail to comprehend its grave implications. . . . We must guard against the acquisition of unwarranted influence, whether sought or unsought, by the military-industrial complex.

. . . We must never let the weight of this combination endanger our liberties or democratic processes. We should take nothing for granted. Only an alert and knowledgeable citizenry can compel the proper meshing of the huge industrial and military machinery of defense with our peaceful methods and goals, so that security and liberty may prosper together.

YET IN ENTERING "military-industrial complex" firmly into the national lexicon, Eisenhower pointed to a "technological revolution" in the business of cold-war defense, with modern research and development now requiring "hundreds of new electronic computers" at immense cost. Government expenditures in science and technology were growing so rapidly, with the military sparing no expense when it came to computing, that public policy "could itself become the captive of a scientific-technological elite." Three days later, President Eisenhower became a private citizen.

On McNamara's first day on the job at the Pentagon, the number of men and women who worked for the nation's military establishment was 3.5 million, more than the total employed by the nation's top twenty corporations combined. The task of modernizing the Department of Defense, with its countless departments and procurement systems, had logically fallen to a man who had done the same for the nation's second-largest automaker. But unlike General Motors' William Knudsen, who had taken over the entire task of producing the nation's weapons during World War II, McNamara did not come from the production side. After graduating from Berkeley in the 1930s, he went on to Harvard Business School, where he exhibited a deep understanding of accounting systems and financial controls. A year after graduating, he returned to Harvard to teach. During the war, he was one of a group of men who had put together a massive system of organizing wartime information into useful, actionable data. After the war, several members of this group were hired by Ford to modernize the then-beleaguered automaker. The group was known as the Whiz Kids, young men with no specific industry training but who embodied the supreme technocratic idea that all organizations were simply vast collections of quantifiable information that changed minute by minute, day to day—if it could be measured, it could be managed. Of this talented group, McNamara was seen as the most brilliant, a rational man among rational men. Senator Barry Goldwater would call him "an IBM machine with legs."

It was only fitting that such a man should be entrusted with overseeing the "military-industrial complex."

OF ALL COMPANIES, IBM had been the primary beneficiary of the military's growing investment in computing research. Its 1960 revenues had grown to just a notch under $2 billion, a staggering increase from ten years earlier.

Yet the company's roots, and in a sense computing itself, could be traced back to a constitutional function as basic as national defense. One of the few tasks relegated to the federal government in the Constitution, in addition to maintaining the postal system and navy, was to carry out a census every ten years. When the Republic was founded, the framers of its governing document sought to limit the federal government's power to a highly finite set of roles, reserving for the individual American states the bulk of governing authority. But as each state was vested with proportional representation at the federal level based on its population, the entire system of government—the Electoral College that decided the presidency and the congressional representation of each state in the Union—depended first on getting an accurate count of who lived where. Even those who were owned by others, counting for three fifths of a person, lent their states the arithmetic of their humanity.

For one hundred years, as the population grew from under three million huddled together on the eastern seaboard to tens of millions across the entire continent, the collection of the census had incrementally improved. But compared with the vitality of the Industrial Revolution in America, with its advances in steelmaking, oil production, manufactured goods, telephones, and electricity, the collection of the people's vital statistics by hand seemed anachronistic. A tally of millions of people conducted by an army of clerks, no matter how efficient, was not commensurate with advances such as telegraphing a message to London via underwater cables.

The census of 1890 changed this, seeding an information revolution that would one day become as significant as the industrial variety then under way. The idea for a more efficient census came from a young Census Office employee named Herman Hollerith. In 1880 Hollerith came into contact with an army surgeon who had been tasked with finding causes of death during the Civil War. The doctor, John Shaw Billings, shared with Hollerith his ideas on using holes in punch cards to signify and store information, rather than keeping handwritten records that required human observation to understand. A simple piece of light cardboard, a punch card, could support rows of holes like the fields on a multiple-choice exam. For such a system to work for the national census, there would be a punch card for every person in America. In the fields on each person's card, different attributes could be marked. On one row there could be six holes for race: If hole 1 was marked, it could signify white. A row could be assigned to age: If hole 3 was punched, it could mean the person was between eighteen and thirty. Rows could be assigned to marital status, children in the household, income range—indeed, a row on a punch card could be purposed for any data item worth collecting.

Building on Billings's theories, the twenty-one-year-old Hollerith began conceptualizing a machine that could seek out the punched holes on a set of punch cards and add the results mechanically without human observation. For all of the punch cards from Iowa, say, the machine could be set up to count the number of people between the ages of zero and eighteen by checking whether the appropriate hole was punched in each card. To execute this function, Hollerith made full use of the electrical knowledge of the time. Each card, rapidly fed through a mechanical sorter, would be placed against a metallic surface. Electrified pins corresponding to a particular hole on the punch card would be placed on top of the card. The punch card, being nonconducting, would prevent electricity from being passed through if the hole was not punched. Then the machine would be set up to determine if a particular hole location was punched over a series of thousands of cards. For every card with that specific punched hole, the electrical circuit would complete momentarily, and the mechanical counter would add +1 in affirmation.

Hollerith's machine for counting what was on the cards was a breakthrough that would last decades. And the benefits went beyond mere addition. The Hollerith machine could be used to repeatedly sort the cards to compile subsets within the data. Finding out how many widows lived in Nebraska or how many households in Connecticut had four children could reveal new insights. By the time preparations were under way for the 1890 census, backed by three patents, Hollerith had devised a practical system for large-scale data management. The Census Office, seeing the dramatic efficiency and accuracy of the Hollerith machines in tabulating the results, agreed to lease fifty of his machines at a rate of $1,000 per year. Soon after, the Department of the Interior reported to the Senate that 62,622,250 punch cards had been created: one for every American reported to be living.

WITH HOLLERITH'S CENSUS success came acclaim—*Scientific American* placed his machine on a cover in 1890—and with acclaim came opportunity. Hollerith formed the Tabulating Machine Company to commercialize his electric information system further.

At the turn of the century, several lines of business machines and instruments had greater commercial viability than the still-nascent field of tabulating data using the Hollerith machine. The Computing Scale Company had consolidated a number of regional companies specializing in weighing commodities from meat to metals—computing, at the time, largely meant measuring weight. In the field of time recording, the International Time Recording Company had consolidated the manufacture of punch clocks and time instruments used for tasks from stamping the time for shift workers to issuing freight confirmations. In 1911 the three companies, Computing Scale, International Time, and Hollerith's Tabulating Machine Company, were consolidated into a new company called Computing-Tabulating-Recording, or C-T-R. Eventually, managing the information collected by functions like weighing, measuring, and counting the products of American industry would become its own industry.

For now, C-T-R needed a boss. The banker behind the organization, Charles Flint, looked to hire an executive from a category of machines that was used by far more businesses than any other. Over the years, tens of thousands of small merchants and retail locations had bought the machines of National Cash Register. But NCR had run into regulatory difficulties due to its hard-charging ways. The federal government criminally indicted over thirty executives for everything from intimidating customers to setting up fake competitors to undermine rivals. One of National Cash Register's highest-ranking sales executives, Thomas Watson, approaching forty, was both indicted and fired.

Undeterred, Watson was hired to run C-T-R. Though C-T-R's punch card business was its smallest line of business, Watson claimed to have understood its potential from the beginning. By the 1920s, the punch card business was growing rapidly, helping businesses keep track of everything from customer orders to employee information, just as the Census Office continued to do. To signify the product line's broad appeal and the company's global ambitions, the company changed its name to International Business Machines.

With each passing year, IBM's punch card implementations grew in complexity. Businesses such as Time Inc. had floors of Manhattan real estate devoted to housing punch cards—each carrying subscription dates, renewals, and billing terms for its millions of subscribers. Banks and insurance companies turned to punch cards to keep track of accounts and policyholders. IBM soon introduced sophisticated processes such as payroll, with the tabulating machines making the necessary deductions for taxes and preparing the checks. It was a stunning combination of holes in cardboard serving as data storage, electricity used for sorting and screening, and mechanical parts used to calculate and output results.

But in the 1930s, one customer provided the biggest opportunity. As recalled by Watson's son Thomas Watson Jr., all of "Roosevelt's welfare, price control, and public works programs" needed "IBM machines by the hundreds." And the biggest of all, Social Security, made "Uncle Sam IBM's biggest customer." The benefits of harnessing this mechanical intelligence were not lost on international customers either. Less than a year before signing the Munich Agreement, Hitler summoned Watson to a private meeting, offering assurances of peace and prosperity that he surmised would find their way back to the White House. Days later, in a further show of respect, Hitler's finance minister presented Watson with the Merit Cross of the German Eagle, adorned with swastikas. To be fair, IBM was an equal-opportunity servicer. Not too long afterward, Watson Jr. was dispatched on a mission to the East, traveling through the Soviet Union, through Japanese-controlled Manchuria, and into Tokyo to evaluate geopolitical conditions firsthand. There was much to protect: In addition to servicing the New Deal and the Nazis, IBM's Moscow office helped the Soviets "manage vast quantities of statistics for their Five Year Plans," as Watson Jr. noted in his memoir.

Once the war started, the data-management needs of the military took center stage. For every man inducted into the army, his IBM punch card "followed him through induction, classification, training, and service" to his discharge.

But scientific advances during the war would change computing from an electromechanical process to a fully electronic one. Namely, magnetic tape used for storing sounds was recognized as a method for storing and retrieving data. Instead of holes in paper punch cards, the same marks could be written on tape, with a sound taking the place of a punched hole. Magnetic tape held far more data in a given amount of space than punch cards. This was no trivial matter. Companies like

Time Inc. and MetLife, which had cards for all of its policyholders, would realize significant savings in real estate and access costs by embracing tape storage. For the right types of customers in corporate America, this new technology delivered real and immediate cost savings.

At the same time, advances in electrical circuits during the war threatened the tabulating machinery. Rather than elaborate gears and mechanical counters, computing processes that could be observed, these "electronic brains" did the processing work invisibly. In explaining computers to customers, Watson Jr. explained that what electrons moving at the speed of light really did was "add one and one," just as the mechanical punch card readers did. At IBM business calculations were broken down into "simple steps of arithmetic and logic such as adding, subtracting, comparing, and making lists. But to amount to anything, these steps have to repeated millions of times." After observing that the fastest mechanisms of the punch card machines could do four additions per second, while the most primitive electronic circuits could do five thousand, IBM began to rapidly reinvent itself.

In the fifties the cold war provided the opportunity. Compared with the computational needs of physicists, engineers, and mathematicians, most business-management functions, like adding up payroll, were primitive. In contrast, the aerial defense needs of the United States, exacerbated by the Soviets successfully testing their own nuclear bomb in 1949, became a fertile ground for computing research and discovery. One of the most expensive projects underwritten in the era was a computing system known as SAGE, which stood for Semi-Autonomous Ground Environment.

Once a radar station picked up an enemy aircraft entering American airspace, SAGE would calculate the incoming flight path based on speed, altitude, and direction and determine which fighter jets should be dispatched to intercept the threat. Other times SAGE might advise that a surface-to-air missile be fired instead. The computers, which were the size of buildings, needed to make recommendations that generals would follow. SAGE went beyond harnessing computing power; it also introduced networking. Through telephone connections, SAGE divided the country into geographic sectors, with a facility in each sector pulling in information from ground radar, naval vessels, and surveillance aircraft. Each facility's computer was networked with the other facilities' computers to transmit and receive data as to which combat facilities should be deployed in the event of an attack. Getting the contract to build computing centers for SAGE accounted for fully half of IBM's computing revenues until the late fifties, subsidizing the transition from the days of punch cards to the new era of computing.

Unfortunately, the Reds couldn't be trusted to sit still. Almost as soon as SAGE became operational, the Soviets upped the ante by putting the first satellite in space. Just like that, the capitalists' SAGE was obsolete. The communists not only had eyes in space, circling the globe from far above, but also had the superior rocket technology to put them there.

WITH THE ADVENT of the computer and the dawn of the space race, the sixties brought futuristic visions of life to the mainstream consciousness. The Soviet satellite *Sputnik* had led to the formation of NASA to oversee America's space program. In prime time on ABC, Americans could tune in to catch the animated cartoon *The Jetsons*, about a space-age family who lived with their housekeeping robot, Rosie, and dog, Astro. A couple of years later, Desilu, *I Love Lucy's* production company, premiered *Star Trek* on CBS. Stanley Kubrick's *2001: A Space Odyssey* had a near-omniscient computer named Hal manipulating its astronauts. By the midsixties, the concepts of artificial intelligence and self-driving cars were no longer in the realm of magic or science fiction—they were seen as the logical, inevitable outcome of the American trajectory.

Modernity and sophistication looked like American Airlines. A leader in the fast-growing field of jet travel, the airline brought in IBM to develop flight plans. With the help of the computer, the company projected that its meteorologists and dispatchers would use weather data to save up to three minutes per cross-country flight—at $15 per minute of flight time, the savings justified leasing an IBM computer. Such were the incremental advantages and applications in corporate America that drew customers to IBM.

The company even drew unlikely customers. From rural Arkansas, operating just five comically cheap-looking stores—a rounding error compared with the largest retailers—Sam Walton made his way to an IBM conference for retailers. While he shied away from investing anything in any emotional aspect of retailing, delivering the lowest prices meant mastering logistics and information. To one speaker at the conference, Abe Marks, modern retailing meant knowing exactly "how much merchandise is in the store? What's selling and what's not? What is to be ordered, marked down or replaced? . . . The more you turn your inventory, the less capital is required." Altering his first impression, Marks found that Walton's simpleton comportment masked his genius as a retailer, eventually calling him the "best utilizer of information that there's ever been." A little over two decades later, Sam Walton would become the richest man in America; he would attribute his competitive advantage to his investment in computing systems in his early days. The small-town merchant who expected that knowing his customers' names or sponsoring the local Little League team would give him some enduring advantage simply didn't understand the sport. American consumers, technocrats at heart, rewarded efficiency as reflected by the prices on the shelves, not the quaint sentiments of a friendly proprietor. To gain this efficiency, information systems were seen as vital.

Corporate demand was so strong in 1962 that Ross Perot, a young IBM salesman, made his annual quota by the middle of January. He sensed that his customers, enthusiastic as they were about buying IBM's latest computers, often lacked the expertise to maximize the value of their investments. Later that year, he quit to found Electronic Data Systems. Knowing the names of customers that had purchased large installations of hardware from him, he now looked to sell them programming services. After adding blue-chip corporate clients for six years, EDS readied itself to go public in the heady climate of 1968.

In a decade filled with dramatic moments—the Bay of Pigs invasion, Martin Luther King Jr.'s "I have a dream" speech, the Cuban missile crisis, Kennedy's assassination, civil rights legislation, and the protests against the Vietnam War—it is easy to imagine an unsettled country on the verge of some revolution. A look at the business pages, however, shows a country in the midst of one of its great economic booms. Given the dominant historical narrative, reviewing the economics of the sixties seems like an investigation into a parallel universe. Yet it also exposes the central paradoxes of the time and the pitfalls of blind faith in modernity.

Indeed, the once-celebrated Robert McNamara learned firsthand the tragic limits of objective facts and figures, the danger of data failing to tell the whole story or, worse, obfuscating the most basic insights of human judgment. Here was America with satellites, computers, jet fighters, and billions of dollars dedicated to defense, yet the conduct of the Vietnam War itself looked far less modern than the terms such as "military-industrial complex," "space race," or "electronic brains" would seem to imply. A simple count of money and weapons pointed to victory. But the intransigent North Vietnamese, with barely one foot removed from their rice paddies and agrarian roots in terms of economic development, refused to open their hearts and minds to the twin virtues of democracy and capitalism and were somehow fighting a superpower to a stalemate.

Equally confounding, in 1968, a year marked by the assassinations of Martin Luther King Jr. and Robert Kennedy and the peak of American casualties in Vietnam, with over ten thousand deaths that year—"Hey, hey, LBJ, how many kids have you killed today?" was a chant making the rounds at rallies—the U.S. stock market seemed an untroubled oasis, climbing to new highs.

The "Go-Go" years made stars out of money managers. New mutual fund companies, especially those calling themselves "performance funds," seemed to replace the old guard with their new techniques for flipping stocks and earning eye-popping returns. In a climate that could have served as a warm-up act for the dot-com bubble of the late nineties, stocks in individual categories like computing or electronics were the coveted companies of Wall Street's ball.

Of all the Cinderellas, the Dallas headquarters of the six-year-old EDS became a favored stop of Wall Street investment bankers. Over a dozen investment banks visited Perot and urged him to take the company's stock public. Conservative firms, given EDS's $1.5 million of income, estimated an initial public offering price that would value the company at thirty times its earnings. Others offered to market it at fifty times earnings. A banker at a smaller firm, Ken Langone at R. W. Pressprich, was less modest and suggested to Perot an offering price of one hundred times earnings, a price that would mean six-year-old EDS was worth $150 million. EDS, after all, did have the unbeatable trifecta of "electronic," "data," and "systems" embedded in its brand. After Perot did some soul-searching, Langone's suggestion seemed inviting. EDS would go public.

IBM's Watsons, who had entered the company as employees, never owned much of IBM at any point. In contrast, Perot was the majority shareholder of EDS, owning 9.5 million shares. His employees were allocated 1.5 million shares. For the IPO, Perot agreed to issue 325,000 new shares and sell 325,000 of his own shares to the public. With the limited float and the public investor's insatiable demand for anything electronic, Langone's company priced the shares at $16.50 per share—a full 118 times EDS's earnings at the time. Perot emerged at the end of the offering with a net worth close to $200 million on paper. *Fortune* declared him "the fastest richest Texan ever." Within two years, his paper net worth would top $1.5 billion, making him technology's first billionaire.

The financial enthusiasm of 1968 Wall Street was felt far from Texas and lower Manhattan. Just fifty miles south of both the flower children of San Francisco's Haight-Ashbury and the hippies of Berkeley, a valley was being transformed. Here too the people would adopt the language of revolution and disruption, of overthrowing the establishment, but for quite different purposes. The evolution from punch cards to mainframe computers had seen the replacement of mechanical processes with electrons moving through vacuum tubes. The tubes had rapidly given way to the modern marvel of the transistor and the semiconductor. The best material to make semiconductors turned out to be the element known as silicon.

Thirty-one

START-UPS

In July 1969 hundreds of millions of people on Earth huddled around television screens to witness a new world come within reach, a pinnacle of human achievement. When Christopher Columbus or Vasco da Gama set off on their respective voyages to explore new worlds, there were likely no more than a few dozen spectators waving them farewell. But the moon landing was a collective journey, made awe inspiring with live images from outer space transmitted through television, putting much of humanity in a collective trance. It was so momentous that the entire first section of the *New York Times* was dedicated to the smallest details and broadest implications of this most highly anticipated event of the space age.

At the time, people expected the moon to be settled, at the very least in some minimal way, in the not-too-distant future. Optimistic speculations suggested that shuttle services for passengers were just a decade away. This impending reality, prompted by the American moon landing, raised interesting questions. One editorial in the next day's issue, written by a member of the *Times* editorial board, asked in a bold headline, CAPITALIST MOON OR SOCIALIST MOON? In it the writer asked, since no one yet owned the moon, how should mineral rights or property rights for lunar hotels one day be allocated? Since it was the American flag that now waved so proudly on the moon's surface, not the Soviet hammer and sickle, did this mean that the moon was by default now open to free-market forces? But the questions were rhetorical devices. The editorial went on to dispute the notion that the "race to the moon was in any sense a test" or competition "between American capitalism and Soviet socialism." Given that the entire effort was financed by the U.S. Treasury and American taxpayers, the writer argued that "the triumphant United States moon program was as socialistic in its central direction and financing" as the space program of the Soviets, and that this should be taken into account when it came to formulating the system of property rights on the moon. Since the moon landing was a triumph of American ingenuity but not of American capitalism, why should anyone assume that the moon would be a free-market moon? This seemed a debate of some consequence in the afterglow of the landing.

But still, there was a fundamental difference between the Americans and the Soviets. And the difference in approach would leave the Americans with compounding economic benefits for decades, none of which involved hotels on the moon. While both the Soviet and American programs were financed by the state, the American program relied on contracts with private suppliers for the vast variety of components, services, and technologies. These contracts, in every sense, subsidized research and development on a scale that no profit-seeking company would have engaged in without the firm revenues of a government contract, which, fairly or unfairly, allowed private entities to retain and benefit from the knowledge gained through the public dollar. So while the initial effort was centrally planned, the residual and serendipitous effects were left to the free market to discover. Communism did not allow this vital second step of allowing fortuitous, profitable accidents to take place.

No place was this more evident than in the business of semiconductors. The use of silicon-based semiconductors, at the most fundamental level, allowed for easier, faster, and more reliable manipulation of electricity, which is central to the execution of all computing processes. In the fifties and sixties, given the nature of their missions, the customers that needed the most reliable, costliest semiconductors—the early adopters—were the air force and, later, NASA.

The story of Silicon Valley starts with the story of the semiconductor. In the late fifties, a group of eight engineers working for William Shockley at Shockley Semiconductor—Shockley won the Nobel Prize in 1956 for inventing the transistor—looked to leave their mercurial, brilliant boss. The men initially thought about pursuing an employment opportunity that would hire them collectively as a team. While brainstorming possible options, the group was connected with a New York banker at the firm of Hayden, Stone & Co. by the father of one of the eight men. The banker, Arthur Rock, proposed that the men form a company rather than move as a roving guild. The group suggested to Rock that they needed around $750,000 to build next-generation semiconductors. After a fruitless search among dozens of prospective joint-venture partners, nearly all of them defense contractors, Rock called Fairchild Camera and Instrument. Sherman Fairchild, the controlling shareholder, agreed to invest, putting in $1.38 million.

Fairchild, incidentally, was also the largest shareholder of IBM—his father had preceded Thomas Watson Sr. when IBM was still the Computing-Tabulating-Recording Company. But the new investment carried a condition: Fairchild would have an option to buy all of the eight men's and Hayden Stone's stakes for $3 million collectively if things went well. Officially, the eight men founded Fairchild Semiconductor. Predictably, given the Fairchild connection, their first customer was IBM, servicing the military. Before long, Fairchild exercised his option to buy all of Fairchild Semiconductor. While the eight men made substantial windfalls, the investment structure lacked the unlimited-upside element now intrinsic to the idea of the Silicon Valley start-up.

In 1968 two of the original eight, Bob Noyce and Gordon Moore, looked to start another company. Given the optimism of the capital markets about anything to do with electronics and computing at the time—the same conditions that valued Ross Perot's six-year-old EDS at over $200 million—the pair were able to forgo a corporate sponsor this time in setting up their new venture. They again turned to Arthur Rock as their banker to help raise the money. The easiest call was to Grinnell College in Iowa, where Noyce was on the board of trustees. The trustees, who included a young money manager named Warren Buffett, approved $300,000 of the college's funds to be invested in the new company, which later that year changed its name to Intel, short for "integrated electronics." With a total of

$2.5 million, including a substantial amount from the Rockefellers as passive investors, Noyce and Moore began their operations.

As its name implied, Intel's business plan was to build the multiple functions of electronic circuitry within a single processing unit, with the goal of continually expanding its power and reducing its size. Intel's microprocessor would enable significant new computing applications in smaller forms—scientific calculators, for instance—as time went on. But an equally enduring and impactful aspect of Intel was on the financial side. In 1971, on track for just $9 million in revenues for the year, Intel filed for what is now the successful start-up's final rite of passage: an initial public offering. Intel's IPO, taking place within three years of the company's founding, helped formalize the financial playbook of Silicon Valley.

While Intel is one of Silicon Valley's most storied brands, its initial fund-raising method was not a typical venture capital round, as the money was collected separately from wealthy individuals and families, including Grinnell College, and the founders. However, as start-ups had no financial histories, institutional investors such as pension funds, university endowments, and foundations were not equipped for the task of evaluating the strength of these new companies as investment prospects. And without operating records, the investments fell far outside their mandate to make safe, prudent investments. Yet with the stock market's reception to companies like Intel and EDS, the prospect of investing early in the dominant companies of tomorrow became increasingly enticing to larger investors.

Before the stock market's demonstrable appetite for tech stocks made itself known in the late sixties, an investor in a promising technology company needed to wait for the company to actually begin delivering the hoped-for operating results to achieve profitable returns. But the public market's willingness to bet on a hot company's future changed this equation: It allowed the investor who risked money at an embryonic stage to achieve financial returns well before the company reached financial maturity or even profitability. Once the shares traded publicly, the early-stage investor could sell a block of his shares to the public to reduce his risk. In turn, the public investor received the opportunity to invest in a company much earlier in its history. The success of Intel's IPO, which proved that the time frame from start-up to IPO could be compressed to three years, gave rise to a new formalized vehicle dedicated to investing in multiple start-ups: the venture capital fund.

The investors in the venture capital funds received the benefits of diversification, where the staggering gains from one hit would ostensibly offset losses from a handful of others. It helped that the venture capital firms that managed the funds were themselves entrepreneurial—the firms raised money from outside investors to invest in start-ups—with the firm usually entitled to 20 percent of the investment gains for finding, screening, and nurturing start-ups. This brave new world of high-risk start-up investing started attracting the families of old industrial wealth, university endowments, and pension funds.

At the same time, many of the pioneering venture capitalists were not moneymen but graduates of the semiconductor industry. One of the eight men who had formed Fairchild Semiconductor, Eugene Kleiner, would found the venture capital firm Kleiner Perkins in 1972, not coincidentally the year after the Intel IPO. In the same year, Don Valentine, a former Fairchild sales executive, founded Sequoia Capital. Kleiner Perkins and Sequoia would become as intrinsic to Silicon Valley as the entrepreneurs themselves—the equivalent of the grand Hollywood studios, with the entrepreneurs analogous to actors, directors, and producers. Over the next forty-five years, several of America's most valuable corporations, including three of the top four, would be funded early on by Kleiner Perkins or Sequoia or both.

This birth of venture capital—a rebirth, really—was a return to the most American of roots, older than its founders' democracy. The organizers of the Virginia Company had called upon "adventurers" to risk capital. A few years later, the Merchant Adventurers in London coffeehouses had agreed to finance the voyage of a large molasses ship known as the *Mayflower*. Three hundred fifty years later, an improved concept of venture capital was being applied to the next era of American discovery.

WITHOUT VENTURE CAPITAL, the Silicon Valley of popular imagination wouldn't exist. Just as ventures to the New World needed more than ships and sailors, the financing mechanism of start-ups is central to their formation. As most new businesses fail, saying start-ups have a very high rate of failure is by itself not particularly revelatory. But a start-up is not a small business. A start-up is designed from the beginning to either become very big or completely fail—the modern-day equivalent of an uncertain, cross-ocean voyage to the New World as opposed to, say, a predictable, moderately profitable seventeenth-century trading voyage from London to Amsterdam. Stakeholders in a start-up are more interested in increasing the potential magnitude of a spectacular out-come than in bettering the probability of modest returns. Thus, the financial ecosystem's willingness to accept a high risk of capital loss made venture capital accessible to outliers and eccentrics.

One such outlier would do much to converge the idea of space travel and the power of computing and put it in the consumer's hands. In the sixties, programmers working on Pentagon-backed projects had come up with a game. On the first generation of computer screens, given the intensity of graphics processing, the game, called Spacewar!, was built to illustrate the value of computing power. A small pixelated spaceship, in the shape of a triangle, was set against a backdrop of stars—keyboard controls rotated the ship, with trajectory, speed, and position of the stars calculated simultaneously. This impressive bit of research and development helped to kill countless hours for programmers with access to the game, among them a University of Utah engineering student, Nolan Bushnell.

In addition to understanding technology, Bushnell had a working knowledge of carnivals and amusement parks. Over summers, he had worked at the types of booths where knocking over milk bottles with baseballs won a stuffed animal. He also knew of the world of coin-operated pinball machines, where a heavy metal ball made its way down through a maze, picking up points as it struck obstacles. After graduating, Bushnell moved to the Bay Area to begin working at Ampex, a large electronics company. In 1971 he decided to build on a wider scale what he had witnessed with Spacewar!.

The unit Bushnell envisioned was a television in a wood case, where a standing player would be able to control objects on the screen. The advances in computing electronics had been so dramatic that processes that had once required $100,000 mainframes could now be accomplished with processors that cost mere hundreds of dollars. Bushnell's game, Computer Space, was a pioneer in the category of what would become known as arcade games. While Computer Space itself was not a hit, Bushnell, sensing success in the overall category, officially formed his business, Atari Inc., the following year to introduce his next product.

His game, Pong, was activated by inserting a quarter. With two players, the game's objective was to prevent the ball from going through a goal. Each player's on-screen "paddle" was a vertical line that could be moved up and down. When a paddle touched the ball, the ball moved toward the other player. Incredibly simple and easy to play, it set off a sensation. The unit, integrating a television, cabinetry, controls, coin counter, and computing hardware, retailed for a few thousand dollars. Initially bars, pool halls, and restaurants started carrying the units, often next to the cigarette machines or jukebox. Distributors would place the machines on location and share the earnings of the unit with the establishment. As countless entrepreneurs entered the market with their own games, arcades that carried a large variety of the standing consoles became a phenomenon that drew in boys and young men competing for points on a screen; the *Times* called the consoles the "space age pinball machine."

By 1974 Atari was booming when America wasn't. Vietnam, after 58,000 American deaths, was on the verge of falling to the communists. Nixon, disgraced for different reasons, became the first president to resign the office. The oil-producing countries tightened supplies dramatically, leading to shortages and price increases at home, a crisis entirely self-inflicted, given that America remained a top-three oil producer—its insatiable demand exposed its economic destiny to the deserts of Arabia. Even America's manufacturing prowess, its industrial might, seemed to be in question, with the efficient Japanese making inroads.

But Silicon Valley was filling up newspapers with dozens of pages of employment ads. One Atari ad in 1974 read simply, "Have Fun, Make Money." The day the ad ran, an unkempt eighteen-year-old who had grown up in nearby Cupertino showed up at the front desk of the game maker. He refused to leave without a job. The receptionist relayed the message to a senior engineer and asked whether she should call the cops.

Instead the engineer, Al Alcorn, engaged with the "hippie-looking kid," learning that he was a dropout from the literary Reed College with no formal engineering background but deep enthusiasm for technology. Despite the negatives, Alcorn hired Steve Jobs as a technician at $5 an hour.

Atari's unconventional hiring practices didn't dissuade Sequoia Capital from making an investment. Neither did Atari's manufacturing floor: "You go on the factory tour and the marijuana in the air would knock you to your knees—where they were manufacturing the product!" Sequoia's Don Valentine would note later. Japanese quality control it wasn't. Still, the venture capitalist took the big picture view to his board duties, suggesting that prudishness would have been futile: "What would I say, get a higher brand of marijuana?" This too was a fundamental shift, the counterculture of San Francisco and Berkeley permeating south. The Silicon Valley of the semiconductor companies, with their engineering prowess, hired men with esteemed academic pedigrees. The male employees wore ties and sold to defense contractors. Their manufacturing processes, given the precision, quality, and reliability needed for aerospace, mirrored the practices of medical laboratories. Now the beneficial effects of the investments of the military-industrial complex were being fused with the live-free culture of antiwar protesters and hippies. At Atari this meant conducting board meetings in hot tubs.

This flexibility was soon embedded in the employment culture found in Silicon Valley. In other industries, both the white-collar worker, as described in *The Organization Man*, and the blue-collar worker, represented through unions, tended to exhibit a deep sense of loyalty to their companies, expecting to stay for the entirety of their working lifetimes. And their companies reciprocated the sentiment through pensions, retirement benefits, perks, and job security. But the start-up was the land of mercenaries, young men whose spirits ran counter to traditional corporate culture but who were vastly capitalistic in their personal financial ambitions and their sacrifices. As risky as start-ups were, given that most failed, these employees had little notion or expectation of stability. In addition, start-ups often paid less than comparable corporate jobs but required more hours. To offset the low compensation and lack of job security, start-ups offered equity in the form of stock options. And if the

stock options paid off, the newly rich early employee often became difficult to manage. The dynamics were more similar to joining a pirate ship
than the Royal Navy.

But some employees, even before becoming rich, were harder to manage
than others. Employees at Atari couldn't stand Steve Jobs. He smelled, and
he routinely treated coworkers like "dumb shits." Given that Atari itself
didn't exactly conform to generally accepted standards of the workplace,
Jobs was shifted around to make it work. But after just six months, Jobs
decided to go to India on a pilgrimage. He passed a year experiencing
India, dropping acid, and spending time at a commune, and just as
dramatically as when he had first joined Atari, Jobs showed up unan-
nounced again, asking for his job back, this time with saffron robes, a
shaved head, and sandals. He wouldn't leave the commercial world again
in his lifetime, but he wouldn't stay at Atari much longer this time either.

IN THE SUMMER of 1975, in Albuquerque, New Mexico, unit 114 in
the Portals apartment complex was becoming increasingly crowded. The
formation of this makeshift operation could be traced back a few months
earlier to a newsstand on the East Coast. It was early winter in Cambridge, Massachusetts, when two old high school friends from Seattle
excitedly pored over the January edition of *Popular Electronics* magazine.
The magazine had partnered with a small builder of electronic components to offer a build-it-yourself computer kit called the Altair, named
for a fictional destination from an episode of *Star Trek*. One of the young
men, Bill Gates, was in his freshman year at Harvard, and Paul Allen
was visiting. For years the duo had talked excitedly about opportunities
in the burgeoning world of computers. Now this simple, crude home
computer kit, selling for $360, seemed to represent a revolutionary change
in computing's price point.

Gates and Allen, however, had ambitions beyond simply ordering the
kit to play with it. Using stationery from a defunct business from their
high school days, Traf-o-Data, they reached out to the company that
actually built the Altair. Traf-o-Data had been founded to help count
cars on the road for public traffic departments, but its value now was that

the young men could seem more official without spending anything extra for letterhead. Addressing the letter to Micro Instrumentation Telemetry Systems, or MITS, located in New Mexico, the pair offered to write a programming language that would increase the Altair's utility and appeal. A programming language is what allows the computer's hardware to understand a programmer's instructions. Receiving the letter, MITS offered to meet the executives of Traf-o-Data. MITS agreed to meet.

Gates and Allen went to work writing a version of BASIC, a programming language, for the Altair in preparation for the meeting. After a successful demonstration, Allen received a job offer from MITS and rented an apartment in the Portals complex. In addition, MITS wanted new versions of BASIC for its upcoming products. To deliver, Gates and Allen set up Micro-Soft, derived from "software for micro-computers." The pair quickly hired several of their programmer friends to move into Allen's apartment for the summer, with Gates joining when spring classes ended at Harvard. When September came around, Gates decided to stay.

The Altair, at the time, was causing significant excitement among early adopters—enthusiasts known as hobbyists—including some in Silicon Valley. At the Homebrew Computer Club, formed just weeks after the *Popular Electronics* issue premiered the Altair, Steve Wozniak made it to the first meeting, which he would later call "one of the most important nights" of his life. There he saw the Altair demonstrated, beginning to understand the implications and flexibility of low-cost microprocessors. Wozniak spent the next few months hacking together the functions of a keyboard and a microprocessor that could show keystrokes on a television screen—which, in Wozniak's telling, was an achievement that had never been accomplished outside large corporate mainframes costing tens or often hundreds of thousands of dollars. At a subsequent Homebrew meeting where Wozniak showed his creation, everyone seemed impressed, including Wozniak's friend Steve Jobs.

Around that time, Jobs was given a freelance project at Atari, having altered the terms of his employment. Atari's founder had tasked Jobs with designing a single-player version of Pong, in which the ball could be simply hit against a wall back to the player. Jobs called on Wozniak, who was working at Hewlett-Packard, to help. Over the course of less than a week, Jobs and Wozniak delivered a single-player version of Pong. Jobs was in a rush. He needed to go back to a commune in Oregon, where the apple-picking season was about to begin.

But Wozniak's keyboard demonstration was not far from either of their minds. At Atari Jobs had seen the tactile experience of the end user seeing his intentions appear on a screen. It was intuitive. The video games of the era almost universally had one joystick and one button as the central inputs. Millions of boys interacted with the world of computer chips for the first time through Atari without the least bit of technical knowledge. And on a personal level, Jobs saw the iconoclastic Atari founder in action with his showmanship. The smoothness of Atari's functions served as Jobs's inspiration to shape Wozniak's product. This wasn't their first time working together. Wozniak and Jobs had operated another hardware business once when Jobs was still in high school and Wozniak was at Berkeley, but that one had involved rigging the telephone system to enable free long-distance calls. This time, no federal crimes would be involved.

While Gates and Allen were holed up in an apartment in the first few months of Microsoft's existence, Jobs and Wozniak started Apple Computer. To seed Apple, Jobs sold his VW minibus and Wozniak sold his HP scientific calculator. And thus commenced the origins of what would become one of the great rivalries in American business: one company started with the sale of the automotive symbol of hippies everywhere, the other by a Harvard student with a near-perfect SAT score.

APPLE WAS THE ARCHETYPAL VALLEY START-UP. The company's headquarters were Jobs's parents' garage. Incidentally, the idea of starting in the garage was not due to its cheapness in terms of office space, though this was a factor. More so, garages were natural places to assemble, solder, screw, and wire hardware. After Wozniak's improvements to his initial keyboard and processor, the Homebrew received a demonstration of an improved version. Seeing this, the proprietor of a just-opened computer electronics store agreed to buy fifty units for $500 each—the product would come to be known as the Apple I.

Apple was also the age-old *American* start-up. Just as unschooled men of humble beginnings with endless, bold hustle—*Luck and Pluck*, as one Horatio Alger title went—found American capitalism the ladder to conquest, this was the start of another example for the American storybook. Democracy was only a political equalizer; this free market was Darwinian competition. In the earliest days of the Republic, when men first learned to navigate upstream with steam power, it was the gritty, unschooled Vanderbilt who conquered the market. The thirteen-year-old Carnegie—fresh off the boat from Scotland, having seen his father displaced there as a casualty of the Industrial Revolution—worked in a boiler room without seeing the sun for days on end, made his way up as a messenger boy at a telegraph office, and eventually dominated the American steel industry. During trial testimony taken well after he was established as a titan, Henry Ford couldn't identify the decade of the American Revolution, speculating that it might have happened in the 1800s. But who cared? The market was not an exam for scholars—the right answer was when the customer paid.

Now this burgeoning field of personal computers was open to another American son of humble beginnings. Jobs had been adopted by working-class parents who couldn't have children of their own. His unwed but college-educated birth mother—a rarity on both counts when she gave birth to him in 1955—extracted the promise that her son would be raised to attend college before allowing him to be adopted. His biological father was a Syrian attending graduate school in Wisconsin. Jobs, as a child, once cried his way back home after a neighborhood girl suggested his biological parents didn't want him. But his adoptive home provided great love: As a young adult, to avoid hurting his parents' feelings, he didn't search for his origins. And yet Silicon Valley seemed as open to him as it was to William Henry Gates III, a scion of a wealthy family from Seattle who had served as a congressional page during high school, who had access to a mainframe computer in his posh Seattle private school, who had made it to Harvard.

Indeed, Jobs reached the economic pinnacle much faster than Gates. The accelerants were venture capital, geographic location, and access to

Silicon Valley's tight ecosystem. When Jobs sensed he had a product that worked in the market, he reached out to Atari's founder, Nolan Bushnell. Bushnell was flush from the $28 million sale of his company to Warner Communications, the parent firm of the Warner Brothers studio that had once risked everything on the first talking picture. But Bushnell said no, referring Jobs to Sequoia Capital instead. Sequoia gave him a conditional no, suggesting Jobs first get an executive on board, referring him to Mike Markkula. Markkula, a young marketing veteran from pre-IPO Intel who had made a fortune from its climbing stock, agreed to provide $250,000 through a combination of a credit line and an equity investment. In turn Markkula received a one-third share, equal to those of Jobs and Wozniak, and turned their entity into a legal corporation.

Through the first nine months of 1977, Apple sold 570 units of a new and improved product, the Apple II. Markkula then helped raise a little over $500,000. The bulk of this round, however, came not from Silicon Valley but from the venture capital arm of the Rockefeller family—a small piece of the great oil fortune had circulated into Intel and now into Apple. In 1978 sales grew to $8 million. Then $48 million. In 1980 sales exceeded $100 million for a company that had yet to see its four-year anniversary. Despite the high inflation and deep economic uncertainties of 1980, which contributed to Reagan's overwhelming victory over Jimmy Carter, the stock market eagerly awaited Apple's IPO. On December 12, 1980, when the stock opened for trading, twenty-four-year-old Jobs's shares were worth $250 million by the end of the afternoon.

When Jobs arrived on the national stage, few people would have heard of the equally young Bill Gates. Microsoft didn't sell a sexy product like a computer—it sold software to other hardware makers. It got paid royalty fees from the sale of hardware or sold programming services. Seeing Apple's triumphant success, countless others tried to enter the personal computer business. Because it was new, it was the one area of electronics manufacturing where fast-rising Japan didn't completely dominate—by the late 1970s, Japan controlled market share in everything from TVs to radios to the new VCRs. One particularly eager entrant, IBM, had heard of Gates and Microsoft. The computing giant had an effort, named the Manhattan Project to reflect its seriousness, under way to build a personal computer. IBM reached out to Microsoft about programming languages to be bundled with its new machine. In addition, IBM mentioned that it needed a "disk operating system" or DOS, the central nervous system of its planned computer, upon which all other software programs would run. After first referring IBM to a company in Monterey, Microsoft agreed to deliver the operating system. At the same time, IBM allowed Microsoft to retain the rights to license the same operating system to other computer makers.

When IBM announced its PC, Apple mocked the late arrival of the corporate giant. But over time, Apple would soon see that IBM wasn't the competitor. The operating system turned out to be Microsoft's Trojan horse. With IBM's entry, application developers wanted to write compatible software, anticipating strong sales of the IBM PC. Other hardware makers, including Hitachi, NEC, and Compaq, anticipating the wide availability of software for the IBM PC, figured it would be better to manufacture computers that could also run the same software—IBM "clones." To make their machines work exactly like IBM's PC, everyone needed to turn to Microsoft to license MS-DOS. For software companies, it was far easier to write a program once for a large market than to write separate versions, so Microsoft became the de facto industry standard for which everyone wrote programs. This reinforcing efficiency, where one standard was cost-effective for both the hardware makers and the software makers, turned Microsoft's operating system into a natural monopoly. Microsoft would so commoditize the hardware part, since all IBM PCs worked the same on it, that IBM would eventually exit the personal computer business, seeing its diminished profitability. The largest profits in the computer business turned out to be in software—Microsoft made money each time a computer was sold with its operating system, which the vast majority of computers sold over the next twenty years would have—and the benefits of this natural monopoly would accrue to the man who never built computers.

Yet Microsoft's eventual rise was in many ways a stark contrast to the archetypal Silicon Valley start-up. Gates's company was profitable from the beginning. Its headquarters moved from New Mexico not to the Bay Area, but to a Seattle suburb. Gates himself was financially conservative, preferring independence to the involvement of venture capitalists. When Microsoft finally did relent to the overtures of Silicon Valley, it raised $1 million for a meager 5 percent of the company in 1981—this at a time when the company was already on track to generate $15 million in revenues that year. Microsoft was so removed from the IPO track of Silicon Valley, it wasn't even a corporation for the first five years, organized instead as a partnership. The lack of much outside investment allowed Gates and Allen to hold the vast majority of their company's stock through the mideighties. Jobs, while his net worth had climbed into a significant fortune with Apple's rise, didn't own enough to control his destiny and was fired. It was a cruel irony: For all his counterculture spirit and brilliance, he suffered the mercenary's fate, left with money but no kingdom. Gates, however, remained reluctant to go public even ten years after Microsoft's founding. Eventually, due to the number of Microsoft employees who owned shares, and U.S. securities laws obligating any company with more than 500 shareholders to be registered, which Microsoft expected to soon pass, Gates agreed to list his shares. But as a final symbol of resistance, he did try to fly coach during the IPO roadshow—one last ode to parsimony—until his underwriters insisted otherwise.

Thirty-two

FINANCE

I n 1965 in the small town of New Bedford, Massachusetts, word had spread of a shareholder coup of sorts at the town's largest employer, Berkshire Hathaway. But few could have foreseen the full implications of what had transpired. A century earlier, New Bedford was the whaling capital of America; it saw its fortunes change when whale oil gave way to oil from the fields of Pennsylvania. The hardy New England town then reinvented itself as a textile manufacturer, joining the dozens of other towns in New England that had a textile operation as their main employer. Not long after the end of World War II, New England had a combined 400,000 workers in the trade. But the industry soon began to face pressure from new operations in southern states, where labor was cheaper.

Some mills combined with others to cut costs and extract efficiencies. The pressure on wages often led to strikes. In the postwar boom, New England textile workers were not the most indulged participants, certainly nothing like the fortunate autoworkers with their gilded pensions and high wage rates. Nor were these towns suburban in character. These were small industrial towns with smokestacks. So when the workers at Berkshire Hathaway learned that the Stanton family, who had operated the company for decades, had lost control of what seemed to be their fiefdom, there must have been a degree of shock at how such a thing could have happened. But Berkshire Hathaway, as small as it was, was a public company. People as far away as Omaha could buy its stock. And thirty-five-year-old Warren Buffett did, thinking of it as a discarded "cigar butt"—something nearly free but of value in that it had a few puffs left before extinguishing. Soon even Buffett would learn that the stock had been valued that way for a reason.

For Buffett the business presented an interesting human dilemma that played out for him into the eighties but that had a clear-cut economic answer from the start. Textiles were a dying business. While the former managers of Berkshire attempted to keep up by buying the latest equipment, so did everyone else, eliminating any competitive advantage. Since the writing was on the wall, the best way forward was to maximize the profits of the operation and not invest any further capital in the American textile business. An American worker, in terms of labor costs, in the North or the South, was not going to be as cheap as an Asian worker anytime in the near future. Going forward, Buffett would close down unprofitable facilities, take Berkshire's capital and deploy it elsewhere, and continue to invest in businesses that had nothing to do with textiles. For Berkshire shareholders, this was the prudent thing to do. For employees in New Bedford, this force of capitalism would end livelihoods.

Of course, the ultimate decision maker in all this was not Warren Buffett but the American consumer: She wanted cheaper clothing for herself, not job security for workers of a challenged business. Sympathies from the heart, yes, maybe; actual dollars from her purse, no. She was no more or less pragmatic than the new chairman of Berkshire Hathaway. None of this made it any less painful for workers. To the displaced, it seemed a zero-sum game in which someone else was gaining at their expense. Who could explain to them that to increase the overall standard of living required the occasional rise and death of businesses and industries, and that to complain, in the grand scheme of things, was the mark of poor economic sportsmanship?

For centuries people in most of the world had barely left their villages over the course of a lifetime. Now entire industries, such as whaling and textiles, came and went within two or three generations. Owners—thousands of shareholders—were everywhere and mostly anonymous. Just as Silicon Valley was rising, giving birth to new giants, the textile mills of New England were dying. And there was no simple formula for labor mobility: A middle-aged textile worker could not pick up and get a job at a Silicon Valley company.

By the midseventies, though, it wasn't just textiles in trouble. American manufacturing at large seemed to be caught in a downward spiral, much of it caused by the nature of postwar American growth. For decades American oil companies had strong supply relationships in the Middle East to supplement their production at home; then several countries began to take greater control of their affairs and sharply cut supply to raise prices. Within weeks in 1973, oil crossed over $10 a barrel and into the teens. American policy makers reacted to the shock with rationing and by lowering the speed limit to fifty-five. But higher prices were here to stay. American households, given that formerly cheap gas was now a larger share of their income, experienced the equivalent of a pay cut. The effects reverberated.

Compounding this, the two-decade expansion of defense work had ended, along with the withdrawal in Vietnam. Television makers such as RCA and Magnavox seemed to be overmatched by the color TVs from Sony and Sanyo, as were American manufacturers in all categories of electronics. The oil crisis opened the door for small, light, fuel-efficient Japanese cars that Ford, GM, and Chrysler had no experience building. With American automakers caught flat-footed by the sudden crosswinds of Japan and the Middle East, related industries such as steel began to feel the effects. The once-thriving crescent-shaped region around Lake Erie that included Buffalo, Pittsburgh, and Cleveland became the Rust Belt, a corroding reminder of America's past industrial glory with large factories left hauntingly vacant. Chrysler, by 1980, was insolvent, needing substantial government loans to survive. At the time when Apple was going public, Chrysler was getting bailed out.

In this industrial funeral procession, Wall Street assumed the roles of underwriter and undertaker.

AT THE HEIGHT of 1980s finance, the epicenter of Wall Street was at the corner of Rodeo Drive and Wilshire Boulevard in Beverly Hills. On one of the floors of the nondescript building, sitting at an X-shaped desk with traders all around him, Michael Milken operated in a once-sleepy backwater of the corporate bond market. His salary at his peak in the eighties was $550 million in cash for one year's work. The work, in his case, required being in total control of the American junk bond market, the fuel that had transformed corporate America into a giant chessboard. And he did it while living three time zones away from lower Manhattan. He had ended up in his position by carefully observing the wreckage of the seventies, especially the corporations that had large debts. Milken was a student first and foremost.

Unlike the stock market, which had the excitement of dramatic rises and falls, the bond market had been its boring, conservative cousin for decades. A bond, whether issued by a city, state, federal government, or corporation, was simply a loan. Corporations issued bonds to borrow money. People and institutions that bought bonds expected a predictable stream of interest and eventually the principal amount back, 100 cents on the dollar. Predictability made it boring—the best outcome was to simply get back one's money along with the promised interest. No news was good news.

There was only one small area of distinction. Some companies were riskier to lend to than others. For investors to buy bonds of a less creditworthy company, they simply required a higher rate of interest to justify the risk, just as individuals with poor credit ratings pay higher rates. Not much was ever made of this until Michael Milken arrived on Wall Street.

As an undergrad at Berkeley in the 1960s, Milken had come across a study by an economist named Walter Braddock Hickman. In a look at nearly every corporate bond that had existed between 1900 and 1945, Hickman's research revealed that a diversified portfolio of the lowest-rated bonds, the bonds that seemed to present the most risk, returned substantially more than a portfolio of middle-grade bonds. There were, as is the case now, very few companies at the highest tier of credit known as triple-A, but this middle grade of bonds was the bulk of the corporate bond market. However, investors mistakenly assumed that the middle tier of companies was safer than it really was and that the bottom tier was riskier than it actually was. In this basic insight, that the lower-rated bonds presented the best value, Milken found religion.

By the seventies, after attending Wharton business school, he was working in the corporate bond department of Drexel Firestone, which soon merged with Burnham & Company. Even after the merger, Drexel Burnham was a third-tier investment bank. From his corner of the trading floor, Milken scouted for companies that the bond market thought were too risky but that he felt had the cash flow to service their debts and were thus unfairly discredited. In the carnage after the oil crisis, there were plenty of companies that had fallen on hard times but still had cash to pay the interest owed on bonds. But bond investors, being conservative, tended to lump all troubled companies together. As a result, the bonds of these companies traded at substantial discounts—30, 40, 50 cents on the dollar. And once they fell out of favor, few banks helped facilitate trading in these bonds, which discouraged investors from buying them since an investor could not sell them easily if the need arose. Armed with an encyclopedic memory of nearly every company and bond issue in this universe, Milken made his case to institutional investors such as pension funds, insurance companies, and savings banks to buy the bonds of these troubled companies. By the late seventies, Milken's clients had made substantial returns, and Milken was a top player in the high-yield bond market. In one account, a loyal Milken client joked that a particular high-yield bond was priced like it was "junk." The pejorative term stuck.

But there was an unlikely competitor at the turn of the decade. The bonds of the government itself seemed to bear interest like junk bonds. When Ronald Reagan took office in January 1981, America was in the midst of a recession and a period of severe inflation, a rare combination. American Treasury notes were paying over 13 percent annually—rates on six-month FDIC-insured certificates of deposits, CDs, were nearly as high. In the first month of Reagan's presidency, Chrysler came out with a $400 million bond issue fully guaranteed by the federal government— even with the full faith and credit of the U.S. government backing them, Chrysler's bonds carried an interest rate of 14.9 percent.

When the dust settled and interest rates normalized, investors continued to have an appetite for the types of interest rates that they had just seen. But there were only so many companies in the bond market that were solvent enough to make their payments but troubled enough to be traded like "junk." Milken's institutional investors wanted much more product than the market had. The solution was both bold and simple: More high-yield bonds needed to be created.

To satiate his market, Milken sought out two types of candidates. The first were entrepreneurs of smaller businesses that wanted to become much, much larger. Milken's entrepreneurs were in capital-intensive businesses or in industries that Wall Street at the time didn't touch. Steve Wynn first met Milken when he owned a gambling hall that generated a few million dollars in annual revenue. He wanted to borrow $100 million to build a casino in the next big thing, Atlantic City, calling it the Golden Nugget. Eventually Milken would raise hundreds of millions of dollars for Wynn when he left to focus on Las Vegas, reinventing America's gambling mecca.

Australian entrepreneur Rupert Murdoch, who owned a hodgepodge of newspapers, wanted to reinvent himself and buy a series of television stations in America, his first serious foray into the medium. Using little cash, assuming well over $1 billion in debt, and issuing additional junk bonds, Murdoch over the course of twelve months in 1985 bought Twentieth Century Fox in one transaction and followed up by buying seven local television stations from Metromedia. Supported by Milken's operation, traders and bankers played multiple roles in financing Murdoch's transactions and in creating the Fox brand on television to compete with CBS, NBC, and ABC.

Similarly, the capital-intensive nature of cable, the next big thing within television, was an especially good fit for junk bond financing. Starting in the early eighties, American homes had rapidly started subscribing to pay television. Cable television, bringing a multitude of channels via wires buried in the ground, needed tens of billions of dollars to wire homes in America. The channels that had proliferated in less than five years, including MTV, TBS, CNN, and ESPN, were in great demand. Cable operators such as Tele-Communications, Inc., or TCI, issued bonds through Milken to facilitate the wiring with the hope that monthly revenues from cable subscribers would pay the interest on the bonds.

Other entrepreneurs, from Ted Turner with his acquisition of the MGM film library to Leonard Riggio and his growing Barnes & Noble chain of bookstores, turned to Milken's operation. But the appetites of investors willing to lend large sums of money for high rates of interest were endless. This gave rise to an entirely new class of individualistic, iconoclastic borrower, who had no particular line of business or vision, like Murdoch or Wynn or Turner, but saw great opportunities to menace corporate America.

FROM OMAHA, WARREN BUFFETT operated in a parallel universe to Milken's, but he embodied many of the forces that led to the heightened role of American finance in the mideighties. Twenty years after assuming control of Berkshire Hathaway, he decided that it was time to shut down the last of the textile mills. For years, Berkshire Hathaway had used its profits to invest in insurance companies like GEICO, the chocolate maker See's Candies, and newspapers like the *Buffalo News*, and had become a holding company that owned a wide variety of disparate assets rather than a simple textile maker, as it had once been for decades. By the eighties, Berkshire Hathaway owned large stakes in companies like American Express and the *Washington Post*. But this raised an interesting dilemma for Buffett and American business in general: What exactly is the role of a company? Is it simply to maximize profits for shareholders? If so, Buffett reasoned that Berkshire should have shut down its textile operations in the seventies, draining all of the capital that was left in textiles, liquidating the remaining assets, and investing it elsewhere. But he didn't.

To his shareholders he argued in a 1978 letter that "despite more attractive uses" for capital, Berkshire Hathaway's textile operations in New England "were very important employers in their communities," and as long as they returned to marginally profitable status, he would keep them open. But the writing was on the wall, and in early 1986, despite the best efforts of the textile operation's management, he admitted to share-holders that "in the end, nothing worked and I should be faulted for not quitting sooner." Berkshire Hathaway at the time was extraordinarily profitable, but to Buffett, investing in a loss-making textile operation that had no prospect of turning around was financial malpractice. On why he had not shut it down in the seventies due to community considerations but now was shutting it down entirely due to financial ones, Buffett told his shareholders, "Adam Smith would disagree with my first" decision and "Karl Marx would disagree with my second; but the middle ground is the only position that leaves me comfortable."

But the fact remained that the greatest investor of the twentieth century had taken a textile business that had employed thousands of people in factories in Massachusetts and converted it into a set of finan-cial holdings operated from a bland headquarters in Nebraska with a few administrative staff. The slow pace of its demise and his nuanced manner of thinking had provided him with insulation from criticism, but as the death of the textile mills was inevitable, what difference would it have really made had the shutdown occurred immediately once it no longer made financial sense? This was the position of the financial mercenar-ies who saw sentimentality as wasteful and inefficient, a destroyer of shareholder wealth. Corporations, on the other hand, sometimes saw themselves as serving more than just the owners who owned them on paper; they had constituencies of stakeholders including employees, ven-dors, and communities. This divergence pitted two forces of profit against each other: corporations and capitalists.

The evolution of this discontent was decades in the making. When the modern corporation came of age at the turn of the century with the trust movement, the largest shareholders of the large corporations then were former business owners, many of whom had taken stock in ex-change for selling their companies to form the larger entity. As time went on, through inheritance or sales of stock, the shares dissipated into ever more hands. With the mutual fund boom of the sixties, the shareholder base of America diversified even further to include in-stitutional investors, creating another layer of separation between small investors and the corporations they ostensibly owned. By the eighties, shareholdings were so widely distributed that the central power of the corporation shifted from the owners to the executives. A CEO who owned a negligible amount of a company's stock was more powerful in his incumbency than any one shareholder. Thus, shareholders had limited ability to check an entrenched management's power. Unlike the conflict between management and labor over wages, eighties finance was a battleground between owners and management.

To represent the interest of shareholders, incongruously, emerged the predatory, gleeful financial entrepreneur of the eighties. It required swashbuckling, swaggering change agents to take on powerful CEOs. Buttoned-up mutual fund managers and diligent Wall Street analysts were no match for the alpha males who had climbed to the top of their respective corporate ladders, but these new men, often denigrated as green-mailers and corporate raiders, seemed to be fully up to the task. With their rise, American culture had new villains, icons, movie characters, and caricatures that remain one part of the enduring imagery of the eighties.

The best juxtaposition of the opposing viewpoints of the essential purpose of the corporation came from American cinema. In *Other People's Money*, Gregory Peck starred as the gentle, patrician chief of New England Wire and Cable, headquartered in a fictional town similar to New Bedford in character. Danny DeVito played the part of the ex-uberant, amoral Larry the Liquidator. Larry finds the company's stock to be cheap, surmises that liquidating the assets of New England Wire and Cable would fetch him more than what he could buy the company for, and asks other shareholders to join him in killing the company. In the final closing scenes, in a large hall convening both workers and share-holders, Peck's character argues that this was the equivalent of murdering communities, "only on Wall Street, they call it maximizing shareholder value, and they call it legal, and they substitute dollars bills where a con-science should be." Then he implores, losing his temper, "Damn it, a business is worth more than its stock. . . . It is where we earn our living . . . dream our dreams. In every sense, it is what binds our communities together." In other words, everyone there has a stake in the company, even people who don't actually own any shares.

This, of course, is where the Liquidator disagrees. "Amen," he says, because "you always say amen after you hear a prayer." To a rapt and hostile audience, he continues, "This company is dead. Don't blame me. It was dead when I got here." Due to new technologies—fiber optics—the wire business is obsolete. "We're just not broke. And you know the best way to go broke: Keep getting an increasing share of a shrinking market." Then he takes a long pause for effect. "You know at one time there must have been dozens of companies making buggy whips. And I'll bet the last company around made the best goddamn buggy whip you ever saw." Businesses die. And it was the owners' right, such as the Liquidator's, to say when.

The ethos of Larry the Liquidator, in many ways, was the exact opposite of the start-up entrepreneur's. Whereas the start-up entrepreneur was starting with a blank slate to build new things, the financial entrepreneur saw himself as playing a vital, natural role in cleaning up the carcasses of old things in corporate America. There was some truth to this. Yet the logic of the argument was alone not enough. Just as Silicon Valley entrepreneurs needed venture capital, their equivalents on Wall Street needed their own specialized financing. The best and the brightest among them looked west to Beverly Hills, where Michael Milken could raise billions of dollars when the need arose, junk bonds becoming the pirate ship on which the corporate raiders sailed.

IF THERE WAS A COMPETITION to find a real-life equivalent to Larry the Liquidator, who relished the persona of financial agitator in the 1980s, the award would have gone to Carl Icahn. Raised in a middle-class home in Queens, Icahn went to Princeton and then enrolled at NYU School of Medicine for two years. He dropped out and joined the army, where his main contribution seems to have been playing poker. After these detours, he found himself on Wall Street through his uncle. He thrived in short order in the abstract world of options trading, where his primary activity consisted of arbitrage, finding mathematical discrepancies in pricing that allowed risk-free profits.

By the late 1960s, Icahn had branched out on his own, forming Icahn and Company with a few hundred thousand dollars from his uncle. Icahn was soon earning substantial annual returns from his activities in the options market. A few years later, Icahn expanded to look at bigger opportunities in undervalued securities, buying larger stakes with longer-term horizons. Once Icahn established a position in a company, the formula was to make some noise challenging the management. This also had the benefit of calling other investors' attention to the thesis that the company was undervalued. Initially, Icahn had no interest in acquiring or running any of the companies, helpfully telling one paper company CEO, "I don't know anything about the paper business. I don't care anything about the paper business. All I care about is the money. And I want it quick."

In the late 1970s and early 1980s, Icahn was able to add a wrinkle to his game. In several attempts in the early 1980s, the companies Icahn targeted bought his positions out at higher prices—succumbing to the practice known as greenmail—to neutralize his overtures. The companies bought out Icahn to quiet him, but such maneuvers did not benefit any other shareholder. Congress didn't like greenmail either. Any practice that derived its name from the color of money and "blackmail" was unlikely to endure. Other times greenmail tactics backfired for investors like Icahn. Larger companies began to sense that these nuisance investors could be ignored—after all, investors like Icahn did not have enough money to take over the entire company, so what could they do but gripe?

Here Drexel Burnham, Milken's firm, sensed opportunity. With Milken's capacity to raise virtually unlimited amounts of money by placing bonds with his loyal investors, what if Drexel could finance financial entrepreneurs with small companies or minor trading operations to buy giant American companies? It was an audacious strategy. With backing from Drexel, an investor that could afford to buy 5 or 10 percent of a company's stock could now finance the other 90 or 95 percent by issuing junk bonds and acquire the entire company. The earnings of the company, or a partial sale of its assets, would then be used to pay the interest on the bonds. Junk bond financing was the equivalent of taking out a mortgage on a rental property and having the rent cover the mortgage payment, only instead of a rental property, the targets were companies like Revlon or Disney. The ability for insurgents like Icahn to leverage a small bit of capital and borrow a large amount set in motion years of high corporate drama, showdowns that featured old, established companies, with their pedigreed executives under assault by these up-starts financed by Milken and Drexel Burnham.

But a vital question remained: What did men like Icahn, who had little professional management experience, know about operating large *Fortune* 500 companies? The answer was found in one trend of the late sixties and seventies. As the values of companies languished, they gave rise to an interesting form of corporate acquisitiveness, where a company like Berkshire Hathaway bought businesses that had nothing to do with the other businesses it owned, like its chain of chocolate shops and its insurance business. Unlike consolidations where a steelmaker buys another steelmaker to gain efficiency or economies of scale from multiple holdings working together, the conglomerate didn't look to extract any synergies. International Telephone & Telegraph was operating the Sheraton Hotel chain. A funeral home operator ended up in control of Warner Brothers, then bought companies like Atari. General Motors bought Ross Perot's EDS. The rise of the perception that a large corporation was merely in the business of making money, rather than in any particular line of work, prepared the ground for the emergence of a hyperactive era of leveraged buyouts and corporate raiding. What did Warren Buffett know about chocolate or newspapers? If an acquisitive CEO of a large corporation could buy and hold a business that he knew nothing about, why couldn't a smart entrepreneur like Icahn, with access to financing, also buy and hold a business he knew nothing about? It seemed that business principles were fairly universal and applicable across the board. This hypothesis would be tested.

In the spring of 1985, the nation's fifth-largest airline, TWA, found itself the target of such evolutionary changes in behavior. Through a securities filing known as a 13D, Carl Icahn had declared that he had accumulated a 20 percent stake in TWA. TWA's management panicked. To ward off a raider like Icahn, TWA agreed to be acquired by Texas Air. The acquisition by Texas Air would have left Icahn with a profit in the tens of millions on his holdings. But to the surprise and dismay of corporate America, Icahn actually wanted to own the company. To many this seemed akin to an aggressive dog catching up to the mail truck rather than simply enjoying a thrilling chase: What happens next?

The answer was that neither Texas Air nor TWA could have predicted the strange bedfellows that corporate raiding made. Texas Air's CEO, Frank Lorenzo, had notoriously bad relations with his unions: pilots, crew, machinists, flight attendants, baggage handlers—any group that did the actual work of the airline. TWA's management, like most, also had its share of union acrimony. Enter Icahn. To win the support of the unions for his bid, Icahn made a series of concessions that he would live up to if he gained control. The unions, shockingly, threw their full support behind Icahn's bid. In the court of public opinion, this effectively neutralized any notion of the airline's management as victims. As far as the unions were concerned, in one of the most visible hostile takeovers, their white knight was the corporate raider. By the fall, Icahn ended up in control of TWA, functioning as the actual CEO, a feat he would be loath to repeat in the future.

But the actions of men like Icahn also set the template for a new type of acquirer, men who were decidedly less rough around the edges or, at the very least, smart enough to appear so. This new category, the leveraged buyout, also required borrowing money to buy a company's stock, but it was not hostile and often required the complicity of the company's management. Among the pioneers were two cousins from Oklahoma, Henry Kravis and George Roberts, who had left the firm Bear Stearns in the late 1970s. Along with a senior Bear partner, Jerome Kohlberg, they formed KKR. The business of KKR was to take public companies private—the opposite of an IPO. The rationale for the business model was that private ownership would bring an unwieldy public company needed operating discipline. The new owners, with huge junk bond debt loads, had to cut frivolous expenses to pay the interest. In this telling, debt was a great disciplinarian. Yet the logic contained an irony: It suggested that large, for-profit, publicly traded companies, despite the forces of free-market capitalism, could be highly inefficient and wasteful if left to their own devices.

By the end of the 1980s, KKR would successfully complete the largest leveraged buyout in American corporate history. Using junk bonds, it would buy the tobacco and snack maker RJR Nabisco for nearly $25 billion. In most ways the KKR purchase marked the end of an era. But the end didn't mean death. Over the years, the leveraged buyout would be rebranded as private equity—the private equity firm provided the down payment and borrowed the rest—and men like Icahn would be rebranded as activist investors, with specialized hedge funds in a later era becoming practiced in the art of publicly excoriating company CEOs. The labels changed, but the game remained the same.

But in the heady atmosphere of the 1980s, Milken slipped in his activities as the junk bond king. He was accused of passing along inside information of pending deals, holding stock for favored clients to mask the identities of the true owners, and engaging in myriad technical securities violations—all to ensure the smooth functioning of his market. Smooth functioning, in this case, meant astounding profits and total disruption of American corporate finance. In 1988 a grand jury returned a ninety-eight-count indictment against him. Drexel, as a firm, would be engulfed as well and soon fail. Milken would plead guilty to six counts and be sentenced to ten years in prison.

Remarkably, as complex a subject as finance was, story lines of trading desks and boardroom aspirations found themselves expressed fully in pop culture. *Family Ties*, the second-highest-rated show on television in the mid-1980s, starred Michael J. Fox as Alex P. Keaton, a precocious and charming ball of comically moneyed ambition. Tom Wolfe's *The Bonfire of the Vanities* spent several weeks at number one on the *New York Times* best-seller list in 1988. Its main character was a top-producing bond trader, a "Master of the Universe" in Wolfe's telling. Oliver Stone's *Wall Street* gave American cinema one of its most memorable antiheroes in Gordon Gekko, played by Michael Douglas. The fall of Gekko starts with his attempt to take over an airline, a story line loosely based on Icahn's efforts at TWA. Douglas would lament the fact that even decades later, men would approach him in restaurants to tell him how inspired they were by his role—*to pursue a career on Wall Street*. Even romantic films found finance to be fertile ground for character redemption. Through the power of love, Julia Roberts in *Pretty Woman* was able to transform Richard Gere from an avaricious corporate raider without a heart into a company builder. For jaded American audiences, it was entirely plausible that a call girl could serve as the moral compass for a financier.

Thirty-three

SHOES

In the hours past midnight on a humid August night in 1988, a canary yellow Rolls-Royce Corniche was parked outside a storefront on 125th Street in Harlem. Inside the store, heavyweight champion Mike Tyson was picking up a custom-made jacket with the rap group Public Enemy's line "Don't believe the hype" embroidered on it. Given the late hour, word of Tyson's late-night shopping excursion had somehow reached the ear of another heavyweight, Mitch Green. Green had once faced Tyson in the ring and, at the time, remained one of the very few opponents who hadn't been annihilated at the champion's hands. But Green had lost the fight nonetheless and had fallen on hard times. Convinced that he had been financially wronged in the deal-making process of the fight, Green took the opportunity to confront Tyson. The argument spilled out into the street and escalated. Green got the worst of it with a bruise that closed one eye. Tyson broke his hand punching Green. The Rolls-Royce lost a side-view mirror as Tyson sped away.

But another victim of the night was the owner of the boutique, Dapper Dan's. As news footage repeatedly showed the storefront in the background, curiosity led to inquiries about exactly what sort of clothing store stayed open at 4:00 a.m.

Daniel Day (the proprietor's given name) specialized in creating a specific type of custom clothing. He used materials from the world of high fashion, from brands like Fendi, Gucci, Louis Vuitton, and Chanel, to create his own designs. When Dan started out in the business, he would simply buy purses from Louis Vuitton sixty blocks south on Fifth Avenue, deconstruct the materials, and stitch them back together to make whatever outlandish creation suited his clients. Before long, Dan decided to cut out the middleman and start screening the logos himself. Soon rappers requiring an entire Mercedes 560SEL decked out in Gucci-logoed seat covers had a reliable supplier. A convertible top made to look like a Louis Vuitton suitcase? No problem. It wasn't legal, but it wasn't a well-kept secret either. Dan's creations regularly appeared in magazines and on the backs of his celebrity clients. Everyone, including the companies infringed upon, knew the products weren't authentic—Louis Vuitton knew that it didn't make full-body jumpsuits—but they were better than authentic: They were from Dapper Dan's.

For young black men with aspirations to the high life, wearing something from Dan signaled success. The two familiar but improbable paths to get there were sports and music. But another kind of star of the street had always been a strong source of Dapper Dan's business: local drug kingpins and high-level dealers. As these men grew in stature—running blocks or taking over entire buildings in the crack trade—self-congratulation often meant commissioning one of Dan's creations.

By the eighties, whites had largely fled the urban core of every major city in America with the exception of a few Manhattan neighborhoods. Large public housing projects, which had eliminated the wide variety of stores and sidewalk life around them, resembled prisons inside cities. Declining populations meant departing businesses. Departing businesses meant loss of jobs and local capital. It was a tall order to ask a people enslaved for two hundred years, legally segregated for another hundred, then blocked from housing options by developers, landlords, real estate agents, mortgage lenders, and local customs to pick themselves up by their bootstraps quickly now that everything was even. And despite the 1968 Fair Housing Act, which outlawed discrimination in housing, the 1970s hit the inner city as hard as they did the dying factory towns, and crime soared.

By the mideighties, the black murder rate in America was worse than the peak of the Mexican murder rate during its cartel wars, with much of it attributed to the drug trade in the inner city. Tragically, and remark-ably, the bleakness of drug-based criminality was one of the sparks that led to the black takeover of wide swaths of American pop culture. Dapper Dan's trifecta of rap stars, athletes, and street kings were on the cusp of becoming tastemakers and trendsetters for an entire generation.

For most of the eighties, "blackness" on television and in music had been dialed down. Television's highest-rated show, *The Cosby Show*, fea-tured an affluent African American family, the Huxtables, headed by a doctor husband and lawyer wife in a posh brownstone. Michael Jackson, pop music's biggest star, was black, but his music didn't have a strong racial component. But the Huxtables didn't reflect the reality for young blacks: By the early nineties, a black male between the ages of eighteen and twenty-four had nearly a one-in-five-hundred chance of being killed over the course of a year. A young black man in 1991 was almost ten times more likely to kill someone, usually another young black man, than any other demographic in America. The climate was more aptly captured in rap lyrics from groups like N.W.A., standing for "Niggas with Attitude," than from Jackson's "Beat It."

Hip-hop, rap music, became the proprietary voice of urban America. The songs were stories about gang life, girls, cars and clothes, and illicit opportunities. In mining the rich reservoir of material from violence and the drug trade, hip-hop's biggest stars veered toward outrageous boastful-ness, openly relishing their success and endlessly chanting of their pur-suit of money. This new poetry of the streets became, ironically, the most overtly capitalistic art form in American history.

Commercialism was central to the genre. In addition to name-dropping status-signifying brands in their lyrics, rappers routinely re-placed the *S* in their stage names with a dollar sign: the five-foot-seven Todd Anthony Shaw became Too $hort, his 1990 album cover featuring sketches of Mercedes-Benzes and a Ferrari. Not since Ayn Rand's *Atlas Shrugged* had the symbolism of the dollar taken on such worshipful connotations.

The reverence of money stood in stark contrast to hard rock and alternative music. For rockers, selling too many records often carried the risk of a band being labeled commercial, of their very success calling into question the authenticity of the music. Pearl Jam and Nirvana would never sing about how much money they made, only endless pain and suffering, no matter how rich they were. For hip-hop's black fans, the celebration of consumerism was an escape from gritty realities—a feeling of one of their own being triumphant, of vicariously enjoying financial success that was so often elusive, of seeing themselves not as victims or as emasculated but as masters of their own destiny. Set to lush, energetic beats, the best hip-hop anthems were as aspirational as the rags-to-riches Horatio Alger stories of the nineteenth century. Since success was key to the art, the genre's biggest stars, such as Christopher Wallace, known as Notorious B.I.G., boasted about their origins in and onetime mastery of the crack trade. Wallace even looked to pass down his rules of business with the instructional song "Ten Crack Commandments." Shawn Carter, the rapper Jay Z, followed suit, suggesting in one song that while he had entered the music business "a hundred grand strong"—money earned from selling drugs—he was now chasing millions instead, boasting, "Put me anywhere on God's green earth—I'll triple my worth." His gilded ambitions extended to the name of his record label, Roc-A-Fella, a phonetic homage to the most storied fortune in American history.

THE RISE OF HIP-HOP paralleled a cultural transformation from the world of sports. One star changed a vital commercial equation.

Michael Jordan first came to the attention of the American public as a college freshman with his performance in the 1982 NCAA championship game, hitting the game-winning shot for the University of North Carolina over Georgetown. Two years later, Jordan decided to forgo his senior year and declared himself eligible for the National Basketball Association's draft, becoming the third player selected, behind Hakeem Olajuwon and Sam Bowie.

While he hadn't been selected number one overall, Jordan's high-flying talent was regarded as uniquely sublime. As was routine, his agent looked to get his player a shoe deal as an ancillary source of income. Endorsement deals were common enough but minor for most. Numerous college teams by this time wore Nikes, with the coaches receiving the endorsement money. Tennis stars, given that it was a single-player sport, had some of the biggest shoe deals. Nike had John McEnroe. But most other types of athletes had relatively modest deals. The biggest shoe deal for a basketball player belonged to Jordan's onetime teammate at the University of North Carolina, James Worthy, who had an eight-year deal with New Balance at $150,000 per year.

As a fan of the brand, Jordan wanted to sign with Adidas. After being pressed by both his agent and his father, Jordan relented and made a trip to Oregon to Nike's headquarters. There Nike made a pitch to Jordan, offering him $500,000 per year for five years, along with royalties from shoe sales. In addition, Nike offered to design a special shoe branded for Jordan with his design input.

All this was a part of a revolutionary leap forward for African Americans. When Jordan was a toddler in 1966, North Carolina didn't allow blacks on its team. The tremendous running back Herschel Walker, celebrated in the South in 1980, wouldn't have been able to play on the University of Georgia's football team just ten years earlier. And now here was a company offering nearly the equivalent of Jordan's basketball salary to market shoes.

This did not necessarily have a liberating effect on Jordan. It had its own set of pressures that Jordan never fully acknowledged publicly. The great black athletes in American history had been regarded as either defiant or respectfully compliant. Jack Johnson, the first black heavyweight champion, was both flamboyant and highly literate, qualities that led Americans to wish for the "Great White Hope" to beat him. Successors, having seen the treatment of Johnson, stayed deferential until Cassius Clay, who not only was brash but also became a Muslim and changed his name to Muhammad Ali. So did the best player in college basketball history, UCLA's Lew Alcindor, who later became Kareem Abdul-Jabbar. Mentioning civil rights too loudly was never in an athlete's financial interests. Some bit their tongues. Others didn't. In twentieth-century athletics, the free market did not automatically mean a meritocracy.

But by 1984 the civil rights era had passed. Black athletes played all the major team sports, except hockey—no colleges openly discriminated against black athletes. But there were still traces of racism. For instance, the most important and cerebral position in pro and college football, quarterback, was still mostly reserved for whites, especially if the offensive scheme involved throwing, which meant decision making. The Houston Oilers' Warren Moon would be the only black starting quarterback in the NFL that year, and he had to take a circuitous route through the Canadian Football League to prove himself. So when Jordan accepted the deal from Nike, regardless of whether he realized it or not, he became responsible for opening the door for other black endorsers and ushering in an era of commercial opportunity.

To justify the expenditure, Nike expected $3 million in first-year sales. The company designed a bold red and white shoe with a black swoosh. When Jordan suited up for his first game, the NBA banned the custom-designed shoe on the grounds that it didn't match the Bulls' uniform. Jordan wore it anyway. The league fined him $5,000 per game. For Nike this became the perfect marketing campaign. When the shoe finally went on sale to the public six months after it premiered on Jordan's feet, the demand was frenzied. Sales of the first Air Jordan exceeded $100 million by the time it was replaced by the Air Jordan II in 1986.

But even when this tremendous success seemed clear, a profile of Jordan in the *New York Times Magazine* in November 1986 didn't fully validate the nature of the achievement. "Conventional advertising wisdom holds that it is very hard for a black athlete to be convincing to white middle-class consumers. There are, of course, those who have crossed this boundary, such as the former football star O. J. Simpson and Arthur Ashe. They are both charismatic and articulate." Pointing out that surveys showed Simpson and Ashe were "perceived as 'beyond race,'" the article held that advertisers were betting that "Jordan has this elusive quality also."

But Simpson and Ashe were anomalies. Ashe played tennis—a sport that was identified with country clubs and affluent society. Simpson, from the seventies, had marketed Hertz, a rental car company aimed at business travelers. He lived in Brentwood, he golfed, and he was embraced by Hollywood. As important, Ashe and Simpson had lighter skin tones and spoke English with white diction, factors that no doubt increased their marketability to whites. However, any black player accepted by whites as safe lacked the urban authenticity required for street appeal. This was where Jordan differed.

He played the game of the inner city. Housing projects didn't have tennis courts or verdant lawns, but they did have a blacktop and an iron hoop. Jordan's style of play, with fast cuts, slashes to the basket, and authoritative dunks, would have won him glory on any court in Bedford-Stuyvesant or Harlem. He had swagger on the court and was smooth and silent off the court. For new marketers interested in Jordan, he had all-American appeal from being a part of the 1984 Olympic team, which, combined with his Nike exposure and his lack of persona off the court, made him safe to brands looking to appeal to whites. According to the *Times*, "his modesty appealed to all of them"—meaning Jordan's new sponsors, including Coca-Cola, Chevrolet dealers in Illinois, and McDonald's. As any basketball fan now knows, humility was not particularly Jordan's strong suit, but in 1986 this interpretation of his smiling silence paved the path for more endorsement deals.

And he did pave the path for others. By 1988 Nike had arguably an even bigger star than Michael Jordan on its roster: two-sport athlete Bo Jackson. Jackson was the best college football player in the country and was the first player selected in the NFL draft, but he felt that the Tampa Bay Buccaneers had tricked him, causing him to lose his collegiate eligibility in baseball to force him into professional football. Rather than sign a lucrative NFL contract, Jackson decided to play baseball, signing with the Kansas City Royals. It was a bit of defiance that would have been unthinkable for a black athlete to attempt ten years earlier, and perhaps even then for anyone besides him, but Jackson's talent was undeniable. Then at the end of his second baseball season, Jackson made arrangements to play football starting midseason for the Los Angeles Raiders, casually calling this part-time second career his hobby. This bit of cockiness only furthered the intrigue. And Jackson delivered. In one of his first NFL games, Jackson ran for over two hundred yards on *Monday Night Football*. Less than two years later, at the Major League Baseball All-Star Game, Jackson, as the first batter of the game, crushed a pitch deep into the stands. Former president Reagan, who was visiting the broadcast booth at the time, could be heard breathlessly gasping, "Oh!" as the ball sailed past the outfield. As if on cue, during the next commercial break of the All-Star Game, Nike debuted a minutelong "Bo Knows" commercial, which became one of the most famous advertisements of all time.

These two stars, packaged by Nike, both born in the American South months apart in 1962 and 1963 and just months old when Martin Luther King Jr. delivered his "I have a dream" speech, were now the two most marketable men in America. It was a feat of commerce breaking and resetting racial boundaries. Two years later, Gatorade aired its "Be Like Mike" commercial, in which a chorus of children of all races could be heard singing about how they dreamed of being like Jordan.

WHILE NIKE'S MARKETING was a cultural story made in America, the manufacturing of its shoes was an Asian story.

Nike's origins dated back to an assignment at the Stanford Graduate School of Business in 1962. A student with a background in track and field, Phil Knight, had written up a business plan to import low-cost athletic shoes from Japan. After a one-year hiatus after graduating with his MBA, Knight remained committed to the idea he had outlined at Stanford and made his way to Japan to explore his idea further. Presenting himself as the president of the company he had set up on paper, Blue Ribbon Sports, he arranged for a meeting and factory visit with a shoemaker named Onitsuka. Like many fledgling Japanese companies at the time, Onitsuka was looking for a strategy to enter the American market.

At the meeting with Knight, Onitsuka representatives presented several prototypes, including the "Limber Up," the "Spring Up," and the memorable "Throw Up." Hearing this, Knight felt he could help Onitsuka better understand the language of the American market. At the time, Americans had great pride in the quality of American goods and viewed Japanese imports to be of vastly inferior quality. But Japanese manufacturers had one significant advantage: Labor costs were significantly lower, which allowed Japanese goods to be priced much lower. Knight assumed that the impression of Japanese quality would change over time and ordered a few samples.

Knight then reached out to his former track coach at the University of Oregon, Bill Bowerman. Investing $500 each to form Blue Ribbon Sports, the men started importing Onitsukas from Japan. For both men, the venture was a side project. Knight started a day job at Price Water-house as a CPA. After four years, he was able to earn enough from Blue Ribbon sales to quit his job. By 1972 Blue Ribbon was selling nearly $2 million worth of Onitsuka shoes in America. But soon after that, Onitsuka decided to cut Knight out as a middleman and handle its own U.S. distribution.

Needing to salvage their operation, Knight and Bowerman looked to draw on their understanding of the needs of runners—Bowerman during this time was serving as the track coach of the 1972 U.S. Olympic team. The pair decided to develop their own shoes, naming their brand Nike, after the Greek goddess of victory. For $35 Blue Ribbon got local student Carolyn Davidson to design a logo. Her eventual design became the fa-mous Nike "swoosh."

In the early seventies, athletic shoes were largely reserved for athletic activities—only one in twelve pairs of shoes sold in America were sneak-ers. By the end of the seventies, it would be one in four. Nike was a primary beneficiary of a boom in jogging and running that had captured America at the time. By 1977, Nike sales had reached $28 million. While Knight had initially been attracted to Japan by its combination of low labor costs and high quality, the rise of Japan also meant the rise of labor costs. Japan's rapid ascent and rising standard of living meant that it could not afford to produce low-value goods like shoes. To counter this, in addition to utilizing other Asian alternatives, Nike started its own factories in New England. In 1979, with 1,500 employees across three factories, Nike became one of the larger employers in Maine and New Hampshire. By 1981 Nike's annual sales had grown to $457 million. Its scorching growth rate from 1977 to 1981 mimicked closely that of Apple. As chance would have it, Nike's IPO occurred just a few days before the computer maker's.

Manufacturing athletic shoes in America, however, turned out to be temporary for Nike. While noting in its first annual report as a public company that it was increasing production in America, Nike enthusiastically mentioned the start of production in Thailand, Malaysia, and the Philippines. Japan's very success in rising to first-world status meant that lower-skilled manufacturing activities it had engaged in just two decades earlier were being transitioned to less-developed Asian countries. But far more meaningful was another Nike disclosure, almost an afterthought, that few at the time could have recognized for the full breadth of its implications: "Also, we began the long process of establishing the People's Republic of China as a source of production." It was among the first signs of the reforms leader Deng Xiaoping had initiated.

Unlike the Soviets, who prided themselves on meeting the Americans as military equals, the Chinese communists decided to deploy their nearly one billion people to become a giant factory to the capitalist world. This entry of one of the poorest countries in the world, which China was in 1980, into the global markets was a silent, unseen narrative throughout a decade overshadowed by the Japanese economic miracle and anti-Japan paranoia.

At the same time, Nike was transforming into a global company and calling into question the definition of national identity for profit-oriented entities. At the time of its first annual report, the majority of Nike's 2,700 employees actually made shoes in America. But eventually the shoemaker's business was not to make shoes but to design, test, and brand shoes. The hands required to stitch the soles to the shell, insert laces into the holes, and push paper into the shoe to hold its shape in transit all worked for a distant factory owner, who made the shoes for Nike on a piecemeal basis. Once the last of the American factories was closed in 1985, Nike ordered shoes from whoever could achieve its sought-after quality most cheaply. But Nike held in America its most valuable asset, its swoosh, the great abstraction of modern capitalism known as a trademark, enabling it to accrue profits at home even as its Chinese-made shoes sold in all corners of the world. Nike, as a new symbol of Americana, was a potent mix of high-margin, high-value American intellectual property and low-margin, low-value foreign labor. Critical to this formula was American marketing.

. . .

A s   h e   s t a r t e d to emerge as a global icon, Jordan wanted to be seen as "neither black nor white." Therefore, he didn't take stances on racial issues when they did come up. He couldn't. The embrace of the black athlete among white shoe buyers was based on his dominance on the athletic court. Using this goodwill to call attention to the victimhood of his people, which whites would invariably take to mean blaming them for the predicament of blacks, would undermine his marketability. Paying nearly $100 a pair, consumers didn't need a civics lesson with their Air Jordans. And Jordan's position was not all that calculated or complicated. He genuinely felt beyond race. At least, he wanted to be.

But the other rising aspect of African-American culture, hip-hop, reveled in its blackness as a most intrinsic condition of the art. In the late eighties, casual use of the word "nigga" found its way into an ever-increasing number of songs and albums. The term that slaveholders had used to describe blacks, the term the NAACP had successfully lobbied to not have mentioned in *Gone with the Wind*, the term that had assaulted the basic dignity of prior generations when they were prevented from using a simple water fountain, the term that sometimes prohibited classic books from being assigned as school reading, was now put forth in casual tones, often accompanied by allusions to violence. For white teenagers in the suburbs, the lyrics were excitingly defiant of all social norms. In the inner city, they were reflections of reality.

This duality between shoe marketing and hip-hop did not and could not coexist gently. There was no escaping the streets. Not for Jordan. Not for Nike. In black America, Jordan's success was becoming a liability. In a sensational 1990 *Sports Illustrated* cover depicting a gun and blaring "Your Shoes or Your Life," the magazine called attention to the rise of street crime associated with sports apparel. The story opened with the strangulation of fifteen-year-old Michael Thomas by a seventeen-year-old acquaintance. The motive was stealing the pair of Air Jordans that Thomas had been wearing. Michael Thomas treasured his Jordans, polishing them every night before placing them back in their box. He had even kept the receipt: $115.50. For children from working-class homes or economically challenged communities, Jordans were a coveted item that conferred instant prestige on its possessor. The writer, Rick Telander, blamed Jordan for how he had "carefully nurtured his image as the All-American role model," for staying quiet, for selling "apparel that Jordan and other athlete endorsers have encouraged American youth to buy." Four years earlier, the *New York Times* questioned the "elusive quality" of black athletes in appealing to whites. Now *Sports Illustrated* was blaming this wave of materialistic criminality on the irresistible appeal of black endorsers.

Complicating matters, the black athlete was being blamed for appearing to be squeaky clean to sell shoes while black artists were portraying themselves as killers and drug dealers to sell records. It was a tragic contrast on multiple levels. On top of this, America was at a generational peak in terms of crime; it was a political issue for both parties. Liberals agreed to tough sentencing laws. Conservatives agreed to limits on assault weapons. Even liberal New York City began a run in which it elected twenty straight years of Republican or Republican-Independent mayors, a direct reaction to high crime rates. Over these two decades, murders would fall nationally by 70 percent.

But Jordan soon understood the senseless nature of crime better than any writer. On August 3, 1993, the body of an older African American man was found floating in a South Carolina creek. It was Jordan's father. Two weeks earlier, James Jordan had pulled over at a rest stop, and he had been missing since. His burgundy Lexus coupe had caught the attention of two young black men. They robbed him, killed him, and disposed of his body. The car was recovered in North Carolina stripped of its tires and stereo. The young men who had allegedly killed him were found with the older man's jewelry weeks later. In contrast to the charge leveled at Jordan by *Sports Illustrated*, no one seemed to blame Toyota's Lexus division for making coveted luxury cars.

There was, however, an unacknowledged dignity, and consistency, to Jordan's silence. Jordan, being an immense star in North Carolina, could have used his platform to press for his father's killers to be executed. But he said nothing and stayed away from the eventual trial. He had wanted to transcend race, yet for all his fame and fortune, not even he could escape the fate that befell so many thousands of black families every year. Less than three months after his father's death, he retired from basketball.

Eventually he would return to his mastery on the court, and the silhouette of him flying through the air would become a global symbol of its own: the Jordan brand, another coveted piece of modern Americana. It would make him a billionaire. And perhaps more important, it would enable him to become a team owner, making him the commercial equal of those who had once employed him on the basketball court.

Thirty-four

INTERNET

From the *New York Times* headline BUSH ENCOUNTERS THE SUPERMARKET, AMAZED followed a story that would not have seemed out of place in the satirical paper the *Onion*. A few days after a visit with the new Russian president Boris Yeltsin, during the early months of his 1992 reelection campaign, Bush had attended the annual convention of the National Grocers Association. At a demonstration, the president grabbed a quart of milk, a bag of candy, and lightbulbs, and as the items ran over an electronic scanner at the checkout, "a look of wonder flickered across his face" as the price registered on a screen. The then decade-old mainstay of the American grocery store had him asking, "This is for checking out?"

Here he was: sixty-seven-year-old George Herbert Walker Bush—with a résumé that included naval aviator in his teens during World War II once shot down over the Pacific, baseball player at Yale, oilman in Texas, congressman, U.S. ambassador to the United Nations, director of the Central Intelligence Agency, vice president under Reagan, commander in chief and coalition builder during the Persian Gulf War, and president of the United States as the Soviet Union dissolved—stumped by a mundane bit of technology, adding one more element to the central narrative that he was out of touch.

In contrast, the Democratic ticket that would emerge, Bill Clinton and Al Gore, both in their forties, talked about an "information superhighway" that would connect homes in unimaginable ways. At the same time, computing's first billionaire, H. Ross Perot, played the role of wild card, denying both traditional parties a majority. It was a prophetic transition: This president of patrician bearing, possessing unrivaled experience in matters of statecraft, was undone by two technocratic men, each of whom seemed to understand the economic future better than he did. With the cold war over, the American century's victory march into the next millennium, capitalism's undisputed hour of triumph, would be presided over by Clinton.

In Clinton's first year in office, this information superhighway started coming into view. Nothing in the commercial history of the world would converge the multiple fine threads of commerce, information, and industry as this new system of communication and computing would. Every old big thing would soon be pulled into this new big thing: electricity, telephone wires, mainframes, personal computers, cable, mail, television, music, film, banking, travel, brokerage, real estate and shopping. Even the short, several-word bursts of the telegraph would again find a place in this new world.

The notion of computers talking to one another via telephone wires was decades old. The U.S. military had built networks in the fifties to coordinate missile defense. Business applications such as airline reservation systems soon followed in the sixties; the automated teller machine was the first direct interaction with a networked machine for millions of Americans. Even the postal service had funded research into a vision of "Speed Mail" in the 1960s. Academics and scientists had used terminals to communicate and remotely access research since the seventies. As personal computers entered society, even consumer services were starting to become available online. In the early eighties, newspapers including the *New York Times*, *Washington Post*, and *Los Angeles Times* looked to follow the *Columbus Dispatch* by making their entire editorial content available to computer terminals via the online service CompuServe. But at $5 per hour for access, the novelty did not lead to immediate commercial viability.

Still, other services soon entered the market. Some arrived at the concept accidentally. A Virginia entrepreneur, William von Meister, had come up with an idea to beam music into people's homes via satellite. Von Meister was successful enough to elicit an early commitment from Warner Bros. music to license its library, but Warner Bros. backtracked, worried about the wrath of the retail stores that sold its records. As consolation, it offered him an opportunity through its Atari division. Von Meister soon formed Control Video Corp. to make modems for the Atari gaming console where games could be downloaded remotely. As Atari by now had millions of home gaming units in American living rooms, von Meister was able to raise millions of dollars from major investors to launch his GameLine service. It was announced with great fanfare in January 1983, but when the units finally went on sale for Christmas later that year, it was a total failure.

Control Video went through a reorganization and was reincorporated as Quantum Computer Services in 1985. Quantum then abandoned the modem idea and began focusing on creating online services for existing computer makers. It found a taker in Commodore and its wildly popular Commodore 64, which connected to a TV screen. The service was text based, but it allowed people to chat and check news, weather, and sports scores. By the end of 1986, Quantum had nearly fifty thousand subscribers for its Q-Link service. It added Apple Computer as a partner and built it a custom online service called AppleLink. But soon afterward, the deal with Apple hit a rocky patch and was terminated, and Quantum decided to focus on one online service rather than operate in partnership with computer makers. It renamed its service America Online.

By the time Clinton took office, America Online, or AOL, was a successful public company with over 150,000 subscribers and $30 million in annual revenue. Its users had access to newspapers, magazines, sports scores, weather, TV listings, and e-mail. Other online services, such as CompuServe and Prodigy, boasted similar offerings that met with marketplace success. Like AOL, these online services brought the consumer into a closed environment that was neatly organized and entirely controlled in terms of content. AOL paid publishers and other content providers for information, then assembled the information for its subscribers.

But these services were not quite what the *Time* cover story in 1993 implied when it discussed the information superhighway. It imagined a consumer equivalent of the "Internet, the sprawling computer grid for students, scientists, and the Pentagon." The reporter presented an industry vision where cable companies and phone companies would build high-speed wires into the home, with major media companies providing full libraries of music and movies and banks, airlines, and restaurants directly interfacing with consumers in their living rooms without a gatekeeper such as AOL or CompuServe. There remained, however, a gulf between visualizing the possibilities and manifesting them in reality. For any American who had seen an episode of *The Jetsons* when it first aired in the early sixties, housekeeping robots and flying cars had once been easy to imagine as well. But the critical breakthrough would come.

IF HUMANITY IS ever eclipsed by an era of self-aware machines, history will place the birth point of this new civilization at the dawn of the Internet—the initial transfer point of the entire documented knowledge of humanity, along with the electronic footprint of each individual's behavior, transactions, curiosities, and physical movements and the endless communications and intrigues reflecting the full range of human emotions, onto the network.

The Internet was designed to be an open network where any connected computer could access another computer speaking a standard language, a protocol. In this decentralized system, academics in one university could publish a set of papers or experimental data and researchers in any other university could access the information. Secure communications and e-mails could be exchanged as well. By the late 1980s, the utility of the Internet was fairly established, with academia and the military its primary users. What launched the consumer Internet, however, was a visual method of organizing and accessing all of the information on the network.

Starting in 1980, a young Englishman named Tim Berners-Lee with a physics degree from Oxford was on a software consulting job at the European Council for Nuclear Research in Switzerland. CERN was financed by a consortium of European countries to conduct experimental research in physics. With thousands of affiliated researchers carrying out experiments at the facility, Berners-Lee saw firsthand the volume of papers and results at the laboratory. What troubled him was that the vast majority of insights and happenstance was lost—researchers published the most formal results, but the best conversations happened in the cafeteria and other informal, unstructured settings. Since "the human mind has the special ability to link random bits of data," the linear limitations of storing research papers, even on a computer network, did not allow for cross-pollination of ideas. These serendipitous associations that the human brain uses as the basis for creativity were lost on the network. He wanted to link ideas within the documents themselves with other documents, online conversations, and messages.

By the mideighties, Berners-Lee had familiarized himself with men who had been equally perplexed by the challenge of organizing information. At the end of World War II, Vannevar Bush, the wartime director of the Office of Scientific Research and Development, published an article in the *Atlantic Monthly* titled "As We May Think." Bush had overseen thousands of scientists rapidly applying science to warfare, and he feared the loss of billions of dollars' worth of findings. He pointed out how "Mendel's concept of the laws of genetics was lost to the world for a generation" because the right people could not access it and asserted that "this sort of catastrophe is undoubtedly being repeated all about us." He proposed a theoretical system he called "Memex" to create a new kind of cataloging system "ready made with a mesh of associate trails running through them." But this Bush was too far ahead of his time.

Another thinker followed up in 1965 as the age of computing arrived. A self-proclaimed "poet, philosopher, and rogue," Ted Nelson conceptualized and coined the term "hypertext" to mean words within documents that linked to other documents. But Nelson, lacking a science or computing background, could not make hypertext a reality. In addition to Bush and Nelson, Berners-Lee credited Doug Engelbart at Stanford for his sixties demonstration of a "mouse," a wooden block with sensors and a ball under it, with which he clicked on words to explore information spatially.

In 1989 Berners-Lee pulled all of the lessons of history together, dreaming up a visual layer—an interface—for the Internet. After going through several permutations, he settled on calling it the World Wide Web, a spiderweb of endless hypertext links. Using Nelson's term "hypertext," he called his way of retrieving information through the links "hypertext transfer protocol" (http). For a researcher or academic to create pages transferable by http, Berners-Lee created hypertext markup language (HTML). Clicking on a word linked as hypertext could take the reader to another part of the Internet. The locations would be referred through a uniform resource locator (URL). He then became an evangelist for his World Wide Web, which technically was owned by CERN and the Europeans.

But his most receptive audience was across the ocean in America. By 1992 knowledge of his World Wide Web concept had grown dramatically in computing circles. At the federally funded National Center for Super-computing Applications at the University of Illinois, a group of student programmers had set out to create a new interface, a browser, to navigate the Web. Introduced as Mosaic in 1993, the browser quickly became the leader in the nascent category of Internet navigation. As Berners-Lee had committed to working on open standards for the Web in a nonprofit manner, CERN agreed to release for free all of the intellectual underpinnings to the public domain.

Given that the best kind of R&D is the kind one doesn't have to pay for, Silicon Valley took notice.

FIFTY YEARS OLD, James Clark was clearing out his office in January 1994. More than a decade after founding Silicon Graphics, a maker of high-end computers used by Hollywood studios and others, Clark had lost an internal political battle and resigned. While Silicon Graphics was worth billions of dollars, Clark ruefully estimated his share in the company to be worth about $20 million. With his forced exit looming, Clark decided he needed to better control his fate next time around, which in Silicon Valley meant he needed to get really rich. One sympathetic colleague suggested to Clark that he take a look at Mosaic. After clicking around, he found the e-mail address of Mosaic's most energetic programmer: twenty-three-year-old Marc Andreessen. Clark wrote Andreessen an e-mail and introduced himself. Andreessen wrote back almost immediately. As it turned out, Andreessen had left Illinois and recently joined a company in Palo Alto.

They met the next day at Caffe Verona in Palo Alto. Ironically, at the dawn of hyperlinks and global connectivity, geographic proximity and a face-to-face meeting were the catalysts. Over breakfast, Clark discussed his desire to start another company, and the men agreed to search for an idea to execute together. In Clark's account, seemingly burned out from his earlier efforts, Andreessen had only one limitation: "I'm finished with all that Mosaic shit."

After a frustrating couple of months, however, Andreessen came to his senses: "Well, we could always build a Mosaic killer." To Clark "the idea seemed instantly right." Clark put in $3 million and authorized Andreessen to hire key members of the Mosaic team graduating from the University of Illinois at Urbana-Champaign that coming spring. This company would soon be named Netscape and would build a commercial Web browser. And the events that this would set into motion would resemble a modern version of the Gold Rush, the Industrial Revolution, and the best of all stock market manias—all compressed within a space of five years.

WHY DID THIS beautifully conceived system of information navigation need America as a catalyst? The World Wide Web had both British and European roots. One answer is that America had the unique capability to finance ideas at the earliest stages, and an ecosystem in Silicon Valley that allowed embryonic companies in nascent markets to develop quickly. It had venture capitalists who could tolerate, even encourage, operating losses for years with the understanding that eventual market dominance meant much larger profits. It had a public stock market that was willing to absorb risk at much earlier stages than European and Asian markets.

A part of this had to do with market size. While Western Europe was developed in standard-of-living terms, its market was not unified. Between French, Spanish, English, Portuguese, Italian, and German, no single language made up a market of even 100 million people. At the time, the countries had different currencies. The strength of their individual cultures limited the size of their market. India and China, the only two countries with more people than America, were not wealthy enough to constitute large markets in dollar terms. And indeed, for much of the world, English was a second language—an international protocol in itself—that allowed American companies to more readily find foreign markets for software products in a way a French or German company could not.

In addition to having a capital market that embraced risk and the largest consumer market in the world in terms of purchasing power, American culture loved the hustler. Americans were suspicious of finance and banking and had no great love for faceless corporations, but they had a soft spot in their hearts for the men who leave everything to pursue dreams, especially dreams of making money. The culture assigned little stigma to failure. Indeed, doing as one pleased—dropping out of college, for instance, as Jobs and Gates did—to follow an uncharted, independent path, was the exercise of a most intrinsic form of freedom. In Europe and England, still conditioned by centuries of aristocracy, the open pursuit of financial success conflicted with the appearance of refinement. In America refinement was considered elitist a wholly impractical trait for the rugged job of selling, organizing, convincing, and doing. It was a remarkable sign of energy and dynamism that even after nearly a century as the world's richest country, the scent of the next big thing could still cause men—upstarts and established men alike—to drop everything and chase gold.

Employed at a New York hedge fund, Jeff Bezos was a well-paid twenty-nine-year-old with a computer science degree from Princeton. Through a newsletter, Bezos learned that the World Wide Web had grown by one thousand times over the previous year. Seeing the growth of the Web as a once-in-a-lifetime "revolutionizing event," Bezos quit his job midyear, forgoing his year-end Wall Street bonus. To participate in this revolution, Bezos decided to sell books via the Internet. Books were small enough to ship cheaply—there were far more titles than any physical store could stock, giving the endless catalog an advantage—and the early adopters to the Internet were presumed to be literate. So he made his way west in a Chevy Blazer. Registering Amazon.com as a domain on November 1, 1994, Bezos raced to build a Web site and raise capital to begin selling books.

Other men left even more lucrative positions. Thirty-three-year-old Rob Glaser was a rising star at Microsoft with multiple degrees from Yale. Rather than continue as one of two dozen or so highly compensated executives, Glaser incorporated Progressive Networks to develop software to stream audio and video files over the Internet. His 1994 migration west consisted of only the twelve miles from suburban Redmond to his new outpost in Seattle's Pioneer Square.

Down in Silicon Valley, Jim Clark and Marc Andreessen signed a lease on eleven thousand square feet of office space. Andreessen's fellow engineers at the University of Illinois started their flights out west to join Mosaic Communications. Each received a compensation package of $65,000 and options on 100,000 shares of stock in the new venture—Andreessen had a much larger stake as a cofounder, with a total of one million shares. By the summer of 1994, Clark had started getting moderately nervous. The burn rate, the rate at which a start-up spends in its quest to become a viable business, was higher than Clark had anticipated. This was partly by design. Sensing the need to move as fast as possible, Clark spent freely to speed progress toward the first commercial Web browser. He then turned to Sand Hill Road, the famed road in Silicon Valley where the major venture capital firms were located. Kleiner Perkins, one of the pioneers in formal venture capital, agreed to put in $5 million for 20 percent of the company.

With the money Netscape was able to launch its browser into the marketplace. It was immediately clear that Netscape had a hit. In the first three months, its revenues were nearly $5 million. Its consumer product, a new advanced Web browser, was made available for $39 to $45. It then charged software makers and computer makers for server tools—the software that allows for hosting Web sites. Then a small miracle happened. The investing public, hyped up by visions of the information superhighway in years past, could sense that something big was afoot. This presented the possibility of Netscape going public through an IPO. Even in Silicon Valley, the idea of taking public a company little more than a year old, with barely one full quarter of actual revenues, was a stretch. Apple and Microsoft had taken years from formation to public offering, and both were highly profitable.

Even with a pending public offering, no one was quite clear on what the Internet or this World Wide Web was actually good for. In its offering documents, Netscape detailed that "companies are expected to use the Internet to publish corporate product and support information as 'electronic brochures.'" A few of these "electronic brochures" did exist, but most companies did not have Web sites or domain names. The vast majority of American households didn't even have a computer yet. But it seemed that a new commercial order was on the brink of emerging.

In the summer of 1995, Netscape pushed forward its IPO. After a road show where Netscape's new CEO, Jim Barksdale, and Marc Andreessen met with the largest mutual funds and institutions, the investment bank Morgan Stanley saw a stunning reception for the fifteen-month-old company. Netscape's second quarter alone had revealed $22 million in revenues, a growth rate that gave the bankers latitude to privately proclaim Netscape "the fastest-growing software company in history."

On the day of the initial public offering, predictably, the vast majority of investors who wanted in were denied the ability to buy at the $28 offering price. When the shares opened at 11:00 a.m. on August 9, with the order book backed up with demand, the first shares changed hands at $71. Investors who were allotted shares in the IPO at $28 could have effectively doubled their money before even having paid for the shares. The *New York Times* called it an "investor frenzy." Jim Clark's stake, 9.7 million shares, was worth as much as $700 million at one point in the trading day. Kleiner Perkins showed paper gains of over 4,000 percent on its investment of a year earlier—its $5 million was worth more than $200 million. Netscape's CEO had the best return of all: After all of seven months on the job, Barksdale had a claim on 4.2 million shares through options and grants. Dozens of employees were sitting on millions of dollars in paper profits on their options. This fundamental idea of employee participation, which enabled scenarios where rewards could far outstrip any possible contribution or expertise, added another dimension of euphoria, attracting thousands to the Bay Area.

Twenty-four-year-old Andreessen made it to an especially iconic cover of *Time* magazine. Barefoot, appearing to sit on a golden throne, Andreessen was dubbed the archetype of "The Golden Geeks." In the story, the historian Alan Brinkley noted that when compared with the railroads, steel, and oil—fortunes that took lifetimes to acquire—the instantaneous nature of this type of wealth creation was unprecedented.

And the mania had barely started.

AT THE MOST fundamental level, the mania was based on a great truth that everyone saw at once. The Internet's impact seemed like a compressed historical inevitability, an immediate transformation of society that would unfold rapidly before everyone's eyes. The only question was the depth and nature of the change.

Expedia started selling airline tickets and hotel reservations online. Banks like Wells Fargo delivered the ability to pay bills without an envelope or stamp. Rebranded for the Internet era, discount brokerages like E*Trade that had once offered voice services now rushed to offer online trading. Newspapers across the country began publishing their entire contents online. All this was happening seemingly overnight. Often this imperative was driven by a desire to preempt new insurgents, unburdened by legacy businesses, from entering the markets serviced by incumbents.

Just about every major brand and corporation, it seemed, had bought a suitable domain and added its Web site address to its marketing materials. Throughout 1996 the change was not something consumers and institutional investors were limited to reading about. They were living it; they were seeing it. Even for those without Internet access, it was hard not to notice strange sets of characters such as "http://" or "www" or "@" on the sides of buses and taxi tops or in television commercials.

With this level of excitement in the air, Silicon Valley and Wall Street knew what to do: Take more companies public. The strategy was partly driven by Netscape's continued reception. After Netscape's IPO, despite the initial shock, or glee, caused by the first day's price appreciation, the company had continued to dazzle. It finished 1995 with over $80 million in revenues, having started from $0 in March 1994. Six months after the stock's dizzying open, the price had more than doubled, trading as high as $172. On good days Jim Clark was a billionaire.

With a total of $1.3 million in revenues, the backers of nine-month-old Yahoo! decided the climate was right to go public in early 1996. They were right. By the end of the offering, its two founders were worth over $100 million on paper—its venture capital firm, Sequoia Capital, achieved a return greater than 10,000 percent on its original $1 million. Not to be outdone, Yahoo!'s three erstwhile competitors in search and Web directories—Excite, Infoseek, and Lycos—all went public within months. Silicon Valley venture capitalists, sensing the speed with which private illiquid investments turned into publicly tradable securities, dramatically turned up their rate of funding start-ups. The compressed time frame from funding to IPO reduced risk. In addition, investors who had made fortunes in earlier Internet start-ups now added to the invest-able capital available for the next wave.

Kleiner Perkins invested $8 million in Amazon.com. An IPO followed. Benchmark Capital invested in eBay, the online auctioneer. eBay was notable in that there was no similar real-world corollary—a real-time nationwide auction for Aunt Mae's dining chairs was not possible without the Internet. Hundreds of start-ups in e-commerce of every conceivable category were funded: Pets.com in pet goods, CDNow and Music Boulevard in music CDs, Buy.com in electronics, and so on. Hotmail, a free e-mail service, received venture funding and quickly grew to ten million users before being acquired by Microsoft for $350 million a little over one year after its founding.

In many ways Microsoft was perhaps the most overlooked beneficiary of the Internet. The arrival of the Internet was a significant boost to computer makers as American households rushed to get online. And they were primarily buying PCs powered by Microsoft Windows, generating revenue for the software maker. Seeing that the first thing that millions of these new computer users did was to get online and use their Netscape browser, Microsoft built its own browser, Internet

Explorer. Rather than sell it as Netscape did, Microsoft gave it away for free bundled with every PC sold in America, along with its vital operating system, which it charged for. Microsoft argued that all of this was a legitimate free-market practice. Others disagreed. It would eventually lead to a major federal antitrust action where much of Silicon Valley, with all its market libertarians, would be rooting for the government.

But for Netscape it was too late. Despite its incredible rise, which had started and defined the era, the market perceived the Microsoft threat to be too much. So while the bubble was still far from its peak, Netscape's best days seemed behind it.

In the days of the first Internet IPOs, prudent investors derided Internet companies for their lack of revenues. Then, as companies like Amazon.com and Yahoo! grew to hundreds of millions of dollars in revenue, the criticism turned to the lack of profits. Though these veterans knew that the Internet was transformative, they liked to see things like growth in the customer base, revenues, and profits, often at the same time. For hard-nosed moneymen, entering 1999, only one Internet company seemed to truly fit the criteria: AOL.

AOL had a relatively long history of revenues—it had brought people online before the Web browser. As an Internet Service Provider (ISP), the service that an online user dialed up with their modem, AOL collected around $20 per month or more from millions of households. Its revenues had grown from $38 million in 1992 to over $1 billion in 1996, almost all from monthly dial-up subscriptions. After successfully dialing onto America Online, the user was subjected to advertising on the service, giving AOL a second revenue stream. By 1999 subscription revenues had grown to $3 billion—by then AOL was selling online advertising so successfully that this category added another $1 billion in revenues. That year it made over $750 million in net income. AOL was so dominant that its iconic greeting "You've got mail" became the title of a movie starring Tom Hanks and Meg Ryan.

The company's value reflected all this. In the summer of 1999, the market deemed AOL to be worth over $175 billion, approaching $200 billion some days. Its stock price had grown by well over one hundred times since Netscape's IPO. Indeed, AOL had even acquired Netscape to add to its arsenal. Such glory eluded media companies. Cable providers, television networks, movie studios, record labels, and magazine publishers could only look on with envy. To be sure, all of the major media companies sprinkled investments online, but they themselves were not seen as game changers in this brave new world.

With the world seeming to pass it by, Time Warner looked to make a grand move. At the time, Time Warner owned HBO, CNN, TBS, and TNT; magazines including *Time*, *People*, and *Sports Illustrated*; the Warner Bros. studio and record label; and a cable television system for which over ten million subscribers paid monthly. Its revenues and profits vastly exceeded AOL's. Yet it fell to the illusion of the Internet bubble, putting too much faith in the wisdom of the stock market: Time Warner agreed to merge with AOL on a 45/55 basis. AOL shareholders received 55 percent of the new entity, Time Warner 45 percent. It was the greatest heist by one set of shareholders of another in the history of mergers.

It also turned out to be the finest irony of the dot-com boom. The one company that had the strongest financial metrics made its money from a dial-up service, but the *whoosh-shiii-whoosh* sound of slow phone modems connecting to AOL was not the future. Adding to the cruelty, Time Warner already owned its part of the high-speed broadband future—it controlled actual wires into millions of homes through Time Warner Cable. Within years, AOL's subscriber growth, revenues, and profits proved to be a blip—the dial-up leader being the equivalent of Oldsmobile, the largest automobile manufacturer of 1904—as broadband connections through cable and phone companies were right on the verge of eradicating AOL's entire business. The sane, hard men with accounting and financial backgrounds had sought safety by counting what could be counted: revenues and profits. But it was the New Yorkers who were fooled.

The midnight hour struck a few weeks into the new millennium. The bursting of the bubble started with investor appetite cooling after a scorching run-up in stock prices. The private market reacted, sensing that they couldn't quickly take companies public. Online companies could not raise additional rounds of funding. Without new capital, the companies could no longer spend on advertising or the services of other dot-coms; these companies' best customers were often other dot-coms. When this became clear, Wall Street headed for the exits all at once.

But there was a fundamental belief that misled otherwise clear thinkers—it was their faith in the rationality of markets. Analysts, bankers, and fund managers had for decades been gripped by the concept of the efficient market hypothesis. This theory held that the market price of a given stock at any point served as the perfect expression of the collective insight and wisdom of all of the participants—nature's perfect algorithm for capitalism. Even among those who gave this theory less than full credence, the view was that the market price could be off by only a bit; few thought the market could misprice an asset by a factor of one hundred. But of course it could, and it did. When the collective irrationality of the market came to bear, several of the highest-profile dot-com companies shed 99 percent of their value.

This collapse was evident with AOL Time Warner. After AOL shareholders received the majority interest in the merged company, a decade later AOL was spun off again as an independent company. This time the market gave it a value of $2 billion, $198 billion below AOL's peak at the height of the bubble. Yet for AOL, the company that owned HBO, CNN, TBS, a storied Hollywood studio, a record label, and a cable system had given up 55 percent of itself to avoid missing out on the Internet boom. But now, even the languishing print magazine assets of Time Warner, like *People*, *Time*, and *Sports Illustrated*, were worth more than the new independent AOL.

But it was not all a speculative, destructive racket. Viable companies like Amazon.com and eBay did emerge from the volatility and carnage. Much of consumer behavior, from online banking to online flight reservations, changed completely within a span of five years. The entire classified section of newspapers and the yellow pages started to fade into irrelevance. By 2000 the majority of American households had computers and access to the Internet. What made the Internet bubble unique was that the cycle of creation and destruction played out so quickly, so visibly, where everyone could see the wastefulness of the experimentation inherent in capitalism, the large-scale trials and errors needed to find what actually worked.

And in the Valley, a place that mystifies and frustrates outsiders with its seemingly imprudent bets, there was a counterexample to AOL's fleeting dominance. The biggest winner of the dot-com era didn't have an IPO in the nineties. It barely had any revenues. And its investors, Kleiner Perkins and Sequoia Capital, ignoring the noise of the market, decided to back a site that was nothing more than a simple, minimalist search box, plenty of white space, and a logo. Indeed, the rush to maximize revenues and retain Wall Street's favor had led Yahoo! and the other early search engines to abandon the field. As the dot-com frenzy played out, Google quietly and patiently grew its audience without the slightest concern for revenues, investors, or journalists.

But after the excitement, there was a sense of loss. In secular Silicon Valley, after the crash, this sentiment was best expressed by the bumper sticker that asked, "Please God, Just One More Bubble."

Thirty-five

MOBILE

It was clear to almost all that Apple Computer's time had passed. Microsoft dominated the personal computer. Upstarts dominated Internet services. Computer manufacturers like Dell made fortunes from machines that ran Windows, Microsoft's ubiquitous operating system. In comparison, Apple's world in 1997 was not just niche but a dying niche. Steve Jobs's company had lost the war.

Jobs himself had been a founder in absentia for twelve years, having been fired in 1985. His failure with the launch of the Macintosh, underwhelming in its initial sales, had been the final death knell. Apple's story then became a classic tale of an enigmatic, iconoclastic founder making way for seasoned business leadership. Eccentricity and imagination produced the initial inspiration and momentum, perhaps, but once a company had achieved scale and hundreds of millions of dollars in sales, business building required devotion to the bottom line, and the founder's capabilities were inadequate for the needs of shareholders. Or so the thinking went. Managing hard reality, not conjuring dreams, was the rational basis upon which investor returns were maximized.

Pushed out, Jobs moved on to other things. In early 1986 he bought an animation studio for $10 million from George Lucas, the creator of *Star Wars*, and then invested tens of millions of dollars of his rapidly disappearing fortune from Apple into it. He founded another computer maker called NeXT to spite Apple. While NeXT didn't live up to Jobs's ambitions, it had its moments—Tim Berners-Lee attributed his development of HTTP, HTML, and the World Wide Web to his use of NeXT's features. Jobs's animation studio, Pixar, created the hit movie *Toy Story* using computer animation rather than the hand-drawing techniques pioneered by Walt Disney. After *Toy Story* Pixar had a public offering in 1995, making Jobs a billionaire for the first time in his life, this second fortune vastly outstripping his first. But being the CEO of a studio making one film a year was far removed from the stature he had once enjoyed, especially as he had little to do with creating the stories or overseeing the animation. He had an opening. Jobs's challenges with NeXT coincided with the failure of management at Apple. For the boost in morale from the return of Jobs as much as the gain of any technology, Apple agreed to buy NeXT in 1996 for a little over $400 million. Jobs came back into the Apple fold as an adviser.

In the dot-com nineties, Jobs's return was regarded as quaint and ceremonial—an aging star evincing glimpses of past glory that he had no hope of recapturing—by everyone but a segment of Apple's most rabid customers. Apple's place in the technology ecosystem seemed trivial at a time when just about everyone was thriving. In the summer of 1997, the only thing that was not trivial was that Apple was poised to lose over $1 billion for the second year in a row, a feat of annual unprofitability that no dot-com had yet attempted. Its bond ratings were lowered to junk. It even began selling manufacturing facilities in America and overseas to raise cash—capacity now unneeded due to the drop in sales. Jobs even solicited an investment of $150 million from Microsoft as part of a deal making Internet Explorer the default browser on Macs, among other things. Appearing ominously on a large screen at the annual Macworld, his image overshadowing Jobs on stage, Gates gave a few words of support. But what was unsaid was even more clear: Microsoft had won so thoroughly, so conclusively, that supporting a competing operating system on life support was of little consequence. Others took less pity: Asked what he would do with Apple, Michael Dell of Dell Computers quipped, "I'd shut it down and give the money back to shareholders."

But the heady days for all of the computer makers, including Dell, and all of the Internet companies would be over soon. After peaking in

2000—perfectly timed to close what had been the American century—the NASDAQ stock market index of America's largest technology companies dropped 80 percent. Wall Street analysts who had been especially exuberant were discredited. In other sectors, large companies including Enron and WorldCom were outed as perpetrators of accounting fraud. Then 9/11 introduced a new sense of vulnerability. Over nineteen months, the sure-footed, euphoric America at the millennium's turn had become a distant memory.

Yet the implosion of the Internet companies had a liberating effect on Jobs and Apple. The seeming new stars of the age, like Netscape and AOL, were gone or damaged. While Apple also had a substantial decline in sales from 2000 to 2001—$8 billion to $5.3 billion—the fallout had created an unforeseeable benefit. In 2001 Apple carried out a considerable amount of its manufacturing in America, maintaining a 748,000-square-foot facility in Sacramento. It also owned facilities in Ireland and Singapore. With the drop-off, Apple began to close its own capabilities in favor of contract manufacturers, foreign third parties that could build new Apple products to the company's specifications.

While it gave up on making its own products, it took an entirely different approach when it came to selling them. Rather than rely solely on third-party retailers, Apple started rolling out its own retail stores to showcase and sell its products directly to consumers. In a world that was pivoting toward online commerce, Apple started moving into shopping malls. Starting with its first store in 2001, Apple grew to sixty-five stores within two years. At a point when retail chains that sold software and hardware were on the verge of collapse, this move was especially bold. It is unlikely that any other chief executive would have been granted such strategic control in the midst of a 33 percent sales decline.

At the same time, in an effort to expand beyond computers, the company began looking into a category that continued to thrive even after the dot-com crash: music piracy. Into the new millennium, millions of young people had taken to sharing songs online, a phenomenon that the music industry and recording artists considered theft. With the growth of the new high-speed broadband connection, the network had made it possible for users to exchange music files within a couple of minutes. It would have impacted Hollywood as well, but movies and shows were much larger files, requiring more time to download and occupying more disk space on hard drives. With music, anyone could copy a song from a CD onto their computer and make it available on the Internet. As the record labels refused to sell music digitally, the technology for sharing music surpassed the music industry's ability to invent a business model to keep up. This piracy was an early look into the next iteration of Internet technologies beyond simple Web sites.

Peer-to-peer networks allowed a single individual's computer to act as a server. Rather than have the entire library of millions of songs on a set of centralized servers controlled by one company, which would have made it easy for the courts and law enforcement to shut music sharing down, peer-to-peer technology now meant anyone could upload or download a song directly to or from another individual. With millions of people uploading songs, the entire recording industry's catalog was dispersed across millions of computers for downloading by millions of others. Needless to say, the music industry was not pleased by this development. Electronics manufacturers, however, unable to resist the opportunity, rushed to produce miniature players capable of storing hundreds of songs. So did Apple. In the same year that it announced the launch of its Apple retail stores, it introduced the iPod.

Here Jobs had a unique credibility that gave Apple a critical opening. Unlike the technocrats behind the device manufacturers or the renegades behind file-sharing services like Napster, Jobs was trusted by media companies for a simple reason: He was one of them. In Hollywood circles, he was still the billionaire chief executive of an animation studio. His other company, Pixar, made money when people went to the theaters to watch *Finding Nemo* and bought *Toy Story* DVDs at Wal-Mart. Jobs had risked tens of millions of dollars over years to develop Pixar's first movie. He didn't believe that the clean dogma of rational algorithms alone dictated the future of the world. There was a place for art in his universe. And he understood that the creators of art, shareable or not, deserved to be compensated. And there was ample precedent for this view, however unpopular it may have been with the kids. The entire modern American experiment depended on respecting and demarcating abstract property rights: trademarks, copyrights, patents, zoning laws, frequencies, airspace. The value of American assets was intellectual as much as it was physical. Theft of the intangible, no matter how convenient or cool or efficient, called into question the sanctity of property itself—possession of a song did not mean unlimited ownership.

But the future was inevitable. Just as cassettes and vinyl records had given way to CDs, consumers had selected music's next medium. Technology companies, including Napster, relied on this consumer power as a form of leverage. If Napster's audience became large enough, no matter how illicit its origins, its founders and backers assumed that the record labels would be compelled to cooperate rather than litigate against the future. But this strategic arrogance caused record labels and artists to dig their heels in further against piracy. Without the cooperation of record labels, Napster was forced out of business. In Jobs, however, the record labels had a trusted, if imposing, negotiating partner, a man with star power who understood both the technology and media worlds, running a company in each. Starting in 2003, Jobs got the major record labels to offer individual songs via Apple for 99 cents. To accommodate Jobs, the record labels essentially gave up the ability to bundle ten or twelve songs in an album to be sold on the strength of one or two hit songs. Apple's iTunes service enhanced its cool, small piece of handheld hardware with the first widespread method of buying songs online.

With the youthful halo effect of music extending to its brand, Apple's new television campaign for the Mac started mocking Microsoft-based PCs as stodgy, nerdy, and awkward. At the same time, Apple's resurgence via handheld electronics came at the expense of another giant. Since the transistor radio, the Japanese had focused on producing basic technologies at cheaper price points. By the seventies, it had made the majority of the color televisions sold in America. In 1981, when Sony brought out the Walkman, its personal cassette player, the Japanese company had become known for cutting-edge, small-form factors in electronics. For two decades, quality electronics had been associated with Sony specifically and Japan generally. With the iPod, the product that would kick-start the company into personal electronics, Apple challenged Sony's dominance and firmly closed this chapter of the postwar Japanese economic miracle.

THE REBIRTH OF Apple and its impending rise to become the world's most valuable corporation were incongruously rooted in the fluidity of modern communism. In the second half of the twentieth century, there were two perfect experiments that pitted communism against capitalism, central planning against market-based systems. In Korea the stalemate resulted in two countries: North Korea, bordering communist China, became a totalitarian state. South Korea, with a permanent American military presence, was market oriented. The results were clear. By the end of the century, South Korea had first-world living standards. North Korea didn't. There were no cultural or ethnic differences: The divergent economic results of the two Koreas were mostly the result of differences in political systems. In Germany at the end of World War II, the two major victors had each taken a portion of the country. East Germany had allegiances to and was modeled on the Soviet state. West Germany had an American military base, free elections, and free markets. Again, the evidence of capitalism's superiority was clear.

When the Berlin Wall fell in 1989, unifying Germany, and the Soviet Union soon after, freeing Eastern Europe's communist bloc to align with the West, few suspected that the rising economic power of the 2000s would be a country firmly controlled by the Communist Party. In 1989, when student protesters took to Beijing's Tiananmen Square, it was seen in the West as one more step in the world's inevitable movement toward democracy. But of course it wasn't. China did not transform much politically afterward, but it did continue its rapid transformation economically. Unlike the Soviets, with rigid ideas of militarism, totalitarianism, and state ownership of the economy, the Chinese modified their version to fit geopolitical realities. Indeed, they had more flexibility. China didn't have the expense of a global military presence that being a superpower entailed. It had no ideological purity to maintain for the sake of unity among its overseas partners in countering America. The

Chinese government calculated that the most pragmatic method of defusing dissent and tension would be to raise the standard of living. Rather than try to export communism as an ideology, as the Soviets did, the Chinese looked to export products to customers in Western democracies. With each incremental success, China was able to decouple capitalism from democracy, two value systems that Americans saw as inseparable—free markets, free speech, free press, and free elections were all a part of the same democratic package. But the Communist Party, in making China the factory to the Western world, offered a counterargument.

Conversely, the Chinese could have argued that American capitalism itself was not simply a set of free market forces organically at work. The strong central government in Beijing was setting the economic trajectory for over a billion people the same way Washington had done for over a century. The tariff on steel was central to the success of Carnegie and other domestic producers during the Gilded Age. Federally guaranteed home loans were and remain the backbone of the housing industry, and with it, the construction industry. Consumer bank deposits were similarly federally insured. Vital developments in radio, television, satellites, mainframe computing, and the Internet had been achieved through military expenditures. America, the leading food producer in the world, had pages of farm subsidies on the books. The automakers had essentially been taken over during the Second World War—they weren't allowed to make cars for private sale for nearly three years. Later, automakers would receive significant bailouts and government-backed loans. And indeed, the participants in the American economy were largely educated at public schools and colleges. Retirement was taken care of for Americans through Social Security. Capitalism in America was not arms-length ideology; it was an endlessly calibrated balance between state subsidies, social programs, government contracts, regulation, free will, entrepreneurship, and free markets. The Chinese looked to do the same thing, albeit with one less political party than the Americans had.

Since capitalism seemed a pragmatic system where profit-motivated entrepreneurs could execute broad government directives, the Chinese communists became devoted practitioners. In so doing, this sparked the early momentum of Chinese growth, making it the great overlooked story of the last two decades of the twentieth century. By the first decade of the 2000s, China had arrived. And it had moved up the production value chain. By being able to manufacture products to the exacting standards of Jobs and Apple, the People's Republic of China would encroach on a citadel of Japanese capitalism, elevating the "Made in China" label from simple products like Nike shoes and plastic toys to increasingly sophisticated ones. In the eighties, Japan had looked so modern, so unstoppable that it was predicted to supplant America as the world's most powerful economy despite having fewer than half as many people. The Soviets had such firm control of a vast sphere of influence that meetings in the mideighties between the American president and the Soviet premier seemed to be those of equals. Yet it was Mao's China—his giant image still overlooks Tiananmen Square—that transitioned into the next century as the ascending power.

The end of the cold war was a moment of triumph on two fronts for the American century: capitalism and democracy. Yet as the forces of capitalism spread further into mainland China, victory ironically proved to be a source of growing anxiety in the United States.

A FEW MONTHS short of his tenth anniversary back at Apple, Jobs took the stage at 2007 Macworld and announced, "We're going to make some history today."

He had reason to feel confident. For the 2006 fiscal year, Apple's revenues from the iPod had surpassed its entire sales of laptop and desktop computers combined—$7.7 billion versus $7.4 billion—making the company as much a handheld electronics maker as anything else. The $200 price of the average iPod had put the Apple brand in over eighty million hands—primarily those of younger consumers—in the six years since it was launched. The iPod was accessible in ways that the premium Macintosh products, retailing for over $1,000, had never been.

"Every once in a while a revolutionary product comes along that changes everything," said Jobs to wild applause before revealing the product. For nearly a decade, Internet companies and phone manufacturers had attempted to combine the Web with the basic cellular telephone.

Comparing the iPhone to the "so-called smartphones" of the day, Jobs pointed to the full keyboards on many of them and scoffed, hinting at his breakthrough: "We're just going to get rid of all these buttons and make it a giant screen." Then he unveiled the gleaming metal and glass iPhone.

It is hard to overstate the stunning difference in functionality between the iPhone and the phones then on the market. The most popular phone in America at the time was the Motorola RAZR, which had much the same utility as the flip phones of 1997. The first iPhone, however, played movies, took high-resolution photographs, offered maps, navigated the Web, and stored music just like the iPod. Some competitors didn't quite get it. Hearing the proposed price, Microsoft's CEO, Steve Ballmer, laughed out loud. "$500! That is the most expensive phone in the world. And it doesn't appeal to business customers because it doesn't have a key-board, which makes it not a very good e-mail machine." Fortunately for Apple, the form appealed to just about everyone else in the world. In less than eight years after the launch, Apple would sell more than 600 million units of various iPhone versions—made in China—bringing in more than half a trillion dollars in revenue and counting, over 230 million iPhones grossing over $155 billion in 2015 alone. The iPhone turned Apple into the world's most valuable corporation.

This degree of success was perplexing. At launch, the iPhone was nearly five times more expensive than the most popular phone of 2007. Less than a year later, America entered a period that would come to be known as the Great Recession, arguably the most serious economic crisis since the Depression. Housing prices collapsed. A significant financial crisis ensued, causing the U.S. government to step in with trillions of dollars in subsidies, bailouts, and outright majority ownership stakes in major companies, including General Motors and the insurance giant AIG. The unemployment rate climbed to 10 percent in 2009. Reactionary populism took hold on the right in the form of the Tea Party and on the left as Occupy Wall Street. Yet the luxury iPhone—a decadent, shiny technological marvel—started selling at a rate of tens of billions of dol-lars per year during this time of great economic deprivation.

For many consumers, the smartphone replaced the computer—many users in third-world countries skipped the personal computer altogether, with the smartphone their first introduction to the Internet. Undoubtedly, a couple of innovations from Silicon Valley provided the boost. Social networks, led by Facebook, had connected people's entire history of acquaintances, friends, and family members. The tactile intimacy of the phone's microscreen and camera, along with the convenience of portability, made the smartphone a natural fit for this form of social behavior. Online services and applications that offered peer reviews of restaurants and hotels, movie times, on-demand car services, traffic updates, and a vast variety of other mobile utilities made the smartphone a must-have.

But the question remained: How was it possible for the cutting-edge future to be so readily and rapidly accessible to most people yet coexist with the narrative that Americans were being left behind? How much of economic satisfaction was simply a matter of perspective? Did it make sense that elements of both the Left and the Right were taking to the streets to voice their economic anger while filming it in high-definition with their new iPhones and posting it to Facebook? A part of the answer was that Americans had lost their traditional narratives, the framework that helped explain how their system worked.

Just as church and state and press and government were separate spheres in the American identity, business and government were as well. But the massive rescue of individual businesses by the government made the system seem far more opaque, complex, and abstract. The simple rules of the marketplace seemed to have been subverted. Even Silicon Valley's Tesla, in 2009, received a several-hundred-million-dollar lifeline when venture capital refused to finance its plans to produce the Model S, its first car meant for mass production. Insolvent banks received hundreds of billions of dollars, yet some bankers walked away with millions. To many Americans, it seemed that the system was rigged, with profits on the upside privatized for a few to enjoy and losses on the downside socialized for all to bear. The economic meltdown came as America was involved in two wars in Iraq and Afghanistan, neither the resounding success expected for a country that saw itself as the greatest military power ever assembled.

There was also a fundamental disruption in the economic equation that the iPhone particularly revealed. Nearly a century earlier, when Henry Ford had announced the $5 workday, the next big thing, a new car, had become accessible to the worker for the equivalent of three months' wages. Both the men working with their hands and the men in the office wielding the pen were integral to the success of American enterprise, together pushing the boundaries of what was possible. But the new age of technology had altered this. A great American product like the iPhone had Silicon Valley brains but was built with Chinese sweat. And the Chinese worker at Apple's massive, dedicated Chinese-owned factories earned around $200 per month. Where was the place for the American worker in this global marketplace when the Chinese worker earned so little but was making the most modern products? American stores were full of cheap Chinese goods, but there was unease as to how such a one-sided equation would ultimately play out. Even Sam Walton in the mideighties had been concerned about how much he was buying from overseas and attempted to encourage sourcing in America—his memoir was titled *Sam Walton: Made in America.* Yet the American consumer had become addicted to low prices, and the fear of trade deficits had remarkably subsided. The political messaging had turned from "Buy American" to extolling the merits of free trade.

And the trade deficit grew to record levels. America now bought $500 billion more from the rest of the world than it sold, an annual imbalance of more than $1,500 per capita caused by the influx of foreign goods. But even services were not safe. Customer-service representatives and certain types of programmers couldn't take their jobs for granted either. Millions of college-educated, English-speaking Indians starting at less than $500 per month were willing to do for white-collar work what the Chinese had done for blue-collar work.

There was little middle ground. The nativist saw jobs leaving due to free trade while the globalist saw the standard of living improving due to the same. America didn't produce anything anymore, one common view held. But it did. It certainly built its own houses—the American enjoyed more square footage than anyone else in the free world. It grew its own food—it remained the largest producer of agricultural products. Starting in the eighties, major automakers including Mercedes-Benz, BMW, Honda, Nissan, and Toyota built factories in America to produce best-selling cars including the Camry and Accord—America was the third-largest automaker in the world. America had been the world's top oil producer from the first drilling in Pennsylvania in 1859 until the early seventies, remained in the top three, then climbed back to the top with new methods of drilling. Boeing still made planes. Its pharmaceutical companies and medical device makers were among the best in the world. John Deere and Caterpillar remained leaders in farm and construction equipment. And it dominated in technology, shaping the world's future in terms of what came next, like self-driving cars and trucks.

For many, the lingering American discontent had roots in nostalgia about some former era of glory—but the thirties had the Depression; the forties, World War II; the idyllic fifties, over thirty thousand battlefield deaths in the Korean War and schoolchildren doing drills to prepare for a nuclear war; the sixties, Vietnam and three political assassinations; the seventies, the oil crisis, economic malaise, and high inflation; the eighties, the fear of AIDS, street crime, and paranoia about Japan. Even the good old days had their share of trauma. And pure measurements such as income inequality and wage levels risked missing the bigger picture of American life, neglecting to note the dramatic progress in quality of life that affected people of all classes. For instance, the lives saved by air bags and seat belts. At one point in the new millennium, murders had dropped by nearly 70 percent from twenty years earlier, the poorest neighborhoods being the biggest beneficiaries. Property crime, such as burglary, which tends to go up in distressed economic times, had dropped dramatically over thirty years. The nation had made tremendous racial progress—a white-majority country elected a black president with the middle name "Hussein." At the same time, the computer, Internet access, mobile phones, and high-definition televisions—the next big things of the past quarter century—were within the reach of the majority of Americans. If anything, the lag between the earliest adopters and the broad consumer market had been compressed, making technological progress as egalitarian as it had always been, if not more so.

BUT THERE WAS a problem with the next big things of America's past, each additional automobile or television set or ton of rolled steel still required the efforts of American laborers. The technological progress of the past forty-five years, while beneficial to most Americans as consumers, shut the vast majority of American laborers out of participation in terms of production. The hard labor was done overseas for around $1 an hour, and the high-income jobs of the next big things were open only to a sliver of highly educated technology workers on the coasts. For a century the American experiment had equalized the worker and the consumer in a way that no society had ever done—every household had pride that it was both consumer and producer—but increasingly, progress was leaving the American worker behind. How long could a global system allow him to fully enjoy the fruits of such progress if his ability to meaningfully contribute to it was nil? Could he remain a high-value consumer without being a high-value producer forever?

This was the paradox of America, a nation that resembled a perpetual construction zone, with old ways demolished to make way for the new, with change creating winners and losers, with the promise that any pain felt was merely temporary, a Darwinian prompt to adapt. It demanded faith based on its historical success. Even among the most strident cynics and critics of American capitalism, the benefits of this volatility were implicitly acknowledged, sometimes at inopportune times. Throughout September 2011, social media was flooded with videos and reports from lower Manhattan. The young protesters of Occupy Wall Street, displaying a combination of "social media savvy, carnival mood, and deep sense of frustration and disenfranchisement," had taken to the streets, using Twitter and Facebook to organize against malevolent economic actors.

On an early October evening, however, the mood among them suddenly shifted from one of defiance to one of sadness. The gathered crowds learned that Steve Jobs, the founder of the world's most valuable corporation, had died. Taking a break from their protests, they instead took to their made-in-China iPhones and two multibillion-dollar social networks to express their sorrow at the loss of a leading architect of global capitalism, mourning a man who had made it so that a customer in India could buy a product made in China, which never entered American airspace or physically touched an American hand but simply said that it was designed in California. But perhaps the sincerity of their vigil in the midst of their cynicism was not as much of a contradiction as it seemed. Americans have always understood the material progress owed to capitalism, but for just as long, they have also insisted upon their democratic right to curb its excesses. Opposing forces and motivations, starting from the venture financing of the religious separatists of the *Mayflower*, were intrinsic to the fusion of the American idea, the ongoing synthesis of capitalism and democracy.

Acknowledgments

This project started as a series of doodles, sketches, random thoughts, and sentences in a journal more than seven years ago. I didn't expect to actually write a book, nor did I think I was capable of it. And I was sure the circumstances of my business and family life would not in any way have allowed it. But the endless intrigues of the subject, which had filled my personal library over the years, gradually pulled a rough outline out of me. Still, I resisted. I thought that it would make for the foundation of a digital project or documentary series more than a book. But this lack of confidence had a benefit: Visualizing the story episodically in my mind gave the book its final structure. It solved the biggest and most frustrating challenge, which was how to approach assembling four hundred years of capitalism into a coherent narrative.

After nearly a year and half of intense research, I sought out the professor who had sparked my imagination as an eighteen-year-old. Now at Stanford, Richard White graciously gave me his time and provided me with the exact boost of confidence that I needed. A month later, energized, the narrative started coming together on paper.

A book such as this one, covering the span that it does, would not be possible without building upon the collective effort of countless others. There are far too many scholars, journalists, biographers, and writers to thank individually who have either directly or indirectly helped me in understanding the various dimensions of the American experience. While many generously offered access and time, my respect for their scholarship led me to spend more time with their published works rather than indulgently impose on their schedules. Nearly all are listed in the bibliography, but they deserve special gratitude here for their service to the historical record.

At the same time, there are many who helped me personally or professionally through the years who were instrumental in more ways than can be counted, including Shanker Srinivasan, Les Sufrin, Kasey B. P. Thompson, David Eraker, Zack Alcyone, Anne Alcyone, Frank O'Brien, Kevin Watson, Peter Kuhn, Ryan Lee, Bob Bagga, Andrew Hergert, Margaret Drain, Sarah Colt, Jordan Hyman, Eric Raskin, John Morley, Dave Schappell, and Eve Claxton. Jack Loop and Bruce Wilson unfailingly offered encouraging words at just the right times. Over several lunches, I discussed the idea of this book with the late Jim Lebenthal, who would have been delighted to see it come to fruition.

In the process of storyboarding and executing ideas on the interactive elements of *Americana*, which often served as a creative reprieve and helped clarify thoughts while writing, Jason Curry, Daniel Salazar, Kristy Curry, Malini Suri, and Grisha Alasadi always came through.

When the book was only partially developed, my agent, Emma Parry at Janklow & Nesbit, showed great faith and commitment from our first conversation and deftly led the way thereafter. In addition, Mort Janklow offered me the generosity of his counsel, which aided me immensely in keeping my focus on the task at hand. Bruce Vinokour and Pierre Brogan at the Creative Artists Agency gave the project energy and introduced exciting possibilities.

Ann Godoff and Scott Moyers cannot be thanked enough for taking a big chance on signing an unproven, first-time author. Remarkably, the enthusiasm that Penguin Press showed me on the day that we met has been sustained all the way through to the completion of the book with the help of their colleagues, including Matt Boyd, Sarah Hutson, Liz Calamari, and Colleen Boyle.

Eric Wechter and Hilary Roberts applied their diligence to fine-tune and copyedit the work. To my great relief in the final weeks before submission, Tyler Bray took years of sources, notes, and scraps of paper, and efficiently assembled endnotes into the manuscript.

At Penguin Press, my editor Emily Cunningham brought great insight, intellect, precision, and tirelessness in helping me shape and chisel the narrative. I consider myself very lucky to have been able to work with her.

Sucha Sudarsanam and Alice Hilal have never failed to read anything of mine, no matter how unpolished, providing unwavering confidence in the process. My father, Marur Venkataraman Srinivasan, has always been a reassuring and calming presence, a grounding force that made the intensity of the writing process far smoother than it otherwise would have been. My mother, Subha Srinivasan, has always encouraged me in all my endeavors, this one being no exception.

While writing passages covering economics, I was often reminded of my late grandfather's refusal to accept conventional arguments without all of the underlying logic laid out for him. A tough debater into his nineties, Balasankar would have turned 100 in the year of this book's publication.

The Srinivasan children, Meera, Ashok, Alex, and Maya, have been wonderful and sweet, tolerating their father's stretches of work with exceptionally good cheer.

Finally, words cannot express the love and gratitude I feel for my wife, Dina, whose support, patience, and counsel continue to carry me forward.

Notes

Chapter 1: Venture

3 **"fair and beautiful":** William Bradford, *Of Plymouth Plantation: 1620–1647*, ed. Samuel Eliot Morison (New York: Knopf, 1989), 17.

3 **one account held:** Ibid., 19–20.

4 **the hard toil:** Ibid., 23.

4 **"some preferred and chose":** Ibid., 24.

4 **"dishonor to God":** Ibid., 25.

4 **"vast and unpeopled":** Ibid., 25, 26.

4 **"Spaniards might prove":** Ibid., 27.

5 **it had lost all:** Edward Duffield Neill, *History of the Virginia Company of London* (Albany, NY: Joel Munsell, 1869), 24–25.

5 **beleaguered state of affairs:** Ibid., 65.

5 **aspects of their practice:** Bradford, *Of Plymouth Plantation*, 30.

5 **His Majesty's sovereignty:** Ibid., 31.

6 **"induce his friends":** Ibid., 38.

6 **Fellowship of the Merchants:** Ibid., 1, 9.

6 **implying shareholders with:** Ibid., 17.

7 **The final push:** William Robert Scott, *The Constitution and Finance of English, Scottish and Irish Joint-Stock Companies to 1720*, vol. 1 (New York: Cornell University Library Digital Collections, 2015), 18.

8 **Sir Francis Drake's:** Ibid., 77.

8 **"Suppose, for instance":** Ibid., 73.

8 **forty-seven times the capital:** Ibid., 81.

8 **"very loving and gentle":** Robert Johnson, "Nova Britannia: Offering Most Excellent Fruits by Planting in Virginia," *American Colonial Tracts*, October 1897, 10. Originally printed for Samuel Macham in 1609.

8 **"Navigation into all parts":** Ibid., 17, 18.

9 **twelve pounds ten shillings:** Ibid., 23.

9 **For many impoverished:** Douglass C. North and Robert Paul Thomas, *The Growth of the American Economy to 1860* (New York: Harper & Row, 1968), 31.

9 **lawyer, Richard Martin:** Neill, *History of the Virginia Company*, 69–70.

10 **priced at ten pounds:** Bradford, *Of Plymouth Plantation*, 40.

10 **In the original terms:** Ibid., 41.

10 **"fishing, trading, etc.":** John Robinson to John Carver, June 14, 1620, quoted in Bradford, *Of Plymouth Plantation*, 43.

10 **"a day's freedom":** Ibid., 44.

10 **moved to salting beef:** Robert Cushman to John Carver, June 10, 1620, quoted in Bradford, *Of Plymouth Plantation*, 45.

11 **"abundance of tears":** Ibid., 47–48.

11 **"to have the conditions confirmed":** Dissenting Pilgrims to Leyden Congregation, August 3, 1620, quoted in Bradford, *Of Plymouth Plantation*, 49.

11 **"one special motive":** Ibid.

12 **"the Speedwell was abandoned":** Nathaniel Philbrick, *Mayflower* (New York: Viking, 2006), 29.

12 **called for landing:** Ibid., 36.

12 **officials in England separated:** Neill, *History of the Virginia Company*, 206.

13 **"but six or seven persons":** Bradford, *Of Plymouth Plantation*, 77.

13 **"That you sent no lading":** Thomas Weston to John Carver, July 6, 1621, quoted in Bradford, *Of Plymouth Plantation*, 93.

14 **to first greet them:** Philbrick, *Mayflower*, 92.

14 **Adept at hunting:** Eric Jay Dolin, *Fur, Fortune, and Empire* (New York: W. W. Norton, 2007), 45.

15 **hunting and preparing:** Ibid., 42.

15 **"few trifling commodities":** Bradford, *Of Plymouth Plantation*, 94.

15 **between £1,200 and £1,600:** Ruth A. McIntyre, *Debts Hopeful and Desperate: Financing the Plymouth Colony* (Plymouth, MA: Plimouth Plantation, 1963), 19.

15 **constrained Weston's credibility:** Ibid., 27.

15 **"This had very good success":** Bradford, *Of Plymouth Plantation*, 120.

16 **"this way is now":** James Sherley et al. to William Bradford, December 18, 1624, quoted in Bradford, *Of Plymouth Plantation*, 120.

16 **exceeding 50 percent:** Bradford, *Of Plymouth Plantation*, 178.

17 **nine annual installments:** Ibid., 194.

17 **building trading posts:** Dolin, *Fur, Fortune, and Empire*, 66.

17 **low reproductive rates:** Ibid., 44.

17 **renegotiations for Bradford:** McIntyre, *Debts Hopeful and Desperate*, 60.

Chapter 2: Tobacco

18 **one hundred shiploads:** Charles C. Mann, *1493: Uncovering the New World Columbus Created* (New York: Alfred A. Knopf, 2011), 68.

18 **population of Virginia:** Arthur Woodnoth, *A Short Collection of the Most Remarkable Passages from the Original to the Dissolution of the Virginia Company*, cited in William Robert Scott, *The Constitution and Finance of English, Scottish and Irish Joint-Stock Companies to 1720*, vol. 1 (New York: Cornell University Library Digital Collections, 2015), 287.

19 **seen with curiosity:** Joseph C. Robert, *The Story of Tobacco in America* (New York: Alfred A. Knopf, 1952), 3–5.

19 **an account to the Queen:** Firsthand account from Thomas Hariot to Sir Walter Raleigh, 1885, Virtual Jamestown Archive, Virginia Center for Digital History, University of Virginia.

19 **"sinne of drunkennesse":** King James I, *A Counter-Blaste to Tobacco* (London: R. B., 1884), 12, 27.

19 **"poor and weak":** William Strachey, "The Voyages to Virginia, 1609–1610," cited in Mann, *1493*, 33.

19 **"marriage of soil":** Robert, *Story of Tobacco in America*, 8.

20 **"tillage of corn":** John Rolfe, "A True Relation of the State of Virginia Lefte by Sir Thomas Dale Knight in May Last 1616," in *Jamestown Narratives: Eyewitness Accounts of the Virginia Colony, the First Decade, 1607–1617*, ed. Edward Wright Haile (Champlain, VA: Roundhouse, 1988), 871.

20 **half of English America:** Edward Duffield Neill, *History of the Virginia Company of London* (Albany, NY: Joel Munsell, 1869), 174.

21 **"Dutch man of war":** John Smith, *The Generall Historie of Virginia, New-England, and the Summer Isles* (New York: Readex Microprint, 1966), 126.

21 **"furnish us again":** Sir Edwin Sandys, Treasurer of Virginia, to Sir William Cockaine, Knight Lord Maior of the City of London, November 17, 1619, quoted in Neill, *History of the Virginia Company of London*, 161.

21 **"transport these children":** Sir Edwin Sandys to Sir Robert Naughton, January, 28, 1620, cited in Neill, *History of the Virginia Company of London*, 160–61.

21 **1625 population of Virginia:** Bureau of the Census, "Historical Statistics of the United States, 1789–1945," Washington DC, 1949, series Z 24–132 (Population Censuses Taken in the Colonies and States During the Colonial Period and Pre-Federal Period), 1171.

21 **"appalling epidemiological environment":** Betty Wood, *The Origins of American Slavery: Freedom and Bondage in the English Colonies* (New York: Hill and Wang, 1997), 43.

22 **thousands of slaves:** Robert William Fogel and Stanley L. Engerman, *Time on the Cross: The Economics of American Negro Slavery* (Boston: Little, Brown, 1974), 16.

23 **young King Charles's:** Alan Taylor, *American Colonies* (New York: Viking, 2001), 136–37.

23 **272,000 pounds of tobacco:** Bureau of the Census, "Historical Statistics of the United States, 1789–1945," Washington DC, 1949, series Z 457–59 (American Tobacco Imported by England: 1616 to 1695), 1191.

23 **75 percent came as servants:** Wesley Frank Craven, *White, Red, and Black* (New York: W. W. Norton, 1977), 5.
23 **additional fifty acres:** Taylor, *American Colonies*, 142.
23 **as the tobacco country had spread:** Ibid., 143.
23 **Royal African Company:** Scott, *Constitution and Finance of English*, 283.
24 **more slaves were imported:** Bureau of the Census, "Historical Statistics of the United States, 1789–1945," Washington DC, 1949, series Z 146–49 (Slave Trade in Virginia: 1619–1767), 1172.
24 **averaged around twenty:** Ibid.
24 **grow to sixteen thousand:** Bureau of the Census, "Historical Statistics of the United States, 1789–1945," Washington DC, 1949, series Z 1–19 (Estimated Population of the American Colonies: 1610 to 1780), 1168.
24 **speculation in tulips:** Edward Chancellor, *Devil Take the Hindmost: A History of Financial Speculation* (New York: Plume, 2000), 15.
24 **"homeless Polish, Lithuanian":** Eric Jay Dolin, *Fur, Fortune, and Empire* (New York: W. W. Norton, 2010), 91.
25 **45,000 square miles:** Taylor, *American Colonies*, 264.
25 **rules of Sabbath** and **The Lords Proprietors:** Ibid., 340, 224.
26 **American colonial exports:** Bureau of the Census, "Historical Statistics of the United States, 1789–1945," Washington DC, 1949, series Z 213–26 (Value of Export to and Imports from England by American Colonies: 1697–1791), 1176–77.
26 **300,000 acres of tobacco:** Robert, *Story of Tobacco in America*, 23; Allan Kulikoff, *Tobacco and Slaves: The Development of Southern Cultures in the Chesapeake, 1680–1800* (Chapel Hill: University of North Carolina Press, 1986), 265.
27 **majority of men:** Kulikoff, *Tobacco and Slaves*, 268.
27 **vice such as tobacco:** Robert, *Story of Tobacco in America*, 24.
28 **"the tobacco planter":** Ibid., 25.
28 **English luxury goods:** Kulikoff, *Tobacco and Slaves*, 276.
28 **clutches of their factors:** Jon Meacham, *Thomas Jefferson: The Art of Power* (New York: Random House, 2012), 69–70; George Washington to Robert Cary & Company, September 20, 1765, George Washington Papers at the Library of Congress, account book I.
29 **80 percent of American exports:** Bureau of the Census, "Historical Statistics of the United States, 1789–1945," Washington DC, 1949, series Z 213–26 (Value of Exports to and Imports from England by American Colonies and States 1897–1791), 1176–77.

Chapter 3: Taxes

30 **against a common enemy:** "Join, or Die," *Pennsylvania Gazette*, May 9, 1754.
30 **right to settle:** Ron Chernow, *Washington: A Life* (New York: Penguin, 2010), 20–21.
31 **Virginians built their own:** Eric Jay Dolin, *Fur, Fortune, and Empire* (New York: W. W. Norton, 2010), 114–15.
31 **Robert Dinwiddie entrusted:** Chernow, *Washington*, 31.
31 **morning of May 28:** Ibid., 42.
31 **"the disunited states":** Benjamin Franklin to Richard Partridge, May 8, 1754, printed in the *Pennsylvania Gazette*, Public Record Office, London.
32 **to the Penn family:** Ron Taylor, *Colonial America: A Very Short Introduction* (New York: Oxford University Press, 2012), 264.
32 **45,000 square miles:** Ibid.
32 **The Penns balked:** Walter Isaacson, *Benjamin Franklin: An American Life* (New York: Simon & Schuster, 2004), 192.
32 **Franklin headed to England:** Ibid., 175–76.
33 **debts of over £60 million:** Paul Kennedy, *The Rise and Fall of Great Powers: Economic Change and Military Conflict from 1500 to 2000* (New York: Random House, 1987), 81.
33 **maintain a standing army:** Edmund S. Morgan and Helen M. Morgan, *The Stamp Act Crisis: Prologue to Revolution* (Chapel Hill: University of North Carolina Press, 1995), 20–21.
33 **passed the Stamp Act:** George III, "Duties in American Colonies Act 1765," March 22, 1765, Avalon Project, Lillian Goldman Law Library, Yale University.

33 **"Monarchy, Aristocracy, and Democracy":** Daniel Dulany, *Considerations on the Propriety of Imposing Taxes in the British Colonies*, 2nd ed. (Annapolis, MD: Jonas Green, 1765), 5.

34 **"an essential principle":** Ibid., 11.

34 **"against a Burthensome Taxation":** "Morgan and Morgan, *Stamp Act Crisis*, 99.

34 **"Declarations of our humble opinions":** "Resolutions of the Continental Congress," October 19, 1765, Avalon Project, Lillian Goldman Law Library, Yale University.

35 **House of Commons:** Benjamin Franklin, Testimony before the House of Commons, August 1766, described in William Jennings Bryan, *The World's Famous Orations: America, 1761–1837*, vol. 7 (New York: Funk & Wagnalls, 1906), 37–52.

36 **"a most dangerous nature":** House of Lords, *Protest Against the Bill to Repeal the American Stamp Act* (Paris: J. W. Imprimeur, 1766), 4.

36 **percent of annual wages:** Ibid., 7.

36 **extracting tax revenues:** Benjamin Woods Labaree, *The Boston Tea Party* (London: Oxford University Press, 1975), 20.

36 **the Sugar Act:** Text of the act, Avalon Project, Lillian Goldman Law Library, Yale University.

37 **to favor British merchants:** Morgan and Morgan, *Stamp Act Crisis*, 25.

38 **were able to lobby Parliament:** Labaree, *Boston Tea Party*, 42–43.

38 **a vast area:** Ibid., 58.

38 **loan of £1.4 million:** Ibid., 63.

39 **ship's twentieth day:** Ibid., 137.

39 **as much tea as the *Dartmouth*:** Ibid., 139–43.

40 **Many in England:** Ibid., 178–79.

40 **raised to be aristocrats:** Jon Meacham, *Thomas Jefferson: The Art of Power* (New York: Random House, 2012), 13–20.

41 **thousands of pounds:** Chernow, *Washington*, 77.

41 **To continental Europeans:** Gordon S. Wood, *The Radicalism of the American Revolution* (New York: Alfred A. Knopf, 1992), 13–15.

42 **planters of Tidewater:** Chernow, *Washington*, 107; Joseph C. Robert, *The Story of Tobacco in America* (New York, Alfred A. Knopf, 1952), 44.

42 **"an irksome thing":** George Washington to Robert Cary & Company, August 10, 1764, in John Rhodehamel, ed., *George Washington: Writings* (New York: Library of America, 1997), 111.

42 **This state of affairs:** Robert, *Story of Tobacco in America*, 45.

42 **"the chief officer":** Thomas Jefferson, *A Summary View of the Rights of British America* (Williamsburg, VA: Clementina Rind, 1774), 6.

43 **"individual adventurers":** Ibid., 11.

43 **made its way:** Meacham, *Thomas Jefferson*, 74–77.

44 **liberate Virginia's slaves:** Alan Taylor, *The Internal Enemy: Slavery and War in Virginia, 1772–1832* (New York, W. W. Norton, 2014), 23.

44 **The liberation of slaves:** *Howell's State Trials* (London: Longman, 1816), Vol. 20, 79–82, in "Black Presence: Asian and Black History in Britain," National Archives, United Kingdom.

44 **the more progressive view:** Taylor, *Internal Enemy*, 21–22.

44 **skilled in the letters:** Chernow, *Washington*, 186; Meacham, *Thomas Jefferson*, 86.

44 **a number of Jefferson's slaves:** Taylor, *Internal Enemy*, 24.

44 **eight of Washington's escaped slaves:** Chernow, *Washington*, 441.

Chapter 4: Cotton

47 **for the steam:** James Watt, *Specification of James Watt: Steam Engines* (London: G. E. Eyre, 1855), 2–7.

47 **valued for millennia:** Sven Beckert, *Empire of Cotton: A Global History* (New York: Alfred A. Knopf, 2014), 5.

48 **new ways replaced old:** Adam Smith, *An Inquiry into the Nature and Causes of the Wealth of Nations*, vol. 1 (1776; repr., Indianapolis, IN: Liberty Fund, 1981), 18–20.

49 **home to South Carolina:** "Notes of Catharine Greene," quoted in Edward T. James et al., *Notable American Women, 1607–1950: A Biographical Dictionary*, vol. 3 (Boston: Harvard University Press, 1971), 85–86.

49 **Whitney had arranged:** Jeannette Mirsky and Allan Nevins, *The World of Eli Whitney* (New York: Macmillan, 1952), 46–47.

49 **letter of explanation:** Eli Whitney Jr. to Eli Whitney, September 11, 1793, Eli Whitney Papers, Yale University Manuscripts & Archives.

49 **One account has it:** Denison Olmsted, *Memoir of Eli Whitney* (New Haven, CT: Durrie & Peck, 1846).

50 **the cotton gin was a simple:** Whitney, "Patent for Cotton Gin," issued March 14, 1794, Records of the Patent and Trademark Office, Group 241, National Archives.

50 **3,000 bales of cotton:** Bureau of the Census, "Historical Statistics of the United States, 1789–1945," Washington DC, 1949, series E 211–44 (Crop Statistics—Hay and Cotton), 109.

51 **"sciences and useful arts":** U.S. Constitution, art. 1, sec. 8, cl. 8 ("Copyright Clause").

51 **"one of our great embarrassments":** Thomas Jefferson to Eli Whitney Jr., November 16, 1793, Thomas Jefferson Papers, Library of Congress.

52 **the cotton from the seed:** Olmsted, *Memoir of Eli Whitney*, 19.

52 **widespread patent infringement:** Ibid., 18.

52 **"vultures called brokers":** Ibid., 19.

52 **"fifty to one hundred gins":** Phineas Miller to Eli Whitney Jr., October 26, 1794, in Olmsted, *Memoir of Eli Whitney*, 20.

52 **"It will be very extraordinary":** Ibid., 22.

53 **"the prospect of large gains":** Ibid.

54 **"We will not go into":** Phineas Miller and Eli Whitney Jr. to the joint committee of both Houses of the Legislature of South Carolina, December 20, 1801, quoted in Olmsted, *Memoir of Eli Whitney*, 29.

54 **$20,000 up front:** Eli Whitney to J. Stebbins from Columbia, South Carolina, December 20, 1801, quoted in Olmstead, *Memoir of Eli Whitney*, 30.

54 **"felon, a swindler, and a villain":** Ibid., 37.

54 **It accused Whitney's:** Speech before the Georgia House of Representatives by James Jackson, 1800, quoted in Mirskey and Nevins, *The World of Eli Whitney*, 148.

54 **ten thousand muskets:** Olmstead, *Memoir of Eli Whitney*, 47.

55 **dispatch James Monroe:** Jon Meacham, *Thomas Jefferson: The Art of Power* (New York: Random House, 2012), 387.

56 **surplus of idle hands:** Frederic Bancroft, *Slave Trading in the Old South* (Columbia: University of South Carolina Press, 1996), 6.

56 **"choice Gold Coast negroes":** Ibid., 4.

56 **producers were added:** Beckert, *Empire of Cotton*, 104.

56 **the world's raw cotton:** Bureau of the Census, "Historical Statistics of the United States, 1789–1945," Washington DC, 1949, series E 211–44 (Crop Statistics—Hay and Cotton), 109.

56 **one billion pounds:** U.S. House of Representatives, "Communication from the Secretary of the Treasury," 32nd Cong., 2nd sess. (1853), 818, 824–27.

56 **thousands of slaves:** Robert William Fogel and Stanley L. Engerman, *Time on the Cross: The Economics of American Negro Slavery* (Boston: Little, Brown, 1974), 47.

57 **"The old rule":** *Milledgeville Federal Union*, January 17, 1860, quoted in John Rogers Commons et al., *A Documentary History of American Industrial Society*, vol. 2 (Cleveland: A. H. Clark, 1910), 73–74; also quoted in U. B. Phillips, *Life and Labor in the Old South* (New York: Grosset & Dunlap, 1929), 180; Phillips, *The Economic Cost of Slave-holding in the Cotton Belt*, 177–78.

57 **price of cloth dropped:** Beckert, *Empire of Cotton*, 141.

Chapter 5: Steam

58 **an obsessive inventor:** Thomas Boyd, *Poor John Fitch* (New York: G. P. Putnam's Sons, 1935), 142–45.

58 **Investors supplied the capital:** Ibid., 152, 211.

58 **state legislature granted Fitch:** New York State Senate, *Journal of the Senate of the State of New-York*, 40th sess. (January 25, 1817), 109.

59 **meant little money:** Boyd, *Poor John Fitch*, 221.

59 **"made any attempt":** New York State Senate, *Journal of the Senate of the State*, 109.

60 **twenty-year term:** Ibid., 109–10.

60 **time to meet the conditions:** Ibid.

60 **many things Fulton touched:** Robert Henry Thurston, *Robert Fulton: His Life and Its Results* (New York: Dodd, Mead, 1891), 53–54; Cadwallader David Colden, *The Life of Robert Fulton* (New York: Kirk & Mercein, 1817), 69, 294, 305.

61 **"put a stop":** Robert Fulton to the Governor and Mayor and Corporation of New York, 1810, quoted in Thurston, *Robert Fulton*, 98.

62 **"that the fault":** Thurston, *Robert Fulton*, 106.

62 **with a tonnage of 160:** Ibid., 126.

62 **Fulton heard the snickers:** Robert Fulton to Joel Barlow, 1807, in Colden, *Life of Robert Fulton*, 176.

63 **"Having employed much time":** Ibid.

63 **almost twice the tonnage:** Thurston, *Robert Fulton*, 135.

63 **at a cost of $320,000:** Ibid., 138.

64 **front-page news:** Cynthia Owen Philip, *Robert Fulton: A Biography* (New York: Franklin Watts, 1985), 1.

64 **and physically imposing:** T. J. Stiles, *The First Tycoon* (New York: Alfred A. Knopf, 2009), 43.

64 **refused to duel:** Herbert A. Johnson, *Gibbons v. Ogden: John Marshall, Steamboats, and the Commerce Clause* (Lawrence: University Press of Kansas, 2010), 42–43.

65 **"strongest I ever knew":** Cornelius Vanderbilt, in *Den D. Trumbull et al. v. Gibbons*, April 10, 1849, quoted in Stiles, *First Tycoon*, 37.

65 **his young captain:** Memorandum of Agreement between Thomas Gibbons and Cornelius Vanderbilt, June 26, 1818, Gibbons Family Papers, Archives and Special Collections, Drew University, Madison, New Jersey, quoted in Stiles, *First Tycoon*, 46.

66 **advice from Aaron Burr:** Aaron Burr, "Of the Validity of the Laws Granting Livingston & Fulton the Exclusive Right of Using Fire and Steam to Propel Boats or Vessels," Gilder Lehrman Institute of American History, New York Historical Society, quoted in Stiles, *First Tycoon*, 47.

66 **"Truly a creature":** Stiles, *First Tycoon*, 58.

67 **income from Bellona Hall:** *New York Times*, November 13, 1877, 2.

67 **or even 75 percent:** Stiles, *First Tycoon*, 102.

67   **avoid price wars:** Ibid., 85.

68 **back into his fold:** William Gibbons to E. Hall, February 6, 1829, cited in Stiles, *First Tycoon*, 612.

68 **with a cut-rate fare:** Advertisements in *Albany Argus*, September 2 and 3, 1843, and *Albany Evening Journal*, November 7, 1834, and March 27, 1835, cited in Stiles, *First Tycoon*, 103, 617.

68 **guaranteed him $5,000:** Stiles, *First Tycoon*, 103.

Chapter 6: Canals

69 **land-based commerce between:** Robert Fulton to Governor Thomas Mifflin, March 1796, quoted in Robert Fulton, *A Treatise on the Improvement of Canal Navigation* (London: I. and J. Taylor, 1796), 133–34.

70 **Pittsburgh to New Orleans:** Albert Gallatin, *Report of the Secretary of the Treasury on the Subject of Public Roads and Canals* (Washington DC: R. C. Weightman, 1808), 35.

70 **fragile political bonds:** George Washington to Benjamin Harrison, January 18, 1784, Washington Papers, National Archives.

70 **acres for speculation:** Ron Chernow, *Washington: A Life* (New York: Penguin, 2010), 479.

71 **"monuments of his glory":** "An Act for vesting in George Washington, Esq. a certain interest in the companies established for opening and extending the navigation of Potomac and James Rivers," State of Virginia, October 1784, found in *Acts of the states of Virginia, Maryland, and Pennsylvania, and the Congress of the United States, in relation to the Chesapeake & Ohio Canal Company* (Washington: Gales & Seaton, 1828), 101.

71 **bequeath his shares:** George Washington to Edmund Randolph, August 13, 1785, Washington Papers, National Archives; George Washington to Patrick Henry, October 29, 1785, Washington Papers, National Archives.

71 **above material interests:** George Washington to Benjamin Harrison, January 22, 1785, Washington Papers, National Archives.

71 **Washington's ownership stake:** General Assembly of Maryland, *Report to the House of Delegates by the Committee to Whom Was Referred the Executive Communication Relating to the Appointment of Commissioners to Inspect the Potomac River*, December sess., 1821 (Annapolis, MD: Jehu Chandler, 1821), 11.

72 **imposing penalties on investors:** General Assembly of Virginia, *An Act Giving a More Speedy Remedy Against Delinquent Subscribers to the Potomac and James River Companies*, Acts of 1787, ch. 24, pa. 21, December 1, 1787 (Richmond, VA: Samuel Pleasants Junior, 1808).

72 **exceeding twenty tons:** Robert Fulton to Governor Thomas Mifflin from London, March 1796, quoted in Fulton, *A Treatise on the Improvement of Canal Navigation*, 132.

73 **"in less than a century"**: Robert Fulton to President George Washington, February 5, 1797, George Washington Papers, series 4, Library of Congress.

74 **large budget surpluses**: Bureau of the Census, "Historical Statistics of the United States, 1789–1945," Washington DC, 1949, series P 99–108 (Federal Government Finances—Treasury Expenditures: 1789 to 1945), 300.

74 **digging cost of $20,000**: Gallatin, *Report of the Secretary of the Treasury.*

75 **For six months**: Peter L. Bernstein, *Wedding of the Waters: The Erie Canal and the Making of a Great Nation* (New York: W. W. Norton, 2006), 104.

75 **"magnitude of this improvement"**: "Introductory Essay by Jesse Hawley," in David Hosack, *Memoir of De Witt Clinton* (New York: J. Seymour, 1829), 208.

75 **"The common purpose"**: Hercules, "Observations on Canals," in Hosack, *Memoir of De Witt Clinton*, 311.

75 **"making a canal"**: Bernstein, *Wedding of the Waters*, 125.

75 **raise a mere $200,000**: Ibid., 124.

76 **budget for 1811**: Bureau of the Census, "Historical Statistics of the United States, 1789–1945," Washington DC, 1949, series P 99–108 (Federal Government Finances—Treasury Expenditures: 1789 to 1945), 301.

77 **had slaves digging**: State of Maryland, "An Act in favour of the president and directors of the Patowmack company, and the commissioners of the federal buildings," November, 1794, in *The Laws of Maryland* (Baltimore, MD: Phillip H. Nicklin & Co., 1811), 272.

77 **Delaware outfit named**: Bernstein, *Wedding of the Waters*, 204.

77 **known as eminent domain**: New York State Legislature, *An Act Respecting Navigable Communications, Between the Great Western and Northern Lakes, and the Atlantic Ocean*, April 15, 1817, *Laws of the State of New York in Relation to the Champlain Canals*, vol. 1 (Albany, NY: E. Hosford, 1825), 360.

77 **plan projected 500,000 tons**: *Report of the Commissioner Under the Act of April 8, 1812*, April 15, 1817, *Laws of the State of New York in Relation to the Champlain Canals*, vol. 1, 80.

77 **stood at $7.8 million**: Don Conger Sowers, *The Financial History of New York State from 1789 to 1912* (New York: Longmans, Green, 1914), 70.

77 **exceeded within ten**: New York State Legislature, *Annual Report of the Commissioners of the Canal Fund of New York Respecting the Tolls Collected and the Property Transported on the Canals, During the Year of 1841* (Albany, NY: Thurlow Weed, 1842), 14.

78 **the Main Line**: Ronald E. Shaw, *Canals for a Nation: The Canal Era in the United States, 1790–1860* (Lexington: University Press of Kentucky, 1990), 62.

78 **formed interior arteries**: Ibid., 160–61.

79 **The canals had opened**: Bureau of the Census, "Historical Statistics of the United States, 1789–1945," Washington DC, 1949, series B 48–71 (Population—Race by Regions: 1790 to 1940), 27.

79 **leading capital market**: Bernstein, *Wedding of the Waters*, 364–69.

Chapter 7: Railroads

80 **ceding its role**: Robert A. Fulton, *A Treatise on the Improvement of Canal Navigation* (London: I. and J. Taylor, 1796), 17.

80 **"great multiplication of"**: Smith, *An Inquiry into the Nature and Causes of the Wealth of Nations*, vol. 1 (1776; repr., Indianapolis, IN: Liberty Fund, 1981), 22.

81 **on farm animals** and **tried hybrid approaches**: Nichols Wood, *A Practical Treatise on Rail-Roads, and Interior Communication in General* (London: Longman, Orme, Brown, Green & Longmans, 1838), 1, 2.

81 **Fourth of July**: Christian Wolmar, *The Great Railroad Revolution* (New York: Public Affairs, 2013), 1; Ronald E. Shaw, *Canals for a Nation: The Canal Era in the United States, 1790–1860* (Lexington: University Press of Kentucky, 1990), 101.

81 **public/private partnership**: B & O Railroad Company, *Report of the Directors of the Baltimore and Ohio Rail Road Company to the Legislature of Maryland* (Annapolis, MD: John Green Printer, 1831).

82 **to raise $1.5 million**: Baltimore and Ohio Rail Road Company, "Report of the Select Committee Appointed to Prepare an Exposition in Reference to so Much of the Governor's Message of January 2, 1840," January 13, 1840, 6, 7.

82 **engineer Horatio Allen**: Alba B. Johnson, "Locomotive and Engine Works," in Chauncey Mitchell Depew, *One Hundred Years of American Commerce, 1795–1897*, vol. 2 (New York: D. O. Haynes, 1895), 337.

82 **until the wooden tracks**: Wood, *Practical Treatise on Rail-Roads*, 20–24.

82 **the West Point Foundry:** Johnson, "Locomotive and Engine Works," 337.

82 **shareholders and politicians on board:** Wolmar, *Great Railroad Revolution*, 20.

82 **longest line in the world:** Ibid., 22.

83 **time cost prohibitive:** Dorothy R. Adler, *British Investment in American Railways, 1834–1898*, ed. Muriel E. Hidy (Charlottesville: University Press of Virginia, 1970), 28.

83 **fifteen hundred miles:** Bureau of the Census, "Historical Statistics of the United States, 1789–1945," Washington DC, 1949, series K 1–17 (Railroads Before 1890—Mileage, Equipment, and Passenger and Freight Service: 1830 to 1890), 200.

83 **$20,000 per mile:** B & O Railroad company, *Report of the Directors of the Baltimore and Ohio*, 42.

83 **sixty miles per hour:** Johnson, "Locomotive and Engine Works," 338.

84 **right to force:** New York State Senate and Assembly, *An Act to Incorporate the New-York and Erie Rail-road Company*, April 24, 1832 (New York: George P. Scott, 1835), 9.

85 **1,497 miles of track:** Bureau of the Census, "Historical Statistics of the United States, 1789–1945," Washington DC, 1949, series K 1–17 (Railroads Before 1890—Mileage, Equipment, and Passenger and Freight Service: 1830 to 1890), 200.

85 **the Panic of 1837:** Wolmar, *Great Railroad Revolution*, 51–52.

86 **"capable of combining":** Smith, *Inquiry into the Nature and Causes*, 21.

86 **estimated at half a million:** T. J. Stiles, *The First Tycoon* (New York: Alfred A. Knopf, 2009), 133.

86 **Rhode Island, and Boston Harbor:** Ibid., 107–9.

87 **"The first time":** Ibid., 120.

87 **three of his steamboats:** Ibid., 142.

89 **"illiterate and boorish":** Records of R. G. Dun & Co., Baker Library, Harvard Business School (New York City), Vol. 1, Entry 1, 374, cited in Stiles, *The First Tycoon*, 165.

89 **"sleeping on a volcano":** Alexis de Tocqueville, "Speech in the Chamber of Deputies Before Outbreak of Revolution in Europe," January 29, 1848, published by *Le Moniteur*, January 30, 1848, quoted in Alexis de Tocqueville, *Recollections: The French Revolution and Its Aftermath*, ed. Olivier Zunz, trans. Arthur Goldhammer (Richmond: University of Virginia Press, 2016).

89 **overturned in time:** Eric Hobsbawm, *The Age of Capital: 1848–1875* (New York: Vintage Books, 1996), 9.

89 **half a million Germans:** Bureau of the Census, "Historical Statistics of the United States, 1789–1945," Washington DC, 1949, series B 304–330 (Immigration—Immigrants by Country: 1820–1945), 34.

90 **to nearly 25,000:** Bureau of the Census, "Historical Statistics of the United States, 1789–1945," Washington DC, 1949, series K 1–17 (Railroads Before 1298—Mileage, Equipment, and Passenger and Freight Service: 1830 to 1890), 200.

90 **$5 million in bonds:** John F. Stover, *History of the Illinois Central Railroad* (New York: Macmillan, 1975), 38.

90 **Paper circulars screamed** and **"This is a rare chance":** Ibid., 46–47.

91 **one thousand new immigrants:** Bureau of the Census, "Historical Statistics of the United States, 1789–1945," Washington DC, 1949, series B 304–330 (Immigration—Immigrants by Country: 1820–1945), 34.

91 **longest railroad in America:** Stover, *History of the Illinois Central Railroad*, 38.

91 **four million people:** Bureau of the Census, "Historical Statistics of the United States, 1789–1945," Washington DC, 1949, series B 48–71 (Population—Race by Regions: 1790 to 1940), 27.

91 **local country lawyer:** David Herbert Donald, *Lincoln* (New York: Simon & Schuster, 1995), 157.

Chapter 8: Telegraph

93 **Dutch town of Leyden:** William Bradford, *Of Plymouth Plantation: 1620–1647*, ed. Samuel Eliot Morison (New York: Alfred A. Knopf, 1989), 47.

93 **a way to store electricity:** Jill Jonnes, *Empires of Light: Edison, Tesla, Westinghouse, and the Race to Electrify the World* (New York: Random House, 2004), 23–24.

94 **letters to his father:** Kenneth Silverman, *Lightning Man: The Accursed Life of Samuel F. B. Morse* (New York: Alfred A. Knopf, 2003), 13.

94 **paint the sitting president:** Ibid., 55.

95 *Gallery of the Louvre:* Ibid., 154.

95 **two Frenchmen announced:** James D. Reid, *The Telegraph in America and Morse Memorial* (New York: Derby Brothers, 1879), 87.

95 **stretching one third of a mile:** Samuel B. Morse to the editors of the *Journal of Commerce*, September 4, 1837, quoted in Taliaferro P. Shaffner, *Shaffner's Telegraph Companion*, vol. 1 (New York: Pudney & Russell, 1854), 292.

95 **a ten-mile circuit:** Samuel B. Morse to Levi Woodbury, Secretary of Treasury, November 28, 1837, quoted in Shaffner, *Shaffner's Telegraph Companion*, 29.

96 **"impossible and visionary":** Alfred Vail to Stephen Vail, February 17, 1838, Alfred Vail Transcripts, New York Historical Society, cited in Silverman, *Lightning Man*, 169.

96 **allow Morse to build:** General Thomas T. Eckert, "The Telegraph," in Chauncey Mitchell Depew, *One Hundred Years of American Commerce, 1795–1895*, vol. 1 (New York: D. O. Haynes, 1895), 127.

96 **British journal had published:** *London Mechanic's Magazine*, February 18, 1838, cited in Reid, *Telegraph in America*, 91.

96 **Czar of Russia:** Silverman, *Lightning Man*, 194.

96 **"This is my first meal":** Notes of General Strother, 1841, quoted in Samuel Finley Breese Morse, *Samuel F. B. Morse: His Letters and Journals*, ed. Edward Lind Morse (New York: Houghton Mifflin, 1914), 164.

97 **grant Morse $30,000:** U.S. Senate, *Government Ownership of electrical means of communication*, Document No. 399, 63rd Congress, 2nd sess. (Washington DC: Government Printing Office, 1914), Appendix A, 18–19.

97 **salary of $2,000:** Ibid.

97 **named Ezra Cornell:** Silverman, *Lightning Man*, 225.

98 **wiring resulted in failure:** Morse to Ferris.

98 **"rapidity almost of common":** Silverman, *Lightning Man*, 234.

98 **Morse biographer noted:** Ibid., 241.

99 **Kendall then licensed the patent:** General Thomas T. Eckert, "The Telegraph," in Depew, *One Hundred Years of Commerce*, 128.

99 **less than $20,000:** Ibid.

100 **miles of wires:** John Moody, *The Truth About Trusts* (New York: Moody, 1904), 382.

100 **he provided $500,000:** Silverman, *Lightning Man*, 406.

101 **"neat, accurate and hard-working"** and **their wages were:** "Women Who Work," *Pall Mall Budget* 32, no. 816 (May 16, 1884): 12.

101 **"From the dark cellar":** Andrew Carnegie, *The Autobiography of Andrew Carnegie* (Boston: Northeastern University Press, 1986), 37–38.

102 **"My father was usually shy":** Ibid., 60.

Chapter 9: Gold

103 **"The bourgeoisie, during":** Karl Marx and Friedrich Engels, *Manifesto of the Communist Party* (Peking: Foreign Language Press, 1968), 37.

103 **"Subjection of Nature's"** and **"no other nexus":** Ibid.

103 **their fellow man:** Ibid., 33.

103 **"everlasting uncertainty":** Ibid., 34.

103 **"the patriarchal master":** Ibid., 39.

104 **"extensive use of machinery":** Ibid.

104 **"appendage of the machine":** Ibid., 40.

104 **the events of 1848:** Eric Hobsbawm, *The Age of Capital: 1848–1875* (New York: Vintage Books, 1996), 10.

105 **Monroe administration acquired Florida:** Treaty of Amity, Settlement, and Limits Between the United States of America and His Catholic Majesty," February 22, 1819, Avalon Project, Lillian Goldman Law Library, Yale University.

105 **With Spain agreeing:** Daniel Walker Howe, *What Hath God Wrought: The Transformation of America, 1815–1848* (New York: Oxford University Press, 2007), 108–11.

105 **encouraged white settlers:** Ibid., 659–60.

106 **General Zachary Taylor:** Ibid., 734.

106 **"our manifest destiny":** James L. O'Sullivan, "Annexation," *The United States Democratic Review*, 17 (85) (July-August 1845): 5.

106 **formed the Associated Press:** Frank Luther Mott, *American Journalism: A History, 1690–1960*, 3rd ed. (New York: Macmillan, 1962), 251.

106 **proponents of Manifest Destiny:** Howe, *What Hath God Wrought*, 703.
107 **John Sutter had made:** H. W. Brands, *The Age of Gold: The California Gold Rush and the New American Dream* (New York: Doubleday, 2002), 3.
108 **"Gold! Gold! Gold!":** Ibid.
108 **$20 per day:** William Tecumseh Sherman to Major H. S. Turner, August 25, 1848, quoted in *The Sherman Letters: Correspondence Between General and Senator Sherman from 1837 to 1891*, ed. Rachel Sherman Thorndike (London: Sampson Low, Marston, & Company, 1894), 42, 52.
108 **two hundred ounces:** Brands, *Age of Gold*, 46.
108 **"I have no hesitation":** William Tecumseh Sherman to John Sherman, August 1, 1848, quoted in Brands, *Age of Gold*, 46.
108 **"abundance of gold":** James K. Polk, "Fourth Annual Address to the House of Representatives," December 5, 1848, American Presidency Project, University of California, Santa Barbara.
109 **Over a dozen whaling ships:** Eric Jay Dolin, *Leviathan: The History of Whaling in America* (New York: W. W. Norton, 2007), 211.
109 **a steamer to Panama:** T. J. Stiles, *The First Tycoon* (New York: Alfred A. Knopf, 2009), 205.
109 **"Many men have already become rich":** William Tecumseh Sherman to his family, August 1848, quoted in Thorndike, *Sherman Letters*, 40.
110 **gambling and women:** William T. Sherman, *Memoirs of General W. T. Sherman*, vol. 1 (New York: D. Appleton, 1875), 67.
110 **"stores were being opened":** Ibid., 54.
110 **"I have seen blankets":** Sherman to his family, August 1848.
110 **used hydraulic pressure** and **Chinese immigrants who:** Brands, *Age of Gold*, 63, 230.
110 **immigrant Levi Strauss:** Ibid., 345.
110 **Henry Wells and his partner:** "Wells, Fargo, & Co.: The Origin and Development of a Great Institution," *Cincinnati Express Gazette*, September 15, 1896.
111 **Hearst learned of a silver strike:** David Nasaw, *The Chief: The Life of William Randolph Hearst* (Boston: Houghton Mifflin Company, 2001), 4–6.
111 **on the Comstock Load:** Ibid., 6–8.
112 **raising private capital:** Stiles, *First Tycoon*, 191.
113 **one bit of evidence:** Bureau of the Census, "Historical Statistics of the United States, 1789–1945," Washington DC, 1949, series K 18–27 (Railroads Before 1890—Capital, Property Investment, Income and Expenses: 1850 to 1890), 201.
113 **world's gold supply:** Byron Webber Holt, *Gold Supply and Prosperity* (New York: Moody, 1904), 76.
114 **more or less equivalent:** Bureau of the Census, "Historical Statistics of the United States, 1789–1945," Washington DC, 1949, series B 48–71 (Population—Race by Regions: 1790 to 1940), 27.
114 **Great debates ensued:** Merrill D. Peterson, *The Great Triumvirate: Webster, Clay, and Calhoun* (New York: Oxford University Press, 1987), 448–49.
115 **Compromise of 1850:** "Fugitive Slave Act 1850," September 18, 1850, Avalon Project, Lillian Goldman Law Library, Yale University.

Chapter 10: Slavery

116 **stood Butler Island:** Mortimer Thomson, "Great Auction Sale of Slaves at Savannah, Georgia," *New York Tribune*, March 2 and 3, 1859.
117 **four million slaves:** Bureau of the Census, "Historical Statistics of the United States, 1789–1945," Washington DC, 1949, series B 48–71 (Population—Race by Regions: 1790 to 1940), 27.
117 **"Fugitive slaves and servants":** "Notes on Constitutional Convention by James Madison," August 28, 1787, Avalon Project, Lillian Goldman Law Library, Yale University.
118 **total of two captures:** Merrill D. Peterson, *The Great Triumvirate: Webster, Clay, and Calhoun* (New York: Oxford University Press, 1987), 470.
118 **"a moment of the highest":** Frederick Douglass, *Narrative of the Life of Frederick Douglass, an American Slave* (1845; repr., New York: Anchor, 1989), 105–6.
119 **"In no trial or hearing":** "Fugitive Slave Act of 1850," September 18, 1850, Avalon Project, Lillian Goldman Law Library, Yale University.
119 **300,000 in its first year:** David Goldfield, *America Aflame: How the Civil War Created a Nation* (New York: Bloomsbury, 2011), 80.
119 **hopes of settling:** Eric Foner, *Free Soil, Free Labor, Free Men: The Ideology of the Republican Party Before the Civil War* (New York: Oxford University Press, 1995), 57–58.

120 **"work is connected":** Alexis de Tocqueville, *Democracy in America and Two Essays on America*, ed. Isaac Kramnick, trans. Gerald Bevan (London: Penguin Books, 2003), 406.

120 **preceding nine years:** Bureau of the Census, "Historical Statistics of the United States, 1789–1945," Washington DC, 1949, series B 304–330 (Immigration—Immigrants by Country: 1820 to 1945), 34.

120 **the "Know Nothings":** Goldfield, *America Aflame,* 90.

121 **Kansas-Nebraska Act:** "An Act to Organize the Territories of Nebraska and Kansas," May 30, 1854, Avalon Project, Lillian Goldman Law Library, Yale University.

121 **senator Charles Sumner:** Goldfield, *America Aflame*, 115.

121 **"mute testimony to":** Ibid., 116.

121 **the exclusionary politics:** David Herbert Donald, *Lincoln* (New York: Simon & Schuster, 1995), 191.

121 **"Free soil and Fremont":** Goldfield, *America Aflame*, 124.

121 **personally notified him:** Ibid., 138.

122 **recognized forever as property:** U.S. Supreme Court, *Scott v. Sandford*, 60 U.S. 393, opinion of Roger B. Taney; "The Ordinance of 1787 and the Missouri Compromise Declared Unconstitutional," *New York Times*, March 6, 1857.

122 **"government cannot endure":** Abraham Lincoln, "House Divided Speech," Text of the address, 1856–57, The Gilder Lehrman Institute of American History.

123 **Richmond, and points in between:** Frederic Bancroft, *Slave Trading in the Old South* (Columbia: University of South Carolina Press, 1996), 234.

123 **details of the sale:** Thomson, "Great Auction Sale of Slaves."

123 **"Nothing was heard for days":** Ibid.

124 **"knew all about":** Ibid.

126 **$2.8 billion collectively:** Bureau of the Census, "Historical Statistics of the United States, 1789–1945," Washington DC, 1949, series B 48–71 (Population—Race by Regions: 1790 to 1940), 27.

126 **cost of $25 million:** *History of the Illinois Central Railroad* (New York: Macmillan, 1975), 64.

126 **American railroad track:** Bureau of the Census, "Historical Statistics of the United States, 1789–1945," Washington DC, 1949, series K 1–17 (Railroad Before 1890—Mileage, Equipment, and Passenger and Freight Service: 1830 to 1890), 200.

126 **was $69 million:** Bureau of the Census, "Historical Statistics of the United States, 1789–1945," Washington DC, 1949, series P 99–108 (Federal Government Finances—Treasury Expenditures: 1789 to 1945), 300.

126 **defending at all costs:** Bancroft, *Slave Trading in the Old South*, 339.

126 **well over half:** Bureau of the Census, "Historical Statistics of the United States, 1789–1945," Washington DC, 1949, series E 211–224 (Crop Statistics—Hay and Cotton, Acreage, Production and Price: 1790 to 1945), 109; and series M 56–67 (Foreign Trade—Value of Merchandise Exports and Imports by Economic Classes: 1821 to 1945), 247.

127 **in increasing quantities:** Dorothy R. Adler, *British Investment in American Railways, 1834–1898*, ed. Muriel E. Hidy (Charlottesville: University Press of Virginia, 1970), 27 (table 3).

127 **capital for the North:** Ibid., 48–49.

127 **better form of collateral:** Richard Holcombe Kilbourne, *Debt, Investment, Slaves: Credit Relations in East Feliciana Parish, Louisiana, 1825–1885* (Tuscaloosa: University of Alabama Press, 1995), 56.

128 **"between negroes and cotton":** "Cotton and Negroes," *De Bow's Review* 28 (August 1860).

128 **$250 million annually:** Bureau of the Census, "Historical Statistics of the United States, 1789–1945," Washington DC, 1949, series P 99–108 (Federal Government Finances—Treasury Expenditures: 1789 to 1945), 300; and series E 211–224 (Crop Statistics—Hay and Cotton, Acreage, Production and Price: 1790 to 1945), 109.

128 **men known as factors:** Edward E. Baptist, *The Half Has Never Been Told: Slavery and the Making of American Capitalism* (New York: Basic Books, 2014), 353; Walter Johnson, *River of Dark Dreams: Slavery and Empire in the Cotton Kingdom* (Cambridge, MA: Harvard University Press, 2013), 261.

129 **wide secondary market:** Johnson, *River of Dark Dreams*, 261.

129 **had slave-holding pens:** Maurie D. McInnis, *Slaves Waiting for Sale: Abolitionist Art and the American Slave Trade* (Chicago: University of Chicago Press, 2001), 87.

130 **"the best investment":** Bancroft, *Slave Trading in the Old South*, 343.

130 **over 500 slaves:** Ibid., 353.

130 **total of $580,150:** Ibid., 355.

130 **worth $4 billion:** Ibid., 351.

130 **Roger B. Taney, the Supreme Court:** Timothy S. Huebner, "Roger B. Taney and the Slavery Issue: Looking Beyond—and Before—*Dred Scott*," *Journal of American History* (June 2010): 17–37.

Chapter 11: War

135 **a generic Bill Smith:** "Negro Insurrection," *New York Times*, October 19, 1859.
136 **"release your slaves":** Ibid.
136 **"the insane undertakings":** Ibid.
136 **"pervades all classes":** "30,000 Federal Troops in Charlestown," *New York Times*, November 30, 1859.
136 **"A man who will not suffer":** "Sermon by Henry Ward Beecher," *New York Times*, November 28, 1859.
137 **their opposition to slavery:** Doris Kearns Goodwin, *Team of Rivals: The Political Genius of Abraham Lincoln* (New York: Simon & Schuster, 2005), 225.
137 **"If slavery is right":** Abraham Lincoln, "Cooper Union Speech," *New York Times*, February 28, 1860.
137 **"election of a man":** "Confederate States of America—Declaration of the Immediate Causes Which Induce and Justify the Secession of South Carolina from the Federal Union," December, 24, 1860, Avalon Project, Lillian Goldman Law Library, Yale University.
138 **"submit to degradation":** "A Declaration of the Immediate Causes which Induce and Justify the Secession of the State of Mississippi from the Federal Union," January 9, 1861, Avalon Project, Lillian Goldman Law Library, Yale University.
138 **"$3,000,000,000 of our property":** "Confederate States of America—Georgia Secession," January 29, 1861, Avalon Project, Lillian Goldman Law Library, Yale University.
139 **"in your hands":** "First Inaugural Address of Abraham Lincoln," March 4, 1861, Avalon Project, Lillian Goldman Law Library, Yale University.
139 **"peace, or a sword?":** David Herbert Donald, *Lincoln* (New York: Simon & Schuster, 1995), 283.
139 **run out of food:** Ibid., 285.
140 **the Pennsylvania Railroad:** David Homer Bates, *Lincoln in the Telegraph Office* (Lincoln: University of Nebraska Press, 1995), 20.
140 **Carnegie was tasked:** Ibid., 20.
140 **rails across Long Bridge:** Ibid., 22.
141 **being track gauge:** Richard White, *Railroaded* (New York: W. W. Norton, 2012), 8; Christopher R. Gabel, *Rails to Oblivion: The Decline of Confederate Railroads in the Civil War* (Fort Leavenworth, KS: Combat Studies Institute, 2002), 5–6.
141 **"widely separated armies":** Bates, *Lincoln in the Telegraph Office*, 11.
141 **reports from the battlefield:** Ibid., 9.
141 **"When defeated, an army":** Christopher R. Gabel, *Railroad Generalship: Foundations of Civil War Strategy* (Fort Leavenworth, KS: Combat Studies Institute, 1997), 8.
141 **"had the war ended":** Gabel, *Rails to Oblivion*, 9–11.
142 **replace worn-out tracks:** Ibid., 11–12.
142 **"rail was wearing out":** Ibid., 13.
142 **in 1860 alone:** Dorothy R. Adler, *British Investment in American Railways, 1834–1898*, ed. Muriel E. Hidy (Charlottesville: University Press of Virginia, 1970), 27 (table 3).
142 **America's prewar exports:** U. S. Congress, "Communication from the Secretary of the Treasury Transmitting the Report of Israel D. Andrews," 32nd Cong., 2nd sess., 1853, quoted in Douglass C. North and Robert Paul Thomas, *The Growth of the American Economy to 1860* (New York: Harper & Row, 1968), 190; Douglass C. North, *The Economic Growth of the United States 1790-1860* (New York: W. W. Norton, 1966), 233, Table A-VIII.
143 **grew increasingly vitriolic:** "Seizure of the Trent," *London Times*, November 28, 1861.
143 **one confident Southern posture:** Sven Beckert, *Empire of Cotton: A Global History* (New York: Alfred A. Knopf, 2014), 256–63.
143 **the British steamship:** Donald, *Lincoln*, 322; Andrew Carnegie, *The Autobiography of Andrew Carnegie* (Boston: Northeastern University Press, 1986), 98.
144 **"rapid way it is being":** Harold B. Hancock and Norman B. Wilkinson, "The Devil to Pay," *Civil War History* 10, no. 1 (March 1964): 24.
144 **London newspapers called for war:** Thomas L. Harris, *The Trent Affair* (Indianapolis, IN: The Bobbs-Merrill Company, 1896), 141.

144 **4.4 million bales:** Bureau of the Census, "Historical Statistics of the United States, 1789–1945," Washington DC, 1949, series E 211–224 (Crop Statistics—Hay and Cotton, Acreage, Production and Price: 1790 to 1945), 109.

145 **"twice before been forced":** Donald, *Lincoln*, 321.

145 **British industry suffered:** Beckert, *Empire of Cotton*, 263–64.

145 **iron exports to America:** Adler, *British Investment in American Railways*, 27 (table 3).

145 **"blind to their own welfare":** William H. Seward to William Thayer, December 15, 1862, quoted in Beckert, *Empire of Cotton*, 264.

145 **"gold for its purchase":** Ibid., 257.

145 **"historians of Egypt":** Ibid., 256.

146 **year's $68 million:** Bureau of the Census, "Historical Statistics of the United States, 1789–1945," Washington DC, 1949, series P 99–108 (Federal Government Finances—Treasury Expenditures: 1789 to 1945), 300.

146 **issue of $150 million:** U.S. Congress, *An Act to Authorize the Issue of United States Notes, and for the Redemption or Funding Thereof, and for Funding the Floating Debt of the United States*, 37th Cong., 2nd sess. (February 25, 1862), Library of Congress.

146 **Legal Tender Act:** Ellis Paxson Oberholtzer, *Jay Cooke: Financier of the Civil War*, vol. 1 (Philadelphia: George W. Jacobs, 1907), 173–74.

146 **to $474 million:** Bureau of the Census, "Historical Statistics of the United States, 1789–1945," Washington DC, 1949, series P 99–108 (Federal Government Finances—Treasury Expenditures: 1789 to 1945), 300.

147 **operate the postal service:** David Goldfield, *America Aflame: How the Civil War Created a Nation* (New York: Bloomsbury, 2011), 302.

147 **bonds to local savers:** Oberholtzer, *Jay Cooke*, 170; White, *Railroaded*, 11.

147 **grow to nearly $3 billion:** Bureau of the Census, "Historical Statistics of the United States, 1789–1945," Washington DC, 1949, series P 132–143 (Federal Government Finances—Public Debt: 1791 to 1945), 306.

147 **Collis Hunington and Leland Stanford:** White, *Railroaded*, 18.

147 **over $100 million worth:** Bureau of the Census, "Historical Statistics of the United States, 1789–1945," Washington DC, 1949, series M 42–55 (Foreign Trade—Value of Exports and Imports: 1790 to 1945), 244.

147 **imports of British iron:** Adler, *British Investment in American Railways*, 27 (table 3).

148 **personal wartime income:** Joseph Frazier Wall, *Andrew Carnegie* (New York: Oxford University Press, 1970), 189.

148 **One $300 man:** Iver Bernstein, *The New York City Draft Riots* (New York: Oxford University Press, 1990), 10.

148 **in his account book:** Jean Strouse, *Morgan: American Financier* (New York: Random House, 1999), 109.

Chapter 12: Oil

149 **owners had sold:** Eric Jay Dolin, *Fur, Fortune, and Empire* (New York: W. W. Norton, 2010), 310.

149 **"terror and dismay":** "The Great Stone Fleet," *New York Times*, November 22, 1861.

150 **entrepreneur, Samuel Kier:** Ida M. Tarbell, *The History of the Standard Oil Company*, ed. David M. Chalmers (New York: Dover, 2003), 2.

150 **"Kier's Petroleum or Rock Oil":** *The Derrick's Handbook of Petroleum* (Oil City, PA: Derrick, 1898), 11.

150 **Pennsylvania Rock Oil Company:** Ibid., 12.

150 **Kerosene Oil Company:** Ibid., 17.

150 **two million coal-oil lamps:** Daniel Boorstin, *The Americans: The Democratic Experience* (New York: Random House, 1973), 43; Catharine E. Beecher and Harriet Beecher Stowe, *The American Woman's Home* (1869; repr., New Brunswick, NJ: Rutgers University Press, 2004), 267.

150 **50 cents per gallon:** *Derrick's Handbook of Petroleum*, 14.

151 **to over 60 feet:** Ibid., 17.

151 **pocket of oil:** Tarbell, *History of the Standard Oil Company*, 5.

151 **"every rocky farm":** Ibid., 6.

152 **"not enough barrels" and "the school teacher":** Ibid.

152 **"not even a shotgun":** Ibid., 7.

152 **2,500 barrels of oil:** *Derrick's Handbook of Petroleum*, 20.

153 **$20-per-barrel:** Tarbell, *History of the Standard Oil Company*, 6.

153 **"They loved the game":** Ibid., 12.

154 **Beginning with $4,000:** John D. Rockefeller, *Random Reminiscences of Men and Events* (Garden City, NY: Doubleday, Page, 1913), 41–42.

154 **profits for the year were $17,000:** Grace Goulder, *John D. Rockefeller: The Cleveland Years* (Cleveland: Western Reserve Historical Society, 1972), 59.

154 **"a cast-iron still":** Rockefeller, *Random Reminiscences of Men and Events*, 81.

155 **"respect for figures":** Ibid., 21.

155 **yet another set:** Goulder, *John D. Rockefeller*, 76.

155 **"I bid a thousand":** Rockefeller, *Random Reminiscences of Men and Events*, 78.

155 **"Finally, it advanced":** Ibid., 79.

155 **"I'll go no higher":** Ibid., 79.

156 **five hundred barrels:** Ron Chernow, *Titan: The Life of John D. Rockefeller, Sr.* (New York: Vintage Books, 1999), 87.

156 **provided by the teamsters:** Tarbell, *History of the Standard Oil Company*, 7.

157 **Samuel Van Syckel:** Ibid., 9.

157 **two-inch pipe:** *Derrick's Handbook of Petroleum*, 34.

157 **"the many wonders":** Ibid., 29.

157 **ten hours a day:** Ibid., 52 (item 16).

157 **the upcoming era's template:** Tarbell, *History of the Standard Oil Company*, 10.

158 **45,000 barrels of oil:** Ibid., 30.

158 **1,500 barrels of this capacity:** Ibid., 26.

159 **27.5 percent to Jay Gould's Erie:** Chernow, *Titan*, 136.

160 **daily refining capacity:** Ibid., 142–43.

160 **sixty railroad cars:** Chernow, *Titan*, 113.

160 **yielding the modern brands:** Ibid., 558.

161 **tissue paper fit:** Eric Jay Dolin, *Leviathan: The History of Whaling in America* (New York: W. W. Norton, 2007), 112.

Chapter 13: Steel

163 **Gould engaged in:** Maury Klein, *The Life and Legend of Jay Gould* (Baltimore: Johns Hopkins University Press, 1997), 92–97.

164 **"for the first time":** Horatio Alger, *Ragged Dick; or, Street Life in New York with the Boot-Blacks* (Philadelphia: John C. Winston, 1910), 140.

164 **Carnegie became a conduit:** Joseph Frazier Wall, *Andrew Carnegie* (New York: Oxford University Press, 1970), 192.

165 **leverage his connections:** Andrew Carnegie, *The Autobiography of Andrew Carnegie* (Boston: Northeastern University Press, 1986), 136.

165 **Keystone Bridge Company:** Wall, *Andrew Carnegie*, 229.

165 **business too volatile:** Ibid., 198.

165 **"taking the lead":** Ibid., 232.

166 **on the bond sales:** Ibid., 272.

166 **assets of $400,000** and **"Beyond this never earn":** Andrew Carnegie to himself at the St. Nicholas Hotel in New York, December 1868, quoted in Wall, *Andrew Carnegie*, 224–25.

167 **Steel was far superior:** Charles Huston, "The Iron and Steel Industry," in Chauncey Mitchell Depew, *One Hundred Years of American Commerce, 1795–1895*, vol. 1 (New York: D. O. Haynes, 1895), 320–26.

167 **apply a steel coating:** Wall, *Andrew Carnegie*, 234.

167 **wore out within months:** Carnegie, *Autobiography of Andrew Carnegie*, 178.

167 **Union Iron Mills:** David Nasaw, *Andrew Carnegie* (New York: Penguin, 2006), 138.

167 **increased by over 70 percent:** Bureau of the Census, "Historical Statistics of the United States, 1789–1945," Washington DC, 1949, series K 1–17 (Railroads Before 1890—Mileage, Equipment, and Passenger and Freight Service: 1830 to 1890), 200.

167 **removing impurities from:** Isaac Lowthian Bell, *Principles of the Manufacture of Iron and Steel* (New York: George Routledge & Sons, 1884), 9–18.

168 **Bessemer had invented:** Ibid., 20.

168 **"the pride of a mother":** Wall, *Andrew Carnegie*, 264–65.

169 **$250,000 was Carnegie's personally:** Ibid., 309.

169 **"All was going well":** Carnegie, *Autobiography of Andrew Carnegie*, 182.

169 **"the failure of Jay Cooke":** "Another Panic," *New York Times*, September 19, 1873.

169 **the patriotic pitchman:** Richard White, *Railroaded* (New York: W. W. Norton, 2012), 10–11.

169 **"Almost every hour":** Nasaw, *Andrew Carnegie*, 151.

170 **enter crisis mode:** White, *Railroaded*, 80–83.

170 **where the tracks were:** Wall, *Andrew Carnegie*, 317.

170 **construction had to be suspended:** Ibid., 319.

170 **able to stay solvent:** Carnegie, *Autobiography of Andrew Carnegie*, 183–84.

170 **his personal cash balance:** Charles R. Morris, *The Tycoons* (New York: Owl Books, 2006), 130.

170 **"the proper policy":** Carnegie, *Autobiography of Andrew Carnegie*, 170.

171 **well over $100,000:** Wall, *Andrew Carnegie*, 324.

171 **In an accompanying note:** William P. Shinn (general manager), note to Andrew Carnegie, quoted in Wall, *Andrew Carnegie*, 326. It is likely Carnegie or his manager mistakenly wrote $9.86 rather than $9.68. The addition of the figures is also incorrect in the original source.

172 **Bessemer Steel Association:** Wall, *Andrew Carnegie*, 331; Nasaw, *Andrew Carnegie*, 169.

172 **large steel operation:** Wall, *Andrew Carnegie*, 333–35.

173 **$28 per ton:** Carnegie, *Autobiography of Andrew Carnegie*, 141.

173 **"has played a great part":** Ibid., 141.

173 **"patriotic duty to develop":** Ibid.

Chapter 14: Machines

174 **"survival of the fittest":** Herbert Spencer, *The Principles of Biology*, vol. 2 (New York: D. Appleton, 1891), 455.

174 **"the irrational doctrines"** and **"the carpenter-theory":** Herbert Spencer, *First Principles* (London: Williams and Norgate, 1862), 120.

174 **"despotism capable of":** Ibid., 119.

175 **"through a single sound"** . . . **"civilized races express":** Ibid., 162.

175 **"hunter, toolmaker, builder":** Ibid., 158.

176 **cotton production even higher:** Bureau of the Census, "Historical Statistics of the United States, 1789–1945," Washington DC, 1949, series E 211–224 (Crop Statistics—Hay and Cotton, Acreage, Production and Price: 1790 to 1945), 109.

176 **final stakes were driven:** Richard White, *Railroaded* (New York: W. W. Norton, 2012), 37.

176 **tens of millions of buffalo:** Eric Jay Dolin, *Fur, Fortune, and Empire* (New York: W. W. Norton, 2010), 295.

176 **"they must be exterminated":** William Tecumseh Sherman to John Sherman, July 16, 1867, in William Tecumseh Sherman and John Sherman, *The Sherman Letters*, ed. Rachel Sherman Thorndike (New York: Charles Scribner's Sons, 1894), 291.

177 **Cody, "Buffalo Bill"** . . . **killed 4,280 buffalo:** Dolin, *Fur, Fortune, and Empire*, 304.

177 **a few hundred in total:** Ibid., 306–9.

177 **2.5 million Germans:** Bureau of the Census, "Historical Statistics of the United States, 1789–1945," Washington DC, 1949, series B 304–340 (Immigration—Immigrants by Country: 1820 to 1945), 34.

177 **Indian population living:** Historical Statistics of the United States, 1789–1945," Washington DC, 1949, series B 48–71 (Population—Race by Regions: 1790 to 1940), 27.

177 **Germans escaping their political crisis:** David Goldfield, *America Aflame: How the Civil War Created a Nation* (New York: Bloomsbury, 2011), 88–89.

178 **"drunkards are in the majority":** Alexis de Tocqueville, *Democracy in America and Two Essays on America*, ed. Isaac Kramnick, trans. Gerald Bevan (London: Penguin Books, 2003), 263.

178 **"spirituous liquor capable":** "Lager Beer Case," *New York Times*, May 21, 1862.

179 **pasteurization allowed for:** Fred Pabst, "The Brewing Industry," in Chauncey Mitchell Depew, *One Hundred Years of Commerce, 1795–1895*, vol. 2 (New York: D. O. Haynes, 1895), 416.

179 **success was bottling:** "Adolphus Busch Dies in Prussia," *New York Times*, October 11, 1913.

179 **Pabst in Milwaukee:** Maureen Ogle, *Ambitious Brew: The Story of American Beer* (Orlando, FL: Harcourt, 2006), 79–80.

180 **Conrad's argument was:** Ibid., 80–81.

181 **especially skilled machinists:** P. G. Hubert Jr., "The Typewriter: Its Growth and Uses," *Cataquan* 8, series 10 (April 1888).

181 **"theoretical writing machine":** "Type Writing Machine," *Scientific American*, July 6, 1867, 3.

181 **C. Latham Sholes:** Clarence W. Seamans, "American Typewriters," in Depew, *One Hundred Years of American Commerce*, vol. 2, 544.
181 **"sewing machine is to the needle":** Hubert, "The Typewriter."
182 **500,000 machines per year:** Seamans, "American Typewriters," 530.
182 **$15 to $20 per week:** Hubert, "The Typewriter."
182 **"The excellent feature":** Ibid.
183 **Women's Christian Temperance Union:** Daniel Okrent, *Last Call: The Rise and Fall of Prohibition* (New York: Scribner, 2011), 12, 16–18.
183 **workingman's living room:** Ibid., 28.
183 **saloons of the nineteenth century:** Madelon Powers, *Faces Along the Bar: Lore and Order in the Workingman's Saloon, 1870–1920* (Chicago: University of Chicago Press, 1999), 65, 55.
183 **24 million barrels:** Pabst, "Brewing Industry," 415.
184 **new "national beverage":** Okrent, *Last Call*, 26.

Chapter 15: Light

185 **inventor named Charles Brush:** "Charles Francis Brush," *Harper's Weekly*, July 26, 1890.
186 **known as arc lighting:** "The Brush Electric Lighting," *Scientific American* 44, no. 274 (April 2, 1881).
187 **"within a two-mile radius":** Ibid.
187 **six thousand individual lights:** Ibid.
187 **"monopolized the field":** Ibid.
188 **Menlo Park section:** Jill Jonnes, *Empires of Light: Edison, Tesla, Westinghouse, and the Race to Electrify the World* (New York: Random House, 2004), 52.
188 **"unstable at times":** "The Risks of Electric Lighting," *New York Times*, March 26, 1882; Jonnes, *Empires of Light*, 142–43.
188 **monthly $75 paycheck:** Robert E. Conot, *A Streak of Luck: The Life and Legend of Thomas Alva Edison* (New York: Seaview Books, 1979), 19.
189 **battery acid spilled:** Ibid., 24–25.
189 **Edison developed a breakthrough:** Ibid., 23; "Annual Report of the Western Union Telegraph Company," *New York Times*, October 15, 1874.
190 **sixty thousand miles of additional wire:** John Moody, *The Truth About Trusts* (New York: Moody, 1904), 384.
191 **a significant breakthrough:** Ibid.
191 **close to $500,000:** Conot, *Streak of Luck*, 64.
191 **the Atlantic & Pacific:** Ibid., 66; "Annual Report of the Western Union."
191 **a cash and stock deal:** Maury Klein, *The Life and Legend of Jay Gould* (Baltimore: Johns Hopkins University Press, 1997), 200–201.
192 **95 percent of his father's fortune:** T. J. Stiles, *The First Tycoon* (New York: Alfred A. Knopf, 2009), 549, 557.
192 **J. P. Morgan took a special interest:** Jean Strouse, *Morgan: American Financier* (New York: Random House, 1999), 232–33.
193 **building on Pearl Street:** Ibid., 233.
193 **newspapers turned skeptical:** Conot, *Streak of Luck*, 138.
193 **the fourteen miles:** Jonnes, *Empires of Light*, 82.
193 **Vanderbilt asked Edison:** Ibid., 13.
194 **library caught on fire:** Strouse, *Morgan*, 232.
194 **by an additional $320,000:** Conot, *A Streak of Luck*, 192.
194 **eight hundred lamps:** Ibid., 198.
194 **an entire system of electricity:** "Edison Electric Light," *New York Times*, September 5, 1882, 8.
194 **Fort Wayne, Indiana:** "Base-Ball by Electric Light," *New York Times*, May 29, 1883.
194 **Jay Gould's grand yacht:** "Jay Gould's Yacht Atalanta," *New York Times*, June 23, 1883.
194 **United States Illuminating Company:** "The Brooklyn Bridge, Bids for Lighting the Structure by Electricity," *New York Times*, February 13, 1883; David McCullough, *The Great Bridge* (New York: Simon & Schuster, 1972), 515.
195 **headlines in 1883:** "Too Much Electricity for Comfort," *New York Times*, April 20, 1883.
195 **headlines in 1883:** "The Horse Injured by Electricity," *New York Times*, November 28, 1883.
195 **headlines in 1883:** "Nuisance of Poles and Wires," *New York Times*, December 1, 1883.
195 **headlines in 1883:** "Almost a Panic at Ridley's," *New York Times*, February 11, 1883.

195 **full-scale infrastructure:** Emerson McMillin, "American Gas Interests," in Chauncey Mitchell Depew, *One Hundred Years of American Commerce, 1795–1895*, vol. 1 (New York: D. O. Haynes, 1895), 297–99.

196 **more cost-effective:** Jonnes, *Empires of Light*, 218.

196 **New Jersey had just passed:** Naomi R. Lamoreaux, *The Great Merger Movement in American Business, 1895–1904* (Cambridge: Cambridge University Press, 1988), 1.

196 **raised a few million dollars:** Strouse, *Morgan*, 312–13.

196 **fewer than 650,000:** Bureau of the Census, "Historical Statistics of the United States, 1789–1945," Washington DC, 1949, series G 224–233 (Power—Electric Utilities, Sales to Ultimate Consumers: 1902 to 1945), 159.

Chapter 16: Retail

198 **"a science and art":** Catharine Esther Beecher, "How to Redeem Woman's Profession from Dishonor," *Harper's*, November 1865.

199 **clean, healthy Christian living:** Catharine E. Beecher and Harriet Beecher Stowe, *The American Woman's Home* (1869; repr., New Brunswick, NJ: Rutgers University Press, 2004), 25.

199 **poor Irish Catholics:** Ibid., 232.

200 **"Alexander Turney Stewart died":** "Obituary of A. T. Stewart," *New York Times*, April 11, 1876.

201 **specializing in Irish linens:** Robert Hendrickson, *The Grand Emporiums: The Illustrated History of America's Great Department Stores* (New York: Stein and Day, 1980), 34.

201 **such as Mary Lincoln:** Ibid., 36.

201 **the First Lady:** Doris Kearns Goodwin, *Team of Rivals: The Political Genius of Abraham Lincoln* (New York: Simon & Schuster, 2005), 401–2.

201 **special Congressional appropriation:** David Herbert Donald, *Lincoln* (New York: Simon & Schuster, 1995), 312.

201 **"absolute honesty between" . . . "any one could wander":** "Obituary of A. T. Stewart."

202 **estimating Stewart's fortune:** Ibid.

202 **as leisurely entertainment:** Hendrickson, *The Grand Emporiums*, 35.

203 **christened Ladies' Mile:** Ibid., 40.

203 **steam-powered elevator:** Ibid., 41.

203 **Wanamaker had visited with Stewart:** Ibid., 38.

203 **primacy of newspaper advertising:** "Wanamaker, America's Master Merchant, Never Takes Vacation from Advertising," *Editor & Publisher*, September 18, 1919.

203 **each day's sales receipts:** Ibid.

204 **Rural Free Delivery:** John Wanamaker, "Report to the President," *New York Times*, December 6, 1892.

205 **Losing his first name:** Charles R. Morris, *The Tycoons* (New York: Owl Books, 2006), 174.

206 **elicited cries of fraud:** "Grangers Beware," *Chicago Tribune*, November 8, 1873.

206 **"the idea of each side":** *Catalogue and Buyers' Guide, Spring and Summer 1895, Montgomery Ward & Co.* (New York: Skyhorse, 2008), 235.

206 **"possibilities of picture":** Ibid., 217.

207 **"when doctors fail" . . . "never fails to fit":** Ibid.

207 **Richard Sears was a freight agent:** "Richard W. Sears Dies," *New York Times*, September 29, 1914.

207 **five hundred gold watches:** Hendrickson, *Grand Emporiums*, 218, 238.

208 **In 1886 Sears decided:** Ibid., 238.

208 **"twice the exuberance":** *Sears, Roebuck & Co. Consumer Guide for 1894* (New York: Skyhorse, 2013), 37.

208 **"Hampden Watches Slaughtered" . . . "Down with Monopoly!":** Ibid., 29.

208 **"We do not guarantee":** Ibid., 17.

208 **no room for comparison:** Ibid., 181.

209 **Pure Food and Drug Act:** "The 'Wiley Act': Federal Food and Drugs Act of 1906," June 30, 1906, U.S. Food and Drug Administration Archives.

209 **"be perfectly harmless":** *The 1902 Edition of the Sears, Roebuck Catalogue* (New York: Gramercy Books, 1993), 441.

209 **"taken in the manner":** Ibid., 447.

209 **Heidelberg Electric Belt:** Ibid., 476.

209 **on moral grounds:** Ibid., 440.

Chapter 17: Unions

211 **a bomb was thrown:** "A Hellish Deed": A Dynamite Bomb Thrown into a Crop of Policemen," *Chicago Tribune*, May 5, 1886.

211 **dynamite and revolution:** James Green, *Death in the Haymarket: A Story of Chicago, the First Labor Movement, and the Bombing That Divided Gilded Age America* (New York: Pantheon, 2006), 140–41.

212 **majority of laboring men:** Richard Theodore Ely, *The Labor Movement in America* (New York: T. Y. Crowell, 1886), 94–96.

213 **"remove disadvantages under":** Ibid., 96.

213 **"overthrow of bourgeois supremacy":** Karl Marx and Friedrich Engels, *Manifesto of the Communist Party* (Peking: Foreign Language Press, 1968), 33, 27.

213 **aims of rival socialist groups:** Ely, *Labor Movement in America*, 232.

214 **fired a group of workers:** Green, *Death in the Haymarket*, 148.

215 **hundreds of Chicago policemen:** Ibid., 151.

215 **52,000 members in 1883:** Ely, *Labor Movement in America*, 74–75.

215 **the English-language *Alarm*:** Green, *Death in the Haymarket*, 126.

215 **called for a general strike:** Ibid., 145–46.

216 **collective action in Chicago:** Ibid., 157.

216 **took the Saturday off:** Green, *Death in the Haymarket*, 160–65.

216 **Spies was enraged:** *Chicago Tribune*, May 4, 1886.

217 **"dynamite bomb" would:** Green, *Death in the Haymarket*, 178.

217 **flyer circulated calling:** Ibid., 179.

217 **next day's headline:** *New York Times*, May 5, 1886.

217 **guilt by association:** "The Anarchists and Labor," *New York Times*, May 7, 1886.

217 **"How Will It End":** *Chicago Tribune*, May 5, 1886.

217 **"Violated Law Vindicated"** and **"that the murderous spirit":** *New York Times*, November 12, 1887.

218 **"The Socialist or Anarchist":** Andrew Carnegie, "Wealth," *North American Review* 148 (July 1889).

219 **John D. Rockefeller:** Ron Chernow, *Titan: The Life of John D. Rockefeller, Sr.* (New York: Vintage Books, 1999), 312–13.

219 **Atlanta's Spelman Seminary:** Ibid., 240.

219 **Stanford's wife had to:** Richard White, *Railroaded* (New York: W. W. Norton, 2012), 402–3.

220 **Vanderbilt had given more:** T. J. Stiles, *The First Tycoon* (New York: Alfred A. Knopf, 2009), 549.

220 **Frick slowly sold:** David Nasaw, *Andrew Carnegie* (New York: Penguin, 2006), 290.

221 **market price of steel:** Bureau of the Census, "Historical Statistics of the United States, Colonial Times to 1970," Washington DC, September 1975, series J 165–180 (Physical Output, Annual Data—Selected Manufactured Commodities: 1840 to 1945), 187.

221 **"simple, uncomplicated attitude":** Joseph Frazier Wall, *Andrew Carnegie* (New York: Oxford University Press, 1970), 522.

221 **"11-foot-high-fences":** Nasaw, *Andrew Carnegie*, 415.

221 **twelve thousand people:** Wall, *Andrew Carnegie*, 164.

222 **Pinkerton dispatched three hundred:** Ibid., 559.

222 **these industrial mercenaries:** Ibid.

222 **eight thousand troops:** Ibid.

222 **fired two bullets:** Ibid., 562.

223 **he finished his workday:** Ibid., 563.

223 **one-word message to Carnegie:** Ibid., 556.

Chapter 18: Papers

225 **this "foreign pauper":** "The Democratic Platform," *Chicago Tribune*, June 23, 1892, 12.

225 **and the tariff:** Bureau of the Census, "Historical Statistics of the United States, 1789–1945," Washington DC, 1949, series P 89–98 (Federal Government Finances—Treasury Receipts, and Surplus or Deficit: 1789 to 1945), 295–96.

225 **tax on the consumer:** Grover Cleveland, "Third Annual Message to Congress," December 6, 1887, American Presidency Project, University of California, Santa Barbara.

225 **bill spearheaded in 1890:** "The Tariff and Taxation," *New York Times*, October 21, 1890, 9.

225 **Even Carnegie, usually:** Joseph Frazier Wall, *Andrew Carnegie* (New York: Oxford University Press, 1970), 450–52.

226 **exporters of grains:** Bureau of the Census, "Historical Statistics of the United States, 1789–1945," Washington DC, 1949, series D 32–46 (Labor Force—Sex and Age of Persons 16 Years Old and Over in Labor Force, 1940, and Gainful Workers, 1890 to 1930), 64.

226 **sales to overseas markets:** Bureau of the Census, "Historical Statistics of the United States, 1789–1945," Washington DC, 1949, series M 56–67 (Foreign Trade—Value of Merchandise Exports and Imports by Economic Classes: 1821 to 1945), 246.

226 **farmers increasingly saw:** "The Farmers' Demands," *New York Times*, July 29, 1890.

226 **"tariff for revenue only":** "A Tariff for Revenue Only," *Chicago Tribune*, June 6, 1892.

226 **an angered Japanese man:** "Chinamen Cut by a Jap," *World* (New York), November 5, 1888.

227 **260,030 copies had been sold:** Ibid., 2.

227 **he bought a stake:** James McGrath Morris, *Pulitzer: A Life in Politics, Print, and Power* (New York: Harper, 2010), 92–93.

227 **seize the new opportunity:** Ibid., 155.

227 *St. Louis Post-Dispatch*: Ibid., 161.

227 **Pulitzer and Jay Gould:** Ibid., 205.

228 **"Mr. Pulitzer quickly succeeded":** "Joseph Pulitzer Dies Suddenly," *New York Times*, October 30, 1911.

228 **working class and immigrants:** Morris, *Pulitzer*, 215.

228 **"city's heat or cold":** "Broiling Human Beings—No Relief to Be Expected," *World* (New York), July 8, 1892.

229 **"If you were a millionaire?":** "$1,000,000: What Would You Do with Your Money and Yourself," *World* (New York), November 5, 1888, 2.

229 **lead to his blindness:** Morris, *Pulitzer*, 4.

230 **gold could be minted:** Irwin Unger, *The Greenback Era: A Social and Political History of American Finance, 1865–1879* (Princeton, NJ: Princeton University Press, 1964), 330–31.

230 **discoveries of silver:** Ibid., 335.

231 **"eastern banking interests":** "The Democratic Platform," *Chicago Tribune*, June 23, 1892, 12.

231 **Cleveland then ordered:** James Green, *Death in the Haymarket: A Story of Chicago, the First Labor Movement, and the Bombing That Divided Gilded Age America* (New York: Pantheon, 2006), 295.

231 **personal income tax:** "The Income-Tax Provisions," *New York Times*, August 17, 1894, 12.

232 **President Cleveland's health:** Wall, *Andrew Carnegie*, 456–65.

232 **William Randolph Hearst:** David Nasaw, *The Chief: The Life of William Randolph Hearst* (Boston: Houghton Mifflin, 2001), 28.

232 **silver mines of Nevada:** Ibid., 11.

232 **literary and cultured:** Ibid., 24.

232 **to appoint him:** Ibid., 61.

232 **changed its masthead:** Ibid., 63.

233 **added fiction, sports, and news:** Ibid., 76–79.

233 **$150,000 in the fall:** Ibid., 97–98.

233 **"Revolution in Journalism":** *New York Times*, April 14, 1895.

234 **"elixir of inflation":** "Bryan Is Notified Again," *New York Times*, September 9, 1896.

234 **strong dollars lent out:** "The Debtor States," *New York Times*, June 3, 1896.

235 **the party establishment:** *Official Proceedings of the Democratic National Convention Held in Chicago, Illinois, July 7, 8, 9, 10, and 11, 1896* (Logansport, IN: 1896), 226–34, reprinted in *The Annals of America, 1895–1904: Populism, Imperialism, and Reform* (Chicago: Encyclopedia Britannica, Inc., 1968), 100–105.

237 **Adolph Ochs was:** Susan E. Tifft and Alex S. Jones, *The Trust* (New York: Little, Brown, 2000), 15–17.

237 **$250 as a down payment:** Ibid., 37.

238 **if he managed:** Ibid.

238 **secretly retain a call:** Ibid., 75.

239 **if Ochs had been:** Ibid., 35.

239 **personal balance sheet:** Willis J. Abbot, *Watching the World Go By* (Boston: Little, Brown, 1933), 148–49.

239 **New York campaign headquarters:** Nasaw, *Chief*, 118.

239 **resisted all temptations:** Abbot, *Watching the World Go By*, 148–49.

Chapter 19: Trusts

240 **"inflated monster rise":** *World* (New York), November 3, 1896.

240 **He sold 1.5 million papers:** David Nasaw, *The Chief: The Life of William Randolph Hearst* (Boston: Houghton Mifflin, 2001), 119.

241 **Pulitzer's shock and dismay:** James McGrath Morris, *Pulitzer: A Life in Politics, Print, and Power* (New York: Harper, 2010), 328.

242 **irrational price wars:** Jean Strouse, *Morgan: American Financier* (New York: Random House, 1999), 313.

242 **dangerously low on gold:** Ibid., 345–49.

242 **fortuitous and succinct headline:** *Seattle Post-Intelligencer*, July 17, 1867.

243 **riches of the passengers:** "Wealth of the Klondike," *New York Times*, July 18, 1897.

243 **$657 million by 1898:** Bureau of the Census, "Historical Statistics of the United States, 1789–1945," Washington DC, 1949, series N 152–165 (Currency and Gold—Money in Circulation by Kind: 1860 to 1945), 275.

244 **Production of pig iron:** Bureau of the Census, "Historical Statistics of the United States, 1789–1945," Washington DC, 1949, series G 93–101 (Metals, Ferrous—Iron Ore, Pig Iron, and Ferro-Alloys: 1810 to 1945), 149.

244 **the workable method:** John Moody, *The Truth About Trusts* (New York: Moody, 1904), 5–11.

244 **The trust then owned:** Ron Chernow, *Titan: The Life of John D. Rockefeller, Sr.* (New York: Vintage Books, 1999), 227.

245 **the "Thread Trust":** Moody, *Truth About Trusts*, 234.

245 **the "Sewer Pipe Trust":** Ibid., 232.

245 **the "Cracker Trust":** Ibid., 259.

245 **entity's desired dominance:** Naomi R. Lamoreaux, *The Great Merger Movement in American Business, 1895–1904* (Cambridge: Cambridge University Press, 1988), 3.

245 **banker or entrepreneur:** Edward Sherwood Mead, *Trust Finance: A Study of the Genesis, Organization, and Management of Industrial Combinations* (New York: D. Appleton, 1913), 88–94.

246 **largest economy in the world:** Harold Underwood Faulkner, *The Decline of Laissez Faire, 1897–1917* (White Plains, NY: M. E. Sharpe, 1951), 69.

246 **Hearst implored Bryan:** Louis W. Koenig, *Bryan: A Political Biography of William Jennings Bryan* (New York: G. P. Putnam's Sons, 1971), 442.

246 **emphasize his anti-imperialism:** Ibid., 300–301.

247 **Capitalized at $40 million:** Moody, *Truth About Trusts*, 157.

247 **Federal Steel, even:** Ibid., 155–56.

247 **American Tin Plate Company:** Ibid., 157–59.

247 **National Tube Company:** Ibid., 161.

247 **Federal Steel consolidation:** Mead, *Trust Finance*, 198–209.

247 **"manufacturing stock certificates":** Strouse, *Morgan*, 399.

248 **Filipinos their independence:** Wall, *Andrew Carnegie*, 695.

248 **wrote out his terms:** Strouse, *Morgan*, 403.

248 **"being the richest man":** Wall, *Andrew Carnegie*, 789.

249 **Morgan's firm deposited:** Moody, *Truth About Trusts*, 135–37.

249 **major steel consolidation:** Ibid., 142.

249 **first company to be valued:** "U.S. Steel Corporation, Preliminary Report to Stockholders," February 17, 1902.

249 **"deep debt I owe":** Andrew Carnegie to employees of Carnegie Steel, March 12, 1901.

249 **libraries in New York City:** Carnegie, *The Autobiography of Andrew Carnegie* (Boston: Northeastern University Press, 1986), 249.

249 **the Carnegie Institution:** Ibid., 257.

249 **"promote the elevation":** Ibid.

250 **given Roosevelt's upbringing:** Edmund Morris, *Theodore Rex* (New York: Modern Library, 2002), 6–7.

251 **after McKinley's death:** "Peace Follows War in Northern Pacific," *New York Times*, November 14, 1901.

251 **over twenty thousand miles:** Moody, *Truth About Trusts*, 435.

251 **80 percent of the railroad mileage:** Bureau of the Census, "Historical Statistics of the United States, 1789–1945," Washington DC, 1949, series K 28–42 (Mileage, Equipment, and Passenger Service; Operating Steam Railways: 1890 to 1945), 201; Moody, *Truth About Trusts*, 439.

252 **Roosevelt delivered the era's:** "First Annual Message," December 3, 1901, American Presidency Project, University of California, Santa Barbara.

254 **Navy Department's budget:** Bureau of the Census, "Historical Statistics of the United States, 1789–1945," Washington DC, 1949, series P 99–108 (Federal Government Finances—Treasury Expenditures: 1789 to 1945), 299.

254 **"done anything wrong":** Morris, *Theodore Rex*, 91–92.

255 **"big rival operator":** Ibid., 92.

255 **"U.S. Steel's revenues":** U.S. Steel Corporation, Preliminary Report to Stockholders."

255 **workers from the coal mines:** "Anthracite Strike's Effect," *New York Times*, May 6, 1902.

255 **anthracite coal production:** Bureau of the Census, "Historical Statistics of the United States, 1789–1945," Washington DC, 1949, series G 13–18 (Bituminous and Anthracite Coal, Production: 1807 to 1945), 141.

256 **British or German mines:** Anthracite Coal Strike Commission, *Report to the President on the Anthracite Coal Strike* (Washington DC: Government Printing Office, 1903), 28–31.

256 **513 died at work:** Ibid., 29.

257 **"Mitchell's monopolistic power":** Morris, *Theodore Rex*, 154.

257 **the White House:** Technically, the negotiations took place in a temporary White House across the street while the West Wing was under construction.

257 **force of ten thousand:** Morris, *Theodore Rex*, 164–65.

258 **a wage increase:** Anthracite Coal Strike Commission, *Report to the President*, 80–83.

Chapter 20: Food

259 **only financial distress:** Nettie Leitch Major, *C. W. Post: The Hour and the Man* (Washington DC: Press of Judd and Detweiler, 1963), 14.

259 **Battle Creek Sanitarium:** Ibid., 2.

259 **Kellogg's spelling of:** John Harvey Kellogg, *The Battle Creek Sanitarium System: History, Organization, Methods* (Battle Creek, MI: Gage Printing, 1908), 13.

259 **Kellogg's medical education:** Ronald L. Numbers, *Prophetess of Health: A Study of Ellen G. White* (Grand Rapids, MI: Wm. B. Eerdmans, 2008), 179.

260 **forms of human sexuality:** John Harvey Kellogg, *Plain Facts for Old and Young* (Burlington, IA: Segner & Condit, 1881), v–viii.

260 **"Infanticide and Abortion":** Ibid., 271.

260 **"Indulgence during pregnancy":** Ibid., 241.

260 **"night after night":** Ibid., 226.

260 **"indulgence may increase":** Ibid., 227.

260 **"purpose of producing":** Ibid., 221.

260 **attributed to meat eating:** Ibid., 202.

260 **"no parallel except"** and **"back or the abdomen":** Genesis 19:5, cited in Kellogg, *Plain Facts for Old and Young*, 315, 330.

260 **"Candies, spices, cinnamon":** Kellogg, *Plain Facts for Old and Young*, 330.

261 **Look at Rome:** Ibid., 288.

261 **Battle Creek philosophy:** Kellogg, *Battle Creek Sanitarium*, 137.

261 **"toasted flaked cereal":** Ibid., 137.

261 **at Kellogg's facility:** Major, *C. W. Post*, 30–31.

261 **To promote Grape-Nuts:** Ibid., 51–57.

262 **best brain food:** Testimony of Floyd W. Robinson, state chemist of the state of Michigan, quoted in Robert Joseph Collier, *The $50,000 Verdict* (New York: P. F. Collier & Son, 1911), 41, 30.

262 **interests ultimately prevailing:** "Digest of Michigan Supreme Court Decision on 'Kelloggs,'" *Spice Mill* 44, no. 2 (February 1921).

262 **"the numerous imitations":** Kellogg, *Battle Creek Sanitarium*, 137.

263 **the "Greatest Discovery":** Samuel Hopkins Adams, *The Great American Fraud* (New York: P. F. Collier & Son, 1905), 48–49.

263 **to cure deafness:** Ibid., 48.

263 **bankruptcy, fires, and failures:** Mark Pendergrast, *For God, Country & Coca-Cola* (New York: Basic Books, 2000), 20.

263 **Dr. Sanford's Great Invigorator:** Ibid., 21.

263 **rather miraculous properties:** Ibid.

264 **marketed as Vin Mariani:** Ibid., 22.

264 **a prohibition law:** Ibid., 27.

264 **Pemberton's "temperance drink":** Ibid., 29, 30.

264 **labyrinth of transactions:** Ibid., 36.

264 **"ideal brain tonic" . . . :** Ibid., 60.

265 **Ida Tarbell had eviscerated:** Ida M. Tarbell, *The History of the Standard Oil Company*, ed. David M. Chalmers (New York: Dover, 2003).

265 **the industry's revenue:** Ibid., 73.

266 **"It is mutually agreed":** Ibid., 6.

266 **"when you touch":** Ibid., 90.

267 **arrived in America:** Bureau of the Census, "Historical Statistics of the United States, 1789–1945," Washington DC, 1949, series B 304–330 (Immigration—Immigrants by Country: 1820 to 1945), 33.

268 **population of Ireland:** Ibid.

268 **all U.S. exports:** Bureau of the Census, "Historical Statistics of the United States, 1789–1945," Washington DC, 1949, series M 56–67 (Foreign Trade—Value of Merchandise Exports and Imports, by Economic Classes: 1821 to 1945), 246.

268 **advent of refrigeration:** Philip D. Armour, "The Packing Industry," in Chauncey Mitchell Depew, *One Hundred Years of American Commerce, 1795–1895*, vol. 2 (New York: D. O. Haynes, 1895), 338.

269 **13 million cattle:** Bureau of the Census, "Historical Statistics of the United States, 1789–1945," Washington DC, 1949, series E 136–151 (Meat—Slaughtering, Production, and Price: 1899 to 1945), 102.

269 **"twenty-five years ago":** Armour, "Packing Industry," 338.

269 **"Here was the chute":** Upton Sinclair, *The Jungle* (1906; repr., Ann Arbor, MI: Borders Classics, 2006), 37.

270 **"organic matter was wasted":** Ibid., 44.

270 **"eat his dinner":** Ibid., 89.

270 **"did not shiver":** Ibid., 90.

271 **"Scraps of meat":** Ibid., 67.

271 **"grade of lard":** Ibid., 107.

271 **"fat of pork":** Ibid., 108.

271 **"this ingenious mixture":** Ibid., 109.

272 **did not mention:** "Jurdis Rudkus and 'The Jungle,'" *New York Times*, March 3, 1906.

272 **"man with the muckrake:"** Theodore Roosevelt, "Fifth Annual Message," December 1905, American Presidency Project, University of California, Santa Barbara.

273 **"misbranded and adulterated":** Ibid.

273 **"I would suggest":** Upton Sinclair to President Theodore Roosevelt, March 10, 1906, National Archives, Identifier: 301981, Record Group 16.

274 **"possession of the facts":** "Sinclair Gives Proof of Meat Trust Frauds," *New York Times*, May 28, 1906, 2.

274 **"displayed a disregard":** "Horrifying Conditions in Packing Houses," *Eugene Register-Guard*, June 4, 1906.

Chapter 21: Automobiles

279 **that "revolutionary inventions":** "The Evolution of the Industry," *Horseless Age* 6, no. 1 (April 4, 1900).

279 **four thousand were sold:** Bureau of the Census, "Historical Statistics of the United States, 1789–1945," Washington DC, 1949, series K 225–235 (Production, Registrations, and Motor Fuel Usage: 1900 to 1945), 223.

279 **achieving speeds of:** "A Gasoline Steam Carriage," *Scientific American* 66 (May 21, 1892).

280 **Francis Times Company in India:** Arthur Pound, *The Turning Wheel: The Story of General Motors Through Twenty-five Years, 1908–1933* (London: Forgotten Books, 2012), 47.

280 **lack of battery storage:** Allan Nevins, *Ford: The Times, the Man, the Company* (New York: Charles Scribner's Sons, 1954), 175.

280 **priced at $650:** "Advertising Supplement," *Horseless Age* 6, no. 3 (April 18, 1900).

280 **one third of:** Pound, *Turning Wheel*, 54.

280 **$200,000 in capital:** Ibid., 51.

280 **sixteen cars in 1903:** Ibid., 76.

280 **control of Buick:** Ibid., 79.

281 **"a money-making concern":** Henry Ford and Samuel Crowther, *My Life and Work* (Garden City, NY: Doubleday, Page, 1922), 36, cited in Nevins, *Ford*, 211.

281 **"a first-class car":** Ford and Crowther, *My Life and Work*, 50.

282 **"life to a car" and "kill a man":** Ibid.

282 **Ford entered Oldfield:** Nevins, *Ford*, 218.

282 **Oldfield would set:** Ibid.

282 **formalized in 1903:** Ibid., 238.

284 **"persons who buy":** "Proposal to License Owners," *New York Times*, December 4, 1910.

284 **"He was contemptuous":** Charles E. Sorensen, *My Forty Years with Ford* (Detroit: Wayne State University Press, 2006), 11.

284 **the Model A:** Nevins, *Ford*, 241.

285 **"habit of grabbing":** Ford and Crowther, *My Life and Work*, 49.

285 **profit of $98,851:** Nevins, *Ford*, 246.

285 **introduced new models:** Ford Motor Co., advertisement, *Motor Age* 6, no. 25 (December 22, 1904).

285 **almost $2 million:** Nevins, *Ford*, 647 (Appendix VI: Net Income of Ford Motor Company).

285 **Ford's net income:** Ibid., 287 (Appendix IV: Dollar Sales of Ford Cars).

285 **a new model:** Ibid., 324.

285 **travel as fast:** Ibid., 327.

285 **bought out Malcomson's:** Ibid., 330.

286 **the industrial artist:** Ibid., 574–77.

286 **over eight thousand:** Pound, *Turning Wheel*, 90.

286 **Buick's production exceeded:** Ibid.; Nevins, *Ford*, 644–45.

287 **incorporate General Motors:** "General Motors Company Starts Rumors Anew," *New York Times*, December 29, 1908.

287 **grow from a little:** Bureau of the Census, "Historical Statistics of the United States, 1789–1945," Washington DC, 1949, series K 225–235 (Production, Registrations, and Motor Fuel Usage: 1900 to 1945), 223.

287 **It included parts:** Pound, *Turning Wheel*, 119.

287 **sold more than:** Ibid., 108–9.

287 **stellar first year:** Ibid., 123.

288 **"had four cylinders":** "Ford 1908 Features," *Horseless Age* 21 (April 1, 1908).

288 **of vanadium steel:** Henry Ford, "Special Automobile Steels," *Harper's*, March 16, 1907, cited in Nevins, *Ford*, 349.

288 **Sears Catalog had:** Nevins, *Ford*, 409.

288 **200,000 vehicles purchased:** Bureau of the Census, "Historical Statistics of the United States, 1789–1945," Washington DC, 1949, series K 225–235 (Production, Registrations, and Motor Fuel Usage: 1900 to 1945), 223.

288 **over ten million:** Ibid.

289 **Ford would sell:** Pound, *Turning Wheel*, 644 (Appendix III: Total Sales of Ford Cars).

289 **"the overhead trolley":** Ford and Crowther, *My Life and Work*, 81.

289 **"With one workman":** Ibid.

290 **"In the chassis":** Ibid., 82.

290 **26 cents per hour:** Pound, *Turning Wheel*, 529.

290 **generous eighteen-day vacation:** Nevins, *Ford*, 531.

290 **but women excluded:** Ibid., 534.

290 **captured front-page headlines:** "Gives $10,000,000 to 26,000 Employees," *New York Times*, January 6, 1914; "Henry Ford Gives $10,000,000 in 1914 Profits to His Employees," *Detroit Journal*, January 6, 1914.

290 **a sociological department:** Nevins, *Ford*, 533, 556–58.

291 **sharecropping in the South:** Christopher L. Foote, Warren C. Whatley, and Gavin Wright, "Arbitraging a Discriminatory Labor Market: Black Workers at the Ford Motor Company, 1918–1947," *Journal of Labor Economics* 21, no. 3 (July 2003): 493–532.

Chapter 22: Radio

292 **a floor exhibit:** Gleason Leonard Archer, *History of the Radio to 1926* (New York: American Historical Society, 1938), 110–11.

292 **messages transmitted everything:** "Statement of Lieut. S. C. Hooper, US Navy," *Hearings Before the Committee on the Merchant Marine and Fisheries on H. R. 19350, A Bill to Regulate Radio*

Communication, 64th Cong., 2nd sess., January 16, 1970 (Washington DC: Government Printing Office, 1917), 120–21.

293 **had expanded significantly:** Bureau of the Census, "Historical Statistics of the United States, 1789–1945," Washington DC, 1949, series P 99–108 (Federal Government Finances—Treasury Expenditures: 1789 to 1945), 299.

293 **with wireless transmitters:** Edmund Morris, *Theodore Rex* (New York: Modern Library, 2002), 455.

293 **Marconi Wireless station:** "Allan Liner Virginian Now Speeding Toward the Big Ship," *New York Times*, April 15, 1912.

294 **lighted bulletin board:** "Times Bulletins Sent Far and Wide," *New York Times*, April 17, 1912.

294 **Straus and John Jacob Astor:** Stephen Birmingham, *The Rest of Us: The Rise of America's Eastern European Jews* (Syracuse, NY: Syracuse University Press, 1999), 104.

294 **Lloyd's of London:** "A $5,000,000 Risk Carried by Lloyd's," *New York Times*, April 16, 1912.

294 **jumped from $170 to $245:** "Marconi Stock $10,000,000," *New York Times*, April 19, 1912.

295 **under federal control:** "President Taft Early Wired for News of Major Butt," *New York Times*, April 17, 1912.

296 **undisputed economic power:** Paul Kennedy, *The Rise and Fall of the Great Powers: Economic Change and Military Conflict from 1500 to 2000* (New York: Random House, 1987), 279–82.

297 **Archduke Ferdinand and:** "Heir to Austria's Throne Is Slain with His Wife by Bosnian Youth to Avenge Seizure of His Country, *New York Times*, June 29, 1914.

298 **Teddy Roosevelt seethed:** A. Scott Berg, *Wilson* (New York: G. P. Putnam's Sons, 2013), 362–63.

298 **in physical gold:** Bureau of the Census, "Historical Statistics of the United States, 1789–1945," Washington DC, 1949, series M 42–55 (Foreign Trade—Value of Exports and Imports: 1790 to 1945), 244.

298 **manufactures of all kinds:** Bureau of the Census, "Historical Statistics of the United States, 1789–1945," Washington DC, 1949, series M 56–67 (Foreign Trade—Value of Merchandise Exports and Imports by Economic Classes: 1821 to 1945), 246.

299 **the balance of forces:** Berg, *Wilson*, 431–37.

299 **total federal expenditures:** Bureau of the Census, "Historical Statistics of the United States, 1789–1945," Washington DC, 1949, series P 99–108 (Federal Government Finances—Treasury Expenditures: 1789 to 1945), 299.

300 **tax quickly exceeded:** Bureau of the Census, "Historical Statistics of the United States, 1789–1945," Washington DC, 1949, series P 89–98 (Federal Government Finances—Treasury Receipts and Surplus or Deficit: 1789 to 1945), 296–98.

300 **aircraft were produced:** Bureau of the Census, "Historical Statistics of the United States, 1789–1945," Washington DC, 1949, series K 239–245 (Air Transport—Aircraft Production and Exports: 1913 to 1945), 224.

300 **the Liberty motor:** Henry Ford and Samuel Crowther, *My Life and Work* (Garden City, NY: Doubleday, Page, 1922), 246.

300 **worldwide death toll:** Kennedy, *Rise and Fall of the Great Powers*, 278.

301 **largest industrial user:** Gleason Leonard Archer, *Big Business and Radio* (New York: American Historical Company, 1939), 6–8.

302 **Marconi wanted to license:** Tom Lewis, *Empire of the Air: The Men Who Made Radio* (New York: Edward Burlingame Books, 1991), 142.

302 **into foreign hands:** Archer, *Big Business and Radio*, 5.

302 **Radio Corporation of America:** Ibid., 8; Lewis, *Empire of the Air*, 145–47.

303 **generate $45 million:** David Sarnoff to Owen D. Young, January 31, 1920, quoted in Archer, *Big Business and Radio*, 19.

303 **Goldsmith's "radiola" had:** Ibid., 13–16.

304 **listen to the fight:** "Times Square Roars for Both," *New York Times*, July 3, 1921, 5.

304 **fifteen important minutes:** Lewis, *Empire of the Air*, 159.

304 **25,000 amateur broadcasters:** "25,000 Transmitting Stations," *Radio Dealer* 1 (April 1922), 19.

305 **"Any attempts to":** "Air Advertising Can't Be Sold Now," *Radio Dealer* 1 (April 1922), 30.

305 **job for "specialists":** David Sarnoff to E. W. Rice Jr., June 17, 1922, quoted in Archer, *Big Business and Radio*, 29.

305 **advanced wiring system:** Archer, *Big Business and Radio*, 282.

306 **other local stations:** Ibid.

307 **National Broadcasting Company:** Ibid., 280.

307 **half of American homes:** Bureau of the Census, "Historical Statistics of the United States, 1789–1945," Washington DC, 1949, series G 217 (Power—Installed Generating Capacity by Class of Ownership: 1902 to 1945), 158–59.

Chapter 23: Bootlegging

307 **storm of political forces:** Daniel Okrent, *Last Call: The Rise and Fall of Prohibition* (New York: Charles Scribner's Sons, 2011), 27.

308 **the entire budget:** Bureau of the Census, "Historical Statistics of the United States, 1789–1945," Washington DC, 1949, series P 120–131 (Federal Government Finances—Internal Revenue Collections, Income, Excess Profits, Capital Stock, Gift Taxes, etc.: 1863 to 1945), 304.

308 **liquor and beer:** Bureau of the Census, "Historical Statistics of the United States, 1789–1945," Washington DC, 1949, series P 109–119 (Federal Government Finances—Internal Revenue Collections, Total and Selected Tax Sources: 1863 to 1945), 302.

308 **revenues in the billions:** Bureau of the Census, "Historical Statistics of the United States, 1789–1945," Washington DC, 1949, series P 120–131 (Federal Government Finances—Internal Revenue Collections, Income, Excess Profits, Capital Stock, Gift Taxes, etc.: 1863 to 1945), 304.

308 **United States Brewers' Association:** Irving Fisher, *Prohibition at Its Worst* (New York: Macmillan, 1927), 9–11; Okrent, *Last Call*, 85.

308 **spoken and written German:** Okrent, *Last Call*, 30.

308 **the Kaiser's birthday:** Ibid., 85.

308 **six million women:** "Women Ask Ban on Beer," *New York Times*, March 1, 1919.

308 **beer in Parliament:** "Noted Man to Fight Dry Amendment," *New York Times*, March 16, 1919.

309 **and anti-German sentiment:** Okrent, *Last Call*, 100–101.

309 **first states to ratify:** Ibid., 104.

309 **"manufacture, sale, or transportation":** Eighteenth Amendment to the United States Constitution, passed December 18, 1917, ratified January 16, 1919, Avalon Project, Lillian Goldman Law Library, Yale University.

309 **Sacramental wine, lobbied:** Okrent, *Last Call*, 186–89.

310 **"How to Finance":** Italian-American Bank, advertisement in *California Grape Grower* 2, no. 7 (June 1, 1921), 10.

310 **people in the East:** Leo G. Altmayer, advertisement in *California Grape Grower* 2, no. 7 (June 1, 1921), 14.

310 **"as if by magic" . . . :** H. F. Stoll, "Have Prohibition Laws Made Growers Prosperous?," *California Grape Grower* 2, no. 2 (January 1, 1921), 1.

310 **"otherwise law-abiding citizens":** "Modifying the Volstead Law," *California Grape Grower* 2, no. 2 (January 1, 1921), 8.

311 **"winning trade names":** "Selection of a Winning Trade Name: Some Popular New Brands," *California Grape Grower* 2, no. 2 (January 1, 1921), 11.

311 **"consumers remained woefully ignorant":** "Campaign of Education Necessary: Homebrewers Do Not Know All Our Wine Grapes," *California Grape Grower* 2, no. 12 (November 1, 1921), 3.

311 **"some euphoric poetry":** "Our Grape-Season Swan Song," *California Grape Grower* 2, no. 12 (November 1, 1921), 6.

311 **the pre-Prohibition level:** Jeffrey A. Miron and Jeffrey Zwiebel, "Alcohol Consumption During Prohibition" (working paper no. 3675, National Bureau of Economic Research, April 1991), 1–2.

312 **had personal caches:** Okrent, *Last Call*, 120.

312 **the temperance movement:** Ibid., 74.

312 **the czar's restrictions:** Ibid., 75.

313 **"Great White Hope":** David Wallace, *Capital of the World: A Portrait of New York City in the Roaring Twenties* (Guilford, CT: Lyons, 2012), 224.

313 **"the greatest Negro city":** James Weldon Johnson, "The Making of Harlem," *Survey Graphic* 6, no. 6 (March 1925).

313 **"city within a city":** Ibid.

314 **vibrant art form:** Stanley Walker, *The Night Club Era* (Baltimore: Johns Hopkins University Press, 1999), 94–95.

314 **one was expected:** Wallace, *Capital of the World*, 224.

314 **frequent contact with:** Mark Pendergrast, *For God, Country & Coca-Cola* (New York: Basic Books, 2000), 163.

314 **its addictive properties:** Ibid., 158.

315 **The drugstore chain Walgreens:** Okrent, *Last Call*, 197.
316 **authorities on the payroll:** "State Enforcement Law Unnecessary," *California Grape Grower* 2, no. 12 (November 1, 1921), 6.
316 **the article headlined:** "The Free Kingdom of Torrio," *Chicago Tribune*, November 21, 1924.
316 **Next door at 2222:** John Kobler, *Capone: The Life and World of Al Capone* (Cambridge, MA: Da Capo, 2003), 67.
317 **in a flower shop:** John H. Lyle, "Kill Dion O'Banion—The Mob Says It with Flowers: Prohibition Era's Worst Gang War Lay Ahead," excerpt from *The Dry and Lawless Years* (Englewood Cliffs, NJ: Prentice Hall, 1960), printed in the *Chicago Tribune*, November 26, 1960.
317 **six Genna brothers:** "Death Marked for 3 More of Genna Family," *Chicago Tribune*, July 10, 1925.
317 **Angelo Genna's funeral:** "Our Genna's Funeral," *Chicago Tribune*, June 1, 1925.
318 **"the worthy citizens":** "'You Can All Go Thirsty' Is Al Capone's Adieu," *Chicago Tribune*, December 6, 1927.
318 **total of $1 million:** Selwyn Rabb, *Five Families* (New York: St. Martin's Press, 2006), 42.
319 **a cautionary tale:** Ibid., 43.
319 **made it to the cover:** "Al Capone," *Time*, March 24, 1930.
319 **a ruling family:** Peter Maas, *The Valachi Papers* (New York: Harper Collins, 2003), 15–17.

Chapter 24: Banking

320 **"The country is":** Calvin Coolidge, "Final Address to Congress," December 7, 1928, American Presidency Project, University of California, Santa Barbara.
320 **26 million registered vehicles:** Bureau of the Census, "Historical Statistics of the United States, 1789–1945," Washington DC, 1949, series K 225–235 (Motor Vehicles—Production, Registrations, and Motor Fuel Usage: 1900 to 1945), 223.
320 **electrified American homes:** Bureau of the Census, "Historical Statistics of the United States, 1789–1945," Washington DC, 1949, series G 225–233 (Power—Electric Utilities, Sales to Ultimate Consumers: 1902 to 1945), 159.
320 **postwar budget surpluses:** Bureau of the Census, "Historical Statistics of the United States, 1789–1945," Washington DC, 1949, series P 89–98 (Federal Government Finances—Treasury Receipts, and Surplus or Deficit: 1789 to 1945), 296.
321 **world's great creditor:** Paul Kennedy, *The Rise and Fall of the Great Powers: Economic Change and Military Conflict from 1500 to 2000* (New York: Random House, 1987), 281.
321 **Germany owed reparations:** Liaquat Ahamed, *Lords of Finance: The Bankers Who Broke the World* (New York: Penguin Books, 2009), 207.
321 **"deeply indebted to":** "Britain Warns Dec. 15 Payment Imperils Lausanne," "Paris Note Pleads France Is Bulwark," *New York Times*, December 2, 1932.
321 **"species of legalized larceny":** Calvin Coolidge, "Inaugural Address," March 4, 1925, American Presidency Project, University of California, Santa Barbara.
322 **"master of the market":** I. B. N. Gnaedinger, "Radio Has Made a New Millionaire," *New York Times*, March 18, 1928.
322 **Women's magazines contained:** John Kenneth Galbraith, *The Great Crash, 1929* (Boston: Mariner Books, 1997), 52, 76.
322 **sponsored new vehicles:** Ibid., 46–48.
322 **those margin accounts:** "Stock Exchange Practices," Senate Report, 1934, cited in Galbraith, *Great Crash*, 78.
322 **in hard dollars:** Milton Friedman and Anna Jacobson Schwartz, *The Great Contraction, 1929–1933* (Princeton, NJ: Princeton University Press, 2009), 21.
322 **worth $4 billion:** "A.T.&T. Valued in Market at $4,047,241,500, Up $138,198,500 in Day, with Shares 307½," *New York Times*, September 19, 1929.
323 **"long dance of":** Galbraith, *Great Crash*, 179.
323 **language masking desperation:** "Bankers Halt Stock Debacle," *Wall Street Journal*, October 25, 1929.
324 **comparisons to Alexander Hamilton:** David Cannadine, *Mellon: An American Life* (New York: Alfred A. Knopf, 2006), 396.
324 **banking fortune made:** Ibid., 277.

325 **deposits of $28 billion:** Bureau of the Census, "Historical Statistics of the United States, 1789–1945," Washington DC, 1949, series N 99–106 (Savings Banks and Deposits—Savings and Other Time Deposits and Depositors: 1910 to 1942), 271.
325 **256 small banks:** Friedman and Schwartz, *Great Contraction*, 25.
325 **Bank of America:** Kenneth S. Davis, *FDR: The New Deal Years 1933–1937* (New York: Random House, 1986), 62.
326 **New York buildings:** "Bank of U.S. Closes Doors; State Takes Over Affairs; Aid Offered to Depositors," *New York Times*, December 12, 1930, 2.
326 **"most colossal mistake":** *Annual Report of Superintendent of Banks*, State of New York, December 31, 1931, quoted in Friedman and Schwartz, *Great Contraction*, 26.
326 **Broderick announced that:** "Bank of U.S. Closes Doors."
326 **"large crowds of bewildered":** "Throngs Are Calm as Branches Close," *New York Times*, December 12, 1930.
326 **the official impression:** Friedman and Schwartz, *Great Contraction*, 26.
327 **and French counterparts:** Ahamed, *Lords of Finance*, 333.
327 **Germans agreed to pay:** Ibid., 199, 336.
327 **the gold standard:** Ben Bernanke and Harold James, "The Gold Standard, Deflation, and Financial Crisis in the Great Depression: An International Comparison," in Ben S. Bernanke, *Essays on the Great Depression* (Princeton: Princeton University Press, 2004), 77–78.
328 **Religiously adhering to:** Freidman and Schwartz, *Great Contraction*, 169–82.
328 **England left the:** Bernanke and James, "The Gold Standard," 74 (table 1).
328 **small banks had failed:** Bureau of the Census, "Historical Statistics of the United States, 1789–1945," Washington DC, 1949, series N 135–140 (Bank Suspensions—Number of Suspensions: 1864 to 1945), 273.
328 **breadwinners out of work:** Bureau of the Census, "Historical Statistics of the United States, 1789–1945," Washington DC, 1949, series D 62–76 (Labor Force—Industrial Distribution of Employed (NICB): 1900 to 1945), 65.
328 **Total income in:** Bureau of the Census, "Historical Statistics of the United States, 1789–1945," Washington DC, 1949, series 101–116 (Gross National Product or Expenditures (Revised, July 1947): 1929 to 1945), 12.
328 **plummeted to a value:** Bureau of the Census, "Historical Statistics of the United States, 1789–1945," Washington DC, 1949, series H 1–26 (Construction Expenditures—Estimates: 1915 to 1945), 168.
329 **Automobile production had:** Bureau of the Census, "Historical Statistics of the United States, 1789–1945," Washington DC, 1949, series K 225–235 (Motor Vehicles—Production, Registrations, and Motor Fuel Usage: 1900 to 1945), 223.
329 **Revenues on American farms:** Bureau of the Census, "Historical Statistics of the United States, 1789–1945," Washington DC, 1949, series E 88–104 (General Statistics—Farm Income, Prices Received and Paid: 1910 to 1945), 99.
329 **number of declared farms:** Bureau of the Census, "Historical Statistics of the United States, 1789–1945," Washington DC, 1949, series E 43–60 (General Statistics—Farm Tenure, by Color and Tenure of Operator: 1900 to 1945), 96.
329 **prices were half:** Bureau of the Census, "Historical Statistics of the United States, 1789–1945," Washington DC, 1949, series E 117–134 (Livestock—Number, Value Per Head, Production and Prices: 1867 to 1945), 101; Bureau of the Census, "Historical Statistics of the United States, 1789–1945," Washington DC, 1949, series E 152–164 (Dairying—Cows Kept for Milk on Farms, Milk Produced and Sold, Manufactured Dairy Products: 1849 to 1945), 103.
329 **The harvested acreage:** Bureau of the Census, "Historical Statistics of the United States, 1789–1945," Washington DC, 1949, series E 181–195 (Crop Statistics—Corn and Wheat: 1859 to 1945), 106; Bureau of the Census, "Historical Statistics of the United States, 1789–1945," Washington DC, 1949, series E 231–243 (Crop Statistics—Oats, Barley, Flaxseed, and Soybeans: 1839 to 1945), 107.
329 **yield of pears:** Bureau of the Census, "Historical Statistics of the United States, 1789–1945," Washington DC, 1949, series E 231–243 (Fruits and Vegetables—Apples, Peaches, Pears, Grapes, Oranges, and Grapefruit: 1889 to 1945), 110.
329 **debt owed collectively:** Bureau of the Census, "Historical Statistics of the United States, 1789–1945," Washington DC, 1949, series E 244–255 (Farm Credit—Farm-Mortgage Debt, Loans, Interest: 1910 to 1945), 111.
329 **"I'm not complaining":** "Capone Moralizes on Eve of Sentence," *New York Times*, July 30, 1931.

330 **unemployment headed to:** Bureau of the Census, "Historical Statistics of the United States, 1789–1945," Washington DC, 1949, series D 62–76 (Labor Force—Industrial Distribution of Employed (NICB): 1900 to 1945), 65.

330 **withdraw printed currency:** Friedman and Schwartz, *Great Contraction*, 37.

330 **raised income taxes:** Ibid., 47.

330 **"The fundamental issue":** Herbert Hoover, "Address in Indianapolis, Indiana," October 28, 1932, American Presidency Project, University of California, Santa Barbara.

331 **Luther Marr, who:** "Buyer of Farm Slain After Forced Sale," *New York Times*, February 1, 1933.

331 **"revolution in the countryside":** Davis, *FDR*, 71.

331 **moratorium on foreclosures:** "Farm Moratorium Made Nation-Wide," *New York Times*, February 1, 1933.

332 **the situation worsened:** Davis, *FDR*, 25.

332 **"only thing we have to fear":** Franklin Roosevelt, "First Inaugural Address," March 3, 1933, Presidency Project, University of California, Santa Barbara.

333 **issued a presidential proclamation:** "Roosevelt Orders 4-Day Bank Holiday, Puts Embargo on Gold, Calls Congress," *New York Times*, March 6, 1933.

333 **to compel "hoarders":** "Gold Inflow Brings $20,000,000 in Day," *New York Times*, March 11, 1933.

333 **"the simple fact":** Franklin Roosevelt, "First Fireside Chat," March 12, 1933, Franklin D. Roosevelt Presidential Library, Marist College.

334 **"beer with alcohol":** "Roosevelt Asks for Beer to Provide Needed Revenue," *New York Times*, March 14, 1833.

334 **total market value:** "Record Rise in Shares," *New York Times*, March 16, 1933.

334 **"increase purchasing power":** "Text of the Administration Farm Relief Bill Submitted to Congress," *New York Times*, March 17, 1933.

335 **Automobile production doubled:** Bureau of the Census, "Historical Statistics of the United States, 1789–1945," Washington DC, 1949, series K 225–235 (Motor Vehicles—Production, Registrations, and Motor Fuel Usage: 1900 to 1945), 223.

335 **Gross national product:** Bureau of the Census, "Historical Statistics of the United States, 1789–1945," Washington DC, 1949, series 101–116 (Gross National Product or Expenditures (Revised, July 1947): 1929 to 1945), 12.

Chapter 25: Film

337 **"the most remarkable":** "A Fine Novel of the Civil War," *New York Times*, July 5, 1936.

337 **over 500,000 copies:** Richard Harwell, "Since 1936, a Landmark in American Fiction," *Chicago Tribune*, July 2, 1961.

337 **"I beg, urge, coax":** Telegram to David Selznick from Kay Brown, quoted in Thomas Schatz, *The Genius of the System: Hollywood Filmmaking in the Studio Era* (Minneapolis: University of Minnesota Press, 2010), 180.

337 **But Selznick waited:** David O. Selznick, *The Creation of "Gone with the Wind" and Other Motion Picture Classics*, ed. Rudy Behlmer (New York: Viking, 1972) 138–39.

337 **one million copies:** Harwell, "Since 1936, a Landmark."

337 **his own productions:** Schatz, *The Genius of the System*, 176.

338 **going to exceed $2 million:** David O. Selznick to Edward W. Butcher (production manager), September 23, 1938, quoted in David O. Selznick, *Memo from David O. Selznick*, ed. Rudy Behlmer (New York: Viking Press, 1972), 164; Scott Eyman, *Lion of Hollywood: The Life and Legend of Louis B. Mayer* (New York: Simon & Schuster, 2005), 258.

339 **Forty-fifth and Broadway:** Douglas Gomery, *The Hollywood Studio System* (London: Palgrave, 2015), 30–31.

339 **strong distribution operation:** Ibid., 30.

339 **offered Goldwyn Pictures:** Schatz, *Genius of the System*, 30.

340 **For $75,000 Loew's:** Ibid., 30–31.

340 **grossed $3 million:** Ibid., 63.

340 **leading the restructuring:** Michael Conant, *Antitrust in the Motion Picture Industry* (Berkeley: University of California Press, 1960), 31.

341 **a company spun:** Ibid.

342 **for 50 percent:** Eyman, *Lion of Hollywood*, 260.

342 **Selznick had to make:** David O. Selznick to Daniel T O'Shea, November 18, 1938, in Selznick, *Memo from David O. Selznick*, 171–73.

342 **"occasional accented word":** David O. Selznick to Will Price, March 25, 1939, in Selznick, *Memo from David O. Selznick*, 199.

343 **slovenliness of Rhett's suits:** David O. Selznick to Mr. Klune and Mr. Lambert, April 17, 1939, in Selznick, *Memo from David O. Selznick*, 203.

343 **exceeded $4 million:** David O. Selznick to Howard Dietz, May 2, 1939, in Selznick, *Memo from David O. Selznick*, 204.

343 **"the largest gross":** Ibid.

343 **"the Horatio Alger":** Douglas W. Churchill, "Now Mickey Mouse Enters Art's Temple," *New York Times*, June 3, 1934.

343 **Mickey Mouse's licensed image:** L. H. Robbins, "Mickey Mouse Emerges as Economist," *New York Times*, March 10, 1935.

343 **Mickey Mouse watches:** "Watch Concern Credits Mickey Mouse with $5,000,000 Sales in Year and a Half," *New York Times*, January 27, 1935.

344 **Walt Disney's cartoons:** "Mr. Shumiatsky on American Films," *New York Times*, August 4, 1935.

344 **"Disney is really showing":** "Mickey Mouse Portrays Capitalist, Reds Assert," *New York Times*, December 11, 1935.

344 **might cost as much:** Churchill, "Now Mickey Mouse Enters Art's Temple."

344 **scientific art school:** Neal Gabler, *Walt Disney: The Triumph of the American Imagination* (New York: Vintage Books, 2006), 258.

345 **wiping away tears:** Ibid., 272.

345 **total audience at:** "'Snow White,' First to Remain for Fourth Week at the Music Hall, Expected to Draw 800,000," *New York Times*, January 31, 1938, 15.

346 **set a minimum:** David O. Selznick to Vice President Al Lichtman, October 20, 1939, in Selznick, *Memo from David O. Selznick*, 225–26.

346 **The code had caused:** Gomery, *Hollywood Studio System*, 67.

346 **"Frankly, my dear'":** David O. Selznick to Will H. Hays, October 20, 1939, in Selznick, *Memo from David O. Selznick*, 221.

347 **"to Georgia, it":** "G with the W," *Time*, December 25, 1939.

Chapter 26: Flight

349 **In 1934 defense spending:** Bureau of the Census, "Historical Statistics of the United States, 1789–1945," Washington DC, 1949, series P 99–108 (Government Finances—Treasury Expenditures: 1789 to 1945), 299.

350 **kidnapped from his bedroom:** A. Scott Berg, *Lindbergh* (New York: G. P. Putnam's Sons, 1998), 238–39.

351 **tours of their factories:** Journal entry, October 23, 1938, in Charles A. Lindbergh, *The Wartime Journals of Charles A. Lindbergh* (New York: Harcourt Brace Jovanovich, 1970), 101.

351 **the Munich Agreement:** "Munich Pact," September 29, 1938, Avalon Project, Lillian Goldman Law Library, Yale University.

352 **wild, cheering crowds:** "Peace Aid Pledged," *New York Times*, October 1, 1938.

352 **"the second time":** Chamberlain's reference is to the Treaty of Berlin (1878), which concerned affairs in Eastern Europe after the Russo-Turkish War.

352 **the German Eagle:** Journal entry, October 18, 1938, in Lindbergh, *Wartime Journals of Charles A. Lindbergh*, 102.

352 **Lindbergh's summer visit:** Ibid., 101.

352 **"far ahead of anything":** Ibid.

352 **"I am anxious":** Journal entry, October 25, 1938, in Lindbergh, *Wartime Journals of Charles A. Lindbergh*, 110.

353 **final wartime debts:** Liaquat Ahamed, *Lords of Finance: The Bankers Who Broke the World* (New York: Penguin Books, 2009), 430–31.

353 **American economy was:** Bureau of the Census, "Historical Statistics of the United States, 1789–1945," Washington DC, 1949, series D 62–76 (Labor Force—Industrial Distribution of Employed (NICB): 1900 to 1945), 65.

354 **the Nazis announced:** "Reich Bars Jews in Trade," *New York Times*, November 13, 1938.

354 **"this week's holocaust":** "Arrests Continue," *New York Times*, November 13, 1938.

354 **"these men are building":** "Hoover Protests Brutality in Reich," *New York Times*, November 14, 1938.

354 **terror against Jews** and **"sense of order"**: Journal entry, November 13, 1938, in Lindbergh, *Wartime Journals of Charles A. Lindbergh*, 115.

355 **of a top-secret:** A. J. Baime, *The Arsenal of Democracy* (Boston: Houghton Mifflin Harcourt, 2014), 52–54.

355 **their American owners:** Ibid., 57–62.

355 **"The aggressor country":** Max Werner, *The Military Strength of the Powers*, trans. Edward Fitzgerald (New York: Modern Age Books, 1939), 6.

355 **"The industrial potential":** Ibid., 5.

355 **the American military:** Davis, *FDR: Into the Storm, 1937–1940* (New York: Random House, 1993), 372.

355 **Luftwaffe's potential strength:** H. H. Arnold, *Global Mission* (Blue Ridge Summit, PA: TAB Books, 1989), 177.

356 **"president came straight"** and **"a new barracks":** Ibid.

356 **the sale of arms:** George Gallup, "The American Mind: A Test of Democracy," *New York Times*, April 24, 1938.

357 **"replace those factories":** "Opposition Forms to Neutrality Bill," *New York Times*, June 17, 1938, 5.

357 **"meddling in foreign affairs":** "Roosevelt Decries 'Neutrality' Effect," *New York Times*, August 30, 1939, 3.

357 **Churchill was once again:** Davis, *FDR*, 491.

357 **"England and France":** "Lindbergh's Talk on Arms Embargo," *New York Times*, October 14, 1939.

358 **"more important for":** Ibid.

358 **"I am absolutely convinced":** Davis, *FDR*, 504.

358 **2,600 planes for 1940:** "Neutral Nations Bid for American Planes," *New York Times*, November 5, 1939.

358 **$1.3 billion over:** Davis, *FDR*, 537; Leland C. Speers, "$1,300,000,000 Bill for Navy Will Ask 95 New Warships," *New York Times*, November 5, 1939.

358 **nine hundred planes:** Bureau of the Census, "Historical Statistics of the United States, 1789–1945," Washington DC, 1949, series K 293–245 (Air Transport—Aircraft Production and Exports: 1913 to 1945), 224.

359 **"picture of the Luftwaffe":** Berg, *Lindbergh*, 387.

359 **"The French army":** Arnold, *Global Mission*, 199.

359 **enlisted William Knudsen:** Davis, *FDR*, 553.

360 **"Anybody that knows":** James C. Hagerty, "Republican Holds Rival Exaggerated Picture of Aircraft Output," *New York Times*, November 2, 1940.

360 **Knudsen tasked Ford:** Charles E. Sorensen, *My Forty Years with Ford* (Detroit: Wayne State University Press, 2006), 275.

361 **"On one side":** Ibid., 278.

361 **the "snail's pace"** and **"custom made plane":** Ibid., 280.

362 **increase the production:** Ibid., 282.

362 **"a mile long":** Ibid., 283.

362 **thirty-ton tanks:** "Procurement: 100 Days," *Time*, October 7, 1940.

362 **"fairest price, fastest":** Ibid.

362 **federal government's expenditures:** Bureau of the Census, "Historical Statistics of the United States, 1789–1945," Washington DC, 1949, series P 99–108 (Government Finances—Treasury Expenditures: 1789 to 1945), 299.

363 **were against sin:** Frank L. Kluckhorn, "President Hopes We Can Avoid War," *New York Times*, July 2, 1941.

363 **"troop movements toward Burma":** "New Troop Moves," *New York Times*, December 7, 1941.

363 **"on our own shoulders":** Journal entry, December 8, 1941, in Lindbergh, *Wartime Journals of Charles A. Lindbergh*, 561.

364 **4 million passenger vehicles:** Bureau of the Census, "Historical Statistics of the United States, 1789–1945," Washington DC, 1949, series K 225–235 (Motor Vehicles—Production, Registrations, and Motor Fuel Usage: 1900 to 1945), 223.

364 **and aircraft makers:** Bureau of the Census, "Historical Statistics of the United States, 1789–1945," Washington DC, 1949, series K 239–245 (Air Transport—Aircraft Production and Exports: 1913 to 1945), 224.

364 **no shortages of iron ore:** Bureau of the Census, "Historical Statistics of the United States, 1789–1945," Washington DC, 1949, series G 93–101 (Metals, Ferrous—Iron Ore, Pig Iron, and Ferro-Alloys: 1810 to 1945), 149.

364 **Beef, pork, wheat:** Bureau of the Census, "Historical Statistics of the United States, 1789–1945," Washington DC, 1949, series E 117–134 (Livestock—Number, Value per Head, Production and Prices: 1867 to 1945), 101.

Chapter 27: Suburbia

367 **"many electric refrigerators":** William J. Levitt, "Let's Build Up—Not Tear Down," speech delivered October 23, 1950, at *Herald-Tribune* Forum, in *Vital Speeches of the Day*, vol. 16, 70.

368 **Servicemen's Readjustment Act:** "Roosevelt Signs 'G.I. Bill of Rights,'" *New York Times*, June 23, 1944.

369 **"search for accommodations":** "Helping to Perpetuate the Housing Shortage," *Chicago Tribune*, December 22, 1945.

369 **a full-blown crisis:** Bureau of the Census, "Historical Statistics of the United States, 1789–1945," Washington DC, 1949, series H 81–83 (Housing—Available Housing Units and Total Families, Nonfarm Areas: 1900 to 1938), 173.

369 **Residential construction had peaked:** Bureau of the Census, "Historical Statistics of the United States, 1789–1945," Washington DC, 1949, series H 1–26 (Construction Expenditures—Estimates: 1915 to 1945), 168.

369 **Strathmore at Manhasset was:** "Housing: Up from the Potato Fields," *Time*, July 3, 1950.

369 **Until the New Deal:** Kenneth T. Jackson, *Crabgrass Frontier: The Suburbanization of the United States* (New York: Oxford University Press, 1987), 203–6.

370 **down-payment requirement was waived:** Gordon H. Sellon and Deana VanNahmen, "The Securitization of Housing Finance," *Economic Review* (July 1988).

370 **gambled on 1,200 flat:** "Nation's Biggest Housebuilder," *Life*, August 23, 1948, 74–78.

370 **"You marvel at":** Levitt, "Let's Build Up."

370 **Sears and Montgomery Ward:** Sears, Roebuck and Co., *Sears Modern Homes Catalogue* (New York: Dover, 2006).

371 **"identical piles of":** "Housing: Up from the Potato Fields."

371 **"Pricing each home identically":** "Nation's Biggest Housebuilder."

372 **social and cultural critics:** Jane Jacobs, *The Death and Life of Great American Cities* (New York: Vintage Books, 1992); Herbert J. Gans, *The Levittowners: Ways of Life and Politics in a New Suburban Community* (New York: Columbia University Press, 1982).

372 **"neither the urbanity":** Jackson, *Crabgrass Frontier*, 244.

373 **"proud country home-owners":** Levitt, "Let's Build Up."

373 **700,000 immigrants arrived:** Bureau of the Census, "Historical Statistics of the United States, 1789–1945," Washington DC, 1949, series B 304–330 (Immigration—Immigrants by Country: 1820 to 1945), 32.

374 **The differentiating factors:** William H. Whyte, *The Organization Man* (Philadelphia: University of Pennsylvania Press, 2002), 299.

374 **to "inconspicuous consumption"** and **"impulse toward egalitarianism":** Ibid., 312.

374 **Levittown homes were advertised:** Levitt & Sons, advertisement, *New York Times*, January 10, 1954, section 3.

375 **periodic and opportunistic shifting:** Whyte, *Organization Man*, 303.

376 **"To have a hand":** Alexis de Tocqueville, *Democracy in America and Two Essays on America*, ed. Isaac Kramnick, trans. Gerald Bevan (London: Penguin Books, 2003), 284.

377 **"largest steel expansion":** Thomas E. Mullaney, "Delaware Valley Undergoes a Boom," *New York Times*, February 29, 1952.

377 **"I wanted to make"** and **"like to be associated":** "Housing: Up from the Potato Fields."

377 **"If we sell one house":** David Kushner, *Levittown* (New York: Walker Publishing Company, 2009), 66.

377 **"solve a housing problem":** Jackson, *Crabgrass Frontier*, 241.

378 **vested interest in:** Ibid., 206.

378 **"protection from adverse":** Federal Housing Administration, "Underwriting Manual: Underwriting and Valuation Procedure Under Title II of the National Housing Act," 1936, part 2, section 2, no. 210.

379 **from Walt himself:** Kushner, *Levittown*, 74.

379 **on Deepgreen Lane:** Ibid., 80–82.

379 **buy the home:** Ibid., 82.

379 **"He's probably a nice guy"**: "Integration Troubles Beset Northern Town," *Life*, September 2, 1957, 43–45.

380 **order was restored**: William G. Weart, "Mob Again Chased from Negro Home," *New York Times*, August 21, 1957.

Chapter 28: Television

381 **an overnight success**: "Cinema: Television," *Time*, May 18, 1931.

381 **missiles and torpedoes**: Gary R. Edgerton, *The Columbia History of American Television* (New York: Columbia University Press, 2009), 70–71.

382 **newsreels at movie theaters**: Raymond Fielding, *March of Time, 1935–1951* (New York: Oxford University Press, 1978), 273.

382 **started at $149**: Admiral, advertisement, *New York Times*, October 8, 1950, 63.

382 **26 million households**: Bureau of the Census, "Historical Statistics of the United States, Colonial Times to 1970," Washington DC, September 1975, series R 93–105 (Radio and Television Stations, Sets Produced, and Households with Sets: 1921 to 1970), 796.

383 **play the role**: Boyne Steven Sanders and Tom Gilbert, *Desilu: The Story of Lucille Ball and Desi Arnaz* (New York: Harper Collins, 2011), 27–28.

383 **company, Desilu Productions**: Ibid., 37–39.

383 **Ricky Ricardo was**: "Desi Arnaz, TV Pioneer, Is Dead at 69," *New York Times*, December 3, 1986, D26.

383 **"Lucy, you goh suhm esplainin'"**: Author's phonetic rendering.

383 **revenues to surpass those of radio**: Bureau of the Census, "Historical Statistics of the United States, Colonial Times to 1970," Washington DC, September 1975, series R 106–122 (Radio Advertising Expenditures, Finances, and Employment: 1935 to 1970), 797; and series R 123–139 (Television Advertising Expenditures, Finances, and Employment: 1945 to 1970), 798.

384 **horse-drawn carriage**: Ronald Reagan, *An American Life* (New York: Threshold Editions, 2011), 25.

384 **partial football scholarship**: Ibid., 45.

384 **enthusiastically cast his ballot**: Ibid., 66.

385 **radio sports announcer**: Ibid, 65.

385 **$5 and bus fare**: Ibid., 66.

385 **$200 per week**: Ibid., 105.

386 **"You had seven companies"**: Ibid., 117.

386 **"New Dealer to the core"**: Ibid., 105.

387 **with over 250,000 people**: Ibid., 128.

387 **self-described "liberal Democrat"**: Ibid., 134.

389 **suspected the actress of**: Ibid., 128.

389 **the Senate appropriated**: W. H. Lawrence, "Senate, 85–1, Votes McCarthy $214,000," *New York Times*, February 3, 1954.

389 **Murrow now produced**: Jack Gould, "Television in Review: Murrow vs. McCarthy," *New York Times*, March 11, 1954, 23.

389 **"one man committee" . . .**: Transcript of "A Report on Senator Joseph R. McCarthy," *See It Now*, CBS-TV, March 9, 1954, Moffitt Library, University of California at Berkeley.

390 **television had become**: Robert Bendiner, "How Much Has TV Changed Campaigning?" *New York Times*, November 2, 1952, 276.

391 **turn down the chance**: "Sport: Kickoff," *Time*, September 9, 1940.

391 **were marginally viable**: Michael MacCambridge, *America's Game* (New York: Anchor Books, 2005), 75.

391 **owner had to put up**: Ibid., 79.

392 **"rougher every year"**: "Savagery on Sunday," *Life*, October 24, 1955, 133–38.

392 **1958 championship game**: Louis Effrat, "Colts Beat Giants, Win in Overtime," *New York Times*, December 29, 1958, 1.

392 **Forty-five million people**: MacCambridge, *America's Game*, 112.

393 **Hunt reached out**: Ibid., 118–19.

393 **oil man in Texas**: Ibid., 121.

393 **American Football League**: Ibid., 124–25.

393 **team slated for Dallas**: Ibid., 125.

393 **share of financial woes**: Ibid., 132.

393 **$170,00 per season; $75,000 from theirs:** Ibid., 171.

394 **deal with CBS:** "Each Club to Get $320,000 a Year," *New York Times*, January 11, 1962, 39.

394 **$36 million deal:** MacCambridge, *America's Game*, 200.

Chapter 29: Roads

395 **Shell Oil Company:** Col. Harland Sanders, *Life as I Have Known It Has Been Finger Lickin' Good* (Carol Stream, IL: Creation House, 2011), 51.

395 **caught on fire:** Ibid., 75.

395 **"You can sleep a man":** Ibid., 76.

395 **consequences for the course:** Ibid., 87.

396 **"greatest public works program":** John D. Morris, "Eisenhower Signs Road Bill; Weeks Allocates 1.1 Billion," *New York Times*, June 30, 1956.

396 **1-cent-per-gallon gas tax:** Joseph C. Ingraham, "U.S. Gasoline Tax Up a Penny Today," *New York Times*, July 1, 1956, 31.

396 **$164,000 for his business . . . :** Sanders, *Life as I Have Known It*, 88.

397 **honorific title of "Colonel":** Ibid., 99.

397 **earning Sanders over $100,000:** Ibid., 114.

397 **buy Sanders out for $2 million:** Ibid., 125.

398 **Lily-Tulip Cup Company:** Ray Kroc, *Grinding It Out: The Making of McDonald's* (New York: St. Martin's, 1987), 54–55.

398 **"to go" cup:** Ibid., 42.

398 **Walgreens with its soda:** Ibid., 55.

398 **"monument to capitalism":** Ibid., 61.

399 **McDonald's had three:** Ibid., 9.

399 **"some latter-day Newton":** Ibid., 71.

399 **authorized to charge:** Ibid., 79.

399 **Rolling Green Country Club:** John F. Love, *McDonald's: Behind the Arches* (New York: Bantam, 1995), 75.

400 **initial setup costs:** Ibid., 73.

400 **life savings of $25,000:** Ibid., 80.

400 **profits for the couple:** Ibid., 81–82.

400 **into the burgeoning suburbs:** Ibid., 82–85.

400 **opted for discipline:** Ibid., 85–86.

401 **Franchising revealed a duality:** Ibid., 86.

401 **"294 highway stops":** "Corporations: Meat, Potatoes & Money," *Time*, November 3, 1961.

401 **revenues approaching $1 billion:** "Food: The Burger That Conquered the Country," *Time*, September 17, 1973.

401 **"a wide gash":** John Steinbeck, *Travels with Charley in Search of America* (New York: Penguin Books, 2002), 71.

402 **revenues from shipping:** Bureau of the Census, "Historical Statistics of the United States, Colonial Times to 1970," Washington DC, September 1975, series Q 23–35 (Operating Revenues, by Type of Transport: 1936 to 1970), 708; and series Q 331–345 (Railroad Freight Traffic and Revenue: 1890 to 1970), 732–33.

402 **the new category:** Herbert Brean, "Discount Houses Stir Up a $5 Billion Fuss," *Life*, August 9, 1954, 53–61.

403 **four thousand stores:** Ibid.

404 **The "loss-leader":** Walter Henry Nelson, *The Great Discount Delusion* (New York: David McKay, 1965), 17.

404 **the loss-leading practices:** Ibid., 68.

404 **populations as small:** Sam Walton, *Sam Walton: Made in America* (New York: Bantam, 1993), 59.

405 **"or socially inevitable":** Jane Jacobs, *The Death and Life of Great American Cities* (New York: Vintage Books, 1992), 7.

406 **producer of oil:** Michael Ratner and Carol Glover, "U.S. Energy: Overview and Key Statistics," *Congressional Research Service*, July 27, 2014.

406 **running trade deficits:** Bureau of the Census, "Historical Statistics of the United States, Colonial Times to 1970," Washington DC, September 1975, series U 1–25 (Balance of International Payments: 1790 to 1970), 864.

Chapter 30: Computing

409 **on a cold morning:** Robert S. McNamara, *In Retrospect: The Tragedy and Lessons of Vietnam* (New York: Vintage Books, 1996), 13–16.

410 **"our world conflicts":** "Eisenhower's Farewell Address to the Nation," January 17, 1961, American Presidency Project, University of California, Berkeley.

410 **more than the total:** McNamara, *In Retrospect*, 22.

411 **hired by Ford:** David Halberstam, *The Best and the Brightest*, 20th anniv. ed. (New York: Ballantine Books, 1993), 227–29.

411 **"an IBM machine":** Stephen Braun, "Robert McNamara Dies at 93; Architect of the Vietnam War," *Los Angeles Times*, July 7, 2009.

411 **IBM had been . . . ; 1960 revenues had grown:** 1968 Annual Report.

412 **with an army surgeon; shared with Hollerith:** Leon Edgar Truesdell, *The Development of Punch Card Tabulation in the Bureau of the Census, 1890–1940* (Washington DC: Government Printing Office, 1965), 30.

412 **punch card, could support:** Ibid., 35.

413 **Hollerith made full:** Ibid., 47.

413 **thousands of cards:** Ibid., 48.

413 **backed by three patents:** Ibid., 37–40.

413 **agreed to lease fifty:** John W. Noble, Secretary of the Interior, to the 52nd Congress, in 1st sess., March 28, 1892, "A Report of Examination and Review of the Census Office," Ex. Doc. No. 69, 11.

413 **62,622,250 punch cards:** Ibid.

413 **machine on a cover:** *Scientific American* 63, no. 9 (August 30, 1890).

414 **consolidated into a new:** "Tabulating Concerns Unite," *New York Times*, June 10, 1911, 16.

414 **Computing-Tabulating-Recording:** John Moody, *The Truth About Trusts* (New York: Moody, 1904), 269.

414 **banker behind the organization:** Emerson W. Pugh, *Building IBM* (Cambridge, MA: MIT Press, 1995), 24–25.

414 **into regulatory difficulties:** Ibid., 32–33.

414 **Watson was hired . . . changed its name:** Ibid., 28.

414 **Businesses such as Time Inc.:** Thomas J. Watson, *Father, Son & Co.*, ed. Peter Petre (New York: Bantam, 2000), 195.

415 **"Roosevelt's welfare, price control":** Pugh, *Building IBM*, 33.

415 **summoned Watson to:** Tom Watson Sr. to Adolf Hitler, June 1940, quoted in Watson, *Father, Son & Co.*, 55.

415 **"manage vast quantities":** Ibid., 57.

415 **"followed him through":** Ibid., 112.

416 **cards for all of its policyholders:** Ibid., 195.

416 **these "electronic brains":** "New Giant 'Brain' Does Wizard Work," *New York Times*, August 24, 1947.

416 **"add one and one":** Watson, *Father, Son & Co.*, 189.

416 **Semi-Autonomous Ground Environment:** Pugh, *Building IBM*, 213–19.

416 **it also introduced networking:** Ibid., 218.

417 **first satellite in space:** Dwight D. Eisenhower, *Waging Peace* (Garden City, NY: Doubleday, 1965), 210–11.

417 **formation of NASA:** Ibid., 257–60.

417 **looked like American Airlines:** "Computer Used on Flight Plans to Save Both Time and Money," *New York Times*, March 25, 1962.

418 **"how much merchandise" and "utilizer of information":** Sam Walton, *Sam Walton: Made in America* (New York: Bantam Books, 1993), 110.

418 **made his annual quota:** Ross Perot, *My Life & the Principles for Success* (Arlington, TX: Summit, 1996), 71–72.

418 **found Electronic Data Systems:** Ibid., 73.

418 **readied itself to go public:** John Brooks, *The Go-Go Years* (New York: Weybright & Talley, 1973), 17.

420 **net worth close to $200 million:** "H. Ross Perot: America's First Welfare Billionaire," *Ramparts*, November 1968.

420 ***Fortune* declared him:** Arthur M. Louis, "The Fastest Richest Texan Ever," *Fortune*, November 1968.

Chapter 31: Start-ups

421 **people expected the moon:** George E. Mueller, "In the Next Decade: A Lunar Base, Space Laboratories and a Shuttle Service," *New York Times*, July 21, 1969.

422 **"race to the moon":** Harry Schwartz, "Capitalist Moon or Socialist Moon?" *New York Times*, July 21, 1969.

422 **business of semiconductors:** T. R. Reid, *The Chip* (New York: Random House, 2001), 148–51.

422 **air force, and later, NASA:** Ibid., 150.

423 **at Shockley Semiconductor:** Leslie Berlin, *The Man Behind the Microchip: Robert Noyce and the Invention of Silicon Valley* (New York: Oxford University Press, 2005), 68.

423 **suggested to Rock:** Ibid., 78–79.

423 **Fairchild Camera and Instrument:** Ibid., 82–84.

423 **putting in $1.38 million:** Ibid., 88.

423 **$3 million collectively:** Ibid., 89.

423 **first customer was IBM:** Donald T. Valentine, "Early Bay Area Venture Capitalists: Shaping the Economic and Business Landscape," Regional Oral History Office, Bancroft Library, University of California, Berkeley, 2010.

423 **named Warren Buffett:** Berlin, *Man Behind the Microchip*, 189.

424 **$2.5 million, including:** Ibid.

424 **initial public offering:** Intel Corporation, *1971 Annual Report* (San Jose, CA: Arthur Young, January 24, 1971).

426 **student, Nolan Bushnell:** David A. Kaplan, *The Silicon Boys and Their Valley of Dreams* (New York: Perennial, 2000), 87.

427 **business, Atari Inc.:** Ibid., 88.

427 **"space age pinball machine":** Peter Ross Range, "The Space Age Pinball Machine," *New York Times*, September 15, 1974.

427 **Silicon Valley was filling:** Walter Isaacson, *Steve Jobs* (New York: Simon & Schuster, 2011), 42.

427 **"Have Fun, Make Money"** and **"hippie-looking kid":** Ibid., 43.

428 **"on the factory tour":** "Early Bay Area Venture Capitalists," 33.

428 **sense of loyalty:** William H. Whyte, *The Organization Man* (Philadelphia: University of Pennsylvania Press, 2002), 161.

429 **routinely treated coworkers:** Isaacson, *Steve Jobs*, 43.

429 **freshman year at Harvard:** Stephen Manes and Paul Andrews, *Gates* (New York: Touchstone, 1994), 63.

429 **Using stationery from:** Ibid., 69.

430 **a successful demonstration:** Ibid., 75.

430 **Homebrew Computer Club:** Isaacson, *Steve Jobs*, 59.

430 **"most important nights":** Ibid., 60.

430 **altered the terms:** Ibid., 52–54.

431 **called on Wozniak:** Ibid., 52–54.

431 **rigging the telephone system:** Ibid., 289.

431 **sold his VW minibus:** Ibid., 62.

432 **fifty units for $500:** Ibid., 66–67.

432 **Henry Ford couldn't identify:** Steven Watts, *The People's Tycoon: Henry Ford and the American Century* (New York: Vintage, 2006), 268.

433 **$28 million sale:** Kaplan, *Silicon Boys and Their Valley of Dreams*, 90.

433 **a young marketing veteran:** Isaacson, *Steve Jobs*, 76–77.

433 **equal to those of Jobs and Wozniak:** Apple Computer, Inc., *Initial Public Offering Prospectus* (New York: Morgan Stanley, December 12, 1980).

433 **Apple sold 570 units . . . :** Ibid.

433 **worth $250 million:** Isaacson, *Steve Jobs*, 104.

433 **Japan didn't completely dominate:** Reid, *Chip*, 158–60.

434 **"disk operating system":** Manes and Andrews, *Gates*, 155.

434 **the same software:** Michael Dell, *Direct from Dell* (New York: Harper Collins, 2000), 30.

435 **raised $1 million** and **on track to generate $15 million:** Manes and Andrews, *Gates*, 165, 176.

435 **the IPO roadshow:** Ibid., 305.

Chapter 32: Finance

436 **coup of sorts:** Leonard Sloane, "Textile Concern Changes Control," *New York Times*, May 11, 1965.

436 **400,000 workers in the trade:** Herbert Koshetz, "Recovery Seen in New England," *New York Times*, January 9, 1972.

436 **degree of shock:** Alice Schroeder, *Snowball: Warren Buffett and the Business of Life* (New York: Bantam, 2008), 276–77.

437 **discarded "cigar butt":** Ibid., 277.

437 **human dilemma that:** Chairman Warren E. Buffett to shareholders of Berkshire Hathaway Inc., March 14, 1978.

438 **overmatched by the color TVs:** T. R. Reid, *The Chip* (New York: Random House, 2001), 218.

438 **The oil crisis:** David Halberstam, *The Reckoning* (New York: William Morrow, 1986), 452–59.

438 **Rodeo Drive and Wilshire Boulevard:** Connie Bruck, *The Predators' Ball: The Inside Story of Drexel Burnham and the Rise of the Junk Bond Raiders* (New York: Penguin Books, 1989), 218.

439 **$550 million in cash:** James B. Stewart, *Den of Thieves* (New York: Touchstone, 1992), 243.

439 **Walter Braddock Hickman:** Bruck, *Predators' Ball*, 28.

439 **more than a portfolio:** W. Braddock Hickman, "Measures of Experience on Defaulted Issues," in *Statistical Measures of Corporate Bond Financing Since 1900* (Princeton: Princeton University Press, 1960), 483.

440 **were too risky:** Bruck, *Predators' Ball*, 30–32.

440 **made substantial returns:** Ibid., 34–35.

440 **The pejorative term:** Ibid., 39.

440 **13 percent annually** and **$400 million bond issue:** "15.31% Note Yield Lures Investors for Chrysler," *New York Times*, February 27, 1981.

441 **More high-yield bonds:** Bruck, *Predators' Ball*, 100–101.

441 **wanted to borrow:** Ibid., 59.

441 **entrepreneur Rupert Murdoch:** Ibid., 245.

442 **last of the textile mills:** Warren Buffett to shareholders of Berkshire Hathaway Inc., March 4, 1986.

442 **"more attractive uses":** Warren Buffett to shareholders of Berkshire Hathaway Inc., March 26, 1978.

443 **"end, nothing worked"** and **"Adam Smith would":** Buffett to shareholders, March 4, 1986.

443 **boom of the sixties:** John Brooks, *The Go-Go Years* (New York: Weybright & Talley, 1973), 138–39.

445 **home in Queens:** Bruck, *Predators' Ball*, 150–51.

446 **"I don't know":** Ibid., 157.

446 **known as greenmail:** Ibid.

447 **conglomerate didn't look:** Brooks, *Go-Go Years*, 154–55.

447 **20 percent stake in TWA** and **notoriously bad relations:** Carol J. Loomis, "The Comeuppance of Carl Icahn," *Fortune*, August 18, 2013.

448 **behind Icahn's bid:** Ibid.

448 **they formed KKR:** George Anders, *Merchants of Debt: KKR and the Mortgaging of American Business* (New York: Basic Books, 1993), 45–47.

448 **RJR Nabisco for:** Ibid., 214.

449 **ninety-eight-count indictment:** Ibid., 486–87.

Chapter 33: Shoes

450 **Rolls-Royce Corniche:** Mike Tyson, *Undisputed Truth* (New York: Plume, 2013), 176.

450 **"Don't believe the hype":** Phil Berger, "Tyson Hurts Right Hand in Scuffle with a Boxer," *New York Times*, August 24, 1988.

450 **bruise that closed:** Pat Putnam, "Now the War at the Store," *Sports Illustrated*, September 5, 1988, 30.

451 **screening the logos:** "Dapper Dan's Designs," *Vibe*, March 1998.

451 **local drug kingpins:** Azie Faison, *Game Over: The Rise and Transformation of a Harlem Hustler* (New York: Simon & Schuster, 2007), 102.

451 **public housing projects:** Jane Jacobs, *The Death and Life of Great American Cities* (New York: Vintage Books, 1992), 273–76.

451 **black murder rate:** Alexia Cooper and Erica L. Smith, *Homicide Trends in the United States, 1980–2008* (Washington DC: Bureau of Justice Statistics, 2011).

452 **one-in-five-hundred:** Ibid.

453 **"a hundred grand strong":** Jay Z, "U Don't Know," *The Blueprint* (Roc-A-Fella Records, 2001).

454 **deal with New Balance:** David Falk, *The Bald Truth* (New York: Simon & Schuster, 2009), 51.

454 **special shoe branded:** Ibid.

455 **exceeded $100 million** and **profile of Jordan:** Phil Patton, "The Selling of Michael Jordan," *New York Times*, November 9, 1986, 48.

457 **be heard breathlessly** and **"Bo Knows" commercial:** Michael Bonfiglio, "You Don't Know Bo," *ESPN 30 for 30*, December 8, 2012.

457 **arranged for a meeting . . . :** Phil Knight, "Commencement Speech at the Stanford Graduate School of Business," Palo Alto, California, June 14, 2014.

458 **one in twelve pairs and with 1,500 employees:** Cynthia Jabs, "Nike: The Shoes That Go 'Swoosh,'" *New York Times*, August 19, 1979, F5.

458 **Nike sales had reached . . . grown to $457 million:** Nike Inc., *2011 Annual Report* (Beaverton, OR: Nike Inc., 2011).

459 **"began the long process":** Ibid.

460 **"neither black nor white":** Patton, "Selling of Michael Jordan."

460 **NAACP had successfully lobbied:** Leonard J. Leff, "'Gone with the Wind' and Hollywood's Racial Politics," *Atlantic*, December 1999.

460 **"Your Shoes or Your Life":** Rick Telander, "Senseless," *Sports Illustrated*, May 14, 1990.

461 **murders would fall:** Cooper and Smith, *Homicide Trends in the United States*.

461 **burgundy Lexus coupe:** Michael Janofsky, "Man Shot to Death Is Identified as Father of Jordan," *New York Times*, August 14, 1993, 25.

Chapter 34: Internet

463 **"flickered across his face":** Andrew Rosenthal, "Bush Encounters the Supermarket, Amazed," *New York Times*, February 5, 1992.

464 **postal service had funded:** "Mail Service Drops Facsimile System," *New York Times*, March 8, 1961.

464 **newspapers including the:** See the editorial sections of the aforementioned publications on July 7, 1980.

465 **Von Meister soon formed:** Alec Klein, *Stealing Time: Steve Case, Jerry Levin, and the Collapse of AOL Time Warner* (New York: Simon & Schuster, 2003), 14–16.

465 **with great fanfare:** Ibid., 15–16.

465 **wildly popular Commodore 64:** Ibid., 33.

465 **Quantum had nearly:** Ibid., 35.

465 **service America Online:** Ibid., 45.

465 **$30 million in:** America Online Inc., *1996 Annual Report* (Washington DC: Securities and Exchange Commission, 1996).

466 **"sprawling computer grid":** Philip Elmer-Dewitt, "Take a Trip into the Future on the Electronic Superhighway," *Time*, April 12, 1993.

467 **"the human mind":** Tim Berners-Lee, *Weaving the Web: The Original Design and Ultimate Destiny of the World Wide Web* (San Francisco: Harper, 1999), 3.

467 **"Mendel's concept of":** Vannevar Bush, "As We May Think," *Atlantic*, July 1943.

467 **"poet, philosopher, and rogue":** Theodor Holm Nelson, "My Life and Work, Very Brief," Hyperland.com.

467 **coined the term:** T. H. Nelson, "Complex Information Processing: A File Structure for the Complex, the Changing and the Indeterminate," *ACM '65 Proceedings of the 1965 20th National Conference*, August 24, 1965, 84–100.

467 **credited Doug Engelbart:** Berners-Lee, *Weaving the Web*, 5–6.

468 **calling it the World Wide Web:** Ibid., 23–29.

468 **National Center for Supercomputing:** Ibid., 68–69.

468 **best kind of R&D:** Jim Clark, *Netscape Time* (New York: St. Martin's, 1999), 35.

468 **about $20 million:** Ibid., 32.

469 **Clark wrote Andreesen:** Ibid., 34.

469 **"I'm finished with all that":** Ibid., 42.

469 **"Well, we could always":** Ibid., 49.

469 **Clark put in $3 million:** Ibid., 57.

470 **Through a newsletter:** John S. Quarterman, "Internet Resource Discovery Services by Bytes," *Matrix News* 4, no. 2 (February 1994).

470 **"revolutionizing event":** Brad Stone, *The Everything Store: Jeff Bezos and the Age of Amazon* (New York: Little, Brown, 2013), 27.

471 **west in a Chevy Blazer:** Ibid., 29.

471 **package of $65,000:** Netscape Communications Corporation, *Form S-1 Registration Statement* (Washington DC: Securities and Exchange Commission, 1995).

471 **20 percent of the company:** David A. Kaplan, *The Silicon Boys and Their Valley of Dreams* (New York: Perennial, 2000), 243.

471 **new advanced Web browser:** Netscape Communications Corporation, *Form S-1 Registration Statement.*

472 **these "electronic brochures":** Ibid.

472 **majority of American households:** Thom File, *Computer and Internet Use in the United States* (Washington DC: U.S. Census Bureau, May 2013), figure 1.

472 **$22 million in revenues:** Netscape Communications Corporation, *Form S-1 Registration Statement.*

472 **"the fastest-growing software":** Clark, *Netscape Time,* 219.

472 **an "investor frenzy":** Laurence Zuckerman, "With Internet Cachet, Not Profit, a New Stock Is Wall St.'s Darling," *New York Times,* August 10, 1995.

472 **4.2 million shares:** Netscape Communications Corporation, *Form S-1 Registration Statement.*

472 **worth as much as:** Netscape Communications Corp., *1997 Annual Report* (Washington DC: Securities and Exchange Commission, March 1997).

473 **this type of wealth creation:** "The Golden Geeks," *Time,* February 19, 1996.

474 **its two founders:** Yahoo! Inc., *1999 Annual Report* (Washington DC: Securities and Exchange Commission, 1999).

474 **"Excite, InfoSeek, and Lycos":** Janice Maloney, "Still Searching for Profits on the Internet," *Fortune,* May 26, 2013.

474 **invested $8 million:** Stone, *Everything Store,* 48.

474 **American households rushed:** File, *Computer and Internet Use,* figure 1.

475 **$1 billion in 1996:** America Online Inc., *1996 Annual Report* (Washington DC: Securities and Exchange Commission, 1996).

475 **starring Tom Hanks:** America Online Inc., *2000 Annual Report* (Washington DC: Securities and Exchange Commission, 2000).

476 **the greatest heist:** Nina Munk, *Fools Rush In: Steve Case, Jerry Levin, and the Unmaking of AOL Time Warner* (New York: Harper Business, 2004), 156.

478 **"Just One More Bubble":** "If You Can Make It in Silicon Valley, You Can Make It . . . in Silicon Valley Again," *New York Times,* June 5, 2005.

Chapter 35: Mobile

479 **from George Lucas:** Walter Isaacson, *Steve Jobs* (New York: Simon & Schuster, 2011), 240.

480 **Tim Berners-Lee attributes:** Tim Berners-Lee, *Weaving the Web: The Original Design and Ultimate Destiny of the World Wide Web* (San Francisco, Harper, 1999), 22–23.

480 **making Jobs a billionaire:** John Markoff, "Apple Computer Co-Founder Strikes Gold with New Stock," *New York Times,* November 30, 1995.

480 **Apple agreed to buy:** Isaacson, *Steve Jobs,* 301.

480 **lose over $1 billion:** Apple Computer Inc., *1997 Annual Report* (Washington DC: Securities and Exchange Commission, 1997).

480 **$150 million from Microsoft:** Michele Matassa Flores and Thomas W. Haines, "Microsoft, Apple Join Forces: Disbelief, Boos Greet Today's Stunning Announcement at Macworld Expo," *Seattle Times,* August 6, 1997.

480 **"I'd shut it down":** John Markoff, "Michael Dell Should Eat His Words, Apple Chief Suggests," *New York Times,* January 16, 2006.

481 **$8 billion to $5.3 billion** and **its first store:** Apple Computer Inc., *2001 Annual Report* (Washington DC: Securities and Exchange Commission, 2001).

482 **introduced the iPod:** Ibid.

483 **Napster was forced:** Richard Nieva, "Ashes to Ashes, Peer to Peer: An Oral History of Napster," *Fortune,* September 5, 2013.

483 **individual songs via Apple:** Isaacson, *Steve Jobs,* 402–3.

486 **$7.7 billion versus $7.4 billion** and **80 million hands:** Apple Computer Inc., *2007 Annual Report* (Washington DC: Securities and Exchange Commission, 2007).

486 **Jobs took the stage** and **"Every once in a while":** Steve Jobs, Keynote presentation of the iPhone at Macworld, San Francisco, January 9, 2007.

487 **"the most expensive phone":** Steve Ballmer, interview at Nortel, Innovative Communications Alliance, *Power Lunch,* January 17, 2007.

487 **600 million units:** Apple Computer Inc., *2015 Annual Report* (Washington DC: Securities and Exchange Commission, 2015).

488 **Silicon Valley's Tesla:** Claire Cain Miller, "An All-Electric Sedan, Awaiting Federal Aid," *New York Times,* March 26, 2009.

491 **"social media savvy":** Brian Stelter, "Coverage Grows for Wall Street Protest," *New York Times,* October 5, 2011.

Bibliography

Abbot, Willis J. *Watching the World Go By*. Boston: Little, Brown, 1933.

Achenbach, Joel. *The Grand Idea: George Washington's Potomac and the Race to the West*. New York: Simon & Schuster, 2004.

Adams, John. *Revolutionary Writings, 1775–1783*. Edited by Gordon Wood. New York: Library of America, 2014.

Adams, Samuel Hopkins. *The Great American Fraud*. New York: P. F. Collier & Son, 1905.

Adler, Dorothy R. *British Investment in American Railways, 1834–1898*. Edited by Muriel E. Hidy. Charlottesville: University Press of Virginia, 1970.

Ahamed, Liaquat. *Lords of Finance: The Bankers Who Broke the World*. New York: Penguin Books, 2009.

Alger, Horatio. *Ragged Dick; or, Street Life in New York with the Boot-Blacks*. Philadelphia: John C. Winston, 1910.

Alglave, Emile, J. Boulard, and Charles Marshall Lungren. *The Electric Light: Its History, Production, and Applications*. New York: D. Appleton, 1884.

Amar, Akhil Reed. *America's Constitution: A Biography*. New York: Random House, 2005.

Anders, George. *Merchants of Debt: KKR and the Mortgaging of American Business*. New York: Basic Books, 1993.

Archer, Gleason Leonard. *Big Business and Radio*. New York: American Historical Society, 1939.

———. *The History of Radio to 1926*. New York: American Historical Society, 1938.

Arnold, H. H. *Global Mission*. Blue Ridge Summit, PA: TAB Books, 1989.

Austrian, Geoffrey D. *Herman Hollerith: Forgotten Giants of Information Processing*. New York: Columbia University Press, 1982.

Baime, A. J. *The Arsenal of Democracy*. Boston: Houghton Mifflin Harcourt, 2014.

Bancroft, Frederic. *Slave Trading in the Old South*. Columbia: University of South Carolina Press, 1996.

Baptist, Edward E. *The Half Has Never Been Told: Slavery and the Making of American Capitalism*. New York: Basic Books, 2014.

Barn, David Haward. *Empire Express: Building the First Transcontinental Railroad*. New York: Penguin Books, 2000.

Barnouw, Erik. *Tube of Plenty: The Evolution of American Television*. 2nd edition. New York: Oxford University Press, 1990.

Bartlett, Sarah. *The Money Machine: How KKR Manufactured Power and Profits*. New York: Warner Books, 1992.

Bates, David Homer. *Lincoln in the Telegraph Office*. Lincoln: University of Nebraska Press, 1995.

Beard, Charles A. *Economic Origins of Jeffersonian Democracy*. New York: Free Press, 1965.

———. *The Republic*. New York: Viking, 1962.

Beckert, Sven. *Empire of Cotton: A Global History*. New York: Alfred A. Knopf, 2014.

Beecher, Catharine E., and Harriet Beecher Stowe. *The American Woman's Home*. 1869. Reprint, New Brunswick, NJ: Rutgers University Press, 2004.

Bell, Isaac Lowthian. *Principles of the Manufacture of Iron and Steel*. New York: George Routledge & Sons, 1884.

Berg, A. Scott. *Goldwyn*. New York: Alfred A. Knopf, 1989.

———. *Lindbergh*. New York: G. P. Putnam's Sons, 1998.

———. *Wilson*. New York: Penguin Random House, 2013.

Berlin, Leslie. *The Man Behind the Microchip: Robert Noyce and the Invention of Silicon Valley*. New York: Oxford University Press, 2005.

Bernanke, Ben S. *Essays on the Great Depression*. Princeton, NJ: Princeton University Press, 2004.

Berners-Lee, Tim. *Weaving the Web: The Original Design and Ultimate Destiny of the World Wide Web*. San Francisco: Harper, 1999.

Bernstein, Iver. *The New York City Draft Riots*. New York: Oxford University Press, 1990.

Bernstein, Peter L. *Wedding of the Waters: The Erie Canal and the Making of a Great Nation*. New York: W. W. Norton, 2006.

Bibb, Porter. *Ted Turner*. Boulder, CO: Johnson Books, 1997.

Bigelow, John. *Memoir of the Life and Public Services of John Charles Frémont*. New York: Derby & Jackson, 1856.

Binkley, Christina. *Winner Takes All*. New York: Hyperion, 2008.

Birdwell, Michael E. *Celluloid Soldiers: The Warner Bros. Campaign Against Nazism*. New York: NYU Press, 1999.

Birmingham, Stephen. *"The Rest of Us": The Rise of America's Eastern European Jews*. Syracuse, NY: Syracuse University Press, 1999.

Blassingame, John W. *The Slave Community: Plantation Life in the Antebellum South*. New York: Oxford University Press, 1979.

Bloomberg, Michael R. *Bloomberg by Bloomberg*. New York: Wiley, 2001.

Bloomingdale Brothers. *Bloomingdale's Illustrated 1886 Catalog: Fashions, Dry Goods and Housewares*. New York: Dover, 1988.

Bogart, Ernest Ludlow. *The Economic History of the United States*. New York: Longmans, Green, 1908.

Bonanno, Joseph. *A Man of Honor: The Autobiography of Joseph Bonanno*. New York: St. Martin's, 2003.

Boorstin, Daniel. *The Americans: The Democratic Experience*. New York: Random House, 1973.

Boyd, Thomas. *Poor John Fitch*. New York: G. P. Putnam's Sons, 1935.

Bradford, William. *Of Plymouth Plantation: 1620–1647*. Edited by Samuel Eliot Morison. New York: Alfred A. Knopf, 1989.

Brandeis, Louis D. *Other People's Money and How the Bankers Use It*. Edited by Melvin I. Ufrosky. Boston: Bedford Books, 1995.

Brands, H. W. *The Age of Gold: The California Gold Rush and the New American Dream*. New York: Doubleday, 2002.

Brawley, Benjamin. *A Social History of the American Negro*. New York: Dover, 2001.

Brinkley, Alan. *The Publisher: Henry Luce and His American Century*. New York: Vintage Books, 2011.

Brinkley, Douglas. *Cronkite*. New York: Harper Perennial, 2013.

Brooks, John. *Business Adventures: Twelve Classic Tales from the World of Wall Street*. New York: Open Road, 2014.

———. *The Go-Go Years*. New York: Weybright and Talley, 1973.

———. *Once in Golconda: A True Drama of Wall Street 1920–1938*. New York: Open Road, 2014.

Brown, G. I. *Explosives: History with a Bang*. London: History Press, 2011.

Brown, Glenn. *Glenn Brown's History of the United States Capitol*. Washington DC: Government Printing Office, 1998.

Brown, James. *I Feel Good: A Memoir of a Life of Soul*. New York: New American Library, 2005.

Bruck, Connie. *Master of the Game: Steven Ross and the Creation of Time Warner*. New York: Penguin Books, 1995.

———. *The Predators' Ball: The Inside Story of Drexel Burnham and the Rise of the Junk Bond Raiders*. New York: Penguin Books, 1989.

Bruun, Erik, and Jay Crosby, eds. *Living History America*. New York: Black Dog & Leventhal, 1999.

Bryan, William Jennings. *The World's Famous Orations: America, 1761–1837*. Vol. 7. New York: Funk & Wagnalls, 1906.

Brzezinski, Zbigniew. *Strategic Vision: America and the Crisis of Global Power*. New York: Basic Books, 2012.

Buffalo Evening News. A History of the City of Buffalo. Buffalo, New York: Hausauer-Jones, 1908.

Buffalo Historical Society. *Publications of the Buffalo Historical Society*. Vol. 2. Buffalo, NY: Bigelow Brothers, 1880.

Buffett, Warren E. *The Essays of Warren Buffett: Lessons for Corporate America*. Edited by Lawrence A. Cunningham. New York: Cunningham, 2001.

Bunyan, John. *The Pilgrim's Progress*. Philadelphia: Henry Atemus, 1895.

Calder, Lendol. *Financing the American Dream: A Cultural History of Consumer Credit*. Princeton, NJ: Princeton University Press, 1999.

Calhoun, John Caldwell. *The Works of John C. Calhoun*. Edited by Richard K. Crallé. New York: D. Appleton, 1855.

Cannadine, David. *Mellon: An American Life*. New York: Alfred A. Knopf, 2006.

Carnegie, Andrew. *The Autobiography of Andrew Carnegie*. Boston: Northeastern University Press, 1986.

———. *Gospel of Wealth*. Bedford, MA: Applewood Books, 1998.

———. *James Watt*. Garden City, NY: Doubleday, Page, 1913.

———. *Triumphant Democracy; or, Fifty Years' March of the Republic*. Garden City, NY: Doubleday, Doran, 1933.

Casson, Herbert Newton. *The Romance of Steel: The Story of a Thousand Millionaires*. New York: A. S. Barnes, 1907.

Chancellor, Edward. *Devil Take the Hindmost: A History of Financial Speculation*. New York: Plume, 2000.

Chenoweth, Neil. *Rupert Murdoch*. New York: Crown Business, 2002.

Chernow, Ron. *Alexander Hamilton*. New York: Penguin, 2004.

———. *The House of Morgan: An American Banking Dynasty and the Rise of Modern Finance*. New York: Grove, 1990.

———. *Titan: The Life of John D. Rockefeller, Sr*. New York: Vintage Books, 1999.

———. *Washington: A Life*. New York: Penguin, 2010.

Clark, Jim. *Netscape Time*. New York: St. Martin's, 1999.

Colby, Gerard, and Lyle Stuart. *Du Pont Dynasty: Behind the Nylon Curtain*. Don Mills, ON: Musson Book Company, 1984.

Colden, Cadwallader David. *The Life of Robert Fulton*. New York: Kirk & Mercein, 1817.

Collier, Robert Joseph. *The $50,000 Verdict*. New York: P. F. Collier & Son, 1911.

Commons, John R., Ulrich B. Phillips, Eugene A. Gilmore, Helen L. Sumner, and John B. Andrews, eds. *A Documentary History of American Industrial Society*. Cleveland: Arthur H. Clark, 1910.

Conant, Michael. *Antitrust in the Motion Picture Industry*. Berkeley: University of California Press, 1960.

Conot, Robert E. *A Streak of Luck: The Life and Legend of Thomas Alva Edison*. New York: Seaview Books, 1979.

Cox, Thomas H. *Gibbons v. Ogden, Law, and Society in the Early Republic*. Columbus: Ohio University Press, 2009.

Cramp, Arthur J., ed. *Nostrums and Quackery: Articles on the Nostrum Evil, Quackery and Allied Matters Affecting the Public Health*. Vol. 2. Chicago: American Medical Association, 1921.

Craven, Wesley Frank. *The Colonies in Transition, 1660–1713*. New York: Harper & Row, 1968.

———. *The Southern Colonies in the Seventeenth Century, 1607–1689*. Vol. 1. Baton Rouge: Louisiana State University Press, 1975.

———. *The Virginia Company of London, 1606–1624*. Vol. 1. Baltimore: Genealogical Publishing, 2009.

———. *White, Red, and Black: The Seventeenth-Century Virginian*. New York: W. W. Norton, 1977.

Cronkite, Walter. *A Reporter's Life*. New York: Ballantine Books, 1997.

D'Antonio, Michael. *Hershey*. New York: Simon & Schuster, 2007.

Darwin, Charles. *The Origin of Species*. Vol. 2. New York: P. F. Collier & Son, 1909.

Davis, Kenneth S. *FDR: Into the Storm 1937–1940*. New York: Random House, 1993.

———. *FDR: The New Deal Years 1933–1937*. New York: Random House, 1986.

———. *FDR: The War President, 1940–1943*. New York: Random House, 2000.

Dawkins, Richard. *The Blind Watchmaker*. New York: W. W. Norton, 1987.

Decker, Wilbur Fisk. *The Story of the Engine: From Lever to Liberty Motor*. New York: Charles Scribner's Sons, 1920.

DeGeorge, Gail. *The Making of a Blockbuster*. New York: John Wiley & Sons, 1996.

Dell, Michael. *Direct from Dell*. New York: Harper Collins, 2000.

Depew, Chauncey Mitchell. *One Hundred Years of American Commerce, 1795–1895*. 2 vols. New York: D. O. Haynes, 1895.

The Derrick's Handbook of Petroleum. Oil City, PA: Derrick, 1898.

Diamant, Lincoln. *Chaining the Hudson: The Fight for the River in the Revolution*. New York: Carol, 1989.

Diamond, Jared. *Guns, Germs, and Steel: The Fates of Human Societies*. New York: W. W. Norton, 1999.

Dilts, James D. *The Great Road: The Building of the Baltimore & Ohio, the Nation's First Railroad, 1828–1853*. Stanford, CA: Stanford University Press, 1993.

Dolin, Eric Jay. *Fur, Fortune, and Empire*. New York: W. W. Norton & Company, 2010.

———. *Leviathan: The History of Whaling in America*. New York: W. W. Norton, 2007.

Donald, David Herbert. *Lincoln*. New York: Simon & Schuster, 1995.

Douglas, Alan. *Radio Manufacturers of the 1920's*. Vol. 1. Vestal, NY: Vestal, 1988.

Douglass, Frederick. *Narrative of the Life of Frederick Douglass, an American Slave*. 1845. Reprint, New York: Anchor, 1989.

Drowne, Kathleen. *Spirits of Defiance: National Prohibition & Jazz Age Literature, 1920–1933*. Columbus: Ohio State University Press, 2005.

Du Bois, W. E. B. *Writings*. New York: Library of America College Editions, 1996.

Dulany, Daniel. *Considerations on the Propriety of Imposing Taxes in the British Colonies*. 2nd edition. Annapolis, MD: Jonas Green, 1765.

Edgerton, Gary R. *The Columbia History of American Television*. New York: Columbia University Press, 2009.

Eisenhower, Dwight D. *Mandate for Change*. Garden City, NY: Doubleday, 1963.

———. *Waging Peace*. Garden City, NY: Doubleday, 1965.

Ellison, Thomas. *Slavery and Secession in America: Historical and Economical*. London: Sampson Low, Son, 1862.

Ely, Richard Theodore. *The Labor Movement in America*. New York: T. Y. Crowell, 1886.

Evening News Association. *Men of Progress: Embracing Biographical Sketches of Representative Michigan Men*. Detroit: John F. Eby, 1900.

Eyman, Scott. *Lion of Hollywood: The Life and Legend of Louis B. Mayer*. New York: Simon & Schuster, 2005.

Fabozzi, Frank J. *Fixed Income Mathematics: Analytical and Statistical Techniques*. 4th edition. New York: McGraw-Hill, 2006.

Faison, Azie. *Game Over: The Rise and Transformation of a Harlem Hustler*. New York: Simon & Schuster, 2007.

Falk, David. *The Bald Truth*. New York: Simon & Schuster, 2009.

Faulkner, Harold Underwood. *The Decline of Laissez Faire, 1897–1917*. White Plains, NY: M. E. Sharpe, 1951.

Fielding, Raymond. *The March of Time, 1935–1951*. New York: Oxford University Press, 1978.

Fisher, Irving. *Prohibition at Its Worst*. New York: Macmillan, 1927.

Fitch, George. *The Automobile*. New York: P. F. Collier & Son, 1910.

Fogel, Robert William. *Without Consent or Contract: The Rise and Fall of American Slavery*. New York: W. W. Norton, 1989.

Fogel, Robert William, and Stanley L. Engerman. *Time on the Cross: The Economics of American Negro Slavery*. Boston: Little, Brown, 1974.

Foner, Eric. *Free Soil, Free Labor, Free Men: The Ideology of the Republican Party Before the Civil War.* New York: Oxford University Press, 1995.

Force, Peter, ed. *Tracts and Other Papers Relating Principally to the Origin, Settlement, and Progress of the Colonies in North America.* Washington DC: Wm. Q. Force, 1846.

Ford, Henry, and Samuel Crowther. *My Life and Work.* Garden City, NY: Doubleday, Page, 1922.

Ford, Worthington Chauncey. *The Writings of George Washington.* Vol. 10. New York: G. P. Putnam's Sons, 1891.

Franklin, Benjamin. *The Autobiography of Benjamin Franklin.* Lexington, KY: Tribeca Books, 2011.

Frémont, John Charles. *Memoirs of My Life.* New York: Cooper Square, 2001.

Fridson, Martin S. *How to Be a Billionaire.* New York: John Wiley & Sons, 2000.

Friedman, Milton, and Anna Jacobson Schwartz. *The Great Contraction, 1929–1933.* Princeton, NJ: Princeton University Press, 2009.

Fulton, Robert. *A Treatise on the Improvement of Canal Navigation.* London: I. and J. Taylor, 1796.

Gabel, Christopher R. *Railroad Generalship: Foundations of Civil War Strategy.* Fort Leavenworth, KS: Combat Studies Institute, 1997.

———. *Rails to Oblivion: The Decline of Confederate Railroads in the Civil War.* Fort Leavenworth, KS: Combat Studies Institute, 2002.

Gabler, Neal. *An Empire of Their Own: How the Jews Invented Hollywood.* New York: Anchor Books, 1989.

———. *Walt Disney: The Triumph of the American Imagination.* New York: Vintage Books, 2006.

Galbraith, John Kenneth. *The Affluent Society.* Boston: Mariner Books, 1998.

———. *American Capitalism: The Concept of Countervailing Power.* Boston: Houghton Mifflin, 1956.

———. *The Great Crash, 1929.* Boston: Mariner Books, 1997.

Gans, Herbert J. *The Levittowners: Ways of Life and Politics in a New Suburban Community.* New York: Columbia University Press, 1982.

Garraty, John A., and Peter Gay. *The Columbia History of the World.* New York: Harper & Row, 1987.

Goldfield, David. *America Aflame: How the Civil War Created a Nation.* New York: Bloomsbury, 2011.

Gomery, Douglas. *The Coming of Sound.* New York: Routledge, 2005.

———. *The Hollywood Studio System.* London: Palgrave, 2015.

Goodwin, Doris Kearns. *The Bully Pulpit: Theodore Roosevelt, William Howard Taft, and the Golden Age of Journalism.* New York: Simon & Schuster, 2013.

———. *Team of Rivals: The Political Genius of Abraham Lincoln.* New York: Simon & Schuster, 2005.

Gordon, Sarah H. *Passage to Union: How the Railroads Transformed American Life, 1829–1929.* Chicago: Ivan R. Dee, 1996.

Gordy, Berry. *To Be Loved: The Music, the Magic, the Memories of Motown.* New York: Warner Books, 1994.

Goulder, Grace. *John D. Rockefeller: The Cleveland Years.* Cleveland: Western Reserve Historical Society, 1972.

Graham, Benjamin, and David L. Dodd. *Security Analysis.* New York: McGraw-Hill, 2005.

Greeley, Horace. *Aunt Sally, Come Up! or, the Nigger Sale.* London: Ward and Lock, 1859.

Green, James. *Death in the Haymarket: A Story of Chicago, the First Labor Movement, and the Bombing That Divided Gilded Age America.* New York: Pantheon, 2006.

Greene, Evarts B., and Virginia D. Harrington. *American Population Before the Federal Census of 1790.* New York: Columbia University Press, 1997.

Greenleaf, William. *Monopoly on Wheels: Henry Ford and the Selden Automobile Patent.* Detroit: Wayne State University Press, 2011.

Hack, Richard. *Hughes: The Private Diaries, Memos and Letters.* Beverly Hills, CA: New Millennium, 2001.

Hakluyt, Richard. *The Principal Navigations, Voyages, Traffiques & Discoveries of the English Nation.* Vol. 5. Glasgow, Scotland: J. MacLehose and Sons, 1904.

Halberstam, David. *The Best and the Brightest.* 20th anniversary edition. New York: Ballantine Books, 1993.

———. *The Reckoning.* New York: William Morrow, 1986.

Hale, Nathaniel C. *Pelts and Palisades*. Richmond, VA: Dietz Press, 1959.

Heath, Dwight B. *Mourt's Relation: A Journal of the Pilgrims at Plymouth*. Bedford, MA: Applewood Books, 1963.

Hechinger, Grace, and Fred M. Hechinger. *Teen-Age Tyranny*. New York: Crest Books, 1964.

Hendrick, Burton J. *The Age of Big Business: A Chronicle of the Captains of Industry*. Edited by Allen Johnson. Vol. 29. Oxford: Oxford University Press, 1920.

Henry, J. T. *The Early and Later History of Petroleum*. Philadelphia: J. B. Rodgers, 1873.

Herman, Arthur. *Freedom's Forge: How American Business Produced Victory in World War II*. New York: Random House, 2013.

Hilmes, Michele. *NBC: America's Network*. Berkeley: University of California Press, 2007.

Hobsbawm, Eric. *The Age of Capital: 1848–1875*. New York: Vintage Books, 1996.

Hoge, Cecil C. *The First Hundred Years Are the Toughest*. Berkeley, CA: Ten Speed Press, 1988.

Holbrook, Stewart H. *The Story of American Railroads*. New York: Bonanza Books, 1947.

Holt, Byron Webber, ed. *The Gold Supply and Prosperity*. New York: Moody, 1907.

Horwitz, Morton J. *The Transformation of American Law: 1780–1860*. Cambridge, MA: Harvard University Press, 1977.

Hosack, David. *Memoir of De Witt Clinton*. New York: J. Seymour, 1829.

House of Lords. *Protest Against the Bill to Repeal the American Stamp Act*. Paris: J. W. Imprimeur, 1766.

Howe, Daniel Walker. *What Hath God Wrought: The Transformation of America, 1815–1848*. New York: Oxford University Press, 2007.

Hunter, Rebecca L. *Mail-Order Homes: Sears Homes and Other Kit Houses*. Oxford: Shire, 2012.

Ingrassia, Paul. *Engines of Change: A History of the American Dream in Fifteen Cars*. New York: Simon & Schuster, 2012.

Isaacson, Walter. *Benjamin Franklin: An American Life*. New York: Simon & Schuster, 2004.

———. *Steve Jobs*. New York: Simon & Schuster, 2011.

Jackson, Kenneth T. *Crabgrass Frontier: The Suburbanization of the United States*. New York: Oxford University Press, 1987.

Jacobs, Jane. *The Death and Life of Great American Cities*. New York: Vintage Books, 1992.

James I. *A Counter-Blaste to Tobacco*. London: R. B., 1884.

James, Edward T., Janet Wilson James, and Paul S. Boyer, eds. *Notable American Women, 1607–1950: A Biographical Dictionary*. Cambridge, MA: Harvard University Press, 1971.

Jefferson, Thomas. *A Summary View of the Rights of British America*. Williamsburg, VA: Clementina Rind, 1774.

Johnson, Herbert A. *Gibbons v. Ogden: John Marshall, Steamboats, and the Commerce Clause*. Lawrence: University Press of Kansas, 2010.

Johnson, Robert. *Nova Britannia: Offering Most Excellent Fruits by Planting in Virginia*. London: Sam Macham, 1609.

Johnson, Samuel, Thomas Warton, Bennet Langton, and Sir Joshua Reynolds. *The Idler*. Vol. 1. London: T. Davies, et al., 1767.

Johnson, Walter. *River of Dark Dreams: Slavery and Empire in the Cotton Kingdom*. Cambridge, MA: Harvard University Press, 2013.

Jones, Winfield. *Story of the Ku Klux Klan*. Washington DC: American Newspaper Syndicate, 1921.

Jonnes, Jill. *Empires of Light: Edison, Tesla, Westinghouse, and the Race to Electrify the World*. New York: Random House, 2004.

Josephson, Matthew. *The Robber Barons*. Orlando, FL: Harcourt, Brace, 1995.

Kaplan, David A. *The Silicon Boys and Their Valley of Dreams*. New York: Perennial, 2000.

Kaplan, Gilbert Edmund, and Chris Welles, eds. *The Money Managers*. New York: Random House, 1969.

Kellogg, John Harvey. *The Battle Creek Sanitarium System: History, Organization, Methods*. Battle Creek, MI: Gage, 1908.

———. *Plain Facts for Old and Young*. Burlington, IA: Segner & Condit, 1881.

Kelly, Cynthia C., ed. *The Manhattan Project*. New York: Black Dog & Leventhal, 2007.

Kemble, Fanny. *Fanny Kemble: The American Journals*. Edited by Elizabeth Mavor. London: Weidenfeld & Nicolson, 1990.

Kemble, Frances Anne. *Journal of a Residence on a Georgian Plantation in 1838–1839*. New York: Harper & Brothers, 1864.

Kennedy, Paul. *The Rise and Fall of the Great Powers: Economic Change and Military Conflict from 1500 to 2000*. New York: Random House, 1987.

Keynes, John Maynard. *The General Theory of Employment, Interest, and Money*. San Diego: Harcourt, 1964.

Kilbourne, Richard Holcombe, Jr. *Debt, Investment, Slaves: Credit Relations in East Feliciana Parish, Louisiana, 1825–1885*. Tuscaloosa: University of Alabama Press, 2014.

King, Tom. *The Operator: David Geffen Builds, Buys, and Sells the New Hollywood*. New York: Broadway Books, 2001.

Kissinger, Henry. *White House Years*. New York: Little, Brown, 1979.

Klein, Alec. *Stealing Time: Steve Case, Jerry Levin, and the Collapse of AOL Time Warner*. New York: Simon & Schuster, 2003.

Klein, Maury. *The Life and Legend of Jay Gould*. Baltimore: Johns Hopkins University Press, 1997.

Kobler, John. *Capone: The Life and World of Al Capone*. Cambridge, MA: Da Capo, 2003.

Koenig, Louis W. *Bryan: A Political Biography of William Jennings Bryan*. New York: G. P. Putnam's Sons, 1971.

Koeppel, Gerard. *Bond of Union: Building the Erie Canal and the American Empire*. Cambridge, MA: Da Capo, 2009.

Koester, Nancy. *Harriet Beecher Stowe: A Spiritual Life*. Grand Rapids, MI: William. B. Eerdmans, 2014.

Kroc, Ray. *Grinding It Out: The Making of McDonald's*. New York: St. Martin's, 1987.

Kulikoff, Allan. *Tobacco and Slaves: The Development of Southern Cultures in the Chesapeake, 1680–1800*. Chapel Hill: University of North Carolina Press, 1986.

Kushner, David. *Levittown*. New York: Walker, 2009.

Labaree, Benjamin Woods. *The Boston Tea Party*. London: Oxford University Press, 1975.

Lamoreaux, Naomi R. *The Great Merger Movement in American Business, 1895–1904*. Cambridge: Cambridge University Press, 1988.

Leigh, Frances Butler. *Ten Years on a Georgia Plantation Since the War*. London: R. Bentley & Son, 1883.

Leland, Ottilie M. *Master of Precision: Henry M. Leland*. Detroit: Wayne State University Press, 1966.

Lemann, Nicholas. *The Promised Land*. New York: Alfred A. Knopf, 1991.

Levy, Jonathan. *Freaks of Fortune: The Emerging World of Capitalism and Risk in America*. Cambridge, MA: Harvard University Press, 2014.

Lewis, Michael. *The New New Thing: A Silicon Valley Story*. New York: W. W. Norton, 1999.

Lewis, Tom. *Empire of the Air: The Men Who Made Radio*. New York: Edward Burlingame Books, 1991.

Lind, Michael. *Land of Promise: An Economic History of the United States*. New York: Harper, 2013.

Lindbergh, Charles A. *The Wartime Journals of Charles A. Lindbergh*. New York: Harcourt Brace Jovanovich, 1970.

Livermore, Thomas Leonard. *Numbers and Losses in the Civil War in America, 1861–65*. Boston: Houghton Mifflin, 1900.

Logevall, Fredrik. *Embers of War: The Fall of an Empire and the Making of America's Vietnam*. New York: Random House, 2013.

Love, John F. *McDonald's: Behind the Arches*. New York: Bantam, 1995.

Lowenstein, Roger. *America's Bank*. New York: Penguin, 2015.

———. *Buffett: The Making of an American Capitalist*. New York: Broadway Books, 2001.

———. *Origins of the Crash*. New York: Penguin, 2004.

Lyons, Eugene. *David Sarnoff: A Biography*. New York: Harper & Row, 1966.

Maas, Peter. *The Valachi Papers*. New York: Perennial, 2003.

MacCambridge, Michael. *America's Game*. New York: Anchor Books, 2005.

Mailer, Norman. *The Fight*. New York: Random House, 2013.

Mair, George. *Inside HBO: The Billion Dollar War Between HBO, Hollywood and the Home Video Revolution.* New York: Dodd, Mead, 1988.

Major, Nettie Leitch. *C. W. Post: The Hour and the Man.* Washington DC: Press of Judd & Detweiler, 1963.

Mancall, Peter C., ed. *Envisioning America: English Plans for the Colonization of North America, 1580–1640.* Boston: Bedford Books, 1995.

Manes, Stephen, and Paul Andrews. *Gates.* New York: Touchstone, 1994.

Mann, Charles C. *1493: Uncovering the New World Columbus Created.* New York: Alfred A. Knopf, 2011.

Markoff, John. *What the Dormouse Said: How the 60s Counterculture Shaped the Personal Computer Industry.* New York: Viking, 2005.

Marshall, James Wilson, and Edward Gould Buffum. *From Mexican Days to the Gold Rush.* Chicago: R. R. Donnelley & Sons, 1993.

Marx, Karl, and Friedrich Engels. *Manifesto of the Communist Party.* Peking: Foreign Language Press, 1968.

May, Thomas. *The History of the Parliament of England.* London: Weise, Cockrane, 1812.

McClure, James Baird, ed. *Edison and His Inventions.* Chicago: Rhodes and McClure, 1889.

McColley, Robert. *Slavery and Jeffersonian Virginia.* Urbana: University of Illinois Press, 1978.

McCraw, Thomas K. *The Founders and Finance.* Cambridge, MA: Harvard University Press, 2012.

McCullough, David. *The Great Bridge.* New York: Simon & Schuster, 1972.

———. *John Adams.* New York: Simon & Schuster, 2001.

———. *1776.* New York: Simon & Schuster, 2005.

McInnis, Maurie D. *Slaves Waiting for Sale: Abolitionist Art and the American Slave Trade.* Chicago: University of Chicago Press, 2001.

McIntyre, Ruth A. *Debts Hopeful and Desperate: Financing the Plymouth Colony.* Plymouth, MA: Plimoth Plantation, 1963.

McNamara, Robert S. *In Retrospect: The Tragedy and Lessons of Vietnam.* New York: Vintage Books, 1996.

McNeil, Alex. *Total Television, Including Cable.* New York: Penguin Books, 1991.

Meacham, Jon. *Thomas Jefferson: The Art of Power.* New York: Random House, 2012.

Mead, Edward Sherwood. *Trust Finance: A Study of the Genesis, Organization, and Management of Industrial Combinations.* New York: D. Appleton, 1913.

Melville, Herman. *Moby-Dick; or, The Whale.* 1851. Reprint, New York: Penguin Books, 2003.

Miller, James Andrew, and Tom Shales. *Those Guys Have All the Fun: Inside the World of ESPN.* New York: Back Bay Books, 2011.

Miller, Scott. *The President and the Assassin.* New York: Random House, 2011.

Mirsky, Jeannette, and Allan Nevins. *The World of Eli Whitney.* New York: Macmillan, 1952.

Mitchell, Margaret. *Gone with the Wind.* 1936. Reprint, New York: Charles Scribner's Sons, 2011.

Montefiore, Simon Sebag. *Stalin: The Court of the Red Tsar.* New York: Vintage Books, 2004.

Montgomery Ward. *Montgomery Ward & Co. Catalogue & Buyers Guide, 1895.* New York: Skyhorse, 2008.

Moody, John. *Moody's Manual of Investments: American and Foreign Transportation.* Vol. 3. New York: Moody, 1921.

———. *The Truth About the Trusts.* New York: Moody, 1904.

Morgan, Edmund S., and Helen M. Morgan. *The Stamp Act Crisis: Prologue to Revolution.* Chapel Hill: University of North Carolina Press, 1995.

Morgan, Lewis H. *The American Beaver: A Classic of Natural History and Ecology.* New York: Dover, 1986.

Morris, Charles R. *The Tycoons.* New York: Owl Books, 2006.

Morris, Edmund. *Theodore Rex.* New York: Modern Library, 2002.

Morris, James McGrath. *Pulitzer: A Life in Politics, Print, and Power.* New York: Harper, 2010.

Morse, Samuel Finley Breese. *Samuel F. B. Morse: His Letters and Journals.* Edited by Edward Lind Morse. New York: Houghton Mifflin, 1914.

Mott, Frank Luther. *American Journalism: A History, 1690–1960.* 3rd edition. New York: Macmillan, 1962.

Munk, Nina. *Fools Rush In: Steve Case, Jerry Levin, and the Unmaking of AOL Time Warner.* New York: Harper Business, 2004.

Nasaw, David. *Andrew Carnegie.* New York: Penguin, 2006.

———. *The Chief: The Life of William Randolph Hearst.* Boston: Houghton Mifflin, 2001.

National Commission on the Causes of the Financial and Economic Crisis in the United States. *The Financial Crisis Inquiry Report.* New York: Public Affairs, 2011.

Neill, Edward Duffield. *History of the Virginia Company of London.* Albany, NY: Joel Munsell, 1869.

Nelson, Walter Henry. *The Great Discount Delusion.* New York: David McKay, 1965.

Nevins, Allan. *Ford: The Times, the Man, the Company.* New York: Charles Scribner's Sons, 1954.

Nevins, Allan, and Frank Ernest Hill. *Ford: Decline and Rebirth, 1933–1962.* New York: Charles Scribner's Sons, 1963.

North, Douglass C., and Robert Paul Thomas. *The Growth of the American Economy to 1860.* New York: Harper & Row, 1968.

Numbers, Ronald L. *Prophetess of Health: A Study of Ellen G. White.* Grand Rapids, MI: Wm. B. Eerdmans, 2008.

Oberholtzer, Ellis Paxson. *Jay Cooke: Financier of the Civil War.* Vol. 1. Philadelphia: George W. Jacobs, 1907.

Ogle, Maureen. *Ambitious Brew: The Story of American Beer.* Orlando, FL: Harcourt, 2006.

Okrent, Daniel. *Last Call: The Rise and Fall of Prohibition.* New York: Charles Scribner's Sons, 2011.

Olmstead, Frederick Law. *The Cotton Kingdom.* 2nd edition. Vol. 1. New York: Mason Brothers, 1862.

Olmsted, Denison. *Memoir of Eli Whitney.* New Haven: Durrie & Peck, 1846.

Olson, Lynne. *Those Angry Days: Roosevelt, Lindbergh, and America's Fight over World War II, 1939–1941.* New York: Random House, 2013.

Ozersky, Josh. *Colonel Sanders and the American Dream.* Austin: University of Texas Press, 2012.

Paglin, Max D., James R. Hobson, and Joel Rosenbloom. *The Communications Act: A Legislative History of the Major Amendments, 1934–1996.* Silver Spring, MD: Pike & Fischer, 1999.

Paine, Thomas. *Common Sense.* Edited by Richard Beeman. New York: Penguin Books, 2012.

Paper, Lewis J. *Empire: William S. Paley and the Making of CBS.* New York: St. Martin's, 1987.

Parsons, Patrick R. *Blue Skies: A History of Cable Television.* Philadelphia: Temple University Press, 2008.

Pearce, David W., ed. *The MIT Dictionary of Modern Economics.* 4th edition. London: Macmillan, 1992.

Pendergrast, Mark. *For God, Country & Coca-Cola.* New York: Basic Books, 2000.

Perot, Ross. *My Life & the Principles for Success.* Arlington, TX: Summit, 1996.

Peterson, Merrill D. *The Great Triumvirate: Webster, Clay, and Calhoun.* New York: Oxford University Press, 1987.

Philbrick, Nathaniel. *Mayflower.* New York: Viking, 2006.

Philip, Cynthia Owen. *Robert Fulton: A Biography.* New York: Franklin Watts, 1985.

Phillips, Ulrich Bonnell. *The Economic Cost of Slave-Holding in the Cotton Belt.* Boston: Ginn, 1905.

———. *Life and Labor in the Old South.* New York: Grosset & Dunlap, 1929.

Pitt, William. *Political Debates.* Paris: J. W. Imprimeur, 1766.

Plunkett-Powell, Karen. *Remembering Woolworth's.* New York: St. Martin's, 1999.

Polenberg, Richard. *One Nation Divisible: Class, Race, and Ethnicity in the United States Since 1938.* New York: Penguin Books, 1980.

Pound, Arthur. *The Turning Wheel: The Story of General Motors Through Twenty-Five Years, 1908–1933.* London: Forgotten Books, 2012.

Powers, Madelon. *Faces Along the Bar: Lore and Order in the Workingman's Saloon, 1870–1920.* Chicago: University of Chicago Press, 1999.

Powers, Ron. *Supertube: The Rise of Television Sports.* New York: Coward-McCann, 1984.

Prout, Henry G. *A Life of George Westinghouse.* New York: American Society of Mechanical Engineers, 1921.

Pugh, Emerson W. *Building IBM.* Cambridge, MA: MIT Press, 1995.

Raab, Selwyn. *Five Families*. New York: St. Martin's, 2006.

Rasmussen, Bill. *Sports Junkies Rejoice: The Birth of ESPN*. Bill Rasmussen, 2010.

Ratner, Sidney, James H. Soltow, and Richard Sylla. *The Evolution of the American Economy: Growth, Welfare, and Decision Making*. 2nd edition. New York: Macmillan, 1993.

Reagan, Ronald. *An American Life*. New York: Threshold Editions, 2011.

Redstone, Sumner. *A Passion to Win*. New York: Simon & Schuster, 2001.

Reich, Simon. *The Fruits of Fascism: Postwar Prosperity in Historical Perspective*. Ithaca, NY: Cornell University Press, 1990.

Reid, James D. *The Telegraph in America and Morse Memorial*. New York: Derby Brothers, 1879.

Reid, T. R. *The Chip*. New York: Random House, 2001.

Rhodehamel, John, ed. *George Washington: Writings*. New York: Library of America, 1997.

Richard, Christine S. *Confidence Game: How a Hedge Fund Manager Called Wall Street's Bluff*. Hoboken, NJ: John Wiley & Sons, 2010.

Ripley, William Z. *Railroads: Rates and Regulation*. Washington DC: Beard Books, 1999.

Robert, Joseph C. *The Story of Tobacco in America*. New York: Alfred A. Knopf, 1952.

Rockefeller, John D. *Random Reminiscences of Men and Events*. Garden City, NY: Doubleday, Page, 1913.

Sanders, Boyne Steven, and Tom Gilbert. *Desilu: The Story of Lucille Ball and Desi Arnaz*. New York: HarperCollins, 2011.

Sanders, Col. Harland. *Life as I Have Known It Has Been Finger Lickin' Good*. Carol Stream, IL: Creation House, 1974.

Schatz, Thomas. *The Genius of the System: Hollywood Filmmaking in the Studio Era*. Minneapolis: University of Minnesota Press, 2010.

Schroeder, Alice. *Snowball: Warren Buffett and the Business of Life*. New York: Bantam, 2008.

Schwarz, Richard W. *John Harvey Kellogg*. Hagerstown, MD: Review and Herald, 2006.

Scott, William Robert. *The Constitution and Finance of English, Scottish and Irish Joint-Stock Companies to 1720*. Vol. 1. New York: Cornell University Library Digital Collections, 2015.

Sears, Roebuck & Co. *Consumer Guide for 1894*. Facsimile edition. New York: Skyhorse, 2013.

———. *Sears Modern Homes, 1913*. Facsimile edition. New York: Dover, 2006.

Selznick, David O. *Memo from David O. Selznick*. Edited by Rudy Behlmer. New York: Viking Press, 1972.

Shaffner, Taliaferro P. *Shaffner's Telegraph Companion*. Vol. 1. New York: Pudney & Russell, 1854.

Shaw, Ronald E. *Canals for a Nation: The Canal Era in the United States, 1790–1860*. Lexington: University Press of Kentucky, 1990.

Sherman, William T. *Memoirs of General W. T. Sherman*. New York: D. Appleton, 1875.

Sherman, William Tecumseh, and John Sherman. *The Sherman Letters*. Edited by Rachel Sherman Thorndike. New York: Charles Scribner's Sons, 1894.

Shrader, Charles R. *History of Operations Research in the United States Army, 1961–1973*. Vol. 2. Washington DC: Office of the Deputy Under Secretary of the Army for Operations Research, 2008.

Shunk, William F. *A Practical Treatise on Railway Curves and Location*. Philadelphia: E. H. Butler, 1854.

Silverman, Kenneth. *Lightning Man: The Accursed Life of Samuel F. B. Morse*. New York: Alfred A. Knopf, 2003.

Sinclair, Upton. *The Jungle*. 1906. Reprint, Ann Arbor, MI: Borders Classics, 2006.

———. *The Moneychangers*. 1908. Reprint, Seaside, OR: Watchmaker, 2011.

Sitkoff, Harvard. *Toward Freedom Land: The Long Struggle for Racial Equality in America*. Lexington: University Press of Kentucky, 2010.

Sklar, Martin J. *The Corporate Reconstruction of American Capitalism, 1890–1916*. Cambridge: Cambridge University Press, 1997.

Sloat, Warren. *1929: America Before the Crash*. New York: Cooper Square, 2004.

Smith, Adam. *An Inquiry into the Nature and Causes of the Wealth of Nations*. Vol. 1. 1776. Reprint, Indianapolis, IN: Liberty Fund, 1981.

Smith, Amanda, ed. *Hostage to Fortune: The Letters of Joseph P. Kennedy.* New York: Viking, 2001.

Smith, John. *The Generall Historie of Virginia, New-England, and the Summer Isles.* New York: Readex Microprint, 1966.

———. *A True Relation of Virginia.* Boston: Wiggin and Lunt, 1866.

Smith, Page. *The Rise of Industrial America: A People's History of the Post-Reconstruction Era.* Vol. 6. New York: McGraw-Hill, 1984.

Smith, Ralph Lee. *The Wired Nation.* New York: Harper Colophon Books, 1972.

Smith, Sally Bedell. *In All His Glory: The Life of William S. Paley, the Legendary Tycoon and His Brilliant Circle.* New York: Simon & Schuster, 1990.

Smith, Truman. *Berlin Alert: The Memoirs and Reports of Truman Smith.* Edited by Robert Hessen. Stanford, CA: Hoover Institution Press, 1984.

Sorensen, Charles E. *My Forty Years with Ford.* Detroit: Wayne State University Press, 2006.

Sowers, Don Conger. *The Financial History of New York State from 1789 to 1912.* New York: Longmans, Green, 1914.

Speer, Albert. *Inside the Third Reich: Memoirs.* Translated by Clara Winston and Richard Winston. New York: Galahad Books, 1995.

Spencer, Herbert. *First Principles.* London: Williams and Norgate, 1862.

———. *The Principles of Biology.* New York: D. Appleton, 1891.

Sperber, A. M. *Murrow: His Life and Times.* New York: Freundlich Books, 1986.

Steinbeck, John. *The Grapes of Wrath.* 1939. Reprint, New York: Penguin Books, 2006.

———. *Travels with Charley in Search of America.* 1962. Reprint, New York: Penguin Books, 2002.

Stellman, Louis J. *Sam Brannan: Builder of San Francisco.* New York: Exposition, 1953.

Stevens, Mark. *King Icahn: The Biography of a Renegade Capitalist.* New York: Penguin, 1993.

Stewart, James B. *Den of Thieves.* New York: Touchstone, 1992.

Stiles, T. J. *The First Tycoon.* New York: Alfred A. Knopf, 2009.

Stone, Brad. *The Everything Store: Jeff Bezos and the Age of Amazon.* New York: Little, Brown, 2013.

Stover, John F. *History of the Illinois Central Railroad.* New York: Macmillan, 1975.

Stowe, Harriet Beecher. *Uncle Tom's Cabin; or, Life Among the Lowly.* 1852. Reprint, New York: Modern Library, 2001.

Strouse, Jean. *Morgan: American Financier.* New York: Random House, 1999.

Tarbell, Ida M. *The History of the Standard Oil Company.* Edited by David M. Chalmers. New York: Dover, 2003.

———. *The Tariff in Our Times.* New York: Macmillan, 1911.

Taylor, Alan. *American Colonies.* New York: Viking, 2001.

———. *The Internal Enemy: Slavery and War in Virginia, 1772–1832.* New York: W. W. Norton, 2014.

Thurston, Robert Henry. *Robert Fulton: His Life and Its Results.* New York: Dodd, Mead, 1891.

Tifft, Susan E., and Alex S. Jones. *The Trust.* New York: Little, Brown, 2000.

Tocqueville, Alexis de. *Democracy in America and Two Essays on America.* Edited by Isaac Kramnick. Translated by Gerald Bevan. London: Penguin Books, 2003.

Todd, Richard Cecil. *Confederate Finance.* Athens: University of Georgia Press, 2009.

Truesdell, Leon Edgar. *The Development of Punch Card Tabulation in the Bureau of the Census, 1890–1940.* Washington: Government Printing Office, 1965.

Turner, Orsamus. *Pioneer History of the Holland Purchase of Western New York.* Buffalo, NY: Jewett, Thomas, 1850.

Turner, Ted. *Call Me Ted.* New York: Grand Central, 2008.

Twain, Mark. *A Connecticut Yankee in King Arthur's Court.* 1889. Reprint, New York: Modern Library, 2001.

———. *The Gilded Age: A Tale of Today.* 1873. Reprint, Garden City, NY: Doubleday, 1970.

———. *The Innocents Abroad; or, The New Pilgrims' Progress.* 1869. Reprint, New York: Modern Library, 2003.

Tyson, Mike. *Undisputed Truth*. New York: Plume, 2013.

Unger, Irwin. *The Greenback Era: A Social and Political History of American Finance, 1865–1879*. Princeton, NJ: Princeton University Press, 1964.

Vail, Alfred. *Description of the American Electro Magnetic Telegraph*. Washington DC: J. & G. S. Gideon, 1845.

Veblen, Thorstein. *The Theory of the Leisure Class*. New York: Dover, 1994.

Vogel, Harold L. *Entertainment Industry Economics: A Guide for Financial Analysis*. 7th edition. New York: Cambridge University Press, 2007.

Walker, Stanley. *The Night Club Era*. Baltimore: Johns Hopkins University Press, 1999.

Wall, Joseph Frazier. *Andrew Carnegie*. New York: Oxford University Press, 1970.

Wallace, David. *Capital of the World: A Portrait of New York City in the Roaring Twenties*. Guilford, CT: Lyons, 2012.

Walton, Sam. *Sam Walton: Made in America*. New York: Bantam, 1993.

Wasserstein, Bruce. *Big Deal: 2000 and Beyond*. New York: Warner Books, 2000.

Watson, Elkanah. *History of the Rise, Progress, and Existing Condition of the Western Canals in the State of New York*. Albany, NY: D. Steele, 1820.

Watson, Thomas J. *Father, Son & Co.* Edited by Peter Petre. New York: Bantam, 2000.

Watt, James. *Specification of James Watt: Steam Engines*. London: G. E. Eyre, 1855.

Watts, Steven. *The People's Tycoon: Henry Ford and the American Century*. New York: Vintage, 2006.

Welles, Gideon. *Diary of Gideon Welles, Secretary of the Navy Under Lincoln and Johnson*. Vol. 1. Boston: Houghton Mifflin, 1911.

Wenaas, Eric P. *Radiola: The Golden Age of RCA, 1919–1929*. Chandler, AZ: Sonoran, 2007.

Werner, Max. *The Military Strength of the Powers*. Translated by Edward Fitzgerald. New York: Modern Age Books, 1939.

White, Richard. *Railroaded*. New York: W. W. Norton, 2012.

Whyte, William H. *The Organization Man*. Philadelphia: University of Pennsylvania Press, 2002.

Wilgus, Horace La Fayette. *A Study of the United States Steel Corporation in Its Industrial and Legal Aspects*. Chicago: Callaghan, 1901.

Wilkerson, Isabel. *The Warmth of Other Suns*. New York: Vintage Books, 2011.

Williams, Robert C. *Horace Greeley: Champion of American Freedom*. New York: NYU Press, 2006.

Willis, Carol. *Form Follows Finance: Skyscrapers and Skylines in New York and Chicago*. New York: Princeton Architectural Press, 1995.

Winthrop, John. *Winthrop's Journal, "History of New England."* Vol. 1. New York: Charles Scribner's Sons, 1908.

Wolff, Michael. *The Man Who Owns the News*. New York: Broadway Books, 2008.

Wolmar, Christian. *The Great Railroad Revolution*. New York: Public Affairs, 2013.

Wood, Betty. *The Origins of American Slavery: Freedom and Bondage in the English Colonies*. New York: Hill and Wang, 1997.

Wood, Gordon S. *The Radicalism of the American Revolution*. New York: Alfred A. Knopf, 1992.

Wood, Nicholas. *A Practical Treatise on Rail-Roads, and Interior Communication in General*. London: Longman, Orme, Brown, Green, & Longmans, 1838.

Wright, Gavin. *The Political Economy of the Cotton South: Households, Markets, and Wealth in the Nineteenth Century*. New York: W. W. Norton, 1978.

Yergin, Daniel. *The Prize: The Epic Quest for Oil, Money & Power*. New York: Free Press, 2008.

Yew, Lee Kuan. *From Third World to First: The Singapore Story: 1965–2000*. New York: HarperCollins, 2000.

Young, James Harvey. *Pure Food: Securing the Federal Food and Drugs Act of 1906*. Princeton, NJ: Princeton University Press, 1998.

Zanuck, Darryl F. *Memo from Darryl F. Zanuck: The Golden Years at Twentieth Century-Fox*. Edited by Rudy Behlmer. New York: Grove, 1993.

Index